Beginning Fedora™ 2

Shishir Gundavaram,
Deepak Thomas, Kapil Sharma, Mark Mamone,
Simon Whiting, Pancrazio de Mauro, Sandip Bhattacharya

Wiley Publishing, Inc.

Beginning Fedora™ 2

Published by
Wiley Publishing, Inc.
10475 Crosspoint Boulevard
Indianapolis, IN 46256-5774
`www.wiley.com`

Published simultaneously in Canada

ISBN: 0-7645-6996-1

Library of Congress Cataloging-in-Publication Data: Available from Publisher

For general information on our other products and services please contact our Customer Care Department within the United States at (800) 762-2974, outside the United States at (317) 572-3993 or fax (317) 572-4002.

Wiley also publishes its books in a variety of electronic formats. Some content that appears in print may not be available in electronic books.

About the Authors

Shishir Gundavaram is the Chief Technology Officer for MechanicNet Group, a company that specializes in providing CRM services for the automotive repair and maintenance industry. When he is not dealing with auto mechanics and broken-down cars, Shishir consults for a number of companies, designing architecture and providing technical expertise. He has more than a decade of experience in various aspects of software development and is considered an expert in wireless applications, distributed systems, electronic commerce, and Web backend architecture. He is also the author of various articles and books, including *Professional Perl Development*, *CGI Programming on the World Wide Web*, and *Scripting Languages: Automating the Web*, and he is regularly invited to speak at technical conferences around the world.

Pancrazio "Ezio" de Mauro has been using Red Hat Linux since 1996. He is a Linux consultant specializing in system integration, mobile technologies, and training. He actively supports and advocates the use of free software. Ezio spends most of his free time traveling and backpacking. He welcomes comments and questions at his e-mail address, `pdm@demauro.net`.

Mark Mamone, a Solutions Specialist working for Syntegra Ltd in the UK, has 16 years of experience in the IT industry ranging from Assembler to MS-DOS and now specializing in the development of enterprise and mobile systems using a variety of technologies, including Microsoft .NET, Java, and Linux.

> *I would like to thank my parents for the Commodore Vic-20, without which my life would have never taken this path. I would like to thank my children—Tanya, James, and Cameron—whose love is my foundation and, most important, my girlfriend, Rachel, whose support, love, and never-ending drive enabled me to complete this book!*

Kapil Sharma developed a keen interest in Linux and open source technology in the mid-1990s and has been working on various UNIX systems and Internet security technologies for more than 10 years. He is a postgraduate in Business Computing and has deployed many UNIX, High availability, Clustering, and Internet security projects. He is a Sun Certified System Administrator (SCSA) and Sun Certified Network Administrator (SCNA). Kapil is also actively involved in the open source community and has contributed many technical articles on system and network security. He enjoys working on new challenges in Internet security, Internet architecture design, and various UNIX flavors. He also fancies technical writing and thereby sharing his knowledge with the community. He maintains a consultancy company for providing UNIX and Internet security solutions, and a Web site with loads of security resources at `www.linux4biz.net`.

Apart from his hectic technical life, Kapil also enjoys clubbing, music, and touring the world. He currently lives with his wife, Usha Sharma, in London, U.K., and can be contacted via e-mail at kapil@linux4biz.net.

> *This book is dedicated to my beloved wife, Usha Sharma, for her continuous support, love, and cups of coffee at night, without which this book would have been a dream — and to my little one who will soon be coming into this world. I thank my parents, Girdhari Lal Sharma and Bimla Devi Sharma, and my elder brother Hemant Sharma for providing continuous support and motivation in my life.*

Deepak Thomas lives and works in the San Francisco Bay area. His interests include PHP, Linux, and J2EE technologies. He has coauthored and reviewed several books for Wrox in these areas. In their spare time Deepak and Ansu go bike riding along the many beautiful trails in their part of the country.

Simon Whiting, a graduate of Clare College, University of Cambridge, is a Principal Consultant for AnIX Group Ltd and has been a Unix system administrator. He is an expert in Linux, storage area networks, and C, Perl, and Korn Shell programming.

Sandip Bhattacharya is an independent technology consultant specializing in Open Source technologies. He is a Red Hat Certified Engineer (RHCE), holds degrees in engineering and management, and is the author of a number of books and articles on Open Source software. He currently runs Puroga Technologies, a small startup with a focus on helping businesses use the Open Source revolution to their advantage. He can be contacted at `sandip@puroga.com`. Sandip is an active participant in various Open Source communities in India, especially his local LUG, the Indian Linux Users Group, Delhi (ILUGD).

Credits

Acquisitions Editor
Debra Williams Cauley

Development Editor
Marcia Ellett

Technical Editor
Jason Luster

Production Editor
Eric Newman

Copy Editor
Nancy Rapoport

Editorial Manager
Mary Beth Wakefield

Vice President & Executive Group Publisher
Richard Swadley

Vice President and Executive Publisher
Bob Ipsen

Vice President and Publisher
Joseph B. Wikert

Project Coordinator
Bill Ramsey

Media Development Specialist
Travis Silvers

Proofreader
Michael Koch

Indexer
Johnna VanHoose Dinse

Introduction

The various versions of the Linux operating system, or distributions as they are known, have matured over the years, becoming simpler to install but continuing to offer a comprehensive set of components so that Linux is threatening more mainstream operating systems such as Microsoft Windows and UNIX. Linux is for everybody; it's fast, stable, and free thanks to its open source status. In fact, suppliers such as Oracle are openly touting Linux as one of their preferred platforms for their products, including the latest version of their relational database, Oracle 10g. Red Hat's distribution holds the title of most popular Linux distribution and the company provides other value-added services such as support contracts and training and certification programs. However, as a retail product, compromises had to be made to meet deadlines and customer demand. Red Hat redirected its efforts in creating a community-based project, and the Fedora distribution was born.

This book teaches you how to install, configure, and use the Fedora operating system and the components you have chosen. The basic goals of the book are as follows:

- Provide an understanding of the Fedora operating system, its basic and optional components
- Explain how to install and configure your Fedora installation to provide a well-configured and secure installation
- Teach the reader how to set up a simple network using the Fedora operating system and its optional components, such as Web servers, mail servers, and so on
- Introduce the reader to some of the more advanced system administrator concepts, including best practice guidelines
- Demonstrate how the preceding points and an introduction to the Perl programming language can be applied to create a simple Web site

What Is Fedora?

Fedora, besides being a type of hat, is the name given to the Linux distribution born from Red Hat Linux because Red Hat, Inc., did not want to surrender to the retail compromises that plague commercial products. Warren Togami had already started a community for building high-quality RPM packages for Red Hat Linux, and because the objectives between his and Red Hat's own requirements were similar, the projects were merged and the Fedora distribution was born. Red Hat's open source project, known as the Red Hat Linux Project, merged with the Fedora project. Red Hat, Inc., provided backing and guidance, with a great deal of community involvement. The Fedora release is an open source distribution with the latest packages, while the Red Hat Enterprise distributions are commercially robust distributions.

While some of the community may have been skeptical at such a change, the merge presents a good solution to both parties, and above all, the end user. Red Hat now has a distribution that can feed its commercial offerings, while the end users have a distribution that is not only backed by the ever diligent open source community, but also by a corporation with the standing of Red Hat.

The distribution is based on version 2.6 of the Linux kernel; this itself has a number of improvements that are worthy of mention. In addition, a large number of packages are available for the four installation types that are offered to you when you install. Let's take a look at some of these improvements and packages.

Linux Kernel 2.6

The new kernel now provides support for both much larger and much smaller systems, for example, personal digital assistants (PDAs). This is in part due to the merge of the uCLinux project that has enabled the use of the Linux kernel for embedded systems such as mobile phones, PDAs, and other devices.

Another major change is the ability of the Linux kernel to support much larger systems by embracing support for Non-Uniform Memory Access (NUMA) systems, something now used on systems that typically have multiple processors.

There are numerous other advances that you may wish to read up on (see `www.kniggit.net/wwol26.html`), but we'll warn you now: the concepts mentioned are not for beginners.

SELinux

You may have heard the term *Security-Enhanced Linux (SELinux)*. SELinux was developed by the U.S. National Security Agency (NSA) to separate the permissions for users, programs, processes, files, and devices so that applications may be granted only the permissions they require to function. This level of isolation, termed *Mandatory Access Control (MAC)*, ensures that security can't be circumvented by rogue applications. This removes some of the problems in having an all-powerful root user account, which would otherwise mean that if a hacker had cracked the password for the root user, anything was possible.

Packages

The distribution is split into a number of key areas, including the following:

- **Anaconda Installer:** This is the installation project that during installation identifies the hardware and installs the distribution and files required to run the product. This enables the user to get up and running far more quickly, without having to worry about the intricacies of which particular display adapter he or she has installed.
- **Artwork:** This encapsulates all artwork for the project including icons, backgrounds, and themes. The overall look and feel of the Fedora product is very professional; the clean lines and clear, color icons create a feel that the user is comfortable working in.
- **Configuration Tools:** This project aims to provide user interfaces to common tasks. These include operations such as disk partitioning, general development, and so on.
- **Desktop:** This project includes the X Window system, the desktop shell, and applications. This graphical user interface (GUI) now provides a powerful interface that rivals the likes of Microsoft or Mac.
- **Translations:** This project provides the translation of applications and documentation into the various different languages for which the distribution is to be made available. At the time of writing, this includes some ten languages, including German, French, Spanish, and Italian.

- **Docs:** This project produces text-based documentation that is easy to follow and included with the distribution. This means that documentation for a package is on hand and available to guide you through those tasks that you may find difficult.
- **Packages:** A package is an application or set of applications that offers functionality that you may find useful. For example, Microsoft Office is a set of applications that offers office productivity tools such as a word processor. The same is true of Fedora; a wide range of packages are available out of the box or for download.

Some packages that you are likely to encounter everyday follow:

- **OpenOffice:** OpenOffice offers a comprehensive, out-of-the-box office productivity suite that rivals the Windows equivalent, Microsoft Office. It includes project management, word processing, spreadsheet, and financial applications.
- **Mozilla:** This is the granddaddy of all Internet browsers and arguably still the best.
- **Evolution:** This application offers functionality similar to its Windows counterpart, Microsoft Outlook, managing all your e-mails, contacts, and calendar requirements.
- **Nautilus:** This is a graphical filesystem explorer, offering you Microsoft Explorer–type functionality on the Linux platform.
- **Multimedia applications:** These are in abundance, from playing CDs or MP3s to creating your own DVDs, movies, or digital photograph albums.

We could continue ad infinitum, but we'll leave the fun of discovering the packages and their capabilities to you.

Why Fedora?

The ethos is that Fedora will have regular releases (at around 4- to 6-month intervals), agreed upon by a common committee, which will feature functionality that will often find its way into the Red Hat Linux product.

Why bother? Well, such a change offers a number of benefits to the end user as well as Red Hat, Inc., itself, including the following:

- **Open source model:** This allows the community to contribute to the development of the product without being constrained by retail dependencies. This results in a faster development process.
- **Risk:** It allows the community to introduce and provide a proving ground to new features and technologies that may be incorporated into the product. This is something that would not have been possible with a retail product.
- **Opportunity:** The open source model allows developers to join and participate in the creation of the Fedora code base and the features within. You can even create your own distribution based on Fedora, providing you comply with the trademark rules defined by the open source licenses such as GPL.

Sound too good to be true? Well, there *are* some caveats, mainly focused around the following keys areas:

- Certification in the areas of hardware, software, and independent system vendors
- Release intervals
- Support

As an open source product developed by the developer community for early adopters and enthusiasts, there is no support from the likes of Red Hat, Inc. Support falls to the developer community, which is sufficient for most users but obviously not for corporate customers who need to adhere to service levels. There are other limitations, such as the lack of Independent System Vendor (ISV) certifications and the lack of hardware or standards certifications. Companies such as Dell and HP underwrite the running of Red Hat Linux on certain hardware platforms and components that they supply through thorough testing by them.

However, the audience at which Fedora is aimed is usually not concerned with such limitations, and if users are concerned, they always have the option of looking at commercial distributions such as Red Hat.

What Is Linux?

Before answering the question, we'll introduce its creator and the chronological events that occurred in the development of Linux.

Linus Torvalds and the Birth of Linux

Linus Benedict Torvalds was studying at the University of Helsinki in Finland when his interest in computing made him curious about operating systems and how he could improve upon existing operating systems such as UNIX. The development of the Linux kernel (its core) began, and in October 1991 version 0.02 was released onto the Internet by Linus Torvalds, the author and trademark holder, with the now famous posting:

```
From: torvalds@klaava.Helsinki.FI (Linus Benedict Torvalds)
Newsgroups: comp.os.minix
Subject: Free minix-like kernel sources for 386-AT
Message-ID: 1991Oct5.054106.4647@klaava.Helsinki.FI
Date: 5 Oct 91 05:41:06 GMT
Organization: University of Helsinki
Do you pine for the nice days of minix-1.1, when men were men and wrote their own
device drivers? Are you without a nice project and just dying to cut your teeth on
a OS you can try to modify for your needs? Are you finding it frustrating when
everything works on minix? No more all-nighters to get a nifty program working?
Then this post might be just for you :-)
As I mentioned a month(?) ago, I'm working on a free version of a minix-lookalike
for AT-386 computers. It has finally reached the stage where it's even usable
(though may not be depending on what you want), and I am willing to put out the
sources for wider distribution. It is just version 0.02 (+1 (very small) patch
already), but I've successfully run bash/gcc/gnu-make/gnu-sed/compress etc under
it.
```

```
Sources for this pet project of mine can be found at nic.funet.fi (128.214.6.100)
in the directory /pub/OS/Linux.
The directory also contains some README-file and a couple of binaries to work under
linux (bash, update and gcc, what more can you ask for :-). Full kernel source is
provided, as no minix code has been used. Library sources are only partially free,
so that cannot be distributed currently. The system is able to compile "as-is" and
has been known to work. Heh. Sources to the binaries (bash and gcc) can be found at
the same place in /pub/gnu.
```

As the posting states, the binaries and source code were released under the open source banner using the GNU General Public License, which ensures that the source code would be free to all. This was a very deliberate act; Linus wanted people to use and test the code, to improve upon it, and extend it as they wished. The extensions and modifications were released onto the Internet. In essence, thousands of people were working across the world on creating the Linux operating system and applications that ran on it—free for all to use and distribute.

Why Is Linux Successful?

The Linux operating system program, also known as the kernel, performs many of the same functions as UNIX and the many Windows variants, but it is distinguishable by its power, features, and flexibility. It wasn't the first open source application to be released under the open source movement, but its power and accessibility have led Linux to evolve and continue to evolve to this date into an operating system that rivals commercial operating systems such as Microsoft Windows. The result is that Linux has become the standard platform for open source applications, of which many thousands exist, such as those available from SourceForge (`www.sourceforge.net`), KDE (`www.apps.kde.com`), and Gnome (`www.gnome.org`) sites.

Some of the features available to a Linux distribution and its applications that are either included in the distribution or downloadable from the Internet are as follows:

- **Graphical user interface (GUI):** The interface between you, the user, and the applications, including the operating system, is made enormously easier by a point-and-click graphical interface such as those found on Microsoft Windows and the Macintosh. Unlike these two operating systems, you are free to choose which GUI you wish to use, such as KDE or Gnome, and Fedora goes further by providing *Bluecurve*, a common theme for these environments.
- **Network support:** Linux can be installed as a workstation or as a server and supports a variety of networking applications. It can act as a file server and print server, or connect and use other Network resources, even those that are non-Linux such as Microsoft Windows or UNIX.
- **Office productivity:** A number of office applications are installed by default, such as word processors, spreadsheets, or presentation managers. The OpenOffice suite of applications is one such example and is covered in more detail in Chapter 4.
- **Internet applications:** Linux is released with fast and efficient Internet servers, such as File Transfer Protocol (FTP), Web servers, domain naming servers (DNS), and mail servers.

The reason it is so successful is that, despite being free, it is a fully functional, extremely powerful operating system with all the applications you could ever wish for. If an application does exist, the development tools and languages required to develop an application are also free, that's assuming that such a project is not already underway by one of the virtual development teams across the globe.

What Are Distributions?

So the Linux software is free, and the numerous applications or components that have been developed for it by those around the world are also free. Complexities are introduced when trying to install the operating system, its components, and applications. To address the problem, commercial vendors saw the opportunity to gather the software in a format that could be freely distributed and even developed an installation program that took some of the pain out of installing the software on the various computer configurations that exist, very much as Microsoft Windows does. Some of these vendors include Caldera, Mandrake, Debian, and the topic of this book, Fedora. These are all known as Linux *distributions*.

Who Is Red Hat, Inc.?

Red Hat, Inc., has been providing services to the Linux community since 1993. Its mission is to "provide professional tools to computing professionals." As previously mentioned, various vendors have created distributions that include a collection of components around a specific version of the Linux kernel, complete with an installation program more akin to those found on the Windows platform instead of the more manual process found in earlier versions of Linux. Red Hat is one such vendor that, at the time of writing, holds the majority share of the Linux marketplace (according to various independent studies) and has seen its revenues grow to more than $10 million in the past few years.

Red Hat releases Red Hat Linux in a variety of different versions:

- **Red Hat Enterprise Linux WS:** Ideal for small desktop deployments.
- **Red Hat Enterprise Linux ES:** Ideal for small/mid-range servers.
- **Red Hat Enterprise Linux AS:** Ideal for high-end and mission-critical systems.
- **Red Hat Professional Workstation:** Ideal for single-user desktop deployments.

For more information on these versions and their features, visit Red Hat's Web site at `www.redhat.com/`.

Why Linux?

We've discussed the merits of Linux in terms of its zero cost of ownership and its functionality, but why should you choose it over some of the other commercial operating systems such as Microsoft Windows or the Macintosh?

- **Size and speed:** Linux, when installed, can consume as little as 150MB of hard disk space and will run quite happily in as little as 32MB of RAM. Compare this to UNIX, which often requires more than 500MB, or Microsoft Windows that requires many more megabytes of hard disk space and RAM to install and run effectively.
- **Security:** One significant reason for Linux's excellent reputation as a secure environment is that its source code is completely accessible, and continues to be viewed by many pairs of eyes. Linux's open source standpoint means that people other than the vendor can check for incomplete code or code that has been tampered with. The more people who study Linux's source code, the more bugs (and security flaws) can be spotted.

Of course, that's only half the story—the other half is that infrastructure is in place for easy bug-reporting, discussion, and bug-fixing. The result of all this is that more bugs get spotted more quickly, and they're fixed faster.

In addition to the numerous security applications (such as firewalls) available, many Linux distributions are specifically created to provide a highly secure environment. Examples include the Immunix OS and Bastille Linux.

- **Standard:** Because it complies with both UNIX and Linux standards, Linux can interoperate with a number of different operating systems and filesystems such as Microsoft Windows and UNIX.
- **GNU software support:** As mentioned, a wide variety of software is freely available through the GNU project, which includes development software, office applications, system administration tools, and more.

Want to Participate?

As previously mentioned, the Fedora source and binaries are openly available and are free to distribute providing you comply with the Fedora Project trademark rules. You are also encouraged to participate. How? There are a number of things you can do:

- Contribute code or documentation.
- Report bugs.
- Provide online support through mailing lists.

In the future, Red Hat will be making a source code system (Concurrent Versions System [CVS]) available, allowing you to view its contents and, if an approved contributor, commit changes to various packages. If you have any questions, you can direct them to `fedora-devel-list@redhat.com`.

In addition, reporting bugs or requesting enhancements is another good method for making changes to packages via `http://bugzilla.redhat.com/bugzilla`.

Who Is This Book For?

As its title suggests, this book tackles the Fedora operating system and its components from a beginner's standpoint. However, given the breadth of the operating system alone, not to mention the wealth of applications distributed with it, this book could not attempt to cover all of the topics expected from everybody.

Instead, it is written for those who have used an operating system before, such as Apple's Macintosh, UNIX, or more likely, one of the many versions of the Microsoft Windows operating system. This book builds upon what you already know about operating systems, such as graphical user interfaces, filesystems, and applications, so that you can get up and running with Fedora faster. However, it is a beginner's book and for those of you that have had no prior experience, the book still provides a great insight and starting place for installing and using Fedora 2.

What Is Covered in This Book?

Conceptually, the book breaks down into a number of different sections that don't necessarily run sequentially. The first section covers the installation of the basic operating system, after which the basics are introduced followed by installation of additional optional components. The second section covers configuring your machine to connect to the Internet and introduces some of the applications you may find useful. The third section covers topics necessary for networking your machine, including an introduction to user accounts. The fourth section covers more advanced topics such as security and advanced administration, with the fifth and final section covering how the Linux operating system includes everything necessary to develop a Web site.

Following is a brief description of the chapter structure. Every chapter builds upon the knowledge amassed in the previous chapters and highlights concepts that may be applicable to other operating systems you may have used, such as Microsoft Windows.

- **Chapter 1** provides support to the existing Fedora 2 documentation in taking you through installing the operating system, how to start and stop the operating system, and how to work with it using the bash shell and GUIs provided.
- **Chapter 2** introduces the Linux basics, explaining fundamental topics such as pipes, user accounts, and installing and configuring hardware. The chapter also looks at how to resolve problems and fine-tune your installation for maximum flexibility and performance.
- **Chapter 3** discusses how you configure your installation to connect to the Internet or your own network so you can start to send and receive e-mails and, if necessary, use the Internet to discover and download some of the optional packages we cover in the next chapter.
- **Chapter 4** introduces the applications that you may typically want to use, such as a Web browser and office applications to MP3 players. The similarities to Windows applications that you may be familiar with are highlighted, and this chapter introduces the bewildering array of applications that comes with Fedora 2 and where to find more.
- **Chapter 5** presents a detailed explanation of the filesystem and covers topics such as mounting drives, managing files and directories, and using the shell to generate and manipulate the output from predefined or custom scripts.
- **Chapter 6** tackles the notion of the shell, which you have been using in the first five chapters of the book, to type commands and execute them. We will examine the shell more closely and look at combining commands into a script, build logic into scripts, and get them to run in specific circumstances.
- **Chapter 7** introduces the basics of security, including information on user accounts and how to manage these, and setting permissions and privileges.
- **Chapter 8** introduces the concept of packages, which provide additional components or applications that are not installed by default, and explains how to install and/or remove these. The chapter concludes with an explanation of how you tackle compiling applications when only the source code is available or needs to be tailored.
- **Chapter 9** provides you with the information necessary to install and configure networking components such as File Transfer Protocol (FTP) servers, Web servers, file servers, print servers, and more—all on the same machine.

- **Chapter 10** explores security, a complex topic, but this chapter explains the kinds of problems you should consider and are likely to encounter. It discusses how you can secure your machine using a firewall and how to perform a vulnerability assessment with best practices.
- **Chapter 11** covers advanced administration topics such as analyzing log files to track down problems, backup and archival strategies, how to install applications from source code, and general housekeeping tasks to ensure all is running smoothly.
- **Chapter 12** presents a detailed recipe for rebuilding the Linux kernel, which is at the heart of the Fedora operating system.
- **Chapter 13** covers scripting using the Perl programming language to automate the common task of managing the log files. It does this by providing a Perl primer, followed by some common examples of Perl scripts and a sample application that monitors common logs and provides a Web-based user interface to the application.
- **Chapter 14** discusses how to contribute to the Fedora project, from finding and reporting bugs, to contributing new code and patches, to writing tutorials and documentation.
- **Chapter 15** presents a survey of some of the more interesting applications that are available for Fedora, focusing in particular on system administration software and application development tools.

What You Need to Use This Book

In order to install, configure, and use the Fedora operating system and the applications covered in this book, you need the Fedora distribution, which is freely available from `www.fedora.redhat.com/` or other mirror sites on the Internet. You may also use this book's companion DVD.

Conventions

To help you understand and follow what is going on throughout this text, and to maintain consistency, we have used a number of different styles of text and layout. Here are some examples of these, and what they mean:

> *Note text is a style that is used to display some information aside from the general discussion, such as advice, hints, and other sideline information.*

When *important words* are introduced for the first time, they are displayed in italics to stand out from the page.

We use three styles to display code. The first is used when we are referring to code within the main body of the text. In this case, `code in text` appears in a monospaced font.

```
The second is used when there are full pieces of standalone code you can run, or
when there is code that is new or important to take in.
```

```
The third type of formatting is used when there are snippets of code, or code that
you have seen before.
```

Shading in code is also sometimes used when command lines are shown, with the output of a command being displayed without shading, as in the following example:

```
> ls file.txt
This is the output from the command
```

> **Important pieces of information are highlighted in boxes like this.**

Tell Us What You Think

We have tried to make this book as accurate and enjoyable as possible, but what really matters is what the book actually does for you. Please let us know your views by contacting us via e-mail at `feedback@wrox.com`.

Errata

We have made every effort to make sure there are no errors in the text or the code. However, "to err is human," and as such, we recognize the need to keep you informed of any mistakes as they are spotted and corrected. Errata sheets are available for all our books at `www.wrox.com`. If you find an error that hasn't already been reported, please let us know.

Our Web site acts as a focus for other information and support, including the code from all our books, sample chapters, previews of forthcoming titles, and articles and opinions on related topics.

Contents

1

Installing Fedora 2

Installing an operating system is often a long, drawn-out process that requires a lot of upfront planning. Installation of traditional UNIX-based operating systems seems to have been particularly painful in the past, requiring even experienced administrators to fret about partitions and drivers. Early versions of Linux were no different in this respect. The first version of Linux, back in 1993, could be booted up using only Minix (another UNIX-like operating system). That version of Linux could support only the Finnish keyboard because the author of Linux didn't have access to a U.S. keyboard.

However, since then, Linux has grown by leaps and bounds. Each of the major distributions show that developers have put a lot of thought and effort into the Linux installation process, and, today, installing Linux for desktop use is a no-brainer.

Red Hat, in particular, has caught the attention of the public, breaking away from the standard tradition of distributing disc images and pioneering the concept of distributing software in the form of packages. (Right now, the Red Hat Package Manager, or RPM, is a standard in distribution of precompiled software packages in the Linux world; RPM is further covered in Chapter 4.)

Red Hat has also been improving Linux usability and features in the most daunting area of any operating system—installation. The latest version of Fedora, Core 2 is truly the most user-friendly ever, with extensive inputs from professional usability experts and a new look to attract even the most hardened technophobes.

The Fedora 2 distribution offers four different configurations, and your choice will depend on how you plan to use the operating system:

- **Personal desktop:** This configuration is targeted at users who are new to Linux, or those who like to use Linux for day-to-day applications such as office productivity tools and Internet browsing. This is the option we'll install in this chapter.
- **Workstation:** This configuration is targeted at developers or system administrators. It provides various tools for software development and system management.
- **Server:** This configuration is mainly intended for systems that will not be used directly, but are primarily for offering network-based services such as e-mail, file sharing, network connectivity, and Web resources.

- **Custom:** This configuration is for experienced users who want more control over exactly what is installed on their systems. The user can select which packages are to be installed and how the hard disks are to be used, and has control over various other configuration options that are preselected in the other three configurations.

In several cases, any one of the preceding installation options may not have all the functionality required. These installation options are not set in stone; that is, if you install a particular option, it does not mean that you cannot take advantage of applications available in another option. You may very well install a particular option and then choose to install additional software that you find useful. Installing additional software is covered in detail in Chapter 4.

This chapter takes a look at getting a Personal Desktop installation in place on a new computer. It looks at each step of the installation and the decisions that you would have to take at various stages of the installation to get a working Fedora desktop in place. By the end of the chapter, you will have a desktop up and running that you will be able to use right away for your daily needs, such as Internet browsing, e-mail, and office productivity tools.

Preparing for the Installation

While the installation process is quite straightforward, it is essential that you prepare ahead of time to ensure that the installation process goes smoothly. Of course, you'll need the necessary installation disks to install the system; but it's also worth looking over your hardware, too. This section examines both software and hardware aspects of preparation.

The Software

To begin with, you need to have the necessary *software* for the job. The Fedora 2 distribution can be obtained from a number of sources. Here are a couple of options:

- **The Publisher's Edition DVD included with this book:** This includes all the material that you need for the installation process itself. This chapter looks at installation using the DVD that is included in this pack.
- **The downloadable CD images:** In the true spirit of open source (`www.opensource.org`), Fedora is also available as CDs downloadable for free public use.

  These CD images can be obtained from the official Fedora Web site at `http://fedora.redhat.com`.

  After you have downloaded the CD images, you need to write them onto CD recordable discs (be sure to tell your CD-burning software that you're burning *CD images* or *ISO images*), which you may then use for installation.

If you are using CDs rather than the accompanying DVD, please note that the Personal Desktop configuration requires the first two installation CD discs during the installation. As you begin to explore some of the many applications supplied with the Fedora 2 distribution, you'll need the remaining discs for installing these applications. Therefore, it is worthwhile to hold on to all three binary CDs discs.

The Hardware

Before you start the installation, it's a good idea to make a note of the hardware details of the machine you plan to use for your Linux installation. These details can help you get the most out of the installation process, and even in detecting problems in the hardware configuration itself—problems that can prevent Fedora 2 from installing correctly.

Determining Your Hardware

During the process of installation, Fedora 2 may need some extra help to determine your computer's exact hardware composition. To help it out, it is a good idea to make a note of the details on the following checklist before you begin the installation:

- ❑ **Keyboard type:** The Fedora 2 installation defaults to a standard American English 105-key keyboard. Unless you are using a language-specific keyboard such as those used in many European and East Asian countries, you don't have to worry about this detail.
- ❑ **Mouse type:** Fedora 2 supports two-button and three-button mice, as well as wheel mice and the cordless variety. You should note the exact make and nature of your mouse. Fedora 2 also supports tablets; to verify that your make of tablet is compatible with Fedora 2, check the Hardware Compatibility List.
- ❑ **Hard disk size:** Make a note of the size of the hard disk that you'll be installing Fedora 2 onto. If the installation process fails to detect the hard disk size correctly, it might point to an underlying hardware problem. Also note that a Personal Desktop installation will require around 1.9GB of hard disk space for the programs loaded during installation. If you plan to install other applications, you will need more.
- ❑ **Video (graphics) card:** Note the chipset of the video card and the amount of RAM. While the Red Hat X-server configuration program can usually probe and detect the video card, it sometimes fails. If it does fail, you'll need to tell Fedora 2 the name of your video card chipset. Note that the video RAM is sometimes also displayed on the screen while the machine boots.

If you can't find the name of your video card chipset in the Hardware Compatibility List (described in the next section of this chapter), don't worry. Note that this means only that Fedora 2's GUI is affected. Generally, if you intend to use the computer only as a server system, you're recommended not to install any GUI for reasons of resource load and security. If you do want a GUI, you'll still be able to configure your machine to use the VESA interface for running the X-server. The VESA interface standard is supported by most of the commonly available video cards.

- ❑ **Monitor:** If you have an unusual monitor model, the configuration of the GUI X Server software (during the installation process) might not detect it. Therefore, it's worth noting your monitor's specific information. You'll need the horizontal and vertical sync rates, which can generally be found either in the monitor manual or at the monitor manufacturer's Web site.
- ❑ **Sound card:** While the installation tries to detect the sound card, it sometimes doesn't succeed. Therefore, noting the name of the sound card chipset in advance is a good idea.
- ❑ **Network card:** During installation, Fedora 2 tries to detect the network interface card (NIC) and load the appropriate software driver automatically. You should note the name of the chipset of the NIC in advance of installation, just in case the installation process fails to determine it.

How do you find this information? Well, if you have the technical specification documents that were supplied with your computer, you'll find the information in there. If not, the machine's existing operating system will probably offer some way of browsing the hardware being used. For example:

- In Windows 2000 or Windows XP, you can find out about existing hardware via Start ➪ Settings ➪ Control Panel ➪ System (select the Hardware tab, and click the Device Manager button).
- In other Linux systems, you can find out about existing hardware through various menu options of the GUI. For example, try the options in Programs ➪ Settings or Main Menu ➪ System Tools, depending on which version of Linux you're using.

The Hardware Compatibility List

Red Hat maintains a list of *officially supported hardware*, called the Hardware Compatibility List (HCL). The HCL lists all the hardware components against which the operating system has been checked extensively for proper functioning. The list is available at `http://hardware.redhat.com/hcl/`.

It's worth checking for your own hardware components in this list before buying new hardware for your Fedora desktop; if you find them, it can give you some peace of mind. You shouldn't panic, however, if your hardware *doesn't* appear in the HCL; there's still a good chance that it will work with the Fedora 2 installation. Many hardware components behave using standardized interfaces that can be persuaded to work with Linux (although sometimes in a less efficient way). For example, most modern video cards support the VESA mode of graphic display, which can be used by Fedora 2 to present a GUI front-end to the user. While the VESA mode is not suitable for performance-intensive graphic displays, it is a quick and easy way to persuade an incompatible video card to work with the GUI software in the Linux operating system.

It is well worth using the HCL to check out the compatibility of hardware with Fedora 2 (or, indeed, any distribution of Linux) before investing your money in it. A significant proportion of all queries submitted by new Fedora users relate to hardware for which Red Hat has not confirmed official support.

While any new motherboard or processor should safely work with a Linux basic console mode, the most common problems lie with compatibility of sound and display hardware. Due to the nature of the open source movement, the compatibility of Linux with specific hardware configurations can take some time to develop. Not all hardware manufacturers are quick to offer Linux versions of their driver software.

The Boot Disk

The installation process will also offer you the opportunity to create a *boot disk*. The boot disk can help you to recover gracefully if you have boot problems. While creation of the boot disk is optional, it is recommended—you never know when you might need it.

For creating the boot disk, it's a good idea to have a floppy disk ready during the installation process. Make sure there's nothing important on the disk because the boot disk creation process will overwrite it.

Network Details

We've already talked about compiling a hardware checklist before installation. If you intend to use your new Fedora 2 desktop within an existing network, you should also compile a checklist of network-related information for use during the installation process. You may need to ask your network administrator some of these details:

- **DHCP or fixed IP:** An IP address is essential for any computer to participate in any networking activity. So, you must ask: Is your desktop assigned an IP address dynamically (by a DHCP server), or should it be configured with a static IP address? By default, Fedora 2 will configure your machine to request an IP address from a DHCP server, but if you need to, you can change this either during the installation process itself or after the installation is complete.

If you are installing your Fedora machine to connect to an ISP or if you have a DSL or cable modem connection with a cable or DSL router, your system is most likely to be assigned an IP address by a DHCP server. If you want to run a Web site or other type of server from off of your Fedora installation, you might want to think of obtaining a static IP address. In all likelihood, your ISP will impose an additional charge for a static IP address. You may want to refer to *Chapter 3* for more information on setting up Fedora in different network environments.

If your computer is to be configured to get its IP address dynamically from a DHCP server, you can skip the rest of these questions.

- **IP address:** If your machine is to have a fixed IP address, you need to know what IP address to use. An IP address is always mentioned along with its *network mask*, so make a note of both the IP address and network mask.
- **DNS host and domain names:** You also need to note some domain name service (DNS) details—specifically, the machine's host name and domain name. For example, if your network administrator assigns your machine the DNS name `arwen.acme.com`, your machine host name is `arwen` and your domain name is `acme.com`. The combination of host name and domain name (here `arwen.acme.com`) is called the *fully qualified domain name* (FQDN).

If your office is running an internal DNS server, this host and domain name combination should refer to the IP address previously mentioned. Many network applications perform optimally when a local DNS server is present in the network.

- **DNS servers:** DNS servers are responsible for resolving Internet names to the corresponding IP addresses. You should note the IP address(es) of your network's DNS server(s). If there is no local DNS server, it's possible that an external DNS server is used for Internet name resolution. Fedora 2 allows you to specify up to three DNS servers.
- **Internet gateway:** Finally, you should note the IP address of your machine's Internet gateway. While any network traffic for your local LAN will be sent directly to those local machines, any traffic to other networks (like those of the Internet) will be sent out through this gateway. Failure to set this value will prevent you from accessing the Internet after installation.

Getting Help

If you find problems, there are plenty of ways to get answers. In fact, the open source community boasts of a huge number of avenues that can help you resolve your technical difficulties.

For example, Red Hat itself has an extensive bug reporting and resolution database, freely available for public access at `http://bugzilla.redhat.com`. In addition, there are many Linux user communities worldwide, hungry to share experiences and thriving on a diet of mutual support (see `www.linux.org/groups`). LinuxQuestions.org (`www.linuxquestions.org`) is an excellent online forum for questions on Linux in general, and Fedora in particular.

The Installation

Having collected all the information in your hardware and network checklists, you're ready to begin the installation itself. This section walks you through the graphical installation tool, describing each of the installation steps.

Booting off the CD or DVD

You typically begin the installation process by booting off the DVD or the first CD of the distribution. To do this, insert the accompanying DVD disc into your DVD-ROM drive or insert Disc 1 of your Fedora 2 distribution into your CD-ROM drive, and then restart the machine. The installation process should start automatically, as soon as the computer's power-on self-test is complete.

If you do not see a Fedora boot screen, it is quite likely that your computer is not configured to boot off the DVD-ROM or CD-ROM drive by default. In this case, you may need to adjust your machine's configuration by changing the boot sequence of your computer, so that it begins with the DVD-ROM or CD-ROM drive.

The best way to do this is to reboot your computer, and take it into the BIOS setup menu immediately after bootup. The exact way to access the BIOS setup menu varies from machine to machine, but it usually involves pressing a button such as F2, F10, or Escape. Check your motherboard's manual if you have it, or follow the instructions onscreen immediately after the reboot.

The boot screen dialog box asks you to select whether to install in *graphical* or *text mode*. Text mode is suitable in situations where a minimal configuration is required, or where there is a problem with the display. We will conduct our installation in graphical mode, so just press the *Enter* key.

When you've selected the mode of installation, the boot program proceeds by displaying a flurry of messages on the screen. Don't be alarmed by this—this is perfectly normal in a Linux operating system boot up. When Linux boots up, it stays in text mode briefly to perform a few routine checks and processes, and then launches the installation in graphical mode.

Testing the Media

Fedora presents you with a *media test module* prior to launching the installation process. The purpose of the media test module is to eliminate one of the most frequent sources of installation problems—defects in the DVD or the CDs. As shown in Figure 1-1, the module asks you whether you would like to test the DVD or CD media before proceeding with the installation.

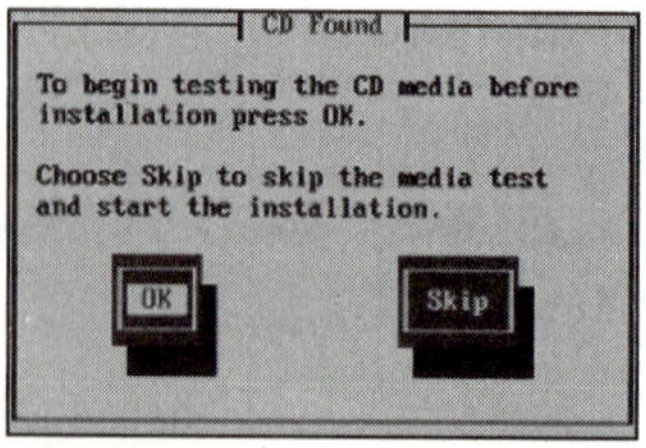

Figure 1-1

This module checks your installation DVD or CDs and informs you if it finds any problems reading their contents. If you have downloaded CD images and burned your own disks, it's definitely a good idea to check the validity of your disks at this point. You should generally have no issues with validity of the media if you are using the accompanying DVD disc.

If you want to skip this test (for example, if you're in a hurry or you already know that the disks are okay), select Skip, and go on to the next section.

Alternatively, to run the media check module (which we recommend if the disks have never been used before), press OK. This takes you to the CD Media Check screen, shown in Figure 1-2.

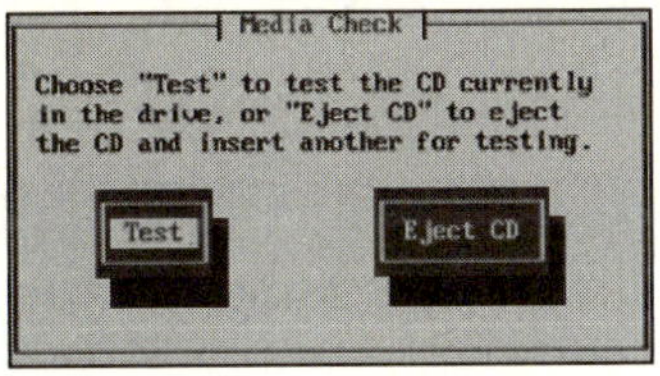

Figure 1-2

If you are using CDs, because the first disc is already in the drive, you can simply press Test to start the media test of the disc right away. If the test completes and doesn't find any errors, you'll see confirmation that the disc passed the test.

If you see an error message instead, it indicates that your CD or DVD is defective. This means that you'll need to arrange to replace it and restart the installation.

If you are using CDs, when Disc 1 has been tested, you will be prompted as to whether you want to insert any other discs for checking (see Figure 1-3).

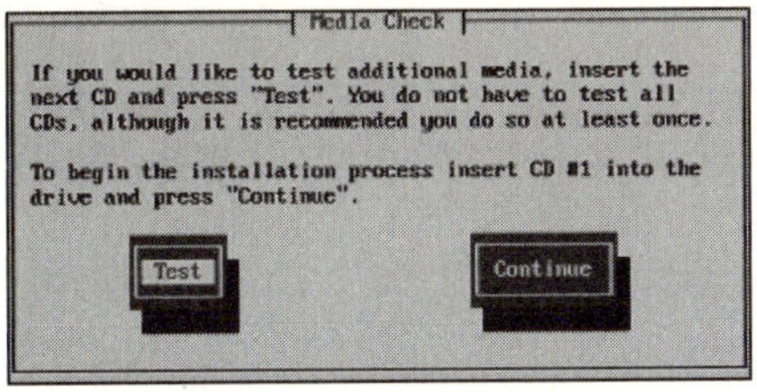

Figure 1-3

If you are using CDs, you should check all the remaining CDs, by pressing the Test button each time. When all of the CDs or the DVD has passed, you can press the Continue button to continue with the remainder of the installation.

The Graphical Installation Launch

Having tested all the CDs or the DVD (or skipped the test altogether), the Fedora 2 installer program, called *Anaconda*, begins, launching the graphical installer. It tries to detect the video card, monitor, and mouse.

> *Note that Anaconda has failed to detect the exact make and model of video card and monitor here, and so has opted for a configuration that it thinks should work. Its choice will probably not give the best performance, but it should at least see you through the installation process to the point at which you can use your checklist to adjust the hardware configuration details more precisely.*

Then it launches into the GUI install screen, as shown in Figure 1-4. Press Next (in the bottom-right corner) to continue to the next screen.

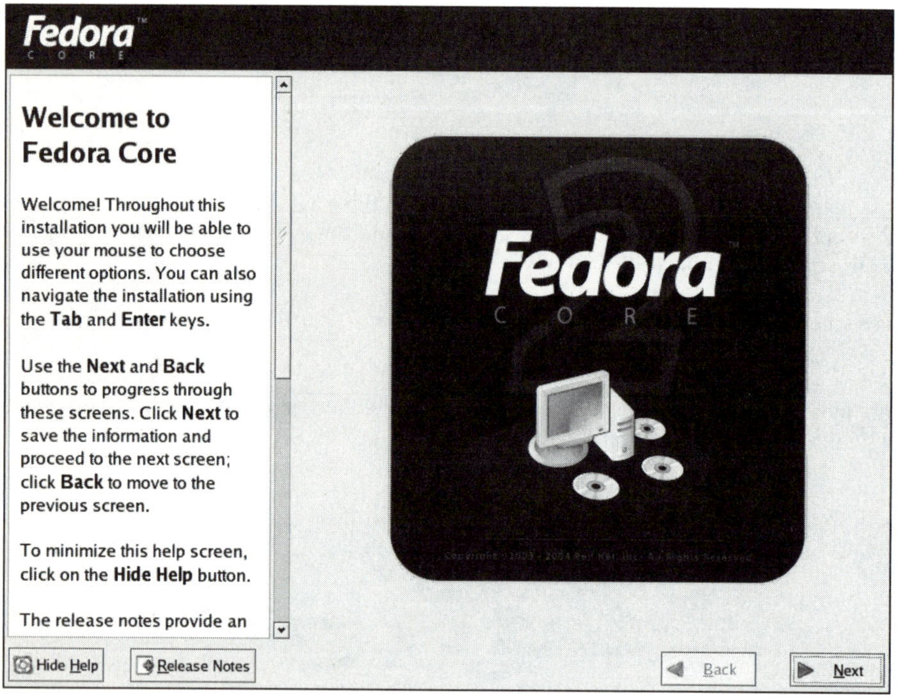

Figure 1-4

Selecting the Default Language

Fedora supports many languages other than English during the installation process. Those more comfortable with their native language can use the screen shown in Figure 1-5 to select a different language.

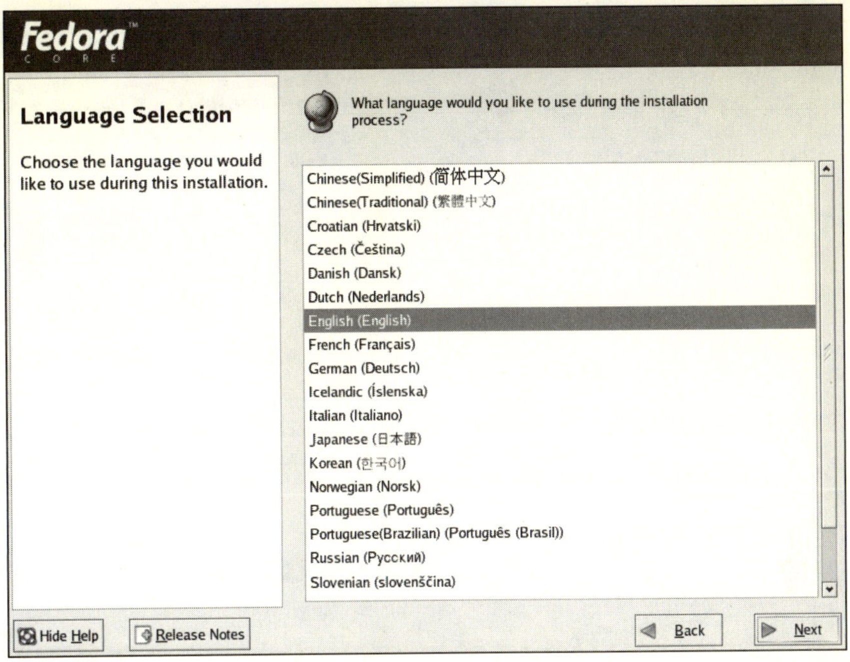

Figure 1-5

Note that many languages, notably those using various Asian Indic scripts, are missing from this list. The GUI toolkit used for developing the installation, GTK+, doesn't support the display of these languages. Fedora developers are continually adding local language support for the installation process and the desktop itself for various localities. If your language of choice is not listed here, you will probably see it added to this list in a future version of the distribution.

Selecting the Keyboard

For many non–English speaking countries, language-specific keyboards are available for the computer. These keyboards facilitate typing in the native language. Fedora 2 allows you to specify the keyboard layout of your choice, as shown in Figure 1-6.

Choose your preferred keyboard option (the screenshot shows a user selecting the default keyboard layout, U.S. English), and click Next to proceed to the next screen.

Selecting the Mouse

In the next screen, shown in Figure 1-7, Red Hat shows the list of mouse types that it supports.

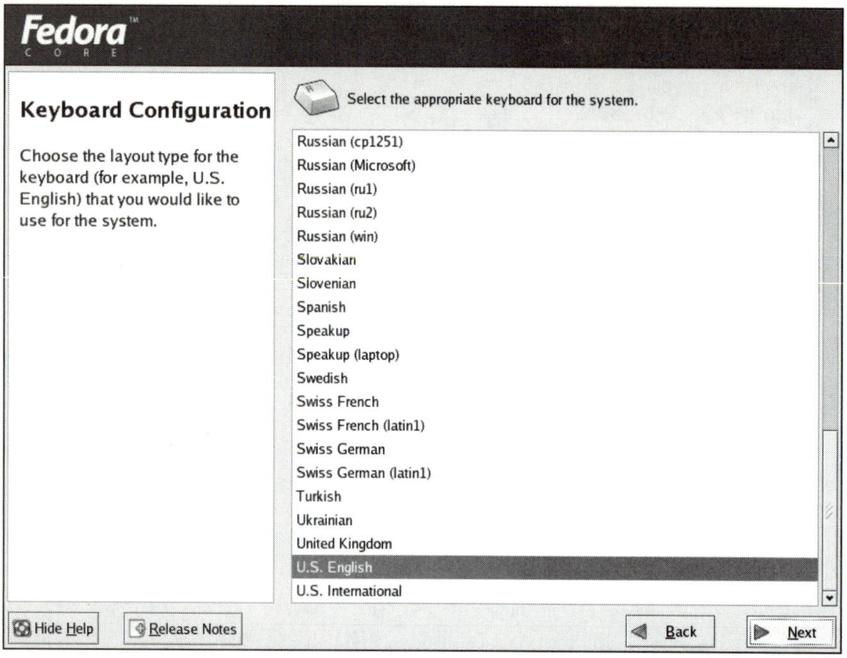

Figure 1-6

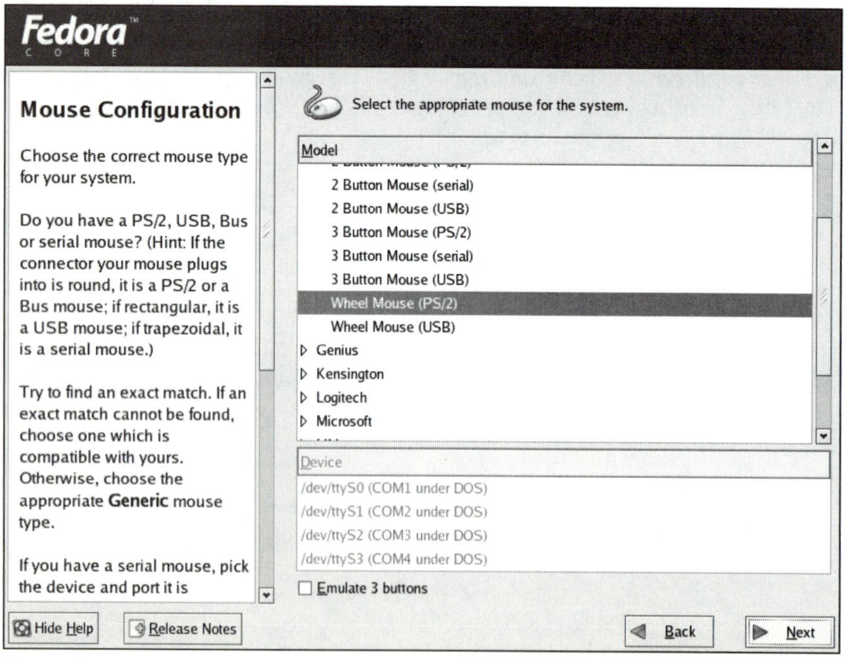

Figure 1-7

Fedora tries to detect and select the correct mouse type automatically for you. If everything goes well, you can just click Next to go on to the next screen.

Selecting an Installation Type

At this stage, the installation looks for an existing version of Fedora on your machine. If it finds one, it will invite you to choose between *upgrading* the existing version and *replacing* it. An upgrade takes less time, and allows you to preserve any existing data on your drives while bringing the software packages up to date with the latest distribution. By contrast, a replacement may overwrite your existing data but will provide a completely up-to-date installation. Here, we'll opt for a completely new installation.

As mentioned at the beginning of this chapter, we will use a Personal Desktop installation for our machine. So, select the Personal Desktop option (see Figure 1-8), and click Next to proceed to the next screen.

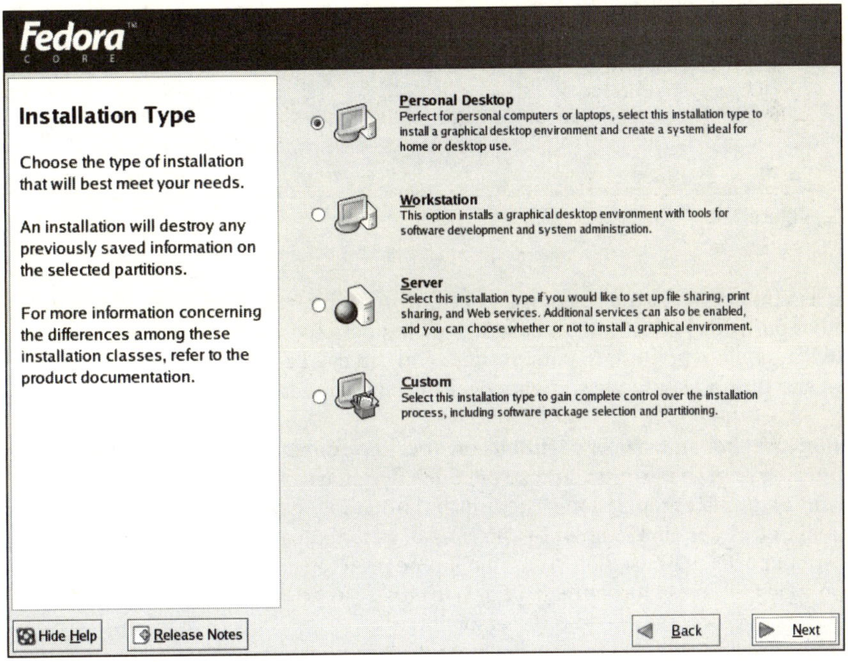

Figure 1-8

Setting Up the Disk Partitions

The next screen allows you to organize the storage space on your machine's hard disk (see Figure 1-9).

The space on your hard disk is normally divided into sections, called *partitions*, for better management of the space. Dividing a hard disk into partitions can help you segregate the available disk space according to its usage.

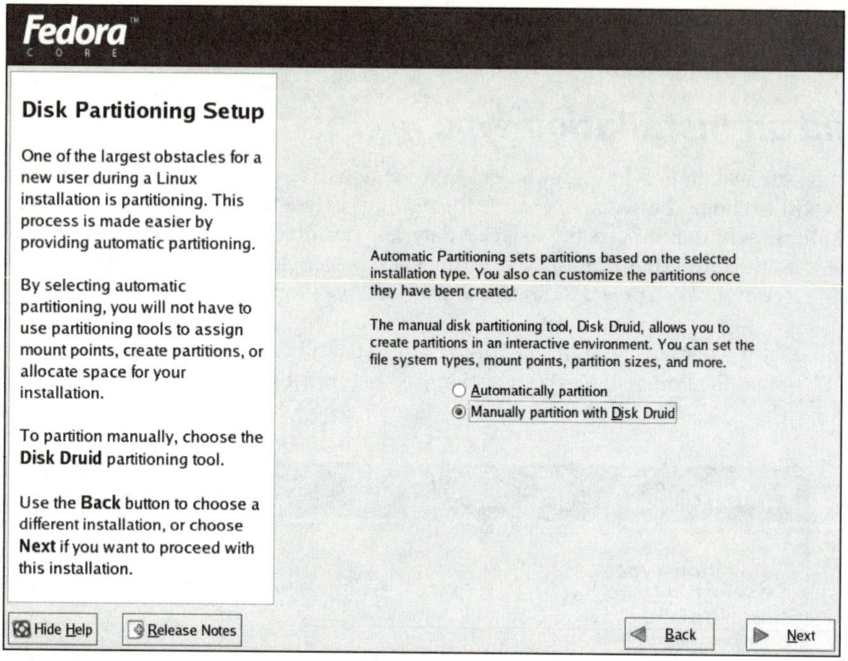

Figure 1-9

For example, you might choose to dedicate one partition solely to your executable programs, and to set aside another partition just to hold your work-related data files. This type of organization has the advantage that when you are upgrading your system, you can ask Fedora 2 to leave the *data* partition of your disk alone, and upgrade only the software packages installed in the *other* partitions.

The optimum number and size of partitions on your disk depends on many factors—the overall disk size, the purpose of each partition, and so on. Such decisions are usually made on anticipated future requirements and data organization structure, and often rely heavily on previous experience. However, Fedora 2 makes this decision simpler by offering an automatic partitioning option, which creates an arrangement of partitions based on your install type preferences. So, if you chose the Personal Desktop installation type in the previous screen, your hard disk can be automatically reorganized into partitions that are likely to be used for day-to-day personal work.

Fedora 2 also offers an option for creating partitions manually, and if you feel comfortable and confident with creating your own partitions, feel free to do so. However, it is normally safe enough to accept the default automatic partition option, and that's what we'll do here.

Installing a Dual-Boot System

Read this section only if you wish to install Fedora such that both Fedora and Microsoft Windows co-exist on the same machine; if not, skip to the next section, "Dealing with Existing Partitions."

WARNING: If you intend to install Fedora 2 on a computer such that it co-exists with either Microsoft Windows 2000 or Microsoft Windows XP, you may run into a bug that could corrupt your computer's Master Boot Record (MBR). Please read the advisory on this issue posted on the Wrox Web site (www.wrox.com) before you proceed any further.

Some of us may want to install Fedora on a computer such that it coexists with another operating system. This is what is known as a dual-boot setup. At boot time, you are presented with a choice of operating systems to boot into. A typical dual-boot system consists of a Microsoft Windows operating system coexisting with a Linux system.

You need to set up the partitions on your hard disk before you can install a dual-boot system. Here are the steps to follow:

1. First of all, you need to make space for the Fedora installation. Typically, Microsoft Windows is already installed on the machine, resulting in a couple of scenarios:

   SCENARIO A: Entire hard disk is occupied by Microsoft Windows partitions: In this case, you need to ensure that there is enough space left on the machine to install Fedora. If the Microsoft Windows installation has multiple partitions, be prepared to give up one or more of them to make space for the Fedora installation. This means copying files from these partitions to the ones that you intend to keep. For example, if the system had a 40GB hard disk, partitioned into drives C: and D:, each a 20GB partition, you could copy all the files from D: to C: to make way for Fedora on the partition currently occupied by drive D:. *Caution:* Remember that all contents of D: in this case will be lost forever once Fedora is installed on that partition. If you do not have enough space to copy all of the content of the second drive (D:, in this case) to the first drive (C:), you may want to use a re-partitioning program such as Partition Magic(`www.powerquest.com/partitionmagic/`) to re-partition the hard disk without loss of data.

   SCENARIO B: Hard disk has Microsoft Windows partitions and some unpartitioned space: In some cases, there may be unpartitioned, free space on the disk. If enough space is left on the system that has not yet been partitioned as a Microsoft Windows drive, you would not need to copy files and free up partitions. You can check the free space information either during the Fedora installation process or from Microsoft Windows. For example, to check the free space available on a drive on Microsoft Windows 2000, go to Start Menu ➪ Programs ➪ Accessories ➪ System Tools ➪ System Information. Expand Components ➪ Storage ➪ Drives and check for the free space available on the drives.

2. Continue with the Fedora installation as previously described. Once you get to the point where the drives need to be partitioned, you need to take appropriate action based on your hard disk layout.

   SCENARIO A: If your hard disk layout resembles Scenario A from Step 1, choose the Manually partition with Disk Druid option (see Figure 1-10) and click Next. Go to Step 3.

   SCENARIO B: If the hard disk layout resembles Scenario B from Step 1, choose the "Automatically partition" option, as shown in Figure 1-11. Go to Step 3.

3. **SCENARIO A:** Figure 1-12 shows a typical layout for this scenario. The hard disk `/dev/hda` has two partitions, `/dev/hda1`, which in this case is the Microsoft Windows C: drive, and `/dev/hda2`, the D: drive, which in this case has been freed up to install Fedora on. You need to delete `/dev/hda2` so that the space used by it is freed up for creating the Fedora partitions. You can delete `/dev/hda2` by highlighting the line corresponding to `/dev/hda2` and clicking the Delete button. Go to Step 4.

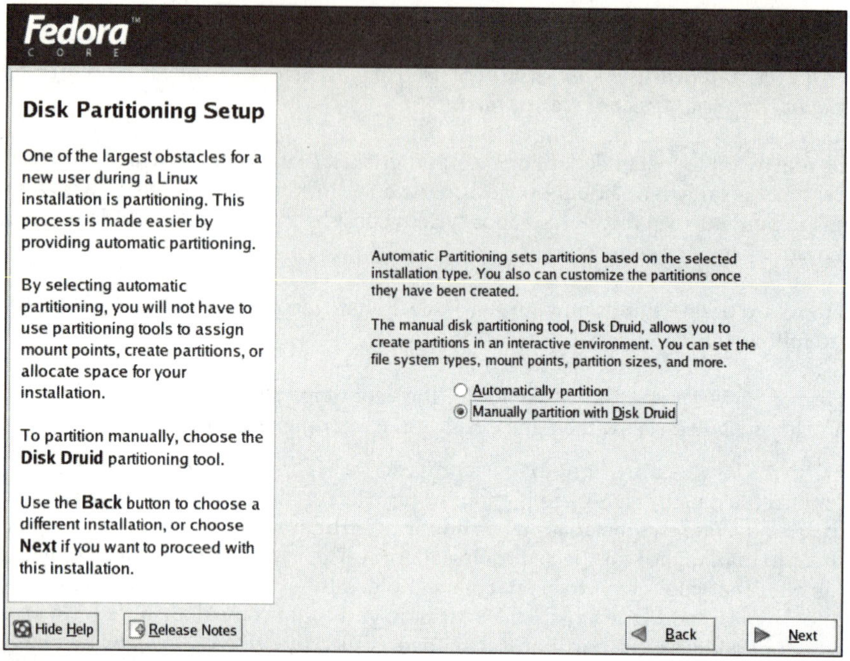

Figure 1-10

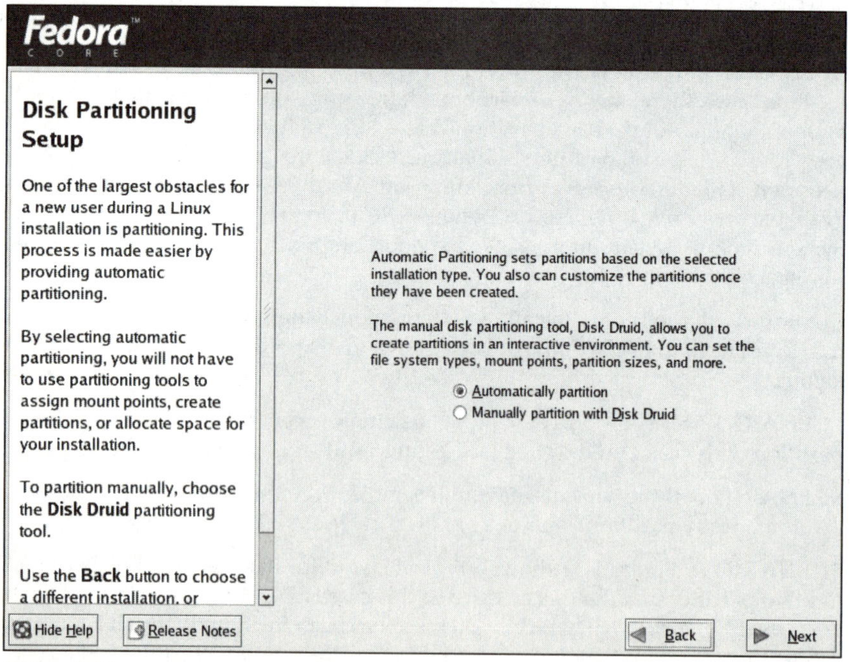

Figure 1-11

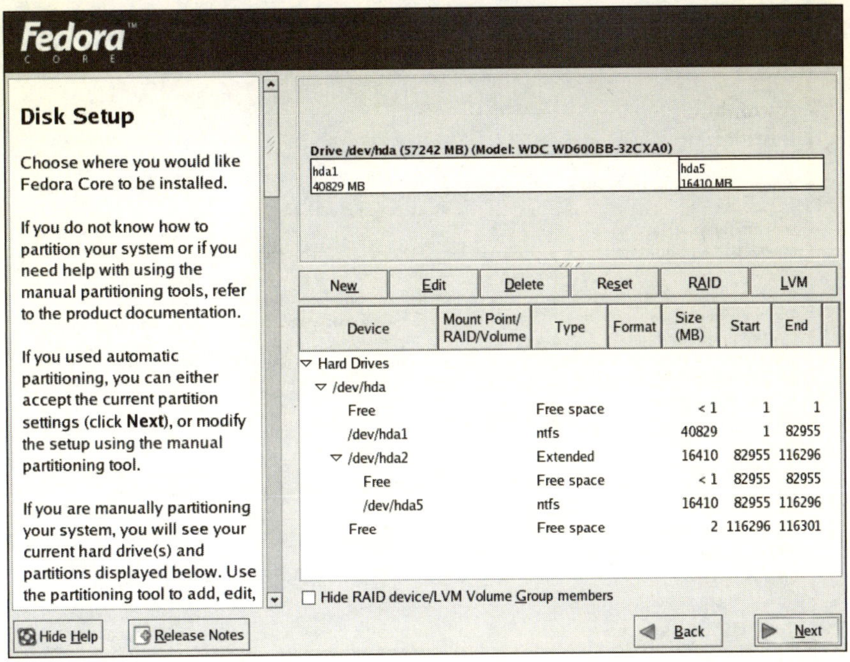

Figure 1-12

SCENARIO B: Choose the "Keep all partitions and reuse existing free space" option and click Next, as shown in Figure 1-13. Accept all the default options until you get to the boot loader screen. In other words, you may skip the rest of this section and go on to the section titled "Setting Up the Boot Loader."

4. **SCENARIO A:** Now you need to create partitions for Fedora to use. Fedora needs at least two partitions, one for the operating system files, also known as the *root partition*, and a second partition known as the *swap partition* for storing some system runtime information when Fedora Linux is booted. Start off by creating the swap partition. To create a new partition, click the New button and specify the File System Type as swap from the drop-down menu (see Figure 1-14). For size, the general rule of thumb is roughly twice the size of the physical memory. So, if you had 0.5GB of RAM, you would allocate a swap partition of 1GB.

   After you finish, a new entry for the swap partition should be created, as shown in Figure 1-15.

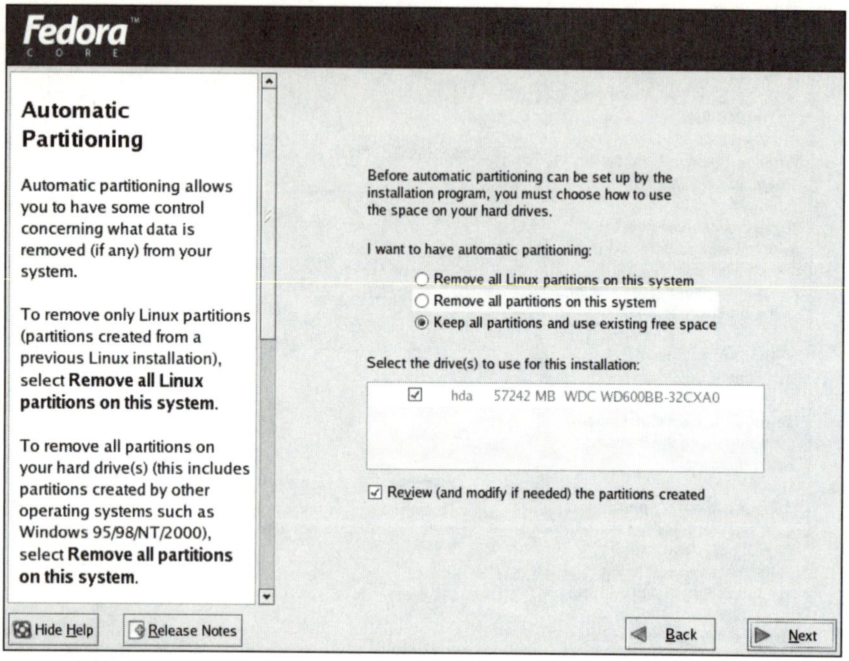

Figure 1-13

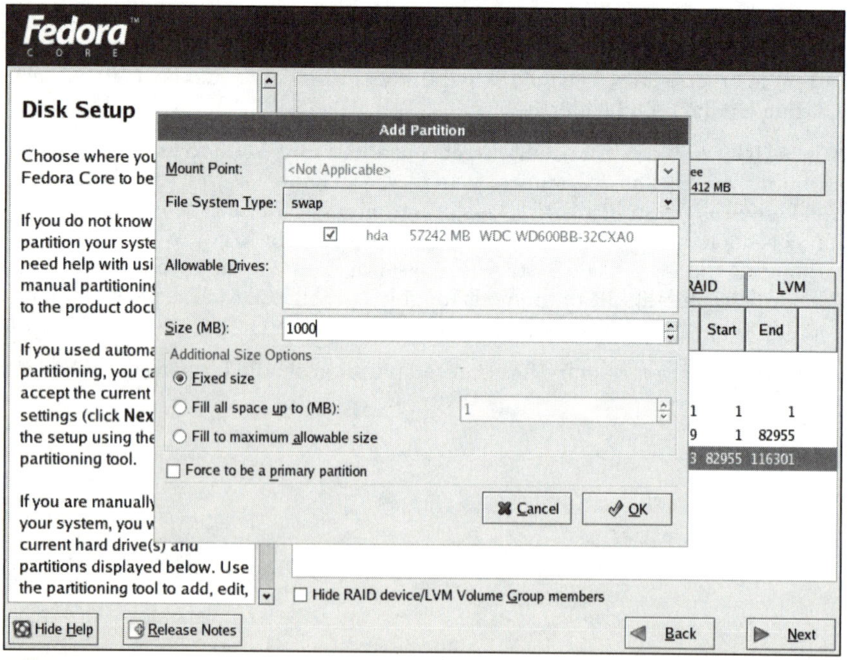

Figure 1-14

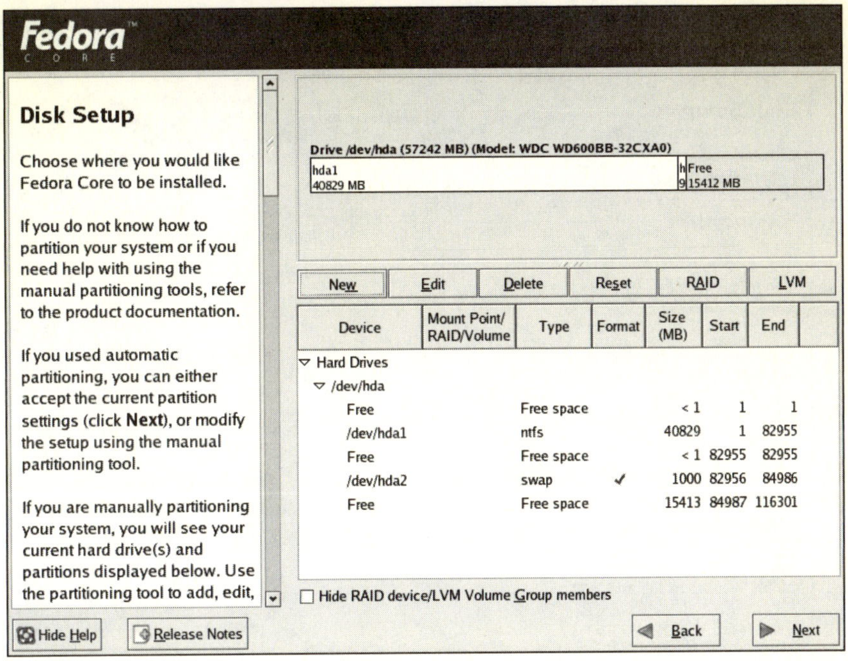

Figure 1-15

5. **SCENARIO A:** Now you need to create the actual partition for the Fedora files to reside on, that is, the /root filesystem. As before, click New, but this time choose ext3 as the File System Type. You can specify the option "Fill to maximum allowable size" to allow the rest of the disk to be used (see Figure 1-16).

   This should result in a screen resembling the one shown in Figure 1-17.

   Click Next until you get to the screen that says Boot Loader Configuration. Once you get to this screen, skip to the section of the chapter titled "Setting the Boot Loader."

Dealing with Existing Partitions

You may skip this section if you are installing a dual-boot system (as explained in the previous section).

If you already have partitions on your disk, you can use the screen shown in Figure 1-18 to remove the older partitions.

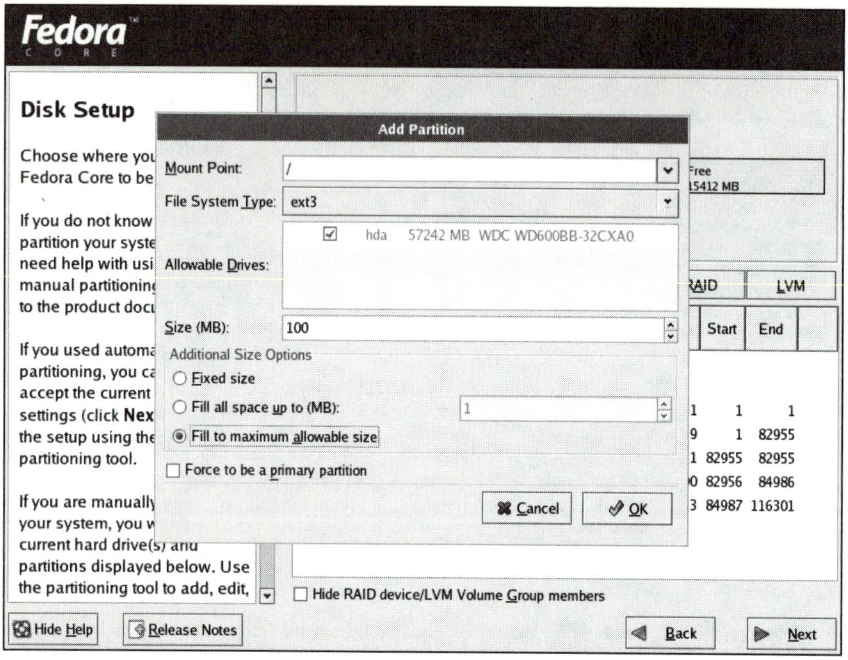

Figure 1-16

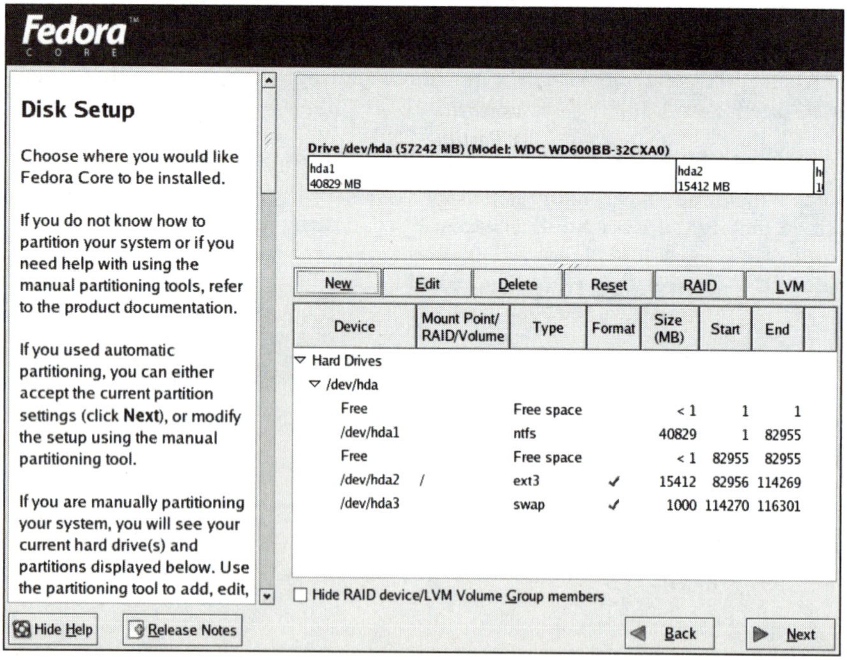

Figure 1-17

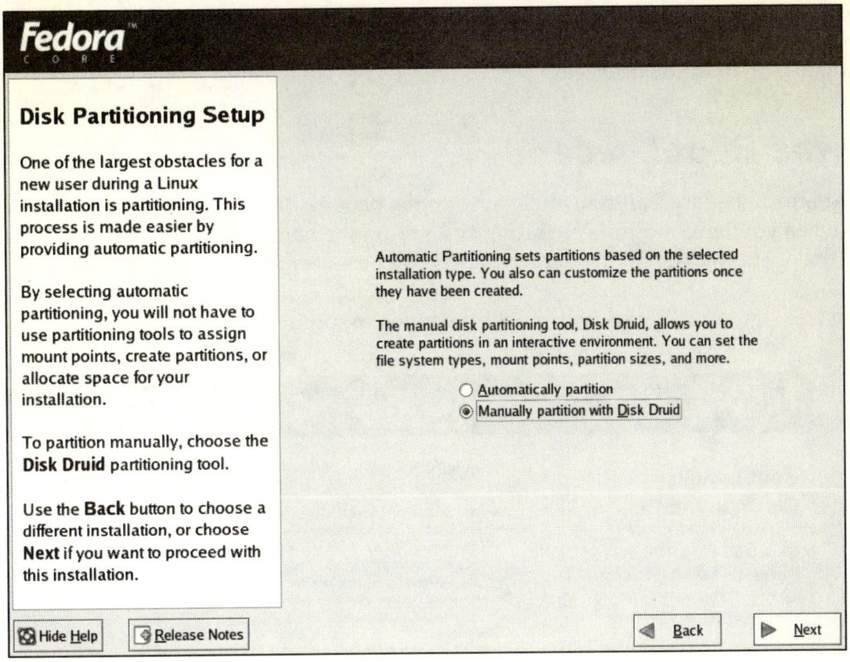

Figure 1-18

Unless you have data left on the disk, it is normally safe to accept the removal of existing partitions on the disk, by clicking the Next button.

> *If your machine has an existing Windows partition that you want to keep, you should note that it's not sufficient to choose the Remove all Linux Partitions option here. Rather, you will need to go back to the Disk Partitioning screen, and configure your partitions manually using the Disk Druid tool. You may even need to resize your Windows partition using a partitioning utility, such as PartitionMagic, to create some free space onto which you can install Fedora 2.*

If you have existing partitions, and you have asked Fedora 2 to remove them for you, you will be asked to confirm your desire to remove the partitions (see Figure 1-19).

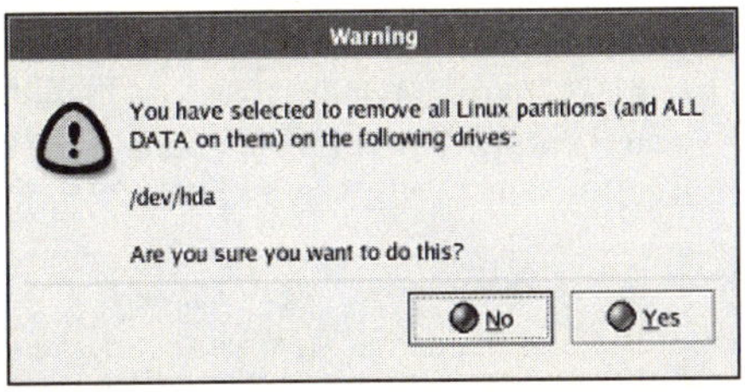

Figure 1-19

Before accepting the removal of the partitions, be aware that removal of partitions leads to complete loss of any existing data on the disk. If you are sure about your decision, confirm the deletion (by clicking Yes), and move on to the next screen.

Setting the Boot Loader

In the next screen, Fedora 2 allows you to set various boot loader options. A *boot loader* is normally required when you have multiple operating systems on the hard disk, and an option (at boot time) for choosing the operating system to boot from. Red Hat provides the *GRUB* boot loader for this purpose.

The screen (see Figure 1-20) provides you with an option to specify the *default* operating system to boot from.

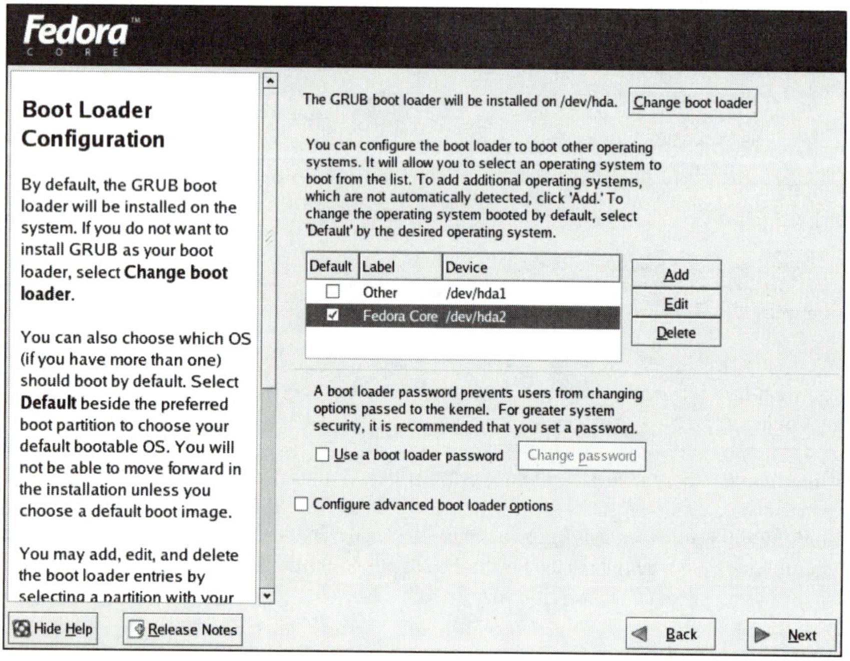

Figure 1-20

In this example, you see two options: Fedora Core and Other. The Other entry represents the Microsoft Windows OS installed on the machine. If you have only Fedora installed on the machine, you would see only the Fedora Core option. If you have the Other entry, you can click Edit and change the name of the option to something more intuitive, such as '"Windows XP" or '"Windows 2000."

You can also set a *boot loader password* in this screen. A boot loader password prevents others from modifying the boot time parameters of the Linux kernel. Any user can, for example, boot the computer into a maintenance mode and then change the root password, thereby taking control of the entire computer. If your computer is unlikely to be handled by others, or if you implicitly trust others who will be using this computer, you can safely ignore this option. If you set a boot loader password, you should keep the password safely in your personal records.

In most situations, you will not need to change anything in this screen. You can just click Next to move on.

Setting the Network Parameters

The installation process now takes you into the Network Configuration section (see Figure 1-21). Your network configuration checklist will come in handy in this section.

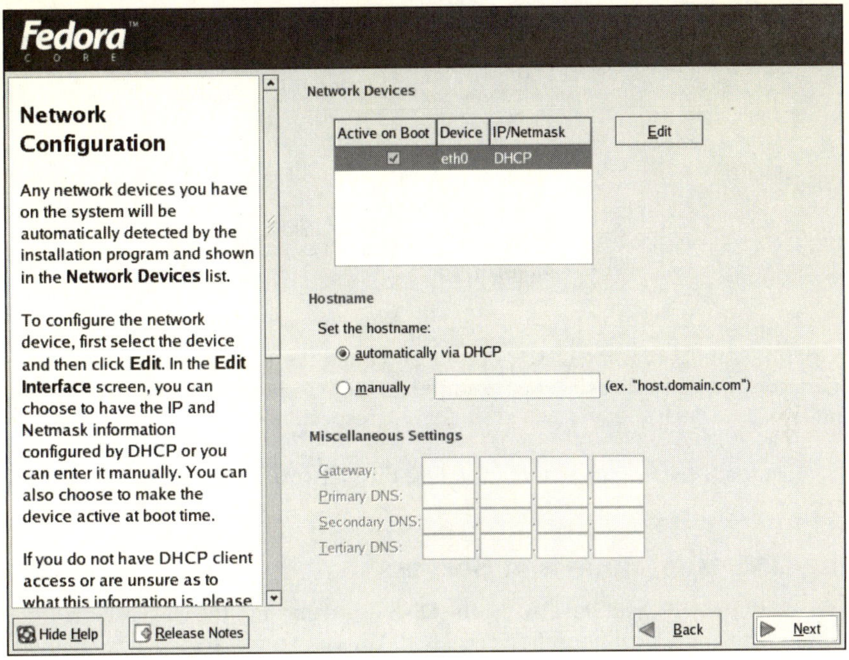

Figure 1-21

Note that if Fedora 2 does not detect your network card automatically, your Network Devices table (at the top of the screen) might be empty. This will prevent you from setting the network parameters for your computer. If that happens, don't panic; all the network parameters on the screen can be configured after the installation process is complete, via the Network Configuration dialog box (Main Menu ➪ System Settings ➪ Network).

By default, Fedora 2 selects automatic network configuration of your computer using the *DHCP protocol*. Therefore, if you have a single desktop at a home or office environment, or if your machine exists in a LAN environment whose IP addresses are provided by a DHCP server, you can skip this screen and proceed to the Firewall screen that comes next.

However, if your machine exists in a LAN environment that requires static IP addresses, you have an opportunity now to set your network configuration.

Again, you don't have to do this now; if you prefer, you can skip the network configuration at this stage and configure your network settings after the installation is complete, via the Network Configuration dialog box.

Manually Configuring the Network Devices

If you choose to do it now, you can use your network configuration checklist to fill up the entries on the screen. First, click the Edit button at the top section of the screen to bring up the network device configuration dialog box (see Figure 1-22).

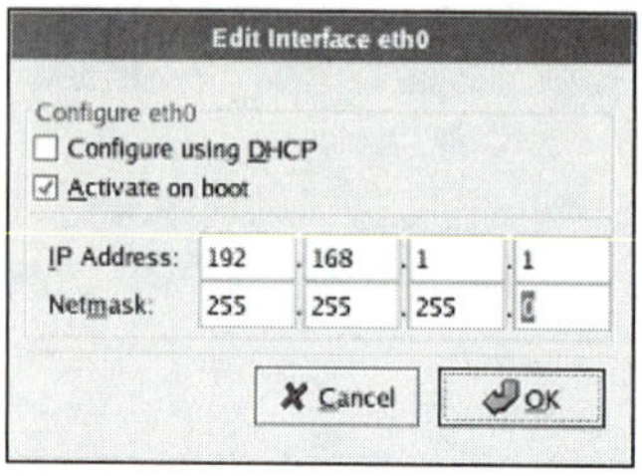

Figure 1-22

Here, deselect the Configure using DHCP option, and enter the IP Address and Netmask details as per your network configuration checklist. For example, in the screenshot we have set the IP address and the network mask to `192.168.1.1` and `255.255.255.0`, respectively.

When you've set the network parameters, click OK; the Network Devices section will now reflect your new settings.

Configuring DNS Hostname and Servers

While you're on this screen, you can also set the DNS hostname and the DNS servers (which you should have noted in your network configuration checklist). You can specify these values in the appropriate entry boxes near the bottom of the screen.

Setting Up the Firewall

The next screen of the installation relates to the setup of a *network firewall* for your machine. A network firewall protects your computer from attacks or intrusions from malicious hackers in the network; you'll learn more about configuring firewalls in Chapter 12. For now, Fedora 2 provides you with two options for network firewall security:

- **Enable firewall:** This option is suitable for those who are quite concerned about their security. Here, all incoming network connections are disallowed unless specifically listed in the services list on the screen. To facilitate normal working, only two exceptions are made—incoming DHCP connections are allowed so that the machine can configure itself, and incoming DNS replies are allowed so that Internet applications can work normally.
- **No firewall:** If you are unlikely to connect to the Internet, or if you are not concerned with hackers and malicious programs, you can select this option (see Figure 1-23). This option doesn't set up any firewall on your machine. In other words, it allows any outside individuals to access network resources on your computer.

Selecting the No firewall option doesn't necessarily mean that all users on the network have direct and unchecked access to your computer's network resources. A firewall is just the first line of defense against intruders. Most network applications have some form of access control that decides who finally gets to use these resources.

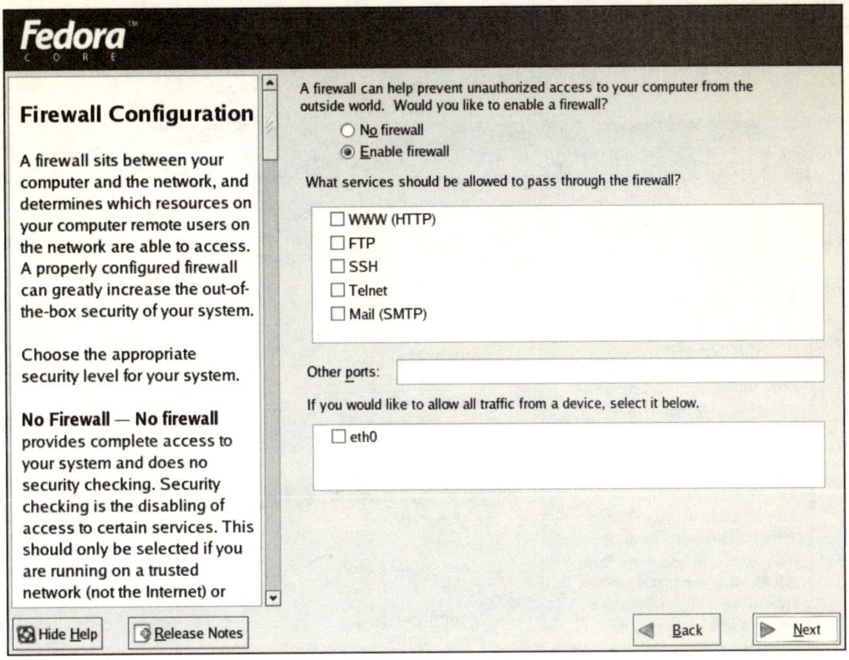

Figure 1-23

You can also customize the firewall rules within these different levels of security. Fedora 2 allows you to select the trusted devices, network interfaces that are expected to carry traffic from sources that you can trust blindly. In a home network this would generally be the interface card connected to the rest of your home network. You should definitely not mark your Internet interfaces as trusted, unless you are absolutely sure about your security needs.

Apart from these devices, this screen also allows you to specify network services that external network identities will be able to access from your computer. To be on the safe side, select only the services that you actually expect to be used, and that do not have insecure software behind them. For example:

- Secure Shell (SSH) allows you to work on a remote machine while ensuring that the data exchanged in the process is kept encrypted and secure. It is generally safe for SSH servers to be open; indeed, this is recommended if you want to be able to access your computer from other machines.
- If you want to use this machine to receive mails from others, you may choose to have an SMTP server on your machine receive these mails. In this case, you should allow incoming connections to the SMTP server.
- Many FTP servers have had a long history of insecurities. It is advisable to leave incoming connections to such FTP services closed, and open them up in the firewall only when you need them. When you've finished, you should immediately cut off their access using the firewall.

Setting Additional Language Support

If you're expecting to use multiple languages, you can select them in the next screen (see Figure 1-24).

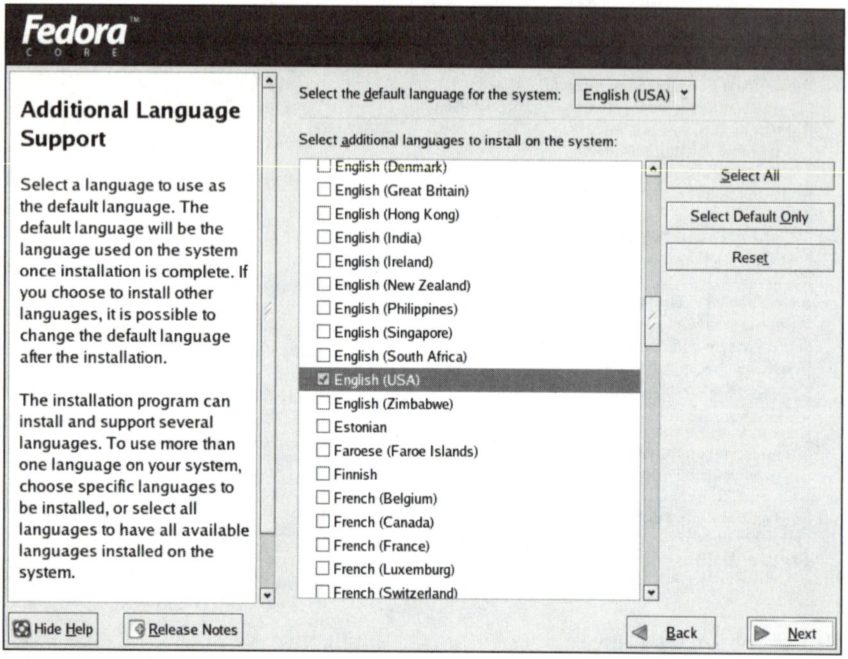

Figure 1-24

Generally, it is safe to continue to the next screen after accepting the defaults that are offered by the Fedora 2 installer.

Setting the Time Zone

In the next screen (see Figure 1-25), you can set the time zone of your location.

Fedora provides a very usable graphical method for selecting your time zone. To use it, bring your cursor to any point on the displayed world map—this allows you to set the time zone of your computer to that of the selected region. A green sticky arrow in the mouse cursor makes the job easier by selecting the city time zone nearest to the cursor. In the preceding screenshot, we have set the time zone to that of New York.

Note the option at the bottom of the screen to enable UTC time in the computer clock. This allows the system to run with correct time zone and daylight saving changes. (Note that you shouldn't use this if you have a dual-boot machine that also boots Windows.)

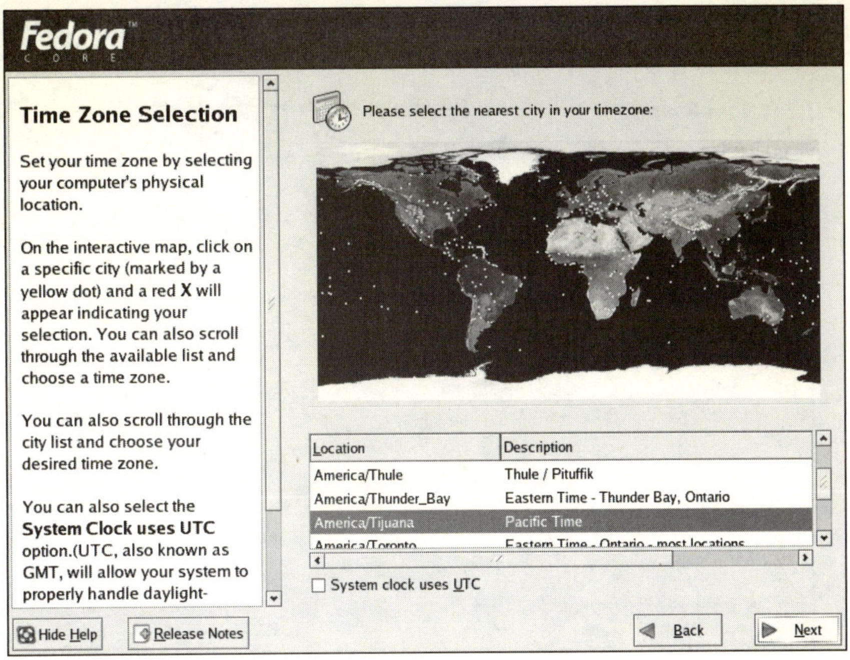

Figure 1-25

Root Account Configuration

By default, the installation process creates a single administrative user account for your machine, called *root*. You'll learn more about the system's users in subsequent chapters of the book, particularly Chapter 8. For now, all you need to know is that whenever you use the system, you do so through the context of a *user account*, and that to do so you log in by specifying the user account's name and a password.

Every user account on the system has its own password, and the root user (or super user) is no different in this respect. In the screen shown in Figure 1-26, you are asked to supply the root user's password.

You are asked to type the password twice, to confirm that you didn't mistype the first time.

You might encounter a message that tells you that the password is too short or too simple. This is a security feature, designed to remind you of the importance of choosing an unguessable password. If you consider your chosen password to be adequate for your needs, you can ignore these messages. However, for the sake of security, you should make an effort to set an uncommon password for the super user account. Password security (and the techniques that people use for breaking passwords) is discussed in greater detail in Chapters 8 and 12.

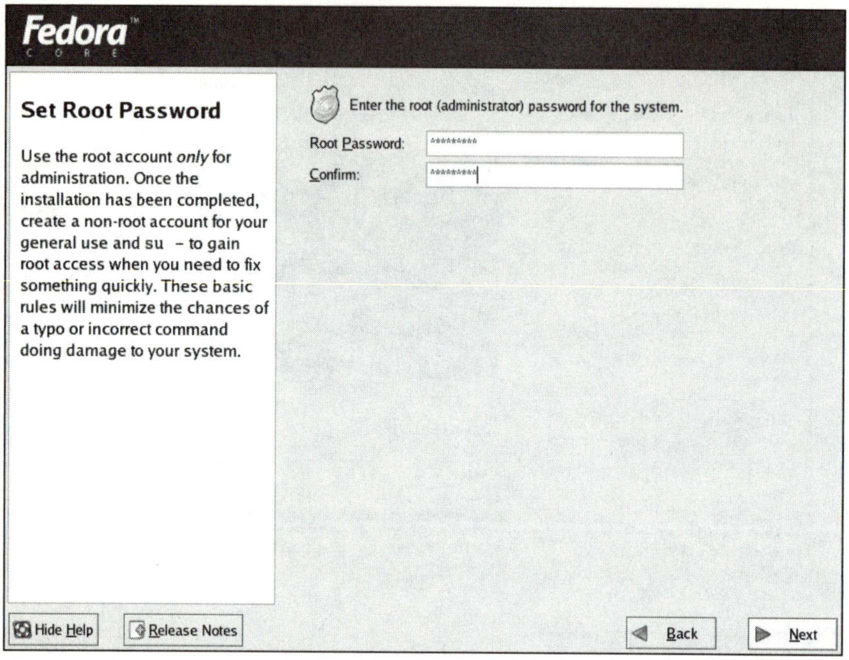

Figure 1-26

Selecting Packages for Installation

Now, you have an opportunity to choose the software packages that you want installed along with the system. Fedora 2 has already chosen a combination of software packages for the installation type that you selected at the beginning of the installation process. If you want to fine-tune the package selection, you can do so here by selecting the "Customize software packages to be installed" option (see Figure 1-27).

You don't have to fiddle with the choice of installed packages here—it's easy to add and remove packages after the installation is complete, as you'll see in Chapter 4. So, to keep things simple, select the Accept the current packages list option here, and proceed to the next screen.

The Automatic Installation Process

The Fedora 2 graphical installation tool has now collected all the information that it needs to begin the installation. The next screen, shown in Figure 1-28, prompts you to begin the software installation.

The software package installation is mostly automatic; the only thing you need to do at this stage, if you are using CDs, is change the CDs a couple of times (when prompted to do so) and admire the photographs that are displayed while the necessary packages are installed.

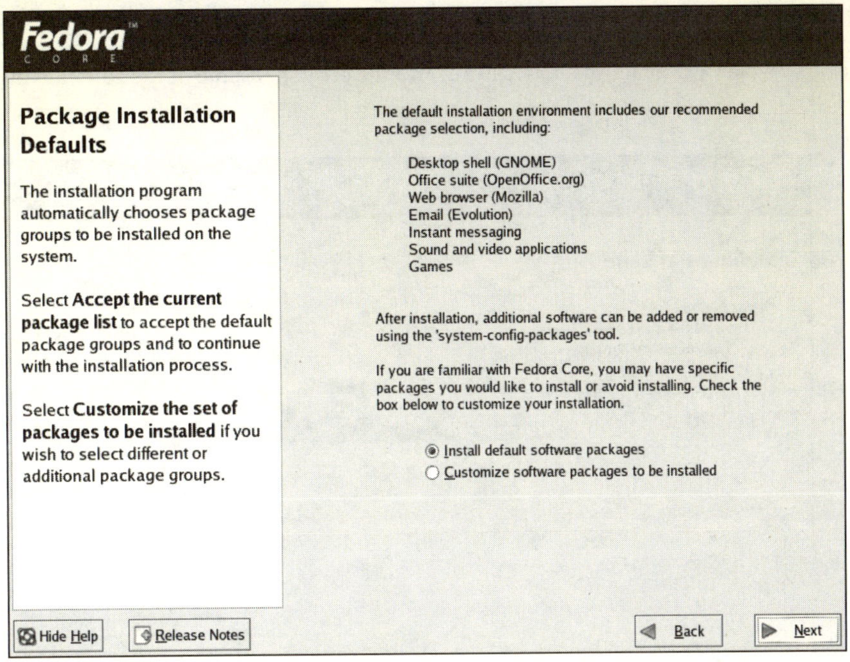

Figure 1-27

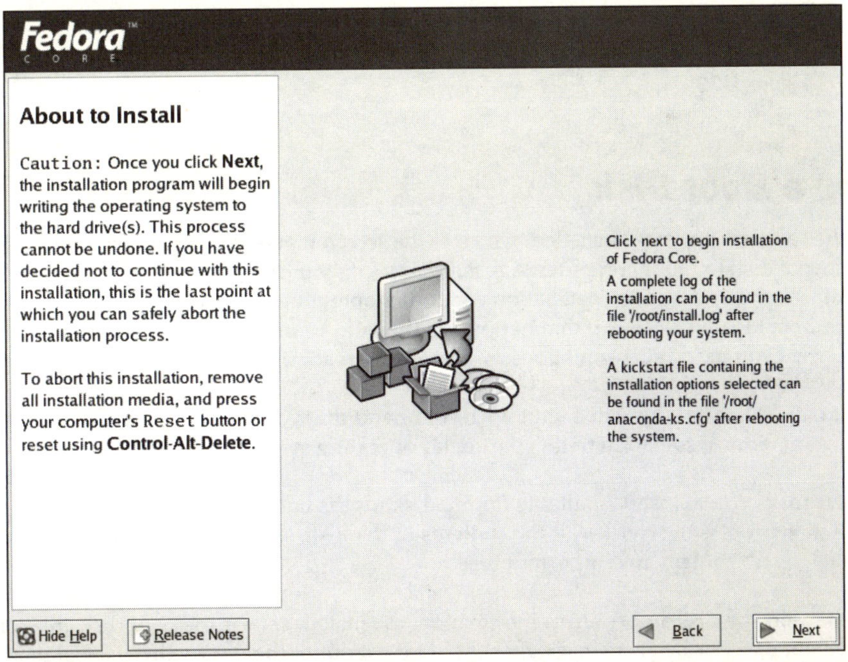

Figure 1-28

Before the software is installed, the installation process formats all the partitions that are supposed to hold these programs. Then, the installation process continues as the software packages are installed. Progress bars display the total time taken so far, and the estimated time of the software installation (see Figure 1-29).

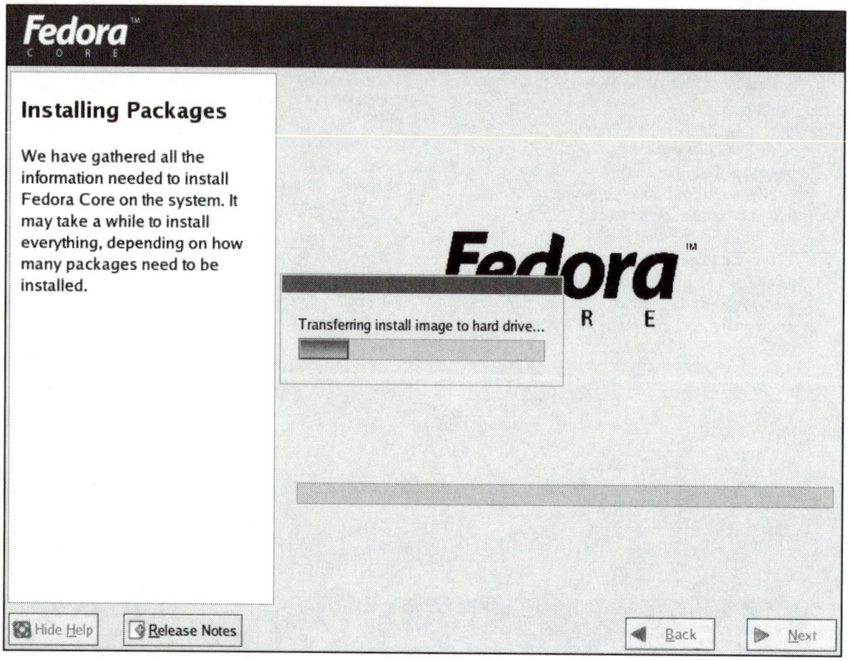

Figure 1-29

Creating a Boot Disk

With all the software packages installed, we go to the screen where you are asked whether you would like to create a boot disk for your computer. A *boot disk* is a safety measure against problems that might occur in the boot loader. For example, installation of another operating system in the computer might overwrite the Fedora 2 boot loader, GRUB; if that happened, it would be impossible to boot back into Linux. The boot disk helps you tackle such situations by providing an alternative way to boot into Linux.

You don't have to create a boot disk, but we recommend that you do (unless you already have a boot disk from a previous installation of this particular operating system).

The installer asks you to insert a suitable floppy disk for the boot disk creation process. Remember that the installation process overwrites all the contents of the disk, so you should provide a blank floppy disk or one that doesn't contain any important files.

When you insert the disk and confirm the creation, the installer starts the boot disk creation process. When the boot disk has been created, you should take it out of the floppy drive, label it, and put it in a safe place.

Finishing

This completes the installation of the Fedora 2 operating system. Now, you need to remove any CDs or DVDs and floppy disks from their respective drives, and click the Reboot button to reboot the machine (see Figure 1-30).

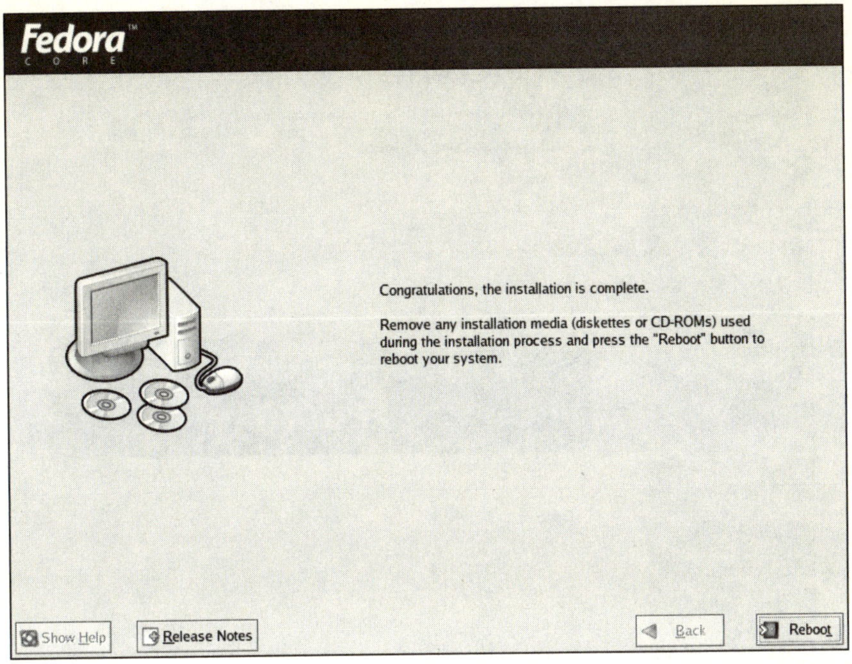

Figure 1-30

Booting Up

When the computer restarts, the boot loader takes over initially.

The boot loader shows the available operating systems to boot from. If you have a dual-boot machine, you would be presented with the choice of booting into either of the operating systems, that is, Microsoft Windows or Fedora. You can change the default choice using the arrow keys. The selected operating system will be booted automatically within a few seconds; you can hasten the process by pressing the *Enter* key. If you choose Fedora, this screen should be followed by a long list of rapidly moving text messages, as Fedora boots into its new installation.

First Boot

Before the new installation is fully usable, Red Hat configures the last few parameters:

- Setting up new user accounts
- Setting the date and time

- ❑ Configuring the system for the Red Hat Network
- ❑ Selecting additional distribution software or documentation to be installed

The Welcome screen (see Figure 1-31) shows the list of parameters to be configured. Click Next to move on to the first of these screens.

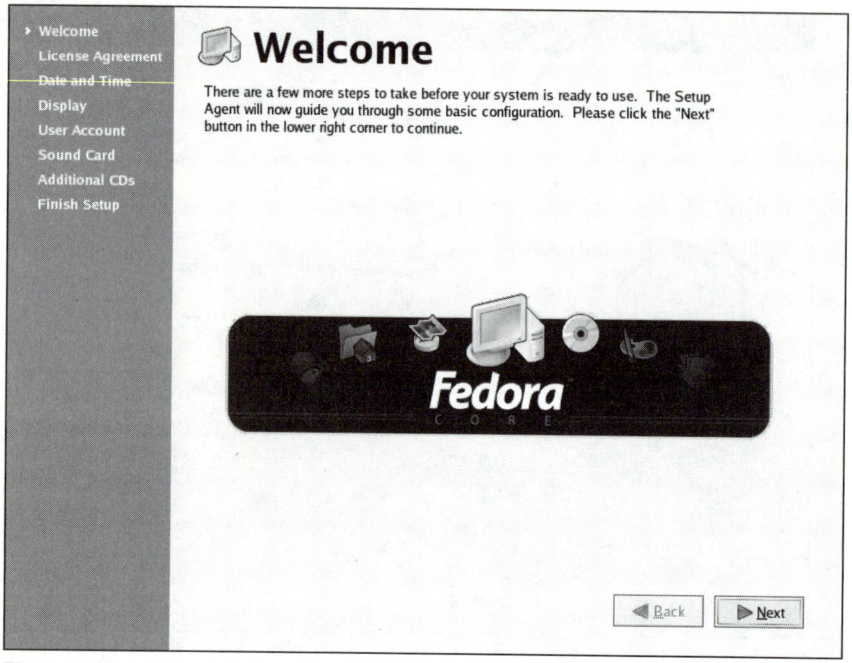

Figure 1-31

Setting the Date and Time

Next, check (and, if necessary, set) the date and time for the computer (see Figure 1-32).

As you can see, this page has a fairly intuitive calendar interface, and you can set the time using the entry fields toward the right of the screen.

Over a period of time, the clock in the computer tends to drift away from the actual time of the computer. To keep the clock in sync, you can use the Network Time Protocol (NTP) option in the same screen—this allows you to specify an NTP server, and the machine will keep in sync with it.

You can find a public NTP server on the Internet at `www.ntp.org`.

Display Settings

Normally, Fedora does a good job of automatically detecting the best resolution and color depth for your display. If you are dissatisfied with automatic settings, you can change the resolution and color depth of your screen display by choosing one of the options from the drop-down menus (see Figure 1-33).

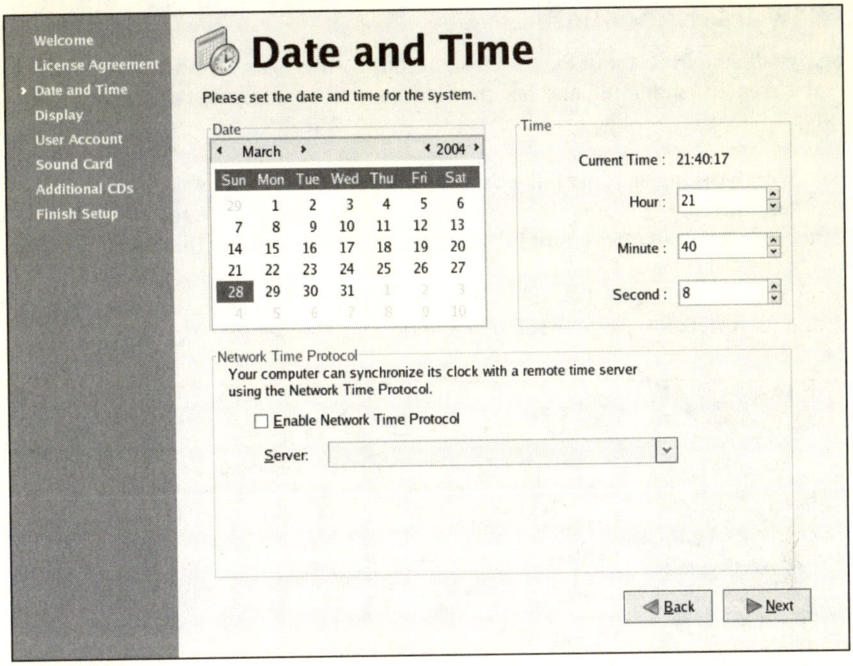

Figure 1-32

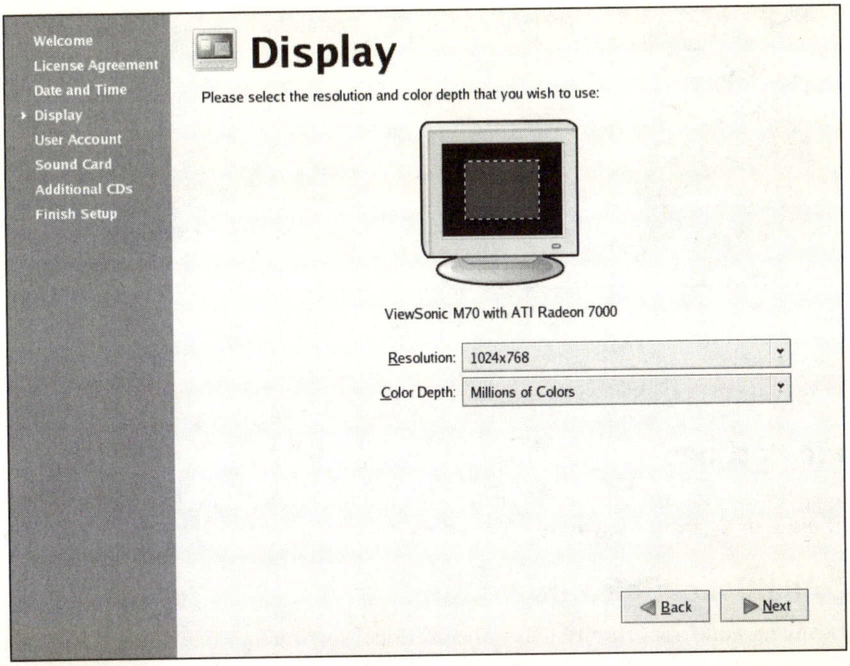

Figure 1-33

Creating New User Accounts

We've already talked a little about the root user account—this is an administrative (or "super user") account that is created by default, and has privileges for performing just about any task that you need on the computer.

The problem with working as root all the time is that these privileges make it very easy to accidentally delete important files that you don't mean to delete. For this reason, we recommend that you create a "normal" (non-administrative) account for your personal use, and use that most of the time.

The following screen (see Figure 1-34) allows you to do that; you just need to choose a username and password, and (if you like) type your full name, too.

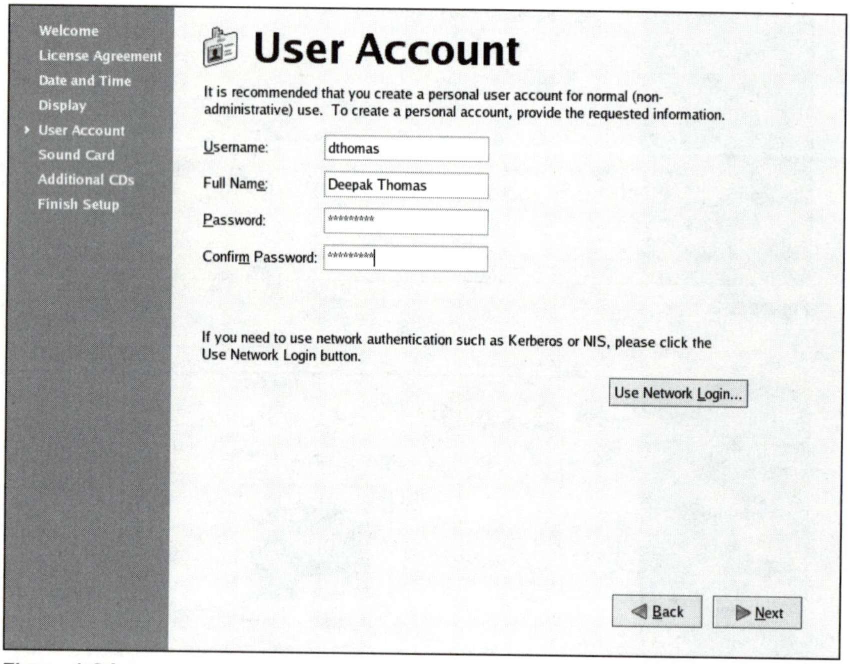

Figure 1-34

When you've done that, click Next to continue.

Sound Card Settings

In this screen the sound card is tested to ensure that it works (see Figure 1-35). Click "Play test sound" to verify that the sound card does work under Fedora 2.

Installing Additional Software

You've already had one opportunity to install additional software and documentation from the range of material available on the Fedora Web site, and now you get another chance (see Figure 1-36).

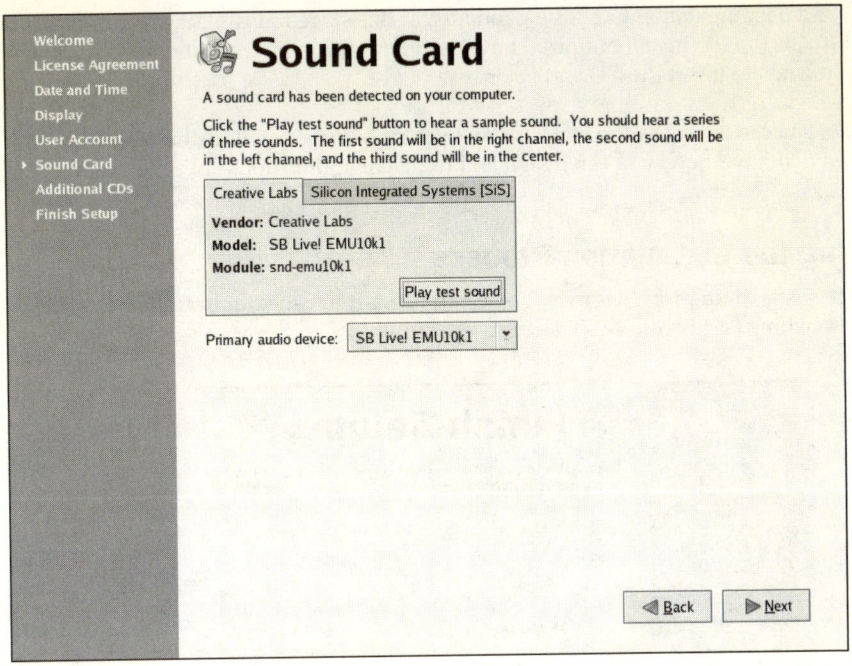

Figure 1-35

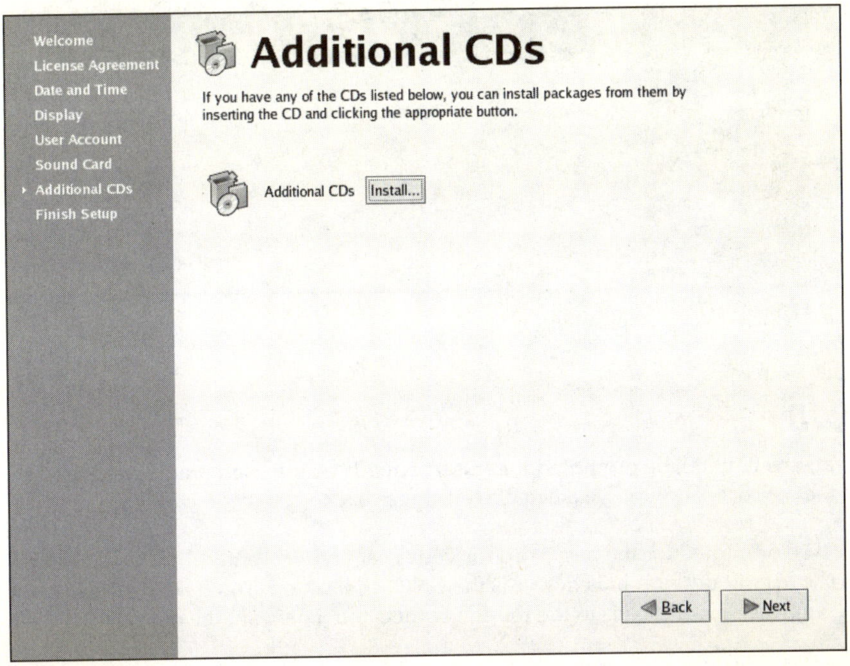

Figure 1-36

If you have a documentation CD, it's a good idea at this stage to install the documentation contained within it (that's the top Install button). The subsequent dialog boxes will talk you through the process, telling you when to insert the CD and so on.

If you like, you can also click the other Install buttons here to install further applications. However, you don't need to do that now; you can install and uninstall applications anytime, via the package manager, as you'll see in Chapter 4.

Completing the Installation Process

Finally, the installation process is over. You can now start to use your brand new desktop—just click Next one last time (see Figure 1-37).

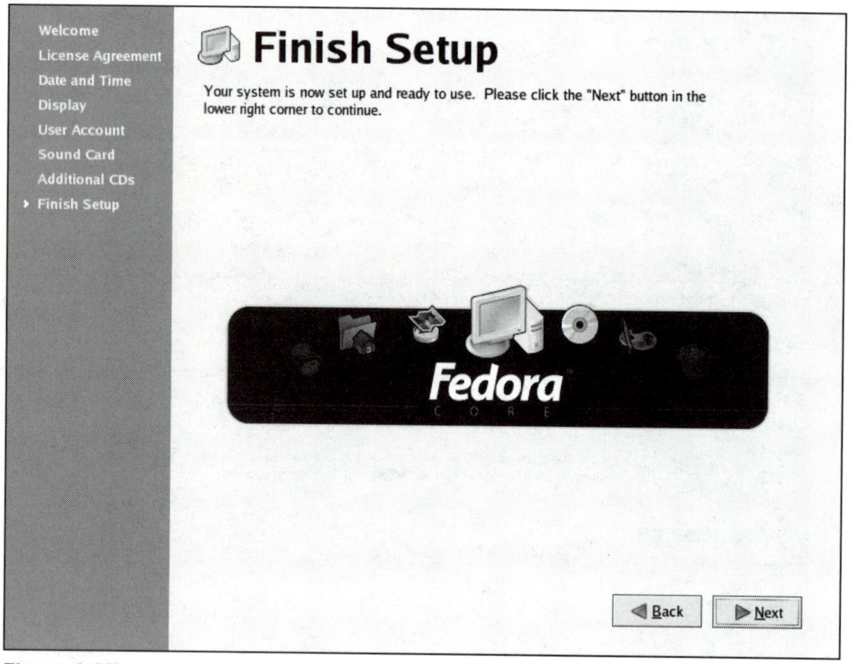

Figure 1-37

Logging In

In the login screen, you'll be prompted for a username. Type the username you created earlier. Here, we'll use the `dthomas` account we created a few pages back.

Then you'll be prompted for the password for your user account; enter that, too. This will start up the desktop. The default desktop in Fedora 2 is the *GNOME* desktop. You'll see a user interface like that shown in Figure 1-38, with icons in the top-left corner, and a panel at the bottom.

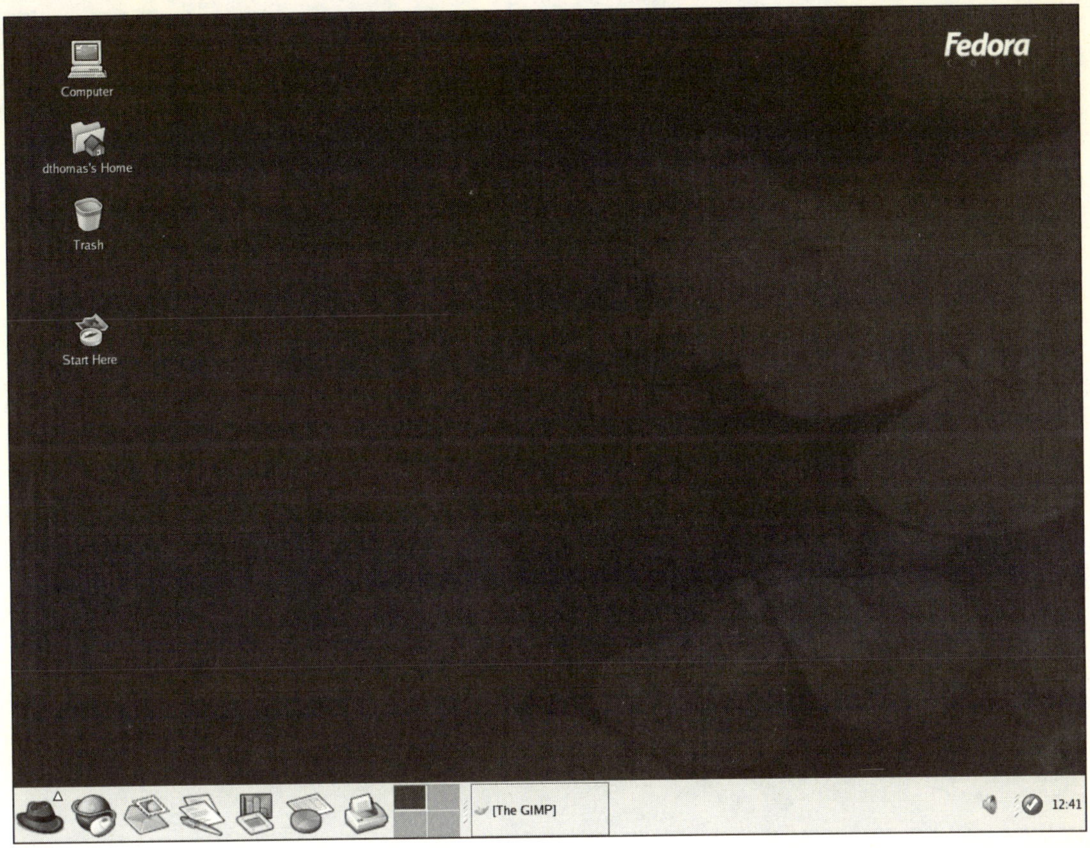

Figure 1-38

The installation is complete, and you're ready to start using the graphical user interface to start making the most out of your Fedora 2 operating system. We'll begin to explore it in the next chapter. Optionally, you may want to go to Chapter 8 to install additional programs and updates to the operating system.

Summary

This chapter looked at the various steps for installing the Fedora 2 operating system.

We began by noting that the installation process requires various pieces of background information about the hardware and network configuration of the computer, and we compiled two checklists of information. The Fedora 2 installation is easier if you prepare these checklists before you start the installation.

After choosing the native language of the installation, the first important choice you make in the installation itself is the installation type. We chose the Personal Desktop installation type for this chapter, although there are four installation types offered by the installation process.

The installation continues with configuration of the keyboard and mouse and searches for existing installations, offering you the opportunity to upgrade an existing installation if it finds one. The next choice relates to disk partitioning—the organization of your hard disk into logical partitions. If you feel comfortable with this, you can configure your own partitions; otherwise, you can allow the installation process to do it for you (as this chapter demonstrated).

After choosing the default boot loader—the software that is used to boot the operating system—we moved on to network configuration options. In single machine situations, it's enough to use the default network configuration, but in situations where you plan to connect to a local area network (LAN) it helps to know whether to choose the default setup (which configures the machine to use a DHCP server), or insert specific static details of the IP address, subnet mask, and so on. Of course, you don't have to get these right the first time—if you're not sure or if you get them wrong, you can reconfigure them using the dialog boxes any time after the installation is complete.

The next decision relates to the firewall options available for the desktop—again, we decided to go ahead with the default standard firewall for this installation. After setting the time zone, selecting a password for the root user, and adding any additional software you choose to add at this stage, the process of collecting information is complete and the installation can proceed.

After the software installation, we did the sensible thing by creating a boot disk (just in case we have problems with the boot loader). Finally, we set up the X-server to give us the desktop's GUI, and reboot the machine, and this completed the initial installation of the Red Hat operating system.

On the first boot of the new installation, Red Hat asks you to create a non-administrative user account, check the date and the time on the computer, and (optionally) register with the Red Hat Update agent; and it gives you yet another chance to install software and documentation. When this is complete, you can log on to the machine and begin your work.

The next chapter looks at how to use the freshly installed desktop. It covers important concepts such as the file hierarchy and devices, which will help you to work effectively in Linux. It looks at various components of the desktop and how to customize them, and explains how to check the hardware configuration of the machine and how to manage and control processes in the system.

Exercises

Now that you have installed Fedora, here are some exercises for you to try.

1. If you add new hardware to your system, how do you configure it?
2. When you switch on a computer on which you've installed a dual-boot system, the boot loader will show you two options to boot into. If you do not choose, it will boot the system into the default choice. How do you change the default choice?

2

Fedora 2 Basics

Now that you have successfully installed Fedora Core 2 on your machine, it is time to familiarize yourself with your new operating system. With Fedora, Red Hat, Inc., has introduced a more aesthetically pleasing interface with improved usability over earlier Red Hat Linux versions. Rather than expose all possible tools available for all tasks, the approach seems to be to expose the best tool for a certain function.

The result is an operating system in which applications are neatly organized according to their function, with a centrally manageable configuration and a uniform interface across all applications that are part of the distribution.

Despite the intuitive nature of the desktop, newcomers to Fedora, specifically Microsoft Windows users, must be aware of several concepts before they can use the desktop effortlessly and customize it to their needs. This chapter quickly familiarizes you with the most frequently used components of the desktop. Many of the concepts covered briefly in this chapter are explained in greater depth in later chapters.

This chapter equips you with the tools and know-how to do the following:

- Navigate throughout the desktop and access the various applications that you require for your day-to-day activities
- Navigate through files and directories (folders) using either a graphical user interface (GUI) or a command line interface (CLI)
- Examine and adjust the hardware and system configuration of your installation
- Manage the various processes running on your system
- Manage the users on your system

Finding Your Way Around the Desktop

The first view of the desktop after you log in is the typical interface of the GNOME desktop with a Bluecurve theme. GNOME is the default desktop interface for Fedora 2, and the one used throughout this book. Figure 2-1 shows what it looks like when you see it for the first time.

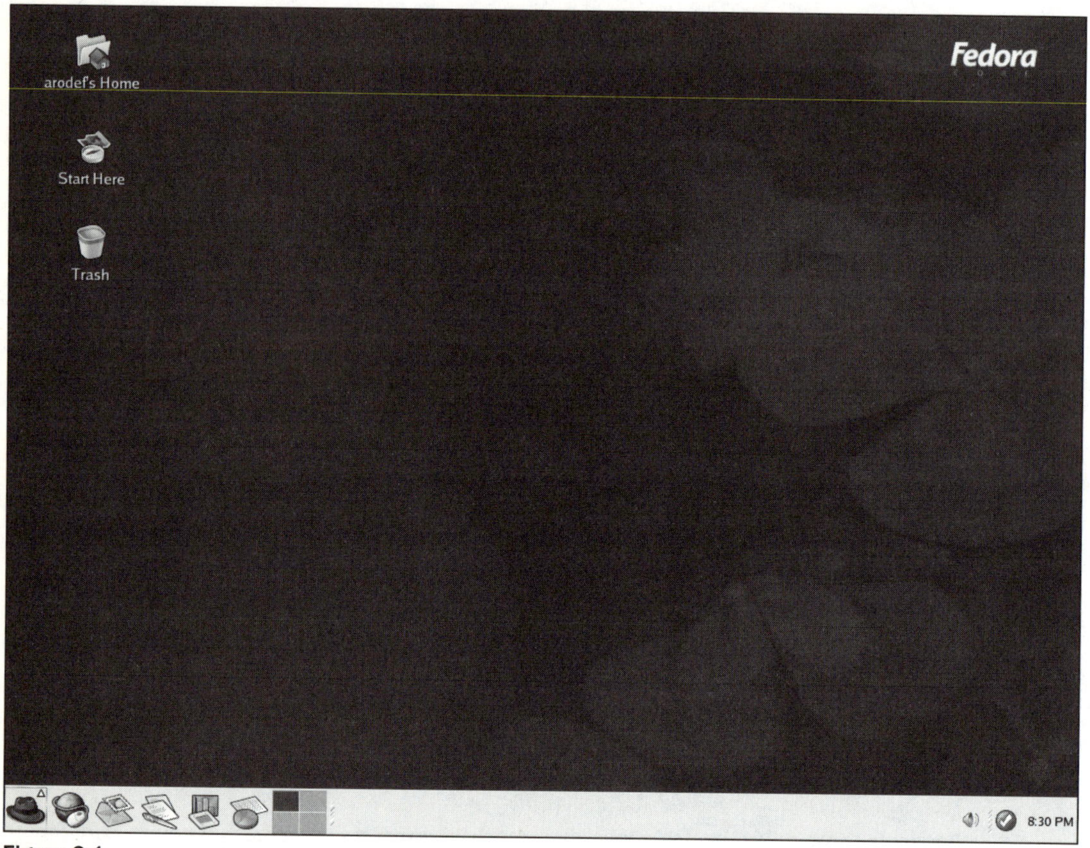

Figure 2-1

There are other desktop interfaces, such as the KDE desktop, which is included in the Fedora 2 distribution but not installed by default. To install it, you must install the necessary KDE packages. Package installation is further discussed in Chapter 4, with GNOME preferred to KDE in this book.

Before we begin discussing the desktop, let us quickly familiarize ourselves with the two main components of this desktop interface:

- **The panel:** This is the gray rectangular box that spans the bottom of the screen. It contains various shortcut buttons (that launch applications when clicked), a menu that provides access to more applications, a workspace switcher, an application tab bar, a status notification bar, and the date-time applet. As you'll soon see, it's easy to modify the panel by adding more options to the menu, more applets, and other application shortcut buttons.

- **The workspace:** The workspace makes up most of the screen. It has a blue background with some artwork. When you run (or *launch*) a GUI application, it is rendered on the workspace. By default, Fedora places a few application shortcuts (or *launchers*) on the workspace—the preceding screenshot shows three such shortcuts in the top-left portion of the workspace. As you'll see later, it's easy to add your own shortcuts to the workspace.

Look at the panel more closely in Figure 2-2. If you click the Red Hat icon at the leftmost end of the panel (the Main Menu button), you bring up the main desktop menu. This menu offers an organized set of applications that can be launched from the desktop.

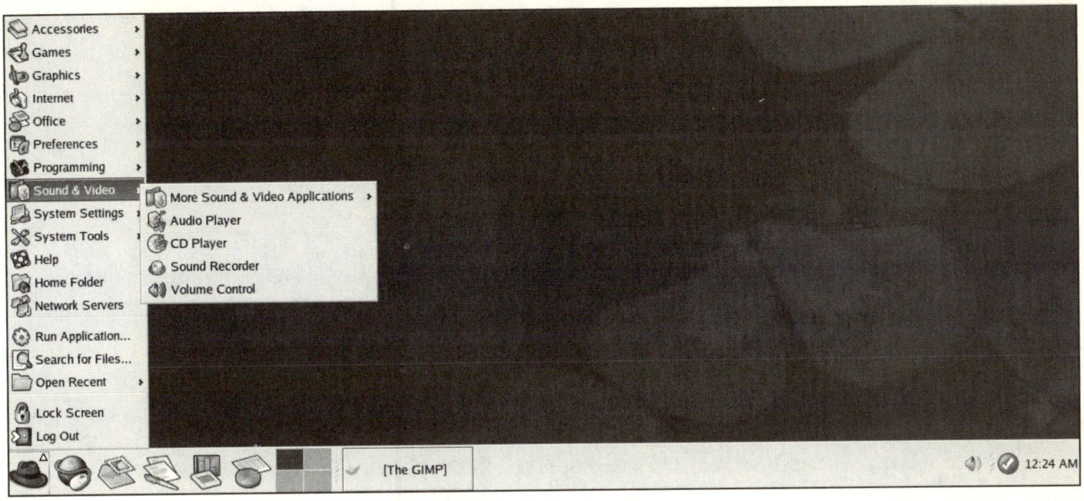

Figure 2-2

Going from left to right along the remainder of the panel, you have the following:

- The next five items of the panel are shortcut buttons for various frequently used applications—browsers, mail applications, word processors, spreadsheets, and a printer manager. We'll return to these shortly, and see how to add our own shortcuts to the panel.
- The curious-looking square (with four equal divisions marked on it) is the *workspace switcher*, explained shortly.
- The application task bars are next. They provide a convenient way of switching between whatever GUI applications are currently running in the workspace. The figure shows two applications running—the Mozilla Web browser, and the Gaim instant messenger application.
- At the right-most end of the panel is *the notification area*, where various applications can indicate their status using icons.
- Finally, the *date and time applet* displays the current date. If you place the mouse cursor on the applet, it displays the date and the day of the week.

The look and feel of this interface should be familiar to users of other GUI-based operating systems. However, Fedora boasts several additional features in this interface, such as the following:

- The main menu can be accessed not only from the panel, but from *anywhere* on the workspace. You can bring up the main menu near the mouse pointer at any time by pressing the *Alt+F1* keys.
- All GUI applications that you execute run in the workspace of the screen, and to switch between GUI applications you can click the corresponding bar on the panel. Of course, it's easy to fill up the workspace with various executing GUI applications, so to avoid overcrowding, Fedora offers you a number of workspaces. By default, you have four such workspaces to work with. The *workspace switcher* (on the panel) allows you to switch from one workspace to another.

  For example, the workplace switcher allows you to have a terminal window and a graphics application (GIMP) open in one workspace, and a spreadsheet open in a different workspace. In such a case, your workspace switcher would give you a tiny preview of the applications running on the various desktops, as shown in Figure 2-3.

Figure 2-3

  The workspace switcher shows the current active workspace by shading it blue, while the others are shaded gray. Only the GUI applications and their respective task bars in the active workspace are visible at any time. You can switch to a different workspace by clicking the corresponding workspace in the switcher.

  Also note that the workspace switcher itself is configurable. If you right-click the workspace switcher and select `Preferences`, you'll get a dialog box that allows you to control the number of workspaces and the way they're displayed in the panel.

- The panel allows you to add small applications (called *applets*) in the panel itself. In fact, the workspace switcher and the date/time sections of the panels are both small applets designed to reside in the panel.

Changing the Appearance of the Desktop

You can customize the desktop fairly easily. You can change the background, the appearance of the panel, or the screen resolution.

Changing the Background

You can change the background theme or color of the workspace by right-clicking the workspace and selecting the Change Desktop Background option, as shown in Figure 2-4.

Customizing the Panel

You can customize the appearance and behavior of the panel by right-clicking the panel and choosing Properties. This menu allows you to specify if applications should be grouped together, what the size of the panel should be, whether to auto-hide the panel, and so on.

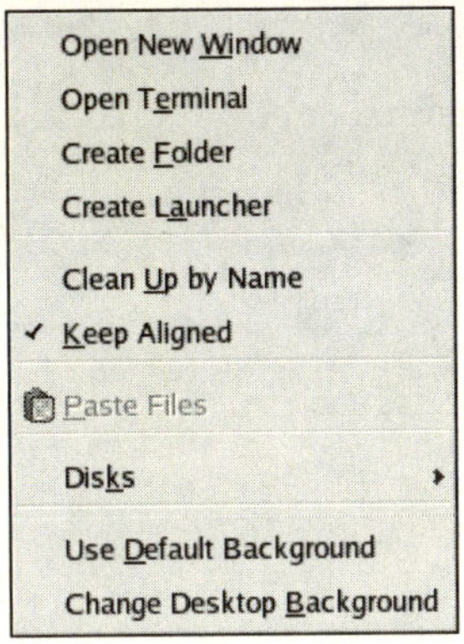

Figure 2-4

Changing the Screen Resolution

New in Fedora, you can now change the screen resolution by clicking the main menu (accessed by clicking the Red Hat icon at the bottom-left corner of the screen) and selecting Preferences ⇨ Screen Resolution. Unlike previous versions, the new screen resolution can take effect immediately without requiring the windowing system to restart. Figure 2-5 shows the Screen Resolution Preferences window.

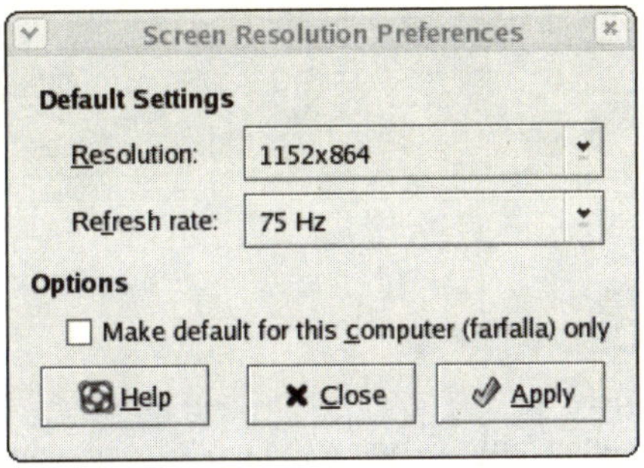

Figure 2-5

Changing the Date and Time

You can change the date and time on your system by clicking the Date & Time applet in the lower-right corner of the screen. If you are not a *root* user, you are prompted for the super user or root password. As you will see later on in the chapter, some operations, including changing the system's Date & Time settings, are privileged operations that only a root user (or super user) can perform. Figure 2-6 shows the Date/Time Properties window.

Other detailed options to configure the display are discussed later in this chapter.

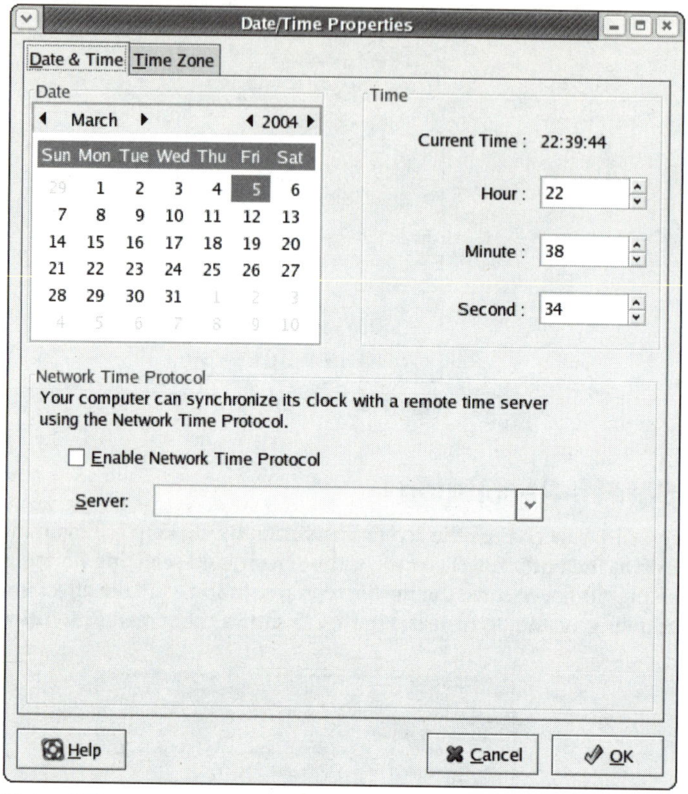

Figure 2-6

The Workspace Right-Click Menu

Fedora keeps a set of frequently used applications at hand by presenting them on the right-click menu on the workspace. If you right-click anywhere on the workspace, you are presented with a menu that allows you to perform some common tasks quickly. These include the ability to launch a new window, open a new terminal, create a new folder, and manage floppy and CD-ROM drives among others. Figure 2-7 shows the right-click menu.

Figure 2-7

Using Applications

A desktop is meant as a place for launching applications for your various needs. Fedora offers you several ways to launch applications; this section discusses four techniques.

Using the Main Menu

Major applications and configuration programs for your desktop have been neatly organized into various categories in the main menu, as shown in Figure 2-8.

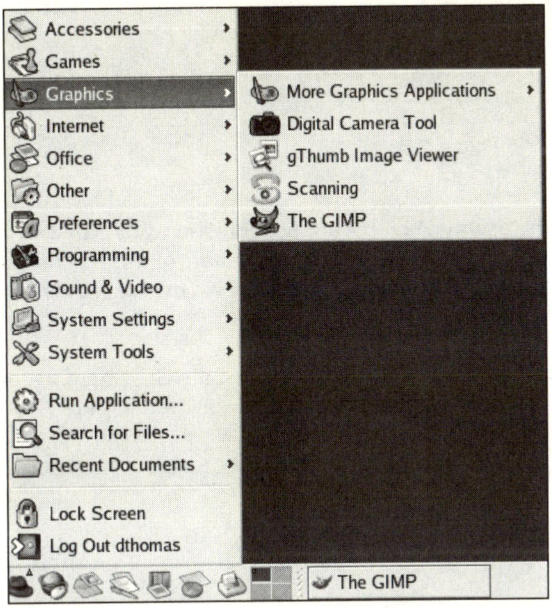

Figure 2-8

The applications that you find here are the applications that Red Hat recommends as the first choice for users. There are many other applications in the distribution, some of which duplicate the functionality of the applications found here. Some of them are installed by default and can be invoked using the other techniques detailed in this list; others must be installed (perhaps using the RPM utility used extensively in Chapter 4). For example, various mail clients are included in the distribution (Evolution, balsa, sylpheed, and others), but only Evolution has been installed and placed in the menu as the mail client to use.

Earlier versions of Fedora listed many similar applications together in the menus. This used to confuse new users because they had no idea which application was the right one to use for a job. To remove such confusion, Fedora 2 lists only one application of each function in the menu.

More than one choice of application exists for every function. In Chapters 4 and 5, you'll learn more about discovering the different applications available in the distribution, and how to install them if necessary.

Using the Run Program Menu Item

You may have noticed the Run Program menu option near the bottom of the main menu in Figure 2-8. When you select this option, you get a dialog box like the one shown in Figure 2-9, within which you type in the name of the application you want to launch.

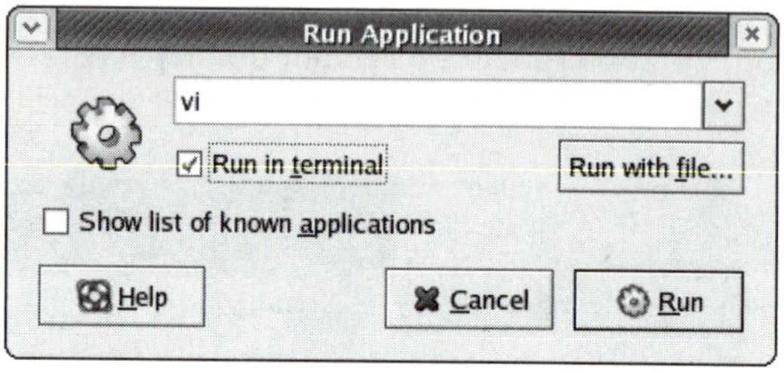

Figure 2-9

This option is particularly useful when the application you want is installed on your machine but not present in the menu. It's also handy if you know the name of the program you want to invoke but you don't know where it is in the desktop menu. You can also invoke the Run Program dialog box by using the shortcut key combination *Alt+F2*.

In addition to typing the name of the application, you may choose from a list of known applications by checking the Show list of known applications option, shown in Figure 2-10.

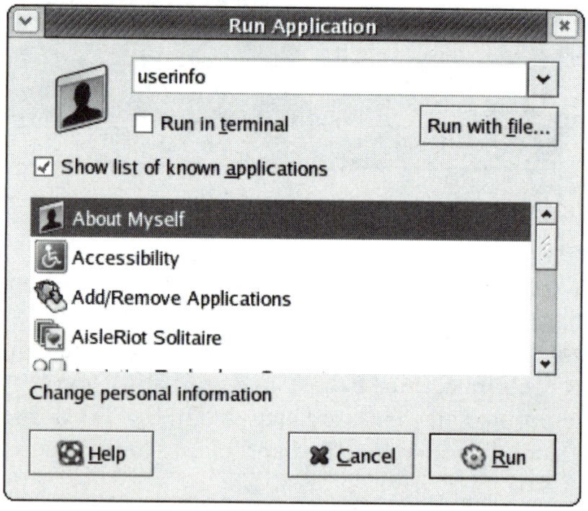

Figure 2-10

Sometimes, it's not sufficient to specify only the name of the application, and you must specify its location as well. This distinction is related to the value of an environment variable called `$PATH`*, which we discuss later in this chapter.*

Using a Panel Shortcut to an Application

You can also create shortcuts to your most frequently used programs and place them on the panel for single-click invocation. As you've seen already, the default Fedora 2 installation comes preconfigured with six such shortcut buttons, as shown in Figure 2-11.

Figure 2-11

The first icon on the panel shown here is that of the Main Menu launcher. The next six icons are shortcuts to six commonly used applications. From left to right these are:

- **GUI Web browser:** This shortcut is preconfigured to launch the Mozilla Web browser for browsing the Internet.
- **Mail client:** The Evolution mail client for accessing your mail.
- **Word processor:** The Open Office Writer word processing program for writing documents.
- **Presentation software:** The Open Office Impress presentation software.
- **Spreadsheet software:** The Open Office Calc spreadsheet application.
- **Print manager:** This shortcut enables you to manage your printer connections and print jobs.

The browser, mail client, and office applications are discussed in more detail in Chapter 5.

Adding New Shortcuts to the Panel

You can add new shortcuts to the panel, too. The easiest way is to right-click with your mouse somewhere on the panel (but not on top of any existing shortcuts or applets), and select **Add to Panel ⇨ Launcher from menu**. This opens up the desktop menu, allowing you to select the application that you want to add to the panel. Figure 2-12 shows how to add a launcher for the Gaim instant messaging client to the panel.

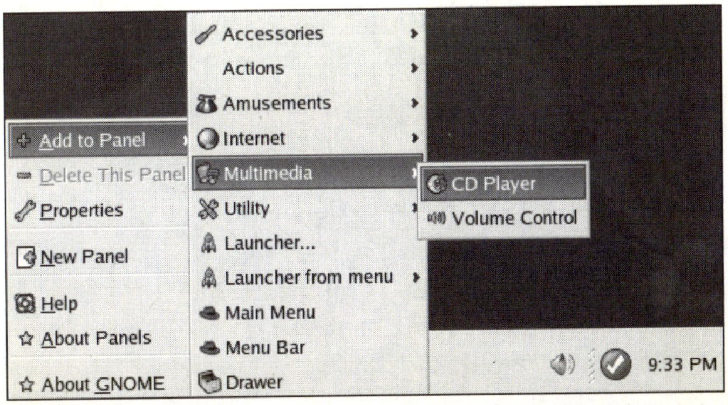

Figure 2-12

This adds the launcher to the panel, as shown in Figure 2-13.

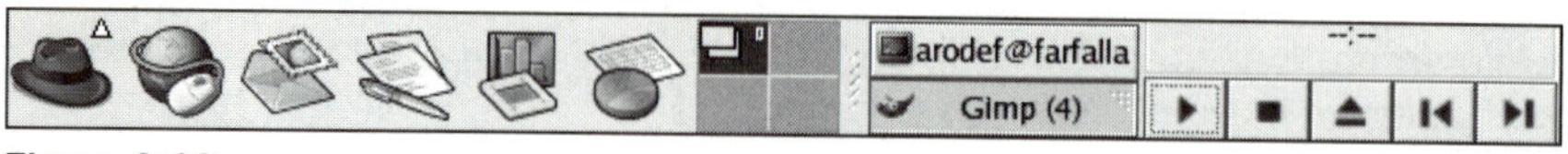

Figure 2-13

The other option to add an application launcher to the panel is to drag and drop an item from the main menu onto the panel.

Changing the Size of the Shortcut Icons

If you're not happy with the size of the shortcut icons in the panel, you can adjust them by right-clicking on the panel and selecting Properties. Then, in the Edge tab of the resulting dialog box, select the appropriate value in the Size field (the default value is Medium).

Using a Terminal Emulator

Perhaps one of the most common methods employed by seasoned Linux users is the terminal emulator interface. This is an interface in which you can invoke GUI and non-GUI applications by typing out the complete command. The interface in a terminal emulator is completely character-based and nongraphical. For users of Microsoft operating systems, this can be considered the equivalent of launching a DOS command prompt. When you invoke a GUI program from the terminal, the operating system opens up a separate GUI window for the program you've invoked.

> *Because all the work done in a terminal emulator requires character-based command input, the terminal emulator is also known as the command line interface (or CLI). It's also often referred to simply as the terminal.*

There are many terminal emulators in existence, such as the gnome-terminal and xterm. This book makes significant use of the gnome-terminal emulator that comes with Fedora. To invoke this particular terminal emulator, you can open up a Run program window (by pressing *Alt+F2*) and type in the name **gnome-terminal**, or you can select Main Menu ➪ System Tools ➪ Terminal.

When you invoke gnome-terminal in this way, you get a terminal-like window that looks like the one shown in Figure 2-14. You can now start typing the names of the programs that you want to execute. In this screenshot you can see that we've executed the program `ls` with the options `-al` to show all the files in the current directory.

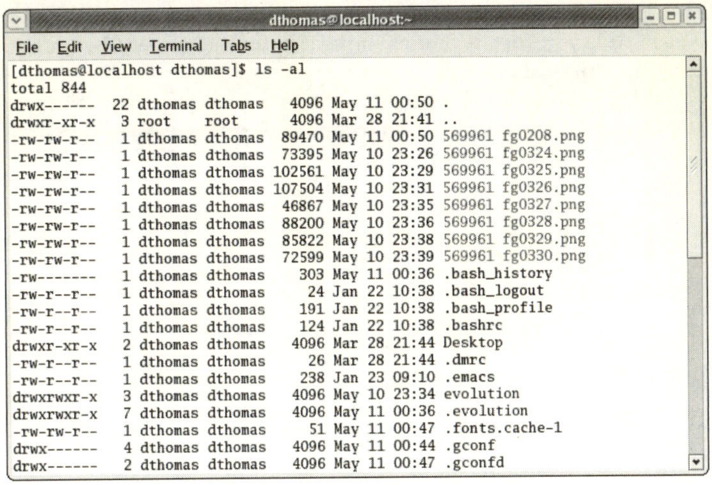

Figure 2-14

Pros and Cons of the CLI

Using a CLI has advantages over the GUI, but it has disadvantages, too:

- To execute programs in this interface, you need to know their names. Unlike a GUI menu interface where the available options are visible, the CLI doesn't offer such ready convenience.
- However, a GUI is generally limited by the amount of space available in the display screen. Even after proper organization using menus, it is difficult to put each and every program of the operating system at your reach, and too many levels of menus make accessing a given program more time-consuming. In contrast, using a CLI, you can easily reach all the programs that are available.
- The CLI can be used to quickly develop powerful scripts on the command prompt. For example, it is fairly simple to type a command that searches for files in subfolders and deletes all files older than a certain date. From a GUI, this is next to impossible to achieve as a single operation.

Ultimately, the CLI offers the strength and the flexibility to give you more complete control over the computer, and if you're performing a lot of similar tasks, it has the potential to improve your productivity over using the GUI. There is a learning curve—mainly related to learning the names of the programs and the appropriate parameters—but this effort generally pays off. To point you in the right direction, here are a couple of handy tools that will help you get started with CLI applications.

Finding the Right Program

Choosing the right program for a particular job is the kind of thing you tend to learn from experience. Of course, to begin with you need help, and there are a number of ways to find out the names of the programs you need.

One handy utility is the apropos program, which can be used to list system commands whose descriptions contain the keywords you specify. For example, Figure 2-15 shows the apropos program being used to find a text editor application.

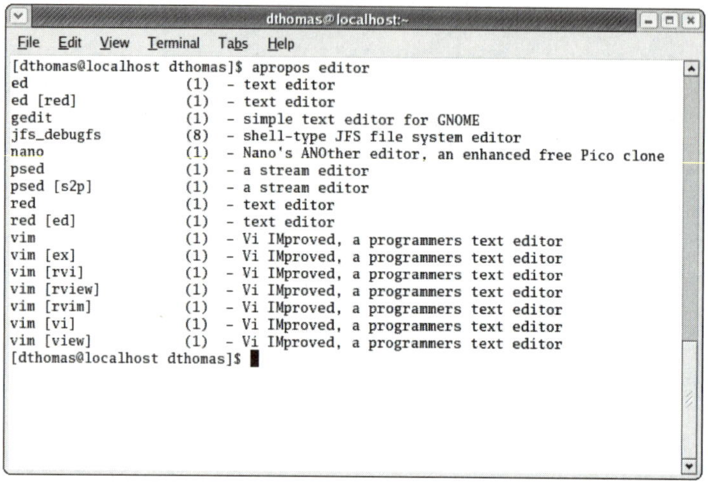

Figure 2-15

As you can see, there are a number of different types of editors here. For example, the text editor program, called vim and shown in the list in the figure, is an extremely powerful and popular editor (in fact, there are a number of incarnations of vim, which is why there are so many entries for it in the list). Later chapters of this book make use of the gedit text editor. Other editors popular with programmers include Emacs and jEdit.

Learning How to Use a Program

To find out more about a command, you can use the `man` command, which gives you a program manual for that command. For example, if you want to know more about the `date` command, you can type the following at the command line:

```
$ man date
```

This generates the output shown in Figure 2-16.

To see the next page of this document, you press the space bar, and you can navigate up and down the document using the arrow keys. To exit the manual (and return to the command line prompt), press *q*.

In fact, the manual comes in a number of sections; some keywords have more than one entry, and, in that case, you may need to specify the correct section. For example, Section 1 covers user commands, and the following gives you the manual page that describes the `passwd` command:

```
$ man 1 passwd
```

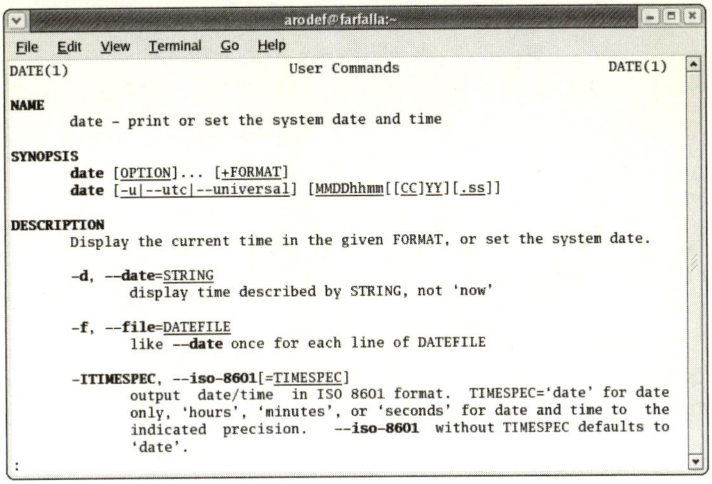

Figure 2-16

By contrast, Section 5 covers file formats, so this next command gives you the manual page that describes the `/etc/passwd` file:

```
$ man 5 passwd
```

For a quick overview of all the sections in the manual, try the following command, where *N* is the section number you are interested in:

```
$ man N intro
```

The more powerful alternative to the `man` command is the `info` command. You can invoke `info` by supplying the name of a program you need help information on. The `info` command displays help text in subpages with the support for commands mapped on to keys in addition to search features. The choice between `man` and `info` is sometimes a matter of personal preference. Figure 2-17 provides an example.

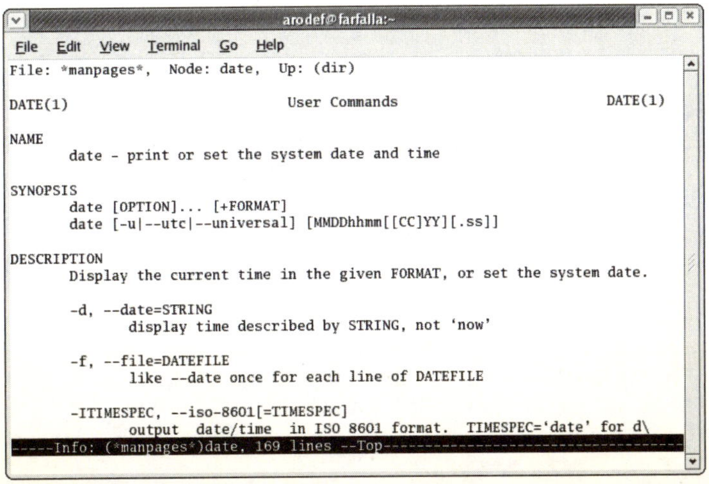

Figure 2-17

Using a Program

Once you understand how to use a program, you can execute it from the terminal. In time, you might find it more convenient to use the terminal than the main menu, in which case you might need to know the program names that correspond to the menu items—so here's a trick that allows you to do that easily:

1. Find the menu item by clicking the Main Menu button and then navigate to the item in question.
2. Don't select the item, but right-click it instead. In the resulting submenu, select the Put in run dialog box option. This opens up a Run program dialog box with the corresponding command name in it.

   Figure 2-18 shows what happens when we use this technique on the Volume Control menu option. The corresponding Run Program dialog box shows that the CLI command to invoke this program is actually `gnome-volume-control`.

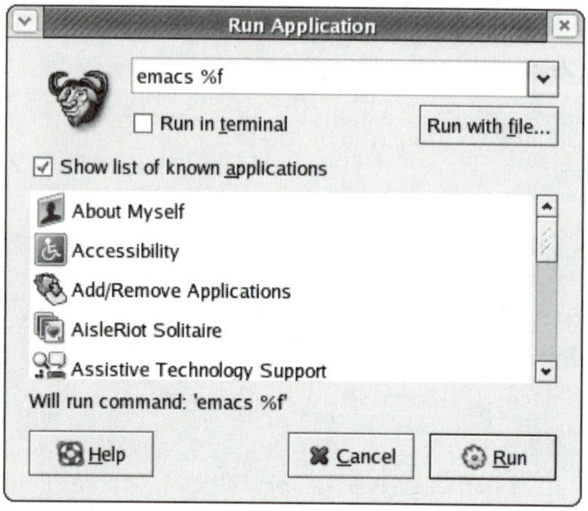

Figure 2-18

3. After you learn the command name for a particular program, use it to execute the program from the terminal.

Shutting Down the Computer

One of your more immediate needs is to find out how to shut down the machine when you are done, or to restart it, if necessary. Moreover, it might be necessary to log out of your desktop when you are finished so that another user can use the computer to log in and do his or her work.

The Main Menu ⇨ Log Out option controls all the options for logging out and shutting down.

If you select Log Out, your current desktop session terminates, and the login screen appears, allowing you or another user to log in and use the desktop. The options Shut Down and Restart are self-explanatory—they allow you to shut down the machine or to restart it.

These are the recommended options for shutting down and restarting the machine to ensure safety of data and to keep the operating system running reliably into the future. It is necessary to shut down the machine properly to avoid data corruption.

Note the Save current setup checkbox at the top of the dialog box. For each of these options, if you select this checkbox, Linux saves the desktop settings before logging you out. The main advantage of this option is that the desktop makes a note of the running applications, and the next time you log in it will try to restart those applications.

You can also use the `shutdown` command to shut the system down. It provides the additional flexibility of specifying when to shut down the system and what to do after shutdown (that is, whether to restart or halt the system). The following command shuts down the system immediately:

```
shutdown -h now
```

The following command reboots the system immediately:

```
shutdown -r now
```

The following command shuts down the system in 40 minutes:

```
shutdown -h +40
```

Please note that only a root user may run the shutdown command.

The Filesystem

For users migrating from a non-UNIX–based operating system (such as any Microsoft Windows OS), Linux's organization of files, directories, disk drivers, and other devices takes a little getting used to. Fedora, being a flavor of UNIX, organizes files the UNIX way—using one grand *hierarchy of directories*. This section looks at the filesystem hierarchy and how to use the filesystem in your work. (The filesystem is covered in further detail in Chapter 7.)

The Filesystem Hierarchy

In the Linux operating system, every file, directory, and device is one part of a grand hierarchy. The topmost member of this hierarchy is the *root directory*, and it is denoted by the symbol `/`. A subdirectory of a given directory is denoted by the concatenation of the names of the parent directory and the child directory. For example:

- There is a subdirectory called `usr` under the root directory, and we denote the full path to that subdirectory by the expression `/usr`.
- A subdirectory of the `usr` directory named `local` can be denoted by the expression `/usr/local`.

This simple hierarchy of directories can be represented by the tree diagram shown in Figure 2-19.

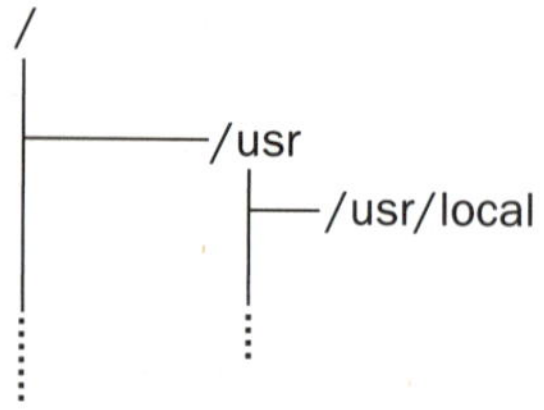

Figure 2-19

Files within a directory are named much like subdirectories. In fact, behind the scenes a directory is just a special kind of file that contains the names of the files inside it and their respective locations on the disk.

Note that the directory separator character in Fedora is `/`*, whereas in Windows it is* `\`*.*

Listing the Contents of a Directory

You can find out the contents of a directory by using the `ls` command. Figure 2-20 shows the output when invoking the `ls` command with the root directory (/) as its argument.

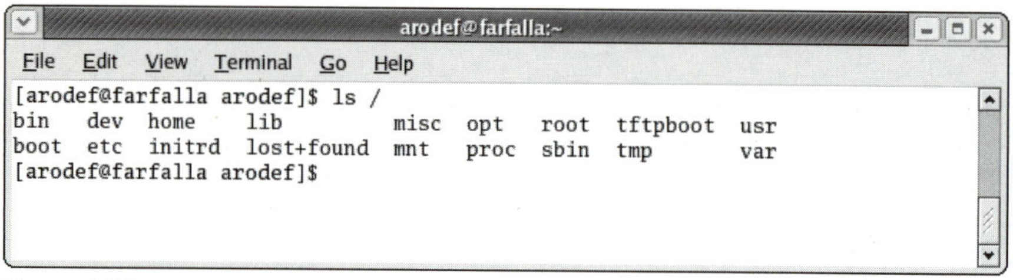

Figure 2-20

The `ls` command takes an argument, which you can use to specify the file or directory to be displayed. If you specify a directory (as we did in the preceding screenshot), the `ls` command displays the files contained in that directory.

For a detailed description of the different ways in which you can customize the output of the `ls` *command, take a look at the program manual by typing* ***man ls*** *at the command line.*

The Fedora filesystem consists of thousands of directories and files arranged in the hierarchy previously described. Within this hierarchy, all the various programs and data files on the system are carefully organized into directories. The directories have generally been organized with the purpose of keeping related programs and files together. For example, the directory /bin contains the essential binary (or executable) programs available to all users, whereas the directory /sbin contains the binary programs essential to the super user (or root user—the user who has complete administrative control of the system).

Of late, Red Hat and all major Linux distributions are trying to conform to the Filesystem Hierarchy Standard (FHS). This standard tries to bring a uniform file organization to the Linux world (which, until some years back, was plagued by different file organizations in the various distributions). You can learn more about FHS at `www.pathname.com/fhs`*.*

The current specification, available at `www.pathname.com/fhs/2.2/`*, explains the various standard directories to expect in a Linux system and the type of files that they are supposed to contain. That said, Red Hat still has some distribution-specific directories that you won't find in other Linux distributions.*

You can see some of the regular directories in the system in the directory tree shown in Figure 2-21.

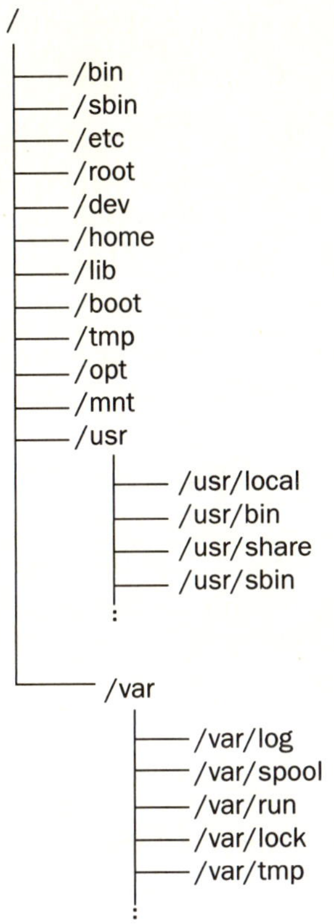

Figure 2-21

The Top-Level Directories

A moment ago, we used the `ls` command to list the contents of the root (`/`) directory, and we found 17 subdirectories. Each of these top-level directories has a very specific purpose, and you will encounter some of them very frequently. Let's take a look at some of these directories in the following table, and find out what they're for.

Directory	Description
/bin/usr/bin	Contains programs available to all users.
/sbin/usr/sbin	Contains programs meant for use by system administrators.
/var/log	Contains the log files made by various applications. The log files are invaluable in keeping track of applications' activities and errors.
/home	Contains all the personal directories of the users of the system.
/boot	Contains the files needed by the operating system to load itself into memory.
/etc	Contains the system configuration files used by various applications.
/mnt	Contains the mount points for any removable devices in the system (such as CD-ROMs, floppy disks, and network drives).
/proc	Contains the system state information. The information in the files of this directory is maintained directly by the operating system kernel.

Invoking a Program by Using Its Path

When you launch a terminal, the terminal in turn executes a command interpreter program called the *shell*. In fact, the command prompt that you see in the terminal is generated by this shell program—the shell outputs this command prompt, and then waits for you to type in a command. When you launch a program from the prompt, the shell searches for it within the filesystem and then executes it.

You can execute programs by typing out their *full path name* at the terminal prompt, like this:

```
$ /bin/ls
```

Alternatively, you can simply use the program's name, like this:

```
$ ls
```

The second of these two commands does not specify the exact location of the `ls` program, so the shell searches for the program among a specific set of locations. These locations are specified by a special environment variable, known as the *search path*. An environment variable consists of a name and a value, and is maintained by the shell for use by programs executed with it. The name of the search path environment variable is `$PATH`, and you can find out its value by executing the following command:

```
$ echo $PATH
/usr/local/bin:/usr/bin:/bin:home/arodef/bin
```

As you can see, the value of `$PATH` consists of a number of directories, separated by `:` characters. If you launch a program by typing only its filename (rather than its full path name), the shell tries to find the program among the directories named in your path.

The value of your `$PATH` variable depends on what account you're using. By default, Linux discourages normal users from executing certain programs, such as the various administrative programs located in the directories /sbin and /usr/sbin that are intended for execution only by the super user. Linux does this by omitting these directories from any normal user's $PATH (as in the preceding example); users cannot invoke these programs without specifying the full path name.

Even if you do try to invoke an administrative program from a non-root account, you will still be challenged to authenticate yourself as a root user before the program will run. This has the added effect of reminding you that you're accessing an administrative program, and to take the appropriate care when doing so.

Finding a Program's Location

The which command allows you to find the location of programs contained within any of the directories listed in the $PATH variable. The following example uses which to find the location of the vim text editor:

```
$ which vim
/usr/bin/vim
```

The whereis command is also useful for locating programs. This command allows you to find the location of programs that are not contained in directories listed in $PATH. In the following example, you can see how which and whereis behave differently:

```
$ which ifconfig
/usr/sbin/which: no ifconfig in /usr/local/bin:/usr/bin:/bin:home/arodef/bin
$ whereis ifconfig
ifconfig: /sbin/ifconfig /usr/share/man/man8/ifconfig.8.gz
```

Here, which is unable to locate the ifconfig program because ifconfig is not located within any of the locations specified by the $PATH. However, whereis locates two files by the name of ifconfig: one (/sbin/ifconfig) is the program we're looking for, and the other is the file that contains the pages of the manual that cover ifconfig.

If a program is not within the scope of your PATH environment variable and you do not know where it is located on the system, you can also use the locate command to find the executable file. The caveat is that using locate as a general-purpose file search program can generate lots of information, and the user may have to sift through it to get to the file of interest. For example, if you used locate to find the location of the date command, it would additionally display the man and info pages for date. The details on using locate are explained in a subsequent section in this chapter.

Navigating the Filesystem

This section helps you navigate the filesystem and all the files in your computer. The filesystem can be navigated using either a GUI file explorer (such as Nautilus) or the terminal.

Navigating Using the GUI

To start the GUI file explorer, you have to execute the Nautilus file manager. A quick way to start Nautilus is to select it from the menu, by choosing Main Menu ⇨ Home Folder. This opens up the Nautilus file manager, which (as you've already seen) resembles Microsoft's Windows Explorer. When you open the Nautilus file manager in this way, the directory shown in the location bar is your home directory, as demonstrated in Figure 2-22.

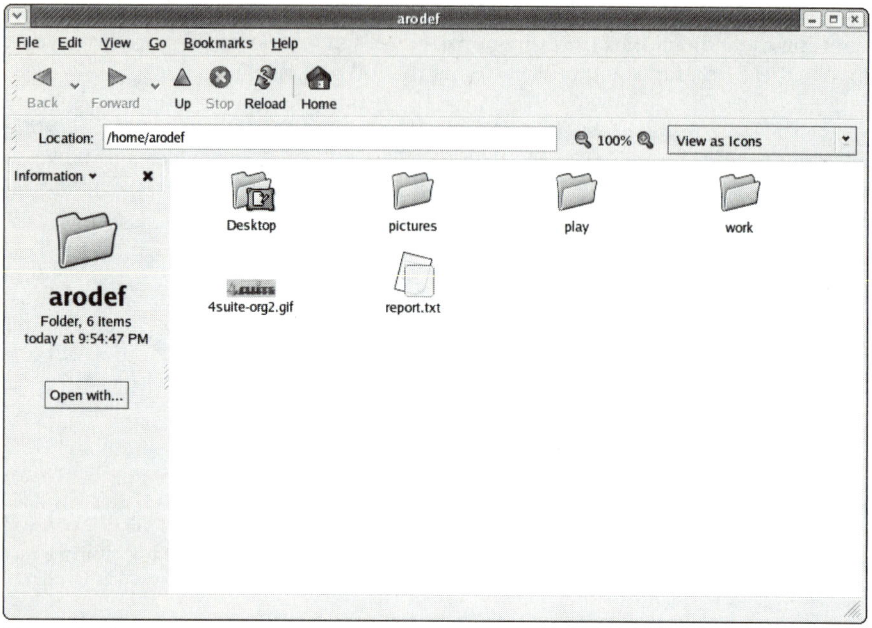

Figure 2-22

A user's ***home directory*** *is the location in the computer where that user can store his or her personal data. Many applications store their user-specific configuration and customization data in the home directory. The user's home directory is by default named after the user login ID and is located under the directory* `/home`. *For example, in this case the figure shows the user account has the login ID* `arodef`; *the home directory of this account is named* `arodef` *and placed under the directory* `/home`. *Thus, the complete path to my home directory is* `/home/arodef`.

Once it's open, you can type any location into the location bar, and Nautilus displays the contents at that location. Alternatively, you can click the button marked Up to make Nautilus display the contents of the parent directory instead. In this way, you can navigate all the way up to the root directory (`/`), where you will find all the computer's top-level directories. You can then double-click the directories here to navigate inside them.

Overall, the navigation of the filesystem using the file manager is very intuitive, and if you have any experience with a GUI-based operating system such as Windows, you'll find yourself right at home with Nautilus.

Navigating Using the Terminal Emulator

Opening up a terminal emulator window places you at the shell prompt, and in your home directory. As already noted, the *shell* is the program that interprets each of the commands that you type at the terminal.

The directory that you are located in at any particular time is called the *current directory* (or *present working directory*). When you first open up the terminal, your current directory is set to be your home directory. At any time, you can find out which directory that is by executing the command `pwd`:

```
$ pwd
/home/arodef
```

This example shows the pwd program being used to confirm that the current directory just after opening the terminal application is the user's home directory.

Please note that the filenames are case sensitive, unlike in Microsoft operating systems.

Displaying the Contents of a Directory

To display the contents of a given directory, you can use the ls program that was introduced earlier in the chapter. If the ls program is executed without any arguments, it displays the files in the present working directory.

If you try this in your home directory just after installation (before you've created any new files in your home directory), the ls program gives no output (to reflect the lack of content in the directory). However, you should note that the ls program's default behavior is to *not* display the *hidden files* in a directory. Hidden files are generally used to store user-specific configuration data, and you can usually spot a hidden file because its name begins with the . (dot) character.

To display these files you must use the -a parameter with the ls command. The following example shows how the -a parameter affects the output of the ls command:

```
$ ls
$ ls -a
.   ..   .bash_logout   .bash_profile   .bashrc   .emacs   .gtkrc   .xauthkIUlWu
```

The lack of output from the first command suggests that the directory is empty. However, the output from the second command reveals the existence of a number of hidden files.

Changing the Current Directory

To change the present working directory to a different directory, you use the cd command. Executing this command without any parameters changes the working directory to be the user's home directory. Adding a directory name as the parameter causes the working directory to be the one specified. The following terminal session provides a good example:

```
$ cd /usr/bin
$ pwd
/usr/bin
$ cd
$ pwd
/home/arodef
```

Here, the first cd command changes the current directory to /usr/bin (as confirmed by the subsequent pwd command). The second cd command changes the current directory to be this user's home directory (which happens to be /home/arodef).

Searching for Files

Two different CLI programs enable you to search for files—`locate` and `find`:

- The `locate` program works by building a daily database of files and their respective locations. When a search is conducted, it simply looks up this database and reports the file locations. (However, this database is updated once a day and, therefore, may not reflect the actual contents of the filesystem if changes have happened in the last 24 hours.)
- The `find` program, by contrast, doesn't use any database and actually looks inside directories and their subdirectories for files matching the given criterion.

The `find` program is more powerful because of the wealth of search criteria that it allows in searches. Both of these commands are used to find a file named `pam.ps` in the following example:

```
$ locate pam.ps
/usr/share/doc/pam-0.75/ps/pam.ps
$ find /usr/share/doc -name pam.ps
/usr/share/doc/pam-0.75/ps/pam.ps
```

The `find` and `locate` commands are explained in more detail in Chapter 7.

Fedora has a separate GUI program for finding files. This program can be executed by selecting the Main Menu ➪ Search for Files option. This opens up the dialog box shown in Figure 2-23.

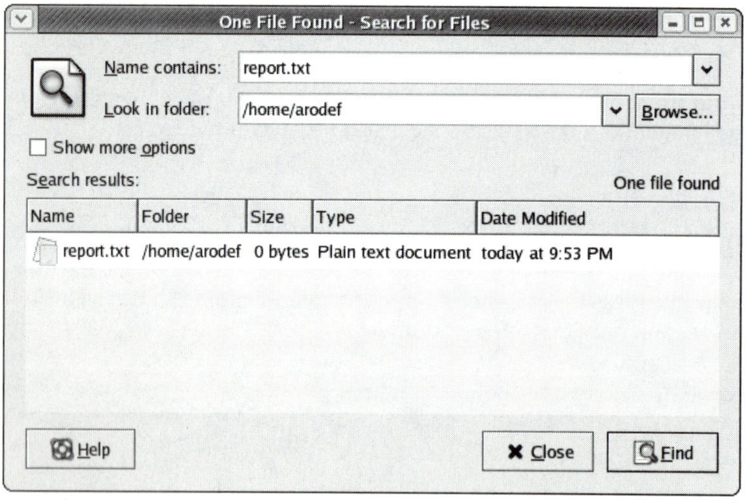

Figure 2-23

In this dialog box you can specify the name of the file that you want to search for and the path in which the search should be performed. By clicking Find, the Search Tool performs a file search based on these criteria and returns the name and location of any files found in the directory mentioned in this box and in any of its subdirectories. For example, the preceding figure shows an attempt to search for a file named `report.txt` in any directory under `/home/arodef`.

The Search Tool also offers more advanced options that allow you to specify more fine-tuned parameters for the search. This mode is selected by clicking the Additional Options caption. You select the options you want from the drop-down list box (shown in Figure 2-24), add them to the list, and then specify the parameter of the restriction.

The preceding screenshot shows that one restriction has already been added, stating that we want the search to return only files exceeding 10Kb in size.

Adding Devices to the Filesystem

In Linux, almost every device is treated as a file. This concept might be a bit unusual to you if you're more familiar with other non-UNIX operating systems such as the Windows family, but you'll quickly get used to it.

The idea behind this is to provide a uniform interface to all resources—whether that resource is a hard disk, a serial device, a floppy disk, the sound card, or even the TV tuner. The notable exceptions in this concept are the network devices, which are handled differently by the operating system.

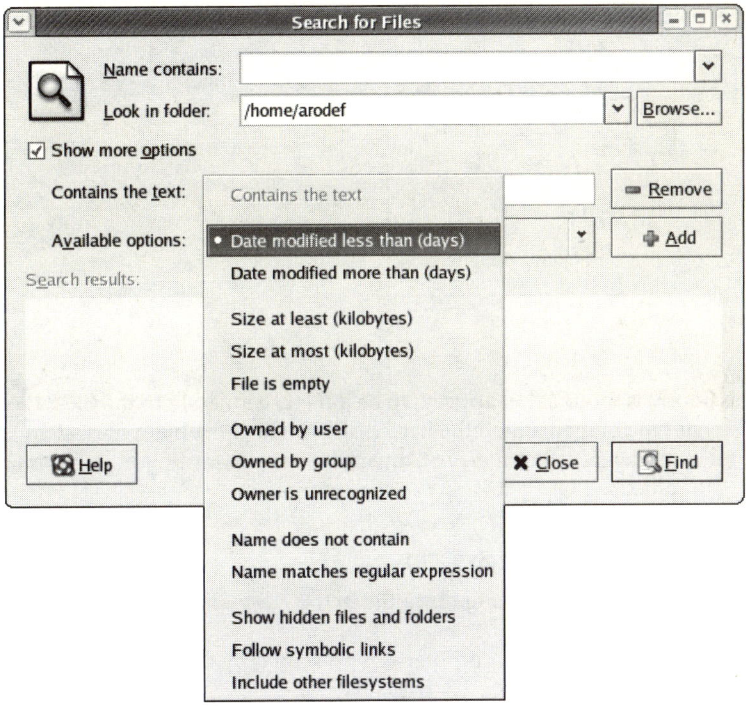

Figure 2-24

Mounting a Device

For users coming from a Windows background, there are some notable differences here. In Linux, the different hard disks and their partitions are not considered different "drives." Instead, when you need to use such a device, it is *mounted* to a directory within the filesystem hierarchy (which is called its *mount point*). Mounting a disk drive causes its own filesystem to appear as a child of the directory on which the device is mounted. Then, you can access the disk drive's content by navigating the directory hierarchy, just like any other file in the filesystem.

For example, suppose you have a floppy disk that contains a single directory, `/doc`, and that this directory contains a single file called `readme.txt`. You can make the contents of this floppy disk accessible by *mounting* the floppy disk (say, to the computer directory `/mnt/floppy`). Then, the file `readme.txt` will be accessible using the path `/mnt/floppy/doc/readme.txt`, as shown in Figure 2-25.

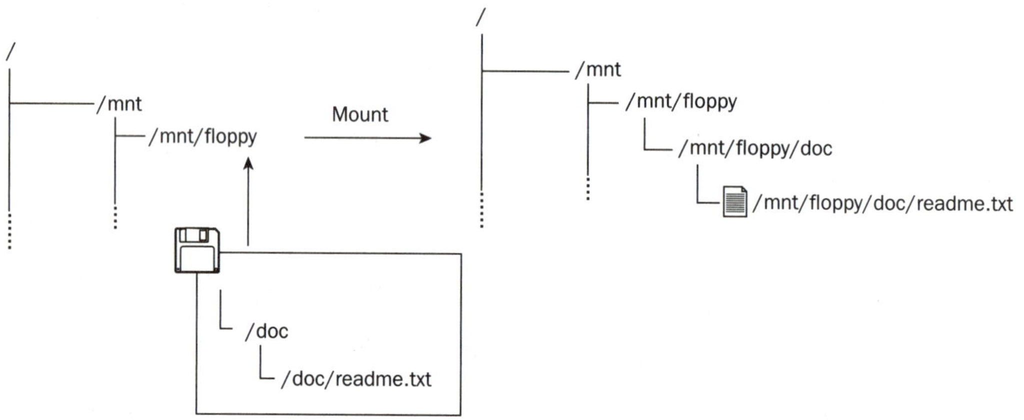

Figure 2-25

Thus, when the floppy is mounted, it appears to be joined seamlessly to the filesystem, even though it is an entirely different type of media than the hard disk on which the main filesystem is situated. By convention, you create mount points in the `/mnt` directory—for example, you might mount a floppy disk onto `/mnt/floppy` or a CD-ROM onto `/mnt/cdrom`.

Representation of Devices on the System

Every device on the system is represented by a file in the `/dev` directory. For example:

- The first floppy drive in the computer is represented by the *device special* file, `/dev/fd0`.
- The first master IDE hard disk or CD-ROM is represented by the file `/dev/hda`.
- The first audio DSP device of the computer is represented by the file `/dev/dsp`.
- The first video capture device is represented by the file `/dev/video`.
- Similarly, the first serial port of the computer is `/dev/ttyS0`.

Only devices that can contain a recognized filesystem are mountable. For example, floppy, CD-ROM, IDE, and SCSI hard disks generally contain filesystems to store their data, and can be mounted onto the computer's filesystem.

Mounting a Device Automatically

The Fedora desktop has an application called `magicdev`, which detects media in the disk drives and mounts them automatically. Whenever you insert a data CD into the CD-ROM drive, `magicdev` does the following:

- Detects it and mounts it on the directory `/mnt/cdrom`
- Opens a GUI filesystem explorer (called Nautilus), with the contents of this directory displayed in it
- Creates a desktop shortcut button for quick access to the contents of the CD

If you were to insert a music CD into the CD-ROM drive, `magicdev` would automatically launch the CD player and play the first track on the CD, as shown in Figure 2-26.

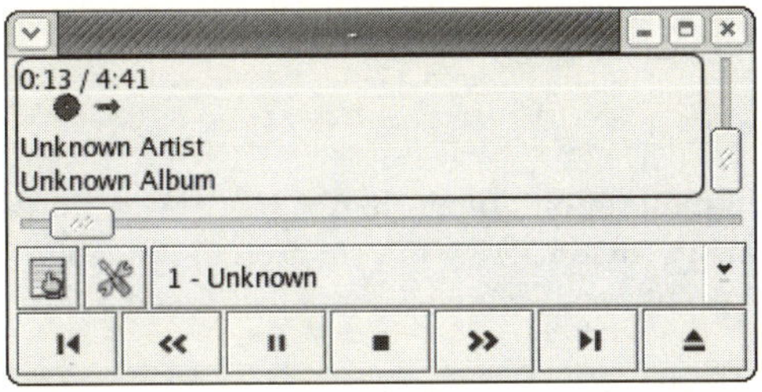

Figure 2-26

Ejecting a Mounted CD

Once the CD-ROM is mounted, the CD-ROM driver *locks* it into the drive. You won't be able to eject the disc by pressing the *Eject* button on the CD-ROM drive. To eject a mounted CD, right-click with your mouse on the CD's desktop shortcut and click the Eject option in the resulting menu, as shown in Figure 2-27. This unmounts the CD from the mount point and ejects the disk.

Figure 2-27

You can also eject a CD by running the eject command from a terminal window. The eject command with no options ejects the CD from the CD-ROM driver.

Mounting and Unmounting from the Command Line

You can also perform the tasks of mounting and unmounting from the command line. To mount a CD-ROM onto the filesystem, you can use the `mount` program. The `mount` program needs to be told the device that has to be mounted, the filesystem that is present on it, and the mount point (the point in the existing filesystem where the device needs to be mounted). For example, the following command takes the CD contained in the CD-ROM drive `/dev/cdrom`, and mounts it at the mount point `/mnt/cdrom`:

```
$ mount -t iso9660 /dev/cdrom /mnt/cdrom
```

Some of the parameters for mounting a CD in a Fedora desktop are preconfigured and stored in the system configuration file `/etc/fstab`. Therefore, you will need to execute only the following command to mount the CD-ROM on the mount point `/mnt/cdrom`:

```
# mount /mnt/cdrom
```

To mount the CD-ROM on a mount point other than `/mnt/cdrom`, you can no longer rely on the preconfigured information; you must provide all the information to the mount program. For example, to mount the CD-ROM on the mount point `/mnt/cdrom1`, you must execute the following command:

```
$ mount -t iso9660 /dev/cdrom /mnt/cdrom1
```

This instructs the mount program to mount the CD-ROM device `/dev/cdrom` onto the mount point `/mnt/cdrom1`. It also specifies the filesystem as `iso9660`, which is present on most standard CD-ROM media.

You can find all the parameters that can be passed to the mount program in the corresponding manual page by executing the command `man mount` *at the terminal.*

To unmount devices from the filesystem, you execute the `umount` program. The `umount` program takes only one parameter—the mount point of the device. For example, the following command unmounts the CD-ROM disc from its mount point:

```
$ umount /mnt/cdrom
```

For unmounting a device from the filesystem, it is absolutely necessary that no application is currently using the device filesystem data. If the device is being used at the time of the unmount process, the process will be unable to unmount the device you specified.

```
$ eject
```

Finally, the eject command ejects the CD from the CD-ROM drive.

Managing the Hardware

The Fedora installation process automatically tries to detect the available hardware and configure it for use in the desktop. However, sometimes this hardware configuration needs to be fine-tuned, or the auto-detection of hardware during the installation process doesn't work as planned. In such cases, it is necessary to know how to adjust the desktop's hardware configuration manually.

Many of the programs shown in this section are executable only by users with administrative privileges. Therefore, you are able to perform the various operations shown in this section only if you have access to the root account of your system.

In fact, this is a security feature of the Linux platform—and you will see it often over the course of this book. If you are using the terminal emulator for executing the command, you can switch to a root shell by using the following command:

```
$ su -
```

When prompted, you'll need to enter the root password. For safety and security reasons, it is advisable to avoid using the root account except when you need to perform administrative tasks. We'll discuss this further when we talk about user accounts in Chapter 8. As mentioned earlier in the section, if you attempt to perform a privileged operation from a GUI, an authentication window prompts you for the root password (as shown in Figure 2-28); this is the same as specifying the password on the command line in response to the `su` *command.*

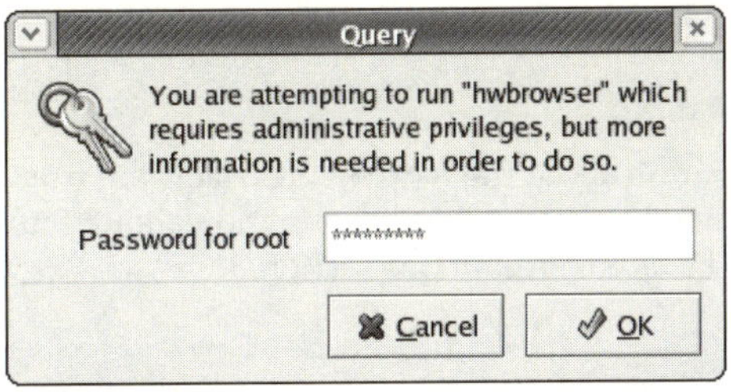

Figure 2-28

Finding the Existing Hardware

You can find out the current major hardware configuration of the system by using the *hardware browser*. To launch the hardware browser, select Main Menu ➪ System Tools ➪ Hardware Browser, or type **hwbrowser** at a command line. The hardware browser searches for the hardware on the system and displays results, as shown in Figure 2-29.

While the depth of information in this program is not great, it is a good indication of whether a particular device has been detected correctly.

Fedora uses the kudzu program to detect new hardware automatically. However, this adds to the amount of time it takes for the system to boot up. Users may choose to disable the checking by running `chkconfig kudzu off`. At a later time, when new hardware is added, they can turn on the checking by running `chkconfig kudzu on`.

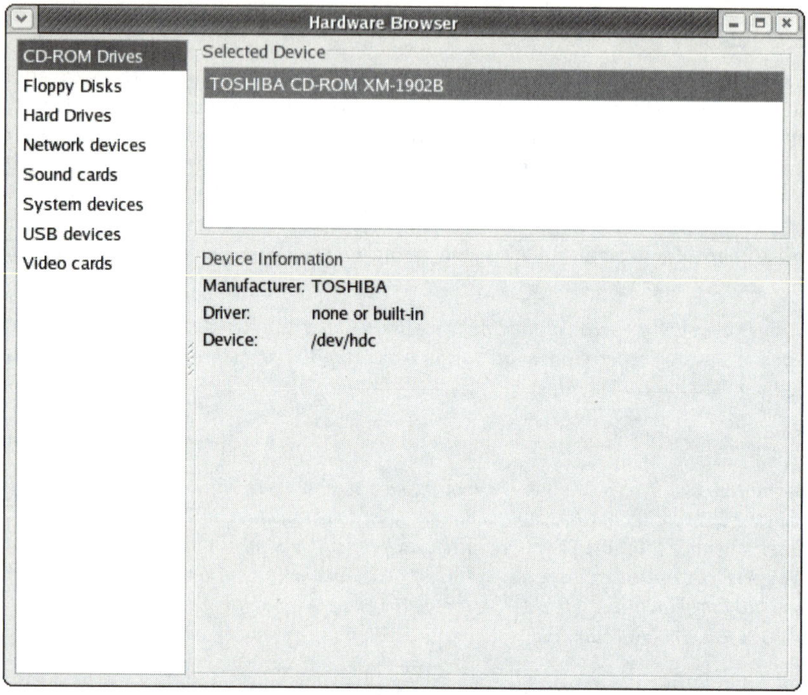

Figure 2-29

You can gather more information about the hardware by working from the terminal itself. The remainder of this section explains how you can gather information about your system using the CLI. The following table lists the major areas covered in this section.

Area	Description
CPU	The type of CPU and the amount of processing load
Memory	The amount of memory installed on the system and its usage pattern
Hard disk, CD-ROM, and floppy drives	The disk capacities and their usage status
Network cards	The network devices that are operational and their usage statistics
Mouse	The kind of mouse being used by the system
Keyboard	The kind of keyboard being used by the system
Display	The display card detected by the system and its current usage status
Various PCI and USB devices	The various devices detected by the system
Sound	The sound card detected and used by the system

You can find much of the information by using special files that are maintained dynamically by the operating system. You can find these files by looking in the `/proc` directory. The files are special because they are generated "on demand" by the operating system, and do not actually exist on the filesystem except when requested (for example, by the `ls /proc` command).

You can view the contents of these files by using the `cat` command (which prints to the screen the contents of any file whose name is passed as a parameter to it, as shown in the next few examples). Alternatively, you could use a text editor such as `gedit`.

CPU-Related Information

You can find the CPU information detected by the operating system by displaying the contents of the file `/proc/cpuinfo` (see Figure 2-30).

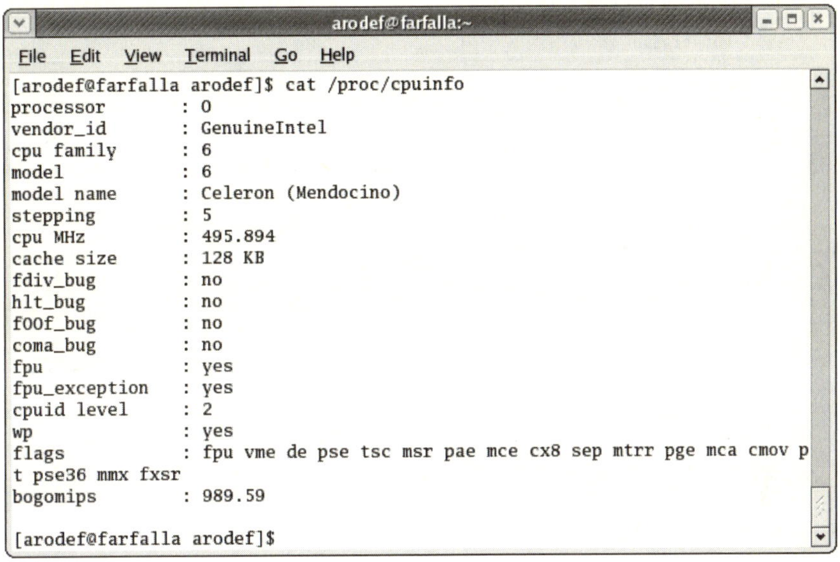

Figure 2-30

The `bogomips` value given at the bottom of the display is a rough calculation of the processor's speed, made by the operating system. This figure can be used to get a rough comparison of the relative speeds of two different computers running different processors.

Memory-Related Information

To find information about the total amount of RAM in the system, the amount of swap memory, and their respective uses, you can look at the System Monitor dialog box (as previously shown in the section on CPU usage). A quick alternative for finding out the status of RAM and swap is to display the contents of the file `/proc/meminfo`, as shown in Figure 2-31.

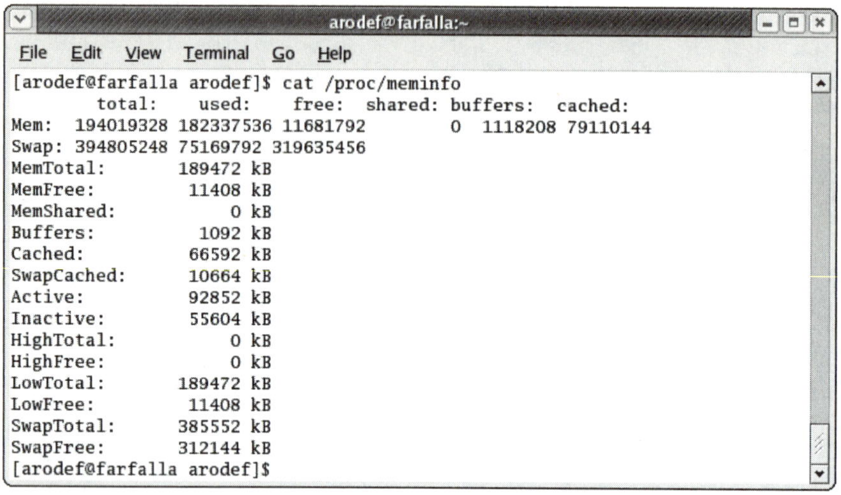

Figure 2-31

The memory usage can also be examined with the System Monitor or the `top` program, as shown previously in the section on CPU usage.

Information About the Filesystem Devices

To find information on the mounted file system in the computer, you can use the graphical interface offered by the System Monitor. However, there is also a quick CLI-based way to find similar information; this involves the `df` program. Figure 2-32 shows a typical usage of the `df` program.

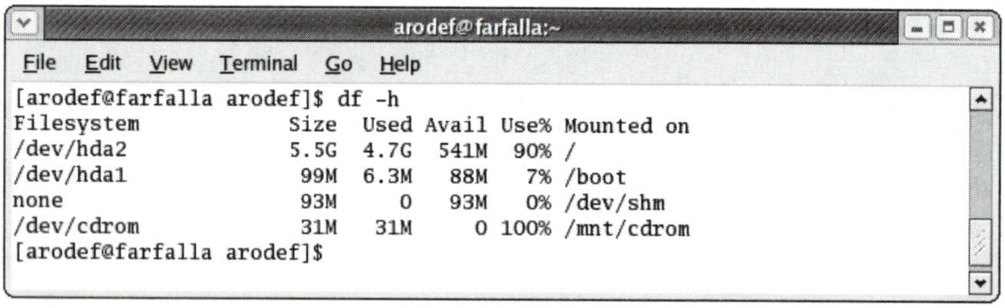

Figure 2-32

Here, the `-h` option displays the output in a more readable format (indicating size in megabytes and gigabytes, rather than bytes).

It is important to know the list of devices that are mounted and their mount points and filesystem types. You can find this information by invoking the `mount` command itself, without any arguments, as shown in Figure 2-33.

If you are using a hard disk with multiple partitions and multiple operating systems, it's handy to be able to check the partition structure of your hard disk and the various partition types existing on it. You can do this with the `fdisk` program, with the `-l` option. Figure 2-34 shows how to use this program.

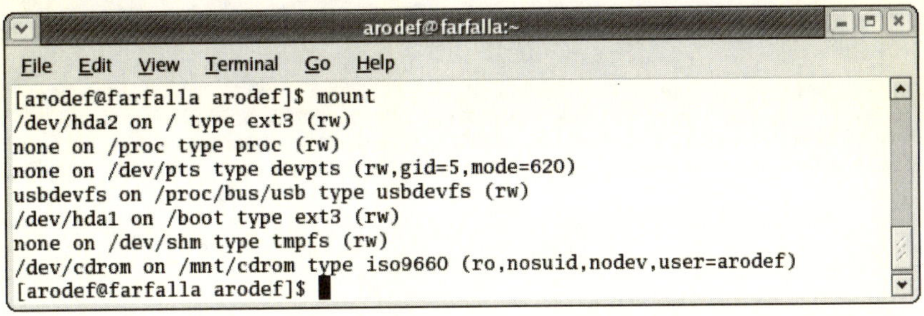

Figure 2-33

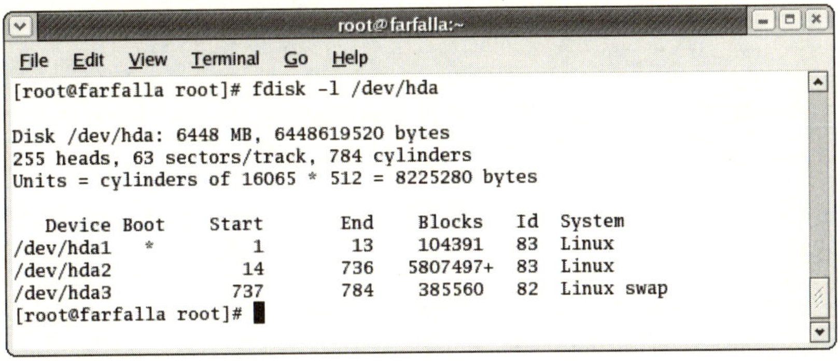

Figure 2-34

Note that you need root permissions to access some of this information, so log in as root using this command:

```
$ su -
```

As you'll recall, the super user mode is indicated by the change in the prompt—the last character of the prompt changing from a dollar ($) sign to a pound (#) sign.

Note that the `-l` option shown in the preceding screenshot is used to query the hard disk structure, and is quite safe. However, other `fdisk` options are designed for manipulating your hard disk partitions, and incorrect usage of these options can destroy your hard disk data.

> **Use the `fdisk` program with caution.**

Information about the Network Devices

To display information about the network devices configured and running in the system, you can use the `ifconfig` utility, as shown in Figure 2-35.

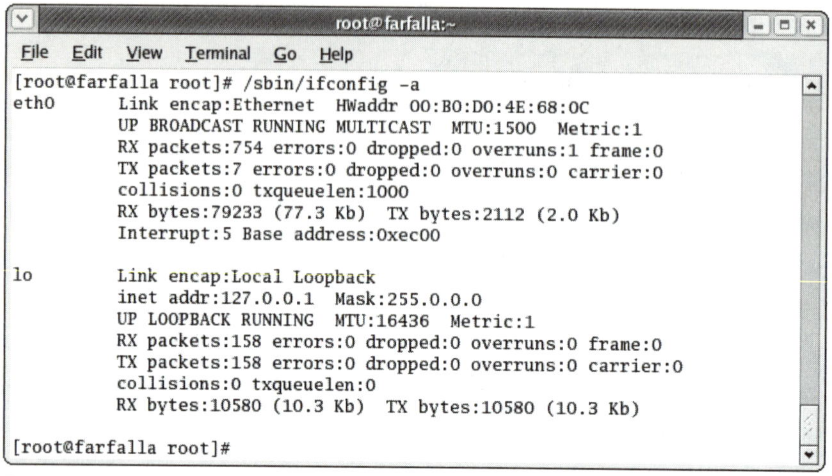

Figure 2-35

The `ifconfig` utility is contained in the `/sbin` directory. This directory is listed as part of the root user's `$PATH`, but is not listed (by default) in the `$PATH` of normal user accounts. Therefore, to run `ifconfig` you need either to specify the full path, `/sbin/ifconfig` (as done here), or switch to the root user's account and launch it from there (as we did with the preceding `fdisk` utility).

As you can see, this command displays a lot of network configuration information about the network devices on the computer. Using the `ifconfig` program without any arguments shows the status of only the network devices that are up and running. Adding the `-a` argument shows all the devices, whether they are running or not.

You can use the output of this command to find out the exact status of these devices. In the preceding example, you see two network devices: `eth0` and `lo`. The first is an Ethernet device, and the second is the local loopback network device. (The loopback device is always present, even when no real network devices exist in the system. This device is necessary for many network applications to work properly.)

So, you can check the *network configuration* of the devices via the `ifconfig` command. If you would like to find more information about the specific network card in use, you can use the Network Device Control program available from the System Tools section of the Red Hat menu.

You can find network details by using the `netstat` and the `route` programs. The `route` program displays the network routes active in the system, including the gateway through which this desktop sends and receives network traffic from the Internet. The `netstat` program shows the currently active network connections and networking services that are available on the machine. You take a look at `netstat` in Chapter 12, and you can learn more about `route` by typing **man route** at the terminal.

Information about the Mouse and the Keyboard

Fedora's tool for configuring the mouse is the program `redhat-config-mouse`—you can run this tool from the command line or by selecting Main Menu ➪ System Settings ➪ Mouse. You have encountered this program already because it was run during the installation process. Figure 2-36 provides a reminder of what that dialog box looks like.

Figure 2-36

The dialog box shows the present mouse configuration in the system. In the preceding screenshot, the mouse is a PS/2-based wheelmouse. The program stores the configuration of the mouse at `/etc/sysconfig/mouse`, which it uses while starting the mouse driver (called `gpm`) at system startup.

For configuring the keyboard layout, the GUI tool to use is the `redhat-config-keyboard` program. Executing this program brings up the dialog box shown in Figure 2-37, which shows your current keyboard layout.

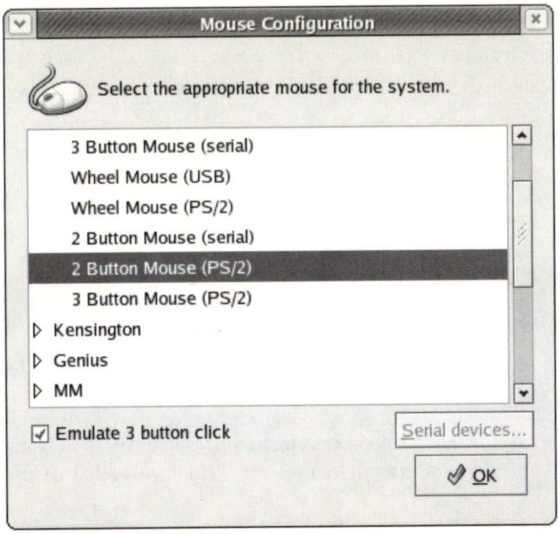

Figure 2-37

You can also change the keyboard layout from this dialog box. The program stores the keyboard's configuration in the file `/etc/sysconfig/keyboard`. The option that you choose here ensures that the appropriate keyboard map is loaded at boot time.

Information About the Display

Information about the display card on the system can be found using the `lspci` command (mentioned earlier). This generally reveals the actual video hardware on the system. In the `lspci` output (also shown earlier), the video hardware was revealed to be a S3 ProSavage card.

The X-Server software is responsible for the basic graphical display of the desktop. This server loads appropriate display drivers according to the video hardware. While recognized good video cards such as S3 have hardware-accelerated drivers, unrecognized video cards are put to use by loading generic display drivers that are low on performance. So, if you see choppiness in the display, it's possible that your video card has been detected incorrectly and that a generic display driver such as Vesa is loaded.

To check or modify the video card and monitor settings of the display, you can use the Red Hat configuration tool `redhat-config-xfree86` (either by typing this command at the command line or by selecting Main Menu ➪ System Settings ➪ Display). Figure 2-38 shows the dialog box that you get when this tool is executed.

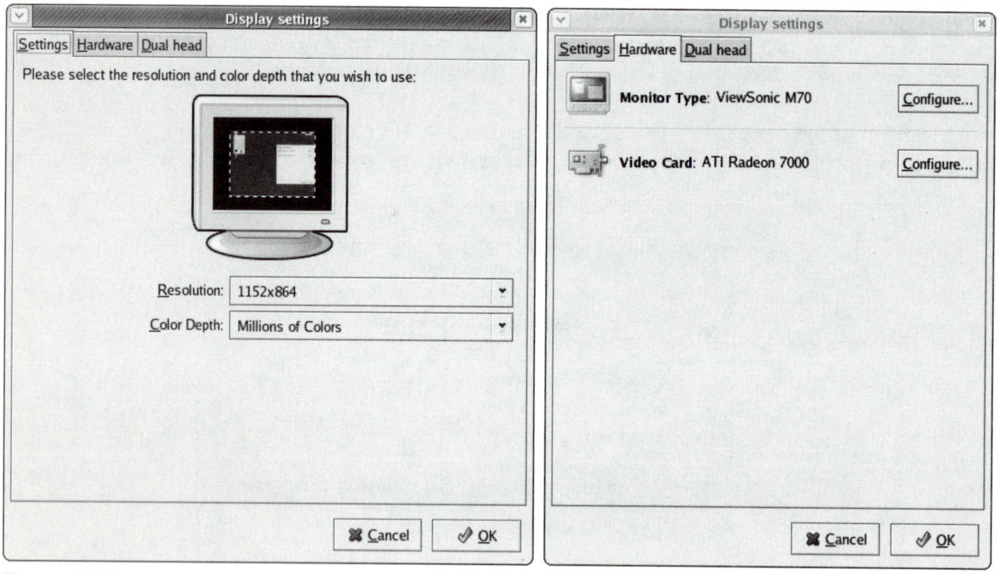

Figure 2-38

These dialog boxes show that the card has been detected correctly and the resolution and color depth are as expected. You can change these values if you want. The changes take effect only when the X server is restarted.

However, they also show that the monitor doesn't seem to be detected correctly. The model name of the monitor is set to a generic Monitor Model, indicating that manual configuration details given during installation are in effect. If you are happy with the display that is generated using these settings, you can just click OK and exit the program. If you want to adjust the settings to try to get something better, click the Configure button to select the precise configuration of the monitor and the video card (as you did to configure X server, during installation).

Information About the Sound Card

The sound card configuration tool is `redhat-config-soundcard` (again, you can run this tool from the command line, or from the menu shortcut Main Menu ➪ System Settings ➪ Soundcard Detection). This program displays a simple dialog box showing the sound card detected on the system and the kernel sound driver loaded, as shown in Figure 2-39.

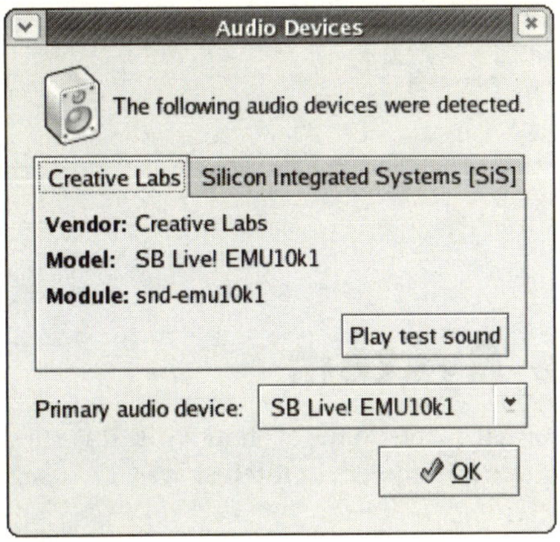

Figure 2-39

You can test the sound configuration by using the Play test sound button.

Information About Various PCI and USB Devices

Information about various other PCI and USB devices can be viewed using the `lspci` and the `lsusb` programs. You looked at the `lspci` program output in an earlier section. As a reminder, Figure 2-40 demonstrates the output you saw earlier.

This output allows you to confirm the PCI-based hardware in xour machine. For example, you can find out the audio controller card (`VT82C686`), the Ethernet network controller card (`RTL-8139`), the video capture card (`Bt878`), and the graphics card (`S3 ProSavage`). These details are extremely useful when hardware auto-detection hasn't happened as planned and you need to tell the configuration program explicitly about the hardware that you want to configure.

The `lsusb` program output lists the characteristics of all the USB devices plugged into the computer. Its output is very verbose and might be too technical for the average user. However, when you hot-plug a USB device, the device characteristics can be verified from the `lspci` output.

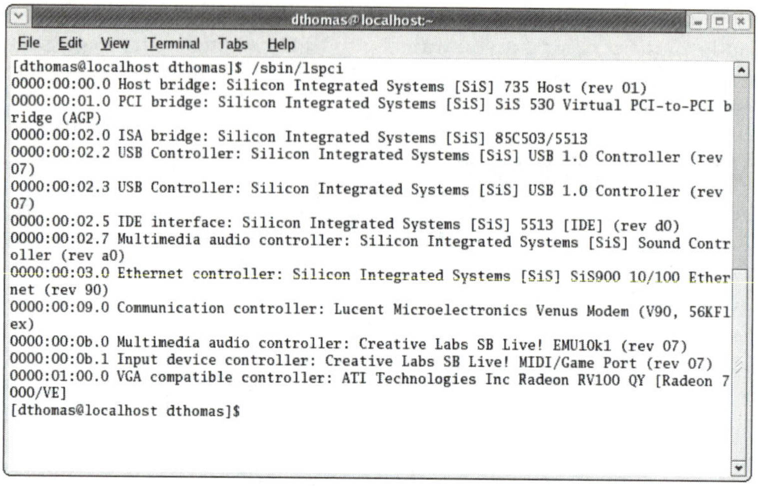

Figure 2-40

Monitoring the System

It is necessary to monitor resource usage on the system while it is running to see if any resource bottlenecks exist. The primary resource parameters of interest are CPU usage and memory usage.

You can check the CPU usage in a number of ways. There is a graphical tool called the System Monitor (you can launch it by selecting Main Menu ➪ System Tools ➪ System Monitor). The System Monitor tab in this application displays the CPU usage over time in a nice graphical format, as shown in Figure 2-41.

Aside from the CPU usage information, the System Monitor tab also provides information on usage of memory (RAM and swap) and mounted filesystems.

Swap memory isn't actually memory in the conventional sense. It's disk space that the operating system uses to store information temporarily—the operating system swaps data from RAM to the swap memory, as necessary. Hence, it functions as if it were extra RAM, and allows the operating system to handle programs and data that require more actual RAM than is installed on the machine. The amount of swap memory available is determined by the size of the `swap` *partition created when installing the operating system.*

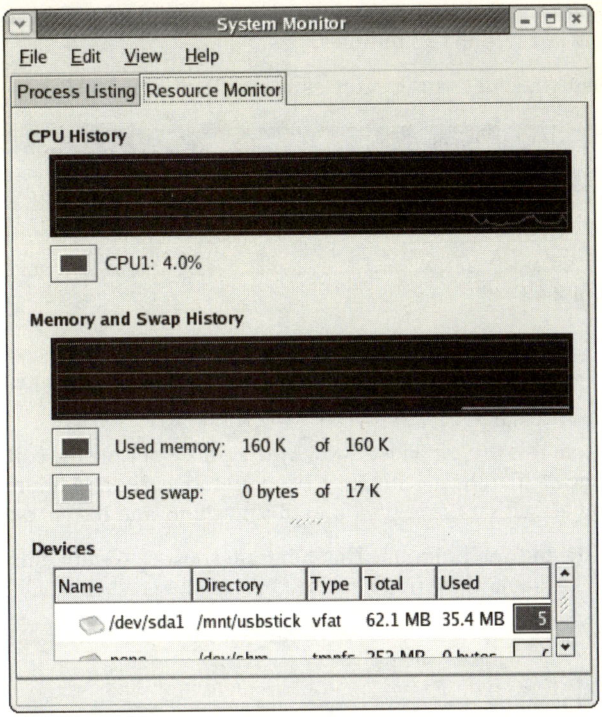

Figure 2-41

Using Load Average to Measure CPU Usage

In Linux and other UNIX-based operating systems, the CPU usage is often measured in terms of *load average*. Load average is displayed using three numerical values. Put simply, the load average is the average number of processes waiting to be executed by the operating system over a given time interval. Over a period of time, these readings give a good indication of the computer's current and recent processing load. You can examine the load average in various ways:

- You can examine the contents of the file `/proc/loadavg`. Figure 2-42 shows a typical `/proc/loadavg` file.

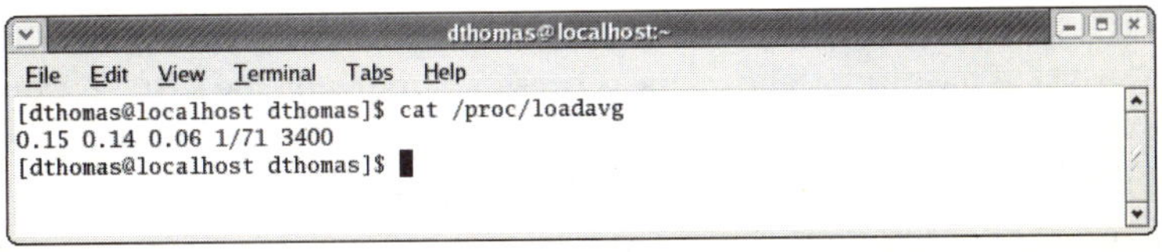

Figure 2-42

In this example, the first three figures (`0.44, 0.29, 0.17`) show the load average of the system taken over the last 1, 5, and 15 minutes.

- You can execute the `uptime` program, as shown in Figure 2-43.

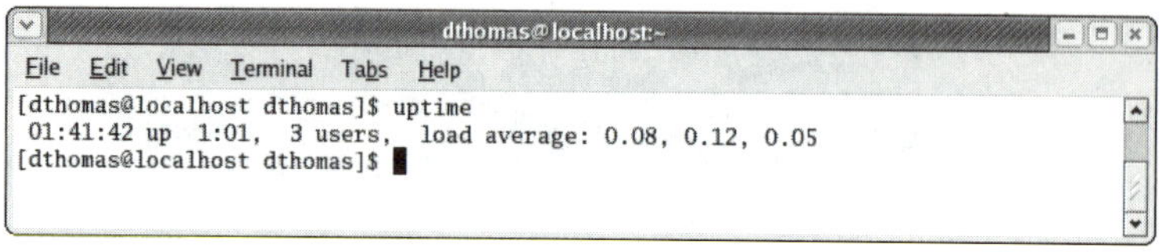

Figure 2-43

Figure 2-43 shows output from a machine whose load average is currently very low, and has actually been decreasing over the last 15 minutes.

The output from this program also shows the amount of time the computer has been running—Figure 2-43 shows that the machine has been up for nearly 15½ hours. It also shows that there are two terminals with users logged into this machine, and the current time on the system.

- You can execute the `top` program. This program shows a wealth of information, as specified in Figure 2-44. The display also updates itself every few seconds.

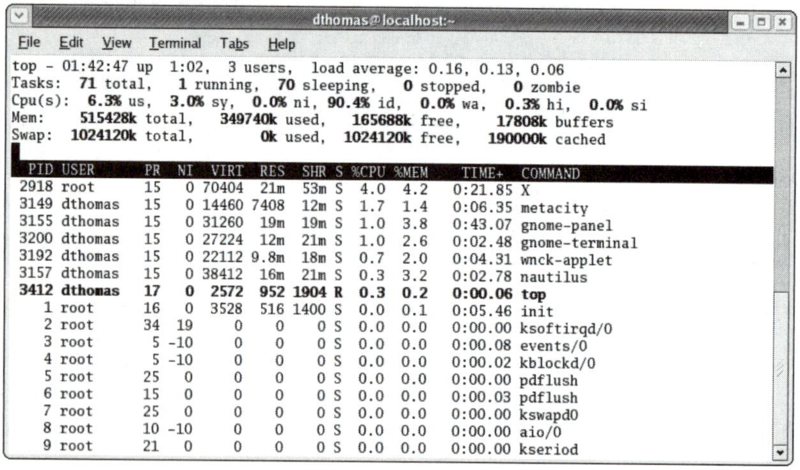

Figure 2-44

The first part of the display shows the system's load average and the memory usage in the system. The rest of the display shows the processes running on the system, along with a wealth of information on each process, such as the user privilege under which the process is running, and the process identifier.

This output is also interactive, allowing you to change various properties of the display and even to kill processes. For more on this, take a look at the Interactive Commands section of the manual (type **man top** at the command line and space down until you find it).

When you want to exit the `top` display, press *q* on your keyboard.

Configuring the Desktop

The workspace and the panel are all part of the desktop environment. The default desktop environment that you have used so far is the *GNOME* desktop environment. This environment controls the behavior of the panel and the application GUI windows, session management, and various other behavioral GUI functions. In Fedora 2, the default GNOME desktop has a new look called the *Bluecurve theme*.

> **This theme covers all the color design in the menus, the panels, the desktop background, and the window decorations. Of course, this is not the only theme available for use on the desktop, but it is certainly the one on which the Red Hat design team has spent most of its effort. The result is a desktop whose look and feel is far superior to and more aesthetically pleasing than that of its predecessors.**

Using the Desktop Control Center

You can control a lot of the features of your desktop using the *GNOME desktop control center*. The control center program displays a number of options to configure the desktop (and if you're familiar with the Windows operating systems, you'll find that the control center is quite similar to the Windows Control Panel).

You can reach the control center by selecting Main Menu ➪ Preferences ➪ Control Center (see Figure 2-45).

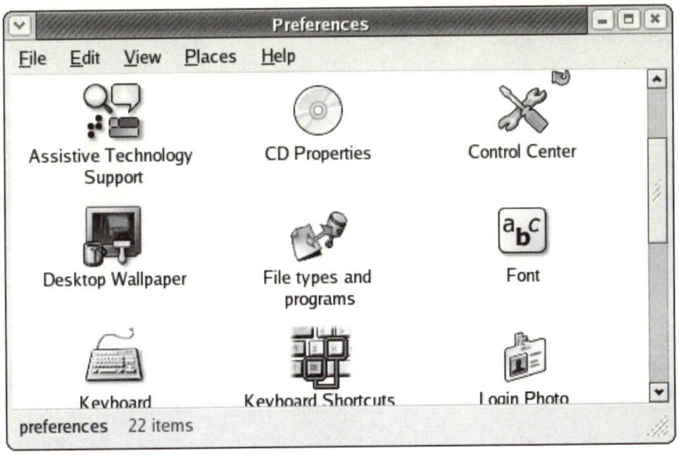

Figure 2-45

Let's look at the options in this configuration program in more detail:

- **About Myself:** This allows you to put additional information about yourself into the system—such as your name, office, and phone numbers. It also allows you to select a *command shell*. The command shell interpreter that is used by default in Fedora is *bash*. The bash shell is covered in greater detail in Chapter 6.

The information entered in this dialog box is stored in the user account database in `/etc/passwd`. You can also enter this information at the terminal by using the `chfn` command. You'll read more about `/etc/passwd` and the `chfn` command in Chapter 8.

- **Accessibility:** This allows you to enter various accessibility options for users with disabilities. If you select the Enable keyboard accessibility checkbox in this dialog box, you reveal various options designed to ease the usability of the GUI. For example:
    - The Enable Mouse Keys option allows you to use the numeric keypad on the keyboard to control mouse movements. This is useful for users who have difficulty handling the mouse.
    - The Enable Bounce Keys option allows you to set the optimum key repeat rate. This is handy for users who have a tendency to hit a key repeatedly when they intend to hit it only once.
    - The Enable Slow Keys option allows one to set the keyboard key acceptance period (the time between the keystroke and its acceptance), for users who type successive keys after unusually long intervals.
    - The Enable Sticky Keys option allows you to configure the keyboard for users who have difficulties in making the simultaneous keystrokes (such as *Alt+F1*) that are required in many applications.
    - The Toggle keys option allows an audible indication to be made whenever a toggle key, such as Num Lock or Caps Lock, is toggled.
- **Desktop Wallpaper:** This allows you to set the background of the desktop. You can set the background to an image file present in the system. Alternatively, you can specify the background to be a simple color or a gradient of two colors.
- **CD Properties:** This allows you to configure the automatic CD detection program `magicdev`. You can ask `magicdev` to mount CD media automatically when the CD is inserted into the drive. You can also specify whether you want to have the file manager open with the CD contents in this case, or whether you want the `autorun` program in the CD to be executed automatically.

  This dialog box also allows you to play audio CDs or DVDs automatically on insertion.
- **Control Center:** This is just a link to the Preferences folder.
- **Menus & Toolbars:** This allows you to change the behavior and appearance of menus and toolbars of windows on the desktop. For instance, you may hide the icons altogether, by selecting the Text Only option from the Toolbar Button Labels drop-down list.
- **File Types and Programs:** This allows you to set program associations for different file types. You can categorize each file type according to its extension (the portion of the filename after the last period), and tell the operating system what application it should use to open files of each type when the user clicks a file of that type in the Nautilus file manager.

Unlike the Windows operating system, filename extensions don't matter in the Linux operating system. A program is considered executable according to the permissions set on the program file, not according to its filename extension. However, in GUI applications such as Nautilus, filename extensions are used not for executing programs, but rather for opening data files in appropriate applications.

- **Font:** This allows you to set the different fonts for the desktop widgets. It also allows you to specify the rendering of fonts on the desktop.
- **Handheld PDA:** For users with Palm or other handheld PDAs, this option allows you to set up synchronization of your local data with that of the PDA. The configuration is done using an easy wizard-like interface.
- **Keyboard:** This allows you to set the behavior of a keyboard key when it's depressed for an extended period (in particular, the length of time that a key must be depressed before it generates repeat signals, and the rate at which a key will repeat). You can also control cursor blinks here.
- **Keyboard Shortcuts:** This allows you to set the various keyboard shortcuts that you can use in the desktop (such as the *Alt+F2* shortcut, which invokes the Run Program dialog box).
- **Login Photo:** This allows you to select an image to be used instead of your name at the initial desktop GUI login screen. To see the effect of this, you also have to make changes in the configuration of the Gnome Desktop Manager (GDM) using the program `gdmconfig`. (In the General tab, you must change the local greeter to be the Standard Greeter rather than the default Graphical Greeter, and in the Standard Greeter tab, check the Show choosable user images checkbox.) The effect of these changes is visible the next time you start GDM. GDM is started at the beginning of each boot.

To be more accurate, GDM is started each time the run level 5 is entered—run levels are further discussed later on in this chapter. You can change run levels to make GDM restart and show you the changes without rebooting. However, the standard greeting is not as attractive as the graphical login, which is endowed with the Bluecurve interface.

- **Menus & Toolbars:** This allows you to specify the look of the menus and the button icons.
- **More Preferences:** This icon opens up a dialog box with three suboptions:
    - **CD Database:** This suboption allows you to specify a CD database server for retrieving CD and track information when you play an audio CD in the computer.
    - **Panel:** This suboption configures the behavior of the panel in the desktop. You can opt to disable the animation of panels in the desktop or to change their animation speed.
    - **Sessions:** This suboption allows you to configure the behavior of the GNOME desktop for maintaining states between successive login sessions. The GNOME desktop can save the open applications and their current settings when you log out. When you log in later, these applications restart with their saved settings. Note that the feature of saving settings works only with applications that are compatible with the GNOME desktop environment.
- **Mouse:** This allows you to control the mouse behavior in the desktop. You can change the mouse pointer, control its speed and double-click delay, and even set it for use for left-handed individuals, in which case the right and the left button functionalities are exchanged.
- **Network Proxy:** For HTTP clients, this allows you to specify the HTTP proxy details and (optionally) the authentication information to use this proxy server.
- **Password:** This allows the current user to change his or her login password. Note that you can also perform this action at the terminal using the `passwd` program.

- **Preferred applications:** This suboption allows you to select preferred applications for opening Web pages and text documents. It also allows you to specify your default terminal emulator application (by default, you can set it to be `gnome-terminal` or `xterm`).

The `gnome-terminal` *is more feature-rich than* `xterm`*, but it's also heavy on memory requirements. When your system is low on RAM, it makes sense to use* `the xterm`*—which has less memory overhead and also loads quickly. However, it can be beneficial to use* `gnome-terminal` *when you need multiple terminals. You can get multiple GNOME terminals with just a single launch of the* `gnome-terminal` *application, but for multiple* `xterm` *terminals you must run* `xterm` *once for each terminal.*

- **Screensaver:** This allows you to configure a screensaver for your desktop. You can set a single screensaver, set multiple screensavers, or disable the screensaver completely.
- **Sound:** This allows you to associate sound events with desktop events, such as opening or closing of applications. By default, sound events are disabled. But if you enable them, you can set individual sound files to be played for each desktop event.
- **Theme:** The GNOME desktop ships with the Red Hat Bluecurve theme. This dialog box enables you to change the theme of the desktop to others available in the menu. Many of these alternative themes are also very attractive and well worth a close look.
- **Window Focus:** This option allows you to define the behavior for working with different windows in the desktop. You can opt to either click a window to work in it, or merely point the mouse pointer inside it to start working in the window.

Managing Processes

To manage a desktop and control its resources, it is very important to grasp the concepts behind *processes* running in the computer. You can think of a process simply as an independent program entity executing and using computer resources such as CPU time and memory. Any application that is executed is started as an independent process. An application may start its own child processes—indeed many applications, such as Web servers and database servers, have multiple processes to tend to the needs of different clients at the same time.

Understanding Processes

Typically, a process is started by a *parent process*. The newly launched process can in turn launch *child processes* if it wants to. When you are working at the desktop, any new program is executed as a child process of the program that is receiving and interpreting your commands. For example, when you are at the terminal prompt, you are interacting with the shell interpreter program (by default, this is bash). The shell itself is running as a process in the computer. Any program that you execute at the bash prompt is launched as a child process of the bash program.

In fact, every executing program on the computer is a process that has been launched by some other parent process; so all the running processes in the computer can be represented in the form of a hierarchical tree. There is only one exception—the first process of the computer. This is the `init` program, which is launched by the operating system itself just after booting. Thereafter `init` *forks* off child processes, which, in turn, may fork off other child processes of their own.

Because of the underlying way new processes are launched, launching a child process in the UNIX environment is also frequently referred to as forking. When launching a child process, the parent process makes a copy of itself by forking, and then executes the child program in the memory space of the new copy.

Viewing Running Processes

The System Monitor program discussed earlier in the chapter also allows you to see the processes running in the machine. You can see this list of processes in Figure 2-46.

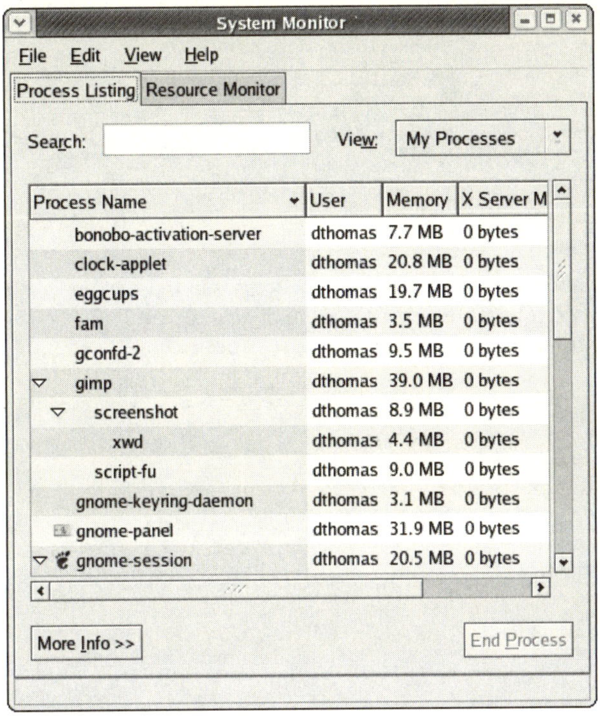

Figure 2-46

You can view the processes sorted by any of the columns on display by clicking the respective column header. Here, you can see that we've sorted the processes according to their memory usage.

At the terminal, you can use the `ps` program to view the processes running in the machine in a non-dynamic way. You can invoke this program in a variety of ways, which are listed on its man page. However, we will mention some commonly used arguments of this program.

To view all the processes running within your current logging session, you can use the `ps` program without any arguments. To view all the processes running in the machine, you can use the command `ps ax`, as demonstrated in Figure 2-47.

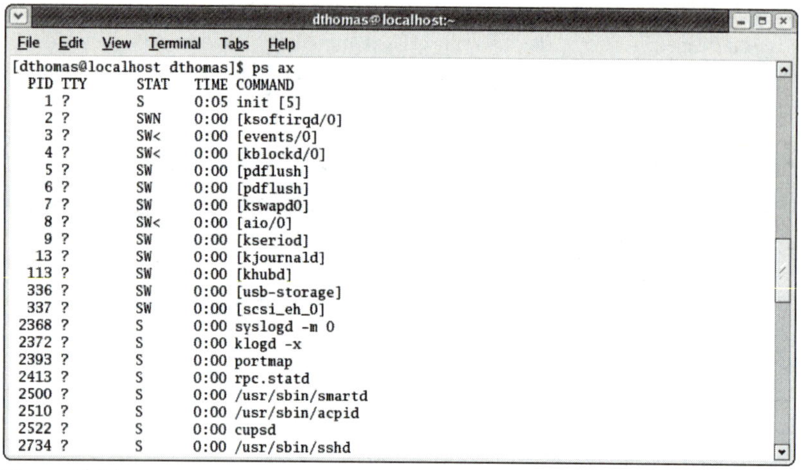

Figure 2-47

The `pstree` program allows you to view all the processes in the system in a tree format, and gives a good idea of the hierarchical nature of processes in the computer. Figure 2-48 shows just a small part of the output of this program, beginning with the `init` process.

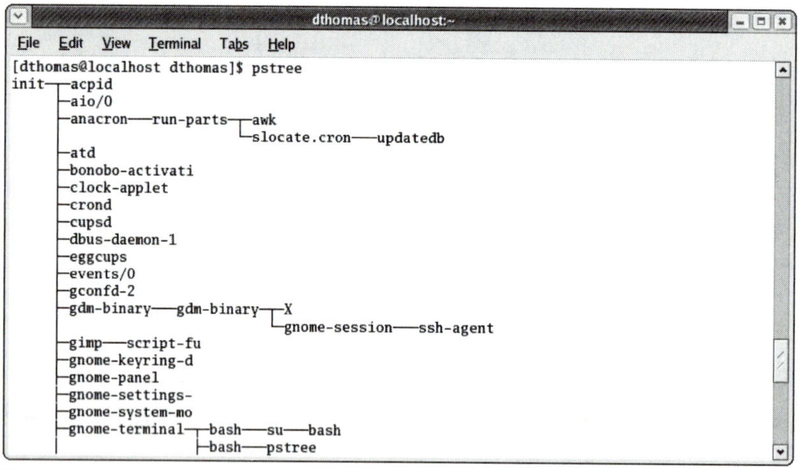

Figure 2-48

As you saw earlier in the chapter, the terminal also provides the top program, which allows you to view the process list in an interactive manner. It shows the process list just as you would see it on the GUI system monitor, and allows you to sort the results by pressing various keystrokes. To get more help on the keys to use for sorting the display, press the help (?) key.

Taking Control of Running Processes

Sometimes you need to exercise some control on a process to keep your memory or CPU resources in check. A process might take up all the available memory in the system and make the system virtually unusable. In such a case, terminating the offending process to regain control of the system might be appropriate. The act of terminating a process is also referred to as *killing* it.

You can use the System Monitor (see the section "Viewing Running Processes") to kill runaway processes. You can select the target process in the list and select the End Process button at the bottom right of the dialog box. Of course, killing a process can result in loss of unsaved data (depending on how you kill it, as explained shortly). For this reason, a confirmation dialog box allows you to confirm your decision to kill the process.

You can also use the `kill` command from a terminal window to kill a running process. The `kill -9 <process id>` command terminates the process abruptly. The *<process id>* corresponds to the actual process id of the process you are attempting to kill. The *–9* indicates that the `SIGKILL` signal is sent to the process causing it to terminate immediately. Other signals may be delivered to running processes from the command line using the `kill` command. For more information on specific signals, run the `man 7 signal` command.

Note that you can kill a process only if you have permission to—that is, if it's running under your user account or if you have permission to take control of another user's processes. This is a security feature that ensures that a user's processes are safe from being terminated by other users of the machine. The only exception is the root (super user).

> *The root user can kill any of the machine's processes; therefore, it is necessary to take precautions to ensure that (as the root user) you don't kill a process by mistake. To prevent this, it's a good idea not to log in as the root user to the machine. Instead, log in using a normal user account. Then, whenever you need to perform a task as the root user, you can assume super user permissions using the following command, as explained earlier in the chapter:*

```
$ su -
```

> *After finishing your immediate job as the root user, log out and return to the login shell of the previous user.*

You can also use the `top` program to kill processes. You can sort the display of the `top` utility by resource usage (in the same way as you can sort the processes using the System Monitor), which is useful when a process is taking up too much CPU or memory resource. Sorting the processes in this way brings the offending program to the top of the list and makes it easy to identify. You can then use the process's process ID to kill it using the `k` command of the `top` program.

Notice that the `top` program asks for a signal number to send to the process. A kill signal is a special message sent to the process by the current process. If you just accept the default option of 15, a signal called `SIGTERM` is sent to the target process asking it to shut down on its own. This allows the target process to shut down cleanly after saving all its unsaved information. However, if the program seems to be ignoring this signal, you can repeat the process sending the signal number of 9 instead; this simply terminates the process without giving it a chance to shut down on its own.

Managing Services

Services on a Linux system are daemon processes; that is, they are alive throughout the time that the system is up and running. Typically, services are configured to start at boot time. Super users may disable a service or start one. Examples of services are telnet, ftp, rlogin, and so on. Services may be managed from the Start menu System Settings ➪ Server Settings ➪ Services (see Figure 2-49).

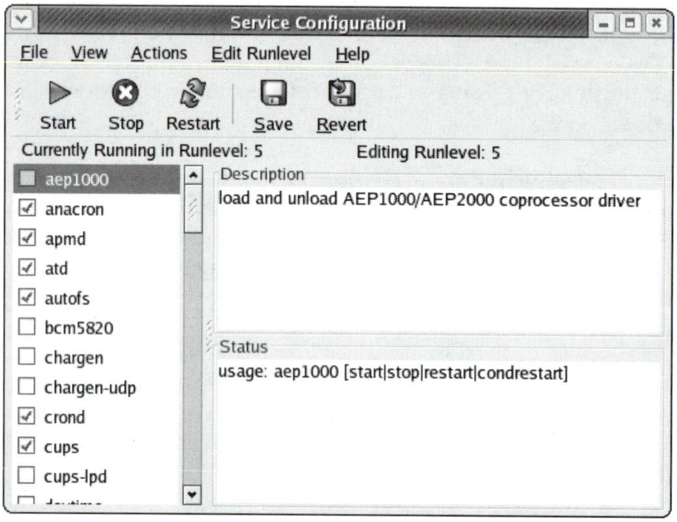

Figure 2-49

Services can be picked from the left panel, and you choose operations to perform on them, such as starting or stopping them, from the buttons on the top panel.

When the computer starts up, the operating system loads and starts off the first process—the `init` process. The `init` process then starts off any required subprocesses before the computer is ready to be used by the user. The processes that the operating system needs to start off after the booting process are specified using *run levels*. A run level is a state of the machine that determines the processes to be run.

The following describes the seven run levels, numbered from 0 to 6:

- *Run level 0* signifies the halted state of a machine. While changing run levels, if you set the new run level to be 0, it effectively halts the machine.
- *Run level 1* stands for the *single user mode*. This brings the machine to a super user mode and disallows external users from using the machine. All networking functions are disabled at this level. This level is also called the *system maintenance mode* because it is generally used to recover from serious system problems. At this level, the root prompt is displayed without any attempt to check the corresponding password. This is necessary to allow for the various maintenance functions that need to be done without the hindrance of an authentication system; however, it also leaves the system open to any malicious users physically present at the computer. Therefore, this run level should be used only when absolutely necessary.

- *Run level 2* allows multiple users to log in to the machine through *virtual terminals* and other login devices, but still doesn't activate any networking functions.
- *Run level 3* finally allows networking processes to be started, and allows the complete resources of the system to be used effectively. However, until this level the interface to the desktop is through a CLI interface. Because the GUI interface uses the computer resources (such as CPU, memory, and hard disk) intensively, this run level is mainly used by server class workstations where precious computer resources are used to deliver networking and other application services more effectively.
- *Run level 4* is unused. You can use it to define your own custom run level.
- *Run level 5* finally allows the X-server process to be started and the accompanying desktop to be loaded to allow users to use the system with a GUI. The desktop that you have been using until now has been working at run level 5.
- *Run level 6* signifies the rebooting state of a machine and is used to restart the machine.

When a machine boots, the `init` program examines the contents of the configuration file `/etc/inittab` to determine the run level to boot the computer to and executes all the processes for that run level. The processes to execute for a particular run level are specified as special program scripts in the directory `/etc/rcx.d/`, where *x* is the run level to boot to.

You can find the computer's present run level by using the program `runlevel`. This outputs two numbers, which represent the previous and current run levels.

You can change the current run level using the `telinit` program. This program needs to be executed as root, and takes a single argument—the run level to boot to. For example, to reboot the system you can execute the command `telinit 6`.

Additionally, run levels and the processes that are part of a run level can be managed from the Services menu discussed previously in this chapter.

Managing Users

Users coming from operating systems such as Windows 9x and Windows Me will find in Fedora a more strict arrangement of permissions that describe what each user can and cannot do. One user's processes and data can't be accessed or modified by other users of the system, unless they are specifically permitted to do so. This concept of user security runs through the heart of the Linux system.

User management is discussed in depth in Chapter 8. However, the key points are summarized here.

Understanding User Management

As previously mentioned, the root user (or super user) has complete access over all the computer's resources. For this reason, various security restrictions are put in place in the system to ensure that this user privilege is not compromised. Even as the administrator of the system, you should attempt to do most of your work as a less privileged user, and assume super user privileges only when they're needed.

Many new users will also find it unusual that the Linux desktop allows many users to work on the system simultaneously. While only one user can work *physically* at the desktop, other users can log in through network services such as telnet and its more secure equivalent, secure shell (ssh).

Linux has a simple way of organizing users. Every user can be part of one or more *groups*. In addition to securing a resource by applying permissions to individual users, you can place users into a group and apply permissions to the group instead.

Understanding Permissions

We have already talked about how privileges are required to control other users' processes; the same applies to *files* and *directories*. Every file and directory is associated with a single user (its owner) and also with a group. Then, specific permissions to access a file are given to the three classes of users:

- The owner
- The group members
- Everyone else

Each of the classes is allowed a combination of three kinds of access permissions, as explained in the following table.

Permission	Meaning when applied to files	Meaning when applied to directories
Read	Enables the user to read the contents of the file	Enables the user to list the contents of the directory
Write	Enables the user to change the contents of the file	Enables the user to create or remove files within the directory
Execute	Enables the user to execute the file	Enables the user to access files and subdirectories

You can find the permissions of a given file using the `ls` program. The following example uses the command `ls -l` to display a "long" version of the file information:

```
$ ls -l /usr/bin/top
-r-xr-xr-x      1  root      root      56406  Aug 12 15:50 /usr/bin/top
```

The read, write, and executable permissions are represented using the characters `r`, `w`, and `x`, respectively. The first part of the file information (in the preceding example, the expression `-r-xr-xr-x`) indicates the file's permission. The first character indicates the file type (directory, character device, and so on), but it is the remaining characters that we're interested in right now. This sequence consists of three sets of three characters—one set each to describe permissions of the owner, the group, and the others. For example, the sequence `r-x` indicates that only the read and execution permissions are set, and no write permission is available. Therefore, this file's permission specifies that all possible users can read and execute the file's content, but they cannot modify the file contents.

You can use the CLI tools chown, chmod, and chgrp to modify the permissions of files and directories in the system. You will learn more about these tools in Chapter 8.

Managing Users

You can add, remove, and modify user accounts on the system in a GUI by using the Red Hat user configuration tool, redhat-config-users, which you can launch using Main Menu ➪ System Settings ➪ Users & Groups. The primary interface of this tool is shown in Figure 2-50.

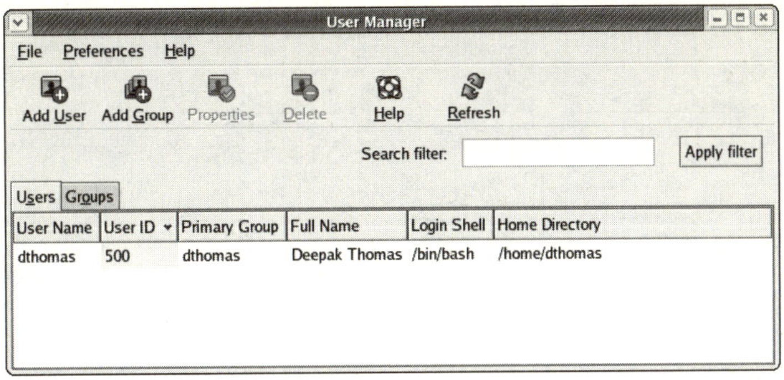

Figure 2-50

You'll need to provide the root password to use this utility. Using this interface you can add, edit, or modify users and groups.

The same operations can be carried out in the CLI, too. The various tools for the job are described in the following table.

Program	Purpose
useradd	Add a user
userdel	Remove a user
chfn, chsh	Modify user details

You can read more about the use of these programs in Chapter 8.

Because Fedora can be a multiuser system, it may be necessary for administrators to monitor the system's users. Unlike Microsoft systems, Linux systems allow multiple users to be logged on to the same system, each with their own account. The who command lists the currently logged-on users of the system. The finger command can be used to perform a lookup of the users of a remote system. This requires the finger daemon to be up and running; finger is disabled by default. The example in Figure 2-51 illustrates the use of the who and finger programs. The last command prints a history of user logins.

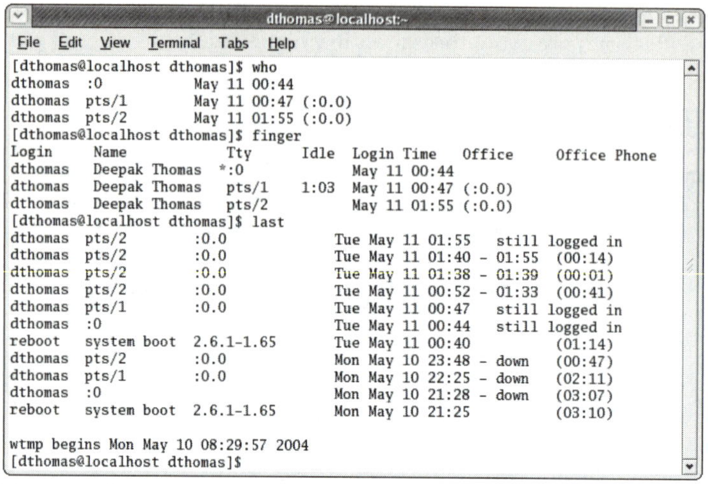

Figure 2-51

Summary

This chapter provided a quick tour of the many features and functionalities available to you when using Fedora. The remainder of the book covers in detail many of the topics that were briefly touched on in this chapter.

The overview began with a look at the basic components of the desktop—the workspace, the panel, and the desktop menu. You saw that there are various methods of launching GUI applications—through the desktop menu, the run dialog box, the shortcuts on the panel, and the terminal emulator.

Moreover, while there is a good deal of functionality available through Fedora's GUI-based utilities, you can achieve more *complete* control over the desktop at the terminal—there are many command line interface (CLI) utilities, and each one offers a plethora of options. You saw how to launch programs via the terminal, and that the `apropos` and `man` commands help you to find out the right program for the job, and how to use that program.

You've seen the hierarchical nature of Fedora's filesystem. There's a single directory (known as the root directory, and denoted by `/`) at the top of the hierarchy, and a subdirectory structure beneath it. To examine the file structure of any external device (such as a CD-ROM, a floppy, or a network drive), you *mount* the device to a directory in this hierarchy, and then treat the device's filesystem as a part of the overall filesystem. You also looked at how to navigate the computer's filesystem using both the CLI and the Nautilus GUI.

It's useful to be able to check the hardware configuration of the machine—CPU, memory, storage and network devices, the display, and peripherals such as the mouse, keyboard, and the sound card. As you saw in Chapter 1, the system attempts to detect hardware automatically during the installation process. This chapter explained the utilities that allow you to check and adjust this configuration manually at any time after installation, including the GUI-based Hardware Browser, and CLI-based utilities such as lspci. You also met the GUI-based System Monitor, and files such as /proc/cpuinfo and /proc/loadavg, and CLI programs such as top that allow you to monitor performance.

You also saw how the desktop control center allows you to customize the Fedora desktop in many ways to suit your convenience and taste.

One important area of desktop usage is process management. The chapter examined the various methods for observing processes and controlling them when necessary. You also looked at run levels, the various states of the machine that determine which processes and services are available in the machine at any given time.

The chapter took a quick look at user management, and at how Fedora allows you to organize a system's users into groups (which is handy for allowing or denying access to system resources). Finally, you took a quick look at the GUI-based User Manager and command line utilities such as useradd and passwd, which allow you to begin managing your accounts; you'll see more of that in Chapter 8.

Exercises

Try the following exercises to increase your skill level.

1. Change the wallpaper (the background) on your desktop.
2. Locate a file called magic on the system. Hint: You can use the locate command to do this.
3. Check your system's load average.

3

Connecting to the Internet

Connecting to a network in general, and to the Internet in particular, has come a long way since the days of manually setting up network cards and hacking modem dialup scripts. Fedora 2 offers a vastly improved configuration interface while retaining the flexibility that enables users to roll up their sleeves and dive into the configuration files should the need arise (rarely, if ever). This chapter looks at the following aspects of connecting to the Internet:

- Connecting to the Internet through an ISP
- Dealing with network devices, connections, and profiles
- Configuring and using the software you need to access the Internet
- Considering the safety of your machine while connected to the Internet
- Contending with common problems related to connecting to the Internet

Connecting to the Internet

Regardless of whether you plan to connect to the Internet using an analog modem, an *x*DSL broadband connection, Ethernet card, or any of a variety of other methods, you need to configure your system before that connection can take place. Enter the *Internet Configuration Wizard* (Main Menu ➪ System Tools ➪ Internet Configuration Wizard).

Of course, sometimes your connection doesn't quite work the first time you set it up, or you need to change something after you've configured it once (perhaps your Internet service provider has changed the dial-up number, or perhaps you've just upgraded to broadband). In this event, you'll need to use the Network Configuration Tool to edit the settings you've already entered.

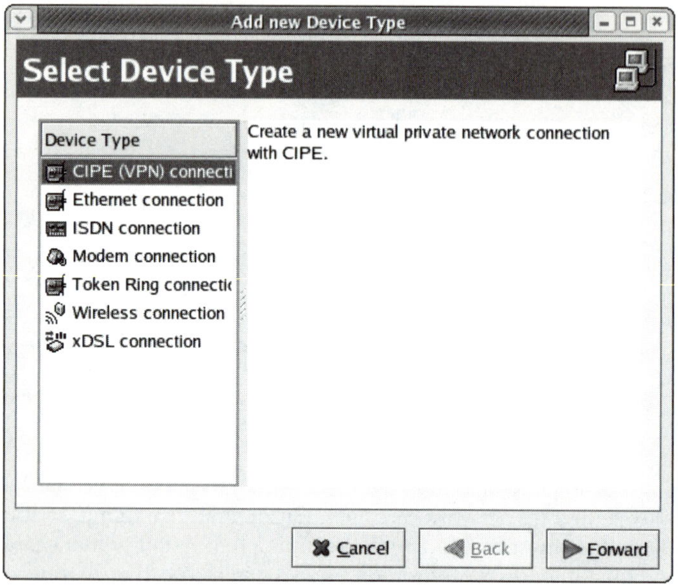

Figure 3-1

Network Configuration Tool

Once you've become reasonably confident setting up connections, you'll probably bypass the connection wizard and come directly to this tool, as your first port of call. You can access it from the Main Menu by selecting System Settings ⇨ Network (see Figure 3-2).

Please note that the Network Configuration Tool is also known as the Network Administration Tool.

Before you look at setting up the different types of connection in detail, let's take a quick tour around this tool so that you know where everything is.

The first thing to notice here is that the panel contains a number of tabs:

- The *Devices* tab is the first of these, and lists the device connections that you have available on your machine. This provides you with very versatile control over the way your machine behaves—we'll come back to it in a later section of this chapter.
- Next is the *Hardware* tab, which allows you to manage the various network devices on the system, such as Ethernet cards, internal modems, and wireless cards.
- The *DNS* (Domain Name Service) tab allows you to specify DNS server information (if this doesn't mean anything to you, don't worry; it applies only to certain types of connection, and is explained in detail later in this chapter). Users of DHCP (more on this later, too) can usually safely leave this alone because DHCP automatically sets up the DNS information.
- Finally, there is the *Hosts* tab, which allows you to modify the hostname of the machine and add aliases to the same host (so the same machine may be called `foo.widgets.com` or `bar.widgets.com`).

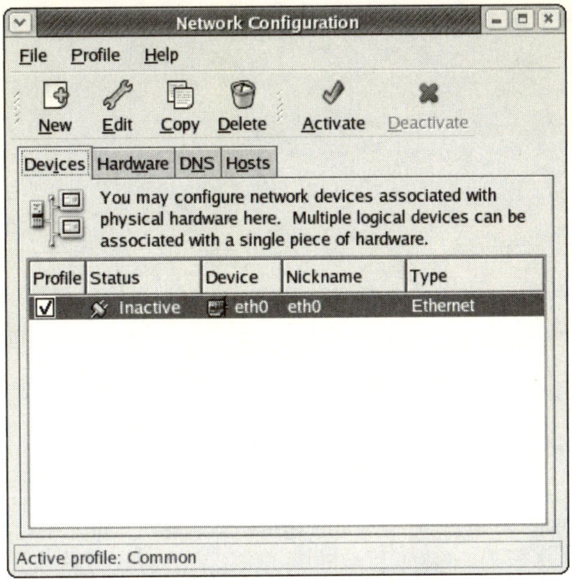

Figure 3-2

The sections that follow discuss the most common methods of connecting to the Internet.

Analog Modem Connections

Despite the advent of easily available and quite affordable high-speed Internet connectivity, using an analog modem attached to a phone line is still the most popular way of connecting to the Internet, particularly for travelers. Most personal computers available today come with an internal modem, usually as a modem card, although some of the cheaper models have them built into the motherboards, or operated through software (so-called "soft-modems").

In the case of soft-modems, there's a chance that they may not operate correctly under Linux, as they rely upon device driver software to operate correctly. If you believe this problem affects you, you should consult your modem's manufacturer to see if a Linux driver is available.

Technical Operation

Before we go into connection details, here's a quick overview of what's actually going on when you use your analog modem to connect to the Internet.

Typically, your modem connects to a phone line and dials out to a phone number provided by your ISP. Most commonly, the underlying protocol used on the wire is point-to-point protocol (PPP). The TCP/IP protocol is then layered on top of this PPP protocol layer. Once your machine has successfully connected to the gateway interface at your ISP, it is then connected to the Internet, and you can send and receive information (see Figure 3-3).

If this seems a little complicated to you, don't worry; like most other modern operating systems, Fedora 2 hides all the details from you (unless you want to look at them) and makes connecting to the Internet a breeze. Simply follow these simple steps.

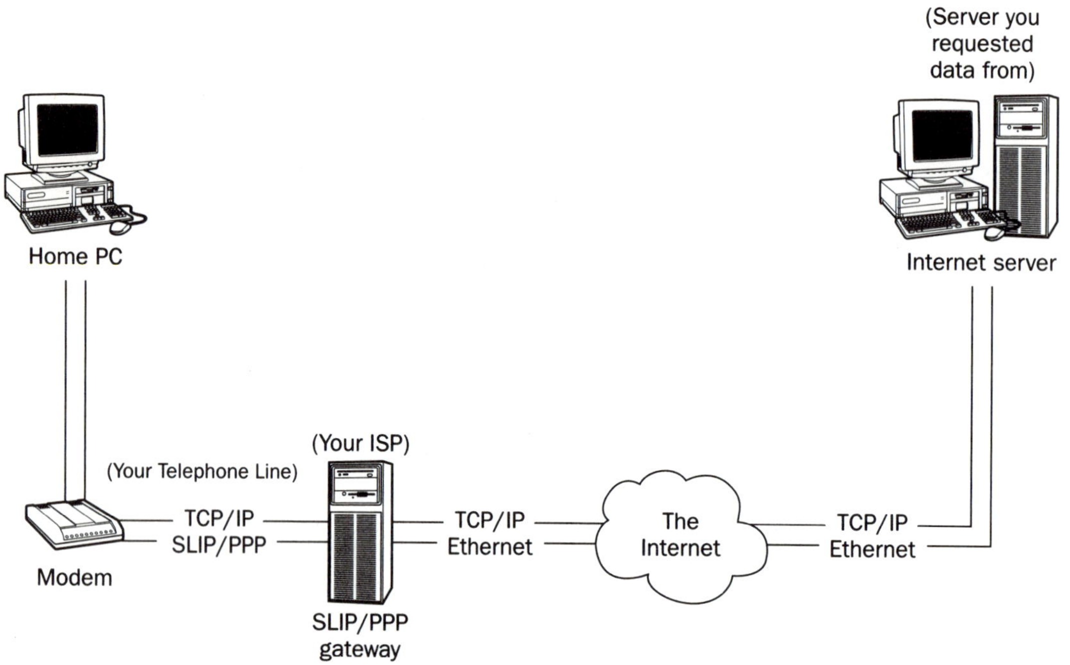

Figure 3-3

Try It Out Connecting an Analog Modem to the Internet

1. Move to the Devices tab, and select New in the Network Configuration Tool (see Figure 3-4).

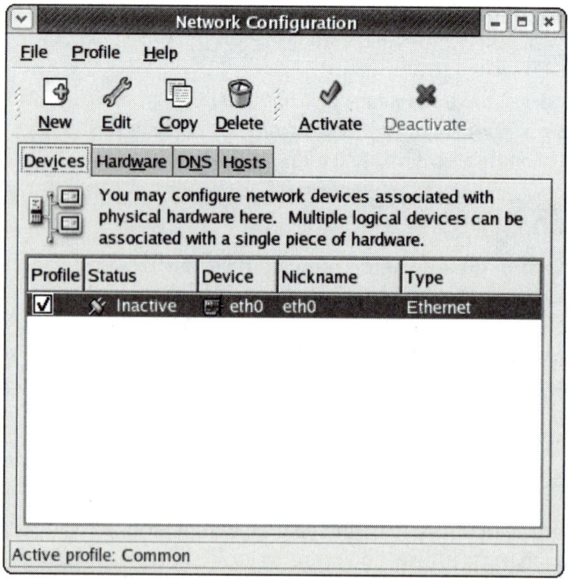

Figure 3-4

2. Choose the Modem connection option, as shown in Figure 3-5.

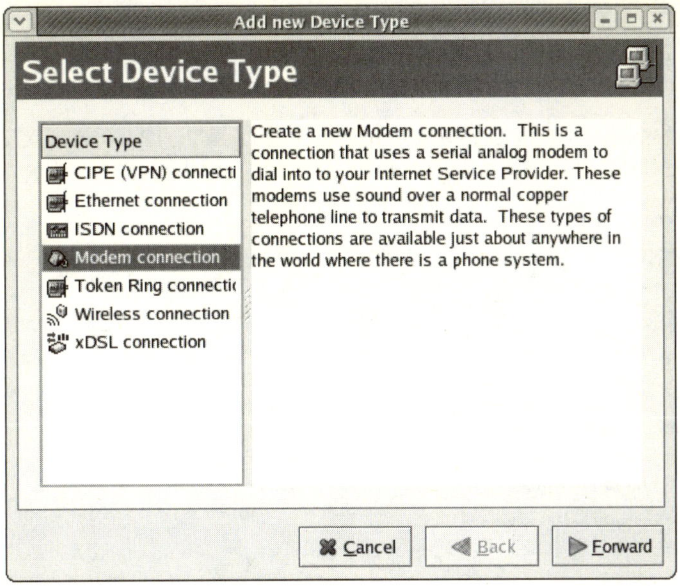

Figure 3-5

Then click Forward to reach the following screen, shown in Figure 3-6.

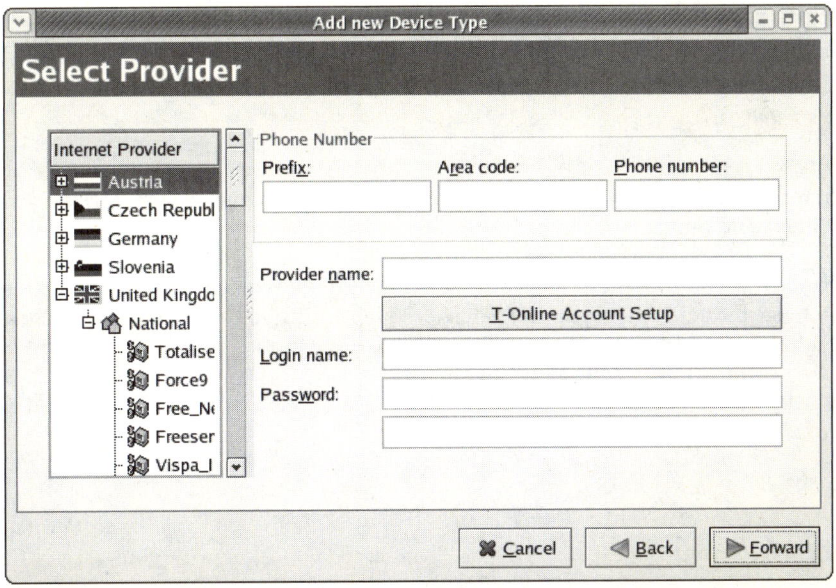

Figure 3-6

In this screen, you can either choose from the expandable list of ISPs on the left, or enter your own dial-up information into the boxes provided on the right. You should do whichever is appropriate for you. Click Forward.

If you wish to connect to the T-Online network, you'll need to press the T-Online Account Setup button, and provide the additional information that you're asked for.

3. In the screen shown in Figure 3-7, you would provide the IP settings. Most, if not all cases of dial-up connections involve automatic IP settings, which means that you need to just click Forward.

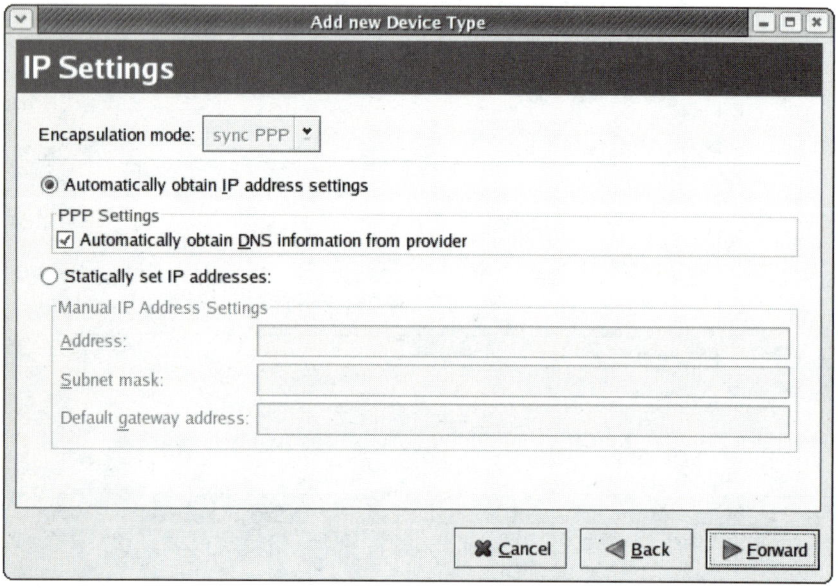

Figure 3-7

4. In the screen shown in Figure 3-8, the connection information is summarized for you. Click Apply to continue.

5. To turn on your Internet connection, select your newly created device, and then click the Activate button at the top of the panel (see Figure 3-9). To turn it off, simply click the Deactivate button that's next to it.

6. Finally, before you close the window, click the Yes option in the dialog box that asks you if you want to save your changes.

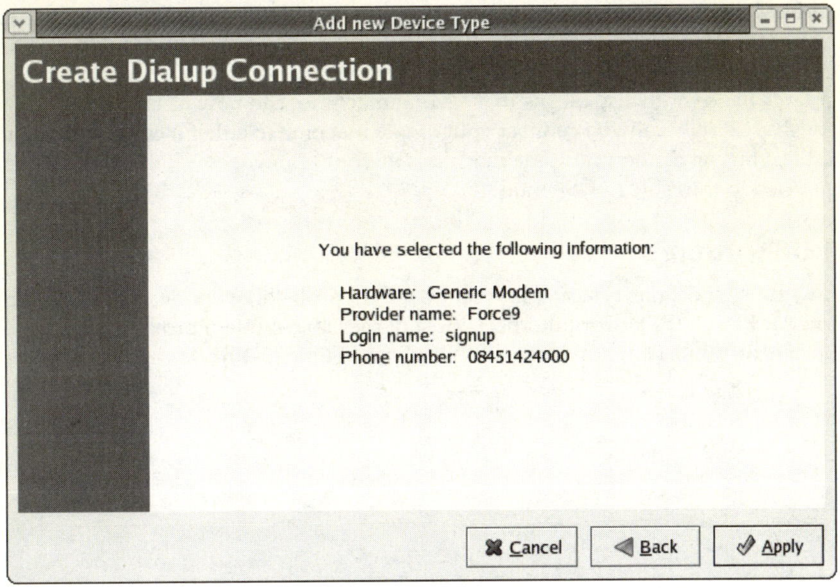

Figure 3-8

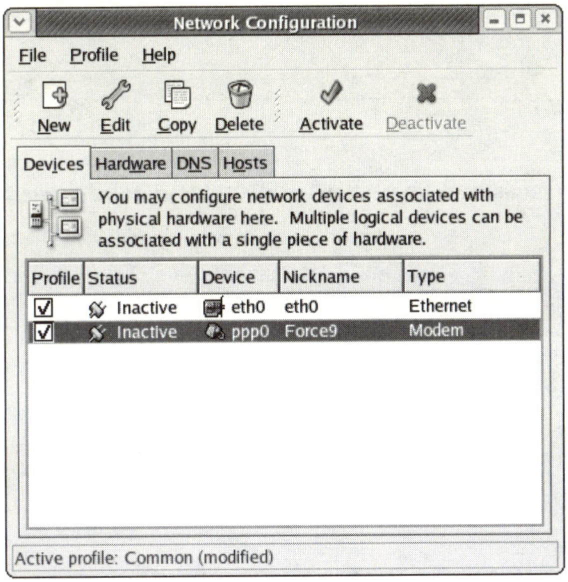

Figure 3-9

High-Bandwidth Connections

While connecting to the Internet using a dial-up modem is sufficient for activities such as checking e-mail or browsing the Web, this technology is not exactly keeping pace with the content offered online. Web sites are offering richer content by the day, and file downloads are getting bigger and bigger. This is where high-bandwidth Internet connections come in. Even though Integrated Services Digital Network (ISDN), the predecessor of today's high-bandwidth solutions, enjoyed only a lukewarm response, cable and Digital Subscriber Line (DSL) modem-based solutions are becoming very popular in many countries. Their large bandwidth also means that several machines can now be connected to the Internet simultaneously. Not only can you connect your single machine to either a cable or DSL modem using an Ethernet cable, you can connect multiple machines in your home network to a network router, which in turn is connected to the cable or DSL modem.

Technical Operation

High-bandwidth connections typically layer the TCP/IP protocol over one of the two hardware protocols: Ethernet or PPPoE (PPP over Ethernet). Most of the cable modem providers use Ethernet as the hardware protocol, while DSL providers use PPPoE (see Figure 3-10).

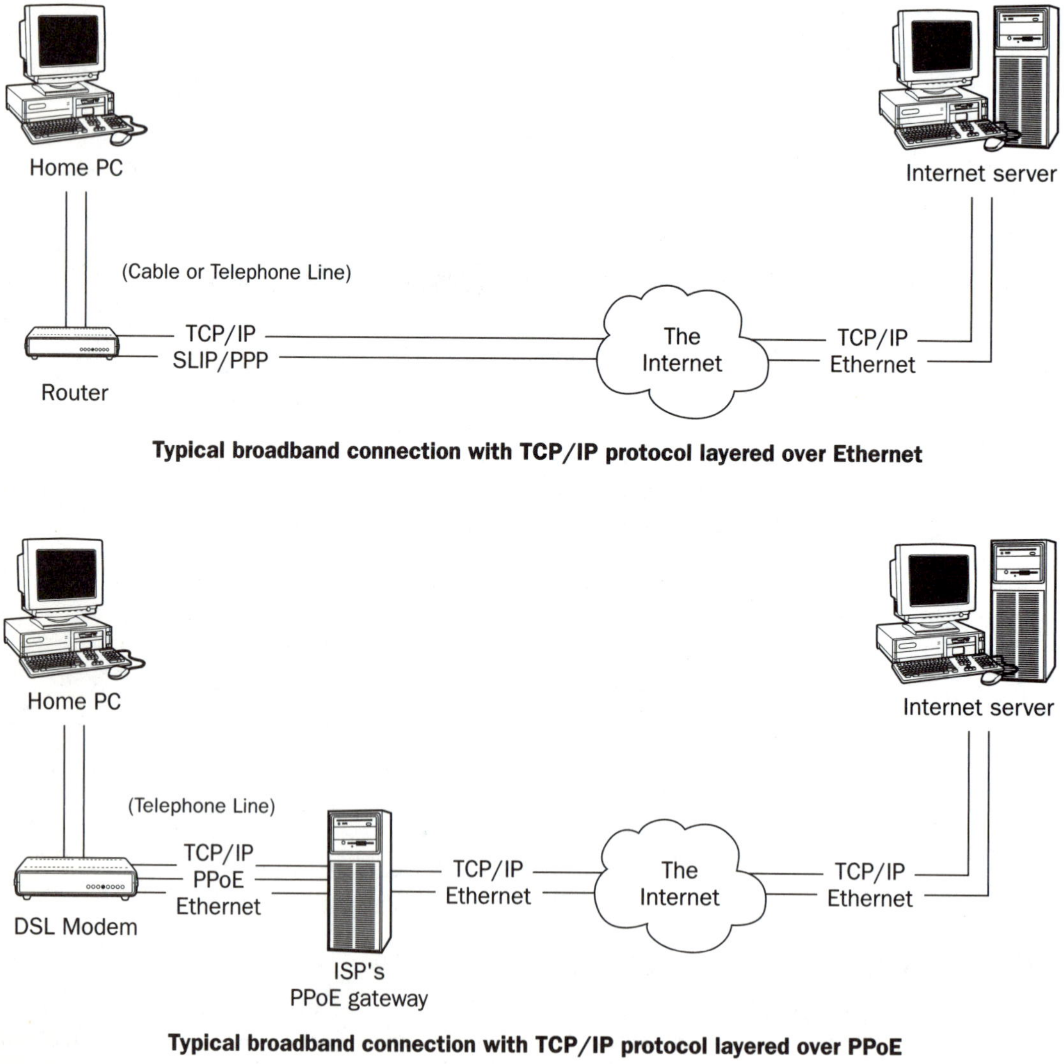

Figure 3-10

Try It Out — Connecting a High-Bandwidth Connection to the Internet

1. Choose xDSL connection from the Internet Configuration Wizard.
2. Enter your account details, such as the Provider Name (which is just an arbitrary name that you can identify the connection by) together with your Login Name and Password (see Figure 3-11). Note that some ISPs may not require a Login name and Password.

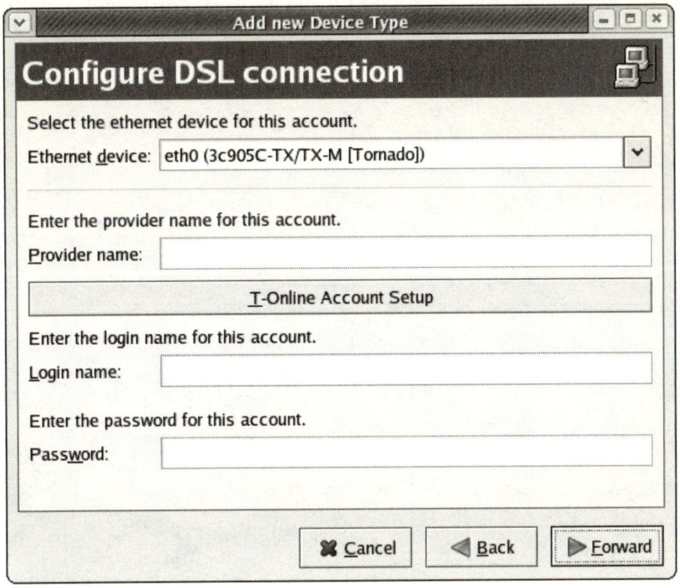

Figure 3-11

If you're connecting to T-Online, you'll need to press the T-Online Account Setup button, and supply the additional information that it asks for.

3. Select Forward, and then Apply, to finalize your configuration.

You can turn your connection on or off using the Activate and Deactivate buttons at the top of the panel. Typically, high-bandwidth connections are "always on." That is, unlike a dial-up connection, there is no need to initialize the device every time a connection is to be made. For a device and the connection associated with it to be activated automatically at boot time, you need to click Edit on the Network Configuration screen, and in the General tab, enable the checkbox that says Activate device when computer starts. Now that you've done this, your connection will come online as soon as you turn your computer on.

Cable modem providers tend to use the Ethernet protocol. As such, connections to their service can be configured in the same manner as for a LAN. We'll discuss this in the next section.

Broadband Routers

It has become increasingly common to connect multiple computers to the Internet such that they share a single broadband connection. This is typically achieved by connecting the DSL modem or cable modem to a broadband router rather than directly to a single computer. Other computers can now be connected to the router. Several of the recent broadband routers are equipped with Wireless LAN (WiFi) capabilities. This allows computers with WiFi cards to share the same broadband connection along with computers that are connected to the broadband router. A typical setup would look like the schematic shown in Figure 3-12.

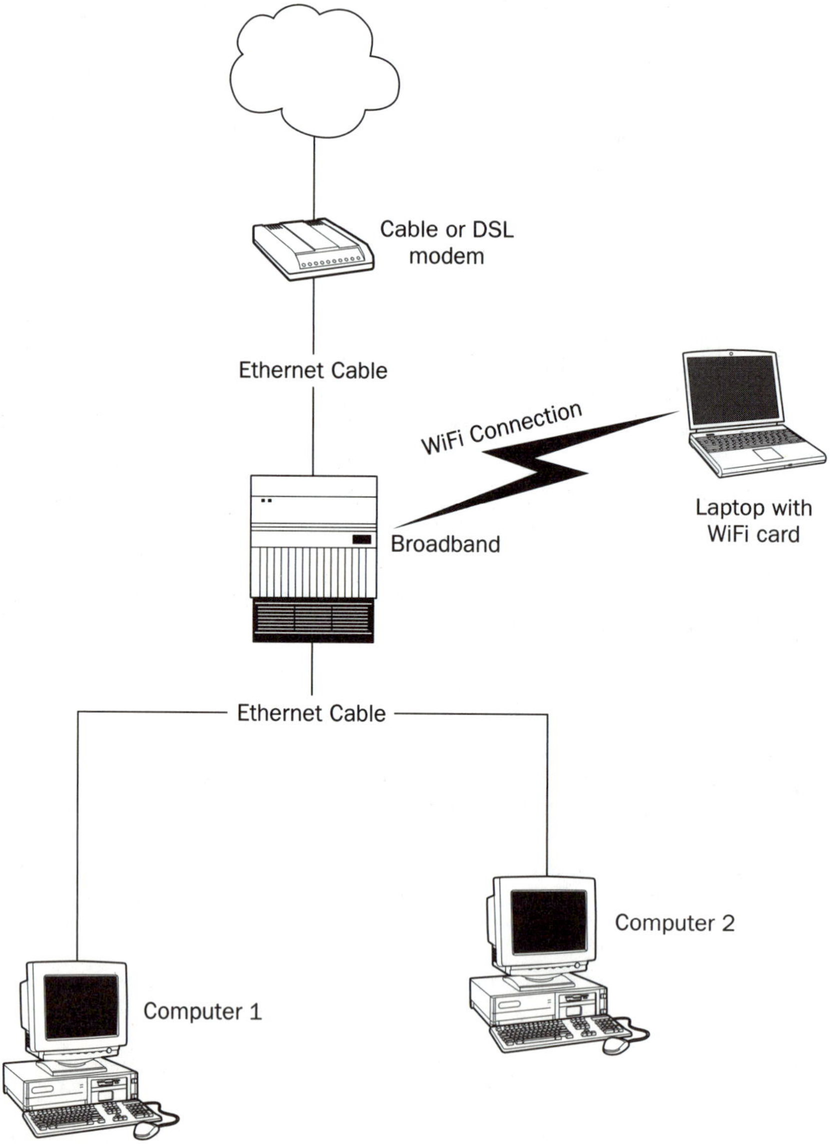

Figure 3-12

Most of the recent broadband routers have a Network Address Translator (NAT). A NAT-enabled router hides from the Internet the machines connected to it from the internal network. The NAT feature along with DHCP effectively frees users from the hassles of configuring IP addresses for each of the machines that they intend to connect to the Internet.

If a machine were to connect directly to the Internet, it would require a globally unique IP address. So your ISP would have to allocate an IP address for every computer that you connect to the Internet. This is neither practical nor cost-effective. Besides, even if you did get an IP address per computer, you would have to configure each of these computers with these addresses. A router with NAT solves the first problem by connecting to the Internet with a unique IP address. All other computers that need to connect to the Internet now connect to the router. These computers may have arbitrary IP addresses assigned to them, and the NAT would take care of translating the connections made by these individual computers to servers on the Internet. The IP address management problem is also taken care of in that most broadband routers come with a DHCP server. So, once your computer connects to the network, it would be allocated an IP address by the DHCP server running on the broadband router. Please be aware that not all broadband routers have NAT and DHCP capabilities; you may want to check your router vendor for details.

In addition to NAT and DHCP, today broadband routers are equipped with a rudimentary firewall. By default, these routers block all incoming connections at all network ports. In other words, your computers connected to the router can make outbound connections to the Internet—to get Web pages or fetch e-mail, for example—but network clients from the Internet cannot connect directly to your computers. In some cases, this may not be desirable because some users may prefer to run a Web server off of one of the machines behind the router, and this would prevent them from doing so. However, routers usually allow you to configure the port settings such that you can allow clients from the Internet to access certain ports, and these connections would be forwarded to certain computers. For example, you could configure your router to allow incoming connections on port 80 (the HTTP, or the Web server port) and to forward these connections to the machine running your Web server. This feature is usually called *port forwarding*; you should consult your router manufacturer's documentation to understand how to configure port forwarding for your specific brand of router.

Connecting to a LAN

This section considers how to connect a Linux machine to a LAN, such as might be found in a home or business office. In these circumstances your machine takes on the role of being a *networked device*. A network device connected to a TCP/IP network (such as the Internet or an intranet LAN) has an IP address associated with it, such as `192.168.100.20`. Using the IP address of a machine, other machines on the network can address it uniquely. An IP address may be *static* or *dynamic*:

- **Static addresses:** These are allotted to machines indefinitely and do not change. Typically, static addresses are allocated to servers.
- **Dynamic addresses:** These are allotted to machines for a specific period with no guarantee that the same address will be available next time the machine connects to the network.

Dynamic IP addresses are distributed and managed via dynamic address allocation protocols. In the case of a machine connected to a LAN using a dynamic IP address (or in the case of an ISP providing TCP/IP over Ethernet), the address is allocated either using the *Dynamic Host Configuration Protocol* (*DHCP*) or the *Bootstrap Protocol* (*BOOTP*). In these cases, you choose either `dhcp` or `bootp` from the drop-down list on your Configure Settings menu. For ISPs that use PPPoE, the address is allotted by the PPPoE protocol, in which case you need to choose `dialup`.

For a machine connected to a LAN or ISP using a static IP address, you need to obtain the network details, such as the IP address, the subnet mask for the network, and the default gateway address, which is the IP address of a router for the network. The local network administrator (or the ISP) should be able to provide these details.

Choose Ethernet connection from the Internet Configuration Wizard. Pick the Ethernet card you want to configure, press Forward, and provide your addressing information in the next screen (see Figure 3-13).

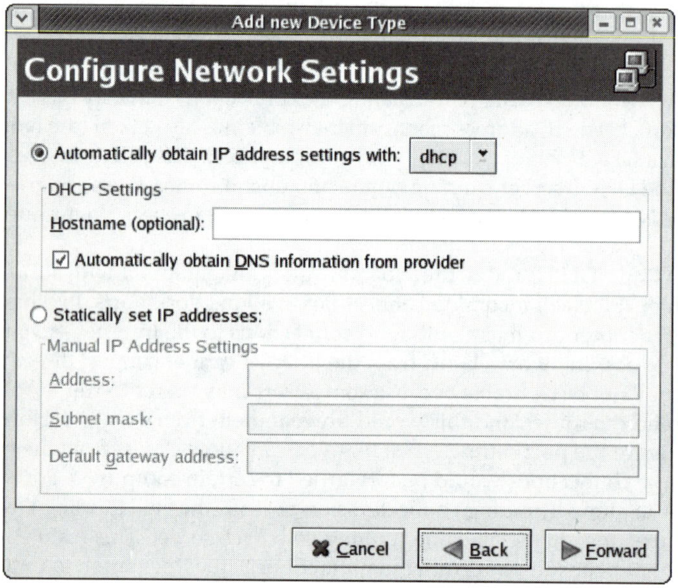

Figure 3-13

If you've performed a LAN-based network configuration during the installation, as detailed in Chapter 1, you can skip the rest of this section because your LAN should already be up and running.

DNS

Rather than remember the IP address of the Wrox Web site, it is easier to remember `www.wrox.com`. *Domain Name System* (*DNS*) servers provide the mapping between human-readable addresses (such as `www.wrox.com`) and the IP addresses of the machines acting as the Web servers for the corresponding Web service. Applications such as Web browsers and e-mail clients require the IP address to connect to a Web site or a mail server, respectively. To get this from the human-readable input that you provide them with, they query a DNS server for the corresponding IP address information. Obviously, this also means that the browser and other clients on the machine need to know the DNS server's IP address. For machines that use DHCP, the information about the DNS server is automatically available when the machine is configured.

Other Connection Types

The Internet Connection Wizard also allows you to configure some of the less common types of connection devices, such as ISDN and Token Ring adapters (see Figure 3-14).

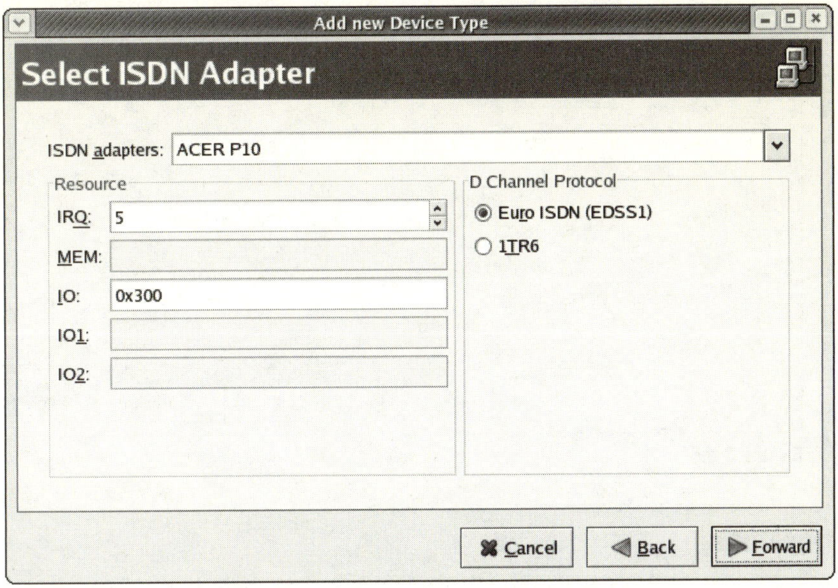

Figure 3-14

External ISDN terminal adapters (the ones that are connected to the serial port on a machine) can be configured just like ordinary analog modems. This discussion deals with ISDN adapters that are *internal ISDN cards*. In this case, you need to know the name of the adapter, its IRQ, the IO address, and the D-Channel protocol used to configure it properly. This information should be available as part of the vendor's documentation for your adapter. Similarly, for configuring a Token Ring adapter, you need to know the name of the adapter you intend to use before you can configure it.

Wireless Connections

The Internet Configuration Wizard allows you to configure a couple of emerging device and connection types: *wireless cards* and *VPN connections* (see Figure 3-15). Most of the popular wireless cards provide connectivity using the 802.11b protocol and are known as Wireless Ethernet devices.

Even though the wizard has a separate option for configuring a Wireless card, it is essentially the same as configuring an Ethernet device (dealt with under LAN) with the added ability to specify some wireless-specific parameters. These parameters are best left set to Auto unless you're sure of what you're doing and wish to alter them to address a performance issue.

These parameters may be specific to the vendor of the card and need to be set based on vendor recommendations.

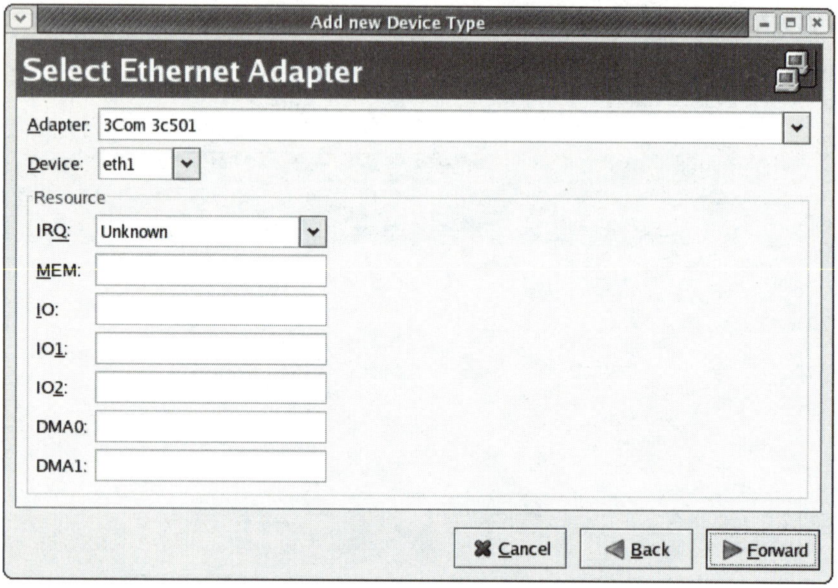

Figure 3-15

VPN Connections

Virtual Private Network (VPN) connections allow you to securely connect to a corporate network via the public Internet. In other words, typical VPN users connect to work over the Internet either from home or while on the road by using a VPN connection, which provides an encrypted channel of communication (see Figure 3-16).

Crypto IP Encapsulation (CIPE) is a Linux implementation of VPN access software. However, you need to have connection information for the particular VPN network that you intend to connect to before you can configure a CIPE connection. *Note that most corporations require that users connect using company-supplied VPN clients that may not necessarily be available for Linux.* In such a situation, using the CIPE-based VPN solution may not work.

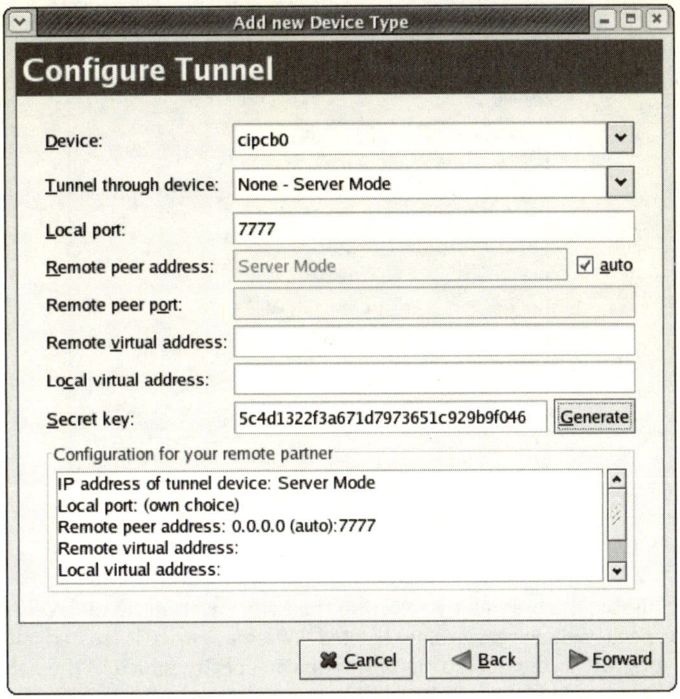

Figure 3-16

Connecting Securely

Most people, particularly home users, connect their computers directly to the Internet. While this allows you to freely access information available on the Internet, it also brings with it some inherent perils. Malicious users and programs will often try to break into your computer, which can result in loss of data and often puts you in a position of liability for actions that are not yours. Therefore, it is necessary to at least take some rudimentary precautions to protect your system. Fortunately, viruses and worms that commonly affect Microsoft platforms in general do not affect Fedora Linux and UNIX systems. However, UNIX systems are still vulnerable to external attack.

The most common mode of attack on a UNIX and therefore a Fedora Linux system is via network services that are available for clients on the network to access. Examples of services include Web servers, FTP service, and the Telnet service. Fortunately, it is possible to secure these services by setting up the firewall feature that is available as part of Fedora Linux. You can access the firewall settings from the Start menu by going to System Settings ➪ Security Level (see Figure 3-17).

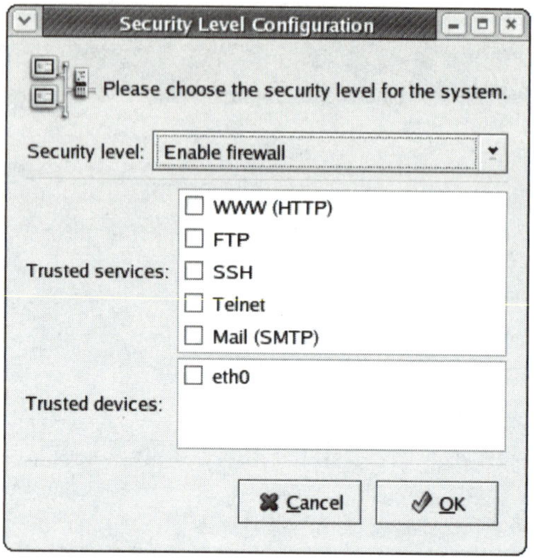

Figure 3-17

You can enable or disable the firewall by selecting the appropriate security level from the drop-down list. You may also specify which services are trusted. When a service is trusted, clients from the Internet or your local network can access it. Additionally, you can specify which of the network devices (for example, network cards or modems) are trusted by you. Network clients cannot connect to any services on an untrusted device.

Be aware that the firewall takes a minimalist approach—that is, it disallows all possible services. It is up to you as the user to specify which services should be accessible. There is always the danger that a service that you assumed to be always running may now be blocked by the firewall. A common technique while troubleshooting network services is to shut down the firewall temporarily during the troubleshooting process. System security is discussed in detail in later chapters.

Managing Multiple ISPs and Connections

Often, you may have a single machine that you would use for different purposes when connected to different networks. You might use the machine to browse the Internet while connected to an ISP, or use it to connect to work and even perhaps take it to work to use on an intranet. Even though it is the same machine, it tends to have different connectivity requirements at different times because different service providers and possibly different devices are involved.

Connection Profiles

Connection profiles help you manage not just multiple ISPs, but also devices that need to behave differently at different times. For physical devices that require different settings at different times, it is possible to associate multiple logical devices with a single physical device. The logical devices can have a variety of settings, the only restriction being that only one logical device associated with a physical device can be used at a time. A *connection profile* is a collection of logical devices and their configurations representing certain connection characteristics. Typical connection profiles could be Work, Home, On the road, and so on.

We touched on connection profiles when looking at the Internet Configuration Wizard at the start of this chapter. Open the Network Configuration Tool again, and, at the bottom of the screen, on the Devices tab you'll see Active Profile followed by details on the profile that's currently active. By default, you are provided with a Common profile, which works well for machines that have fixed connection characteristics.

Before getting started with profiles, you need to configure all the *physical network device* types on the machine. Available network device types are Ethernet, ISDN, Modem, *x*DSL, Token Ring, CIPE, and Wireless.

The following steps take you through the process of creating and managing profiles. The *Try It Out* example that follows should clarify the process even further.

1. Create a new profile by clicking New. A profile is typically associated with a location. Locations have their distinct network configuration requirements. Logical devices describe these network configuration settings. A logical device is just a manifestation of a physical device in a particular profile. For example, if your laptop has a network card, there could be two logical devices based off that network card, perhaps a home network card and a work network card. A profile simply consists of multiple logical devices. However, it is also important to note that a logical device can belong to only one profile at a time.
2. After the profile is created, you create all the logical devices necessary for the profile. The general rule is that if a particular physical device will be used in the context of the new profile, it needs a logical device for that profile.
3. After the logical devices for the new profile are created, you need to associate the logical devices with the profile.
4. You may choose to create more profiles by following Steps 1 through 3, again.

Try It Out — Creating Multiple Profiles and Logical Devices

Let's configure connection profiles for a hypothetical Fedora 2 laptop that you use at work to write articles, at home to browse the Web, and while on the road to read e-mail. At work, the laptop is connected to the company's intranet via an Ethernet card. While on the road, you use the laptop's internal modem to dial an ISP and check your e-mail. At home, you use a wireless Ethernet card so you can browse the Web from the living room couch. On occasions when pets monopolize the couch, you're forced to browse over a cable modem connection from the study, thereby using the same Ethernet card you used at work. To manage all these connections, you'll create four profiles: Work, Home, Road, and Couch.

Before you begin, let's get your machine's hardware profile fresh in you mind. It looks like that shown in Figure 3-18 (with what you've learned so far, you should be able to create this with fictional information if you want to follow along—you can always delete it when you're done):

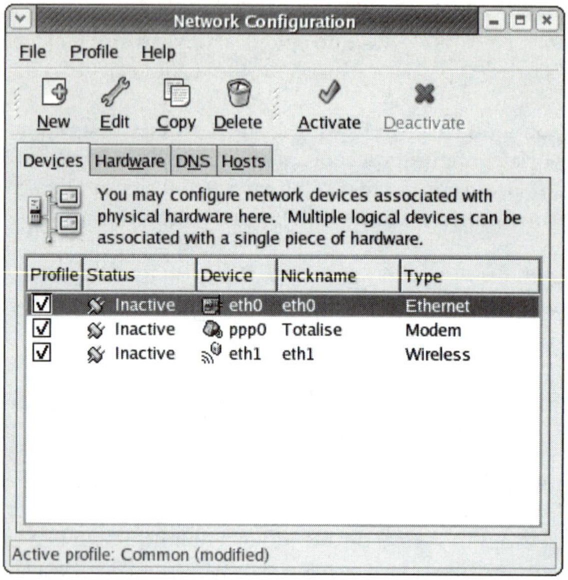

Figure 3-18

Create the required profiles using the following steps:

1. Choose Profile from the drop-down menu, and select New.
2. Enter Work in the pop-up box that appears (see Figure 3-19).

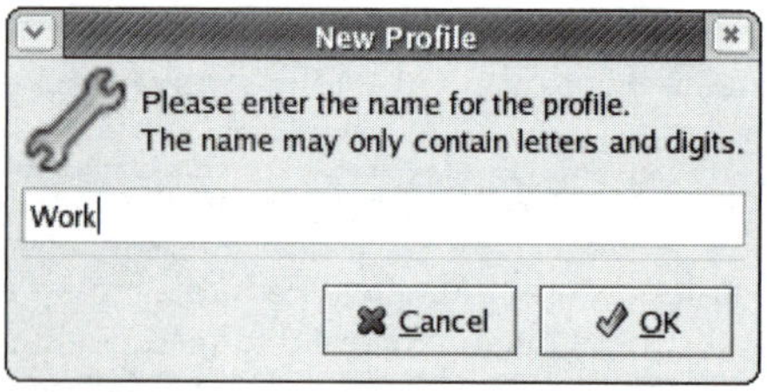

Figure 3-19

3. Now that you have your profile created (look at the bottom of the Network Configuration Tool, and you'll see that it's changed from Common to Work), you need to create a logical device for it based on the physical device `eth0`—the Ethernet card.
4. Highlight the physical device `eth0` and click Copy.

You might be tempted to click the Add button to create a logical device, but this is incorrect. You should use the Copy button after highlighting the physical device in question.

5. Select the copy, click the Edit button, and specify the nickname `eth0_work` along with other properties such as the DNS server to be used and the IP address (you can make these up for the purposes of the demonstration). Click OK.
6. Add the newly created logical device to the Work profile by marking the Profile checkbox on the left side for those logical devices that belong to the profile.
7. To save your changes, click the Apply button. Remember that a logical device can belong to only one profile. The result is shown in Figure 3-20.

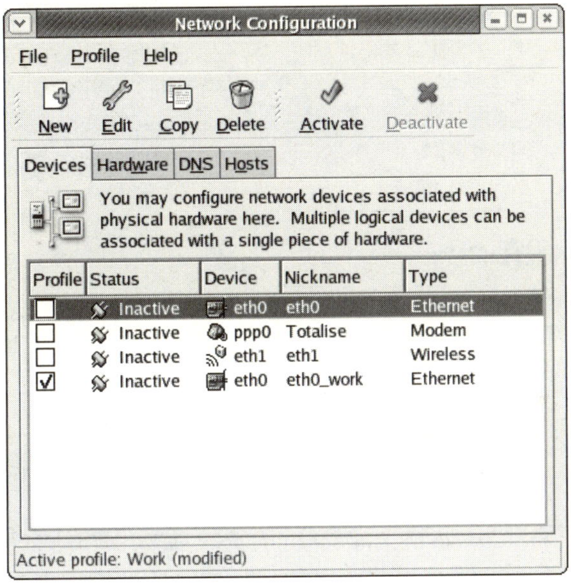

Figure 3-20

8. You can use the same routine to create profiles for the Home, Road, and Couch accounts (see Figure 3-21).

A particular profile can be activated at any time from the Network Configuration Tool by choosing the profile from the drop-down list.

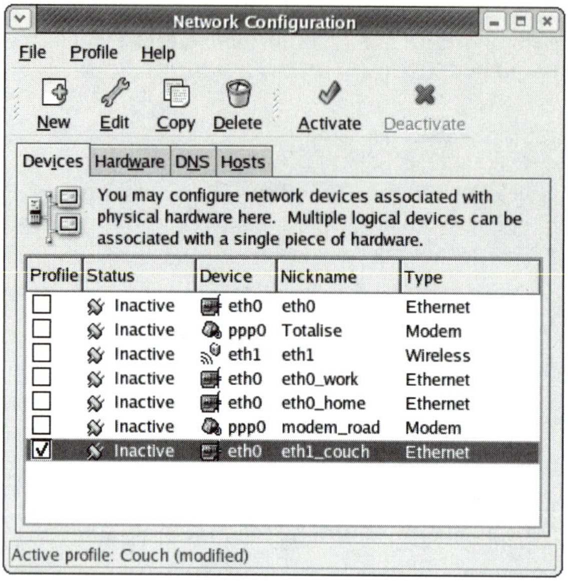

Figure 3-21

Starting Connections

So how do you actually connect to a network using each of these devices? Some of them, such as the Ethernet device, remain connected (or activated) as long as they are physically connected to the network. Others, such as a modem, need to be activated when you need them.

Therefore, to connect using a configured connection, at any time, you could go to the Main Menu and choose System Settings ➪ Network, highlight the appropriate connection, and click Activate (see Figure 3-22).

To activate a connection as soon as the machine starts up, highlight the connection and click Edit, and enable the radio button that says Activate device when computer starts.

It's also possible to configure Fedora 2 to automatically establish a modem connection when needed, using a daemon called `diald`. However, using such a process can make your system considerably less secure than it is at the moment (currently, you have to manually "OK" any modem network connections). We'd advise that you read on a little further through the book and familiarize yourself with the command shell and security issues before deciding if `diald` is right for you. If you decide to proceed, all the configuration information you need can be found at `www.linux.org/docs/ldp/howto/Diald-HOWTO.html`.

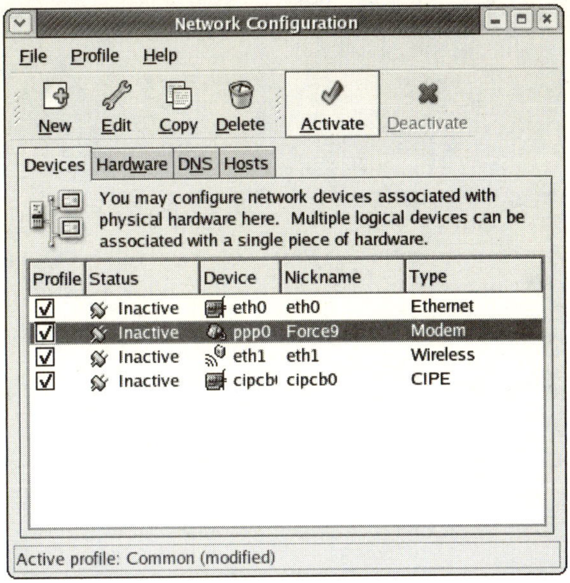

Figure 3-22

Software and Configuration

Now you've got your Internet connection set up, you're ready to fire up your browser and go places. Let's look at the tools that Fedora 2 makes available for you to do this.

Web Browsers

The most common and popular way to access the Internet is by using a Web browser. Fedora 2 comes with the highly functional Mozilla browser installed, by default. You can start it from the Panel at the bottom of your screen, by clicking on the globe and mouse icon. Alternatively, you can type **mozilla** at the command prompt. For those of you who connect directly to the Internet, that's it. Up pops Mozilla, helpfully set to a Welcome to Red Hat page, and you're ready to go (see Figure 3-23).

> *Notice that it's actually browsing HTML pages on your local filesystem at the moment, rather than the Web—just type* ***file:///*** *to explore your machine.*

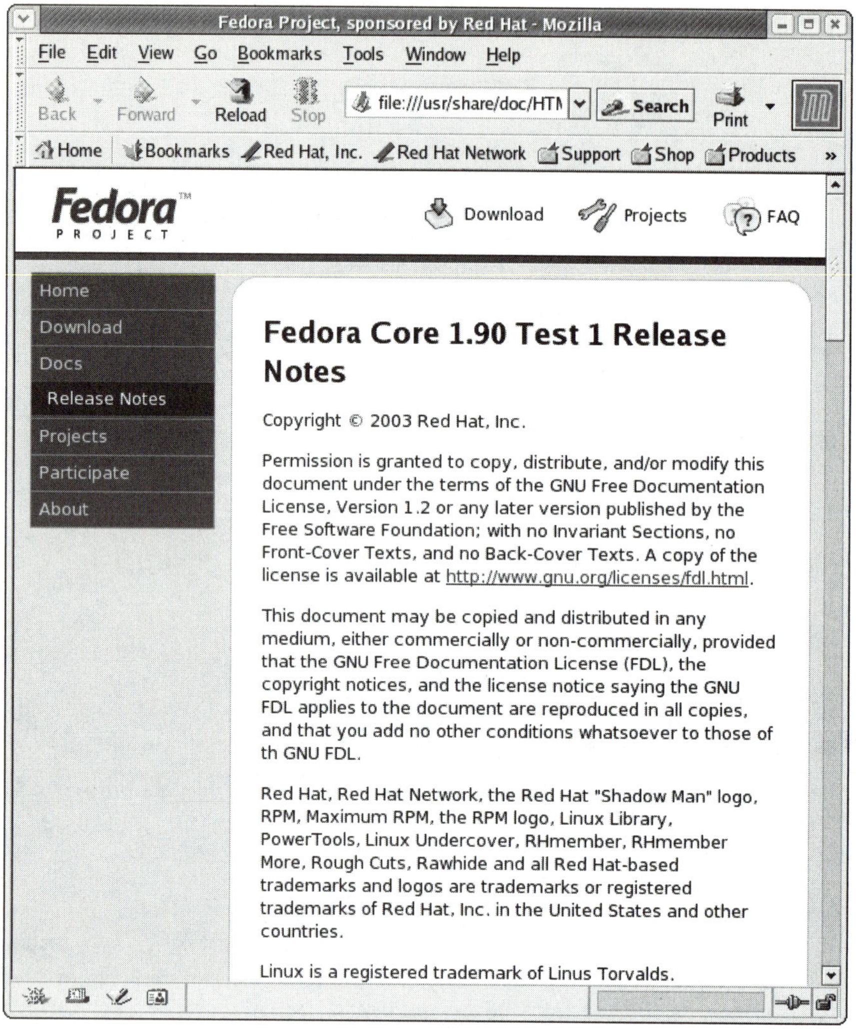

Figure 3-23

Mozilla Proxies

Those of you who connect through an HTTP proxy, however, have a little bit more work to do. First, you need to get hold of the following information from your network administrator:

- The DNS name of the proxy and the port number it listens at for HTTP connections.
- Most of the time, the same proxy server handles other protocols such as SSL, FTP, Gopher, and SOCKS. If you intend to use any of these protocols, you need to get the address of the proxy server for each of these protocols and the port at which they listen for incoming requests.
- Some intranets publish a URL that has JavaScript in it that can configure the proxy settings automatically for the user. In this case, you need to provide that URL.

Once you've got your information, fire up Mozilla, and open Edit ➪ Preferences ➪ Advanced ➪ Proxies (see Figure 3-24).

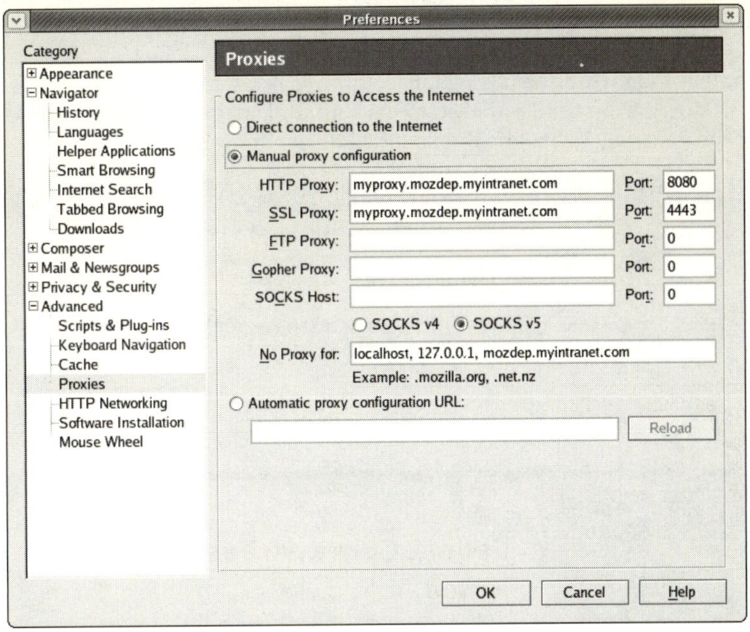

Figure 3-24

Configuring Mozilla

The best thing about Mozilla is that it comes with a horde of functionality to make browsing much more fun. The following sections list a few of the settings that you might find useful.

Privacy and Security Settings

Mozilla comes with a host of privacy and security settings that allow you to browse the Web without being bothered by security concerns or prying eyes.

- **Pop-up ads:** Most, if not all of us are annoyed by the often-distracting pop-up advertisements that appear when we attempt to load a page. These pop-up windows can be blocked by choosing the menu item Edit ➪ Preferences ➪ Advanced ➪ Scripts & Plugins and clearing the Open unrequested windows checkbox.
- **Blocking ad images:** Besides pop-up ads, the other annoying mode of online advertisement is banner advertisements that are served up by online ad-banner companies that embed links to images in Web pages. You can block these ads by right-clicking the ad image and selecting Block images from this server. You can reinstate permissions to allow a blocked server to display its images from the Tools ➪ Image Manager ➪ Manage Image Permissions menu by highlighting the site in question and clicking Remove.

Browsing and Appearance

Mozilla allows you to customize your browsing experience by providing a tabbed browsing interface and the ability to change the appearance of the browser itself. Additionally, several other convenient features exist that make browsing as fast as it is fun.

- **Tabs rather than windows:** Using tabs to browse is faster and results in less clutter than using new windows every time you need to have multiple pages open at the same time (look at the top of the page, just below the Bookmarks line in Figure 3-25).

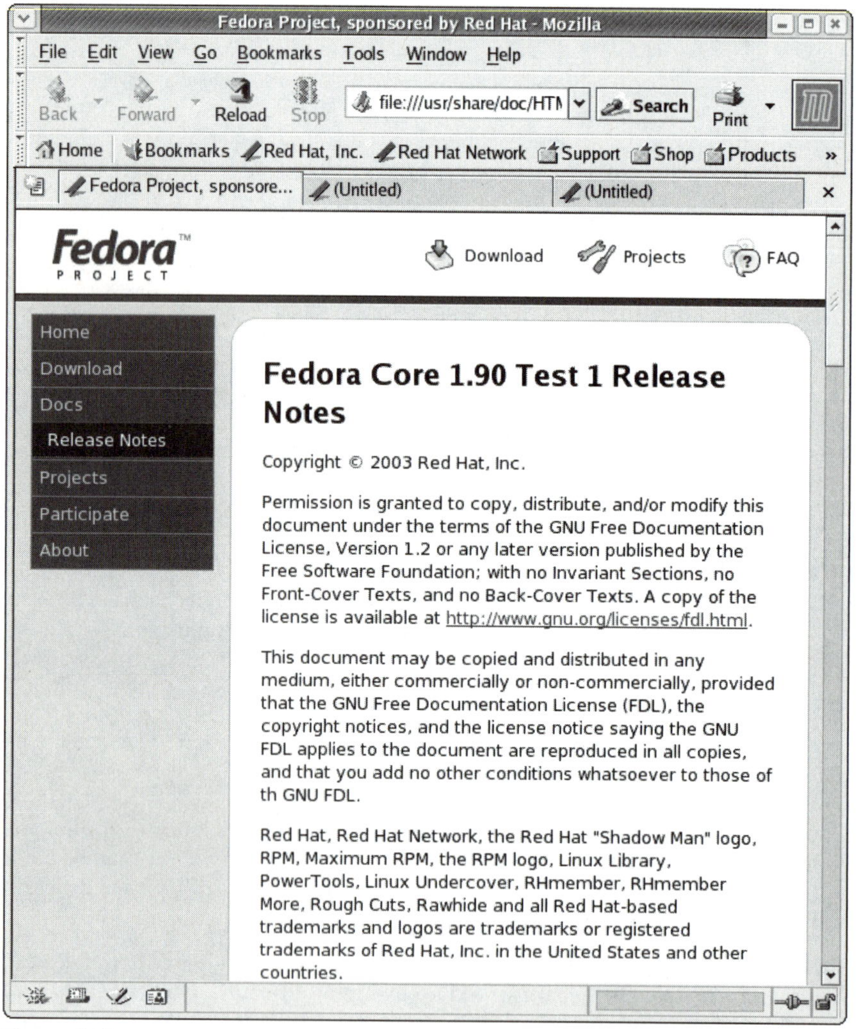

Figure 3-25

You can open a new tab with the *Ctrl+T* key combination, or open a link in a new tab by right-clicking the link and choosing Open Link in New Tab. Further, if you enable the Middle-click or Control-click of links in a Web page option, you can open links in new tabs by clicking links using the middle mouse button or a *Ctrl + left-click* of the mouse. These options are available from the Edit ➪ Preferences ➪ Navigator ➪ Tabbed Browsing menu. From the same menu, by enabling *Ctrl+Enter* in the location bar option, you can open a location in a new tab by typing in the URL followed by *Ctrl+Enter.*

- **Themes**: You can change the appearance of the Mozilla browser by applying themes that change the look-and-feel of the user interface. Mozilla has the classic theme and a modern theme available by default, and you can download new themes from `www.mozdev.org`.

  You can have several themes available and switch between them by choosing the menu option View ➪ Apply Themes and selecting the name of the theme to be applied. Newly selected themes take effect only after restarting Mozilla. In Figure 3-26, the browser's buttons and borders have changed to reflect the new theme.

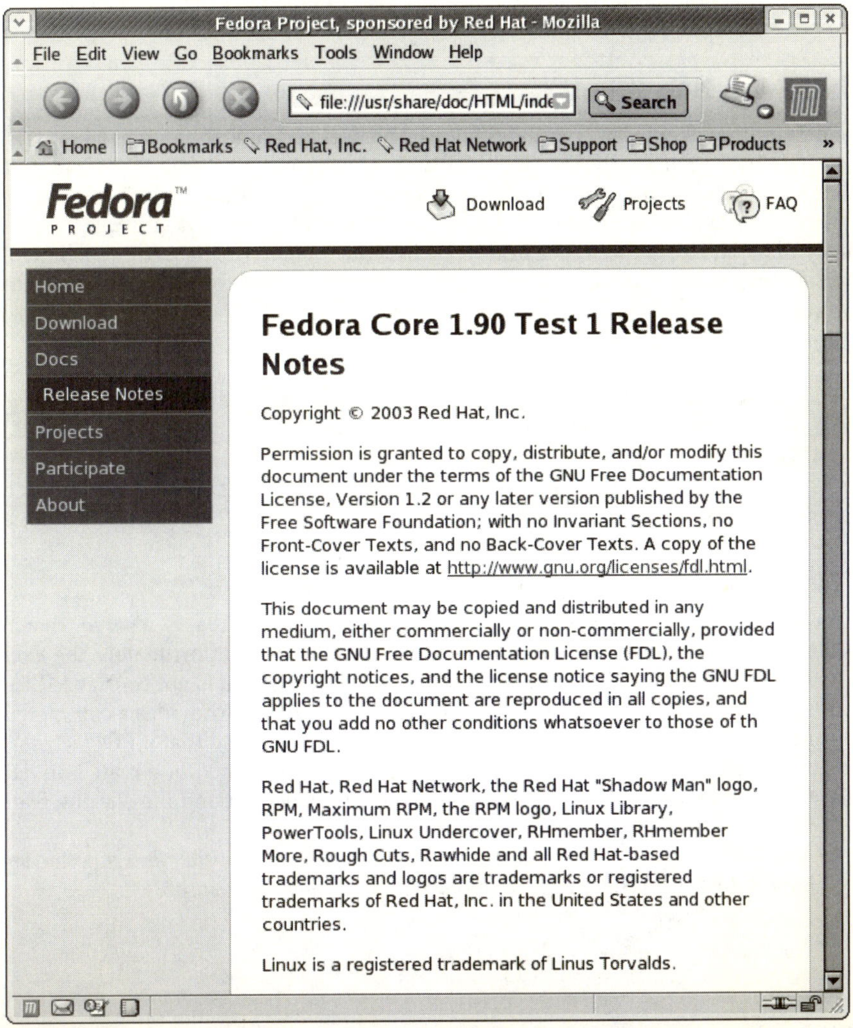

Figure 3-26

- **Auto-completion:** Some users may prefer to have Mozilla automatically complete a URL that they are typing in. This behavior can be enabled by ensuring that the Automatically complete text typed into the Location bar option from the Edit ➪ Preferences ➪ Navigator ➪ Smart Browsing menu is selected.

Installing Plug-ins

Plug-ins, from a generic standpoint, allow the browser to process non-HTML data. Mozilla, by default, does not have plug-ins installed. Details about plug-ins for various software, some of them commercial, are available at the Plugindoc page, `http://plugindoc.mozdev.org/linux.html`. Some of the more interesting plug-ins worth considering include Java, Real Audio, and Macromedia Flash plug-ins.

E-mail and News Clients

Now that you have configured your Web browser, it is time to look at the options Fedora 2 presents for accessing e-mail and newsgroups. The default e-mail client is Ximian Evolution, but your Mozilla installation also has excellent mail client facilities built in, and also functions as an Internet News client.

The Ximian Evolution Client

The Ximian Evolution client is similar in both look-and-feel and functionality to Microsoft Outlook minus the virus issues commonly associated with Microsoft's e-mail clients. The similarity makes it a viable alternative for users moving to Fedora from a Microsoft environment. The Evolution client also integrates calendar and contacts management software. In fact, you can access calendar information hosted on a Microsoft Exchange server from your Evolution client (using a commercially licensed connector available from `www.ximian.com`). When you start Evolution for the first time from the panel, a wizard prompts you to enter account information for your e-mail. Once you've done this, the program starts, and you're able to start using it (see Figure 3-27).

Additional accounts can be added from the Tools ➪ Settings menu while in the Inbox screen by choosing the Mail Accounts tab and clicking Add.

As mentioned previously, Ximian Evolution also comes with an integrated calendar, task manager, and address book that makes mail and schedule management on Fedora 2 simple and intuitive.

Accessing Microsoft Exchange Mail from Ximian

Several corporations use Microsoft Exchange as a groupware server, that is, a server that allows users to manage and share calendar events, contacts, e-mail, and even files. Unfortunately, the Exchange server is designed to work primarily with Microsoft Outlook and quite often it is not configured to allow clients to access e-mail using the POP or IMAP protocols. However, Ximian provides a commercially licensed connector to access e-mail from an Exchange server. It should be noted that if POP access is enabled, the connector is not required if you use the Microsoft Exchange server only for e-mail. You definitely need the connector if you rely on a Microsoft Exchange server for calendar and file-sharing features.

You can download the Ximian connector from `www.ximian.com`*. To install the connector, you also need to download Red Carpet, the Ximian installer, from the same Web site.*

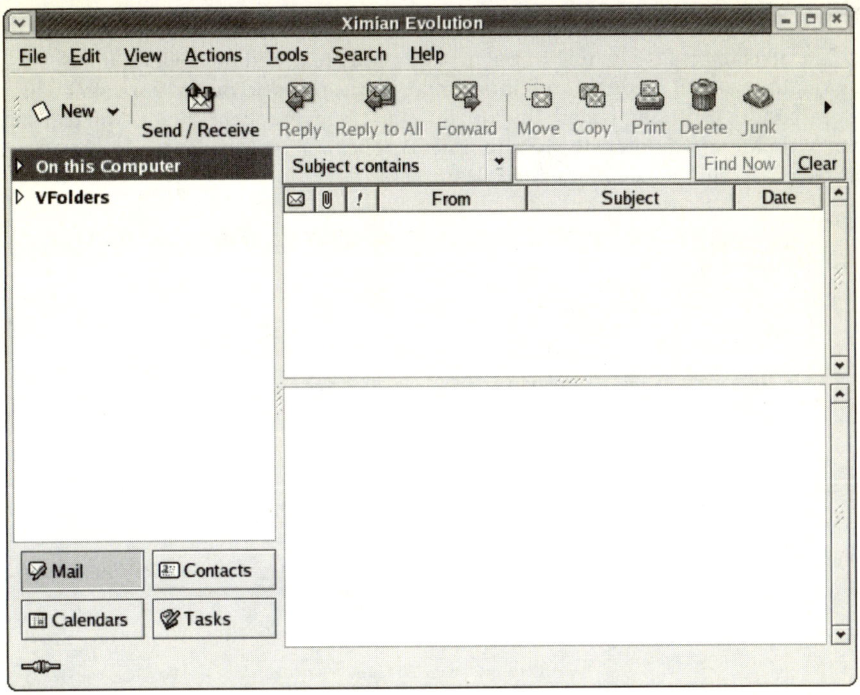

Figure 3-27

To configure Ximian to retrieve and send mail using an Exchange server, from the Tools Mail Settings menu, set the Server Type as Microsoft Exchange and supply the following information:

- The mail user's full name.
- The login name for the Exchange server. This is usually the part of the e-mail ID preceding the @ symbol, also known as the mail user ID. It may also be a different name altogether, depending on how this is configured locally. Some installations have multiple NT domains, in which case the login name is of the format `domainname\login name`.
- If the mail user ID is different from the login name, you need to provide that ID as the mailbox name. In any case, there is no need to prefix the domain name.
- The DNS name of the Exchange server, for example `exchange.foobar.com`.
- If an LDAP-based corporate directory server such as the Netscape Directory Server is deployed locally, the DNS name of the server can be entered to look up contacts using Lightweight Directory Access Protocol (LDAP).

If you're unsure about any of this information, you should speak to the administrator of your Exchange Server.

The Mozilla Mail Client

The Mozilla mail client is fast gaining popularity as a fully featured mail client. It has several features for managing multiple e-mail accounts and, most importantly, news accounts. For users who subscribe to news groups besides accessing e-mail, the Mozilla client is an excellent choice. You can start the Mozilla client from Main Menu ➪ Internet ➪ More Internet Applications ➪ Mozilla mail or by clicking the mail icon (bottom left in Figure 3-28) of the Mozilla browser.

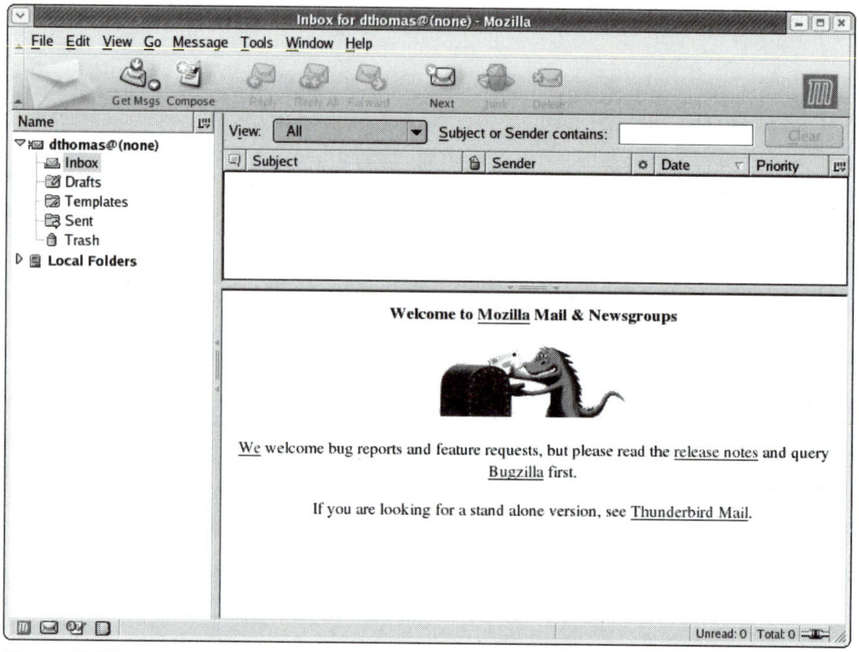

Figure 3-28

When the Mozilla mail client is started for the first time, it prompts you to set up an account for sending and receiving e-mail. Also, a new account can be set up from the Edit ➪ Mail & Newsgroups settings menu by clicking the Add account button. In either case, the settings are similar to the settings for the Ximian Evolution client that you saw in the previous section. The news reader client can be set up from the same menu by specifying the new account as a Newsgroup account and entering the DNS name of the news server (see Figure 3-29).

Other Software

This section looks at the other software beside browsers and mail clients that you can use to access the Internet.

FTP Clients

You often need to download software over the Internet or transfer files between machines. The most popular protocol for this function is the File Transfer Protocol (FTP).

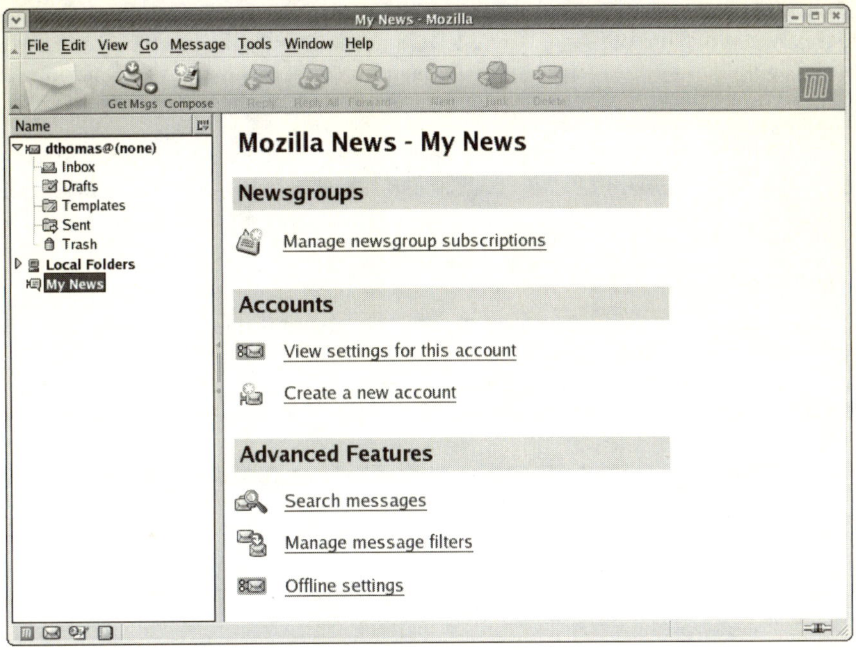

Figure 3-29

The Graphical FTP (gFTP) tool available with Fedora 2 installations has several powerful features that are lacking in the other clients. You can start the gFTP client by selecting Main Menu ➪ Internet ➪ More Internet Applications ➪ gFTP, or by typing **gftp** at the command line prompt (see Figure 3-30).

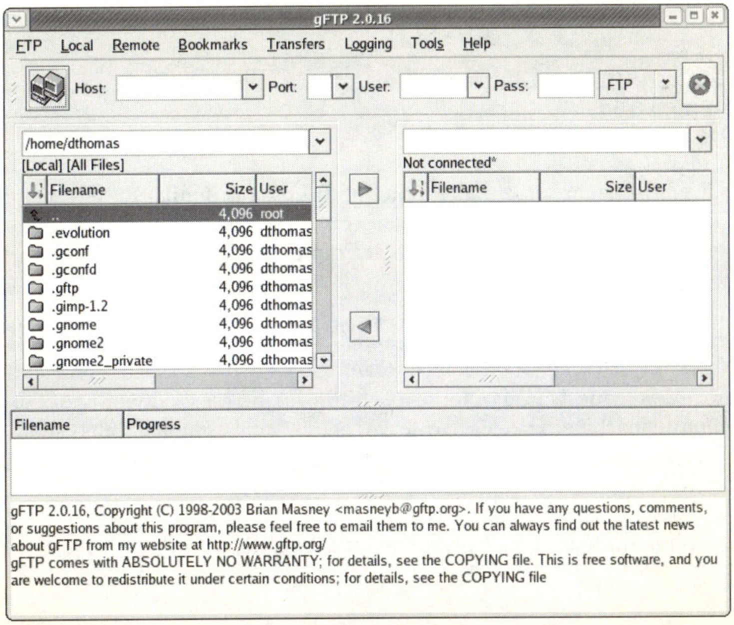

Figure 3-30

The gFTP client is multithreaded, allowing transfer of multiple files simultaneously, and supports transferring files between two remote servers over FTP (that is, not onto the machine you're working on). It also supports downloading entire directories and subdirectories, as well as bookmarking FTP sites, which enables you to quickly reconnect to remote sites. The gFTP client also supports resuming interrupted file transfers.

Traditionally, the most popular FTP client has been the command line FTP tool, simply called `ftp`. The command-line tool is interactive and suitable for quickly fetching a file or two.

Xchat

Internet Relay Chat (IRC) is the predecessor of peer-to-peer and instant messaging systems of today. It has a huge user base and is still one of the major reasons people connect to the Internet. Fedora 2 comes with an IRC client called Xchat that can be accessed from the Main Menu ➪ Internet ➪ More Internet Applications ➪ Xchat menu (see Figure 3-31).

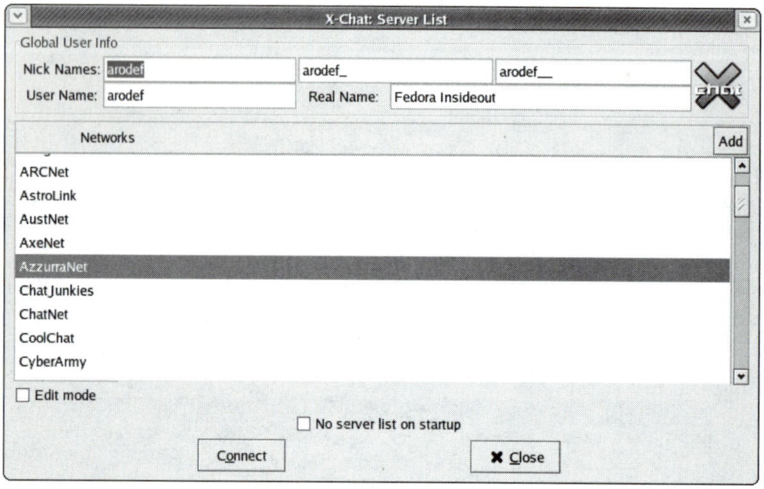

Figure 3-31

IRC consists of *channels* that are essentially topics of discussion, similar to the *chat room* of today's messaging clients. To join a channel, you need to connect to a server that hosts the channel. You can choose a server from the list of servers available by default from the X-Chat ➪ Server list menu, or add some of your own to the list from the same menu.

Most IRC servers expect that you to identify yourself to the server. This is achieved by running the `identd` server on your machine. The `identd` server listens on port 113 for connections using the `identd` protocol and processes requests from remote machines asking for the identity of the user attempting to connect to the remote machine. The `identd` server is available as an RPM that should be installed separately because it is not part of the default installation. Chapter 4 has information on using the package manager for installing RPMs.

Note that, at the present time, Xchat cannot connect to an IRC server through a firewall.

Instant Messaging

Instant messaging is fast emerging as the latest Internet application to connect people together. Most of today's instant messaging applications allow users to chat one-on-one or in a group in real time as well as allowing them to share files. Unfortunately, all of the instant messaging applications are not based on a common protocol, but on proprietary protocols that do not interact with each other. So, a user on AIM (AOL's instant messaging solution) cannot seamlessly connect with a user on a different messaging network, such as Yahoo! Messenger.

This is where Gaim comes in. Gaim is an instant messaging client that supports multiple protocols and also allows a user to be logged on to different networks with different account names simultaneously. In fact, Gaim can even connect to IRC servers. You can invoke Gaim by selecting Main Menu ➪ Internet ➪ Instant Messenger (see Figure 3-32).

Figure 3-32

Before you can use Gaim, you need to set up a couple of things. For Gaim to work with a certain instant messaging network, it needs to have a plug-in for that network loaded. This is a one-time task that you can accomplish by clicking the Plugins button followed by the Load button and choosing the appropriate plug-in—for example, `libyahoo.so` for Yahoo! Messenger or `libicq.so` for ICQ. Once the plug-ins are set up, you need to fill in account information for each of the networks to which you intend to connect. Enter account information by clicking the Accounts button followed by the Add button. The official Gaim Web site is `http://gaim.sourceforge.net`. See Chapter 5 for a more detailed discussion of Gaim configuration.

Summary

This chapter explored the issues associated with connecting your Fedora 2 installation to the Internet. You should now have a working Internet connection, and be able to surf Web pages, check your mail, transfer files by FTP, and use IRC with confidence.

In brief, you have done the following:

- Investigated the use of various wizards such as the Internet Configuration Wizard, and Network Configuration Tool to configure devices and connections in the context of different connection requirements
- Learned how to create logical devices and profiles to better manage your resources
- Explored some of the important Internet access software available with the Fedora installation

Exercises

Try out the following exercises to increase your skill level:

1. What are the different services running on your machine?
2. Determine the Ethernet address of your network card.
3. Web sites use cookies to track your use of the site. Determine which sites are using cookies to track you.

4

Everyday Applications

With the Fedora Operating System now installed, you have probably looked around to see what's new and found that a fair bit has changed. Some of the new additions have already been introduced to you, and a few applications you will find yourself using again and again. For example, at some point, you'll probably be looking for Office-type applications that will allow you to create documents, spreadsheets, and so on. Maybe you'll even want to embed some graphics into your documents that you've either scanned or captured from your digital camera. Finally, while you're drafting your latest masterpiece, you may want to listen to some music either from a CD you've bought or from some MP3s you've downloaded.

Well, the good news is that this and more is available in Fedora, out of the box. This chapter looks at some of the new applications available within the Fedora distribution. While Red Hat already had such a bewildering array of applications out of the box that covering them *all* in a single chapter would be impractical, Fedora has updated or added yet more applications. We'll introduce some of them, concentrating on the applications that we think you're most likely to need to complete those vital everyday tasks, and have some fun, too.

The applications in this chapter are grouped into the following sections:

- Office applications
- Internet applications
- Personal information management applications
- Multimedia applications
- System utilities

Each section will discuss what's required to install the application (if it hasn't already been installed by default), and how to configure the installation to suit your requirements. We'll also point out some of the similarities and differences between these applications and other applications that you may be familiar with—such as those found on the Microsoft operating system.

This chapter also covers emulator technologies, which emulate the Microsoft Windows operating system or interpret Windows applications and allow them to run on Linux. These will be of interest if, for example, you're thinking of developing a cross-platform application and you want to check its compatibility with both Linux *and* Windows operating systems.

As a survey, this chapter is designed to show you what's available, rather than to act as a user guide for individual applications. For most of these applications, the online help is comprehensive and well written, and can be accessed from the application's Help menu. In addition, you'll find URLs of Web sites that provide further documentation and support.

Office Applications

Most of us will spend at least some of our time creating and maintaining office documents such as word-processing documents, spreadsheets, and presentations. Therefore, this chapter begins with an introduction to the *office productivity* applications available within Linux.

Because these office tasks are so important, Fedora comes with a number of different office applications. Some of these applications are rich in functionality and compare very favorably with the likes of Microsoft Office, whereas others are smaller in size but still worthy of mention. These applications should be enough to meet your requirements—and if not, there are even more office application suites for Linux available via the Internet.

This section begins with a brief survey of all the office application suites included with Fedora. We can't cover them all in depth because there isn't room, but you should get an idea of what you can achieve by taking a closer look at *OpenOffice*, the standard office suite in Fedora.

What's Different?

Red Hat Linux shipped with OpenOffice 1.0, so what's new in OpenOffice 1.1? Red Hat put a great deal of effort into fixing bugs, making the latest version of the suite even more reliable. The Office compatibility has been enhanced, allowing for better accuracy when importing and exporting Microsoft Office files. In addition, a number of new features have been added, these including the following:

- Exporting to PDF
- Exporting to Macromedia Flash format
- Support for handicapped users (see `www.sun.com/access`)
- Macro Recorder for reoccurring tasks

For more details, take a look at `www.openoffice.org/dev_docs/features/1.1`.

Fedora and Office Applications

The following office application suites are all available with Fedora:

- The *OpenOffice* suite is installed when you install Fedora using the default settings. OpenOffice consists of a number of applications, including the following:
  - Dia (for structure drawings)
  - OpenOffice Writer (for word processing)
  - OpenOffice Calc (for spreadsheets)
  - OpenOffice Draw (for graphics)
  - OpenOffice Impress (for presentations)
  - OpenOffice Math (for editing formulas)
  - Project Management
  - Ximian Evolution

  OpenOffice is the most functionally capable of the suites listed here, and is explained in more detail in a moment. It's worth mentioning that other Office Suite applications are available, and while they are worth considering, this chapter could hardly do them justice. The suites are listed below with associated links; you can investigate these in more detail at your leisure:

  - **StarOffice:** The latest release at the time of this writing is version 7.0. More information is available at .

OpenOffice is the open source version of StarOffice; they are built on the same code – the only difference between the two is that OpenOffice has fewer text filters, no fonts, no DB, no full clip art library, and no template library. It also doesn't come with tech support or manual – which is why you pay $79 for it, and why OpenOffice is free.

  - **Koffice:** One of the original office suites whose current release is version 1.3. More information is available at `www.koffice.org`.
  - **GNOME Office:** This office suite is built from a variety of technologies used within the Bonoobo framework. More information is available at `www.gnome.org/gnome-office`.

Installing Office Applications

Most of the packages for the default office and productivity applications are listed within the Office/Productivity package group, which you'll find under the Applications category of the *Package Manager* application that is discussed in Chapter 8. (There are one or two exceptions; for example, GIMP is listed in the Graphics package group.)

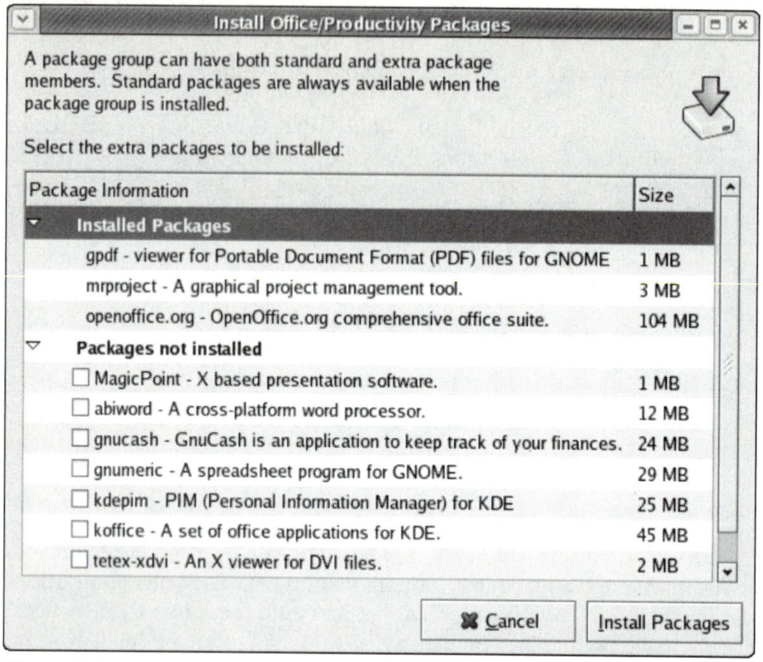

Figure 4-1

As you can see, the Office/Productivity package consists of 12 packages, including one for the OpenOffice suite and one for the Koffice suite. As you can see in the table that follows, three of these packages (including the OpenOffice suite) are installed by default when you install Fedora in any of its versions.

Package Name	Description
mrproject	This is a graphical project management tool. It's similar to Microsoft Project, allowing you to plan project tasks and resources.
openoffice	This is the OpenOffice.org office suite. As previously mentioned, it's a set of office productivity applications.
xpdf	This is a PDF file viewer for the X Window system.

You can safely install any (or all) of the remaining packages alongside OpenOffice simply by selecting the packages you want to install and clicking the Update button. (You'll need the distribution disks to complete the installation.) You can experiment with these applications at your leisure, choose your favorites, and (if you wish) uninstall the others later on.

We'll spend the remainder of this section looking at some of the applications in the OpenOffice suite. Note that you can find the latest information and downloads for OpenOffice at `www.openoffice.org`. This site has OpenOffice downloads for a variety of platforms including Linux, Windows, and Mac OS

X. You'll also find localized dictionaries, documentation, and support facilities to help you get the most from these applications.

Starting an OpenOffice Application

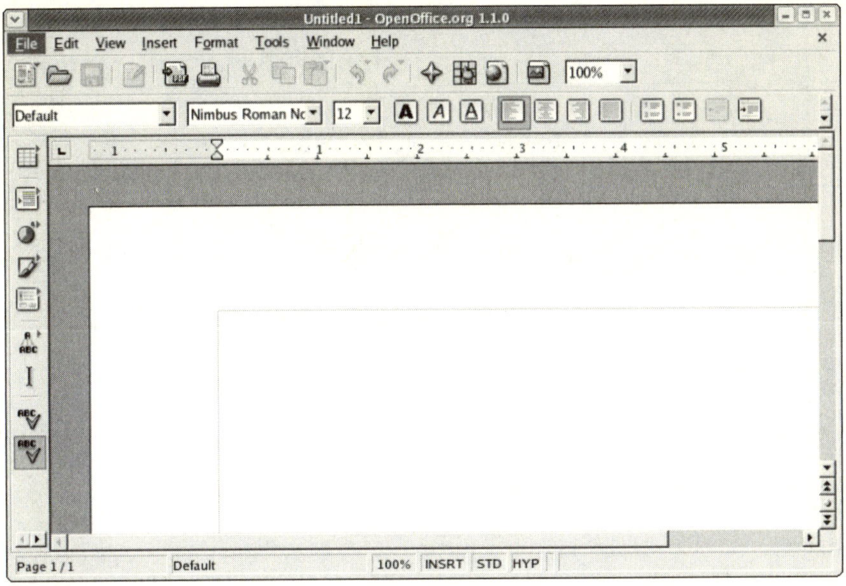

Figure 4-2

In addition to the menu shortcuts, the OpenOffice installation process also places three shortcut icons within the taskbar at the bottom of the screen, as shown in Figure 4-3; these are for the Writer, Impress, and Calc applications, respectively. To invoke any of these applications, just click the icon.

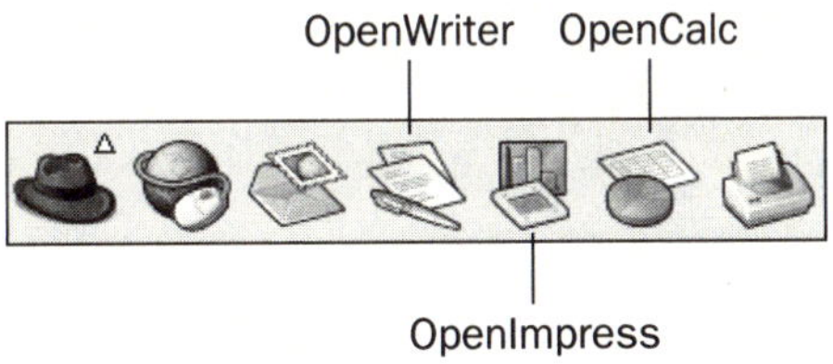

Figure 4-3

It is also possible to run the office applications from the command line. The simplest way of achieving this is to select Run Application from the Main Menu and type the command line you wish to execute. For example, `oocalc` *is the binary file for Calc (see Figure 4-4).*

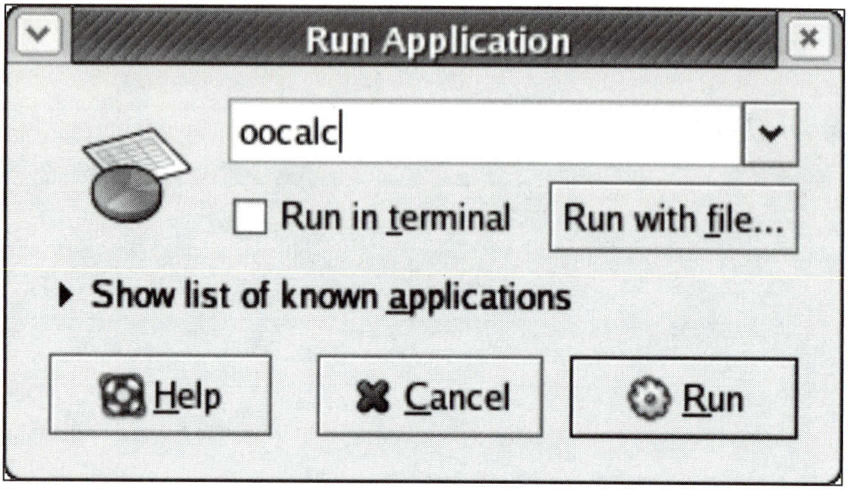

Figure 4-4

You'll notice as you type something that as Fedora recognizes a known application, the icon will change to represent the application recognized (in this case, the Calc icon). Now selecting the Run option will execute the command line and, in this case, the Calc application.

By default, the executable files are installed into the `/usr/bin` directory, which is part of the `$PATH` environment variable. This means that you can run any of these applications simply by typing its name at the command line.

The following table lists the commands for some other applications in the OpenOffice suite.

Executable	Application
`oocalc`	Spreadsheet application
`oodraw`	Drawing application
`oomath`	Mathematical formula composer
`ooimpress`	Presentation application
`oowriter`	Word processor
`ooffice`	The default OpenOffice window for creating any OpenOffice document

Common Functionality

To begin, take a look at some of the elements that are common to all the applications in the OpenOffice suite.

The *layout* of the main window of each application will be familiar to you if you've ever used applications such as Microsoft Word. The top part of the application displays the *menu bar* and a *function bar*. Beneath this are the *object bar* and the *ruler*, with the main working area below that. The *status bar* is at the bottom of the window, and behaves like the Microsoft Word status bar. To the side of the main word area is the *main toolbar*.

The diagram in Figure 4-5 demonstrates these areas as visible within an OpenOffice application.

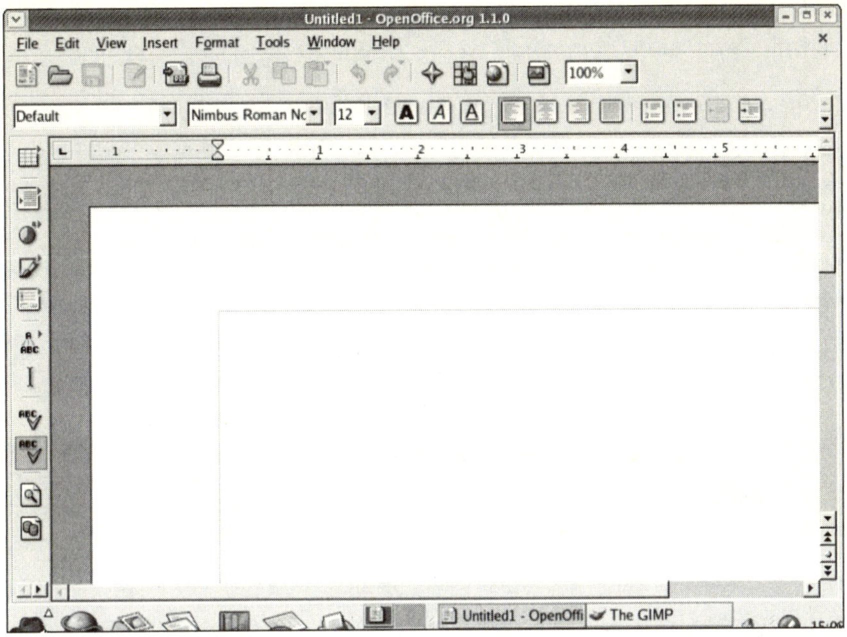

Figure 4-5

You can choose to hide some of these toolbars via the View ➪ Toolbars menu option. Unlike Microsoft Word, OpenOffice doesn't allow you to undock the toolbars or move them around the screen. However, you can customize the contents of a toolbar either by right-clicking a toolbar and selecting Customize, or by selecting View ➪ Toolbars ➪ Customize from the menu.

The toolbars vary from application to application, although the Function, Object, and Main toolbars are common to all the OpenOffice applications.

The menu structure also varies from application to application, and therefore it would be impractical to try and explain all the options here. If you've used Microsoft Office, you'll notice some familiar menu options. Even if you're unfamiliar with Microsoft Office, you'll find these quite self-explanatory:

- The File menu allows you to open, save, and close files, and offers other features such as printer and page-reviewing options.
- The Tools menu allows access to tools that are either incorporated into the application or added via plug-ins. In addition, this menu also usually offers the opportunity to configure various application-specific options.

- The Window menu allows you to switch between different documents that you have open in the application at the same time.
- The Help menu provides access to the built-in help system (which, incidentally, is extremely comprehensive, and should be the first port of call for any problems or information you require).

Compatibility with Microsoft Office

One thing that many first-time Linux users worry about is whether their Microsoft Office documents are compatible with OpenOffice. For example, you may wonder if it is possible to do the following:

- Create a document in Microsoft Word, and then edit it using OpenOffice
- Save a spreadsheet in OpenOffice, and then use it at work within Microsoft Excel

The answer is Yes! OpenOffice's built-in *interoperability* features allow you to use OpenOffice applications to load and save documents using file formats that are compatible with other applications (such as those in Microsoft Office). You must configure OpenOffice to handle features such as object embedding (and other features that are native to Microsoft Office) to ensure their behavior is as you would expect.

You can configure these options by accessing the Options dialog box from the Tools ➪ Options menu from any OpenOffice application (see Figure 4-6).

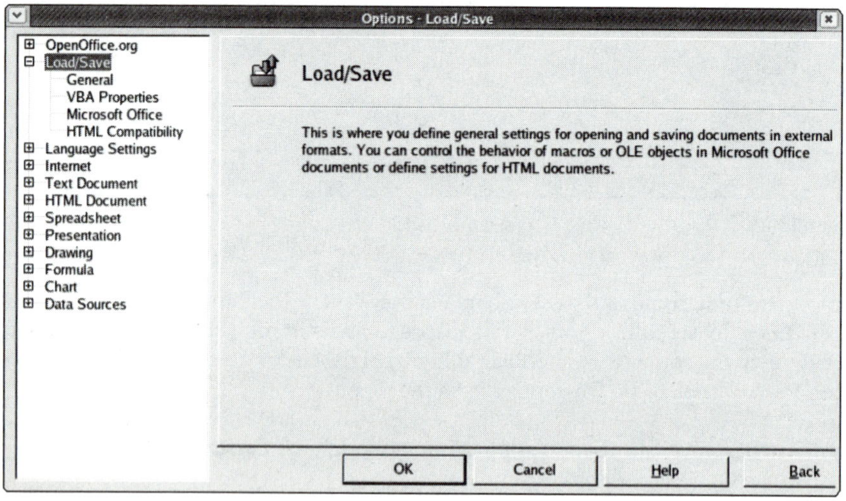

Figure 4-6

Not all OpenOffice applications support specific conversion features (those that do are discussed here), but they all support the ability to load and save between different file formats. You can find out more by looking at each application's documentation.

Of particular interest here are the options found under the Load/Save node on the left of this dialog box. Only those options associated with compatibility with Microsoft Office are covered here.

General Loading and Saving Options

The option of interest here is the default File Format that is used when you save a document. You can see this option at the foot of the General tab, as shown in Figure 4-7.

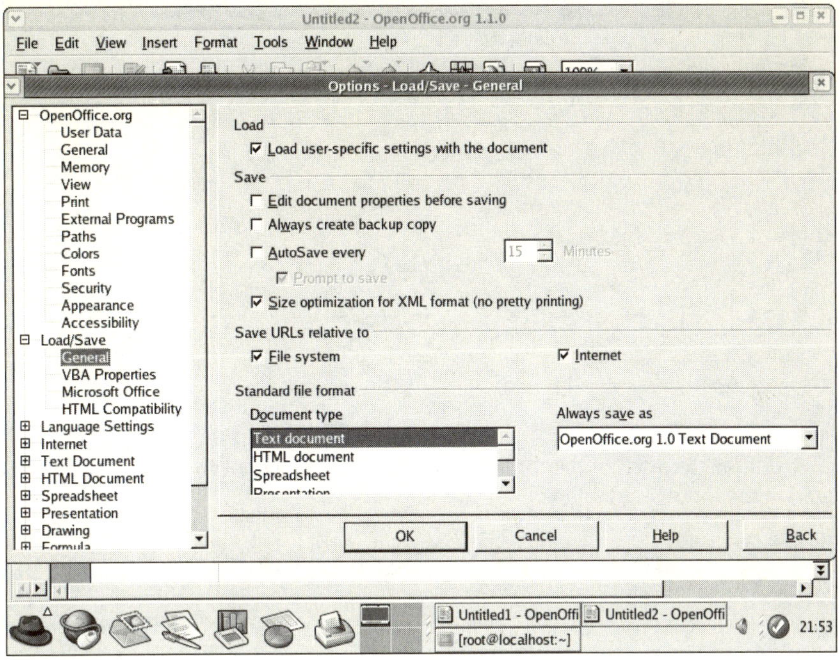

Figure 4-7

It is here that you can select the default format that the application will use whenever you ask it to save your document to disk (for example, using File ⇨ Save). As you can see from the preceding figure, when you first install OpenOffice this default document type is set to the OpenOffice.org.1.0 format.

If you want to work with Microsoft Office file formats only, it is here that you should change this default setting. This can be particularly useful if you transfer files between home and work often, and you don't want to forget to save in the correct format. For example, suppose you use Microsoft Word XP at your place of work and OpenOffice's OpenWriter at home. If you regularly create documents at home for use at work, you can configure OpenWriter to save your documents in Microsoft Word 97/2000/XP format by default, so that these documents are compatible with the software at your place of work.

VBA Options

Your documents might contain code written using *Visual Basic for Applications (VBA)*. OpenOffice applications can handle VBA code in a number of different ways, but support is limited to documents that originated in Microsoft Word 97/2000, Microsoft Excel 97/2000, and Microsoft PowerPoint 97/2000.

OpenOffice supports VBA through the dialog box shown in Figure 4-8.

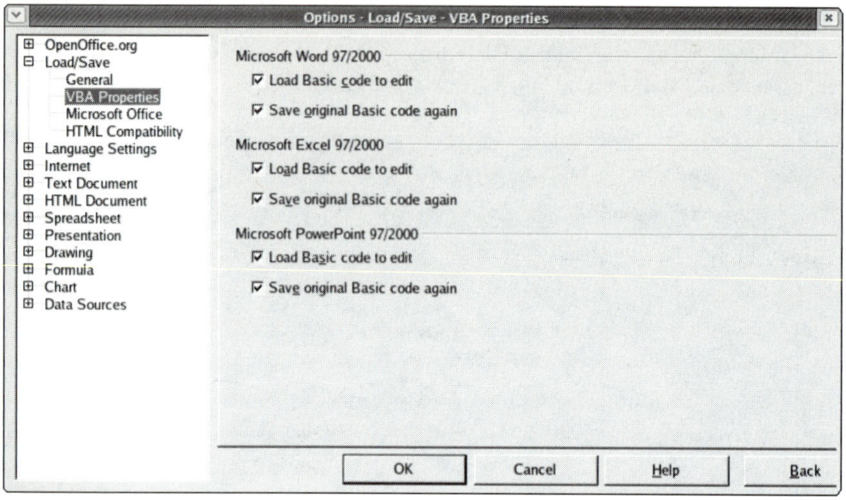

Figure 4-8

There are two options for each of the three office applications that support VBA code embedding. They are explained in the following table.

Option	Description
Load Basic code to edit	When this option is selected, the application loads the VBA code from the original document and embeds it into a special Basic module within OpenOffice. This module preserves the code and allows you to edit it through the application's interface or IDE.
Save Original Basic Code again	When this option is selected, the application saves the code as preserved in the Basic module in the format expected of the Office application, so the code continues to work as expected (assuming its syntax is correct).

It is beyond the scope of this chapter to cover BASIC within OpenOffice. If you want to know more, take a look at `www.engineering.usu.edu/cee/faculty/gurro/Software_Calculators/StarOffice_Docs/StarOfficeBasicManual.zip`*. StarOffice Basic is very similar to OpenOffice Basic, and you can switch between OpenOffice and VBA Help (if you run Windows) to find assistance.*

Microsoft Office Options

Microsoft Office's applications also allow users to embed objects of one type within another. For example, if you want to show sales data from a spreadsheet within your sales report, you can easily embed your Excel spreadsheet within your Word document. In Microsoft parlance, this is known as *Object*

Linking and Embedding (OLE). With OLE, the embedded object inherits the functionality of the application it was created in (so in the example cited here, the embedded Excel spreadsheet inherits the functionality of Microsoft Excel, even though it is embedded into an Microsoft Word file).

The Options dialog box in OpenOffice allows you to select which objects are converted (if at all) and at which stage—when the object is loaded into OpenOffice and/or when saving from OpenOffice into a Microsoft format (see Figure 4-9).

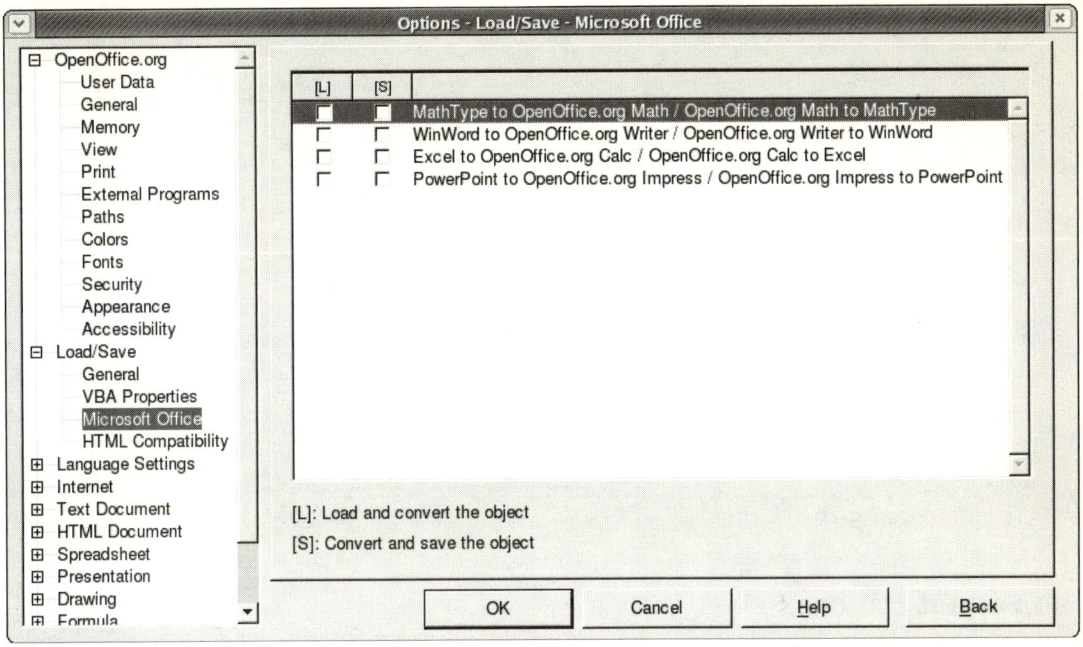

Figure 4-9

The checkboxes in the [L] (for load) column indicate that an object of the specified type should be converted into an OpenOffice object when a Microsoft document is loaded. The checkboxes in the [S] (for save) column indicate that the object should be converted to the specified Microsoft Object when the document is saved to a Microsoft file format. (So, if you leave the [S] checkbox unchecked, the objects will not be converted and will be absent from the resulting file.)

As you can see from Figure 4-9, there are four object types supported, including Microsoft Word (WinWord), Microsoft Excel, Microsoft PowerPoint, and MathType.

MathType is used to represent mathematical formulas. For more on this application, see `www.mathtype.com/mathtype`.

HTML Compatibility Options

This dialog box doesn't offer any features for converting between versions of Microsoft Office, but it does contain the setting that indicates what browser is targeted when exporting a document from an

OpenOffice application in HTML format (see Figure 4-10). OpenOffice supports a number of formats, including the following:

- ❑ Netscape Navigator (version 4.0 and above)
- ❑ Microsoft Internet Explorer (version 4.0 and above)
- ❑ HTML 3.2 (most browsers support this)

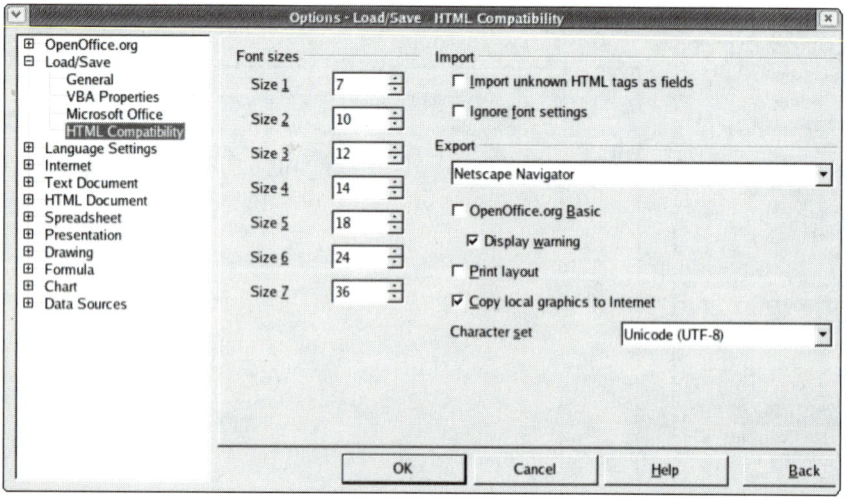

Figure 4-10

File Format Options

In addition to the settings in the Options dialog box, OpenOffice's capability to load from (and save to) different file formats is integral to the applications themselves. These options vary according to the context of the application, and so they are covered within the OpenOffice applications themselves.

However, it's also worth noting the existence of a generic document conversion tool called AutoPilot, which is accessible from all OpenOffice applications. If you select File ➪ AutoPilot ➪ Document Converter, you'll see a dialog box like the one in Figure 4-11.

AutoPilot is actually a batch tool, for which OpenOffice provides a shortcut.

This dialog box provides you with options to convert from StarOffice or Microsoft Office file formats to the new OpenOffice XML (eXtensible Markup Language) format. The preceding figure illustrates the Microsoft Office file formats and a Word document we intend to convert, so the Word documents option is marked.

After pressing Next, you'll see the dialog box shown in Figure 4-12. It prompts you to say whether you wish to convert templates, documents, or both, and whether you are to include subdirectories in your conversion process. In this case, we're converting only Word documents from our working directory and placing the converted files in the same directory.

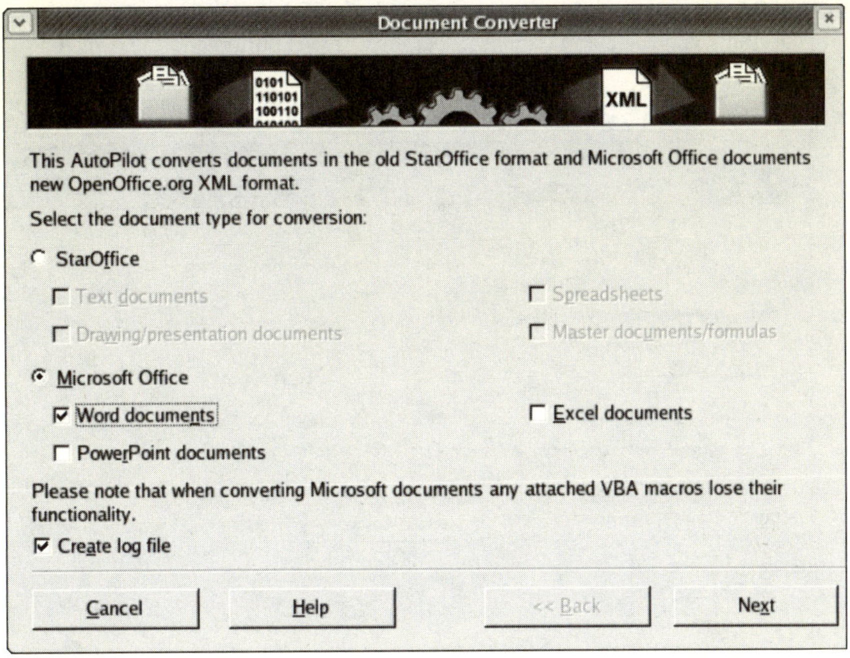

Figure 4-11

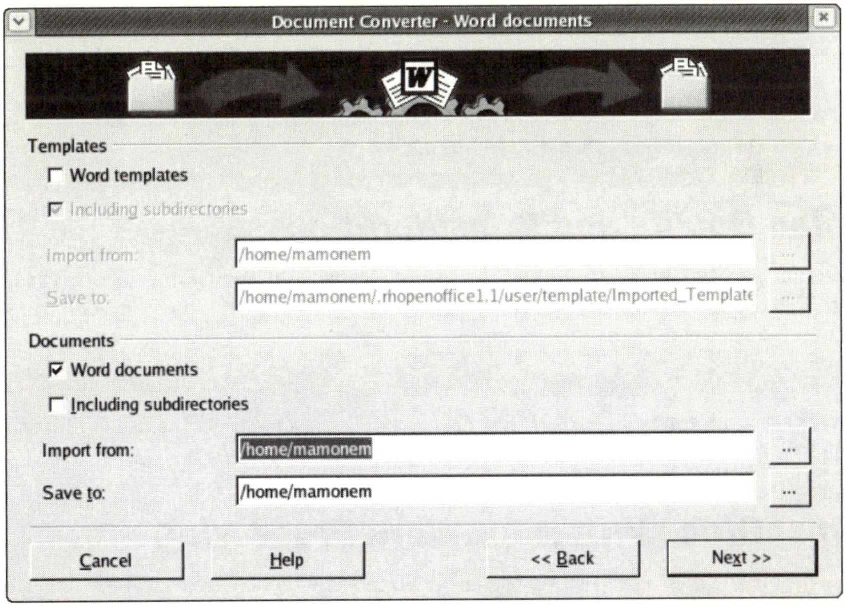

Figure 4-12

When you click the Next button again, you see a confirmation dialog box, shown in Figure 4-13. If you're happy that everything is present and correct, select the Convert button and the conversion process begins.

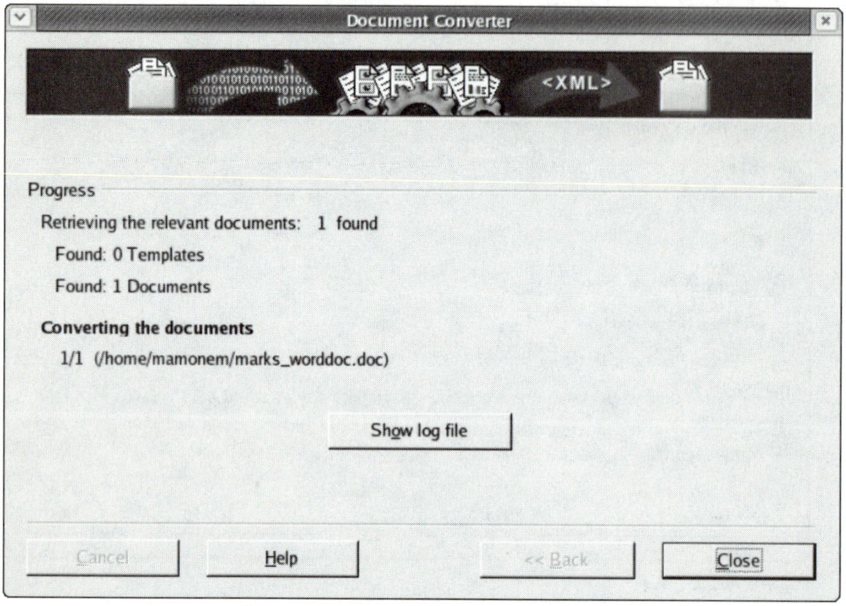

Figure 4-13

When the conversion is complete, the Progress screen displays the results of the conversion process .

Note that this conversion process renders any VBA code invalid. If your documents contain VBA code that you wish to preserve, you should avoid this method.

Conversion Quality and Considerations

The conversion quality between different file formats (especially Microsoft Office) is excellent. The only caveats are that the conversion process from OpenOffice to Microsoft Office can lead to files larger that their original file sizes due to the lack of compression. However, this is likely to change in future releases.

It's worth experimenting with the Rich Text Format (RTF) file format—this will help to avoid potential conversion errors, although at the expense of certain formatting capabilities.

Using OpenOffice Writer for Word Processing

When you start the Writer word processing application (which you can do using Main Menu ⇨ Office ⇨ OpenOffice.org Writer or the shortcut icon from the task bar), you are presented with a window like the one shown in Figure 4-14.

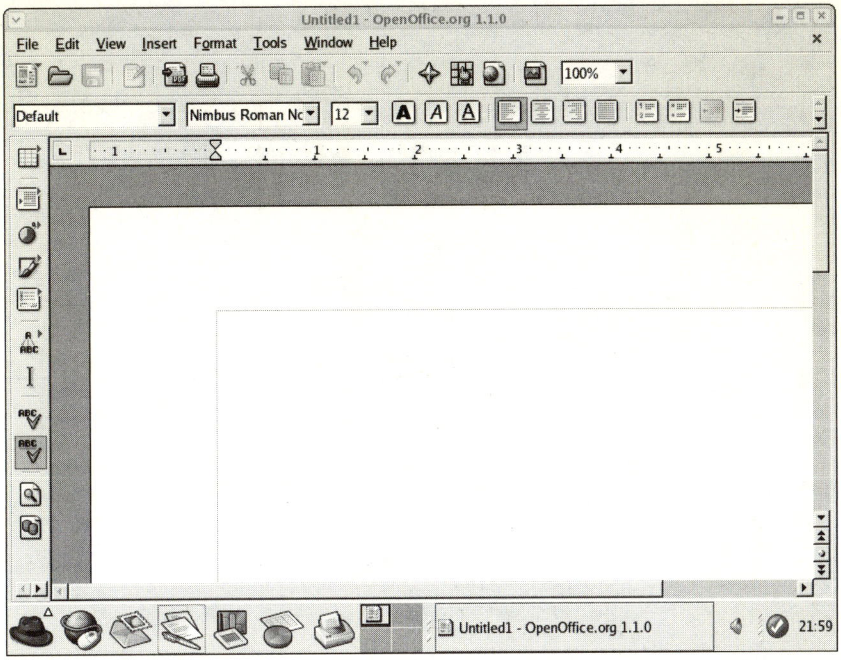

Figure 4-14

Writer provides the wealth of features that one would normally expect to find in a commercial word processing application. We won't list them all here; like the other applications in the suite, it would warrant a book in its own right. However, we will highlight some of the key features included and also describe how interoperability with other applications such as Microsoft Office is achieved. Some of the key features are as follows:

- Styles and style galleries
- Thesaurus
- Spell checker
- Clipart
- Support for other file formats, such as Microsoft Word, StarWriter, and so on

As you've seen, Writer is compatible with Microsoft Word. In particular, it is capable of loading and saving documents and templates in a number of Word file formats, including Microsoft Word 97/2000/XP and Microsoft Word 6.0/95. You can load and save between OpenOffice's native version and any of the other versions listed simply by using the File ➪ Open and File ➪ Save dialog boxes. The File Type drop-down list box allows you to choose the appropriate format (see Figure 4-15).

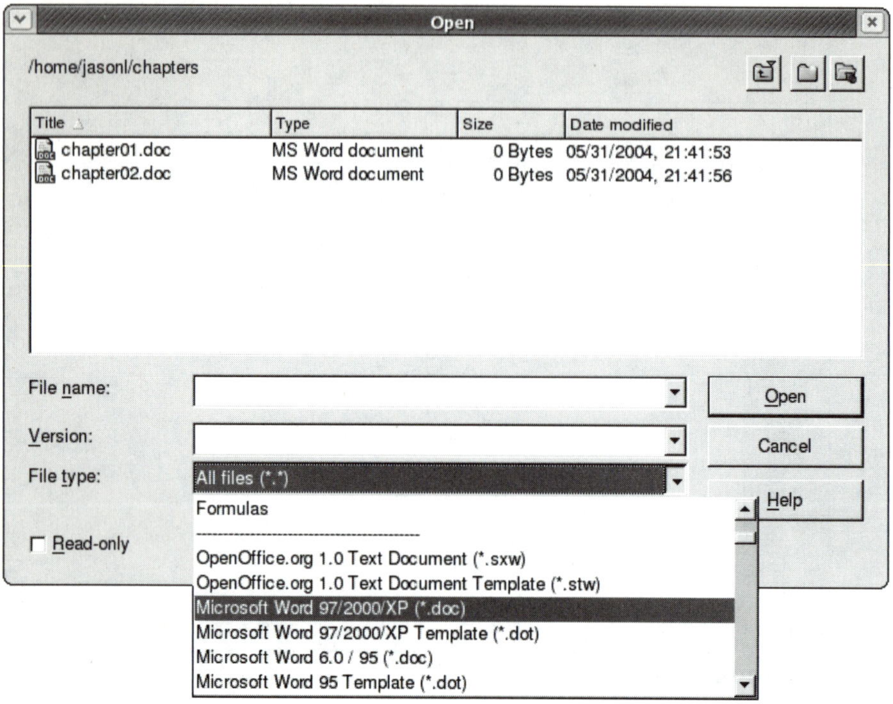

Figure 4-15

Using OpenOffice Calc for Spreadsheets

The *Calc* (or *Calc*) application again provides numerous features that you would expect of a commercial application and is comparable to Microsoft Excel, the spreadsheet application within Microsoft Office. Some of the key features include the following:

- Ability to handle multiple spreadsheets simultaneously
- Embedded graphics and charts
- Cell security
- External data sources
- Data Pilot (this is similar to PivotTables in Excel)

Calc also supports compatibility with Excel through its ability to load and save spreadsheets and templates in a number of Excel file formats, including Microsoft Excel 97/2000/XP and Microsoft Excel 4.*x*–5.0. Other interoperability features include the handling of VBA code and embedded objects (as mentioned earlier in this chapter).

Other, more specific options mimic the behavior of Microsoft Excel, and help to make users with an Excel background feel more comfortable. One specific such option is the ability to indicate that OpenCalc's searching capability should behave in the same manner as Excel's. This option can be found in the Tools ➪ Options dialog box, in the Spreadsheet ➪ Calculate tab (see Figure 4-16).

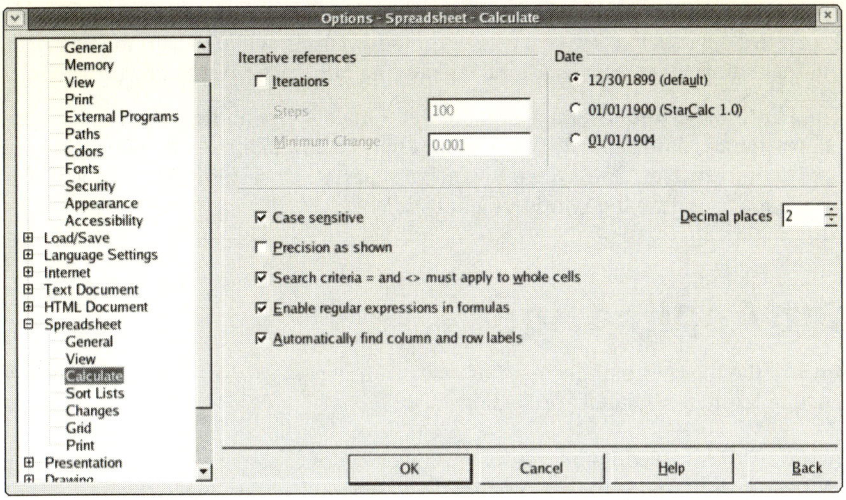

Figure 4-16

Note the "Search criteria = and <> must apply to whole cells" option in this dialog box. When this option is selected, Calc handles searches in the same way as Microsoft Excel, in that the search criteria entered are specific and must match the whole cell. When the option is not selected, the search criteria are matched against *any* position within the cell.

Using OpenOffice Impress for Presentations

The *Impress* (or *Impress*) application again provides many of the features that you would expect of a commercial application, and is comparable to Microsoft PowerPoint, the presentation management application within Microsoft Office. The key features of Impress include the following:

- Master templates
- Slide animation and transition effects
- Notes against slides
- Timing rehearsals

Impress supports compatibility with Microsoft PowerPoint, in its ability to load and save presentations and templates in PowerPoint's file format (PowerPoint 97/2000/XP).

It's worth experimenting with the applications installed within the OpenOffice suite to learn more about what they're capable of doing. Here's a brief summary of each:

- The diagramming tool, *Dia*, is launched through Main Menu ⇨ Office ⇨ Dia Diagrams. This application is used for drawing diagrams based on a variety of templates—from simple boxes and lines to circuit diagrams. It is a primitive (or highly scaled-down) version of the Microsoft Visio diagram application. See `www.lysator.liu.se/~alla/dia/dia.html` for more information.

- The *Draw* application, launched via Main Menu ➪ Office ➪ Openoffice.org Draw, can be used to generate drawings that are of a more graphical nature. It allows you to insert clipart from its internal library or external sources. It draws its influence from Microsoft's Draw application.
- The *Printer Setup* application (Main Menu ➪ Office ➪ Openoffice.org Printer Setup) simply allows you to confirm printer devices that may be available to you, and direct output from applications such as OpenOffice to your printers. Its closest Windows cousin is the Printers option found within the Windows Control Panel.

Internet Applications

The existence of the Internet is at the heart of many of the most exciting Linux applications. This section looks at the Linux Internet-related applications.

The default installation of Fedora includes a number of applications contained in the Graphical Internet package. All these applications have a *graphical user interface (GUI)* to make the user's life easier. The package group contains some 14 applications (of which 8 are installed by default). This section concentrates on just two of them:

- **The Mozilla application:** A Web browser that provides similar functionality to the Netscape Navigator or Microsoft Internet Explorer browsers. Mozilla is a fully functional Web browser, and also supports extensions to add further functionality (such as mail).
- **The Gaim client:** An Instant Messaging client similar to Microsoft Instant Messenger and capable of interfacing with a number of messaging protocols (such as AIM, ICQ, Yahoo!, MSN, IRC, and others) used by various messaging clients.

We'll take a look at these applications in more detail, and discuss their history and interoperability features, leaving you in a position to further explore at your leisure.

The Mozilla Web Browser

The Netscape browser's core source code, known as *Mozilla,* was released to the public under the Netscape Public License (NPL) in 1998. The Mozilla project (a group set up to continue Netscape Communicator as an open source application) used this code as the basis for its own commercial-level browser. The current version of Mozilla, version 1.6, is released under the NPL license for modifications of the core Mozilla code and the Mozilla Public License (MPL) for any new additions.

The Mozilla Web browser is the primary browser for Fedora plus other distributions, and is an X Window system application that provides a very similar look and feel to the Netscape Navigator and Internet Explorer applications. To take a look, fire it up now by clicking the Web Browser icon on the bottom left of your desktop (next to the Main Menu button), or by selecting Main Menu ➪ Internet ➪ Mozilla Web Browser (see Figure 4-17).

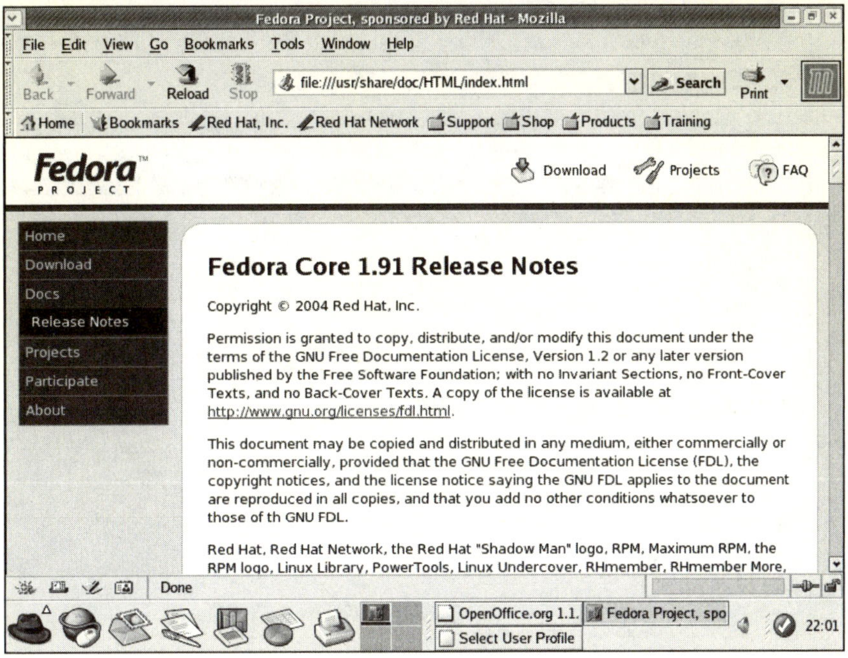

Figure 4-17

The layout of the application is likely familiar to you. The *menu bar* contains all the familiar menus, and the *navigation toolbar* allows you to type in a URL, move backward and forward between recently visited pages, reload a page, and stop a page from loading. The preceding figure also shows a *personal toolbar folder*, which contains shortcuts to your favorite Web sites. You can control the shortcuts on your personal toolbar folder by using the Manage Bookmarks option (which you'll find under the Bookmarks menu; see Figure 4-18).

The features provided by Mozilla (and the look-and-feel of those features) will be familiar if you've used Internet Explorer, and more so if you've used Netscape Navigator (because Mozilla and Navigator are derived from the same original source code).

The Mozilla Mail Client

In addition to its core functionality as a Web browser, you can extend the Mozilla base feature set by installing additional functionality (plug-ins), such as the Mozilla-based *mail client*. In fact, the mail client plug-in is installed as a default extension to Mozilla.

The mail client is accessible from the Mozilla application by selecting the Window ➪ Mail & Newsgroups option from the menu bar. When you first use this, you'll be prompted to create a default account using the information provided by your Internet Services Provider (ISP) or network administrator. When you've successfully entered that information, the main application will start with the screen shown in Figure 4-19.

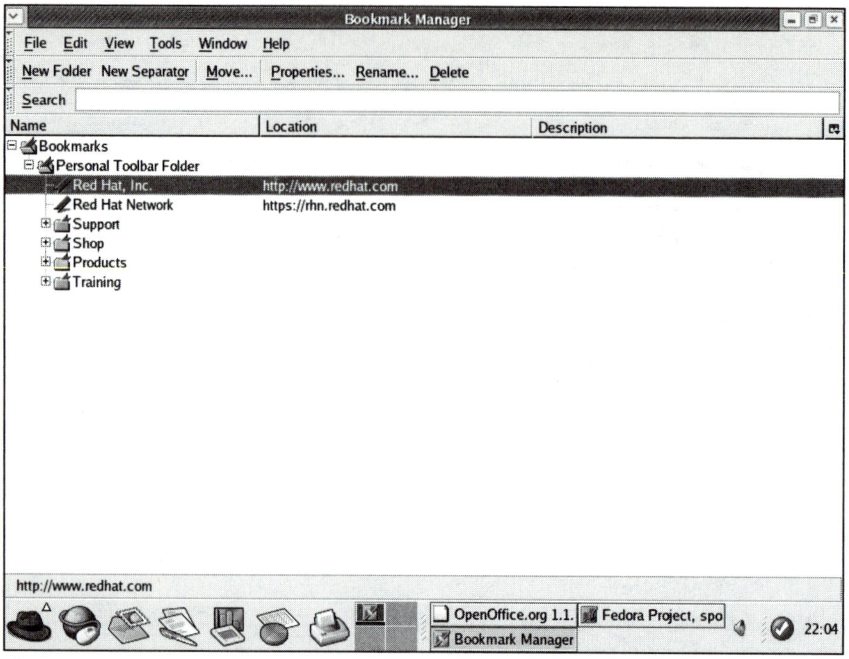

Figure 4-18

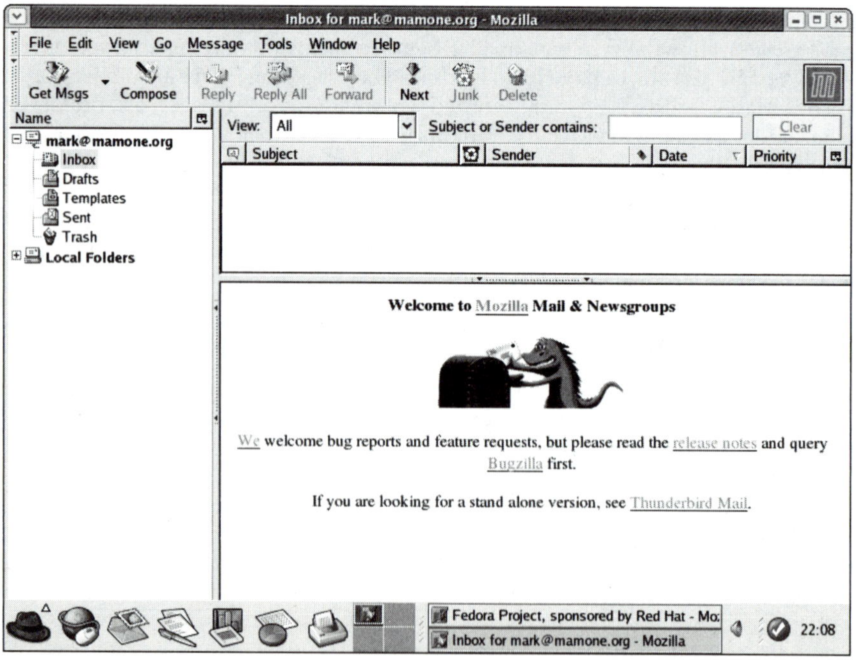

Figure 4-19

This has very similar functionality to that of Microsoft Outlook Express—providing folders for your e-mail and for any newsgroups that you're subscribed to. By default, Mozilla includes support for Internet Security Standards such as Secure Sockets Layer (SSL), which provides encryption of information over the Internet.

Let's have a look at some of the specific interoperability features within Mozilla mail.

Importing from Other Clients

If you have been using another mail client, such as Netscape Communicator, Microsoft Outlook, or Microsoft Outlook Express, you can import your mail messages into Mozilla mail by using the features provided from the Tools ➪ Import menu option..

These features will guide you through the process of importing mail settings and messages, or an address book from another mail client—you simply select the appropriate option and follow the wizard.

You can also *export* an address book to a variety of formats (including Outlook and Outlook Express). To do this, select Window ➪ Address Book and then the address book you want to export, and then click the Tools ➪ Export menu option.

The Gaim Instant Messenger Application

So you can browse the Internet and correspond using e-mail. What about chatting? This technology has suffered from the number of different protocols used by different organizations for transmitting information. However, in true Linux tradition, *Gaim* is flexible enough to cope with this and offers an elegant solution.

Gaim is a utility for supporting online chats; it's similar to the AOL Instant Messenger or Microsoft Messenger application. It provides a single front-end for multiple protocols (including Napster, MSN, ICQ, IRC, and Yahoo!), and so can interoperate with other Instant Messenger applications.

The first thing to do (if you haven't already) is create an account with an Internet messaging service (there are plenty around—MSN and Yahoo! are just two examples). Then, start Gaim (by selecting Main Menu ➪ Internet ➪ Instant Messenger or type **gaim** at the command line). Gaim is shown in Figure 4-20.

By default, a number of protocols are installed:

- AIM/ICQ
- Gadu-Gadu
- IRC
- Jabber
- MSN
- Napster
- TOC
- Yahoo
- Zephyr

Figure 4-20

It's possible that your messaging service uses a different protocol, or you may wish to add additional functionality, such as Notifications, that is not supported by default. Fear not—Gaim is extensible and can support more protocols and additional functionality via plug-ins. To install the protocol support you need, click the Preferences button and use the Plugins option to select the functionality required (see Figure 4-21).

When you've done that, you can tell Gaim about your account. Do so by clicking the Accounts button and supplying the information about your account and the protocol used.

Then, you can sign in and start chatting, as shown in Figure 4-22.

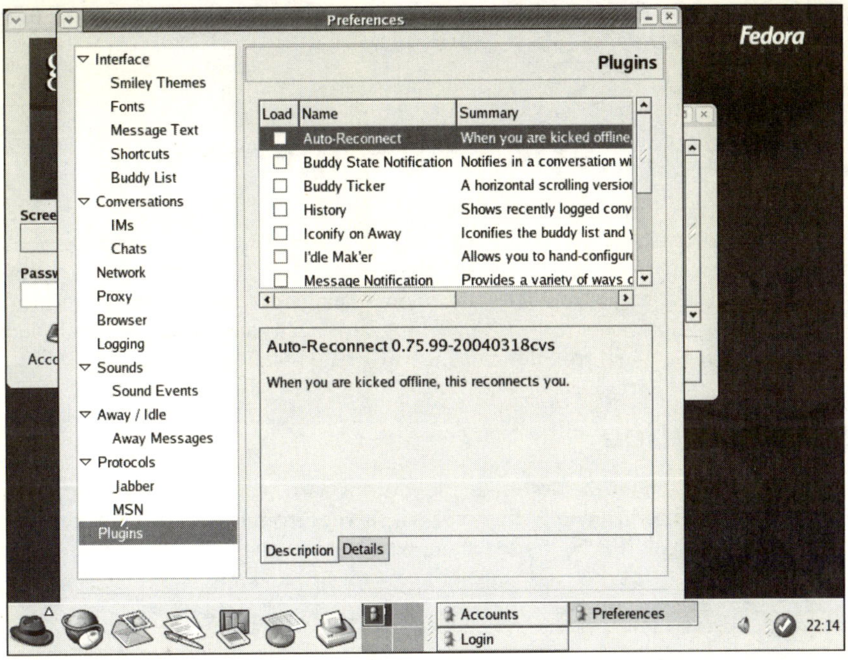

Figure 4-21

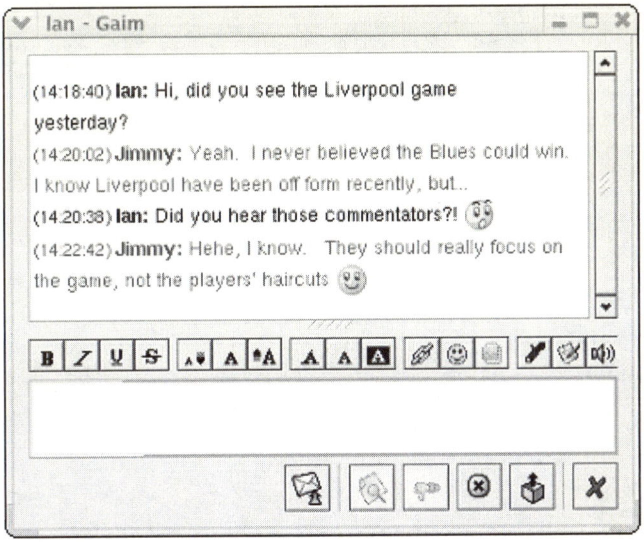

Figure 4-22

You can find the latest updates, documentation, and additional plug-ins to extend the functionality of Gaim at its Web site at `http://gaim.sourceforge.net`.

Personal Information Management

As if the Mozilla plug-ins for tasks such as e-mail management weren't enough, an application to manage e-mail, contacts, and related things is available in the form of Ximian's *Evolution*. The Evolution application is a groupware program, similar to Microsoft Outlook, that provides access to personal information such as e-mail, a calendar, contacts, and so on. Management of this type of information is often known as *personal information management (PIM)*. Programs such as Evolution (and Outlook) allow you to manage all of this personal information within a single application.

Setting Up Evolution

If you are starting Evolution for the first time, the setup wizard will guide you through completing the information to establish a connection with your mail server through your ISP. Figure 4-23 shows one of the early screens in the Evolution Setup Assistant, which starts up the first time you run the application.

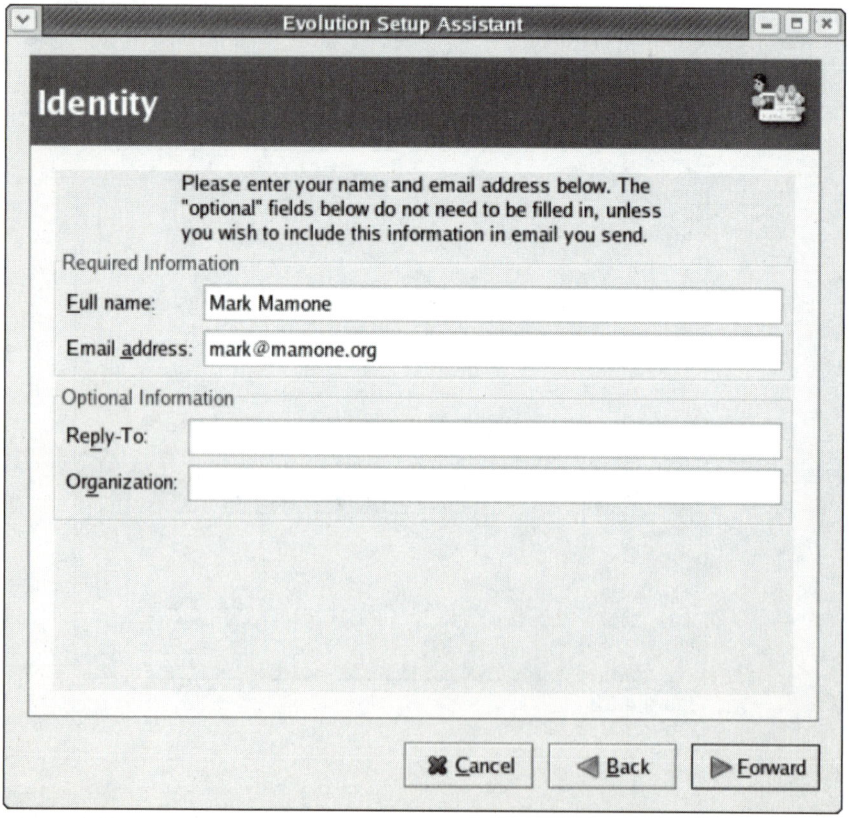

Figure 4-23

Alternatively, you can set up your mailbox properties once the application has started properly. To do this, select Tools ⇨ Settings (this is the starting point for changing most of the Evolution settings), and then select the Mail Accounts tab, which allows you to add new accounts and edit the properties of your existing accounts (see Figure 4-24).

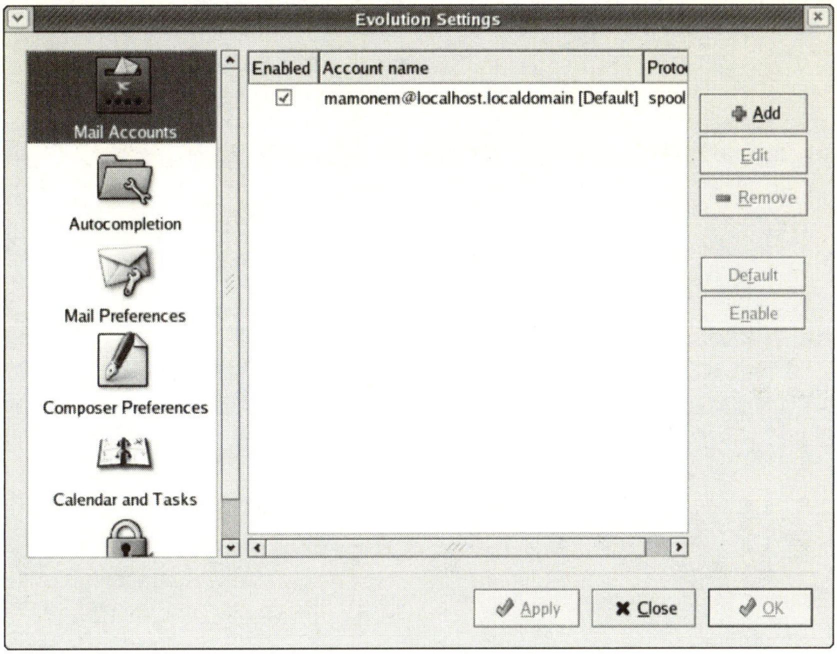

Figure 4-24

The wizard guides you through the process of entering the information that is provided by your ISP to gain access to your Internet account and e-mail subscription: your name, e-mail address, and the name of the server and username assigned by your ISP.

Using Evolution

Selecting this option will start the setup wizard, and when the wizard is complete you'll see the Summary screen by default. You can move to other areas of the application by selecting the icons on the left side of the window. For example, selecting the InBox icon displays the screen shown in Figure 4-25.

The layout of the window consists of the usual *menu bar* and a context-sensitive *toolbar*. The toolbar's icons reflect the application's current mode (Summary, Inbox, Calendar, Tasks, or Contacts). These modes are accessed via the *shortcut toolbar* that runs down the left side of the application.

- The *Inbox* (shown in the preceding figure) provides access to your e-mail account, allowing you to send, receive, and manage your e-mail using features and folders.
- The *Calendar* allows you to manage your schedule, adding forthcoming appointments between one or more people and attaching reminders so you don't forget.

- The *Tasks* feature provides a simple task database, allowing you to record tasks and assign due dates. In addition, you can categorize your tasks for more flexibility when managing them.
- The *Contacts* feature allows you to store your contacts in an address book, which may then be used when sending e-mails. However, it allows you to store far more information than simply an e-mail address such as mailing addresses, Web pages, a variety of telephone numbers, company information, and more.

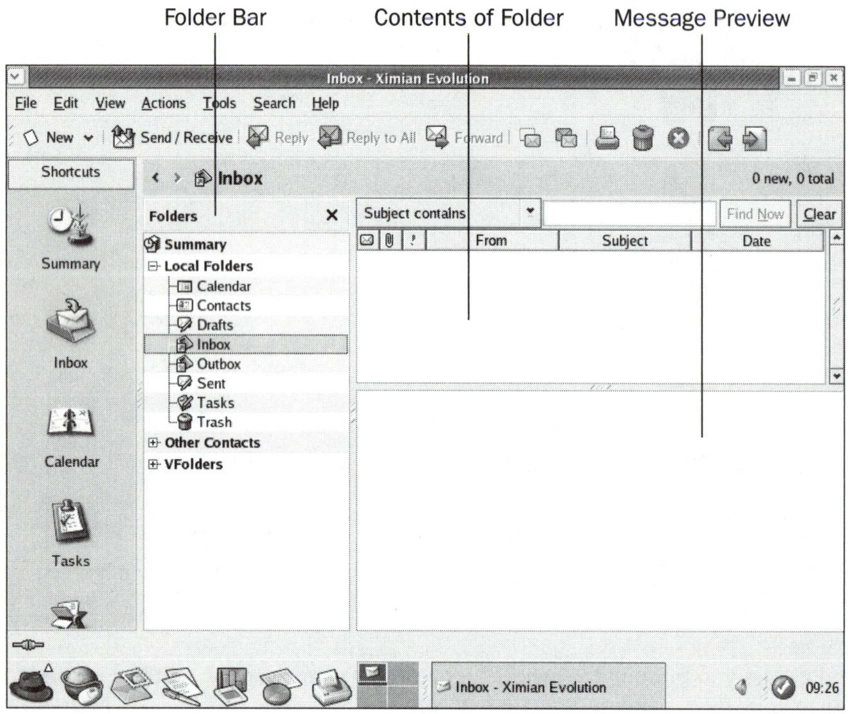

Figure 4-25

Again, check out the online documentation; it is more than sufficient to take you through the details of individual tasks. We'll concentrate on the key features of the application, note some similarities with Microsoft Outlook, and cover some of the features for interoperability with other applications (particularly Microsoft Outlook).

The Inbox Feature

The Inbox screen provides an interface not only to your Inbox folder, but to all your local mail folders. When you first open the Inbox screen, you get to see the Inbox folder, with a list of messages shown in the top panel and the content of the currently selected message shown underneath in the preview panel. The toolbar contains shortcuts to the most popular features—creating, replying to, and deleting messages; printing; navigation; and so on.

The folder bar is a particularly useful feature that's not shown by default. To make it appear, select View ➪ Folder Bar.

As you can see, the folder bar makes it much easier to find your way around your local mail folders. In addition, you can use the folder bar to manage your folders (creating, deleting, moving, copying, renaming folders, and so on). For example, to create a new subfolder you simply select the parent folder in the folder bar and either select File ➪ New ➪ Folder or right-click and select Create New Folder.

Evolution also provides the usual search facilities, which are very similar to those in Microsoft's Outlook. You can apply search criteria against fields held in e-mails, such as the subject or body.

The Calendar Feature

The *Calendar* function provides you with a view that represents a certain time period. It can display a single day, a week (including or excluding weekends), or a month. You can change this setting via the View ➪ Current View menu item. The example in Figure 4-26 shows the Working Week view.

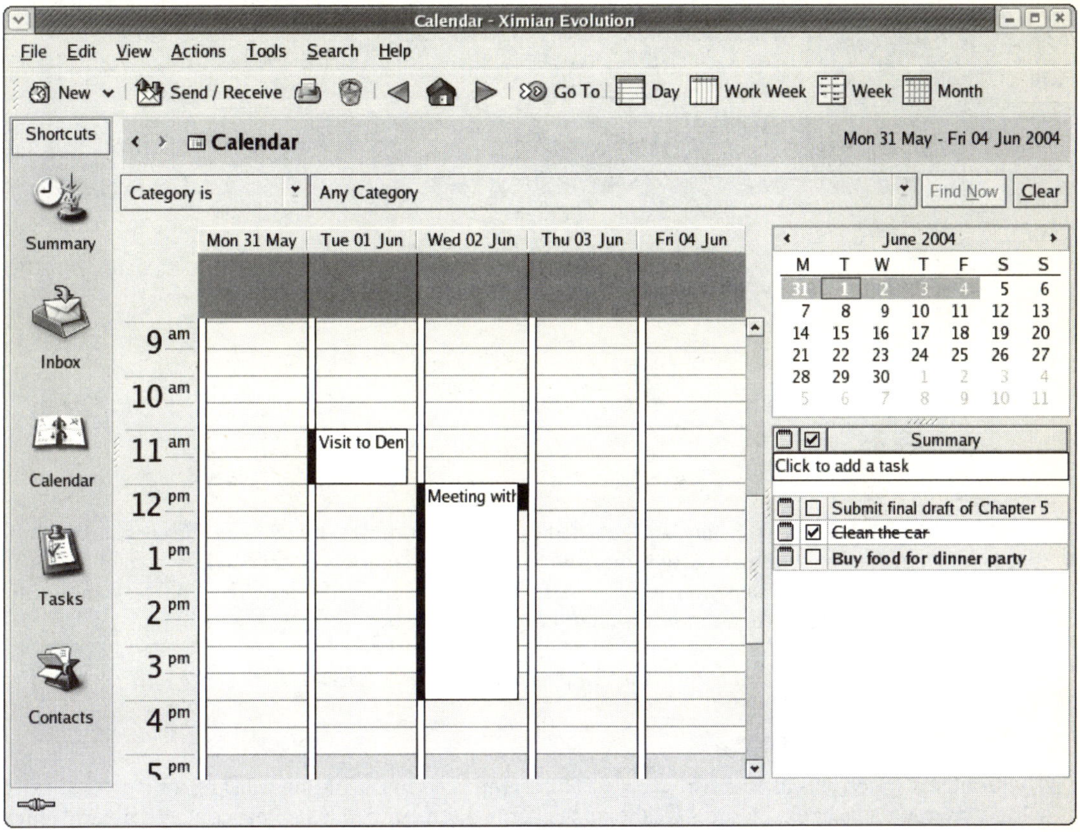

Figure 4-26

It is within these views that you can create Appointments that hold information such as Summary, Location, Start Date/Time, Classification, and so on. You can even add a Reminder to your appointment, and you can create recurring reminders over a period of days, weeks, months, or years. In the preceding figure, you can see that Mark had a couple of appointments, including a visit to the dentist and a meeting with the publisher.

The Tasks Feature

The Tasks screen is a simple but effective list of jobs. To enter a task, you can select New ➪ Task or Click the New Task button to add a task text box. If you want, you can also assign a Due Date, and when the task is complete, you can mark it as finished.

Figure 4-27 shows an example of the Tasks screen with some tasks entered.

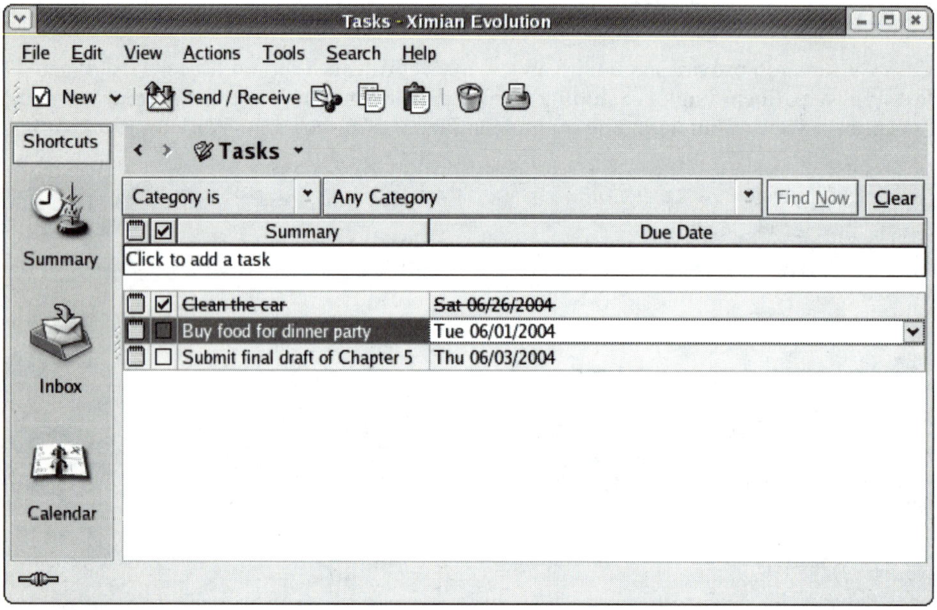

Figure 4-27

So, Mark cleaned the car last Friday, and marked the task as complete by clicking the checkbox next to that task. We're having a dinner party tomorrow (Tuesday), so mark will have to buy some food—the application is showing that task in bold because food has to be bought today. The final task shows that Mark has until February 26 to submit this chapter to the Publisher.

Remember that these tasks can also be displayed on your Summary screen.

The Contacts Feature

The Contacts screen acts as an address book. The screen presents a columnar list of contacts that exist within your address book. Figure 4-28 shows the contact screen with just a few contacts already entered.

You can see here that I have added a few contacts. I've added entries for all the co-authors of this book, and for two companies (Wrox Press and Red Hat). I've also added a distribution list, which I've called Beg RHL9 Authors. This entry has a table icon to the right of it to indicate that it's a distribution list; it contains a list of the entries for the other authors.

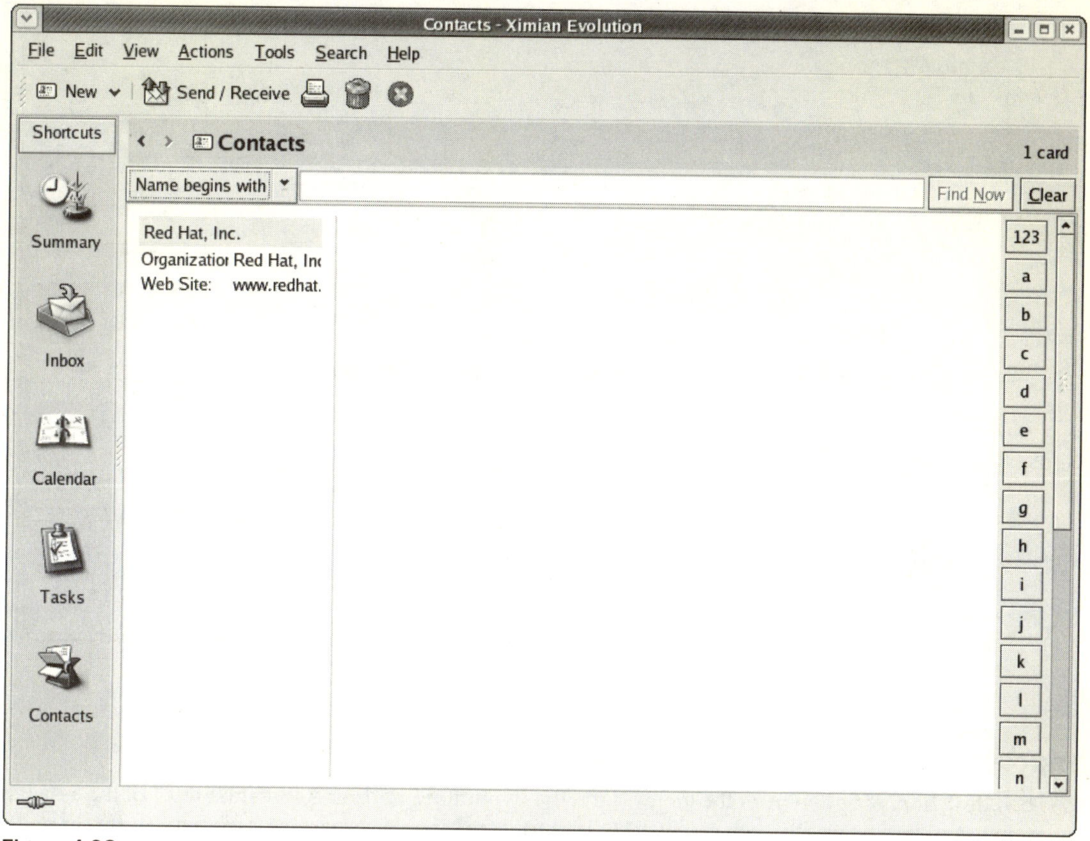

Figure 4-28

To add a contact, you can select New ➪ Contact or the File ➪ New ➪ Contact menu option. When you do so, you get a dialog box in which to enter your information, as shown in Figure 4-29.

Creating distribution lists is equally simple—you select New ➪ Contact List button or the File ➪ New ➪ Contact List menu option to bring up the dialog box, supply a name, and then use your mouse to drag-and-drop contacts into the list.

To the right of the window you'll notice a list of shortcut buttons. Each button acts as a filter on the contacts. So if I selected the W button, only those contacts beginning with W would be shown (in this case, only Simon Whiting and Wrox Press).

Importing E-mail from Other Systems

If you are familiar with Microsoft Outlook (or Outlook Express), you will find Evolution very familiar and comfortable. In fact, you can use Evolution either to import data from a recognized format in the form of a data file or to connect to an e-mail account already held on Microsoft Exchange, such as one within your corporate environment or even at home.

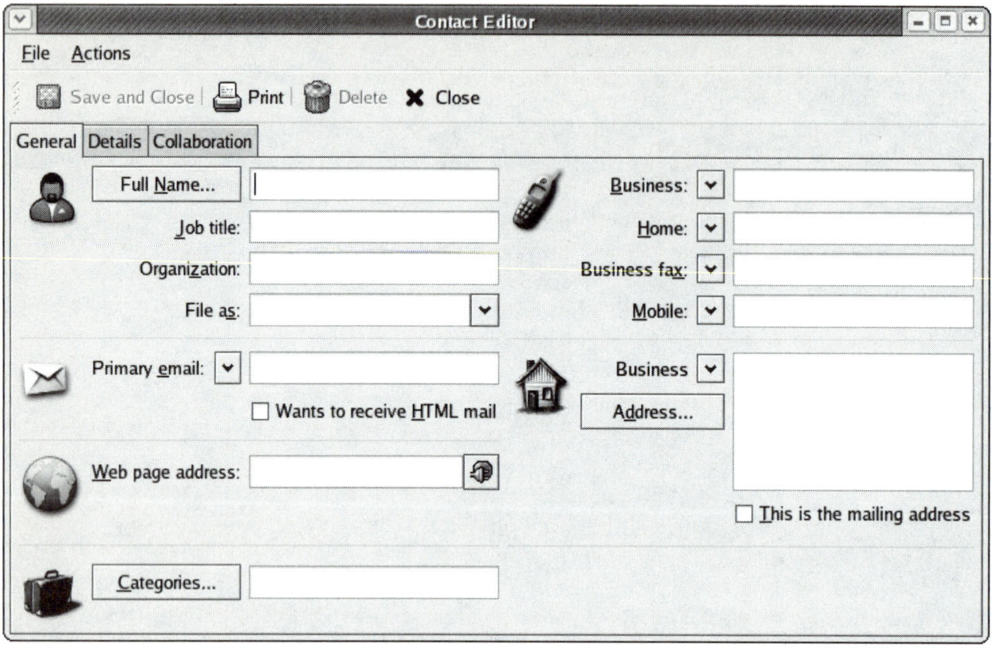

Figure 4-29

Importing from Outlook and Other Formats

The File ➪ Import option from the menu starts the Evolution Importer Assistant. Step 1 of the assistant invites you to indicate whether you want to import from an older program or from a file. If you're importing from a file, Figure 4-30 shows you what Step 2 looks like.

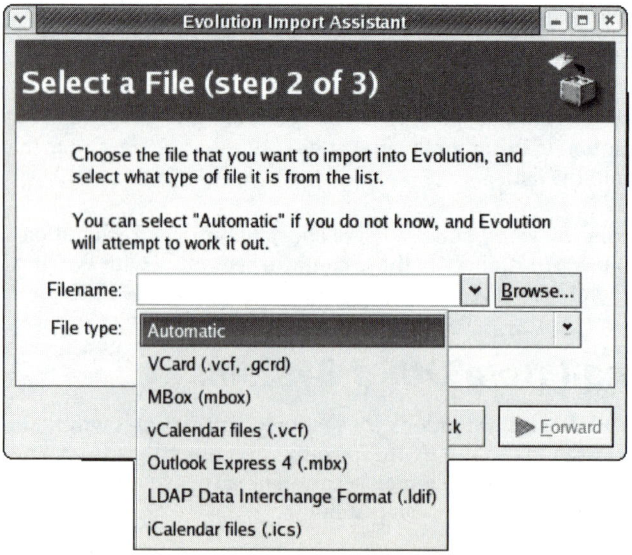

Figure 4-30

You can import from any of six formats listed in the drop-down list box shown in the screenshot. When you've selected the data file you wish to convert, move to Step 3 using the Next button, and select the Import button to begin the import process.

You cannot use this technique when importing information from Microsoft Outlook or Outlook Express version 4 (or later). However, you can convert these files into the standard mbox format that is supported by the preceding method (you can perform this conversion using another mail application such as Mozilla Mail). Alternatively, you can use the Outport tool. For more information, see `http://outport.sourceforge.net` *and* `http://support.ximian.com/cgi-bin/ximian.cfg/php/enduser/std_adp.php?p_faqid=59`.

Connecting to a Microsoft Exchange Mail Server

Connecting your Evolution client to a Microsoft Exchange server is fairly simple, as long as you have purchased the Ximian Connector for Microsoft Exchange. You can find instructions for setting up accounts using this feature within the online documentation, or at the Ximian support desk (try `http://support.ximian.com/cgi-bin/ximian.cfg/php/enduser/popup_adp.php?p_faqid=148`).

You can find additional information about the features and the costs associated with the Ximian Connector at `www.ximian.com/products/connector`.

Multimedia Applications

The category of multimedia applications encompasses a wide variety of applications from playing CDs, to creating your own music library using MP3 files, to creating your own videos. This section covers some of these applications that enable you to create audio or graphical file formats.

Fedora ships with no less than 22 packages packed full of multimedia applications. You'll find these packages in the Sound and Video package group (under the Applications category) in the RPM. There are 16 other package groups installed by default, which cover a variety of audio and graphical functionality, as detailed in the following table.

Package Group	Description
aumix	An ncurses-based audio mixer
sox	Sound file conversion tool
cdda2wav	A utility for converting CD audio tracks to WAV files
cdlabelgen	Utility for generating fontcards and traycards for JewelCases
cdp	Text application for playing audio CDs
cdparanoia	Compact disc digital audio (CDDA) extraction tool (also known as a *ripper*)
cdrecord	Command line–based CD recording program
dvd+rw-tools	Toolchain to master DVD+RW/+R media
dvdrecord	Command line–based CD and DVD recording program

Table continued on following page

Package Group	Description
gtoaster	CD Recording package for both sound and data
rythmbox	Music management application
sound-juicer	Clean and lean CD ripper
tvtime	High quality TV viewer
vorbis-tools	Vorbis general audio compression codec tools
XMMS	Winamp type multimedia player for X Window system
mikmod	MOD file player

In addition, the packages listed in the following table are available but not installed by default, and so are not covered in this chapter. However, you can enjoy discovering on your own what these packages can do.

Package Group	Description
dvgrab	Utility for capturing video from a DV Camera
grip	Front-end user interface for command line CD Rippers
kdemultimedia	Multimedia application for X Window system
XMMS-skins	Skins for XMMS
xcderoast	Utility for creating CDs

The next sections take a look at some of the more useful applications.

Audio Applications

Fedora provides numerous utilities with various features that allow you to play CDs, not to mention the wealth of applications for Linux that will also run on the Fedora release. Some of the most useful and user-friendly audio applications in the Sound and Video package group are covered here, as are some that are included in other packages such as the GNOME desktop:

- Playing audio CDs
- Playing multimedia files
- Burning (writing) and ripping (extracting from) music CDs

Playing Audio CDs

The default application for playing your audio CDs is *Gnome-CD*. You can run Gnome-CD by selecting Main Menu ➪ Sound & Video ➪ CD Player or by typing **gnome-cd** at the command prompt, but you'll find that the application starts automatically if you put an audio CD into your CD drive. It presents you with the following screen (see Figure 4-31).

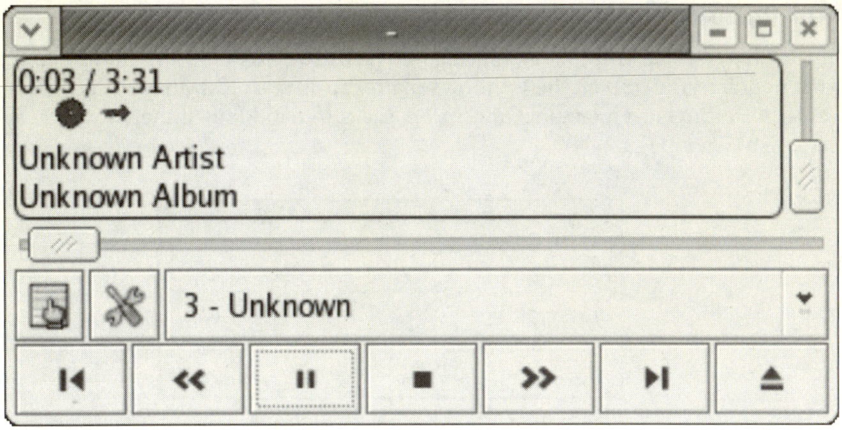

Figure 4-31

The Gnome-cd application will automatically extract the track list and duration from the CD. From here you can play, skip forward, skip backward, adjust the volume, and so on, just as you would on a standard CD player.

The two buttons on the left (just below the words "Unknown Album" in the figure) lead to the Track Editor and Preferences dialog boxes. The Preferences dialog box is particularly useful because it allows you to choose the CD player device and to control the behavior of the application when you start it and close it (see Figure 4-32).

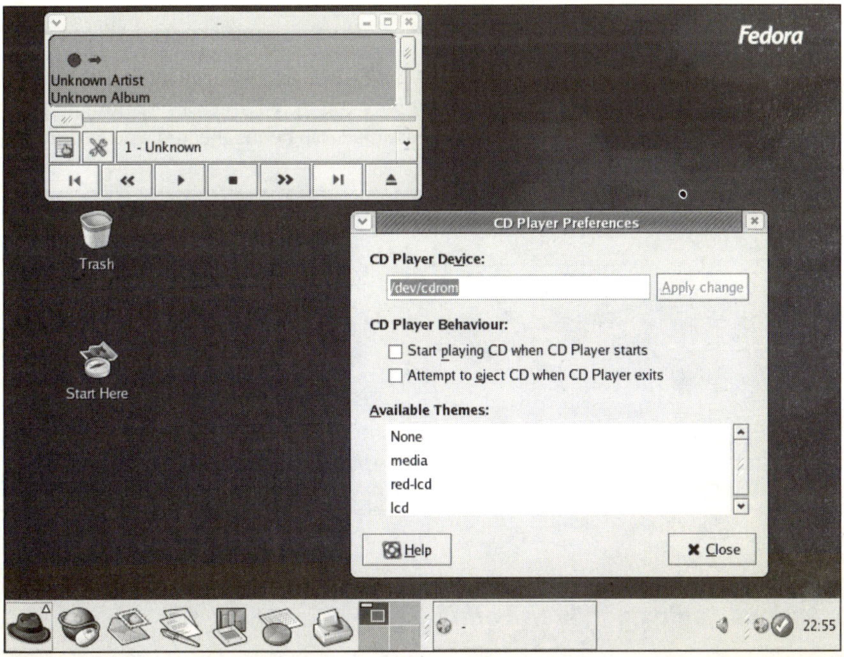

Figure 4-32

Playing Multimedia Files

Fedora ships with a copy of *XMMS* (version 1.2.8), which is a cross-platform multimedia player very similar to the popular WinAmp on the Windows platform. To start XMMS, you can select Main Menu ➪ Sound & Video ➪ Audio Player, or run XMMS from the command line. Either way, you are presented with the screen shown in Figure 4-33.

Figure 4-33

As you will notice, the interface is small and concise, relying on separate windows to encapsulate further features that you may decide to switch on. You can access the XMMS main menu by right-clicking the title bar of the window. This provides you with a menu that allows access to the following:

- Play options (File, Directory, Location)
- Window displayed (Main Window, Playlist Editor, or Graphical Equalizer)
- An Options submenu
- A Playback submenu
- A Visualization submenu

In Figure 4-34, you can see the Main Window, Playlist Editor, and Graphical Equalizer all together. The application has retrieved the tracks from a CD by using the Play Directory option, and selecting `/mnt/cdrom` as the location. You can also see that Track 2 has been selected and is currently playing.

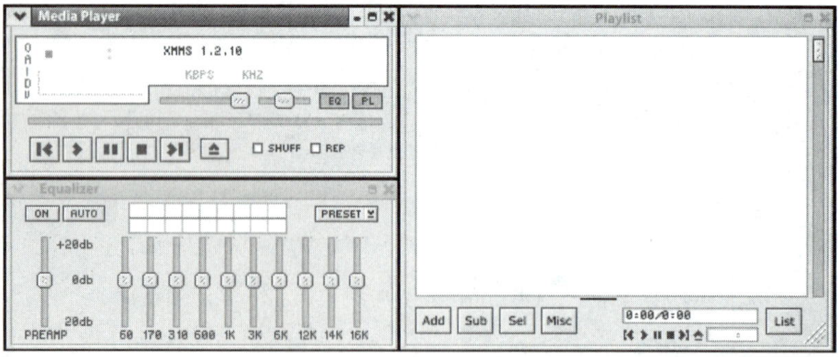

Figure 4-34

Support for Various Audio and Video Formats

So, the XMMS application can be used to play audio CDs in the same way as Gnome-CD. The real benefits come from using the application to play other audio and video formats, such as MP3s, which may exist on media other than a CD. For example, you might keep your MP3 collection on your hard disk, in which case you can use the Play Directory feature of XMMS.

You can extend the capabilities of the XMMS application using plug-ins, which can be enabled and configured using the Preferences dialog box. To get to the Preferences dialog box, right-click the main XMMS window and select Options ➪ Preferences (see Figure 4-35).

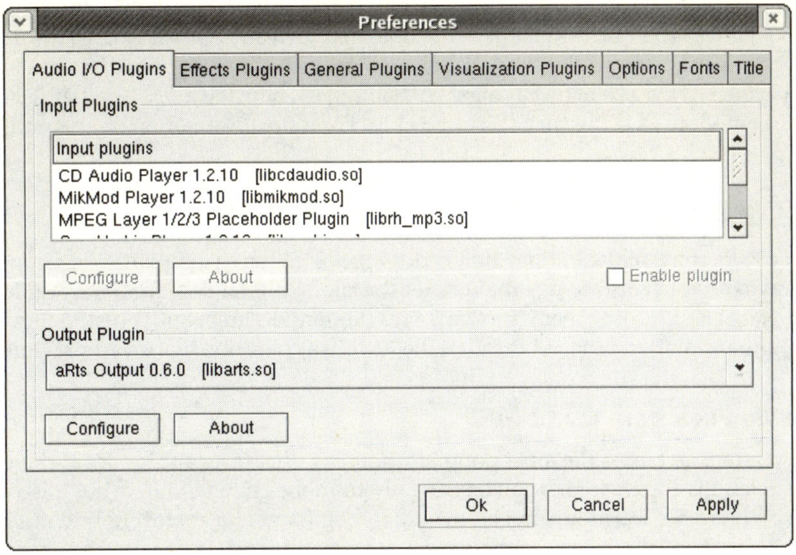

Figure 4-35

Notice that the dialog box contains a number of tabs—these tabs allow you to configure various plug-ins and include Audio, Visualization, and General options. We'll concentrate on Audio plug-ins and allow you to play with the others. A number of plug-ins are already installed, and these plug-ins cover the following audio sources:

- Audio CD-ROMs (using `libcaudio.so`)
- .mod files (using `libmikmod.so`)
- .wav files (using `libwav.so`)
- .ogg files (using `libvorbis.so`)

Support for MP3s

Due to patent and licensing concerns, you'll notice that earlier versions of the Red Hat distribution excluded support for MP3 files. The same is true of Fedora; MP3 support is disabled by default. However, you can reinstate such features by installing the XMMS MP3 update from various Internet sites. You simply need to install the xmms-mp3 RPM, which consists of the files necessary to restore MP3 capability to XMMS.

For Fedora, the source (also known as the SRPM) is also provided from which the binary (the executable) may be built. This is the same XMMS source that shipped with the Red Hat version of the package, except that it uses the unrestricted XMMS source (that is, it has MP3 support), and has been modified to create the XMMS-mp3 sub-package. The package can be downloaded from `www.gurulabs.com/downloads.html`.

You would then install the RPM using a command line similar to the following, depending on the package name:

```
rpm -Uvh XMMS-mp3-1.2.8-33.p.i386.rpm
```

Finally (although we won't discuss them here), note that there are XMMS extensions that provide a number of other features, including visualization, skins, and effect plug-ins (for simulating echo, stereo, and other effects). For the nostalgic amongst us, you can even install a plug-in that will play tunes written for the Commodore 64 using the SID sound chip. For more information on this and other plug-ins, see `www.XMMS.org/`.

CD Burning and Ripping Utilities

This section covers some of the utilities that Fedora provides for writing data to CDs and DVDs (a process known as *burning*). It also covers the utilities for taking digital data from the audio tracks of a CD (known as *ripping*) and turning them into MP3 files (known as *encoding*). The MP3 files can then be stored on your hard disk and played through the XMMS application discussed previously.

Extracting Audio Files from CD to MP3

In previous versions of Linux, the most popular utility for extracting audio files and one that is still installed by default is cdparanoia. It can be run only from the command line, but it is very flexible and you can have a lot of fun learning what all the different parameters are for. To find out about all the different parameters, just type the application name at the command line:

```
$ cdparanoia

USAGE:
  cdparanoia [options] <span> [outfile]
OPTIONS:
 -v --verbose            : extra verbose operation
 -q --quiet              : quiet operation
 -e --stderr-progress    : force output of progress information to
                           stderr (for wrapper scripts)
 ...
```

In its simplest form, the following command line will extract all the tracks on a CD and store them in separate files in the current working directory:

```
$ cdparanoia -B -w "1-"
```

The following table explains how to interpret the parameters in this command.

Parameter	Meaning
`-B`	Indicates that this is a batch and each track will be extracted to a separate file.
`-w`	Indicates that the output file is to be a .wav file.
`"1-"`	Indicates that you wish to extract from the first track to the end of the disc.

You can find out more about cdparanoia at `www.xiph.org/paranoia/` *or use the* `-help` *parameter to provide on onscreen list of all the parameters available.*

A GUI for CD Rippers and MP3 Encoders

To make your CD ripping and MP3 encoding activities easier, Fedora provides you with two options by default. One is the inclusion of the *grip* utility, a graphical front-end to command line utilities. Alternatively, in the More Sound and Video Application submenu, the *Sound Juicer CD Ripper* application is provided as another Graphical CD Ripping utility.

Alternatively, you can use the Grip utility. You can fire up this GUI by selecting Main Menu ➪ Extras ➪ Sound & Video ➪ grip. By default, it's configured to use cdparanoia for extracting the audio files (as .wav files) and the lame executable for encoding the files into MP3 format.

As previously mentioned, the lame encoder is not included by default in Fedora, due to its company's decision to not support MP3 out of the box. However, you can download the lame encoder from `http://dag.wieers.com/packages/lame/`.

Figure 4-36

You can find more information at the Grip's Web site at `http://nostatic.org/grip/`.

Recording Files onto CD

The *cdrecord* utility is a command line utility for recording files onto writable CDs using an appropriate CD-writer drive (CD-R or CD/RW). It is installed by default in Fedora, and its Web site is at `www.fokus.gmd.de/research/cc/glone/employees/joerg.schilling/private/cdrecord.html`.

Like cdparanoia, the cdrecord utility is a very flexible program and, as such, has a large number of parameters. The parameters you need vary according to the type of CD format you are writing (for example, whether you're creating an audio CD or a data CD). For a full list of parameters, you can check the Web site or type the application's name at the command line:

```
$ cdrecord
...
Options:
    -version        print version information and exit
    dev-target      SCSI target to use as CD/DVD-Recorder
    ...
```

The following example command records an audio CD by writing the .wav files created by using the cdparanoia utility:

```
$ cdrecord -v dev=2,0 -dao *.wav
```

This example assumes that the .wav files are located in the current directory, and that a blank CD-R or CD-RW is in the drive. The table that follows shows how the parameters used here affect the application's behavior.

Parameter	Meaning
`-v`	Indicates that progress is displayed via the verbose switch.
`-dev`	Indicates the SCSI target for the device identified. Each SCSI device is assigned an ID; in this case, it's `2,0`.
`-dao`	Indicates that a single session is to be written to the CD and closed when finished.
`*.wav`	Indicates that all files matching this specification should be written to the CD.

You can also use the dvdrecord utility to record information on writable DVD drives such as DVD-RAM. There's more information on this at `www.nongnu.org/dvdrtools/`.

GnomeToaster

If you find all this command line stuff daunting, you can use the *GnomeToaster* application. GnomeToaster is a graphical CD recording utility written for the GNOME environment. You can start this application by selecting Main Menu ⇨ System Tools ⇨ More System Tools ⇨ CD Writer, or by typing **gtoaster** at the command line (see Figure 4-37).

We won't dwell on this application, but note that the user interface is again easy to use and provides a simpler (if less flexible) alternative to the cdrecord option. You simply use the top part of the dialog box to locate the files you want to record, drag them across to the bottom part of the dialog box (which represents the CD-ROM drive), and select the Record option.

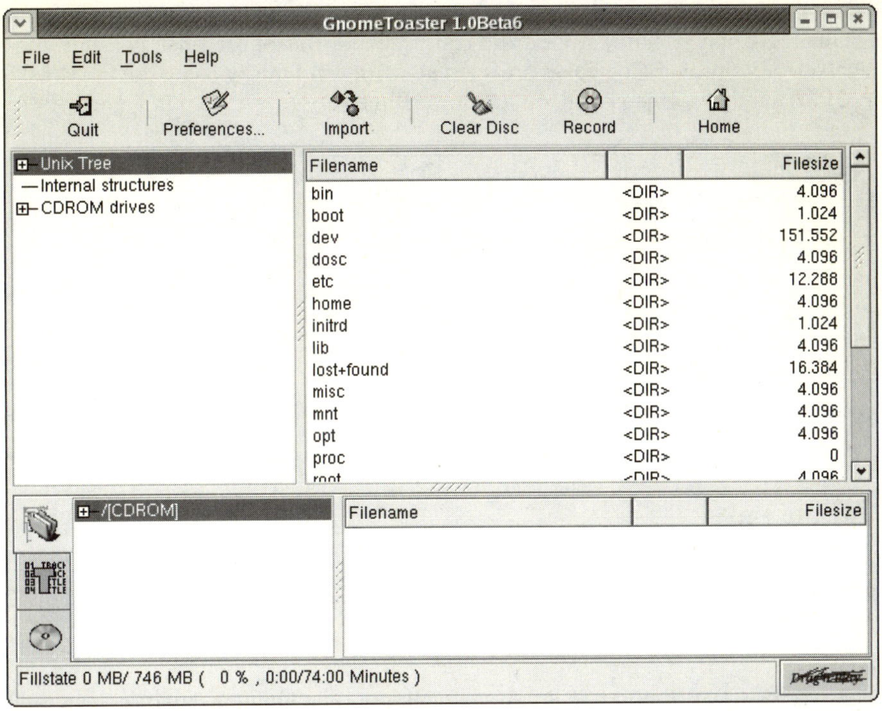

Figure 4-37

Graphics Applications

Numerous graphical applications are installed within Fedora; some exist as part of KDE or GNOME. Others can be found within application suites such as Draw (which is included within OpenOffice), and yet others are standalone applications written for the sole purpose of manipulating images.

This chapter concentrates on the applications that are installed by default with Fedora Desktop: The GIMP, PDF Viewer, GQView, and Draw. Most of these are contained within the Graphics package group (which you'll find under the Applications category of the RPM), and can be found by selecting Main Menu ⇨ Graphics menu.

The GIMP

The *GNU Image Manipulation Program (GIMP)* is a very powerful piece of software used for graphic manipulation. Its flexibility allows you to use it as a simple paint program or for retouching photographic images you may have. It can be extended using the plug-in technology common to a number of Linux applications, but can also be enhanced by using the internal scripting interface that allows you to automate tasks.

The GIMP has been released under the GNU General Public license and is freely distributed software. It is installed by default within Fedora and it has a Web site at `www.gimp.org/`, where you'll find documentation, support, and downloads.

You can start the application by selecting Main Menu ➪ Graphics ➪ The GIMP, or by typing **gimp** at the command line. A variety of configuration and control windows appear when you start the application, and you can control which dialog boxes are open at any given time by using the File ➪ Dialogs menu of the main GIMP window (which is the top left of the three windows shown in Figure 4-38).

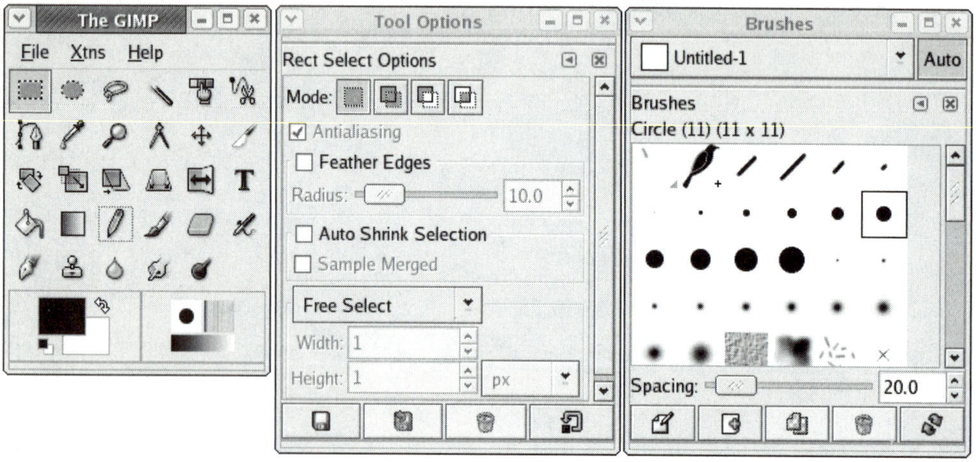

Figure 4-38

As you can see, the GIMP application is a discrete window containing a menu, an icon toolbar, and color information. Each new image is seen in its own separate window (not shown here), which carries its own menu (accessed by right-clicking on the image).

The application is considerably more powerful than Microsoft Paint, and its features are more closely aligned with applications such as Photoshop or Paint Shop Pro. For example, it supports the following:

- ❑ Numerous paint tools
- ❑ Layers, channels and paths
- ❑ Advanced scripting and plug-in capabilities
- ❑ Gradient editor and blend tools
- ❑ Transformation support such as rotate and scale
- ❑ Multiple file formats

The GIMP features are too numerous to list in detail, but the online documentation (`www.gimp.org/docs.html`) is very thorough and this can be supplemented by the documentation found at its main Web site (`www.gimp.org/`). In addition, the resources available from the Web site include patterns, palettes, brushes, gradients, scripts, and fonts, and contain links to other important Web sites for The GIMP (such as a plug-in registry at `http://registry.gimp.org/index.jsp` and the very useful *GIMP User Group*, or GimpForce, at `http://gug.sunsite.dk/`).

Eye of Gnome

Eye of Gnome is a simple application that allows you to view a number of graphical images simultaneously. You start by selecting the directory in which the graphic files exist, and then either selecting the file from the left-hand pane with its image being displayed in the right-hand pane or using the Slideshow feature available on the View menu.

To start this application, select Main Menu ➪ Graphics ➪ More Graphical Applications ➪ Image Viewer. Figure 4-39 shows the utility being used to display screenshots from the Fedora installation process that was covered back in Chapter 1.

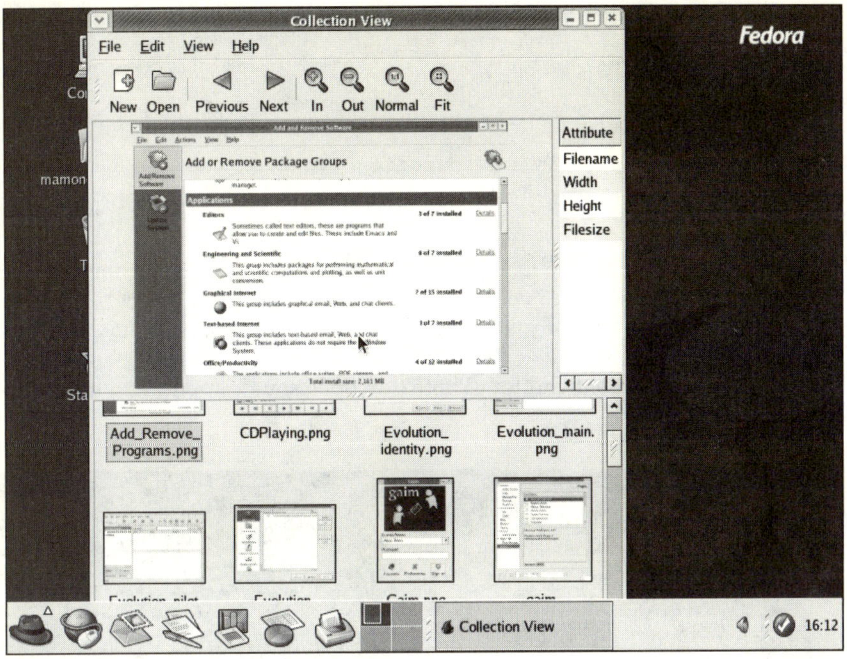

Figure 4-39

PDF Viewer

The GNOME *PDF Viewer* is another simple application, whose functionality is limited to viewing PDF files onscreen. To start the PDF Viewer, select Main Menu ➪ Graphics ➪ PDF Viewer, or run the xpdf application from the command line. To access a file, use the right-hand mouse button and select Open from the menu.

There are a number of ways to convert a document into PDF format. In essence, you convert to the postscript file format, and then use a utility to convert to the PDF file format using the PS2PDF converter supplied with Ghostscript. For more information, see `www.pathcom.com/~kujira/pdf_idx.htm`.

OpenOffice Draw

The *Draw* application is installed as part of the OpenOffice suite, and is similar to the Microsoft Draw application that is now embedded within Microsoft Word. It allows you to draw diagrams using a variety of 2D and 3D objects and shapes, group and color them, and then embed your diagrams into your OpenOffice documents. It also supports the generation of graphs and the manipulation of text within your image.

TVTime Television Viewer

A new application to Fedora is the Television Viewing application called TVTime. This application takes a feed from a TV Capture card and displays this on the computer monitor or an attached projector. It supports features such as the following:

- Widescreen viewing
- Removal of Black Borders via "Overscanning"
- Closed Caption support
- Station Management

For more information. see `http://tvtime.sourceforge.net/`.

Digital Camera

The default installation of Fedora also includes a graphical utility, GTKam, for importing the images taken by a digital camera connected to your machine. To start this utility, select Main Menu ➪ Graphics ➪ Digital Camera, or run the gtkam application from the command line (see Figure 4-40).

The application is a graphical front-end for gPhoto2, an open source application that supports nearly 400 cameras.

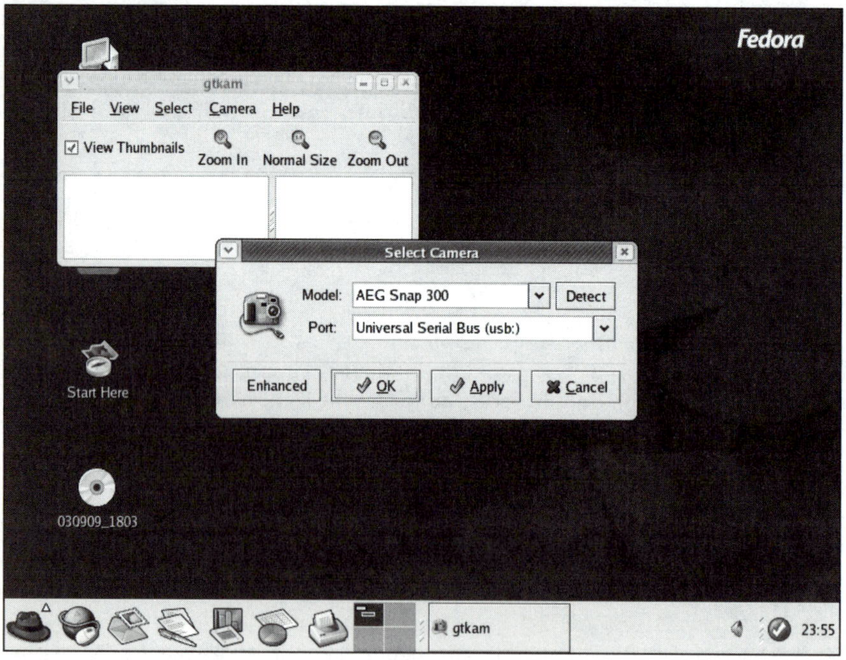

Figure 4-40

System Utilities

Numerous other applications are available and installed with Fedora. Half the fun of a new operating system is exploring all these utilities. There is much that isn't installed by default, but is available on the Internet as freeware.

This section of the chapter covers some of the handy system utilities and bread-and-butter applications that are usually not so exciting but are there to make your life easier. The applications examined here are the file managers, file compression utilities, and emulators.

A Simple Text Editor

For many users, the fact that tasks are accomplished primarily via GUI-based applications is a big attraction. UNIX has always been associated with command line input, and it was not until the X Window system provided a GUI front-end that things became easier. One application that lends itself to this method of input is the simple text editor.

Of course, you could use editors such as Writer to edit documents, but the formatting and functionality provided with applications such as Writer are really overkill for configuration files and similar documents. This is where *gedit* is very useful.

The gedit application is similar to Notepad or Wordpad in Microsoft Windows, and is an effective text editor with a nice graphical user interface. To launch gedit, choose Main Menu ➪ Accessories ➪ Text Editor, or type **gedit** at the command line (see Figure 4-41).

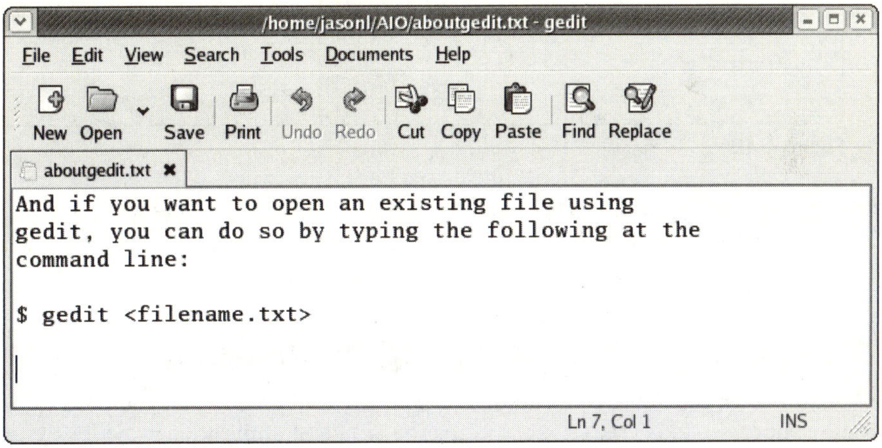

Figure 4-41

A File Management Application

A *file manager* is a GUI that allows you to manage and navigate the various drive types and directory structures on your system and network. Given the size of hard disks today (60GB is normal), and the capacity of CD-ROM drives, DVD-ROM drives, not to mention your local area network, the ability to quickly navigate and manage the files of such devices is extremely important.

To start you off navigating your filesystem, Fedora places a link to your home directory (`/home/<username>`) on your desktop—you could call it Mark's Home, for example. This shortcut fires up Fedora's favored file manager, the *Nautilus* application, allowing you to manage your files and filesystem easily via Nautilus's graphical user interface.

Alternatively, you can start Nautilus by typing **nautilus** at the command line. For example, to start exploring the `/usr` directory you would type the following:

```
$ nautilus /usr
```

Figure 4-42 shows the Nautilus GUI.

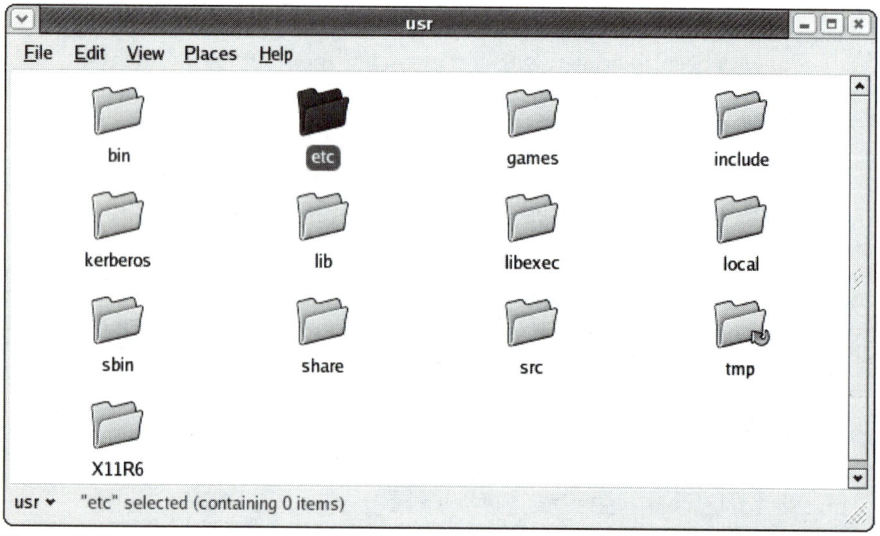

Figure 4-42

This application is very similar to the Windows Explorer application you find in the Microsoft' Windows operating systems. It allows you to move up and down directory trees by double-clicking the icons. It also allows you to create new folders, move files, and cut and paste directories and files.

A File Compression and Archiving Application

While Nautilus allows you to manage your files, you'll also find times when you need to archive files into a single compressed file in the style of PkZip. The *File Roller* application provides a graphical user interface to compressed files, allowing you to archive files and extract items from existing archives. It's very similar to the WinZip utility for Microsoft Windows, which also provides a graphical interface to the PkZip utility.

To start the File Roller application, select Main Menu ➪ Accessories ➪ File Roller, or type **file-roller** at the command line (see Figure 4-43).

File Roller supports a number of compressed file formats, including .zip, .lzh, and so on. It can be used to create new archives using the Archive ➪ New menu option, to open existing archives, and to extract files from these archives.

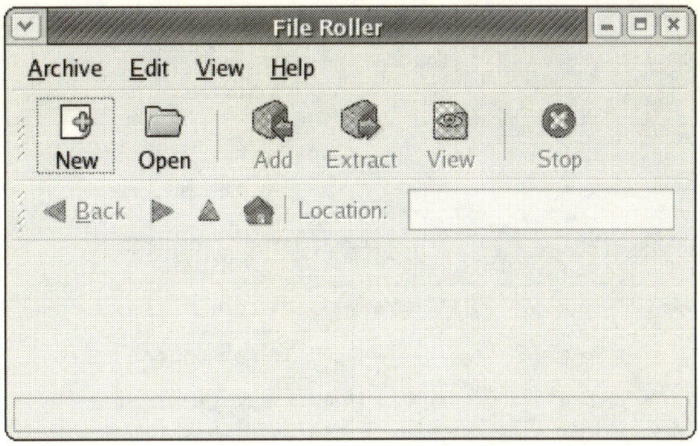

Figure 4-43

For example, to create a new .zip archive, select the Archive ➪ New menu option and enter a filename in the field provided (in Figure 4-44, I'm creating a new file called `/home/markm/screenshots.zip`).

Then you can add files using the Add shortcut icon or the Edit ➪ Add Files menu item. This will prompt you to select the files you wish to add. Figure 4-45 shows the window after adding all the files from the `/root/anaconda-screenshots` directory, which we used in Chapter 1.

This starts the process of adding the files to the archive, compressing as you go.

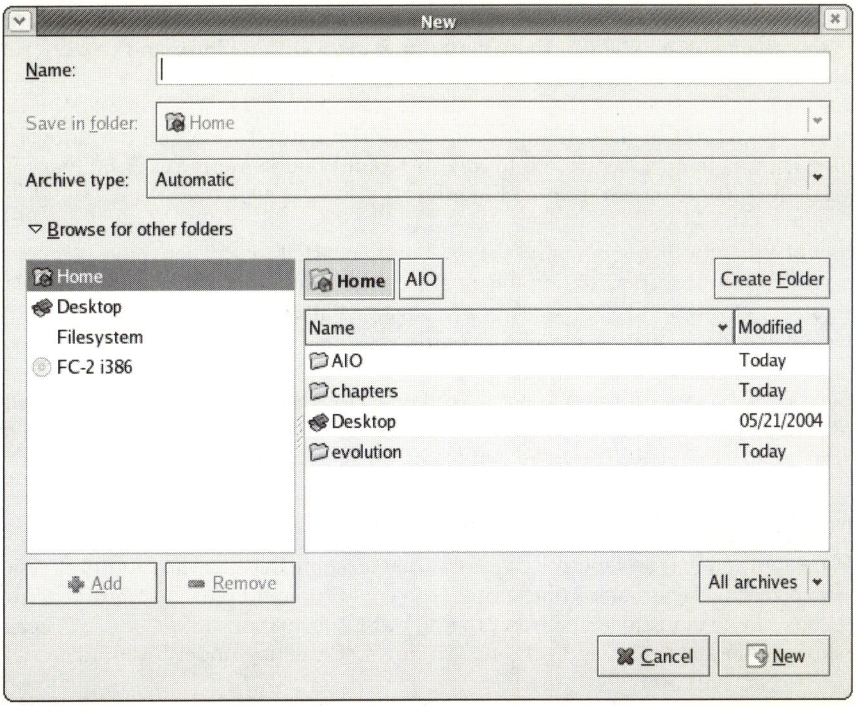

Figure 4-44

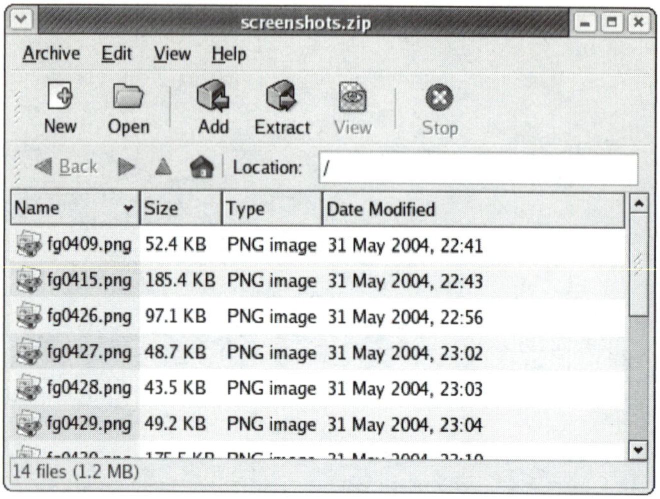

Figure 4-45

Emulators

We've discussed various interoperability features of the applications in this chapter. For example, you've seen how OpenOffice is able to load and save files in formats such as the Microsoft Office formats, and other non-native file formats. In addition to these features, there are a number of *emulators* in existence. An emulator implements another (virtual) operating system within Linux, and you can run executables that are native to that operating system.

For example, you can run an emulator application that simulates the Microsoft Windows operating system running within Linux, allowing you to run Microsoft Windows applications (binary files) untouched in their native format from within Linux.

The concept of emulators is not new, and they're not unique to Linux. There have been many different emulators, for lots of platforms. Among the most common emulators are those that simulate 8-bit home computers such as the Sinclair ZX Spectrum. However, what's far more impressive is the fact that emulators are available for simulating complex operating systems such as Microsoft Windows.

This section discusses some of the emulators available. We won't cover emulators in detail—the online documentation provided by the suppliers of some of these emulators is more than sufficient to get you started—but we will mention a couple of emulators so you can get an idea of what they're about.

VMWare

The VMWare application is an Enterprise Class virtual machine that can run multiple versions of an operating system on a single computer. For example, you could run multiple versions of the Windows operating system on a single Linux machine. You can find more information at `www.vmware.com`. An example screen is shown in Figure 4-46, demonstrating Windows XP running under VMWare on a Linux box.

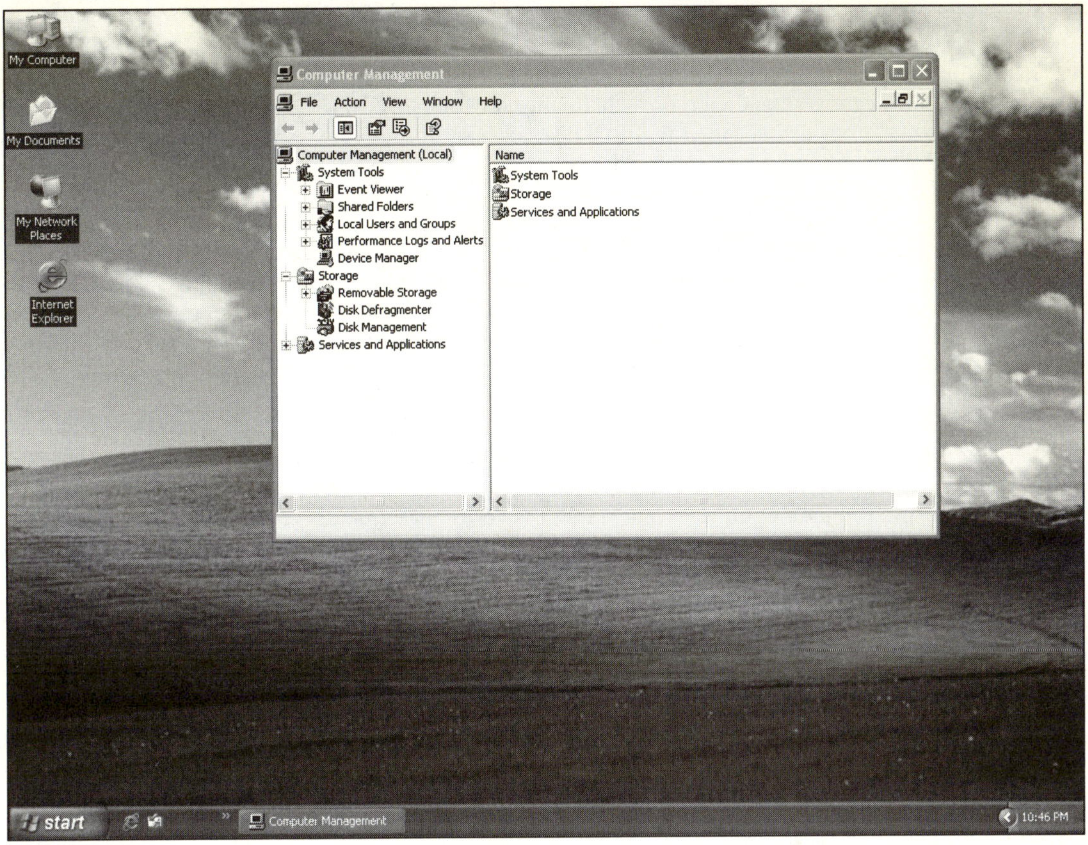

Figure 4-46

Wine

Wine is an application that implements the Windows Application Programming Interface (API) on top of the native X Window system that is used by the GNOME and KDE graphical environments. It's more of a compatibility layer than an emulator, but it does allow Windows applications to run. You can find the latest version and more information at the Wine Web site at `www.winehq.com`.

You can find the most recent release of the Wine RPM packages at `http://mecano.gme.usherb.ca/~vberon/wine`. Instructions for installing Wine and troubleshooting problems that you encounter can be found within the Wine User Guide, at `www.winehq.com/Docs/wine-user`.

Summary

This chapter touched on a variety of applications installed by default in Fedora. In some cases, we discussed how they can be extended to provide further functionality. In fact, there are thousands of quality applications that are available either within the Fedora distribution or via the Internet, in some cases freeware thanks to the Open Source Foundation and the GNU Project. In other cases, shareware is available at a small cost, again via the Internet.

The chapter started by covering the OpenOffice suite of applications commonly used for office productivity. We touched on a couple of Internet applications—the Mozilla browser and the Gaim Instant Messenger application—and the Evolution personal information management tool. We skipped through a number of multimedia applications, which provided various audio and graphical facilities, and took a look at some of the more essential system tools—the gedit text editor, the Nautilus file manager, the File Roller compression tool, and the VMWare emulator.

There is such a wealth of functionality available that you shouldn't have trouble finding the application you need to do the job you want, whether it's included in the Fedora distribution or on the Internet somewhere. And if there's nothing out there that fits your requirements, you can always start off your own open source project. In the end, you can achieve in Linux everything that you'd expect to be able to achieve on other platforms.

Exercises

To further build on the skills you have learned so far, here is an exercise you can use to test yourself. The answers are provided in the back of the book in Appendix A, but keep in mind, there is always more than one way to accomplish a given task, so if you choose to do things a different way and the results display the way you want, more power to you.

Try modifying your php files in the following ways:

1. Create a very simple home page using the word processor as part of Office and then save it as an HTML file so it can be easily viewed by both Microsoft and Netscape browsers.
2. Use the browser shipped with Fedora to open the HTML home page that you created in Exercise 1.
3. Using a tool provided with Fedora, extract tracks from one of your favorite music CDs and save them to an electronic format that can be played from disk without the need to have the CD loaded in the CD drive.
4. Considering that the files you extracted in Exercise 3 can take up valuable disk space, use a Fedora utility to compress them into a single archive and thus free up some disk space.

5

The Filesystem

This chapter discusses the filesystem in depth. In very simple terms, the filesystem is that part of the operating system that takes care of organizing files and directories. Of course, the filesystem does much more than that, and this chapter explores the following aspects of the filesystem:

- Various file and directory attributes and how they relate to everyday tasks
- Filesystem hierarchy and the location of various useful programs
- The concept of supporting multiple filesystems
- Managing and maintaining the filesystem

What Is the Filesystem?

What does the filesystem do for the user? Besides organizing your data files and useful programs, it also manages configuration information required for the operating system to provide you with a consistent environment every time you restart the computer. It also enforces security and allows you to control access to your files. Processes may read, write, append, delete, move, or rename files and directories. The filesystem defines the rules of the game when such operations are performed.

The shell, combined with a host of other programs, allows you to navigate the filesystem and get your tasks done. Depending on the distribution and installed software, you may also use file managers to navigate the filesystem; in the case of Fedora 2, you can use the *Nautilus* file manager.

However, one of the most interesting aspects of the filesystem (and one that is not immediately obvious) is that Linux treats almost all devices as *files*. Hard disks, terminals, printers, and floppy disk drives are all devices—devices that can be read from and written to (mostly). In fact, with the *proc* filesystem, Linux goes so far as to provide a filesystem abstraction to running processes. You will see more about this in the "The Navigating the Filesystem" section. The thing to note is that treating devices as files allows Linux to deal with them in a consistent manner.

Linux supports a wide variety of filesystem types, including Microsoft Windows filesystem types. Some first-time Linux users find it interesting that it is possible to copy a file from a Microsoft Windows filesystem onto a floppy, edit it on a Linux machine, and take it back to Windows. In fact, Linux even allows remote Windows-shared filesystems to be accessed locally using Samba (you'll see more of this in Chapter 9).

The Anatomy of a File

To understand the filesystem better, this section starts off with a close examination of an individual file. Examine the following file with a line of data in it:

```
$ cat >dissectme.txt
Innards of this file
^D
$ ls -l dissectme.txt
```

Now that we have created our file, let's list it with the `ls` command:

```
-rw-r--r--    1 deepakt  users          21 Jan 19 18:40 dissectme.txt
```

In fact the `ls` command is your close ally in the exploration of the filesystem. It is a veritable Swiss army knife when it comes to examining the various attributes of a file. By attributes, we mean the various characteristics of the file including its name, date of creation, permissions to access it, and so on. You also need to remember that file and directory names in Linux are case-sensitive—that is, `bluecurve.txt`, `Bluecurve.txt`, and `BLUECURVE.txt` are all different filenames.

Another curiosity for those coming to Fedora from a Microsoft environment is that filename extensions, such as `.txt` or `.exe` do not matter in Fedora 2 (as is the case with most operating systems with a UNIX parentage). Whether a file is executable or not is determined by its permissions. File permissions are explained in some detail in the following sections. In other words, as long as a file has executable permissions, it may be executed as a program; it does not matter if it has a `.exe` extension or not.

File Types

We start off by analyzing the output of the `ls` command. The first column (that is, the `-rw-r--r--` segment) has information about the type of the file and the permissions to access it. The first hyphen (-) symbol indicates that the file is a regular file and not a directory or other type of file. The first character of the `ls -l` listing always indicates the type of file, to tell you whether it is a regular file, a directory, a FIFO (a mechanism by which programs communicate with each other), a character device (such as a terminal), or a block device (such as a hard disk).

Examples of the various types of files are listed so you understand how they differ from a regular file. In the listing for the `/etc` directory, you see that the first letter indicating the type of the file is the letter *d*, confirming that `/etc` is indeed a directory:

```
$ ls -ld /etc
drwxr-xr-x   59 root     root         8192 Jan 19 18:32 /etc
```

The next two listings initially list one of the first hard disks on the system, `/dev/hda` in this case. You see the letter *b*, which indicates that this is a block device. In the listing for the terminal device, `/dev/tty`, you see that the letter *c* indicates a character device:

```
$ ls -l /dev/hda
brw-rw----    1 root     disk       3,   0 Aug 30 16:31 /dev/hda
$ ls -l /dev/tty
crw-rw-rw-    1 root     root       5,   0 Aug 30 16:31 /dev/tty
```

A *block device* performs input and output in blocks of data; for example, when you read a file from the hard disk, data is read in multiples of a block of (say) 4,096 bytes. By contrast, a *character device* (such as a terminal) reads and writes data one character at a time.

You'll see more about device files in the `/dev` *directory in later sections of this chapter.*

In the listing for the bash shell executable in the `/bin` directory, you see that `sh` is actually a symbolic link to the Bash shell (`/bin/bash`):

```
$ ls -l /bin/sh
lrwxrwxrwx    1 root     root             4 Oct 30 14:46 /bin/sh -> bash
```

A *link* is not really a file by itself; rather, it is a pointer to another file. You'll see more about links in the course of the chapter.

The last two listings are rather exotic from a user's perspective because the user rarely (if ever) deals with them directly. Here, we create a FIFO called `myfifo`, using the `mknod` command; and then we list it. The letter *p* indicates that this is a FIFO:

```
$ mknod myfifo p
$ ls -l myfifo
prw-r--r--    1 deepakt  users            0 Jan 19 19:09 myfifo
$ ls -l /tmp/ssh*
/tmp/ssh-XXiVoKic:
total 0
srwxr-xr-x    1 deepakt  users            0 Jan 19 18:40 agent.996
```

A FIFO is a mechanism used by processes to talk to each other; it is therefore known as an inter-process communication mechanism (IPC). FIFO is an acronym for First In, First Out. Programmers, rather than users, deal with FIFOs.

On listing the Secure Shell (SSH) directories in `/tmp`, you see a file whose listing begins with the letter *s*. This indicates that the file is a *socket*, another IPC mechanism that is often used by processes on remote machines to talk to each other.

SSH comprises a set of programs that are intended to provide a secure alternative to UNIX remote access programs that transmit information including passwords in clear-text.

Another command that is useful in checking the type of files is the `file` command. It does more than just list the type of the file; it is often able to distinguish between files of the same type. That is, it can differentiate between a regular text file and a program file:

```
$ file /etc /dev/hda /dev/tty /bin/sh /bin/bash dissectme.txt myfifo /tmp/ssh-*/*
/etc:                          directory
/dev/hda:                      block special (3/0)
/dev/tty:                      character special (5/0)
/bin/sh:                       symbolic link to bash
/bin/bash:                     ELF 32-bit LSB executable, Intel 80386,
                               version 1 (SYSV), dynamically linked (uses
                               shared libs), stripped
dissectme.txt:                 ASCII text
myfifo:                        fifo (named pipe)
/tmp/ssh-XXiVoKic/agent.996:   socket
```

Note the entry for `/bin/bash`, *which indicates that this file is an executable, compiled to execute on an Intel processor. You'll see more about dynamically linked executables in a later section.*

Linux treats files as a "stream of bytes," without record boundaries; that is, there are no special characters used by the system to distinguish one line from the next. On the other hand, although files on Microsoft Windows operating systems also do not have explicit record boundaries, the operating system uses the convention that text files have a *carriage return–line feed* pair at the end of lines. The operating system also uses different modes for opening files as *text* or *binary* files.

UNIX does not use filename extensions in the way that Windows does. All associations between filenames and extensions are merely based on convention. Typically, UNIX executable files don't have extensions such as `.com` or `.exe`.

Links

In examining the `/bin/sh` file, you noted that it is in fact a link to the file `/bin/bash`. In other words, `/bin/sh` is not really a file itself, but anyone executing `/bin/sh` is actually executing `/bin/bash`. Actually, Bash is a replacement for the `sh` shell, and is nearly 100 percent backward compatible with sh.

Let's illustrate the use of links: consider a hypothetical program `foo`, which has two different modes of operation; in mode one, it copies files, and in mode two, it renames files. One way to switch between the program's modes is to pass it an option; for example, `foo -c file1 file2` would create a copy of `file1` named `file2`. If you pass it the `-m` option (that is, `foo -m file1 file2`), it would create a copy of `file1` named `file2`, but would also remove `file1` (effectively renaming it).

Another way to switch modes is to create two links to the file `foo`, one named `copy` and the other named `rename`. Now the program `foo` needs to figure out only the name it was invoked with to switch to the appropriate mode. In other words, if it was invoked with the name `copy`, `foo` would copy the file, and if it was invoked with the name `rename`, it would copy the file and remove the original.

The concept of a link is analogous to that of a shortcut in Microsoft Windows. A link allows you to refer to a file (or directory) by a different name, even from a different directory altogether. This leads to another use of links—version management of software. Take the case of a program that refers to the `libc.so.6` library in the `/lib` directory. Simply put, a *library* contains common functions that may be used by several programs:

```
$ ls -al /lib/libc.so.6
lrwxrwxrwx  1 root  root  14 Oct 30 14:45 /lib/libc.so.6 -> libc-2.2.93.so
```

Here, you can see that `libc.so.6` is actually a symbolic link to the actual library `libc-2.2.93.so`. This means that if the library is upgraded from version 2.2.93 to 2.2.94, for example, the upgrade process removes the link between `libc.so.6` and `libc-2.2.93.so` and creates a new link between `libc.so.6` and `libc-2.2.94.so`. This ensures that the programs referring to `libc.so.6` need not be modified every time a library they refer to is changed.

This applies not just to libraries, but also to executable programs. Users typically refer to the program by a link, while system administrators can replace the actual executable with a newer version unbeknownst to the user.

Hard Links and Symbolic Links

Links come in two varieties: *hard links* and *symbolic links* (also known as *soft links*). Before you learn more about each of these, you need to understand the concept of *inodes*. Inodes are essentially an indexing mechanism—a number by which the operating system refers to a file. The filename is for us mortals; the operating system mostly refers to a file by its inode number.

> *Linux hard disks are divided into partitions. Partitions allow you to divide the disk into filesystems that have different functionality and are often managed independently of each other. For instance, a system may have a root partition housing all the operating system commands and configuration files and a user partition that houses the directories and files of individual users. You'll see more about partitions in a later section of this chapter.*

The inode number is unique only within a disk partition. In other words, it is possible for two files on different partitions (for example, one on the `/boot` partition and another on the `/` partition) to have the same inode number. The `df` command can be used to list the partitions on your system. To see the inode number of a file, you could use the `ls` command again, this time with the `-i` option:

```
$ ls -li /etc
total 2012
 226972 -rw-r--r--    1 root    root      15228 Aug  5 03:14 a2ps.cfg
 226602 -rw-r--r--    1 root    root       2562 Aug  5 03:14 a2ps-site.cfg
 226336 -rw-r--r--    1 root    root         47 Jan 19 04:00 adjtime
 ...
```

The inode number is listed in the first column. Each file has a unique inode number. While both hard links and symbolic links are used to refer to another file, the real difference is in the inode number:

- Hard links have the same inode number as the original file.
- Symbolic links have their own unique inode number.

Here are examples of both hard links and symbolic links so you can see how they work:

```
$ ln dissectme.txt hard.txt
$ ln -s dissectme.txt soft.txt
```

Both hard links and symbolic links can be created using the `ln` command. While the `-s` option of the `ln` command creates a symbolic link, with no options it creates a hard link. Initially, we create a hard link to the file `dissectme.txt` with the name `hard.txt`. We then create a symbolic link to the same file, called `soft.txt`:

```
$ ls -li dissectme.txt hard.txt soft.txt
131524 -rw-r--r--    2 deepakt  users  21 Jan 19 18:40 dissectme.txt
131524 -rw-r--r--    2 deepakt  users  21 Jan 19 18:40 hard.txt
131528 lrwxrwxrwx    1 deepakt  users  13 Jan 19 20:23 soft.txt ->
                                                          dissectme.txt
```

When we list all three files with the -i option of ls, you see that inode numbers of the hard link and the inode number of the actual file are the same:

```
$ cat dissectme.txt hard.txt soft.txt
Innards of this file
Innards of this file
Innards of this file
```

When we list the contents of the file and the links, you see that the output is just the same, indicating that all three are actually referring to the same file.

Now let's try something else:

```
$ pwd
/home/deepakt
$ ln /boot/boot.b boot.b_hard
ln: creating hard link `boot.b_hard' to `/boot/boot.b': Invalid cross-device link
$ ln -s /boot/boot.b boot.b_soft
$ ls -al boot.b_soft
lrwxrwxrwx  1 deepakt  users   12 Jan 19 20:21 boot.b_soft -> /boot/boot.b
```

When we attempt to create a hard link to a file on a different partition, the operating system does not allow us to do so because inode numbers are unique only within a partition, and a hard link requires the same inode number as the link target, which may not be possible on a different partition. However, you can successfully create a symbolic link to a file on a different partition.

Links are commonly used for organizing shared directories. For example, a project group may choose to share files in a directory called /var/documents. Users who wish to share documents may choose to leave the documents in any subdirectory under their own home for ease of maintenance. This is how a typical directory structure would look in this case:

```
$ ls -l /var/documents
total 0
lrwxrwxrwx    1 deepakt  users    22 Feb 23 23:54 deepakt ->
                                                 /home/deepakt/joe_docs
lrwxrwxrwx    1 zora     users    18 Feb 23 23:55 zora ->
                                                 /home/zora/work/blueprints
lrwxrwxrwx    1 sarah     users   18 Feb 23 23:55 sarah ->
                                                 /home/sarah/deep/down/mydocs
```

Members of the group may choose to maintain their documents in any subdirectory under their home directory. They still have the convenience of referring to a colleague's shared documents by accessing /var/documents/<username>. A new project member, with the username apprentice, would typically execute the following command to add her document directory to this scheme of things:

```
$ ln -s mydocdir /var/documents/apprentice
```

For this scheme to work, the owner of the `/var/documents` directory should allow members of the project group write permissions for the `/var/documents` directory. You'll see more about groups and permissions in the next section.

Ownership of Files

Every file stored on a Linux system has an *owner*—this indicates the creator of the file. Each file also has a *group* associated with it. A group is essentially a group of users (a number of groups exist on the system by default, including the groups `users`, `administrators`, and `daemon`). The file `/etc/group` has a complete list of available groups on the system:

```
$ cat /etc/group
root:x:0:root
bin:x:1:root,bin,daemon
daemon:x:2:root,bin,daemon
sys:x:3:root,bin,adm
...
users:x:100:deepakt
ntp:x:38:
...
```

- The first column indicates the name of the group.
- The second column, indicated by an `x` character, is the password column.
- The third column is the group ID of the group, which is a unique number for the group.
- The last column is a list of users who belong to the group.

In this case, the group `users` has a group ID of 100 and the user `deepakt` belongs to it.

Take another look at the listing of the `dissectme.txt` file:

```
-rw-r--r--    1 deepakt  users          21 Jan 19 18:40 dissectme.txt
```

In the output here, the third column (`deepakt`) indicates that the owner of this file is a user called `deepakt`. The fourth column (users) shows that the file belongs to a group called `users`.

You can assign access control based on group membership. For example, you can arrange for all the members of a certain project to belong to the same group, and set up group access permissions for that group to all the project-related documents on your Linux system. This way, you can allow access to these documents for all users belonging to that group and to no other users. We discuss permissions in the next section.

By default, the file's group is the same as the group that the creator of the file belongs to. However, it is possible to change a file's group so that it is different from that of its owner. To change the ownership of a file, you use the `chown` command; to change its group, you use the `chgrp` command.

File Permissions

In the previous `ls` listing, the `-rw-r--r--` part of the output indicates the *permissions* associated with a file. The *permissions block* is split into three parts:

- The first part indicates the read, write, and execute permissions for the owner.
- The second indicates the read, write, and execute permissions for the group.
- The last part indicates the read, write, and execute permissions for the rest of the world (that is, users who do not belong to this file's group).

You can use a number of different characters here to reflect permissions:

- An `r` indicates read permission.
- A `w` indicates write permission.
- An `x` indicates execute permission.
- A hyphen (-) indicates that a particular permission is denied.

Execute permissions for a file do not automatically mean that a file can be executed—the file also has to be of an executable format (such as an executable binary or a shell script).

Therefore, in the example in the previous section, you see that the owner has permissions to read and write (that is, modify) the file, but no permissions to execute it. Other members of the `users` group can only read the file, but they cannot modify or execute it. The same permissions also hold for all other users of the system.

Directory Permissions

For a directory, "read," "write," and "execute" have slightly different meanings:

- The *read* permission refers to the ability to list the files and subdirectories contained in that directory.
- The *write* permission refers to the ability to create and remove files and subdirectories within it.
- The *execute* permission refers to the ability to enter the directory using the `cd` command (in other words, change the current working directory to be this directory).

You can use the `chmod` command to change permissions for a file by specifying the permissions for the owner, group, and others. An easy way to interpret permissions in the context of directories is to think of directories also as files, the only difference being that these files contain names of files or other directories. Therefore, listing a directory is analogous to reading the contents of a file, and adding or removing contents of a directory is analogous to writing and deleting content from a file.

So what are the default permissions when you create a file? This is controlled by the default file creation mask, which can be set using the `umask` command.

A File and Directory Permissions Experiment

Let's create a file and a directory and experiment with changing permissions and ownership. First, we'll list the current file mask:

```
$ umask -S
u=rwx,g=rw,o=rw
```

Here the -S option prints out the default file mask in rwx form. This mask allows owners to read, write, and execute files; it allows the group and others read and write permissions, but no execute permissions.

Now, let's modify the file mask:

```
$ umask u=rwx,g=r,o=r
$ umask -S
u=rwx,g=r,o=r
```

You do this using the umask command supplying the desired file mask. The new mask allows the owner permission to read, write, and execute, while the group and others have just read permissions. A newly created file reflects the current file mask:

```
$ mkdir widgets
$ ls -ld widgets
drwxr--r--    2 deepakt  users        4096 Jan 20 01:05 widgets
$ cd widgets
$ touch foowidget
$ ls -al
total 8
drwxr--r--    2 deepakt  users        4096 Jan 20 01:05 .
drwx------   13 deepakt  users        4096 Jan 20 01:05 ..
-rw-r--r--    1 deepakt  users           0 Jan 20 01:05 foowidget
```

Here you should notice that (as intended) the foowidget file has just read permissions for the group and others. However, while the file mask reads u=rwx,g=r,o=r, the owner of this file does *not* have execute permissions because foowidget is interpreted by the shell as a text file, and execute permission does not make sense for text files in general. Shell scripts or other text files of scripting languages such as Perl are therefore treated as text files, but need to be manually assigned execute permissions for them to run. (If you were to compile a program to create an executable, you would notice that execute permission for the owner is enabled. Execute permissions are also enabled by default for the owner when creating a directory because the execute permissions for a directory are necessary to allow users to execute the cd command to enter the directory.)

Now, let's modify the files permissions again:

```
$ chmod u=rwx,g=rw,o=rw foowidget
$ ls -al foowidget
-rwxrw-rw-    1 deepakt  users           0 Jan 20 01:05 foowidget
```

This command modifies the permissions of the foowidget file such that the group and others are now allowed to both read and write the file, and the owner is allowed to read, write, and execute it. The file list confirms that the permissions have indeed changed.

Now, let's switch to the root user and change the ownership of the file:

```
$ su
  Password:
# chown nobody:nobody widgets
```

To change the ownership of the widget directory, you use the chown command. The chown command is restricted to the root user, so you must switch to the root user using the su command and *then* change the owner and group of the file to nobody and nobody, respectively.

The chown command takes the name of the new owner followed by the filename. Optionally, you can also modify the group by specifying the name of the new group after the owner, separated by a colon (:) character. In this case, the owner is nobody and the group is also named nobody. Both the user and group name "nobody" are used to assign minimum privileges to programs that are often exposed to the external world such as daemon (or server) processes.

Now let's switch back to being a normal user by typing **exit** in the shell, and try to list the widget directory:

```
# exit
$ ls -al widgets
ls: widgets/.: Permission denied
ls: widgets/..: Permission denied
ls: widgets/foowidget: Permission denied
 total 0
```

Now you can check the impact of the changed ownership of the directory. Without the root user's privileges, it's not possible to enter the directory, although the read permission still allows you to see that the file foowidget exists inside the directory.

Finally, let's finish up by trying to remedy this situation. Switch once again to the root user and change the group ownership of the directory to grant permissions for the group, before changing back to a normal user again:

```
$ ls -ld widgets
drwxr--r--     2 nobody   nobody       4096 Jan 20 01:05 widgets/
$ su
Password:
# chgrp users widgets
# chmod g=rwx widgets
# exit
```

The new group ownership and group permissions once again allow you access to the directory:

```
$ ls -ld widgets
drwxrwxr--     2 nobody   users        4096 Jan 20 01:05 widgets
$ cd widgets
```

Ordinary Users with Extraordinary Privileges

You've already seen in this chapter that when a program executes, it needs to have permissions for performing its tasks (see the attempt in the previous section to list the widgets directory). Often non-root users need to perform functions that may be restricted to root users only. This applies not just to the root and non-root user case; in fact, it applies to any user or group the user belongs to that may not have the permission to perform a certain operation.

Fortunately, there is a way to set permissions so that this can happen, *without* actually elevating the non-privileged user to a privileged status. If a certain command requires root privileges, the superuser can set the `setuid` execute permissions for this program. Once the `setuid` bit has been set, it is possible for non-privileged users to execute the program and have it behave as if it were run by root.

The `passwd` program is a typical example. Regular users can use this program to modify the password they use for logging in. By default on Fedora 2, passwords are encrypted and stored in the `/etc/shadow` file that can be modified only by the root user. From what you have seen so far, when a user executes the `passwd` program, the program assumes just the privileges assigned to that user. So how does the `passwd` program modify this file to update it with the new password? The trick lies in setting the `setuid` bit:

```
$ ls -al /usr/bin/passwd
-r-s--x--x    1 root     root         15368 May 28  2002 /usr/bin/passwd
```

The `s` indicates the `setuid` bit for this program. Thus, when the `passwd` program executes, it assumes the privileges of the root user. Because it is restricted to just updating the `/etc/shadow` file, there is not much of a risk involved. In simple terms, assigning the `setuid` bit by a privileged user to a program owned by them indicates that other users can execute the program with the same privileges as the owner. Along the lines of the `setuid` bit is the `setgid` bit. When set, the program executes with the privileges of the group it belongs to.

Of course, it is not advisable to assign the `setuid` bit arbitrarily to programs. System administrators and programmers must carefully review the program before assigning the `setuid` bit to prevent malicious users from using `setuid` bit-enabled programs to compromise system security. The `setuid` and `setgid` bits can be assigned via the `chmod` command:

```
$ chmod u=rws treasure_key.txt (setting the setuid bit)
$ chmod g=rws treasure_key.txt (setting the setgid bit)
```

Time Attributes

Any file has three different *time attributes* associated with it:

- `mtime` is the time at which the file was last modified.
- `atime` is the time at which the file was last accessed.
- `ctime` is the time at which the file's *attributes* were last changed.

When you list a directory using the `ls -l` command, the output includes the `mtime` (the modification timestamp) of each file. The `ls` command also has a `--time` option; this option takes the argument values `atime` or `ctime` and displays the other two time attributes accordingly. The `touch` command (with a filename as the argument) can be used to update a file's `mtime` and `atime`.

Try It Out — Exploring Time Attributes

Let's create a file and perform a few operations on it. After each operation, we'll check the file's `mtime`, `atime`, and `ctime` to determine how they have been affected by the operation.

1. Let's start by creating a new text file, called `time.txt`. You can use the `cat` command to create the file and to put some text into it. Put in as much text as you like, and use *Ctrl+D* to end the input. Then, use three `ls` command calls to check the `mtime`, `atime`, and `ctime` (as previously described):

```
$ cat > time.txt
Test of time
^D
$ ls -l time.txt; ls -l --time=atime time.txt; ls -l --time=ctime time.txt
-rw-r--r--    1 deepakt  users           13 Jan 20 03:49 time.txt
-rw-r--r--    1 deepakt  users           13 Jan 20 03:49 time.txt
-rw-r--r--    1 deepakt  users           13 Jan 20 03:49 time.txt
```

   You can see that they are all the same. Here, the file was created at 03:49. The file was accessed and modified at that time, and its attributes were all set at that time, so the `mtime`, `atime`, and `ctime` are all the same.

2. Now, let's modify the content of the `time.txt` file by overwriting the existing content with some new content. You can use the `cat` command again, and use *Ctrl+D* to end the input. Then, look at the `mtime`, `atime`, and `ctime` again:

```
$ cat > time.txt
Sands of time
^D
$ ls -l time.txt; ls -l --time=atime time.txt; ls -l --time=ctime time.txt
-rw-r--r--    1 deepakt  users           14 Jan 20 03:51 time.txt
-rw-r--r--    1 deepakt  users           14 Jan 20 03:49 time.txt
-rw-r--r--    1 deepakt  users           14 Jan 20 03:51 time.txt
```

   You can see from this output that the `mtime` (modification time) attribute has changed, as you'd expect because the file has just been modified. More surprisingly, the `ctime`, that is, the timestamp indicating that attributes have been modified, has *also* changed because the modification altered the size of the file.

   Also, note that the `atime` didn't change because we have not accessed (that is, read) the contents of the file in the time since we first created it.

3. Now, let's use `cat` again, but this time to read and list the contents of the file (note the slightly different usage). Then, look at the `mtime`, `atime`, and `ctime` again:

```
$ cat time.txt
Sands of time
$ ls -l time.txt; ls -l --time=atime time.txt; ls -l --time=ctime time.txt
-rw-r--r--    1 deepakt  users           14 Jan 20 03:51 time.txt
-rw-r--r--    1 deepakt  users           14 Jan 20 03:52 time.txt
-rw-r--r--    1 deepakt  users           14 Jan 20 03:51 time.txt
```

   You can see that only the `atime` has changed, reflecting the fact that we accessed the file but didn't change it (or its attributes) in any way.

4. Finally, use `chmod` to change the permissions of the file. Then, look at the `mtime`, `atime`, and `ctime` one more time:

```
$ chmod u=rwx time.txt
$ ls -l time.txt; ls -l --time=atime time.txt; ls -l --time=ctime time.txt
```

```
-rwxr--r--    1 deepakt  users          14 Jan 20 03:51 time.txt
-rwxr--r--    1 deepakt  users          14 Jan 20 03:52 time.txt
-rwxr--r--    1 deepakt  users          14 Jan 20 03:53 time.txt
```

This time, only the `ctime` has changed because we changed the attributes but did not access or modify the file.

5. Finally use the `touch` command to modify a file's timestamps. The `touch` command can be used to change both the modification and access times of a file or directory:

```
$ ls -l time.txt; ls -l --time=atime time.txt; ls -l --time=ctime time.txt
-rwxr--r--    1 deepakt  users          14 Jan 20 03:51 time.txt
-rwxr--r--    1 deepakt  users          14 Jan 20 03:52 time.txt
-rwxr--r--    1 deepakt  users          14 Jan 20 03:53 time.txt
```

The preceding command displays the timestamps (`mtime`, `atime`, and `ctime`, respectively) of the file. Execute the following commands:

```
$ touch -m time.txt
$ ls -l time.txt; ls -l --time=atime time.txt; ls -l --time=ctime time.txt
-rwxr--r--    1 deepakt  users          14 Jan 20 03:54 time.txt
-rwxr--r--    1 deepakt  users          14 Jan 20 03:52 time.txt
-rwxr--r--    1 deepakt  users          14 Jan 20 03:54 time.txt
```

The modification time has changed since the `-m` option to the `touch` command changed the modification time (`atime`). Also notice that, as with the `cat >` command, the `ctime` also changed. Pause for a minute and execute the following commands:

```
$ touch -a time.txt
$ ls -l time.txt; ls -l --time=atime time.txt; ls -l --time=ctime time.txt
-rwxr--r--    1 deepakt  users          14 Jan 20 03:54 time.txt
-rwxr--r--    1 deepakt  users          14 Jan 20 03:55 time.txt
-rwxr--r--    1 deepakt  users          14 Jan 20 03:55 time.txt
```

Using the `-a` option to `touch`, you can modify the file's access time (`atime`). Consequently, the `ctime` has also changed.

The difference between using `touch` and `cat` (or a text editor) is clearer when it comes to modifying the access time. When changing the `atime` with `touch`, the `ctime` is also modified, whereas it is unchanged when using the `cat >` command.

File Size

The *size* of a file is indicated in the file listing with the `-l` option in bytes:

```
$ ls -al dissectme.txt
-rw-r--r--    1 deepakt  users          21 Jan 19 18:40 dissectme.txt
```

To obtain the size of the contents of a directory, you could use the `du` command. The `-h` option prints the size in a human-readable format (that is, in bytes, kilobytes, megabytes, and so on). The `-s` option summarizes the output rather than list the sizes of each of the files and directories in each of the subdirectories:

```
$ du -sh /home/deepakt/
153M /home/deepakt
```

Filenames

The `ls` command always displays filenames, regardless of what options you choose. The `-F` option indicates the various file types with symbols, such as the following:

- A slash (`/`) next to a directory
- An asterisk (`*`) next to an executable file
- A pipe (`|`) next to a FIFO
- An `@` next to a symbolic link

For example:

```
$ ls -F
a.out*          dissectme.txt  foo.txt    new2  ps_auxww.txt  whataboutme.txt@
boot.b_soft@    downloads/     hard.txt   new3  ps.txt        which.txt
crontab.txt     env.txt        hello.c    new4  soft.txt@     widgets/
csh.txt         foobar         myfifo|    new5  testcmd.sh*
```

This command lists a typical directory with all of the different file types in it. Of course, to see the same output, you'd have to create these files using the commands described earlier (that is, `mkdir` for a directory, `chmod` for setting execute permissions on a file, `mknod` for a FIFO, and `ln` for creating a symbolic link).

When the `-d` option is used with a directory name as the argument, the `ls` command prints information *only* about the directory and not about its subdirectories or the files it contains. Another useful option for color terminals is the `--color` option of `ls`, which lists files of each type with a different color.

White Space in Filenames

Linux does away with the traditional UNIX restriction that filenames cannot have white space characters in them. The following example creates a file called `filename with white spaces.txt`:

```
$ cat > "filename with white spaces.txt"
This file has white spaces in its name
```

To read the contents of this file, you can refer to the filename using the slash-space-escape sequence for a white space character:

```
$ cat filename\ with\ white\ spaces.txt
This file has white spaces in its name
```

In fact, you could interchangeably use double quotes or backslashes irrespective of whether you are creating the file or listing its contents. Also, if you use the bash shell, using the *Tab* key for command completion automatically adds the slashes to the filename.

File Search Utilities

Over time, most users tend to accumulate quite a large number of files, so much so that it becomes impractical to search for files merely by listing directories. At other times, you may be trying to execute a program and not finding it because it is not in a directory listed in your `PATH` environment variable. You obviously need something more powerful than `ls` when searching for files.

Searching with the locate Command

The quickest and simplest way to locate files on Linux is to use the `locate` command. It maintains an index of files on the filesystem and is able to return partial and exact matches very quickly. You can specify a complete filename or an expression that uses metacharacters as search criteria for the `locate` command. The `locate` command can also perform case-insensitive searches for filenames.

Try It Out Elementary Searching Using locate

Let's try using the `locate` command to search for a few files.

1. First, try out the `locate` command with no options. Search on the string `moon`, like this:

```
$ locate moon
/usr/share/icons/Bluecurve/16x16/apps/kmoon.png
/usr/share/backgrounds/images/space/clem_full_moon_strtrk.jpg
/usr/share/backgrounds/images/space/gal_earth_moon.jpg
...
```

   As you can see, this searches the system for partial and exact matches, so the output here includes any file whose name contains the string `moon`.

2. Now try searching with an expression that uses a metacharacter. The following command uses the `*` character as a wildcard:

```
$ locate "*.conf"
/etc/sysconfig/networking/profiles/default/resolv.conf
/etc/X11/gdm/factory-gdm.conf
/etc/X11/gdm/gdm.conf
...
```

   This returns any file whose name ends with the `.conf` extension.

3. Now try an example using the `-i` option, to see the difference between case-sensitive and case-insensitive searches. First, without the `-i` option, you have a case-sensitive search:

```
$ locate bluecurve
/usr/lib/gtk-2.0/2.0.0/engines/libbluecurve.la
/usr/lib/gtk-2.0/2.0.0/engines/libbluecurve.so
/usr/lib/gtk/themes/engines/libbluecurve.la
...
```

   Now, run the same command with the `-i` option, to specify case-insensitivity:

```
$ locate -i bluecurve
/usr/lib/gtk-2.0/2.0.0/engines/libbluecurve.la
/usr/lib/gtk-2.0/2.0.0/engines/libbluecurve.so
/usr/lib/gtk/themes/engines/libbluecurve.la
...
/usr/share/pixmaps/nautilus/Bluecurve
/usr/share/pixmaps/nautilus/Bluecurve/desktop-home.png
/usr/share/pixmaps/nautilus/Bluecurve/Bluecurve.xml
...
```

You can see that the search results are different—for example, the second search picked up the file `Bluecurve.xml`, whereas the first did not.

4. The `locate` command maintains an index of files on the system, which is used to quickly look up filenames. This index is updated periodically (automatically) with new files. However, the `-u` option can also be used to update the index explicitly.

   To demonstrate, let's first create a file called `new_file.txt` using the `touch` command:

```
$ touch new_file.txt
```

   We then attempt to search for the file, but it returns no results even though the file has been created in the current directory. This is because the new file has not yet been added to the index of files:

```
$ locate new_file.txt
$
```

   Now change the user to be the root user so that you have privileges to update the `locate` command's index. Run the `locate` command this time with the `-u` option, which updates the index:

```
$ su -
Password: <not displayed>
# locate -u
# exit
```

   Now try to locate the file again from the revised index. This time the `locate` command is able to locate the file `new_file.txt` because it has been added to the index of files by the `-u` option:

```
$ locate new_file.txt
/home/deepakt/new_file.txt
```

Searching with the find Command

While the `locate` command is very useful for finding files quickly anywhere on the system, the search criteria that can be specified with `locate` are quite rudimentary. The `find` command has a much richer array of options. With the `find` command, you can search for files and subdirectories under a certain hierarchy, or specify various criteria such as the access time of the file, the size of the file, and so on. You can also use `find` to execute other commands on files that meet the search criteria. Therefore, while `locate` is very fast with fewer features, `find` is more feature-packed but slower.

Try It Out   Advanced Searching Using find

Let's experiment with the `find` command to execute a number of searches for files, specifying various criteria. The following examples will give you a taste of what is possible with `find`.

Start off by searching for files under the `/etc` directory that end with the `.conf` extension:

```
$ find /etc -name "*.conf" -print
/etc/sysconfig/networking/profiles/default/resolv.conf
/etc/X11/gdm/factory-gdm.conf
/etc/X11/gdm/gdm.conf
```

The first argument to `find` is the directory below which to search for files. Other arguments specify the search criteria to be utilized. In this case, we specify the `-name` option, which takes an expression representing a file or set of files as its argument. The search string may be a simple metacharacter expression or it can be the exact name of the file. Note that you use double quotes to specify the search string; this prevents the shell from interpreting the asterisk literally. Finally, you can specify the action to be performed once the search criteria are met. The `-print` option specifies the action; it indicates that the names of the files or directories matching the criteria should be displayed.

In the next search example, we look for all directories under `/tmp` whose name starts with the string `ssh`:

```
$ find /tmp -type d -name "ssh*" 2>/dev/null
/tmp/ssh-XX18hvoD
/tmp/ssh-XXzdTPki
/tmp/ssh-XX4DYEB5
/tmp/ssh-XX7KJPAN
```

These are temporary directories created by the SSH programs run by various users. The `-type` option specifies the type to search for, in this case `d`, indicating a directory. (Similarly, `f` indicates a file.) You may have permission to list only those SSH temporary directories that belong to you. Hence, to redirect permission errors, use the shell redirection to redirect the error to the `/dev/null` device. The `/dev/null` device is actually a pseudo device that acts as a black hole, accepting input and discarding it at the same time.

This next search is based on the time of last access—you do this by specifying the `-amin` option:

```
$ mkdir foobar
$ date
Mon Jan 20 22:41:29 PST 2003
$ find . -type d -name "foo*" -amin -10 -print
./foobar
$ ls -ld --time=atime foobar/
drwxr-xr-x    2 deepakt  users        4096 Jan 20 22:41 foobar/
```

The `-10` option combined with the `-amin` option specifies a search for files that have been accessed in the last ten minutes. Therefore, you are actually searching for files with names that begin with `foo` that have been accessed in the last ten minutes. The `A +10` option would result in a search for files last accessed more than ten minutes ago.

The next example combines the `-amin` option with the `-or` option:

```
$ mkdir bar
$ find . -type d -name "foo*" -amin -10 -or -name "*bar"
./foobar
./bar
```

The `-or` option is actually the logical OR operator that can be used to combine two specified criteria. In this case, we search for files called `foo*` that have either been accessed in the last ten minutes, or files with names ending in `bar`. (The `-and` option allows you to combine two of the specified criteria in a logical AND expression.)

You can also search by file size, using the `-size` option. By specifying the size with a plus (+) or minus (–) sign before it, you indicate that the file should be greater or smaller in size than the specified number:

```
$ find . -size -20k -and -size +10
./.viminfo
./downloads/nop.txt
./downloads/p.txt
./downloads/curl
./downloads/curl/p.txt
 ...
```

In this case, the search is for files whose size is between 10 bytes and 20 Kilobytes (note that the `-and` option is used to achieve this).

The last search demonstrates the `-exec` flag, which allows you to execute a command when the search criteria are met:

```
$ find /tmp -type f -atime +1000 -exec rm {} \; 2>/dev/null
```

The `-exec` option is followed by the command to be executed, and optionally a pair of curly braces. The command is executed for each file that matches the criteria. The curly braces indicate the matched file. The semicolon (`;`) indicates the end of the command; it is escaped (by a preceding \ character) to prevent the shell from interpreting it. In this case, we search and delete all files under the `/tmp` directory that have not been accessed in the last 1,000 minutes.

Searching with the GNOME Search Tool

The GNOME search tool is a graphical front-end to the `locate` and `find` commands. It can be invoked from the Main Menu by clicking Search for Files (see Figure 5-1).

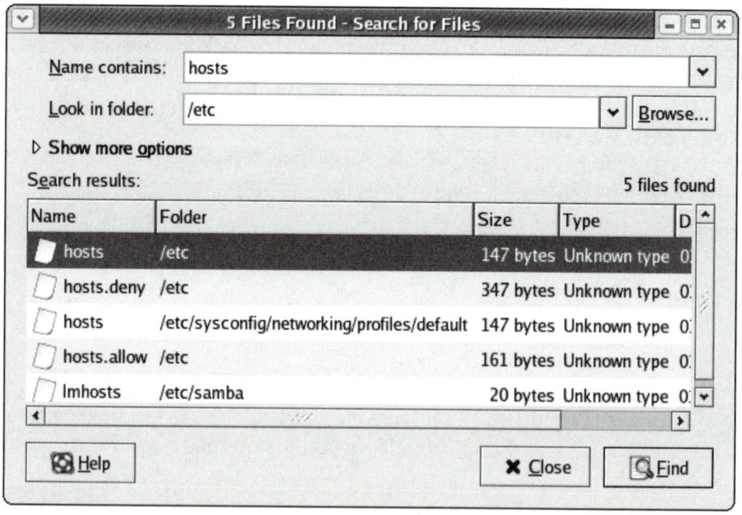

Figure 5-1

Filenames can be entered in the "File is named" text box, and a directory in which to start the search can be specified in the "Look in folder" box. The preceding example shows a search for the file `hosts` in the `/etc` directory.

Wildcard searches are also possible using the expression syntax we used for `locate`. For example, `host*` would search for all files starting with the characters `host` (and followed by one or more characters), and would therefore match `hosts`, `hosts.deny`, `hosts.accept`, and so on.

Clicking the Additional Options button presents an advanced search interface using rules, as described in Chapter 2.

Text Searches

Combining file searches with text searches within files allows you to quickly pinpoint the files that have the text you are looking for. You know how to search for a file by its filename (and also by its location); but how do you search the filesystem for files that contain a particular string of text? This type of search is very useful, but quite different from what you can achieve using `locate` or `find`.

The `grep` command is the most common way to search for a string in a file. In fact, it can search multiple files at the same time. The `grep` command, by default, performs a case-sensitive search, although it can perform a case-insensitive search if required.

The `xargs` command reads its standard input and feeds it as arguments to any command that is supplied as an argument to it. In other words, `xargs` will dynamically create the arguments for a command. This makes it particularly useful for chaining commands using the pipe (`|`) shell operator. As illustrated in Chapter 6, simply using a pipe operator feeds the output of a command as input to another command. The `xargs` command in conjunction with the pipe operator feeds the output of a command as arguments to another command. The following "Try it Out" section illustrates its use.

Try It Out — Using grep and xargs

Let's try out some `grep` searches and combine them with the `xargs` and `find` search utilities.

The `grep` command takes the string or expression to match as the first argument followed by one or more files to search. In the following example, `grep` searches for the string `nobody` in the files `/etc/passwd` and `/etc/group`:

```
$ grep nobody /etc/passwd /etc/group
/etc/passwd:nobody:x:99:99:Nobody:/:/sbin/nologin
/etc/passwd:nfsnobody:x:65534:65534:Anonymous NFS User:/var/lib/nfs:/sbin/nologin
/etc/group:nobody:x:99:
/etc/group:nfsnobody:x:65534:
```

The `grep` command prints the names of the files in which the string was found, followed by a colon character (`:`) and the occurrence of the string within those files.

The `-i` option causes `grep` to search for the string or expression ignoring case. In the next example, the line corresponding to the `Deepak Thomas` user is displayed as a match because the string `Deepak Thomas` matches a case-insensitive search for the expression `de*`:

```
$ grep -i "de*" /etc/passwd
deepakt:x:501:100:Deepak Thomas:/home/deepakt:/bin/bash
```

Finally, look at the combination of the `find`, `xargs`, and `grep` commands to search for files in the `/etc` directory that contain the string `farfalla` (which, in this case, happens to be the name of the machine the command is run on):

```
$ find /etc -type f 2>/dev/null |xargs grep farfalla 2>/dev/null
/etc/sysconfig/networking/profiles/default/network:HOSTNAME=farfalla
/etc/sysconfig/network:HOSTNAME=farfalla
/etc/hosts:127.0.0.1    farfalla        localhost
```

The `find` command locates all the files in the `/etc` directory. This list is piped as the input to the `xargs` command. The `xargs` command in this case has one argument, the `grep` command. The `grep` command also has an argument, that being the string to search for. Internally, the `xargs` command constructs a command line that looks like this:

```
grep farfalla file1 file2 ... filen
```

Here, *`file1, file2, ..., filen`* are the results of the search by the `find` utility.

Other more sophisticated text searching tools exist. For example, the `awk` command is considered to be a language in itself, and allows for rich expressions and control flow. Another command, `sed` (the *stream editor*), is intended to transform input text streams, typically files or the output of commands.

The following `awk` script prints the login names and the actual names of users on the local system:

```
$ awk -F: '{print $1, "-", $5}' /etc/passwd
root - root
bin - bin
daemon - daemon
ftp - FTP User
nobody - Nobody
rpc - Portmapper RPC user
vcsa - virtual console memory owner
nscd - NSCD Daemon
sshd - Privilege-separated SSH
nfsnobody - Anonymous NFS User
xfs - X Font Server
ident - pident user
apache - Apache
webalizer - Webalizer
deepakt - Deepak Thomas
```

The `-F` option here indicates the field separator. In this case, it is the colon (`:`) character that is used to separate fields in the `/etc/passwd` file. The `awk` action prints the first and fifth columns of the file to the standard output (that is, the terminal), with a hyphen (-) character separating column entries on each line.

The following `sed` command line transforms a string in the `seashells.txt` file. The expression `'s;sells;shells;'` indicates that the pattern `sells` should be substituted with the pattern `shells` (the letter `s` indicates substitution):

```
$ cat >seashells.txt
She sells sea shells on the sea shore
^D
$ sed -e 's;sells;shells;' seashells.txt
She shells sea shells on the sea shore
```

The commands awk and sed do not modify the input file directly. Instead, they treat the file as a stream of input and write the output to the standard output (in this case, the terminal). As shown in the next example, it should be possible to capture the output to a file as well; output redirection using the > operator is dealt with in detail in Chapter 6. For now, you need only to understand that the > operator causes any input to it to be directed to the filename following it

```
$ sed -e 's;sells;shells;' seashells.txt > seashells2.txt
$ cat seashells2.txt
She shells sea shells on the sea shore
```

Navigating the Filesystem

This section looks at the file organization of Fedora 2 in general, based on the various utilities that are available and the location of configuration files. The root filesystem is indicated by the `/`. The contents of the root filesystem follow:

```
$ ls -F /
bin/   dev/  home/    lib/          misc/  opt/   root/  tftpboot/  usr/
boot/  etc/  initrd/  lost+found/   mnt/   proc/  sbin/  tmp/       var/
```

The utility programs are organized under the `/bin`, `/usr/bin`, and `/usr/local/bin` directories. The following tables list some of the common programs under these directories. It is very useful to ensure that these directories are set in the `PATH` environment variable.

Remember, you can get full information on each of these by querying their `man` *pages, and abridged details by typing the command followed by* `--help`.

Let's look at each of these directories in some detail.

The table that follows lists commands that are located in the `/bin` directory.

Command	Description
awk	Pattern-scanning and processing language
bash	The Bourne-again shell
cat	Concatenates files and prints on to standard output
chgrp	Changes the group ownership
chmod	Changes file access permissions
chown	Changes file ownership permissions

Table continued on following page

Command	Description
cp	Copies files and directories
cpio	Copies files to and from archives
csh	C-shell
cut	Removes sections from each line of input
date	Prints the current date and timestamp; super user may set the date and time
dd	Converts and copies files
Df	Displays disk usage for filesystems
dmesg	Displays startup messages
echo	Displays a line of text
ed	An old text editor
grep	Regular expression-matching program
gzip	GNU Zip program for compressing files
kill	Terminates running processes
Ln	Creates links to files and directories
Ls	Lists files
mail	Command line mail client
mkdir	Command line mail client
more	Paginates a file
mount	Maps a filesystem to a directory
mv	Moves a file from one location to another; same as renaming a file
netstat	Prints network statistics
ping	Checks for the network reachability of other machines on the network
ps	Lists currently running processes
pwd	Displays current working directory
rm	Removes files
rmdir	Removes directories
sed	Stream editor can be used to programmatically modify files and the output of programs
sh	Bourne shell
sleep	Delays for a specific amount of time
sort	Sorts the lines of input

Command	Description
su	Changes identity of a user
tar	Archiving program
tcsh	Enhanced C shell
touch	Updates the timestamp on a file
umount	Unmounts a currently mounted filesystem
uname	Prints system information
vi	A text editor

The commands in the following table are located in the /usr/bin directory.

Command	Description
At	Queues jobs for later execution
Bc	A bench calculator
Cc	C-compiler (this command is a symbolic link to the GNU C-compiler gcc)
Clear	Clears the screen
Crontab	Maintains a list of tasks to be performed later
Du	Reports disk usage for a directory and subdirectories
Emacs	An editor
F77	Fortran compiler
File	Prints file type
Find	File-searching utility
Finger	Looks up user information
ftp	File transfer program
Gcc	GNU C-compiler
Gdb	GNU debugger
Gftp	Graphical FTP client
Gimp	GNU image manipulation and painting program
Gmake	Maintains a group of programs (this command is a symbolic link to the GNU make command gmake)
Head	Displays the first few lines of a file
Ispell	Interactive spell checker

Table continued on following page

Command	Description
`Lpr`	Spools print jobs
`Man`	Displays manual pages for commands
`Nslookup`	Looks up a host's DNS information
`Passwd`	Changes a user's password
`telnet`	Telnet client allows remote logins
`Wall`	Sends a message to the terminals of all users currently logged on
`Wc`	Counts words, lines, and characters of input text
`Which`	Displays the full path of commands
`Who`	Displays the list of users currently logged on to the system

The next batch of files are system configuration files located in the `/etc` directory and its subdirectories. The following table contains some of the more commonly modified ones.

File	Description
`Exports`	Lists the filesystems to be exported via NFS
`Ftpaccess`	Configuration file for `ftpd`
`Group`	Lists the various groups on the system and each of their members
`Hosts`	Lists the hostname and IP addresses of machines
`host.conf`	Used by the DNS resolver library
`Motd`	Contains the message of the day
`passwd`	Contains user information for all users on the system
`shadow`	Contains the encrypted passwords of the user
`xinetd.conf`	Configuration file for the xinetd daemon

You can find administrative binaries under `/sbin` and `/usr/sbin`. The following table provides a list of commands from the `/sbin` directory.

Binary	Description
`Arp`	Prints a machine's Address Resolution Protocol (ARP) table
`cardmgr`	PCMCIA device manager
`chkconfig`	Manages runlevel information for system services
`debugfs`	Ext2 filesystem debugging utility

Binary	Description
dhclient	DHCP client
e2fsck	Ext filesystem diagnosis and repair tool
fdisk	Disk-partitioning utility
fuser	Displays the IDs of processes using the specified files
ifconfig	Configures network interfaces
insmod	Installs loadable kernel modules
lspci	Lists all PCI devices on this systems
lspnp	Lists all PNP devices on this system
mkfs	Creates a new filesystem on a partition
modprobe	Detects and manages loadable modules
route	Displays and sets system routing table
sysctl	Displays or changes system parameters

The following table lists some of the files from the `/usr/sbin` directory.

Binary	Description
adduser	Creates a new user
automount	Configures mount points for `autofs`
chpasswd	Updates password file in batch mode
chroot	Runs command with the root set to a new root
gpm	Mouse-based cut and paste utility for virtual consoles
groupadd	Adds a new group
in.fingerd	Finger daemon
in.ftpd	FTP daemon
in.identd	`identd` daemon
in.telnetd	Telnet daemon
kudzu	Configures new hardware
pppd	PPP daemon
squid	HTTP caching server
tcpdump	TCP/IP diagnostics tool
vipw	Password file editor
zdump	Dumps time zone information

The /usr/local/bin directory usually houses new programs when they are installed.

Shared libraries (that is, libraries that contain common functions used by multiple programs at the same time without multiple in-memory copies) reside in the /lib, /usr/lib, and /usr/local/lib directories. It is often a good idea to ensure that the LD_LIBRARY_PATH environment variable contains these directories. This variable is not set by default, although it can be set in the .bashrc file or other startup files.

The /boot directory contains bootable images of Linux kernels. Following is an extract from a typical listing (here, the vmlinuz entries are the kernel binaries):

```
$ ls /boot
boot.b
chain.b
config-2.4.18-14
config-2.4.18-17.8.0
...
vmlinuz-2.4.18-14
vmlinuz-2.4.18-17.8.0
vmlinuz-2.4.18-19.8.0
```

Transient and temporary files can be found under /var/tmp and /tmp. The /tmp directory is cleaned up by startup scripts after every reboot, whereas the /var/tmp directory is not. This behavior may dictate for some programmers the choice of using /var/tmp as opposed to /tmp.

Files related to peripherals, such as devices, can be found under the /dev directory. By convention, various peripherals, such as CD-ROM drives and floppy drives, are mounted under the /mnt directory. You'll see more on this directory in a later section.

The /proc directory provides a filesystem abstraction to the processes currently running on the system. Each process has a directory assigned to it and several files under it that contain information about the process. For more details, you should refer to the proc manual page by invoking the command man proc.

And, finally, as you first discovered in Chapter 2, the user's home directories are typically created under /home.

Managing Drives and Partitions

Now that you have seen several aspects of the filesystem from a user's perspective, let's look at some of the administrative aspects of the filesystem, such as the different drives on a system and its partitions. Apart from the hard disks on a system, there is almost always a floppy disk drive and a CD-ROM drive, both of which are treated as filesystem drives. In addition, certain other peripheral devices, such as digital cameras or removable storage devices, may present the storage available on them as filesystem drives. A drive may be *mounted*, making it available for use by the filesystem, or *unmounted*, making it unavailable for the filesystem to use.

You can list the currently mounted drives on a system using the `df` or `mount` commands. Let's look at the output of the `df` command:

```
$ df -k
File system            1K-blocks      Used Available Use% Mounted on
/dev/hda2                5716172   3426868   1998932  64% /
/dev/hda1                 101089     19137     76733  20% /boot
none                       94752         0     94752   0% /dev/shm
/dev/fd0                    1423       105      1318   8% /mnt/floppy
/dev/cdrom                661728    661728         0 100% /mnt/cdrom
```

The `-k` option to `df` causes it to report partition sizes in kilobytes.

In the preceding listing, you see the following:

- The first IDE hard disk, `/dev/had`, has two partitions, `/dev/hda1` and `/dev/hda2`.
- The floppy drive is the `/dev/fd0` drive.
- The `/dev/cdrom` drive represents a CD-ROM drive.

In addition, a drive marked `none` (in this case) represents a temporary filesystem (`tmpfs`) necessary for certain shared-memory operations.

With the other drives, in addition to the space-usage numbers on each of them, the thing to note is the `Mounted on` column. This represents the directory that these filesystems are mapped on to. Therefore, the following is true:

- The `/dev/hda2` partition contains a filesystem that is mapped on to the `/` or the root directory.
- The `/dev/hda1` partition contains another filesystem that is mapped on to the `/boot` directory.

What this means is that each time you execute the `cd /` command or the `cd /etc` command, you are actually accessing a filesystem on the second partition of the only hard disk on this system. Also, executing `ls -l /mnt/cdrom` will list the top-level files and subdirectories of the currently mounted CD in the CD-ROM drive.

Mounting Drives

A device such as a floppy drive may be detected by the operating system when it boots up. However, for the floppy drive to be *usable*, it needs to be mounted first (this is like grafting the drive onto a filesystem entry point).

To mount a drive, you must first create a directory (or use the already available `/mnt/floppy` and `/mnt/cdrom` directories for floppy disks and CD-ROMs, respectively). You then mount the floppy drive `/dev/fd0` to that directory. Drives can be mounted in two different ways:

- Automatic mounting of the drive at boot time
- Manual mounting at any time after the system has come up

For a drive to be mounted automatically by the system, you must make an entry for it in the file `/etc/fstab` or the filesystem table file. Here is a typical `/etc/fstab` file:

```
LABEL=/            /              ext3    defaults         1 1
LABEL=/boot        /boot          ext3    defaults         1 2
none               /dev/pts       devpts  gid=5,mode=620   0 0
none               /proc          proc    defaults         0 0
none               /dev/shm       tmpfs   defaults         0 0
/dev/hda3          swap           swap    defaults         0 0
/dev/cdrom         /mnt/cdrom     iso9660 noauto,owner,kudzu,ro 0 0
/dev/fd0           /mnt/floppy    auto    noauto,owner,kudzu 0 0
```

Notice that there are more entries in this file than were listed by the `df` command because there are drives of several other types that do not have true filesystem characteristics. For example, disk usage of the `proc` filesystem does not make much sense because the `proc` filesystem actually represents a set of processes currently executing on the system. Similarly, the `/dev/pts` entry indicates a pseudo-terminal device, which is not really associated with commonly used files and directories; rather, it is used for managing terminal-based input and output. However, these special types of filesystems are also listed in `/etc/fstab` so that they may be mounted automatically at boot time.

Also, notice that besides the floppy and CD-ROM drives, there is also a `swap` device. This is a device used by the operating system to juggle processes and chunks of memory content between the RAM and the hard disk, therefore allowing arbitrarily large programs to be loaded and executed. In general, `swap` partitions are critical to the operating system because they are necessary for multitasking—that is, running multiple tasks at (almost) the same time.

It is also possible to manage drives at runtime using the Disk Management utility. It may be accessed from the Start Menu ➪ System Tools ➪ Disk Management (see Figure 5-2).

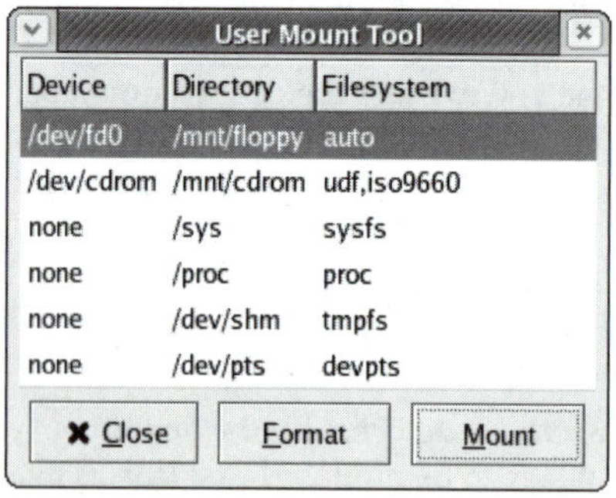

Figure 5-2

You can mount or unmount specific devices or even format a new device from this tool.

The Hardware Browser

You can also check for the hard disks on a system and their partitions by using the Hardware Browser application, which you'll find under the Main Menu ➪ System Tools menu. When you're there, select the Hardware Browser option to view the hard drives on your system, as shown in Figure 5-3.

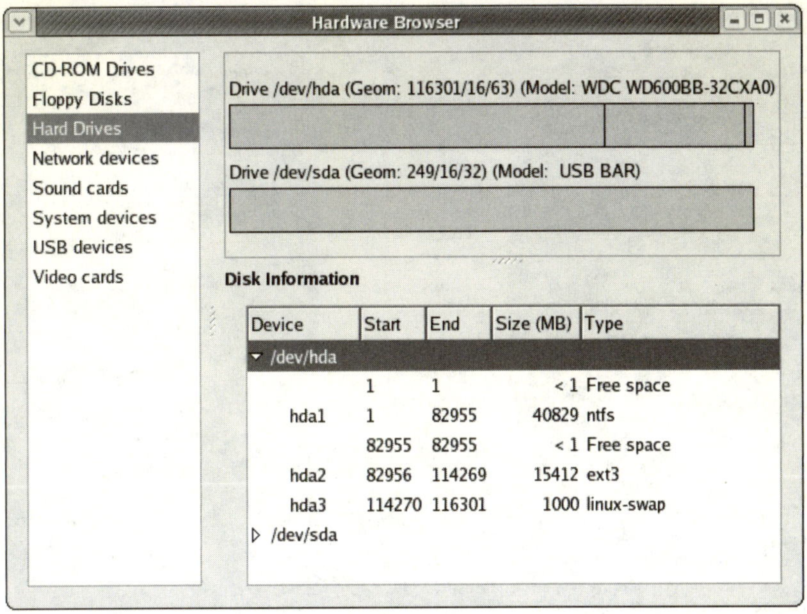

Figure 5-3

In Figure 5-3, you can see that on this machine the disk `/dev/hda` has three partitions: hda1 is an NTFS partition, hda2 is a Linux ext3 partition and hda3 is a Linux swap partition,

Mounting Drives Manually

You can mount a drive (such as the CD-ROM drive) manually by using the `mount` command. To unmount a drive manually, use the `umount` command.

You can also use the Bluecurve desktop to mount floppies and CD-ROMs. To do this, right-click on the workspace, choose Disks from the context menu, and then select the required drive to be mounted (floppy, CD-ROM, USB Flash drive, or all of them), as shown in Figure 5-4.

As a demonstration, let's try to mount a floppy disk using the `mount` command and later unmount it to understand how the process of mounting and unmounting drives works (you'll need a floppy disk for this).

Start out by trying to list the `/mnt/floppy` directory. No files are listed because the floppy drive device has not yet been mounted to `/mnt/floppy`:

```
$ ls /mnt/floppy/    before mounting the floppy drive
no files listed
```

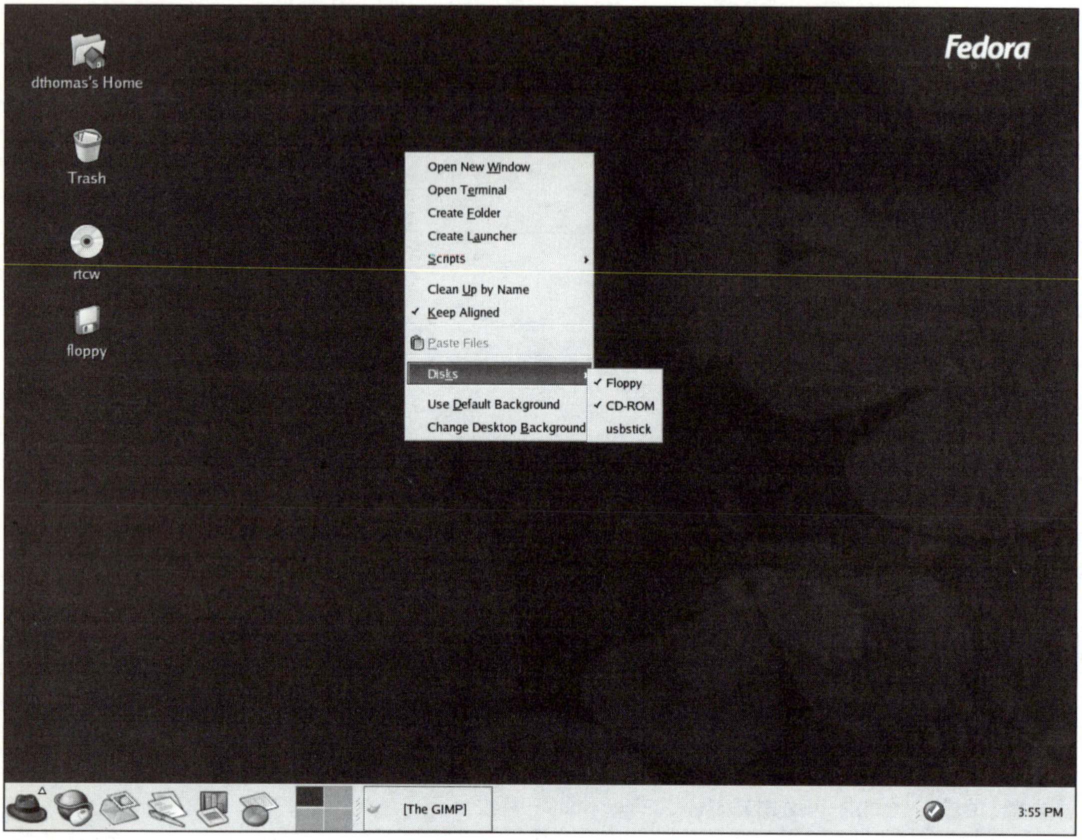

Figure 5-4

We attempt to mount floppy drive device `/dev/fd0 to /mnt/floppy`. However, we are prevented from doing so because this is a privileged operation allowed only for administrators or programs that have the `setuid` bit set. So we switch to the root user and try again to mount the drive. This time we succeed in mounting the `/dev/fd0 device to /mnt/floppy`:

```
$ mount /dev/fd0 /mnt/floppy
mount: only root can do that
$  su
Password:
# mount /dev/fd0 /mnt/floppy
# df -k|grep floppy
/dev/fd0                  1423       105       1318   8% /mnt/floppy
```

The `mount` command minimally takes two arguments. The first is the name of the device containing a filesystem to mount, and the second is a directory to map the device on to. Verify this using the `df` command whose output is piped to the `grep` command, which searches for the string `floppy`; sure enough, the drive is listed as being mounted to `/mnt/floppy`.

Once this is done, non-root users may also access the `/mnt/floppy` directory. You can exit from the root shell and assume your previous identity of a regular user:

```
# exit
$ ls /mnt/floppy/
aliases.txt  df.txt   ff.html     ps_A.txt      testcmd.sh  which.txt
crontab.txt  env.txt  parted.txt  ps_auxww.txt  top.jpeg
```

Now, as a regular user, you can list the files under the `/mnt/floppy` directory:

```
$ umount /dev/fd0
umount: only root can unmount /dev/fd0 from /mnt/floppy
$ su
Password:
# umount /dev/fd0
# exit
exit
$ ls /mnt/floppy/
bash$
```

However, as a regular user, you are not permitted to unmount the device. To do this, you once again must assume the identity of the root user and run the `umount` command. The `umount` command takes the name of the device—`/dev/fd0`, in this case. After the device is unmounted, the `ls` listing is not available any more because there is no device with files and subdirectories grafted to the filesystem at this point.

If a program has a file open on a mounted device or a reference to a directory, the system will not permit the device to be unmounted. This is characterized by an error message that reads as `unmount: /mnt/floppy: device is busy`. If you see this error, ensure that you do not have a shell window open that is accessing a directory or file on the device in question.

In Fedora 2, CDs are mounted automatically; manually mounting them is not required. The Nautilus file manager automatically pops up a dialog box if the CD has a runnable program on it. Another tidbit to take note of is the `eject` command. You can use the `eject` command to unmount the CD and cause the CD-ROM tray to be opened.

Mounting a Flash Drive

Recently, *key-chain storage drives* have gained popularity. These are small, inexpensive (at least the not-so high-end ones) flash memory cards that can be connected to a computer via a USB port. You can use the key drive to copy files back and forth between computers. Because most of them start with a minimum of 32MB, going up to 1GB or more, they are much more practical than floppy disks or burning a CD when you need to carry with you important information such as documents or presentations. Fedora supports these USB mass-storage devices and treats them as storage devices.

To use the USB flash device, you need to mount the USB mass-storage device. After you plug in the device, you can either use the right-click menu as before, or mount the device from the command line using the `mount` command.

```
$ /sbin/mount -t vfat /dev/sda0 /mnt/usbstick
```

You may also choose to mount the drive during boot time by adding the following entry to `/etc/fstab`:

```
/dev/sda0        /mnt/usbstick     vfat    user,noauto,umask=0        0 0
```

If you already have a USB mass-storage device connected to the computer, the system may recognize the device to be `/dev/sda1` and not `/dev/sda0`. Also, if you have a pre-existing SCSI hard disk on the computer, `/dev/sda` will be allotted to the hard disk. In this case, the USB mass-storage device is assigned the device `/dev/sdb`.

Partitions

You can use partitions to divide a disk drive into a number of filesystems. For example, consider the hard disk discussed earlier that had one partition dedicated to the root filesystem (`/`), another for the `/boot` directory (which houses the various kernels that can be used to boot up the system), and the `swap` partition.

On *dual boot systems*, partitions allow you to dedicate certain partitions to one operating system and the remaining to a second operating system. The partitions are indicated as numbers next to the disk drive—for example, `/dev/hda1`, `/dev/hda2`,and so on, or `/dev/sda1`, `/dev/sda2`, and so on. The first IDE hard disk is usually named as `/dev/hda`, the second one as `/dev/hdb`, and so on. SCSI hard disks are named in the order `/dev/sda`, `/dev/sdb`, and so on.

A disk's partition information is stored in a partition table that is read by the operating system. The tools that you can use to manipulate the partition table to change partition information on hard disks are discussed later in this chapter.

Supported Filesystem Types

Now that you know how disks are organized into partitions, it is time to explore *filesystem types*. Various operating systems have their own notion of how data should be organized on disk partitions. For example, Microsoft DOS uses the *file allocation table (FAT)* filesystem to organize files on the disk. With the advent of Windows NT, *NT filesystem (NTFS)* became another filesystem supported by Microsoft operating systems.

The *de facto* filesystem on Linux is the *extended (ext)* filesystem. A second version of this filesystem was called ext2; Fedora 2 supports the latest version, ext3. Usually, when a system is shut down abruptly, (without allowing it to save all of the in-memory filesystem data), the operating system performs a lengthy sanity check of the disk and sometimes also repairs the disk. With ext3, the time taken for the check (and repair) in such an event is significantly reduced due to a new feature supported by ext3 known as *journaling*, which maintains disk consistency by constantly logging disk activity.

Fedora 2 currently supports a host of filesystems, and many simultaneously. For example, it is possible to have a system with one FAT partition and the remaining partitions in the ext3 format. The file `/proc/filesystems` contains a list of the filesystems supported on a particular machine:

```
$ cat /proc/filesystems
nodev   rootfs
nodev   bdev
nodev   proc
nodev   sockfs
```

```
nodev   tmpfs
nodev   shm
nodev   pipefs
        ext2
nodev   ramfs
        iso9660
nodev   devpts
        ext3
nodev   usbdevfs
nodev   usbfs
nodev   autofs
        vfat
```

The `nodev` entry against a filesystem type indicates that no device is currently using that filesystem type (although the filesystem type itself is supported). In the preceding sample listing, the filesystem types currently used by devices are as follows:

- The extended filesystem types, ext2 and ext3, used by the Linux partitions
- The CD-ROM filesystem ISO-9660 for the CD-ROM device
- The VFAT filesystem for the floppy device

Support for additional filesystems can be compiled into the kernel or loaded as a kernel module. Chapter 12 has information on recompiling the kernel and setting up loadable kernel modules.

Compatibility of Filesystems

You might wonder how it is possible that a file residing on a Linux ext3 partition can be copied onto a floppy that uses the VFAT filesystem of Microsoft Windows? Historically, filesystems have been designed with a certain operating system or class of operating systems in mind. For this reason, filesystem types are subject to the idiosyncrasies of the operating systems. However, Linux handles a multitude of filesystems, several of which have been designed to allow interoperation with other operating systems.

Do programmers who write programs on Linux write code to handle each and every supported filesystem that Linux supports? If that were true, wouldn't these programs break when a new filesystem type was supported?

In reality, Linux application programmers do not write filesystem-specific code (this would make most programs too complex and unmaintainable, besides being very hard to extend when a new filesystem type is supported by the operating system). They write code assuming a simple, generic filesystem. The abstraction of multiple filesystems is handled by the *Virtual Filesystem (VFS)*. VFS is not really a filesystem in itself; rather, it is a way to abstract the common aspects of most filesystem types.

For example, almost all of the operations that relate to the manipulation of files can be reduced to a few basic actions: *create*, *delete*, *rename*, *open*, *read*, *write*, and *close*. The VFS layer in the kernel supports these generic interfaces in the form of functions that higher-level programs can use. Internally, VFS figures out the real implementation to invoke.

For example, while attempting to copy a file from a FAT partition to an ext3 partition, the copy program would invoke *system calls* (among other things) such as `read()` and `write()`. Because the VFS layer understands that the target filesystem type is FAT, it ends up invoking a `fat_read()`, and because the destination filesystem type is ext3, it invokes `ext3_write()` (see Figure 5-5).

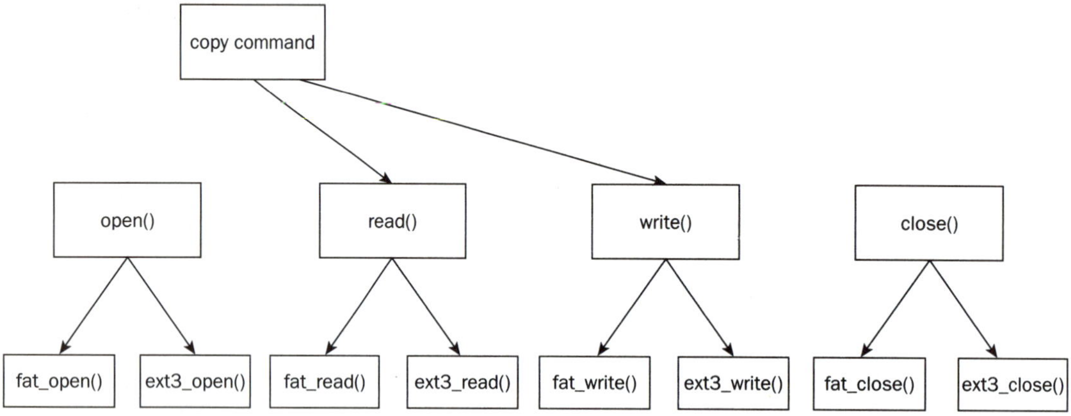

Figure 5-5

In the diagram, the `copy` command invokes the `read()` system call. The `read()` internally translates into the appropriate filesystem specific call, `fat_read()`, for example.

Accessing Microsoft Windows Filesystems

Because Fedora supports and recognizes a large number of filesystem types, including several Microsoft filesystems, it is possible to access files residing on disk partitions formatted as Microsoft filesystems, such as FAT32 or NTFS. Here is what you need to do to mount a FAT32 partition:

```
$ mount -t vfat /dev/hda1 /mnt/winfiles
```

This would effectively mount the `/dev/hda1` device (presumably the C: drive on Microsoft Windows) to the directory `/mnt/winfiles`. From this point, it is possible to work with the Microsoft Windows files using standard Linux commands.

To always mount the drive at boot time, you must add the following entry to `/etc/fstab`:

```
/dev/hda1 /mnt/winfiles auto noauto,users,exec 0 0
```

However, there is a catch when it comes to accessing NTFS filesystems. Fedora does not come with support for NTFS, presumably due to licensing or legal issues concerning this proprietary filesystem. That can, however, be remedied by installing the necessary kernel support for NTFS. The tedious way to achieve this is to recompile the kernel with NTFS support. However, a simpler option exists, which is to install the NTFS support available as RPMS from `http://linux-ntfs.sourceforge.net/rpm/`.

See Chapter 4 for details on installing RPMs.

Once support for NTFS is installed, you can choose to mount an NTFS partition with the `mount` command, as illustrated in the following example:

```
$ mount -t ntfs /dev/hda4 /mnt/myntfs
```

Optionally, you may choose to have the drive mounted at boot time by adding an entry similar to the following to `/etc/fstab`.

```
/dev/hda4 /mnt/myntfs ro              0 0
```

Even after you install NTFS support, there is still a catch; NTFS partitions may be accessed only as read-only partitions. You can copy or open files on NTFS partitions, but you cannot create, modify, delete, or rename files and folders on these partitions.

Accessing Fedora Filesystems from Microsoft Windows

Surprisingly, it is possible to access Linux filesystem partitions from certain Microsoft Windows platforms. This is achieved by plugging in support for reading the ext filesystem of Linux. Explore2fs is one such project that provides support for Microsoft Windows. More details on Explore2fs can be found at `http://uranus.it.swin.edu.au/~jn/linux/explore2fs.htm`. Please note that this software offers write support for Linux filesystems in addition to read support. However, the write support may not be very stable.

Copying Files on a Dual-Boot System

Even with the limitations of the aforementioned drivers, it is possible to copy files between Linux partitions and NTFS partitions. For example, to copy a file from Windows to Linux, you would boot into Linux and, using the NTFS support, copy the file to a Linux partition. To copy a file from a Linux partition, you would boot into Windows and, using the `ext` filesystem support offered by Explore2fs, copy the file from a Linux partition to a Windows partition.

Managing Partitions

This section explains how to manipulate a partition table—to create, verify, delete, and resize partitions, and to manage partitions in general. It is inevitable that sooner or later most people will have to deal with the task of partitioning or repartitioning hard disks, either as part of a fresh installation or a disk upgrade.

You have several tools at your disposal. The `fdisk` command is the oldest of this genre of tools, although these days the `parted` command seems to be the preference of an increasing number of users. The `cfdisk` and `sfdisk` commands are other partition manipulation tools that are available as part of the Fedora 2 distribution. The *disk druid* utility is also supplied by Red Hat, and can be employed if the user chooses to perform custom partitioning.

Try It Out — Editing Partitions with parted

Because `parted` is fast emerging as the popular choice for editing partitions, let's use it here to experiment with partition management. The `parted` program, unlike `fdisk`, does not gather all the modifications during an editing session and apply changes to the partition table at the end.

Inexperienced users of parted need to be aware of the following:

- The parted program writes changes immediately to the partition table, so users are warned against curious experimentation using parted on disks containing any significant information.
- When resizing a partition, the partition in question must not be in use. That is, it must be unmounted using the umount command.

Having said that, parted is definitely much more function-packed and user-friendly in comparison to fdisk.

In the following example, because you will be resizing the root partition, the root partition cannot be mounted. Therefore, you need to run parted from a boot disk, as described here:

1. A boot disk image with parted is available at ftp://ftp.gnu.org/gnu/parted/bootdisk/partboot.img. Download a copy if you're not confident about making a boot disk yourself.
2. Save the image as partboot.img. The image file needs to be written onto a floppy disk (as the root user) by running the dd command, (as shown in the following code) from the same directory as the file:

```
# dd if=partboot.img of=/dev/fd0 bs=1440k
```

   This step prepares the book disk. For more information about this, refer to the Parted manual at www.auth.gr/mirrors/gnu/manual/parted-1.6.1/html_mono/parted.html.

3. The system needs to be shut down and restarted by booting from this boot disk.
4. After the system comes up, run the parted command from the boot disk, as shown. When editing partitions other than the root or boot partitions, you need not use a boot disk. Simply ensure that the partition is unmounted and invoke parted as /sbin/parted.

```
# parted /dev/hda
```

5. Start parted as the root user, specifying the hard disk whose partition table you wish to modify. The parted command allows you to edit the partition table interactively:

```
(parted) print
Disk geometry for /dev/hda: 0.000-6149.882 megabytes
Disk label type: msdos
Minor    Start       End     Type      Filesystem  Flags
1          0.031   101.975  primary   ext3        boot
2        101.975  5773.359  primary   ext3
3       5773.359  6149.882  primary   linux-swap
```

6. The print command prints the current disk geometry with the partition information. Note that parted can specify the size of partitions as a size range (0 to about 100MB for partition 1 and roughly 101MB to about 5,773MB for partition 2). This is a marked improvement over some of the earlier programs that required you to manually calculate disk geometry using cylinders, sectors, and so on. Here, you see that you have two extended filesystem partitions and one swap partition:

```
(parted) resize 2 101.975 5000
(parted) print

Disk geometry for /dev/hda: 0.000-6149.882 megabytes
Disk label type: msdos
Minor    Start       End      Type      Filesystem  Flags
1          0.031   101.975  primary   ext3        boot
2        101.975  4996.779  primary   ext3
3       5773.359  6149.882  primary   linux-swap
```

7. The first thing you do is attempt to resize the biggest partition of the three (that is, the second partition), which currently extends from 101.975MB to 5773.359MB. You use the `resize` command by specifying the partition to resize (Partition 2), and the new size range (101.975 to 5,000). With this resizing, you shrink the partition by 773.395MB (that is 5773.359MB to 5000MB). On printing the partition table, the new disk geometry is evident:

```
(parted) mkpartfs primary ext2 4996.779 5773.359
(parted) print

Disk geometry for /dev/hda: 0.000-6149.882 megabytes
Disk label type: msdos
Minor    Start       End      Type      Filesystem  Flags
1          0.031   101.975  primary   ext3        boot
2        101.975  4996.779  primary   ext3
4       4996.780  5773.359  primary   ext2
3       5773.359  6149.882  primary   linux-swap
```

8. You now create a *new* partition, using the space taken from Partition 2. You use the `mkpartfs` command to do this, indicating that this is a primary partition (partitions can be primary, extended, or logical). You also indicate that this is a partition that will house an ext2 filesystem because ext3 is not yet supported by `parted`. You specify the new partition range from 4996.779MB to 5773.359MB. Printing the partition table confirms that the new partition has been created:

```
(parted) rm 4
(parted) resize 2 101.975 5773.359
```

9. Now that you have learned to resize partitions, you can try and restore things to their original state (at the start of this example). Delete the newly created partition using the `rm` command, specifying the partition number of the partition you wish to remove. Finally, resize Partition 2 to its original size:

```
(parted) print
Disk geometry for /dev/hda: 0.000-6149.882 megabytes
Disk label type: msdos
Minor    Start       End      Type      Filesystem  Flags
1          0.031   101.975  primary   ext3        boot
2        101.975  5773.359  primary   ext3
3       5773.359  6149.882  primary   linux-swap
(parted) quit
```

10. The `print` command confirms the latest attempt to resize the partition. When you are done experimenting, exit the parted program using the `quit` command.

Adding a New Hard Disk

Regardless of the hard disk real estate that you start out with, it is very likely that you will run out of disk space before the end of the lifecycle of our machines. When this happens, you will most likely purchase an additional hard disk or replace the current disk with one that has more storage capacity.

When you first installed Fedora 2 on the system, you did not have to bother about explicitly setting up your hard disk—the installer took care of this behind the scenes. But, if you need to add a disk yourself, there are a few manual steps that you need to perform.

Detecting the Hard Disk

After hooking up the new hard disk to the system, and before going any further, it is necessary to ensure that the disk has been recognized by the operating system. Usually, Red Hat's *kudzu* configuration tool will allow you to configure your new hardware when it is detected during the bootup process.

To ensure that the new disk has been recognized, you need to examine the kernel startup messages—you can view these messages with the `dmesg` command. You need to look for detection messages corresponding to your new hard disk. Here is a typical `dmesg` line, which indicates that the new hard disk has been detected:

```
$ dmesg | grep -i maxtor
hdb: Maxtor 90651U2, ATA DISK drive
```

An alternative is to list the contents of `/proc/partitions`, which lists all the currently available partitions, including those that have not yet been mounted. Here is the listing of a typical `/proc/partitions` file. For our purposes, it is sufficient to look for a new row in the table and note the name column, in this case, hdb.

```
$ cat /proc/partitions
major minor #blocks name rio   rmerge rsect  ruse   wio   wmerge wsect  wuse
running use    aveq
22     0      661728 hdb  40    32     280    500    0     0      0      0      -24865
2297424 1939878
 3     0     6297480 hda  17031 21392  305170 253707 11959 16564  228632 422367 -1
6577905 2337991
 3     1      104391 hda1 35    85     240    408    14    6      40     244    0
636     652
 3     2     5807497 hda2 16967 21086  304394 252974 11788 14238  208776 250927 0
188263  503912
 3     3      385560 hda3 9     25     104    146    157   2320   19816  171195 0
3453    171341
```

If there are no kernel startup messages or listings in `/proc/partitions`, it is quite likely that the disk was not detected. There are several possible reasons for the system's failure to detect the disk. To eliminate the possibility of a hardware setup problem, you should check all hardware settings, such as the master–slave mode settings of the hard disk, and compare them with the manufacturer's recommended settings. The detection failure may have occurred because the correct driver is missing from the kernel; this problem can be remedied by recompiling a kernel, or by using a dynamically loadable kernel module that has support for the new hard disk. Chapter 12 has details on how to perform these steps.

Partitioning the Hard Disk

Once the disk has been detected, it is usually assigned a `/dev` name (such as `/dev/hdb`) automatically by the system. After you know what this name is, as you can see in the `dmesg` output or the `/proc/partitions` file, you need to partition the device.

If you intend to create a `swap` partition on this disk, the rule of thumb is to create a partition that is at least two and a half times the size of the available physical RAM. You can use `parted`, `fdisk`, `sfdisk` (or another similar command) to partition the new drive. During the partitioning process, it is necessary to specify the intended filesystem for this hard disk.

Formatting the Hard Disk

After partitioning, the next logical step is to format the disk. The formatting process prepares the partition for a certain filesystem type to create files and directories. During this process, filesystem-specific information may be created on the partitions. Formatting is very much specific to the filesystem that will be installed on the partition. For example, to format the first partition of the `/dev/hdb` disk to use the ext3 filesystem, the following command is used:

```
#  mkfs.ext3 -c /dev/hdb1
```

The `-c` option forces a check for disk errors.

Mounting the Hard Disk

Now that you have partitioned and formatted the disk, it is ready for use and needs to be mounted to a filesystem mount point. For example, suppose you intend to mount the new partition to the directory `/public`. For this, you can use the following command:

```
# mount -t ext3 /dev/hdb1 /public
```

Although this command mounts the partition for now, it is *not* enough to mount the partition automatically when the system reboots. For automatic mounting, you need to add an entry to the `/etc/fstab` file. A typical entry would look like the following:

```
/dev/hdb1            /public                   ext3    defaults         1 1
```

The first entry (`/dev/hdb1`) represents the partition containing the filesystem to be mounted. The second entry (`/public`) represents the directory that this filesystem should be mounted to. The third entry (`ext3`) indicates the filesystem type. The fourth entry indicates the permissions for the device; permissions determine the type of operations that may be performed on the filesystem. In this case, the default permissions (that is, allowing both read and write access) is in effect. The last two entries indicate operating system parameters (dump frequency and parallel `fsck` number) that may be left set to `1`.

The `parted` *command has a* `copy` *command that enables entire filesystems to be copied from one partition to another. This is particularly useful during disk upgrades that involve the replacement of an existing disk with a larger one. It is possible to add the new disk to the system without removing the older disk—possibly in a master–slave configuration. If you want to set this up, you should look at the disk manufacturer's documentation.*

After both disks are hooked up to the system, you can use the `parted copy` *command to copy the old filesystems to the new partitions. Once the copy is complete, the old disk can be removed from the system or reused (even perhaps as a swap disk) on the same system.*

From this point, you can use the `/public` directory (in this case) just like any other directory on the system.

Filesystem Maintenance

To get optimum performance out of the filesystem, and to guard against data corruption, you need to ensure proper maintenance of the system in general, and the filesystem in particular, as it manages the persistent part of the operating system.

Precautions

When it comes to filesystem maintenance, there are a number of simple precautions that help in preventing costly mishaps. It is extremely important that the system be properly shutdown before restarting the machine. On a typical Linux system, a significant part of the filesystem is always being worked on in memory. In fact, if possible, it is a good idea to run the `sync` command before shutting down the machine, as this will flush unwritten filesystem blocks in memory to the disk and avoid boot time filesystem inconsistencies.

As you'll recall from Chapter 1, during the Fedora 2 installation you are prompted to create a boot disk. This is particularly useful if the partition containing the bootable image of the kernel becomes corrupted. With a boot disk, you can boot up to a minimal shell and run diagnostics and repair tools.

If you have important data on your system, it is always a good idea to use some form of backup utility to back up the system periodically. We look at this in more detail in Chapter 11.

Running fsck

Most UNIX filesystem partitions contain a *super block*, which is essentially a bookkeeping section of that partition. When a system is shut down gracefully (that is, without errors), a flag is set to indicate the graceful shutdown. When the system comes up the next time, it examines this flag to see if the shutdown was graceful or not. If not, the system may require you to run diagnostic and repair tools on that partition.

The most popular diagnostics and repair utility on Linux (and in the UNIX world) is `fsck`. Running `fsck` with the `y` option allows it to proceed with any repairs that need to be performed in the course of diagnostic analysis. The `N` option to `fsck` performs a dry run; the actual repair routines are not performed, but only printed out. Here is a typical output with the `N` option on a partition with a corrupted superblock.

```
$ /sbin/fsck -N /dev/hda
fsck 1.27 (8-Mar-2002)
[/sbin/fsck.ext3 (1) -- /dev/had] fsck.ext3 /dev/hda
$ /sbin/fsck -y /dev/hda
```

```
fsck 1.27 (8-Mar-2002)
e2fsck 1.27 (8-Mar-2002)
Couldn't find ext3 superblock, trying backup blocks...
fsck.ext3: Bad magic number in super-block while trying to open /dev/hda

The superblock could not be read or does not describe a correct ext3
filesystem.  If the device is valid and it really contains an ext3
filesystem (and not swap or ufs or something else), then the superblock
is corrupt, and you might try running e2fsck with an alternate superblock:
    e2fsck -b 8193 <device>
```

Tuning the Filesystem

The `tune2fs` command allows you to set various tunable parameters on the ext2 filesystem partitions. It is commonly used to control the frequency at which `fsck` is automatically run on a filesystem:

- The `fsck` utility can be run once every few days, weeks, or months by specifying the `-i` option. For example, the following command would force an execution of `fsck` once every two weeks:

```
$ tune2fs -i 2w
```

- The `-c` option controls the running of `fsck` based on the number of reboots. For example, `-c 10` indicates that `fsck` will be run once in every ten system reboots.

```
$ tune2fs -c 10
```

Note that these settings also apply to an ext3 filesystem.

Summary

This chapter explored the Fedora 2 filesystem in detail. In summary, the focus was on the following areas:

- Filesystem concepts and the need for a filesystem.
- The various attributes of a file, such as the types of files, ownership, permissions, access privileges, timestamps, file sizes, and filenames. We examined the differences between hard and soft links.
- Various utilities, such as `find` and `locate`, to search for files on the filesystem, and utilities, such as `awk` and `sed`, used in conjunction with `xargs` and the `find` command to search for strings in files.
- The organization of the filesystem in terms of directories, configuration files, and executables.
- Creating and formatting partitions and filesystems, and mounting filesystems on to directories on the system.

You also learned how to add a new hard disk to the system, as well as format and partition it correctly; and, finally, the topics of maintaining the filesystem by taking certain precautions were also discussed, as well as diagnosing and repairing filesystems using `fsck` and tuning the filesystem using `tune2fs`.

The next chapter takes a closer look at how Linux deals with users, groups, permissions, and related issues.

Exercises

Now that you have spent some time exploring various aspects of the filesystem, try out the following exercises to reinforce your understanding:

1. Calculate the size of all files under the `/etc` directory.
2. Create a file called `story.txt` containing the following line of text:

   ```
   The quick brown fox jumps over the lazy dog
   ```

   Use the `sed` command to change the contents of the file to the following:

   ```
   The quick brown dog jumps over the lazy fox
   ```

3. Use the `find` command to list files that are greater than 500KB in size created by users of the system.

6

The Shell

Before graphical user interfaces came into vogue, the only way to interact with an operating system was via the *command line shell* (often known simply as the *shell*). The shell allows users to type in commands for the operating system and the operating system to display the output that results from the execution of these commands.

Despite the rise of GUIs such as GNOME and KDE and predictions of the complete demise of the command line shell, the shell has held steady as the user interface of choice for a large number of users—sometimes as a last resort when the GUI fails, but often simply because it is a very flexible and powerful tool. In fact, the shell has evolved into a tool that allows users to do pretty much *all* that can be done using the operating system, and far beyond what a GUI would permit.

This chapter discusses the following:

- The command line shell and its background
- Shell commands, shortcut keys, and aliases
- The command line syntax
- Managing multiple tasks at the same time
- Using the shell as a scripting language

The Shell as a Command Line Interface

An operating system such as the Linux kernel consists of code written mostly in the low-level programming language C. The kernel is loaded into memory at the time the machine boots up, and sits there awaiting instructions.

You can pass instructions to the kernel in a number of ways. One of the most important is to write programs that interact with it—once a program is written, you can compile and execute it to accomplish the task.

Because programs written to interact with the kernel often have several tasks in common, there is usually a library of these common tasks, which is a collection of C subroutines (or functions) organized into a library. This is simply known as the *C library* (*libc*). While programs that use the C library are powerful and flexible, it is often cumbersome, if not downright impractical, to write a program, compile it, and run it every time you need to do something as simple as copying a file.

What Is the Shell?

The shell is a *declarative and parameterized* mechanism for executing common tasks. What this means is that the shell allows you to execute programs that are generic enough to take parameters. For example, by using the file copy program `cp` and supplying a source file and a destination file as parameters (also known as arguments), it is possible to copy a file from one location to another in the filesystem. The power of the shell comes from the wide gamut of programs that can be executed from it. These programs are commonly known as *UNIX commands*. As you might have guessed by now, the shell itself is just another program.

In addition to allowing you to simply execute commands, the shell enables you to *manage* the execution of commands. It allows users to define shortcuts and abbreviations to refer to these commands and even to serve as a handy tool for knitting together commands to create conglomerates that function as new commands (they're called scripts).

In terms of flexibility, performance, task automation, and repetitive processing of tasks, the shell in the hands of a knowledgeable user still beats a GUI hands down.

Different Types of Shell

The earliest versions of UNIX came with what is today known as the *Bourne shell* (`sh`), named after its inventor, Steve Bourne. Since then, a variety of shell flavors have emerged. However, the core functionality and basic syntax of all of these shells has changed very little.

The *C-shell* (`csh`), distributed as part of BSD UNIX, was the next popular version of the shell to arrive. The C-shell syntax resembles the C programming language (particularly when it comes to writing shell scripts), hence its name. This aspect of the C-shell was intended to popularize it among the UNIX users, who at that time were largely C programmers.

Other popular shells soon arrived, each with more features than the last, and all were backward compatible for the most part. Among them were the *Korn shell* (or `ksh`), which was written by David Korn of AT&T Bell Laboratories, and *tcsh* or the C-shell with command-completion features—that is, the shell "intuitively" completes the commands when you type them in.

The *Born Again shell* (*Bash*) is one of the newer versions of the shell, and is almost completely compatible with its ancestor, the Bourne shell.

Most UNIX systems have `sh` available apart from a preferred flavor of the shell for that UNIX system. In fact, some UNIX systems make several shells available, and the user can switch between them at will. As far as Linux (and therefore Fedora Core 2) is concerned, Bash is the preferred shell, although users may switch to other shell flavors (for example, you can switch to the C-shell by typing **csh** at the Bash prompt). The choice of a shell is often dictated by personal preference, sometimes by the fact that a user started off with a particular version, or sometimes, as in the case of the C-shell, the programming language the user is most comfortable with. This chapter uses the default shell, Bash, to illustrate various features of the shell.

You can figure out what your current shell is by typing the `ps` command in any terminal window at the command prompt. The `ps` command lists the processes—that is, the currently executing programs on your system:

The command prompt is depicted as `$` for brevity; it is usually [user@localhost current directory] by default. You'll learn more about setting the prompt later in this chapter.

```
$ ps
  PID TTY          TIME CMD
 5355 pts/0    00:00:00 bash
 5381 pts/0    00:00:00 ps
```

On executing the `ps` command, you should see an output similar to the one shown. On the last column of the second line of the output you see `bash`. If you were to switch to a different shell, such as `csh`, you would see `csh` in the output beside the Bash shell, which was used to launch it. Try it out by typing **csh**, followed by **ps**. (You look at the `ps` command in more detail in the next section.)

```
$ csh
% ps
  PID TTY          TIME CMD
 5355 pts/0    00:00:00 bash
 5389 pts/0    00:00:00 csh
 5409 pts/0    00:00:00 ps
```

Note that the prompt changed to a percentage sign (`%`) indicating that the current shell is C-shell. It should also be noted that "switching" to another shell doesn't mean you actually exit Bash and start `csh`; rather you use `bash` as the launch pad to start another shell, in this case `csh`.

You can, however, explicitly exit a shell. This can be achieved by using the `exit` command.

```
$ csh
% ps
  PID TTY          TIME CMD
 5355 pts/0    00:00:00 bash
 5389 pts/0    00:00:00 csh
 5409 pts/0    00:00:00 ps
% exit
$ ps
  PID TTY          TIME CMD
 5355 pts/0    00:00:00 bash
 5409 pts/0    00:00:00 ps
```

Note that after you execute the `exit` command, the command-prompt changes back to that of Bash. Also, the `ps` program does not list the C-shell any more because the C-shell terminated due to the `exit` command.

Built-in Programs and External Programs

Two different types of command can be executed from a shell. They are *built-in programs* and *external programs*:

- Built-in programs are inherently built into the shell:
    - All shells share a common set of built-in programs, such as the `cd` command, which enables you to change directory.
    - In addition, there are other built-in commands that are specific to *certain* flavors of the shell. For example, the amend method for setting environment variables usually varies from one flavor of the shell to another (more on setting environment variables later in this chapter).
- External commands are those that are independent of the flavor of shell. They can be executed from any shell and yield more or less the same result. For example, the `date` command would output the date no matter what shell it is executed from.

For the purpose of our discussion, we shall refer to both built-in commands and external commands by the generic term, *command.*

Of course, when you're working within a particular shell, you can use only the built-in commands that are valid for that flavor of shell. As you'll see in the "Shell Scripting" section towards the end of this chapter, this is particularly important when you write a shell script, a file that contains a sequence of shell commands. If you run a shell script within a particular shell, it should contain only commands that are valid for the shell in question.

To this end, it is useful to be able to check whether a given command is a built-in or an external command. For this, you can use the `type` command. This command tells you whether it is a built-in command within the current shell, or (if it is an external program) the location of the command.

For example, in the Bash shell, if you use `type` to query the nature of the `date` and `cd` commands, you'll find that the former is external and the latter is built-in:

```
$ type date
date is /bin/date
$ type cd
cd is a shell builtin
```

Shell scripts are discussed in detail in the "Shell Scripting" section of this chapter.

Some Common Shell Commands

This section examines some of the commands that you can use to find your way around Fedora Core 2 using the command line shell. There are different categories of commands:

- **Filesystem commands**: Used for navigating and manipulating the filesystem
- **Process management commands**: Used to manage processes
- **Administrative commands**: Used to perform various administrative tasks on the system

This section takes a look at these three categories of commands and examines some frequently used examples of each.

Filesystem Commands

Filesystem commands allow you to access and manipulate various parts of the UNIX filesystem tree. In UNIX, the filesystem is organized as a tree structure, in much the same way as in other operating systems (each directory can contain files and subdirectories). For each machine, there is always one *root directory*; this is the topmost directory, and contains subdirectories and files. Refer to the root directory by using the forward slash (`/`).

From this basic structure, there are a number of tasks that you may need to do, such as changing the working directory, establishing the contents of a particular directory, or creating, copying, moving, and deleting files and directories.

Changing and Establishing the Working Directory

The *working directory* is the directory you're currently working in. To change the working directory (that is, to select a particular directory to be the working directory), you use the `cd` (change directory) command.

For example, to select the root directory to be the working directory, you would type the following:

```
$ cd /
```

To select the directory `/home/deepakt` (the home directory of the user `deepakt`) to be the working directory, you could type this:

```
$ cd /home/deepakt
```

Absolute and Relative Paths

In both of the preceding examples, you've specified the absolute path of the directory in question. You can also use relative paths. For example, if you wanted to change the working directory from `/home/deepakt` to its parent directory, `/home`, you could use the absolute path, like this:

```
$ cd /home
```

Or use the relative path, like this:

```
$ cd ..
```

You can use `cd` to change the working directory to any directory that the system allows you to. If you use the `cd` command with no arguments, it will always set the working directory to be the directory that you logged into (often this is `/home/`*`<username>`*).

This is different from the Microsoft DOS command prompt, where the `cd` command with no arguments merely prints the absolute path of the present directory.

Determining the Working Directory

Now comes the question of how to determine your current directory. For this, you use the `pwd` (print working directory) command, which outputs the absolute path of the present working directory. For example:

```
$ cd /home/deepakt
$ pwd
/home/deepakt
```

Listing the Contents of a Directory

You can list the contents of a directory by using the `ls` (list directory contents) command. If you don't specify a directory, `ls` will list the contents of the present working directory:

```
$ ls -al
total 288
drwxr-xr-x    3 deepakt users        4096 Jan 16 14:29 .
drwxr-xr-x   11 deepakt users       16384 Jan 16 14:27 ..
-rw-r--r--    1 deepakt users       49714 Jan 16 14:27 f.html
-rw-r--r--    1 deepakt users       22696 Jan 16 14:29 ff.html
drwxr-xr-x    2 deepakt users           0 Jan 16 17:10 foo
-rw-r--r--    1 deepakt users      131498 Jan 16 14:20 showthread.php.html
```

The `ls` command has a multitude of options. The preceding example uses two options:

- The `-l` option requests that the output is the "long form"—that is, with more details than just the name of the file.
- The `-a` option lists all the files, including those beginning with a dot (`.`). Files beginning with a dot are usually configuration files. For those familiar with Microsoft operating systems, they are vaguely analogous to hidden files in DOS.

As discussed in Chapter 5, each item in the output is either a file or a directory; a directory is denoted by a `d` *in the first position of the 10-character code in the first column. In the output, there are three directories listed:* `foo`*, the present working directory (denoted* `.`*), and the parent directory (denoted* `..`*).*

Creating, Moving, and Removing Files and Directories

When it comes to creation and removal, directories and files are handled differently, so we'll take a couple of subsections to explain.

Creating and Removing Directories

You use `mkdir` (make directory) and `rmdir` (remove directory), respectively, to create or remove directories. The following example creates a subdirectory under the present working directory, called `grapple`:

```
$ mkdir grapple
```

You can also create an entire hierarchy of directories at one go. To do this, use the `-p` option. For example, the following command creates the directory `4wds` (as a subdirectory of the `vehicles/cars` directory), but it *also* creates the `vehicles` and `cars` directories if they do not already exist:

```
$ mkdir -p vehicles/cars/4wds
```

By default, the `rmdir` command can remove only an empty directory, that is, one that has no files in it. This is designed to help you avoid deleting files that you didn't necessarily know were there:

```
$ rmdir grapple
```

To remove a directory and its contents recursively including the subdirectories, you can use the `rm -r` command:

```
$ rm -r vehicles
```

Creating and Removing Files

A quick way to create a file is to use the `touch` command. The actual purpose of the `touch` command is to update the timestamp of an existing file (the idea being that if you touch the file, the OS should update its timestamp). A side effect of this is that if you specify the path of a file that does not yet exist, Linux also creates an empty file:

```
$ touch tigers.txt
```

To remove a file, use the `rm` (remove) command:

```
$ rm tigers.txt
```

Moving Files and Directories

To move a file or directory, use the `mv` (move) command. This requires two arguments: the file or directory to be moved, and the destination:

```
$ mv squidgy.txt squeezy.txt
```

This is a classic example of moving a file. It uses `mv` not to move the file to a different directory, but simply to *change the name* of the file. In Linux, "moving" a file really means changing its path.

It's also possible to move multiple files at the same time. For example, the following command moves the files `squeezy.txt` and `stodgy.txt` from the present working directory to the directory `/etc/textures`:

```
mv squeezy.txt stodgy.txt /etc/textures
```

Try It Out Creating, Moving, and Removing Files and Directories

Let's step through a simple example in which you create a directory with a file in it, and then rename the file. After you are done experimenting, you will clean everything up by deleting both the file and the directory.

1. Change the present working directory to your home directory. For example, if you were logged in with the username `deepakt`, you would simply type this:

```
$ cd
```

2. Just to check that the first step worked, use pwd to check the present working directory:

```
$ pwd
/home/deepakt
```

3. Now create a subdirectory called test, and make it the working directory:

```
$ mkdir test
$ cd test
```

4. Now create a new file called nomme.txt:

```
$ touch nomme.txt
```

5. To prove that the touch command really did create a new file, you can use the ls command to list the contents of the test directory:

```
$ ls -al
total 4
drwxr-xr-x    2 deepakt users           0 Jan 16 17:29 .
drwxr-xr-x    3 deepakt users        4096 Jan 16 17:29 ..
-rw-r--r--    1 deepakt users           0 Jan 16 17:29 nomme.txt
```

6. Now use mv to change the name of the file, and use ls again to check the change:

```
$ mv nomme.txt name.txt; ls -al
total 4
drwxr-xr-x    2 deepakt users           0 Jan 16 17:29 .
drwxr-xr-x    3 deepakt users        4096 Jan 16 17:29 ..
-rw-r--r--    1 deepakt users           0 Jan 16 17:29 name.txt
```

Note that we used a semicolon (;) after the mv *command and typed in the* ls *command. A semicolon is used to separate multiple commands on the same line.*

7. Next, to start the cleanup, use rm to remove the file name.txt, and use ls to check it:

```
$ rm name.txt
$ ls -al
total 4
drwxr-xr-x    2 deepakt users           0 Jan 16 17:29 .
drwxr-xr-x    3 deepakt users        4096 Jan 16 17:29 ..
```

8. Now move back to the parent directory (that is, make your user's home directory the working directory):

```
$ cd ..
$ pwd
/home/deepakt
```

9. Finally, remove the test directory that you created right at the beginning:

```
$ rmdir test
```

Summary of Filesystem Commands

The following table provides a quick summary of common commands necessary for getting around the filesystem:

Command	Description
`cd`	Change directory. Without arguments, this command changes the current working directory to the user's home directory. When a directory name is supplied as an argument, it changes the current working directory to that directory.
`pwd`	Prints the current working directory.
`mkdir`	Creates new directories. Creates one or more directories as specified by arguments to this command. When a hierarchy is specified, the `-p` option creates intermediate directories if they are missing.
`rmdir`	Removes an empty directory.
`cat`	Concatenates the contents of a file. May be used in conjunction with the > operator to create a file or the >> operator to append to a file (see the sub-section on "I/O Redirection" under the "Command-Line Syntax" section for details).
`rm`	Removes a file. The `-i` option prompts the user to confirm whether to proceed with deletion. The `-f` option is the silent remove option. It attempts to remove the file without seeking confirmation; if it is unsuccessful in removing the file, it does not report an error.
`mv`	Moves one or more files or directories supplied as arguments to another directory.
`ls`	Lists the contents of one or more directories supplied as arguments to it. The `-l` option lists the details of a file. The `--color` option lists files with color-coding describing the type of file. The `-t` option lists the timestamps of files and directories. The `-R` option recursively lists the contents of a directory. Several of the important `ls` options to `ls` were discussed in the previous chapter.
`touch`	Modifies the timestamp of files or directories supplied as arguments. If a specified argument does not exist, `touch` creates an empty file by that name in the current directory.

Process Management Commands

UNIX (and therefore Linux) has processes that are essentially tasks running on the operating system infrastructure. Each time a command is invoked, the invocation results in one or more *processes* being spawned. Processes belong to users, and in general are insulated from one another. Often, the only time general users of the system are concerned with processes is when one refuses to respond; this is commonly referred to as a *program hang*.

Listing Processes

To list the current processes spawned that are started from a particular shell or its parent shell, you can use the ps (processes spawned) command:

```
$ ps
PID TTY          TIME CMD
 5355 pts/0    00:00:00 bash
 5381 pts/0    00:00:00 ps
```

To list *all* the processes on the system, you can use the ps command with the -A option:

```
$ ps -A
  PID TTY          TIME CMD
    1 ?        00:00:04 init
    2 ?        00:00:00 keventd
    3 ?        00:00:03 kapmd
    4 ?        00:00:00 ksoftirqd_CPU0
    5 ?        00:00:03 kswapd
    6 ?        00:00:00 bdflush
    7 ?        00:00:00 kupdated
    8 ?        00:00:00 mdrecoveryd
    ...
```

Note that this option is case-sensitive.

Getting the Complete Command Line

Processes represent commands that were executed. But what ps does not tell you (at least not easily) is what the complete command line was when the process was invoked. Sometimes, you need to know what arguments were passed to the command and what options were invoked. To see the complete command line of a process with the name of the owner of the process , you can coax the ps command with the -auxww options:

```
$ ps -auxww

USER       PID %CPU %MEM   VSZ  RSS TTY      STAT START   TIME COMMAND
root         1  0.0  0.2  1336  428 ?        S    Jan15   0:04 init
...
root       449  0.0  0.3  2056  756 ?        S    Jan15   0:00 /sbin/dhclient -1 -q
-lf /var/lib/dhcp/dhclient-eth0.leases -pf /var/run/dhclient-eth0.pid -cf
/etc/dhclient-eth0.conf eth0
root       619  0.0  0.2  1328  412 ?        S    Jan15   0:00 /usr/sbin/apmd -p 10
-w 5 -W -P /etc/sysconfig/apm-scripts/apmscript
ident      657  0.0  0.3 27032  708 ?        S    Jan15   0:00 identd
root       671  0.0  0.4  3276  860 ?        S    Jan15   0:00 /usr/sbin/sshd
root       685  0.0  0.3  2096  752 ?        S    Jan15   0:00 xinetd -stayalive -
reuse -pidfile /var/run/xinetd.pid
deepakt   5270  0.0  3.1 16436 5952 ?        S    12:03   0:04 /usr/bin/gnome-
session
deepakt   5313  0.0  0.3  2900  724 ?        S    12:03   0:00 /usr/bin/ssh-agent
/etc/X11/xinit/Xclients
```

Now, the final column gives the complete command used. For example, the lines shown in bold show the complete command used to invoke the DHCP client daemon. What you should note in all of these cases is the presence of the `PID` column. The *Process ID (PID)* number is used to uniquely identify a process at any given time.

Terminating a Process

You can use the `kill` command to send a signal to a process by specifying the signal to be sent and the Process ID. The signal that most general users are interested in is the `SIGTERM` signal, which terminates the process. This is particularly useful for dealing with a process that is hanging or has run amok:

```
$ ps
PID TTY          TIME CMD
 5355 pts/0    00:00:00 bash
 5365 pts/0    00:00:00 haywire
 5381 pts/0    00:00:00 ps
$ kill -s SIGTERM 5365
$ ps
PID TTY          TIME CMD
 5355 pts/0    00:00:00 bash
 5381 pts/0    00:00:00 ps
```

The `SIGTERM` signal can be *handled* by processes. In other words, it allows processes to *clean up* before exiting; for example, the process may want to close the files it has opened before exiting. If the safer option of `SIGTERM` does not work, you can resort to `SIGKILL`. The `SIGKILL` signal forces a process to terminate immediately—it does not allow it to exit gracefully. The `man 7 signal` command lists and describes the complete set of signals.

Watching System Processes

The `top` command allows you to see which processes consume maximum resources on the system (see Figure 6-1). The `top` command refreshes the screen periodically because the resource consumption on a system usually fluctuates rapidly.

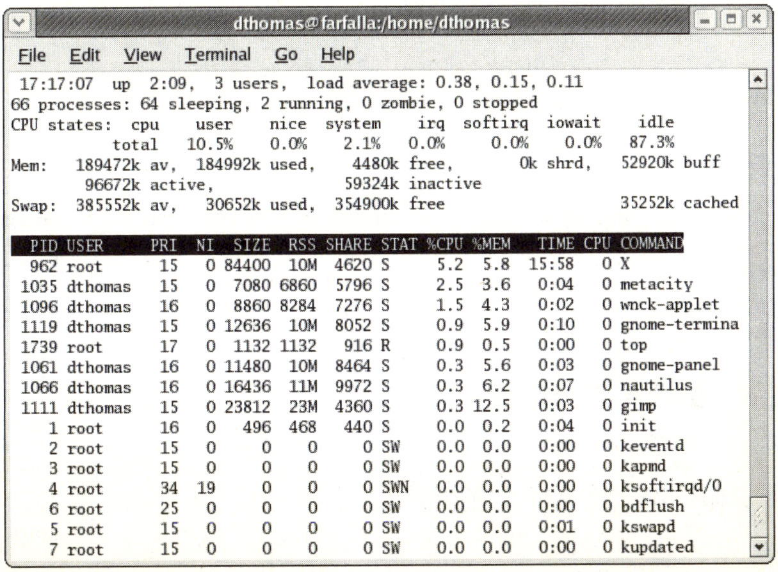

Figure 6-1

Administrative Commands

It is Linux's administrative commands that set it apart from GUI-based operating systems. These commands are as numerous as they are powerful. This section examines only the most important administrative commands (in terms of day-to-day use). More commands will be introduced in later chapters, especially in Chapter 11.

Switching Identities

For day-to-day activity on your Linux system, it's generally a good idea to log in using a regular user account—that is, one that has no administrative privileges. (For example, this protects you from the dangers of accidentally deleting or changing important files and configuration.)

However, to perform certain privileged tasks, such as shutting down the system, you need to assume the identity of an administrator (or root user, in UNIX parlance). In these situations, it's rather inconvenient to have to log out of the system and log back in as a root user. There is a simpler alternative—you can use the `su` command (with no arguments) and supply the root user's password. This provides you with a shell that has the privileges of the root user. When you've completed your administrative tasks, you can switch back to the safety of non-admin privileges by exiting the root shell by typing **exit** or *Ctrl+D*.

The `su` command can also be used to switch identities between two non-root users. The `id` command prints the current user ID of the user:

```
$ id
uid=500(brucewayne) gid=513(users) groups=513(users)
$ su
Password:
bash# id
uid=0(root) gid=0(root) groups=0(root), 1(bin), 2(daemon)
bash# exit
$ id
uid=500(brucewayne) gid=513(users) groups=513(users)
$ su batman
Password:
$ id
uid=800(batman) gid=513(users) groups=513(users)
```

The `uid` field indicates the user ID of the user, which is a unique number, assigned to each and every user on the system. The `gid` is the group ID of the *primary group* that a user belongs to. A group is essentially a collection of users who have some common set of privileges. For example, all members of the engineering group may have access to the blueprints directory on a machine. Each user belongs to at least one group, which is known as the primary group. In addition, they may also belong to other groups as indicated by the `groups` field. Groups, such as `users`, have a number associated with them; in the preceding code, `513` denotes the group ID of the `users` group.

Shutting Down and Rebooting

The `shutdown` command shuts down the system. This command is restricted to root users only. Shutdown can be immediate (in which case the `now` argument is passed), or it can be delayed (by *n* seconds by passing the `-t` *n* option).

If you need to reboot rather than shut down the system, the `reboot` command comes in handy. It is usually a good idea to run the `sync` command before rebooting or shutting down the system. The `sync` command ensures that filesystem objects are in a consistent state.

Disk Usage

The `df` command displays a partition-by-partition summary of disk usage. You can supply arguments such as `-k` to indicate to `df` that it should report disk usage in increments of kilobytes, as shown here:

```
$ df -k
Filesystem           1K-blocks      Used Available Use% Mounted on
/dev/hda2              5716172   3424988   2000812  64% /
/dev/hda1               101089     19137     76733  20% /boot
none                     94752         0     94752   0% /dev/shm
/dev/cdrom              659488    659488         0 100% /mnt/cdrom
```

The `Available` column indicates remaining disk space. In this case, roughly 2GB of disk space remains free on the root partition.

Mounting Disks and Media

Often, you need to read from CD-ROM discs, and to read from and write to floppy disks. Because Linux treats all peripheral devices as filesystems, you must *mount* or associate these physical devices to a filesystem *mount point*—essentially a directory. The `mount` command can be used to mount such media. You must have root user privileges to mount and unmount devices.

Here's an example. Start by trying to use `ls` to list the contents of `/mnt/cdrom`:

```
# ls /mnt/cdrom
```

At this stage, no files are listed because there is no device associated with the `/mnt/cdrom` mount point. Now put a disc in, mount the CD-ROM device to the `/mnt/cdrom` mount point, and list the contents again:

```
# mount /dev/cdrom /mnt/cdrom
# ls /mnt/cdrom
Fedora
Autorun
README
```

The exact listing you get depends on which CD is in your CD-ROM drive.

The complementary command is the `umount` command, which *disassociates* a device from a filesystem mount point:

```
# umount /mnt/cdrom
```

The `eject` command is also handy for CD-ROM devices because it unmounts the device and pops the tray open (on condition that the underlying CD-ROM drive supports this operation).

As you saw in the previous chapter, when you insert a CD into the drive Fedora automatically mounts the CD. The preceding commands may be used to do this manually.

Listing Users

Often, administrators (and even regular users) need to see the list of users currently logged on to the system. (This is a little counterintuitive to users familiar with desktop operating systems because the UNIX model allows users to connect to a system remotely using programs such as `telnet` and `rlogin`.)

You can achieve this with the `who` command, which lists all users currently logged on to a machine:

```
# who
deepakt      :0               Jan 13 12:03
hbatman      192.168.1.100    Jan 11 11:30
```

The `finger` command goes one step further, listing users logged on to a remote system somewhere on the network. For `finger` to work, the remote server should have the `fingerd` daemon running; this is becoming rarer by the day in these times of increased system security.

Special Keys and Shortcuts

The Bash shell comes with numerous special keys and clever shortcuts, which are designed to make your life at the keyboard faster and more efficient. Some of these control process execution, while others simply make it easier to enter your next command.

Control Keystrokes

Many of the following keystrokes are used to interrupt the execution of a process:

- *Ctrl+C* sends a `SIGINT` signal to the currently executing process, causing the process to be interrupted from whatever it was doing. This is useful when a program runs into a condition such as an infinite loop and you decide to terminate the execution of the command.
- *Ctrl+* sends a `SIGSEGV` signal to the currently executing process. By default, the `SIGSEGV` signal causes a process to write the memory image of itself to the disk, often to a file called `core`. Some programmers find this useful because it allows them to interrupt execution of a (possibly faulty) program and then examine its memory image in the core file—and thus determine what the program was doing.

  At other times, *Ctrl+* comes in handy while attempting to terminate programs that do not terminate on *Ctrl+C*. Such programs may actually be handling the `SIGINT` signal for a legitimate purpose, but in a hang state, this prevents the graceful termination of the process.
- *Ctrl+Z* is used to suspend a process that is currently executing. This causes the process to relinquish control, and the shell prompt is returned. This behavior is explored further in the "Job Control" section later in this chapter.
- *Ctrl+D* is used to indicate the end of input. For example, if a program was coded to read in data until it encountered an end-of-file condition, *Ctrl+D* can be used to simulate the end-of-file when a user is typing in the input for the program.

  The classic example for this is the shell itself. If you type *Ctrl+D* at the command prompt, the shell assumes that you have reached the end of your input into the shell, and that you have decided to exit. In fact, for the shell, *Ctrl+D* is synonymous with the `exit` command.

- *Ctrl+V* does not have anything to do with process management, but it is used to input literal values of *Ctrl* keystrokes. For example, if you need to type the character corresponding to *Ctrl+D*, you would type *Ctrl+V* and *Ctrl+D*.
- The erase keystrokes (*Ctrl+W* and *Ctrl+U*) come in handy when editing the command line (a topic covered in the next section of this chapter). *Ctrl+W* erases the entire word to the left of the cursor, and *Ctrl+U* erases everything to the left of the cursor.
- The navigation keystrokes (*Ctrl+A* and *Ctrl+E*) move the cursor to the start and end of the command line, respectively.
- *Ctrl+R* can be used to invoke an interactive search of the history.

Cursor Keys

The *cursor keys* are those that allow you to manipulate the shell's input cursor. Using the *Up* and *Down* arrow keys, it is possible to scroll through a history of commands that were executed, and execute them again (the *Up* arrow key allows you to scroll backward through the history of commands, while the *Down* arrow key allows you to scroll forward through them).

Often, you want to execute a command that is only slightly different from a previous command. In this case, you can use the *Up* and *Down* arrow keys to retrieve the previous command, and then use a number of different keys to position the cursor and edit the command:

- You can use the *Left* and *Right* arrow keys to position the input cursor within the command.
- As previously mentioned, you can also use *Ctrl+A* to jump to the start of the command line and *Ctrl+E* to jump to the end.
- You can use the *Backspace* key to delete characters, and enter new characters simply by typing them in.
- When you are finished, press *Enter* to execute the command.

The history Command

While we're on the subject of the command history, it's worth taking a look at the `history` command. The `history` command prints a history of the commands executed, with a sequential number next to each command in the history:

```
$ history
    1  ls -al
    2  date
    3  pwd
    4  who
    5  touch cellar/maze/labyrinth/passage/foo.txt
$ !2
date
Tue Jan 14 23:03:43  2003
$
```

A previous command at position *n* can be referred to as `!`*n*. So, to execute the `date` command again, you could simply type in `!2` (as shown in the example). While this does not sound like much of a saving, it is a great help when you're working with very lengthy commands.

Other Related Keyboard Shortcuts from the Shell's History

Here are some more useful shortcuts that can be used to invoke commands from the history:

- The double exclamation mark (`!!`) has the effect of telling Bash to execute the last command once again. For example, if you execute the `date` command, and then enter `!!`, the `date` command will be executed again:

```
$ date
Tue Jan 14 23:03:43  2003
$ !!
Tue Jan 14 23:03:45  2003
```

- An exclamation mark (`!`), followed by some text, has the effect of executing the command from the shell's history that begins with that text and has the closest match to it. For example, given the history of five commands shown previously, the command `!p` would result in the `pwd` command being executed. If there was another command starting with the letter `p` in the history (for example, `ps`), you would have to supply a closer match (such as `!pw`) to execute the `pwd` command.
- The `!$` shortcut allows you to reuse the last argument of the previous command. For example, in the fifth command of the previously listed history, a file named `foo.txt` has been created under a deep directory structure. Suppose that you wanted to remove it immediately after; you could do this by typing in `rm !$` as the next command:

```
$ touch cellar/maze/labyrinth/passage/foo.txt
$ rm !$
rm cellar/maze/labyrinth/passage/foo.txt
$
```

The Bash shell automatically substitutes `!$` with the last argument of the previous command, so that the `rm` command shown with the gray background here is equivalent to the one shown with the white background after it.

- An extension of the `!$` shortcut is the `!*` shortcut. This simply translates into *all* of the arguments of the previous command. For example, the following commands create two files and then delete them again:

```
$ touch foo.txt bar.txt
$ rm !*
rm foo.txt bar.txt
$
```

- As mentioned previously, the *Ctrl+R* keystroke can be used to invoke an interactive search of the history. After typing in *Ctrl+R*, you could type in the minimal set of characters that uniquely match the start of a command in history:

```
$ history
    1  ls -al
    2  date
    3  pwd
    4  ps
    5  touch cellar/maze/labyrinth/passage/foo.txt
$ Ctrl-R
(reverse-i-search)'pw': pwd
```

The act of typing in the letters pw uniquely matches the pwd command, successfully distinguishing it from the ps command, which also starts with the letter p.

Auto-Completion

The previous section looked at shortcuts that help to quickly ferret out commands from the history and execute them as such or modify them before executing them. This section explores shortcuts to reference commands and objects in the filesystem. The *Tab* key is your ally in this quest.

Command Completion

To appreciate command completion, you first need to understand how, when you type in a command at the prompt, the shell knows where to look for that command on the filesystem. For example, when you type in the date command, the shell seems to know that you are referring to the date program residing in the /bin directory.

In fact, when Bash starts up, it consults a *startup script*. The startup script contains an environment variable called PATH, the value of which is a list of directories that contain programs. Then, when you type in a command and press *Enter*, Bash automatically searches the directories in this list, in an attempt to locate a program whose name is the same as the command you typed in.

We'll discuss environment variables and startup variables more as we progress through the chapter.

If you type in just the first few letters of a command at the Bash prompt, and then press the *Tab* key, Bash starts searching the PATH (the list of directories) for a unique command that matches the starting letters that you typed in:

- If it finds an exact match, it completes the command automatically:

```
$ da<Tab>
date
Tue Jan 14 23:03:43 2003
```

- If it finds *more* than one match, it beeps and awaits user input. If you press the *Tab* key again, it displays a list of all matches. At this point, you need to type in more letters and hit the *Tab* key again to narrow down the search to the command that you are interested in:

```
$ ta<Tab>
tac tack tail talk tar
tal<Tab>
$ talk
```

- If Bash does not find a single match, it simply beeps every time you press the *Tab* key. So, going by the previous cases, if Bash beeps twice in a row with no choices to display, it is trying to tell you that it found no match for what you typed in.

Filename Completion

Apart from automatically matching and completing the commands to be executed, Bash also features automatic completion of the names of files and directories. For example, the following creates two directories called cistern and cavern, and a file called water.txt. Then, the third command moves the file into the `cistern` directory using the `mv` command, by specifying just enough of the `cistern` directory name followed by the *Tab* key:

```
$ mkdir cistern cavern
$ touch water.txt
$ mv water.txt ci<Tab>stern
```

The *Tab* keystroke causes Bash to look for a unique match and, in this case, it finds one—the `cistern` directory—and thus completes the directory name.

The same rule applies to files, too. The first command here changes the working directory to `cistern`, and the second removes the file `water.txt` (which you specify simply by typing `w` and letting *Tab* and the shell do the rest):

```
$ cd ci<Tab>stern
$ rm w<Tab>ater.txt
```

Command Line Syntax

So far, this chapter has explored techniques that facilitate working with Bash. This section explores the syntax of the command line, including details of what makes Bash such an expressive interface to the operating system. This section also contains several building block concepts that you will use when you program using the shell in the last section.

File Globbing

Often, you want to deal with not one but several files at a time; for example, perhaps you want to copy all the files in a directory to another directory, or you want to copy just a group of files with a certain extension into another directory. To do this, you need a way to address files (and directories) as a group, based on certain characteristics of their names. This is where *file globbing* comes in. *File globbing* is a loose term that describes the technique of grouping files together using simple wildcard or metacharacter expressions.

Three metacharacters are available:

- The asterisk (`*`) represents zero or more matches of any characters.
- The question mark (`?`) represents a match of exactly one character.
- The square brackets (`[ ]`) match any one of the characters between them. The characters to match may also be specified as a hyphen-separated range of characters to match against.

You can also use the exclamation mark (`!`). When you apply `!` to an expression, it indicates that you are looking for the complement of the expression match resulting from the parentheses metacharacters (that is, all results *except* those that match the expression).

Try It Out File Globbing

Perhaps the easiest way to understand the type of things that file globbing allows you to do is to look at an example. So, in this example you create a number of files and then use different globbing expressions to select different subsets of the files for listing.

1. Create a temporary folder called `numberfiles`, and then set it to be the current working directory:

```
$ mkdir /home/<username>/numberfiles
$ cd /home/<username>/numberfiles
```

2. Now create ten files, named after the Italian words for the numbers 1 to 10. Use the `touch` command to do this:

```
$ touch uno due tre quattro cinque sei sette otto nove dieci
```

Use the `ls` command just to list them all (by default, it lists them by name in alphabetical order):

```
$ ls
cinque  dieci  due  nove  otto  quattro  sei  sette  tre  uno
```

3. Now let's group them in a number of different ways, using the metacharacters. First, list all the files that start with the letter `s`:

```
$ ls s*
sei  sette
```

4. Next, use the `?` metacharacter to select all files with three-character filenames:

```
$ ls ???
due  sei  tre  uno
```

5. Next, select all the files that have vowels starting their filename:

```
$ ls [aeiou]*
otto  uno
```

6. Next, select all the files that have any character in the range `a` to `f` beginning their filename:

```
$ ls [a-f]*
cinque  dieci  due
```

7. Finally, select all the files that do not have a vowel as the start of their filename. The exclamation operator must be within the square parentheses.

```
$ ls [!aeiou]*
cinque  dieci  due  nove  quattro  sei  sette  tre
```

How It Works

We've used the `ls` command here to demonstrate file globbing because the output from `ls` shows the effects of the globbing very clearly. However, you should note that you can use file globbing with any command that expects filename or directory name arguments. Let's look at each of the globbing expressions here.

We used the expression `s*` to match all files that begin with the letter `s`:

```
$ ls s*
```

This expression matches the file names `sei` and `sette`, and would even match a file called `s` if there were one because the `*` matches any string of any length (including the 0-length string).

To match filenames with *exactly* three characters, you use a `?` to represent each character:

```
$ ls ???
```

We used the expression `[aeiou]*` to pick up all filenames starting with a vowel. The `*` works in the same way as in the `s*` example, matching any string of any length, so files matching this expression begin with a character `a`, `e`, `i`, `o`, or `u`, followed by any other sequence of characters:

```
$ ls [aeiou]*
```

A similar approach applies for the expression `[a-f]*`, except that you use a hyphen (`-`) within the parentheses to express any one of the characters in a range:

```
$ ls [a-f]*
```

Using a range implies that the characters have an assumed order. In fact, this range encompasses all alphanumeric characters, with numbers (0–9) preceding letters (a–z). (Hence the expression `[0-z]*` would match all filenames that start with either a number or a letter.)

Finally, you use the exclamation mark (`!`) within the square parentheses to negate the result of the vowel-matching expression, thereby arriving at all filenames that start with a consonant:

```
$ ls [!aeiou]*
```

Using Quotes

Over the course of the chapter, you've seen that the shell uses several special characters. Sometimes, you need to use these special characters literally. In this situation, you use *quotation characters* to protect these special characters from being interpreted by the shell or the shell script.

You often use single quote (`'`) characters to protect a string:

```
$ touch 'foo*bar'
```

This creates a file called `foo*bar` on the disk. Without the single quotes, the `*` character would have been interpreted as a wildcard metacharacter.

You use double quote characters when referencing variables. All characters, including `\` and `'`, are interpreted literally except for the dollar sign (`$`), which is used to refer to the value of a variable:

```
$ foo="foo/'"
$ bar="'\bar"
$ echo "$foo$bar"
foo/''\bar
```

The echo command prints its arguments to the standard output. The echo command is discussed again in some detail in the "System-defined Variables and User-Defined Variables" section of this chapter.

The double quotes protected the single quotes and the slashes (both forward and backslashes) when the strings were assigned to variables foo and bar. As expected, when $foo and $bar are enclosed in double quotes in the last command, the $ is interpreted, and the two variables expanded to their values.

The backquote (`) is used to execute commands. The backquote is convenient when the output of a certain command needs to be assigned to a variable:

```
$ datevar=`date`
$ echo $datevar
```

You end up with the following:

```
Tue Jan 14 23:03:43  2003
```

In the first command, the datevar variable is assigned the output of the date command because it is executed within backquotes. The echo commands prints the value of the datevar variable.

Aliases

Aliases are your first step toward customizing Bash. In its simplest form, an alias functions as an abbreviation for a commonly used command. In more complex cases, aliases can define completely new functionality. An alias is easily defined using the notation *<alias_name>=<alias_value>*. When you need it, you invoke it using <alias_name>—the shell substitutes <alias_name> with *<alias_value>*.

In fact, the standard Fedora Core 2 shell already has several aliases defined. You can list the existing aliases using the alias command:

```
$ alias
alias l.='ls -d .* --color=tty'
alias ll='ls -l --color=tty'
alias ls='ls --color=tty'
alias vi='vim'
alias which='alias | /usr/bin/which --tty-only --read-alias --show-dot --show-tilde'
```

Some of the common aliases include aliases for the ls command, to include your favorite options. If you use the ls command without any options, it simply prints the list of files and subdirectories under the current working directory. However, in this case, the ls command is aliased to itself, with the --color option, which allows ls to indicate different file types with different colors.

Aliases may be defined for the lifetime of a shell by specifying the alias mapping at the command line or in a startup file (discussed in the "System-Defined Variables and User-Defined Variables" section) so that the aliases are available every time the shell starts up.

Just as it is possible to set an alias as a synonym to a command with options and arguments, it is possible to disassociate the synonym. This is achieved using the unalias command:

```
$ alias
alias vi='vim'
alias l.='ls -d .* --color=tty'
alias ll='ls -l --color=tty'
alias ls='ls --color=tty'
$ unalias vi
$ alias
alias l.='ls -d .* --color=tty'
alias ll='ls -l --color=tty'
alias ls='ls --color=tty'
```

Notice that on executing the `unalias` command, `vi` is no longer associated with `vim`.

Environment Variables

Like aliases, *environment variables* are name-value pairs that are defined either on the shell prompt or in startup files. A process may also set its own environment variables programmatically (that is, from within the program, rather than declared in a file or as arguments).

Environment variables are most often used either by the shell or by other programs to communicate settings. Some programs communicate information through environment variables to programs that they spawn. There are several environment variables set for you in advance. To list all of them that are currently set, you can use the `env` command, which should display an output similar to the following:

```
$ env
HOSTNAME=localhost.localdomain
SHELL=/bin/bash
TERM=xterm
HISTSIZE=1000
USER=deepakt
MAIL=/var/spool/mail/deepakt
PATH=/usr/local/bin:/usr/bin:/bin:/usr/X11R6/bin:/home/deepakt/bin

...
```

As you can see, the `PATH` variable is one of the environment variables listed here. As described earlier in this chapter, Bash uses the value of the `PATH` variable to search for commands. The `MAIL` variable, also listed here, is used by mail-reading software to determine the location of a user's mailbox.

System-Defined Variables and User-Defined Variables

You may set your own environment variables or modify existing ones:

```
$ echo $PATH
PATH=/usr/local/bin:/usr/bin:/bin:/usr/X11R6/bin:/home/deepakt/bin
$ export MYHOME=/home/deepakt
$ export PATH=$PATH:$MYHOME/mybin
$ echo $PATH
PATH=/usr/local/bin:/usr/bin:/bin:/usr/X11R6/bin:/home/deepakt/bin:/home/
deepakt/mybin
```

Whereas user-defined variables (also known as local variables) can be set as `MYHOME=/home/deepakt`, these variables will not be available to any of the commands spawned by this shell. For local variables to be available to child processes spawned by a process (the shell in this case), you need to use the `export` command. However, to achieve persistence for variables even after you log out and log back in, you must save these settings in startup files.

Environment variables are defined either interactively or in a startup file such as `.bashrc`. These variables are automatically made available to a new shell. Examples of environment variables are `PATH`, `PRINTER`, and `DISPLAY`.

However, local variables do not get automatically propagated to a new shell when it is created. The `MYHOME` variable is an example of a local variable.

The `echo` command, followed by the name of a variable prefixed with a dollar (`$`) symbol, prints the value of the environment variable.

I/O Redirection

Earlier in the chapter, you saw how you can use filesystem commands to manipulate files and directories and process management commands such as `ps` to manage processes. The shell provides you with a powerful set of operators that allow you to manage input, output, and errors while working with files and processes.

I/O Streams

If a process needs to perform any I/O operation, it has to happen through an abstraction known as an *I/O stream*. The process has three streams associated with it: standard input, standard output, and standard error. The process may read input from its standard input, write its output to standard output, and write error messages to its standard error stream.

By default, the standard input is associated with the keyboard; output and error are associated with the terminal, in our case, mostly an `xterm`. Sometimes, you may not want processes to write to or read from a terminal; you may want the process to write to another location, such as a file. In this case, you need to associate the process's standard output (and possibly the standard error) with the file in question. The process is oblivious to this, and continues to read from the standard input and write to the standard output, which in this case happens to be the files you specify. The I/O redirection operators of the shell make this redirection of the streams from the terminal to files extremely simple.

The < Operator

The < *operator* allows programs that read from the standard input to read input from a file. For example, consider the `wc` (word count) program, which reads input from the keyboard (until a *Ctrl+D* is encountered) and then prints the number of lines, words, and characters that were input:

```
$ wc -l
12345
67890
12345
^D
3
```

Note that the `-l` *option is used here, which has* `wc` *print the number of lines only.*

Now consider a case in which you have the input to `wc` available in a file, called `3linefile.txt`. In this case, the following command will produce the same result:

```
$ wc -l < 3linefile.txt
3
```

Here, the standard input is redirected from the keyboard to the file.

The > Operator

The > *operator* is similar to the < operator. Its purpose is to redirect the standard output from the terminal to a file. Consider the following example:

```
$ date > date.txt
```

The `date` command writes its output to the standard output, which is usually the terminal. Here, the > operator indicates to the shell that the output should instead be redirected to a file.

When you write the file out to the terminal (using the `cat` command), you can see the output of the `date` command displayed:

```
$ cat date.txt
Tue Jan 14 23:03:43 2003
```

Try It Out Redirecting Output

Based on what you have learned so far, create a file with some contents in it:

```
$ cat > test.txt
The quick brown fox jumped over the rubber chicken
^D
$ cat test.txt
The quick brown fox jumped over the rubber chicken
```

Using `cat` to create a file in this way is similar to using the Microsoft DOS command `COPY CON TEST.TXT`.

How It Works

The `cat` command, used without any options, is supposed to "echo" back to the standard output anything that it reads from the standard input. In this case, the > operator redirects the standard output of the `cat` command to the file `test.txt`. Whatever was typed on the keyboard (standard input) ends up in the file `test.txt` (standard output redirected by the shell).

The >> Operator

The >> *operator* is essentially the same as the > operator. The only difference is that it does not overwrite an existing file; instead, it appends to it.

```
$ cat >> test.txt
Since rubber chicken makes bad nuggets
^D
$ cat test.txt
The quick brown fox jumped over the rubber chicken
Since rubber chicken makes bad nuggets
```

The | Operator

The | operator is used to feed the output of one command to the input of another command.

```
$ cat test.txt | wc -l
2
$wc -l test.txt
2
```

The output of the `cat` command—that is, the contents of the file `test.txt`—is fed by the shell to the `wc` command. It is the equivalent of running the `wc -l` command against the `test.txt` file. It is also possible to chain multiple commands this way (for example *command1* | *command2* | *command3*).

The & Operator

Often, you may want a program to output both its standard output and error to one file. Typically, this is a requirement when a program has to run unattended, as is the case with programs automatically executed on a schedule, such as a backup program (see the section "Scheduling Tasks" later in this chapter to learn more about scheduling programs to run unattended). You would want to capture the output and error statements of the backup program in one file.

```
$ mybackup -r allnight >/tmp/mybackup.out 2>&1
```

Here, the fictitious program `mybackup` redirects its standard output to the file `/tmp/mybackup.out` due to the > operator. The `2>&1` notation indicates that 2, that is, the standard error, is *dup*-ed to 1, the standard output. This causes the standard output and standard error to be written to the same file.

The xargs Command

The `xargs` command has no life of its own, but it acts as a mechanism to dynamically complete arguments for another command. Look at the following example, which uses the command sequences to find all files with the string `needle` in a hierarchy of directories.

```
$ ls -R .|grep needle
Thimble and needle in hand, undaunted they
The space needle dominated the bleary landscape
```

Unfortunately, you don't know if both of these lines are from the same file. Even worse, you don't know which files they came from. The `xargs` command to the rescue:

```
$ ls -R .|xargs grep needle
sewing101: Thimble and needle in hand, undaunted they
seattledaily: The space needle dominated the bleary landscape
```

Here the xargs command acts as an argument completion mechanism for the grep command. Each line of output from the ls command (that is, individual filenames) is concatenated by xargs into a set of arguments to the grep command. The grep command, on seeing multiple files to search for, prints the filename along with the occurrence of a matching string in a file.

Configuring the Shell

As you saw in the section about aliases, most of us are likely to have our own preferences about how the shell should function. Bash is a highly customizable shell that allows you to set the values of environment variables that change its default behavior. Among other things, users like to change their prompt, their list of aliases, and even perhaps add a welcome message when they log in:

```
$ echo $PS1
$
$ export PS1="Grandpoobah > "
Grandpoobah >
```

Bash uses the value of the PS1 environment variable to display its prompt. Therefore, you could simply change this environment variable to whatever pleases you. However, to ensure that your brand new prompt is still available to you the next time you log in to the system, you need to add the PS1 setting to the .bashrc file.

Try It Out Modifying the .bashrc File

Add some entries to the .bashrc file (save a backup copy first, so you can put it back to normal when you're done):

```
export PS1="Grandpoobah> "
alias ls='ls -al'
banner "Good day"
```

When you log in, you see a banner that displays the silly "Good day" message. If you list your aliases and environment variables, you see that your new settings have taken effect.

How It Works

When a user logs in, Bash reads the /etc/bashrc file (which is a common startup file for all system users). Then it reads the .bashrc file in the user's home directory and executes all commands in it, including creating aliases, setting up environment variables, and running programs (the banner program in this case).

Because the user's .bashrc is read after the system-wide configuration file, this is a good place to override any default settings that may not be to the user's liking.

A user can also create a .bashrc_logout script in his or her home directory, and add programs to it. When the user logs out, Bash reads and executes the commands in the .bashrc_logout file. This is a good location to add that parting message or reminder and simple housekeeping tasks.

A Sample .bashrc

Take a look at a sample `.bashrc` file:

```
export PS1='foobar$ '
export PATH=$PATH:/home/deepakt/games

alias rm='rm -i'
alias psc='ps -auxww'
alias d='date'
alias cls='clear'
alias jump='cd /home/deepakt/dungeon/maze/labyrinth/deep/down'
```

Setting the `PS1` environment variable changes the command prompt. We may have a separate directory in which we store a number of games. We also add this directory to the `PATH` environment variable. In the aliases section, we alias the `rm` command to itself with the `-i` option. The `-i` option forces the `rm` command to confirm with the user if it is all right to delete a file or directory. This is often a useful setting for novice users to prevent accidental deletion of files or directories. We also abbreviate the `ps` command and arguments to display the entire command line of processes with the `psc` alias. The `date` command is abbreviated as `d`. Finally, to save on typing the complete path to a deeply nested directory, we create `jump`, an alias to the `cd` command that changes our current working directory to the deeply nested directory.

As you saw in the "Switching Identities" subsection of the "Administrative Commands" section, the `su` command switches the identity of a user to that of another user. By default, when the switch happens, the new user's `.bashrc` file is not executed. However, if you use the - option to `su`, the new user's `.bashrc` is executed and the current directory is changed to that of the new user:

```
$ su - jmillionaire
```

Setting the Prompt

You can set the command prompt in several interesting formats. This is possible due to several special character sequences that expand dynamically when assigned to the `PS1` variable, as in the following example:

```
$ export PS1='\[\w\]'
[/home/deepakt]
```

Here, the command prompt is now set to the value of the current directory, `/home/deepakt`, because the `\w` character sequence expands to the current working directory.

The following table shows character sequences that may be used to customize the command prompt:

Character Sequence	Description
`\d`	Today's date
`\h`	Host name of the system
`\s`	The name of the current shell
`\t`	Current time
`\u`	User's login name
`\W`	Base name of the current working directory
`\w`	Current working directory
`\!`	History number of the current command

Managing Tasks

The Linux operating system was designed to be a multitasking operating system—that is, to allow multiple tasks to be executed together. Until a few years ago, end users of the system were not directly exposed to this aspect of the operating system.

As far as Linux is concerned, the job-control features of Bash allow users to take advantage of the multitasking features of the operating system. This section looks at managing multiple tasks, both attended and unattended. Let's start with an overview of how processes work in Linux.

Processes

Processes, as you saw in the "Process Management Commands" section, are programs executing in memory. A process may be associated with a terminal (for example, the `date` command is associated with the terminal because it prints its standard output to the terminal). The association of a process with a terminal also means that all the signals delivered to the terminal's group of processes will be delivered to the process in question.

Some processes, such as servers (or daemons), are seldom associated with a terminal. These processes are typically started as part of the system boot process, and they run during the entire time that the system is up and write output to log files. When a user starts a process (that is, when the user runs a command), the command is associated with the terminal and is, therefore, also described as running in the foreground.

While a process is running in the foreground, the shell does not return a prompt until the process has completed execution. However, a process may also be started such that the prompt is returned immediately; in this case, the process is called a *background process*.

To run a process as a background process, use the ampersand (`&`) character after the command:

```
$bash ls -R / &
```

This indicates to the shell that the process must be disassociated from the terminal and executed as a background process. Its output continues to be written to the terminal.

Job Control

Job control is a feature of Bash that allows the user to start and manage multiple programs at the same time rather than sequence their execution. You can suspend a program using *Ctrl+Z*, and you can send it to the background or foreground (using the `bg` and `fg` commands) or even leave it suspended. It is also possible to list all of the jobs (processes) started and terminate some of them.

Try It Out — Managing Processes with Job Control

Try using job control to manage a long-running process, the `ls -R /` command, which recursively lists all the files and directories on the system:

Step 1: Stopping the process

```
$ ls -R /
^Z
[1]+  Stopped       ls -R /
```

Step 2: Listing the jobs

```
$ jobs
[1]+  Stopped       ls -R /
```

Step 3: Sending the job to background

```
$ bg %1
[1]+  ls -R / &
```

Step 4: Bringing the job to foreground and stopping it

```
$ fg %1
ls -R /
^Z
[1]+  Stopped       ls -R /
```

Step 5: Killing a stopped job

```
$ kill -s SIGKILL %1

$
[1]+  Killed       ls -R /
```

How It Works

Start the program `ls` with the `-R` option. After a while, we decide to suspend the program using *Ctrl+Z*. The `jobs` command displays the current jobs and their status.

Use the bg command to send the process to the background. After a while, we decide to bring the process back to the foreground, for which we use the fg command. Both bg and fg take an argument that indicates the job number. The %1 argument indicates that we are referring to job number 1.

Finally, having had enough of the process, we suspend it once again and kill it (using the kill command).

Note that the job control commands are built-in commands, and not external commands.

Scheduling Tasks

Often, it is not necessary (or not possible) for the user to be present when a task needs to execute. For example, if a user wants to have a certain script executed at midnight to take advantage of the spare CPU cycles, what he or she needs is a mechanism by which the task can be scheduled and executed unattended. Alternatively, if a certain task takes hours to complete and may not require any user input, it is not necessary for the user to remain logged on until the task is complete.

Scheduling Processes

You can use the cron utility to execute tasks automatically at arbitrary times, and even repeatedly if required. The cron daemon is a system process that runs at all times in the background, checking to see if any processes need to be started on behalf of users. You can schedule tasks for cron by editing the crontab file.

Try It Out Scheduling a Task

Let's schedule a cron job that needs to be started every Monday and Thursday at 11:55 PM to back up our system:

```
$ crontab -e
No crontab for deepakt - using an empty one
```

This brings up the vi editor, using which we add the following crontab entry:

```
55  23  *  *  1,4  /home/deepakt/mybackup >/home/deepakt/mybackup.out 2>&1
```

Save the file and exit the editor:

```
crontab: installing new crontab
$ crontab -l
# DO NOT EDIT THIS FILE - edit the master and reinstall.
# (/tmp/crontab.6642 installed on Fri Jan 17 05:09:37 2003)
# (Cron version -- $Id: crontab.c,v 2.13 1994/01/17 03:20:37 vixie Exp $)
55      23      *       *       1,4     /home/deepakt/mybackup
/home/deepakt/mybackup.out 2>&1
```

How It Works

We need to use the crontab command to create new cron jobs. The -e option pops up the vi editor that allows us to add the new cron job. The entry for a cron job consists of six columns:

- The first five columns indicate the time at which the job should execute and the frequency—the minute (0–59), the hour (0–23), the day of the month (1–31), the month of the year (1–12), and the day of the week (0–6, with 0 indicating Sunday). An asterisk represents all logical values, so asterisks appear for the day of the month and the month of the year because this job needs to run during all months of the year.
- The last column indicates the actual command to be invoked at these times. You need to specify the full command, with the complete path leading to your backup program, and also redirect the output to a log file.

  The `2>&1` indicates that the standard error is also redirected to the same log file.

Allowing a Process to Continue After Logout

The `nohup` command can be used to execute tasks that need to continue to execute even after the user has logged out:

```
$ nohup ls -R / &
```

The `nohup` command is quite straightforward, in that it takes the program to be executed as the argument. You need to send the whole process to the background by using the `&` operator. The standard output and error of the `nohup` command will be written to the user's home directory in a file called `nohup.out`.

Shell Scripting

As you've seen in this chapter, the shell has extensive capabilities when it comes to providing tools for finding your way around the operating system and getting your job done. But the true power of the shell is in its capacity as a scripting language.

To capture this, we use *shell scripts*. Essentially, a shell script is a sequence of commands and operators listed one after another, stored in a file, and executed as a single entity.

Shell scripting in Bash is a topic that deserves a book by itself. Our objective in this short section is simply to touch upon the salient features of scripting using Bash.

Bash shell script files start with the command interpreter, in this case `bash` itself:

```
#!/bin/bash
```

Or:

```
#!/bin/sh
```

Variables

Like most other programming languages, Bash scripting requires variables to store its data in during the course of execution. Shell scripts' variables are essentially the same as regular environment variables. In fact, they are set and retrieved the same way as environment variables. Certain variables have special meanings:

- `$n` indicates the *n*th argument to the script. Therefore, `$1` would indicate the first argument to the script.
- `$0` indicates the name of the script itself.
- `$*` prints the complete command line.

Try It Out Shell Script using Variables

Try out a program that prints the values of special variables `$n` and `$*`:

Step 1: Creating the script

```
#!/bin/sh

echo "Script name: $0"
echo "First argument: $1"
echo "Second argument: $2"
echo "All arguments : $*"
```

The `echo` command (in this shell script) has the effect of interpreting and writing its arguments to the standard output.

Step 2: Running the script

You need to save this in a file called `testcmd.sh`:

```
$ chmod +x testcmd.sh

$ ./testcmd.sh foo bar
```

```
Script name: ./testcmd.sh
First argument: foo
Second argument: bar
All arguments : foo bar
```

You run the command `testcmd.sh` as `./testcmd.sh` because this indicates the full path of the shell script; in other words, you indicate that the `testcmd.sh` script residing in the current directory needs to be executed. Alternatively, you could add the current working directory to your `PATH`:

```
$ export PATH=$PATH:.
```

Conditional Constructs

Finally, how do you specify the execution path of your code based on conditions? This is more complex than the ideas we've looked at so far, but with that complexity comes a great deal of added flexibility. You can use conditional constructs to create extremely flexible scripts that automate many common tasks on your system.

We will begin by looking at the `if then .. else .. fi` conditional construct used for testing and branching. This command is useful when you need to execute a certain set of statements (commands) if a particular condition is met and a certain other set of commands if the condition is not satisfied.

You could type the following example into a file using your favorite editor and save it as a shell script, say `testif.sh`:

```
#!/bin/sh
x=10
y=5

if [ "$x" -eq "$y" ]
then
  echo x and y are equal
else
  echo x and y are not equal
fi
```

Then issue the following command:

```
$ chmod +x testif.sh; ./testif.sh
```

The `chmod` command sets execution permissions for the shell script; in other words, it makes the script executable. Chapter 5 contains detailed information on setting various permissions for files. The `./testif.sh` command executes the script. You see the following output:

```
x and y are not equal
```

It is not necessary to type a shell script into a file. You can type it in at the command line itself:

```
$ x=10; y=5
$ if [ "$x" -eq "$y" ]
> then
> echo x and y are equal
> else
> echo x and y are not equal
> fi
x and y are not equal
$
```

Note that the shell prompt changes into a > sign because the shell expects more input.

The `if then ... else ... fi` statement has the following syntax:

```
if expression
then
  statement 1
  statement 2
...
  statement n
else
```

```
    statement 1'
    statement 2'
  ...
     statement n'
  fi
```

If the value of the expression turns out to be true, the statements from *statement 1* to *statement n* are executed. If it evaluates to false, the statements from statement 1 to *statement n*are executed. The expression can be formed using operators, in this case the `-eq` operator. The `-eq` operator tests for equality of numbers. It evaluates to true if two numbers are equal and false if they are not.

A shorter form of this construct is the `if then .. fi` construct that follows:

```
if expression
then
  statement 1
  statement 2
  ...
  statement n
fi
```

This construct is useful when you need to execute certain statements only if a certain condition is met. Following is a sample script that uses the `if then .. fi` form:

```
#!/bin/sh
x=10
y=5

if [ "$x" -eq "$y" ]
then
  echo "The two numbers are equal"
fi
```

Note that in both cases the statements are indented to make the code more readable and this is not a requirement.

The previous examples used operators such as `-eq` to evaluate conditions. The following table lists commonly used operators and their functions.

Operator	Example	Tests to See If . . .
`-eq`	`"$x" -eq 3`	Both integer operands are equal.
`-neq`	`"$x" -neq 3`	Both integer operands are not equal.
`=`	`"$str" = "some string"`	Both string operands are the same.
`!=`	`"$str" != "some string"`	Both string operands are not the same.
`-n`	`-n "$x"`	The operand is of non-zero length.
`-z`	`-z "$x"`	The operand is of zero length.

Operator	Example	Tests to See If . . .
`-d`	`-d "/tmp/foo"`	The specified directory exists.
`-f`	`-f "/tmp/foo/bar.txt"`	The file specified exists.
`-lt`	`"$x" -lt "$y"`	First integer operand is lesser than the second integer operand.
`-le`	`"$x" -le "$y"`	First integer operand is lesser than or equal to the second integer operand.
`-gt`	`"$x" -gt "$y"`	First integer operand is greater than the second integer operand.
`-ge`	`"$x" -ge "$y"`	First integer operand is greater than or equal to the second integer operand.

Loops

This section looks at looping constructs that allow you to conditionally execute a set of statements repeatedly.

The `for` loop is essentially a simple looping construct that allows you to specify a set of statements that need to be executed a certain number of times:

```
#!/bin/sh
for fil in `ls *.txt`
do
  cat $fil >> complete.txt
done
```

The preceding script concatenates all the text files in the current directory into a text file, that is, `complete.txt`.

```
#!/bin/sh
for number in 1 2 3 4 5
do
  echo $
done
```

This script prints out the numbers from 1 to 5 producing the following output:

```
1
2
3
4
5
```

The syntax of the `for` construct is as follows:

```
for variable in word
do
  statement 1
  statement 2
  ...
  statement n
done
```

Here, `word` is a set of items that gets assigned to the `variable` one at a time for each iteration of the loop. The loop therefore executes as many times as there are items in the word.

The `while` looping construct tests a logical condition for continuing the looping:

```
#!/bin/sh
x=10
y=5

while [ "$x" -ge "$y" ]
do
  echo $y
  y=`expr $y + 1`
done
```

The preceding script displays the following output:

```
5
6
10
```

The syntax of the `while` construct is as follows:

```
while expression
do
  statement 1
  statement 2
  .
  .
  statement n
done
```

The `while` loop continues as long as the expression evaluates to true.

Going Further

You've had just a taste of the functionality that your Bash shell has to offer. Many good books exist on the subject that you can consult if you wish to learn more about its more complex functionality.

Summary

This chapter has aimed to give you a working knowledge of the Bash command line shell. The history of the shell was explained, providing insight into the various shells and their origin. Some simple yet useful commands for managing processes and the filesystem were dealt with. Commands to perform common administrative tasks were also examined. To assist the power user, some keyboard shortcuts and control key mappings that abbreviate common tasks were examined. Command-line syntax, including the use of quotes and the concept of environment variables, was also examined, as was the ability to redirect input and output. Some job control features, such as the ability of the shell to perform multiple tasks at the same time, were explained. Additionally, this chapter dealt with the ability to run unattended tasks. Finally, the chapter examined the most powerful and flexible aspect of the shell, the ability to construct complex programs from simple shell commands (that is, shell scripting).

Exercises

The chapter on the shell introduced you to basic commands and common tasks performed using them. Test your knowledge of the shell with the following examples:

1. List the complete command lines of all the processes belonging to the root user.
2. Modify the command prompt to display the current working directory.
3. Use `cron` to run the `date` command once every 15 minutes.
4. Write a shell script that will maintain a log of users logged on to the system. Logging should happen every 5 minutes.

7

Managing Your User Accounts

UNIX has always enabled multiple users to work independently and simultaneously on the same computer—right back to the earliest UNIX operating systems, born at the end of the 1960s. Each user in possession of a valid user account could log in to the computer (by supplying a username and password) and work with the desired applications. Users would access the system via a *system console* (which was normally reserved for administrative tasks such as backups) or from one of a number of *serial terminals* (these usually consisted of a keyboard and a monitor, or perhaps even a line printer). Even though networking wasn't part of the original UNIX design, it became available quite early, giving users the ability to interact with a UNIX system from anywhere: locally, via the telephone system and a modem, or via a network connection.

Linux inherited its multiuser nature from those first UNIX systems, just as it inherited a surprising number of other capabilities, such as permissions and file protection. These features haven't changed much over time. What *has* changed is the toolset—tasks such as adding a new user account are now easier than they've ever been. The traditional techniques (using command line tools, or even employing a text editor to alter the relevant configuration files) have been enriched with graphical tools that greatly simplify administrative chores. Fedora Core is just one of a number of Linux distributions that have made developments in this direction.

If you have a single machine that is meant mostly for exclusive use, and you're not planning to share its resources with anyone else, the world of administering user accounts and permissions may seem irrelevant to you. However, the notion of multiple user accounts is quite important in Linux, as it is in many other modern operating systems (such as Mac OS X, other UNIX derivatives such as the BSD family, and Microsoft Windows NT, 2000, or XP).

Whether you share your machine with other users, or it's exclusively for your own personal use, each action you request of it will be denied or allowed in accordance with specific policies. For example, some user accounts will be allowed to install applications, execute certain programs, and access devices such as a CD-ROM drive, while other accounts will not.

Understanding how to manage user accounts and control permissions is a definite advantage when learning Linux. For example, it will allow you to share your computer with other people without compromising privacy; it will help you to protect yourself from accidental damage (such as accidental deletion of system files); it will help you to avoid virus problems; and it will help you prevent secondary users from cluttering the system with unnecessary software installations.

This chapter does the following:

- Formally introduces the notion of the root user, normal users, groups, and home directories
- Demonstrates how to create, modify, and delete users and groups
- Looks at various strategies for granting and denying access to resources
- Reviews a number of valuable commands that are particularly useful when dealing with user accounts
- Shows how to configure your Fedora Core installation so that you can carry out certain administrative tasks via a "non-administrator" user account

The Purpose of Different User Accounts

By now, you're probably used to the fact that, to access your computer through Linux, you must *log in* by providing a *username* and the corresponding *password*. That's the same for each user; every user of the system is able to identify himself by his own unique username.

The existence of different user accounts on a system has a number of important and useful consequences:

- Only authorized users are able to access the system because the operating system allows entry to those users who supply the correct *credentials* (a username and a matching password).
- *Access* to resources, such as files and devices, will be granted accordingly. For example, any authorized user is able to *read* the "message of the day" contained in the `/etc/motd` file, but only some users are permitted to *change* the contents of that file.
- Each user is assigned a separate directory, called their *home directory*, for storing personal data.
- Linux can be configured to execute user-specific setup procedures at the time that user logs in. For example, it might run a program that notifies the user of the arrival of new mail.
- Every program started by the user is associated to that user's account, and can be identified afterward. Moreover, each program will have access only to those resources that the owner can access.

Many large systems make a distinction between an *administrator* (or *super user*) and a *normal user*. In particular, a user is prevented from performing special (often sensitive) tasks, such as the following, unless that user has administrator privileges:

- Global maintenance, personalization, and upgrade of the system
- Global installation of applications, devices, and their drivers
- Periodic backup of data
- User account management

It is the administrator's work that leaves normal users free to carry out their day-to-day tasks. Indeed, in very large environments with many thousands of users, system administration is a full-time job. In these environments, it's easy to see why it makes sense to differentiate between super users and normal users. If administration were left to the individual users, regardless of their expertise or authority, the lack of policy and control could be catastrophic—risking the stability of the system, performance levels, security violations, and so on.

In fact, the distinction between super users and normal users is enforced in *all* Linux installations—even on small Linux computers that are used by only one person, because many of the same arguments that apply on large networks *also* apply on the smallest installations. For example, while the super user account is very useful for performing certain tasks, it's definitely a mistake to work as super user when you're performing more "everyday" tasks, such as reading e-mails. It's not only that you don't *need* super user privileges to read your e-mail, it's also about protecting yourself from accidentally damaging your system integrity.

The administrator account in Fedora Core (as in almost every other operating system of UNIX heritage) is called *root*. The power of root is so extensive that almost no task is forbidden for this account. While it's impossible for a normal user to delete system files, root is able to delete them all too easily.

For this reason, the root account should be used with great care. It is important that you create a personal account as part of the Linux installation, and we did that back in Chapter 1. If you are currently logged into your Linux system using the root account, log out now and log back in with a normal (non-root) account.

In general, don't use the root account unless it is necessary.

If you're worried about the hassle of logging in and out of different accounts, worry no more. Linux allows you to run a root shell from within your normal account, so you can do most of your work under the normal account and switch to the root shell for those sensitive administration-level activities (this is discussed later in the "When root is Not Necessary" section).

The User Manager

This section takes a look at some of the most common tasks in user account management: creating user accounts and groups, and adding a user account to a group. We'll use the graphical User Manager tool to step through some examples. Then, the next section looks at what's happening under the covers—the impact of our actions on the relevant configuration files and how to perform the same (and other) operations via the command line.

To try the User Manager, you'll need to use the root account (and to be extra careful) at each step. We'll assume that you're logged in with a non-root account, which (as previously mentioned) is the safest way to use your operating system.

When you launch any of Fedora Core's graphical administration tools from a non-root account, Linux will (if necessary) prompt you to enter the password to the root account. Figure 7-1 shows the window you'll see every time the root password is required by a graphical tool.

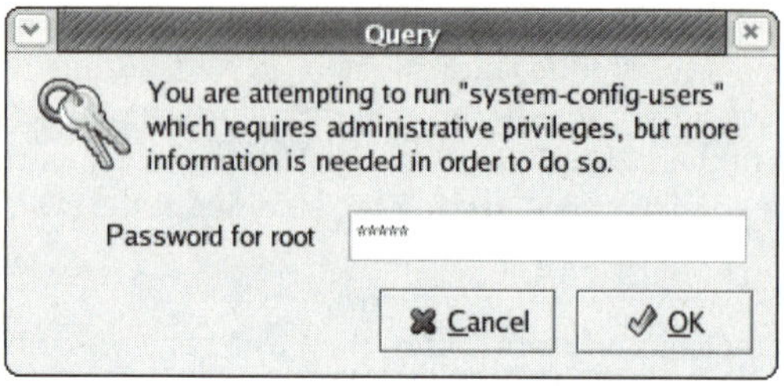

Figure 7-1

If the password is accepted, a key-shaped icon appears in the notification area at the bottom-right corner of the screen. As long as that icon remains displayed, you can start other Fedora Core graphical administration tools without being asked again for the root password. The key icon does not mean that all actions are undertaken with root privileges; it simply means that when an administration tool requires the root account to run, it may skip this step because the user has already provided the password.

Creating a User Account

Let's step through the process of creating user accounts for some of the authors of this book. Assume that one normal user account (eziodm, the account for Pancrazio 'Ezio' de Mauro) was created during the installation process; we'll add a couple more accounts, kapils and deepakt, over the course of the following steps.

Try It Out Creating User Accounts

1. Launch the User Manager (do this by selecting Main Menu ➪ System Settings ➪ User and Groups, or by typing `system-config-users` at a command line). Enter the root password if you're prompted to do so. After this, you'll see the User Manager interface, as shown in Figure 7-2.

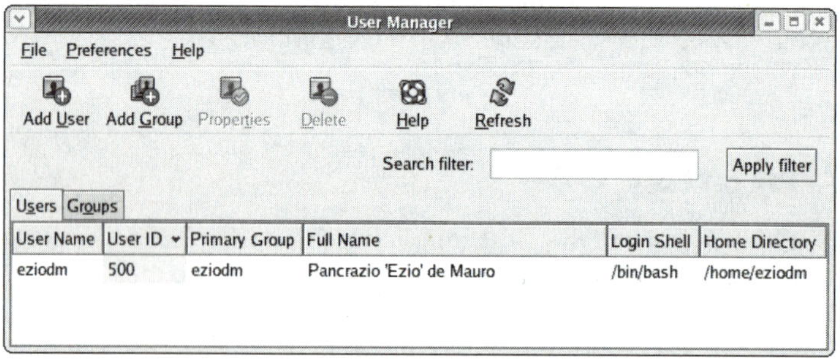

Figure 7-2

Each line contains the details of one user account. By default, system accounts are not shown. If you want to see the system accounts, you can do so by selecting the Preferences menu and disabling the Filter system users and groups option.

2. Click Add User. This opens the Create New User window, as shown in Figure 7-3.

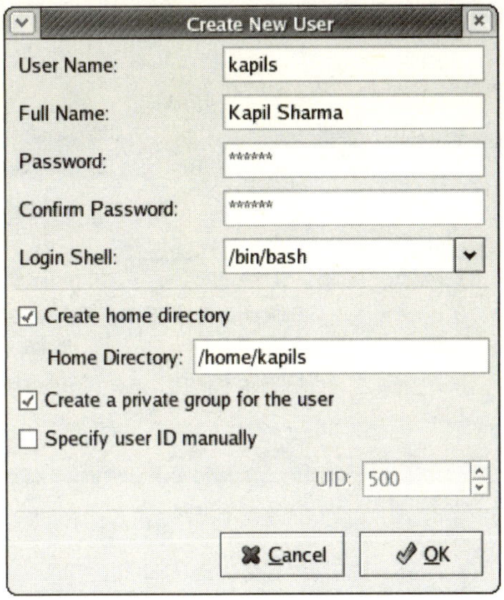

Figure 7-3

As you can see, this looks similar to the Add a User Account dialog box you saw in Chapter 1, when installing Fedora Core. Fill in the necessary values, so that the dialog box looks something like the one shown in the figure. There are a few points to note as you fill in the fields here:

- Remember to choose a unique name for the new account.
- The Login Shell list is taken directly from the `/etc/shells` file. It is possible to type in the location of a shell that doesn't appear in this list. However, the values commonly used here are `/bin/bash` or `/bin/tcsh`. If you don't know the difference between the two, stick to `/bin/bash`—it tends to be more popular.
- You should create a Home Directory, unless the account is for a program and not a person.
- It is a good idea to create a private group for the user at the same time because this will help in setting up good protection schemes. This is the default for Fedora Core and shouldn't be changed without good reason.
- It is best *not* to specify a user ID manually, but to allow the tool to generate one.

After clicking OK, the new user is created and the account is visible on the main window.

3. Click the new account, and then the Properties button to review the information just entered, and check that it's correct. With the three tabs (Account Info, Password Info, and Groups) it is possible to enable account expiration date, lock the account temporarily, enable password expiration, and assign the account to some of the existing groups. Click OK when you're done reviewing or changing.
4. The new account has been created. Now repeat the procedure from Step 2 to create as many more accounts as you like. Figure 7-4 shows what the User Manager looks like after creating accounts called kapils and deepakt.

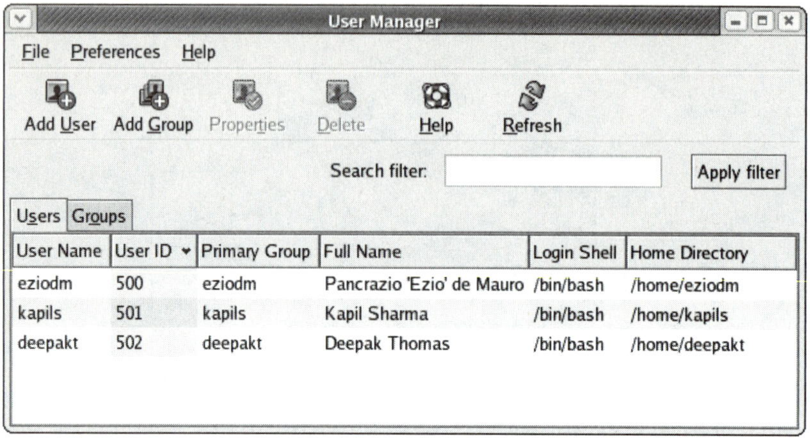

Figure 7-4

Creating a Group

Groups are useful when you need to treat a number of different users the same way. For example, if you want to grant a group of users access to a particular file or directory, you add the users to a group and grant the permission to the group (instead of to the individual user accounts). You'll see more of this later, but first you need to see how to create a group.

We have some user accounts for some of the authors on this book. Let's create a group called authors, and then add these accounts to that group.

Try It Out Creating a New Group

1. You can use the User Manager GUI to manage your groups, too. After you've launched the GUI, press the Groups tab to see which groups are present (see Figure 7-5).

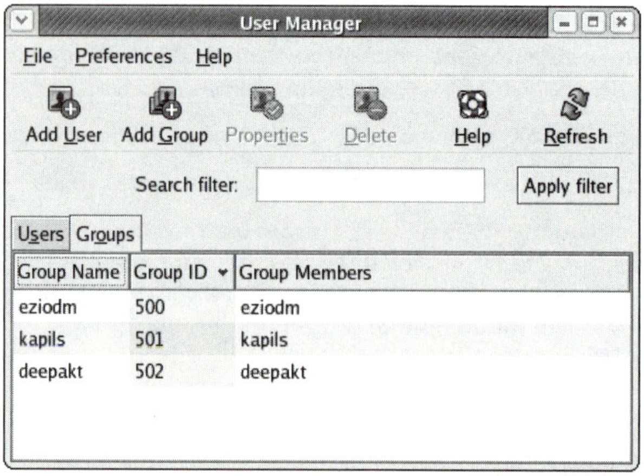

Figure 7-5

Again, the GUI's default behavior is to hide the system groups. You can reveal them by selecting the Preferences menu and then disabling the Filter system users and groups option. In Figure 7-5 you can see a group for each of the user accounts created earlier: this is the effect of the "Create a private group for the user" option you selected when adding the accounts.

2. Now click the Add Group button to create a new group. In the resulting Create New Group dialog box, type the name of the new group. If you know what you're doing, you can specify a certain group identification number; otherwise, you should let the system decide (see Figure 7-6).

Figure 7-6

When you're done, press OK.

3. Now you'll see that the authors group has been created, and is shown in the main User Manager screen. You can create more groups if you like, simply repeating Step 2.

Managing Group Members

After you've created your new group, you can start adding the relevant user accounts to it. Then, when you specify the access rights for your group later on in this chapter, the access rights you set will apply to every member of that particular group.

Group membership is not set in stone when the group is created: you can add accounts to the group and remove members from the group at any time. In fact, there are two ways to manage group membership:

- You can modify a *user's* properties, by specifying which groups that user is a member of.
- You can modify a *group's* properties, by specifying which users belong to that group.

In the following example we'll add the users eziodm, kapils, and deepakt to the authors group. In the process, you'll see both of these techniques.

Try It Out — Managing Group Membership

1. First, modify the membership properties of the eziodm account in the User Manager by selecting the Users tab, and then selecting the eziodm user. Then click the Properties button, and select the Groups tab in the newly created window.

2. In the Groups tab, you can see which groups this user belongs to just by looking at the checkboxes, as shown in Figure 7-7. You can also add the user to (and remove him from) groups simply by clicking the group names.

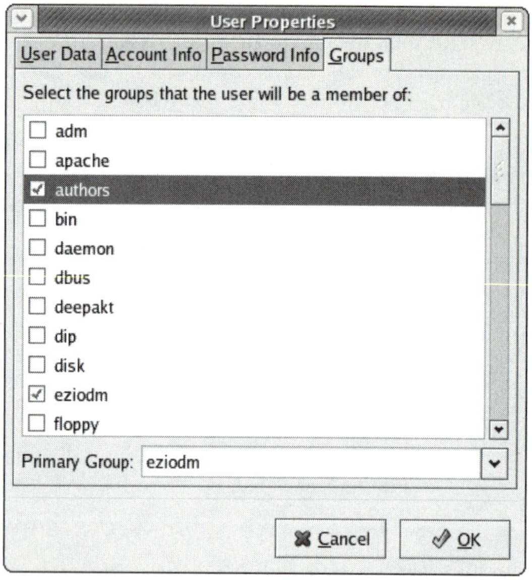

Figure 7-7

In this case, you're managing the eziodm user account's membership of the various system and custom groups that exist on the system. This user is already a member of the private group of the same name, and by selecting the checkbox next to the authors group, you can add the user to that group, too. Click OK to confirm.

3. Now add the other two users to the authors group. In the User Manager dialog box, select the Groups tab and then the authors group, and then click Properties. In the resulting Group Properties dialog box, select the Group Users tab.

   You should find that the eziodm user is already checked because you added this user to the group a moment ago. To add the other two users, just select the checkboxes next to those usernames, as shown in Figure 7-8.

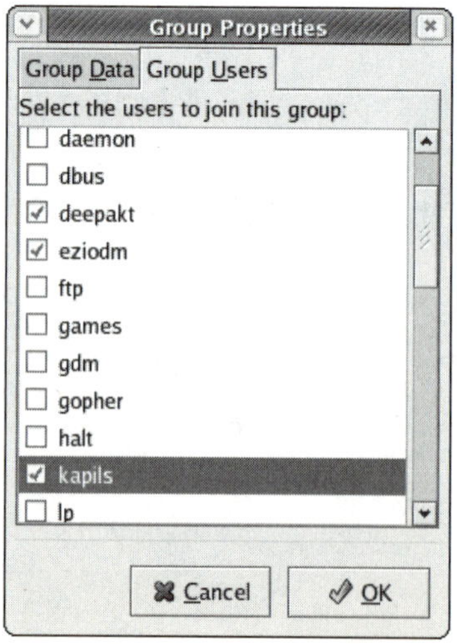

Figure 7-8

4. When you submit this, the User Manager confirms the three new members of the authors group, as shown in Figure 7-9.

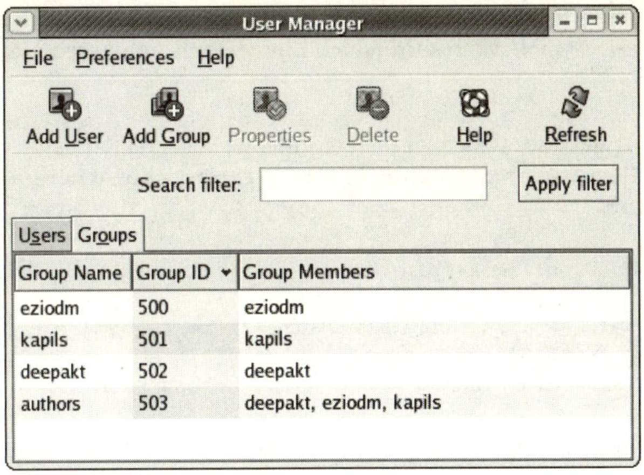

Figure 7-9

How Linux Stores User Account Information

As you've seen, the User Manager makes it really easy to create user accounts and groups, and to define group membership. Having seen it in action, it's a good time to see where account information is stored in the filesystem. By taking a quick look at these files, you'll get a better understanding of what you achieved in the preceding examples, and it will prepare you for using the command line tools that you'll see later in this chapter.

Linux stores its local user account information in the text configuration files shown in the following table.

Configuration File	Purpose
`/etc/passwd`	Contains a list of local users and their data
`/etc/shadow`	Contains encrypted passwords and bookkeeping information such as account expiry
`/etc/group`	Defines groups and associated accounts

There is a fourth file, `/etc/gshadow`*, that we will not cover extensively here. It stores encrypted group passwords. You can find out more by reading the HOWTO file on this subject, which (in the current release) can be found at* `/usr/share/doc/shadow-utils-*/HOWTO`.

User Accounts and Their Properties

To examine in better detail the properties of a user account on your system, you can take a look at your /etc/passwd file (using a text editor such as gedit or a CLI command such as cat). The /etc/passwd file is essentially the *user account database* in which Linux stores valid accounts and related information about these accounts.

The following example includes details of the accounts we just created using the User Manager. Your /etc/passwd file will be similar in structure to the file excerpt shown here, although the exact details may be a little different:

```
root:x:0:0:Super User:/root:/bin/bash
halt:x:7:0:Stop the System:/sbin:/sbin/halt
eziodm:x:500:500:Pancrazio 'Ezio' de Mauro:/home/eziodm:/bin/bash
kapils:x:501:501:Kapil Sharma:/home/kapils:/bin/bash
deepakt:x:502:502:Deepak Thomas:/home/deepakt:/bin/bash
```

Each line of the /etc/passwd file is a single *record* in the user database and represents a single user. The administrator (root) account is usually the first user account defined in the file; it's followed by a number of *system accounts*, and finally the ordinary user accounts (such as the eziodm, kapils, and deepakt accounts here).

Each record is composed of a number of *fields*, which describe the properties of the user account. In this file, adjacent fields are separated by a colon (:). To get a better understanding of the purpose of each field, let's look, for example, at the third record (see Figure 7-10).

Figure 7-10

- The first field contains the *username* (also known as the *account name* or *login name*). When the user logs in, submitting a username, Linux looks up the specified username in this table. Usernames usually begin with an alphabetic character, and can be up to 32 characters long, although some older programs can accept only the first eight characters.

In fact, the eight-character limit for account names is a historic UNIX thing. Sticking to this maximum length is still considered the safest choice, especially when networking with older UNIX computers.

- The second field contains a placeholder for the *password*. In older versions of Linux, this field used to contain an encrypted version of the password itself. For reasons of security, passwords are now stored in the /etc/shadow file (they're still stored in encrypted form); we'll return to this issue in the next section.

- The third field contains the account's *user identification number (UID)*. The UID identifies the user account—each UID is unique to exactly one account within the system. In Fedora Core, UIDs below 500 are reserved for system accounts. For example, the UID 0 (zero) is reserved for the super user, root. If the UID 0 is assigned to another account, it will grant administration rights to that account. Needless to say, that is a very dangerous thing to do.
- The fourth field contains the *group identification number (GID)* of the account's *primary group*. A GID is unique to exactly one group within the system. An account belongs to at least one group (and it may belong to more than one), but the one specified here is the primary group with which the user is associated (and is usually the private group you created at the same time as the account).

  Once again, the GID 0 (zero) should be reserved for root, even though it's not as dangerous as the UID zero.

An account's UID and primary group GID are not necessarily the same values; the preceding example is slightly special. As mentioned, UIDs and GIDs below 500 are reserved for the system; and eziodm was the first non-system account created on this machine. So, when the system created this account, it set the UID to the first available UID value (which was 500), and it assigned the GID of the associated group to the first available GID value (which was also 500).

- The fifth field is the *description* of the user account. In general, the description can be any string. For example, when the account is for a particular person, it usually makes sense to use that person's name for the account description (like the accounts for Ezio, Deepak, and Kapil); when the account is designed to fill a specific role, a description of the role is suitable (like the halt account).

  Later in the chapter, you'll see how the User Information dialog box allows users to enter a name and contact information associated to their account. When they do so, the information is stored in this field, in comma-separated format.
- The sixth field contains the account's *home directory*. This is most commonly used for personal accounts, and provides users with a directory within which they can store their own personal files. By default, a user's home directory is created under the `/home` directory (for example, eziodm's home directory is `/home/eziodm`), but in fact, it is possible to place a user's home directory anywhere on the system.

There is one notable exception: the root account's home directory is always `/root` (or even `/` itself in old systems). This design is to ensure that the directory will be available for use even if `/home` is not available after booting (for example, if the `/home` filesystem lies on a separate partition to the rest of the filesystem, and a disk error prevents Linux from mounting it).

  For an account that is associated with a function or a software program, rather than a user, the notion of using the home directory field to store "personal files" is somewhat lost. In this scenario, the home directory field is sometimes used to specify the directory in which the software is located, or it may point to a general location place such as the `/bin` directory.

- The seventh and final field contains the *login shell* associated with the account. You saw in Chapter 6 that the shell is in charge of executing user commands. The system runs the login shell whenever you log in using text mode, or open a terminal window using graphical mode. A list of valid shells is typically kept in `/etc/shells` (although any program can be used as a

> login shell). There are programs that check the contents of `/etc/shells` to find out whether a user account is an ordinary account (with a shell listed in `/etc/shells`) or a special account. One special account is the halt user: if you log in using the halt account and you supply the correct password, the system will initiate the shutdown sequence to switch the computer off.

You can get more information with the `man 5 passwd` and `man 5 shells` commands from your terminal window or console screen.

User Account Passwords

As it happens, any user has read access to the `/etc/passwd` file—indeed, this access is handy if, for example, you need to match an account name to its UID. But as previously mentioned, older versions of Linux stored account passwords in encrypted format in the second field of the `/etc/passwd` file. A consequence of this was that it was easy for users to access the encrypted versions of the passwords of other users.

Initially, this was not considered a security issue because the passwords were encrypted. However, the storage of encrypted passwords in `/etc/passwd` is no longer considered safe; as we explain in the next subsections, techniques now exist that make it much easier to guess a user's password given its encrypted form and knowledge of the encryption algorithm.

To plug this security hole, Fedora Core stores encrypted passwords in a different file—`/etc/shadow`. This file is accessible to root only. While non-root users can still read from `/etc/passwd`, they do not have permission to read from `/etc/shadow`, and thus do not have access to encrypted passwords.

Password Encryption

While the account passwords are now stored safely in the restricted access `/etc/shadow` file, Linux *still* takes the precaution of storing them in encrypted format.

If you use root privileges to examine the contents of the `/etc/shadow` file, you'll see each encrypted password stored as an incomprehensible string of characters, like this:

```
$1$mWzQxFuT$EWnSiX5hmxiERbUpfwR5V0
```

Fedora Core *never* stores passwords in the clear text form in which the user enters them. Rather, it always encrypts them before storing them or working with them, in such a way that it is not easily possible (or even feasible) to decipher the encrypted version and find out the original password.

In fact, once the password has been encrypted and stored in `/etc/shadow`, there will never be the need to decrypt it again. This is a key point: when a user logs in, the operating system verifies her identity by *encrypting* the submitted password and comparing it with the encrypted string contained in the `/etc/shadow`. If the two strings match, access is granted. It is this process that enables Linux to avoid ever having to decrypt passwords.

A Technique for Guessing Passwords

Unfortunately, the fact that a password is encrypted before storage is not enough to guarantee that it can't be discovered by other means. While it's very difficult to use decryption techniques to discover the original passwords, it is quite possible to use a *brute force* method to find out "weak" passwords. The power of modern computer hardware makes it possible to take large numbers of common passwords, encrypt them using the same algorithm used by the operating system, and check if the encrypted version is the same as the one stored in the password file.

This technique is often called a *dictionary attack* because the attacker can take large numbers of candidate passwords from a dictionary. A surprising number of passwords can be cracked in this way—indeed, Chapter 10 takes a look at a program called crack, which uses this technique to crack passwords.

The existence of such techniques is the motivating factor behind the decision to place passwords in `/etc/shadow`, rather than `/etc/passwd`. Thus, users are prevented from stealing encrypted passwords and then trying to break the weak ones via a dictionary attack.

> *Further discussion of cryptographic techniques is outside the scope of this chapter. However, cryptography is a fascinating science. If you're interested, you could start experimenting with the GNU Privacy Guard (GnuPG)—install the* `gnupg` *package on your system, and then have a look at the* `gpg` *command. The* `gpg` *manual page will certainly be useful, providing information and lists of other documents.*

A Sample /etc/shadow File

Examine the following few lines from a sample `/etc/shadow` file. This example contains the entries for the accounts added via the User Manager earlier in this chapter. Once again, your `/etc/shadow` will probably differ from this, although its structure will be similar:

```
root:$1$eÂúkæÛAÈ$Kv55YOaIHDcPlI1q6igoQ0:11961:0:99999:7:::
halt:*:11961:0:99999:7:::
eziodm:$1$W/RgbXrI$OP9t9IyVmQyvPfxNLUFwQ1:12100:0:99999:7:::
kapils:!!$1$68Q7Ci4g$CqbN8rdCBw4GmxDlouQ2q/:12100:0:99999:7:::
deepakt:$1$sUejrHGF$I3cSo2TRmKIbN55wfLgfB1:12100:0:99999:7:::
```

Just like `/etc/passwd`, each line (or *record*) represents a user, and adjacent fields are separated by a colon. Again, to understand the purpose of the fields in this file, let's look at the third line (see Figure 7-11).

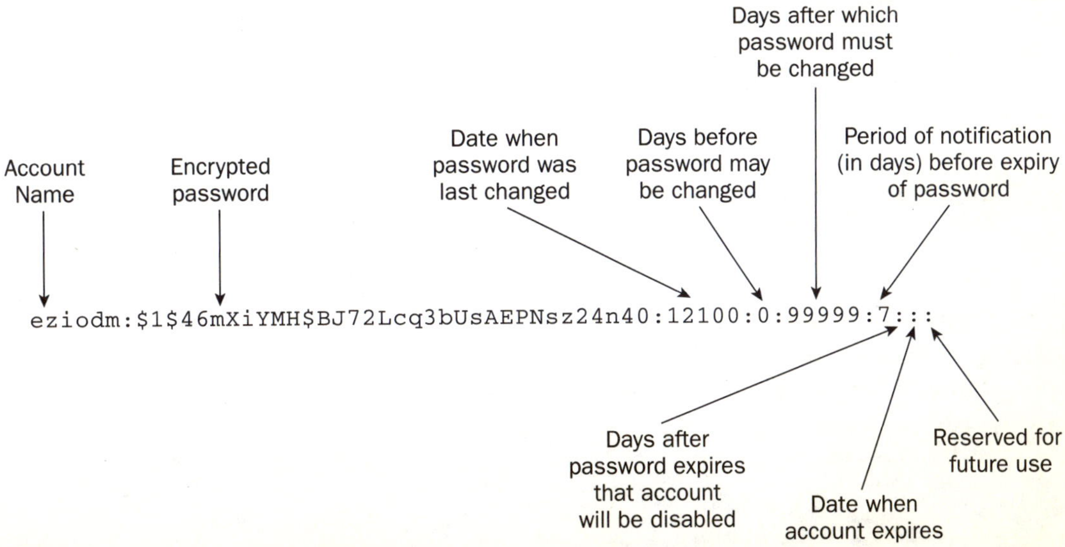

Figure 7-11

- The first field contains the account name. It must match the name found in `/etc/passwd`.
- The second field contains the encrypted password. An asterisk (`*`) here indicates that the account is disabled (that is, the user cannot log in), while a `!!` sequence here (followed by the original encrypted password) indicates that the account is temporarily locked.
- The third field indicates the date when the password was last changed. It is expressed as the number of days elapsed since January 1, 1970. It is very typical, in systems of UNIX descent, to count the number of days or seconds since this date, also known as *the epoch*. In the example, you can see that eziodm's password was last changed 12,100 days after January 1, 1970.
- The fourth field contains a count of the number of days before the password *may* next be changed. The value zero or an empty field (as in the preceding examples) means that it can be changed anytime.
- The fifth field contains a count of the number of days after which the password *must* be changed. This default value means that the password can stay in its place for almost 274 years, which is probably long enough.
- The sixth field specifies the number of days users will be warned that their password is about to expire.
- The seventh field specifies after how many days the account is disabled if its owner does not change the password when requested to.
- The eighth field is the date when the account will be unconditionally disabled, expressed in days since January 1, 1970.
- Finally, at the end of the line is an empty field, reserved for future use.

To get more information about `/etc/shadow`, you can consult its manual page by typing `man 5 shadow` at your shell prompt.

Groups

A user can belong to many groups, but as you've seen, `/etc/passwd` allows membership of only one group (the *primary group*). Membership of additional groups must be specified in the `/etc/groups` file. This file is very similar in structure to the two you've already seen. The following example shows the groups created earlier in this chapter:

```
root:x:0:root
bin:x:1:root,bin,daemon
daemon:x:2:root,bin,daemon
eziodm:x:500:
kapils:x:501:
deepakt:x:502:
authors:x:503:eziodm,kapils,deepakt
```

The structure is quite simple. Let's study the second line of this file to understand the fields (see Figure 7-12).

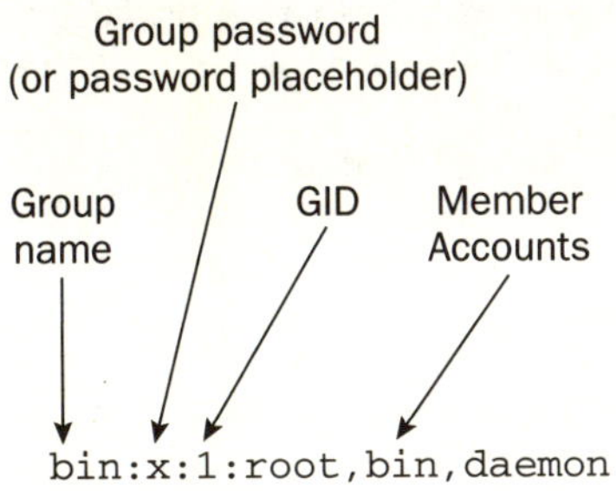

Figure 7-12

- The first field contains the group name.
- The second field contains a placeholder for an optional *group password*. The password, if present, is stored in `/etc/gshadow`. Group passwords are rarely used so they aren't discussed here.
- The third field contains the group identification number (GID). As previously mentioned, every group on the system must have its own unique GID. Recall that `/etc/passwd` refers to primary groups by number, not by name; so when it's necessary, this field is used to match a group number with its corresponding group name.
- The last field contains the list of user accounts that belong to this group.

For more information about `/etc/group`, you can type `man 5 group` at your shell prompt.

Advanced User Account Management

You've also seen how to manage user accounts and groups via the User Manager, and you've seen how Fedora Core stores this user information in the configuration files `/etc/passwd`, `/etc/shadow`, and `/etc/group`.

It's evident that these configuration files are just plain text files, and perhaps you're tempted to put aside the User Manager and edit those files manually, using a text editor such as `gedit`. It is quite possible to manage your user information this way, but it is safer to use the User Manager or the CLI commands instead. First, the files are of critical importance to the successful execution of your Fedora Core installation, and their integrity must be ensured at all times. The tools are designed to ensure the integrity of these files, but if you edit them manually you are on your own. Second, the tools carry out proper *file locking*. This is a mechanism that prevents overwriting problems in a situation where several administrators try to manage users at the same time. It is definitely convenient to be able to examine these configuration files, but when you need to make adjustments to them, it's safest to use the designated tools—the graphical User Manager interface that you've already seen, and the command line tools that are examined next.

Some Useful Command Line Tools

If you plan to use the command line tools to manage your users and groups, you'll need to do so in the context of the root account. Having fired up a terminal window, there are a few clues to remind you which account you're logged in as—remember that the typical root shell prompt is denoted with the # character, while the prompt for an ordinary user account is denoted with $ or >.

You can also use the id command to check your identity:

```
$ id
uid=500(eziodm) gid=500(eziodm) groups=500(eziodm),503(authors)
```

This output shows that the user is logged in as the eziodm account. (Note that it also confirms information about the account's group membership—in particular, that its primary group is also called eziodm and that the user is a member of two groups, eziodm and authors.)

To run in the context of the root account in a terminal window, simply execute the switch user (su) command at the command line:

```
$ su -
Password:
```

You'll be prompted to type the root password, as shown. The effect of the su command is to execute a new shell under a different user account. Note that the new shell isn't a *substitute* for the existing shell. Instead, the new shell runs *on top of* the existing shell. To demonstrate this point, take a look at Figure 7-13, which shows a user switching from eziodm to root, using the root shell, and then leaving it.

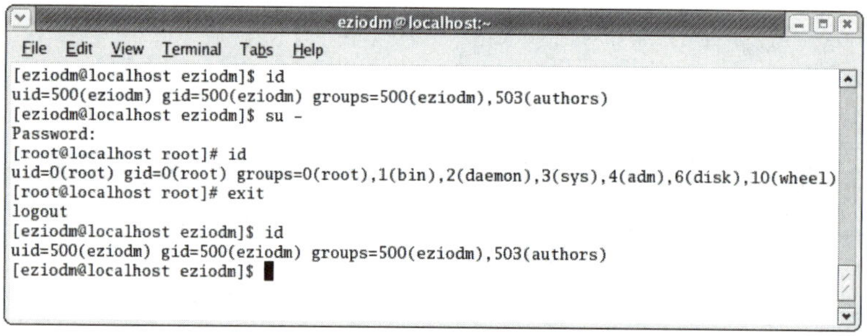

Figure 7-13

As you can see, the new (root) shell terminates (via the exit command), and the terminal window remains open and reverts to the context of the original account.

The default behavior of Fedora Core is to clear the screen after a user types the exit *command; therefore the* /root/.bash_logout *file has been temporarily renamed to avoid executing the* clear *command at the end of the* su *session.*

Note that the su command here is accompanied by a dash (-) symbol. This ensures that the new shell is treated just like any other login shell. In particular, it means that the login scripts associated to the user account (root, in this case) will be executed just as if root were logging in from a terminal. These scripts have a number of effects. For example, in this case, they do the following:

- They set the current working directory to be that of `root`'s home directory.
- They set the `$PATH` environment variable (the search path for executable programs) to the value associated with the root user by adding the directories `/sbin` and `/usr/sbin`. These two directories contain administrative programs that are used only by administrative accounts.
- The user's login and logout scripts are executed.

If the `dash` character (-) is omitted, the `su` command will execute a shell but will not execute the login scripts.

If you use `su` *to switch to the root account, and then find that various administrative commands are "missing," it could be that you omitted the – switch; that is, you typed just* `su` *instead of* `su –`.

Note also that you can use `su` *to execute a shell with an account other than root, as in the following example:*

```
$ su kapils
$ su - kapils
```

We're now ready to add new users to the system using the command line.

Adding Users at the Command Line

Adding users can be a straightforward task on a standalone PC, but when you're a professional system administrator with a lot of settings to get through, the graphical User Manager tool can make the task a time-consuming one.

Hence, it sometimes makes more sense to make use of command line tools instead. Once you've got the hang of the command line tools, it's easy to include them in automated scripts and perform complex or lengthy operations more quickly. As you'd expect, the command line tools also have lots of options and are rather more flexible than their GUI counterparts.

Try It Out Adding Users with the Command Line Interface

In its simplest form, here's the sequence of commands that replicates the behavior of the graphical tool, using default values when possible.

1. At a *root shell* prompt, type the following command to add a new user without having to worry about details such as choosing UID and GID:

```
# useradd -c 'Mark Mamone' -s /bin/bash markm
```

2. Before proceeding, use the `gedit` text editor to examine the configuration files. First, in `/etc/passwd`, you should find the following new entry, for the account you've just created:

```
...
eziodm:x:500:500:Pancrazio 'Ezio' de Mauro:/home/eziodm:/bin/bash
kapils:x:501:501:Kapil Sharma:/home/kapils:/bin/bash
deepakt:x:502:502:Deepak Thomas:/home/deepakt:/bin/bash
markm:x:503:504:Mark Mamone:/home/markm:/bin/bash
```

The UID is 503 and the primary, private GID is 504. Next, from /etc/group, you read the following:

```
...
eziodm:x:500:
kapils:x:501:
deepakt:x:502:
authors:x:503:eziodm,kapils,deepakt
markm:x:504:
```

From this, you can deduce that the group with GID 504 is called markm. Finally, there's a new line in /etc/shadow:

```
...
eziodm:$1$W/RgbXrI$OP9t9IyVmQyvPfxNLUFwQ1:12100:0:99999:7:::
kapils:!!$1$68Q7Ci4g$CqbN8rdCBw4GmxDlouQ2q/:12100:0:99999:7:::
deepakt:$1$sUejrHGF$I3cSo2TRmKIbN55wfLgfB1:12100:0:99999:7:::
markm:!!:12100:0:99999:7:::
```

The !! in the second field means that the account is disabled. In fact, this is the default behavior of useradd—it creates disabled accounts.

3. To enable the newly created account, you must assign a password. Still using the root account, use the passwd command to assign a password for markm:

```
# passwd markm
Changing password for user markm.
New password: (password not shown)
Retype new password: (password not shown)
passwd: all authentication tokens updated successfully.
```

4. Now refresh your view of the /etc/shadow, to see what has changed:

```
...
eziodm:$1$W/RgbXrI$OP9t9IyVmQyvPfxNLUFwQ1:12100:0:99999:7:::
kapils:!!$1$68Q7Ci4g$CqbN8rdCBw4GmxDlouQ2q/:12100:0:99999:7:::
deepakt:$1$sUejrHGF$I3cSo2TRmKIbN55wfLgfB1:12100:0:99999:7:::
markm:$1$3afRsVjz$mg9zGakhspD.fcpDwx4wv0:12100:0:99999:7:::
```

Now the markm account has a password, and is fully operative.

5. To test out the markm account, open a new terminal window as a normal user. Then use the su command to verify that the account works:

```
$ su - markm
Password: (password not shown)
$ id
uid=503(markm) gid=504(markm) groups=504(markm)
```

As you can see, the new user identity is now markm. The new current directory is /home/markm because you used the su - form:

```
$ pwd
/home/markm
$ ls -a
.  ..  .bash_logout  .bash_profile  .bashrc  .emacs  .gtkrc
```

How It Works

The `useradd` command creates a new user called markm. The description, `Mark Mamone`, is delimited by single quotation marks to instruct the shell to keep it as a single parameter. The shell is `/bin/bash`:

```
# useradd -c 'Mark Mamone' -s /bin/bash markm
```

The `passwd` command assigns a password to the account. The password is to be accepted but not displayed:

```
# passwd markm
```

Other aspects of the account are determined automatically from the system defaults and from the arguments specified. By default, the home directory will be `/home/markm`; the UID and GID will be the first available (in this case, 503 and 504, respectively); and the account and password expiration data are taken from `/etc/login.defs` and `/etc/default/useradd`.

You might be surprised to find that the newly created home directory is not empty. Its content is copied from the `/etc/skel` directory, which contains the files and directories that should be added to a new home directory whenever a new user account is created. This is a particularly handy feature for the system administrator: if every user needs a similar setup, it is sufficient to put the desired files in `/etc/skel`.

Other defaults, such as password-aging values, are taken from `/etc/login.defs`.

More on the useradd and passwd Commands

The `useradd` command has several options that you can use when the defaults are not appropriate. More details are available by typing `man useradd` in a terminal. The following table provides a list of the most commonly used options.

Option	Purpose
`-d`	Allows you to specify the user's home directory.
`-e`	Allows you to specify the expiration date of the account in the format DD-MM-YYYY.
`-f`	If the password expires, the operating system will wait a number of days before permanently disabling the account. This option allows you to specify the number of days between these two events.
`-g`	Allows you to specify the GID of this account.
`-G`	Allows you to specify a comma-separated list of other groups to which the user belongs.
`-M`	Allows you to omit the creation of a home directory.
`-u`	Allows you to specify the UID of this account.

You can use the `passwd` command whenever a password needs to be changed or initialized. Of course, normal (non-root) users are allowed to change only their *own* passwords—they can do this via the `passwd` command. Root users can change *anyone*'s password, and to do that they can specify the `passwd` command followed by the account name (as you saw in Step 3 of the "Adding Users with the Command Line Interface" example).

Modifying One's Own User Account

Once a user account has been created, its owner has a certain degree of control over it. Not surprisingly, Fedora Core has graphical and command line tools, and account owners can change things such as the password, account description, and shell.

Modifying One's Own Password

As you'll see in the following two examples, the basic steps for changing your password are identical whether you use the GUI or the command line procedure.

To change your password via the graphical interface, select Main Menu ➪ Preferences ➪ Password or type `userpasswd` in a terminal window. The dialog box shown in Figure 7-14 appears. For security reasons, you'll have to type your old password first.

Figure 7-14

Then you'll be prompted twice for the new password (see Figure 7-15).

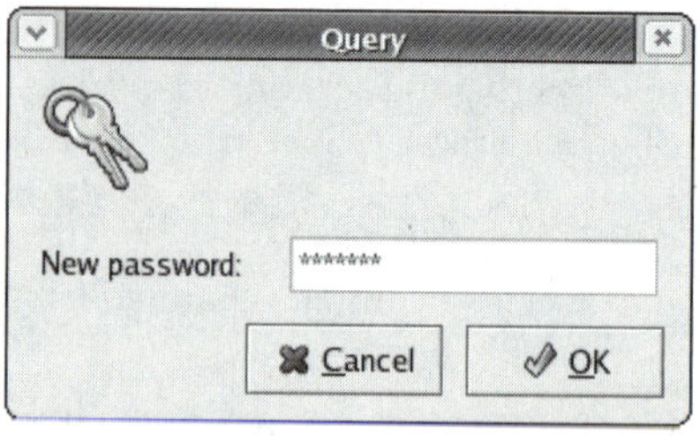

Figure 7-15

If you type the same password twice, and it is not too short or based on a dictionary word, the new password will be accepted. Remember, it is a good idea to change your password regularly, especially if your computer is shared with somebody else, even if the system does not enforce password expiration.

To change your password via the command line, you can use the `passwd` command. You'll first be challenged to enter your current password—again, this is to ensure you have the right to change it:

```
$ passwd
Changing password for user eziodm.
Changing password for eziodm
(current) UNIX password: (password not shown)
```

Then you're asked to enter the new password. You can take this opportunity to find out the sort of passwords that are acceptable. Try typing `ape5` as your new password:

```
New password: (password not shown)
BAD PASSWORD: it is too short
```

Because `ape5` is too short, try `elephant6` instead:

```
New password: (password not shown)
BAD PASSWORD: it is based on a dictionary word
```

The `passwd` command won't accept dictionary-based passwords either: it has a built-in mechanism that prevents you from choosing passwords that can be easily guessed. Try something a little more complex, such as `e!eph4nt`:

```
New password: (password not shown)
Retype new password: (password not shown)
passwd: all authentication tokens updated successfully.
```

As you can see, the steps in the command line procedure are identical to those of the GUI-based procedure.

Finally, remember that if a normal user, such as eziodm, forgets his or her password, root can run the following command to reset it to a known value:

```
# passwd eziodm
```

Changing Your Own Account Description and Shell

Red Hat Linux also provides GUI and CLI utilities that allow users to control other aspects of their account. You can launch the GUI utility by selecting Main Menu ➪ Preferences ➪ About Myself, or by typing `userinfo` at the command line. This brings up the User Information dialog box shown in Figure 7-16.

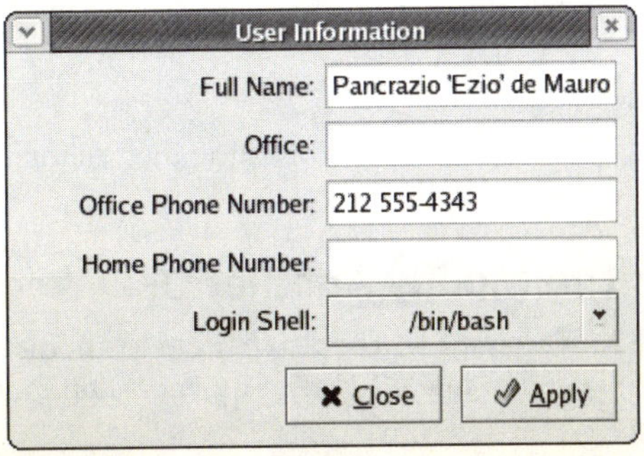

Figure 7-16

With this dialog box, you can edit the system's record of your name and add contact information, if you wish. All this information is then stored (in comma-separated format) in the *description* field of the record in `/etc/passwd`, like this:

```
eziodm:x:500:500:Pancrazio 'Ezio' de Mauro,,212 555-4343,:/home/eziodm:/bin/bash
```

You can also use this dialog box to change your login shell. Note that it is not possible to choose a shell that is not in the list. When you're finished, just click Apply to confirm (if you want to discard your changes, click Close instead). If you modify and confirm anything, the tool asks for your password to verify your identity.

Changing Your Account Description via the Command Line

From the command line, you can use `chfn` to change your personal information and `chsh` to change your shell. Here's an example in which user eziodm uses `chfn` to change personal information:

```
$ chfn
Changing finger information for eziodm.
Password: (password not shown)
Name [Pancrazio 'Ezio' de Mauro]: Pancrazio de Mauro
Office []:
Office Phone [212 555-4343]: +44 20 1234 5678
Home Phone []: +39 02 1234 5678
Finger information changed.
```

The result achieved by this is very similar to that achieved by using the User Information dialog box you saw in the preceding section. You can see that this user was first required to enter a password (to identify themselves), and then changed the account's Name and Office and Home phone numbers.

To change the login shell, you can use the `chsh` command, which works in a very similar way:

```
$ chsh
Changing shell for eziodm.
Password: (password not shown)
New shell [/bin/bash]: /bin/tcsh
Shell changed.
```

If you want to return to your previous shell, just run `chsh` again and specify the original one:

```
$ chsh
Changing shell for eziodm.
Password: (password not shown)
New shell [/bin/tcsh]: /bin/bash
Shell changed.
```

You can find out more about `chfn` and `chsh` by consulting their manuals from a terminal with `man chfn` and `man chsh`.

Using the root Account to Modify Another User Account

When you need to adopt the root account and apply changes to another account, the best tool to use is dependent on the changes you need to make. Some of the more common operations (such as account or password expiry) are easy to perform using the User Manager (you select the account and then press the Properties button).

However, if you need to make more major changes to an account (such as changing the UID), the User Manager is not enough. In fact, you can't even use the CLI-based commands such as the `passwd`, `chfn`, and `chsh` utilities to change the UID of an account.

If you absolutely *must* change an account home directory, UID, GID, or even login name, here's how to do it using `usermod` on the command line. Remember, you have to be logged in as root to do this. Suppose you have the following user in `/etc/passwd`:

```
eziodm:x:500:500:Pancrazio 'Ezio' de Mauro:/home/eziodm:/bin/bash
```

If you want to rename the account from eziodm to eziod, you can run `usermod`, like this:

```
# usermod -l eziod eziodm
```

We've used the `-l` option to indicate that we want to change the login name, and we specify the *new* login name before the existing one. As a result, the record for this user in `/etc/passwd` changes to the following:

```
eziod:x:500:500:Pancrazio 'Ezio' de Mauro:/home/eziodm:/bin/bash
```

As you can see, the account has preserved its UID, description, home directory, and so on. If you want to change the location of the user's home directory, you can run this command after the previous one:

```
# usermod -d /home/eziod -m eziod
```

Here's how to read this command:

- The `-d /home/eziod` option specifies the new home directory.
- The `-m` option instructs `usermod` to *move* the contents of the old directory to the new one. After the move, the old home directory will not be visible anymore.
- The username (eziod) specified at the end of the command is the account on which `usermod` must operate.

You can change an account's UID and GID via `usermod`, using the `-u` and `-g` options, respectively. However, this operation can create undesirable side effects if the user has files outside his or her home directory. In particular, the command does not update the *ownership* of those files accordingly—they have to be changed manually (perhaps with the help of other utilities, such as `find`). The manual page of `usermod` (`man usermod` in a terminal) warns about this and other critical points.

To get a list of files whose owner or group does not exist in `/etc/passwd` *or* `/etc/group`*, you can use the following command as root:*

```
# find / -nouser -o -nogroup
```

The `find` *command is a very powerful and useful command. You can check other options with* `man find` *in a terminal. There's more about it in Chapters 2 and 6.*

Deleting User Accounts

Deleting user accounts is all too easy. In the User Manager graphical interface, you can delete a user simply by selecting the user in the Users tab, and then clicking the Delete button.

Be very careful when deleting accounts via the User Manager: there will be no confirmation! However, the user's home directory will not be destroyed. So, in cases of accidental deletion, it is possible to recover the files and create an account with the same properties of the one just deleted.

From the root command line, you can run `userdel`. Using the command like this will erase the account called test from `/etc/passwd`, but the associated home directory will not be deleted:

```
# userdel markm
```

If you also specify the `-r` option, the account information, home directory, and mailbox will also be destroyed:

```
# userdel -r markm
```

Advanced Group Management

As you've seen, each user account belongs to a primary group (specified in the `/etc/passwd` file) and can be assigned to other groups during the account creation or whenever necessary. Groups are useful when setting permissions on files or directories. You've already seen how to create groups and manage group membership via the Red Hat User Manager; now you'll perform some similar tasks, and more, with the command line. The commands in the following subsections will directly affect `/etc/groups`.

Creating Groups via the Command Line

You need to be logged in as root to create a new group from the command line. The command is `groupadd`, followed by the group name:

```
# groupadd editors
```

Optionally, you can specify the GID, like this:

```
# groupadd -g 1973 editors
```

For further information, you can browse the manual page by executing `man groupadd` from a terminal.

Managing Group Membership from the Command Line

From the command line and with the appropriate permissions, even ordinary users can administer groups and decide which users belong to them. This authorization comes from root, via the `gpasswd` command:

```
# gpasswd -a eziodm authors
Adding user eziodm to group authors
# gpasswd -A eziodm authors
```

The first command uses the -a option to ensure the eziodm account is added to the authors group. The second command uses the -A option to grant eziodm the administration rights for the authors group.

Now, the eziodm user account is permitted to add new users to the authors group, like this:

```
$ gpasswd -a markm authors
Adding user markm to group authors
```

He can also remove users from that group:

```
$ gpasswd -d deepakt authors
Removing user deepakt from group authors
```

Revoking a User's Permission to Manage Membership of a Group

Finally, you can see what happens when root revokes administration rights for eziodm. This can be done by passing an empty list to the -A option:

```
# gpasswd -A '' authors
```

To test that this command has indeed revoked eziodm's right to manage the authors group, we can switch users to eziodm and use that account context to try to reinsert deepakt as a member of the authors group:

```
# su - eziodm
$ gpasswd -a deepakt authors
Permission denied.
```

As you can see, eziodm no longer has the rights to add members to the authors group.

If you want to find out something more about gpasswd, you can check its manual page with man gpasswd at your shell prompt.

When you add new members to a group, or remove members from a group, your changes are not visible until the next login, either via su - *or by logging out completely and logging back in. If you use* su - *followed by your account name (or even* newgrp *followed by a group you've just been given access to), only commands you type in that shell (for example,* id*) will be affected by the new membership.*

Deleting Groups

It is advisable to delete a group only when it doesn't contain any members. It is possible to delete secondary groups with user accounts still associated to it. Moreover, deleting a group (just like deleting a user account) could leave "stale" files whose group no longer exists. You can run the following command periodically as root on your system, to identify these files:

```
# find / -nouser -o -nogroup
```

From there, you can reassign these files to valid users or groups.

To delete a group via the User Manager GUI utility, you need to select the group and click the Delete button.

> **Beware: The group is deleted immediately, and *without confirmation*.**

Deleting Groups via the Command Line

From the command line, as root, use the `groupdel` command followed by the group name:

```
# groupdel authors
```

Just like the graphical tool, `groupdel` will not ask for confirmation.

You can check the manual page for this command via `man groupdel`.

Users, Groups, and Filesystem Permissions

With the help of groups, it is possible to implement some very sophisticated access policies. You'll recall from Chapter 7 that every file or directory in the filesystem defines access rights for three different sets of users (the *owner*, the *group*, and *others*) via a system of access modes that you can see when you use `ls`:

```
$ls -l
drwxr-xr-x    4 eziodm   eziodm      4096  Feb 12 17.40  backup_images
-rw-r--r--    4 eziodm   eziodm   1037238  Feb 12 17.25  picture1.bmp
-rw-r--r--    4 eziodm   eziodm    262314  Feb 12 17.29  picture2.bmp
-rw-r--r--    4 eziodm   eziodm     58398  Feb 12 17.37  picture3.bmp
```

When it comes to user groups, the behavior of Fedora Core is notably different from that of many other UNIX variants, including other Linux distributions. By default, every user belongs to his or her own *private group*, which is not shared with anyone else. Earlier in this chapter, you saw that whenever you create a new user account, the system tools also create a private group for that account that has the same name.

Together with this user/private group scheme, Fedora Core also ensures that the default creation mode for files (the *umask*) grants write permissions to the group. Because the group (like the user account) is private, this does not compromise the security of files that are owned by the user. However, this mechanism becomes quite an advantage when sharing files among users.

In this section you'll see six examples of how to use file protection and file sharing. You can regard them as suggestions on how to set up several protection schemes that suit normal files, directories, or executable programs:

- You can apply these techniques to files to control which documents can be accessed by which accounts and groups.
- You can apply the techniques to directories to control which accounts can access that directory, add files to it, or list its contents.
- You can apply the techniques to executable programs to control which accounts have the rights to execute certain pieces of software on your computer.

First Scenario: Private Files

In this scenario, a user wants to keep his or her files private. Groups are not really relevant here: it is sufficient to remove read, write, and execute permissions for others. The permissions for the group don't really matter because in Fedora Core the primary group is assigned to its primary user only. Thus, a directory with its permissions set as shown in Figure 7-17 guarantees privacy of its contents—that is, the directory's content can't be read, written, or executed by users other than the owner.

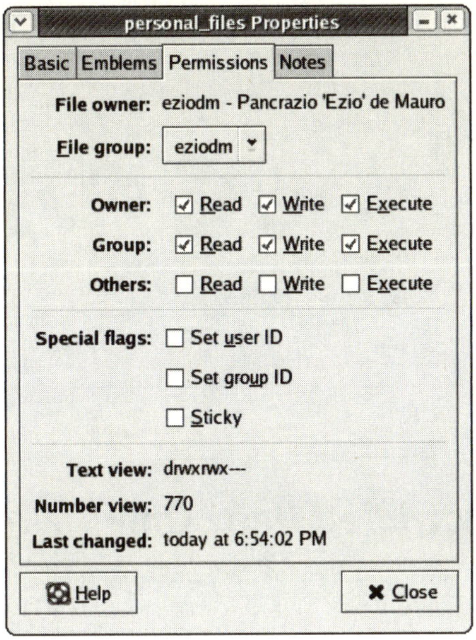

Figure 7-17

Once again, it is important to note that group permissions (Read, Write, Execute) are safe because the group in question is the group called eziodm—and the only member of this group is the user called eziodm.

Second Scenario: Public Read-Only Files

This scenario is quite simple to implement. Suppose you want to give public access to the file, and you want this public access to be read-only. Therefore, all you need to do is to ensure that the Write permission for Others is denied (see Figure 7-18).

The figure shows the permissions applied to a *directory*. You can tell this because the Text view starts with *d* (it's `drwxrwxr-x` here). When applied to a *directory*, the Execute permission refers to the user's authority to search files in that directory.

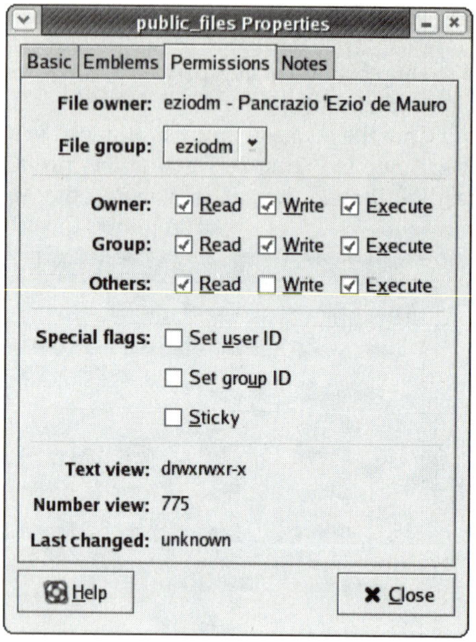

Figure 7-18

Third Scenario: Restricted Read-Only

In this scenario, you want to keep your files private, and open up the possibility of viewing the files to a limited number of users (see Figure 7-19). This is where groups start to make sense.

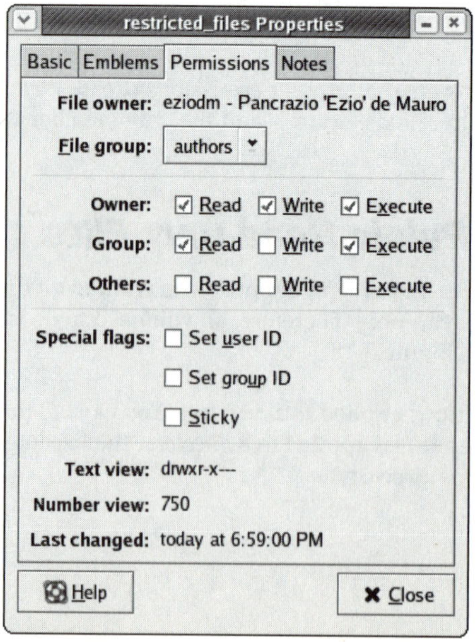

Figure 7-19

Figure 7-19 shows the permissions for a directory that belongs to the authors group. However, group members won't have Write access to the folder. All other users (that is, users who are *not* members of the authors group) are completely barred. To complete your access policy on this directory, all you need to do is add the appropriate users to the authors group. It is a good idea to repeat this for each file contained in the directory. It is a tedious task with the graphical tool, but it can be quickly achieved with the command line:

```
$ chmod -R u=rwx,g=rx,o-rwx restricted_files
```

In this command, `-R` (remember that `-R` and `-r` are not the same thing) instructs `chmod` to update the `restricted_files` directory and its entire contents, as follows:

- Setting the owner's permissions to Read, Write, Execute (`u=rwx`)
- Setting group permissions to Read, Execute (`g=rx`)
- Taking away Read, Write, Execute permissions for all others (`o-rwx`)

For additional techniques for specifying permissions, you may want to review the `chmod` command syntax with `man chmod` in a terminal.

Fourth Scenario: Restricted Write

As you gain confidence in the members of the authors group, you might want to give them Write access to the directory and its contents. This is not as trivial as it seems: you have to remember that each user has a different, personal, primary group. If you don't set up the directory properly, you'll end up with a rather messy situation: each newly created file will be assigned to the user's primary group, not to authors. This makes file sharing a bit difficult, but still possible.

The solution is to add the *Set GID Bit* to the shared directory. The Set GID Bit is a special access right conceived exactly for this scenario: every file created in the directory will belong to the *directory*'s group, not to the user's private group. To activate the Set GID Bit on a directory and fully benefit from it, the owner can create and initialize it with these commands:

```
$ mkdir restricted_directory
$ chgrp authors restricted_directory
$ chmod ug+rwx restricted_directory
$ chmod o-rwx restricted_directory
$ chmod g+s restricted_directory
```

The `mkdir` command creates a directory called `restricted_directory`, and then the `chgrp` command changes its group to authors. Then there are three `chmod` commands:

- The first (`ug+rwx`) ensures that user and group have read, write, and execute permissions.
- The second (`o-rwx`) clears all permissions for others.
- The third (`g+s`) activates the Set GID Bit.

Now you can copy files into the directory, or create files directly in it. No matter what method is used, the group will always be correctly set. Figure 7-20 shows what the directory looks like in the file manager.

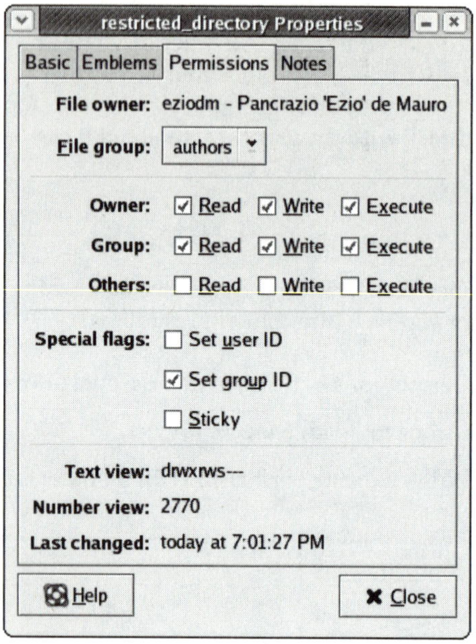

Figure 7-20

Note that the Text view field specifies the letter `s` (instead of `x`) in the group permissions, and in the Number view field, the Set GID Bit appears as a `2` in front of the usual three digits.

Fifth Scenario: Restricted Write, Public Read

To achieve this result, and have a directory that is shared in read-write mode among a restricted group of users and viewable read-only for the public, you need only to add Read and Execute permissions for Others (see Figure 7-21).

Sixth Scenario: Restricted Write, Restricted Read

In this last scenario, you want the contents of the `book` directory to have different permissions for different groups:

- You want to grant Read, Write, Execute for the authors group (they need to *write* the contents).
- You want to grant Read, Execute rights to the lecturers group (they need to *read* the contents to prepare lectures).
- You don't want any other accounts to be able to access the directory (for example, you don't want students to peek at exercises and solutions).

The difficulty here is that you can't set up different protections for different groups on the same directory because only one owner and group can be specified. On the other hand, you don't want to rely on Others for your protection scheme because that would include students as well.

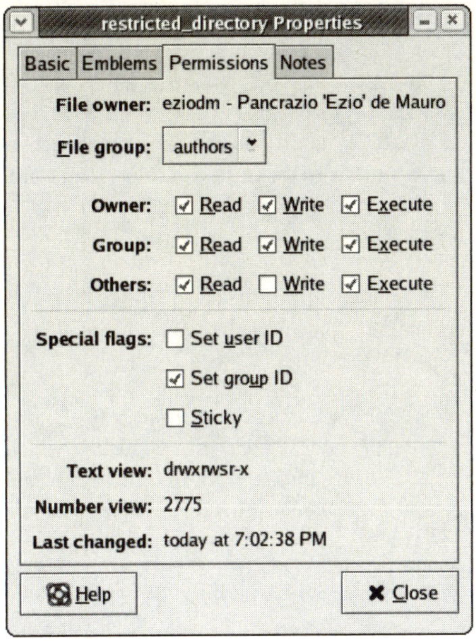

Figure 7-21

Here's a possible way to get around it. You can create a group called course, which inherits all the users from authors and lecturers. Then proceed with creating a `material` directory that is Read, Write, Execute accessible by the owner (probably a lead author) and Read, Execute accessible by the course group. Other users must not have access to it. Here's a possible example:

```
drwxr-x---    2 eziodm    course       4096 Jan 19 11:03 material
```

This means that everyone belonging to the course group, and who *also* belongs to authors or lecturers, will be able to access the `material` directory. No other accounts will be able to access the directory.

Now, create a `book` directory as a subdirectory of the `material` directory. The `book` directory will be Read, Write, Execute accessible by the owner and the authors group. Other users will have only Read, Execute access. This is exactly what you want, because the `material` folder at the immediately above level protects the `book` folder from unwanted access by students, so it is safe to leave Read and Execute access for others: in our case, others can be the lecturers group only. You must not forget to activate the Set GID Bit on the folder to allow your writers to cooperate nicely. So, these are the permissions for the `book` directory:

```
drwxrwsr-x    2 eziodm    writers      4096 Jan 19 11:04 book
```

Another way to decide fine-grained access rights is by setting up an Access Control List (ACL). ACLs are a relatively new feature in Linux and other UNIX variants, and therefore not discussed further here. You can find out more on this topic by looking at the manual pages for `acl`, `chacl`, `getfacl` *and* `setfacl`, *installed with the* `acl` *package.*

When root Is Not Necessary

As previously mentioned, the protection offered by Linux when working as a normal user is a definite advantage. Certainly, working as root all the time is one of the worst habits that a novice Linux user can develop. For example, suppose you're working as the root user, and you're cleaning up some unwanted files in your home directory, so you want to execute the following command:

```
# rm -rf /home/eziodm/tmp/redundant
```

Now, consider what happens if you accidentally insert a space character, like this:

```
# rm -rf /home /eziodm/tmp/redundant
```

Please don't try this out for yourself! The extra space character is almost invisible, but it completely changes the meaning of the command. The first of these commands will attempt to delete only the directory `/home/eziodm/tmp/redundant` *and its contents. But the second command will attempt to seek out and destroy the contents of every home directory on the system!*

If you're working as root, there's no protection—root is allowed to delete these directories, and they'll be wiped out in an instant.

You can protect yourself from accidents like this by working as a normal user. Normal users are prevented from deleting such important directories, and this is what happens when you try:

```
$ rm -rf /home /eziodm/rmp/redundant
rm: cannot remove '/home': Permission denied
```

So, the message is clear: use the root account only when it is really necessary. This generally applied policy has so far prevented viruses from spreading wildly in Linux (and UNIX in general). It's impossible for an ordinary user to infect an executable in the `/bin` directory, quite simply because ordinary users don't have Write access to those files.

In addition, it's possible to protect personal files and directories by disabling write permissions to prevent accidental deletion.

You don't need the root account for those daily tasks such as surfing the net, and you won't miss root's authority. Most of the time, there is simply no advantage in working as root. Naturally, there are times when administration rights are required—for example, when doing (but not limited to) any of the following:

- Adding new users
- Changing a forgotten password
- Connecting to the Internet
- Setting up a local area network connection
- Formatting a floppy disk

Fedora Core comes with an excellent set of tools to perform these tasks graphically, and as you've seen, the system asks you to enter the root password when necessary, so there's no need to be root all the time.

Here are some other tips to improve your normal user experience.

Mounting Devices

Thanks to technologies such as USB, FireWire, and PCMCIA (or PC Card) devices, you have several removable storage media to plug into your computer. In Linux, plugging these devices in can be a tedious job because each device must be mounted, and mounting a device requires administration privileges.

The solution is to update `/etc/fstab` once and for all as root with the correct information. After you've done this, normal users will be able to mount removable (or fixed) media, either graphically or via the command line.

Try It Out — Mounting Devices with Normal User Accounts

Suppose you have a CompactFlash card containing pictures taken with a digital camera. Once inserted, Fedora Core supports this medium, which is considered just as if it were an ordinary hard disk.

1. If you don't know the name of the device associated to your removable media, try to plug it in and have a look at the system logs. To do this, select Main Menu ➪ System Tools ➪ System Logs, or type `system-logviewer` from a terminal window. Authenticate if necessary, and then choose System Log and insert your card. You should see something like that shown in Figure 7-22.

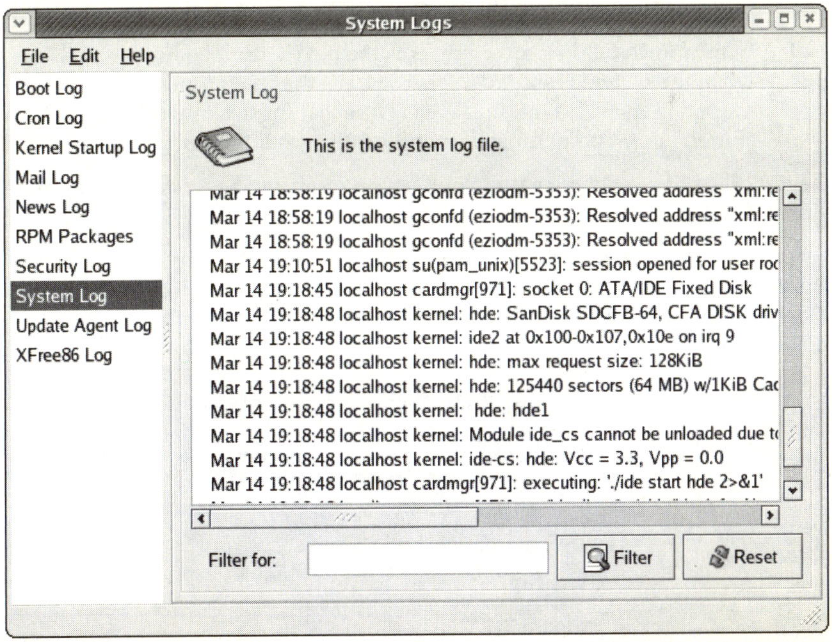

Figure 7-22

You can see the same lines in a root terminal by using the following command:

```
# tail -f /var/log/messages
```

In this output, you can tell that the device has been recognized as an IDE disk, `hde`, with only one partition (`hde1`). Thus, `/dev/hde1` is the device you want to mount.

2. Now you have to choose a *mount point* in the filesystem. Any empty directory, for example `/mnt/flash`, is an appropriate mount point. You can create `/mnt/flash` from the file manager, or from a root shell using the following command:

```
# mkdir /mnt/flash
```

3. The final step to make this device available to normal users is to edit the file `/etc/fstab`. This file contains a list of mountable devices and relative options. As root, open `/etc/fstab` using a text editor such as `gedit`. Add the following (highlighted) line at the end of the file:

```
...
/dev/cdrom    /mnt/cdrom     udf,iso9660  noauto,owner,kudzu,ro 0     0
/dev/fd0      /mnt/floppy    auto      noauto,owner,kudzu     0     0
/dev/hde1     /mnt/flash     auto      noauto,user,kudzu    0     0
```

This is how to read the line:

- The first field (`/dev/hde1`) is the device to be mounted.
- The second field (`/mnt/flash`) is the mount point.
- The third field (`auto`) will try to detect automatically the *filesystem type* on the device, for example `vfat` (very likely) or `ext3`.
- In the fourth field, `noauto` prevents the device from being mounted automatically when the system is started. Also, `owner` is the *crucial* option: it is this setting that allows normal users to mount the device. Note that for this to work, `/mnt/flash` or your chosen mount point must be mentioned in `/etc/security/console.perms`.

The rest of the line is not relevant to our example and can be ignored. You can find out more with `man fstab`.

4. Now the CompactFlash card can be mounted and unmounted by normal users without root's intervention. To test this out, log in as a normal user and select Main Menu ➪ System Tools ➪ Disk Management. The User Mount Tool dialog box appears with the newly added device, as shown in Figure 7-23.

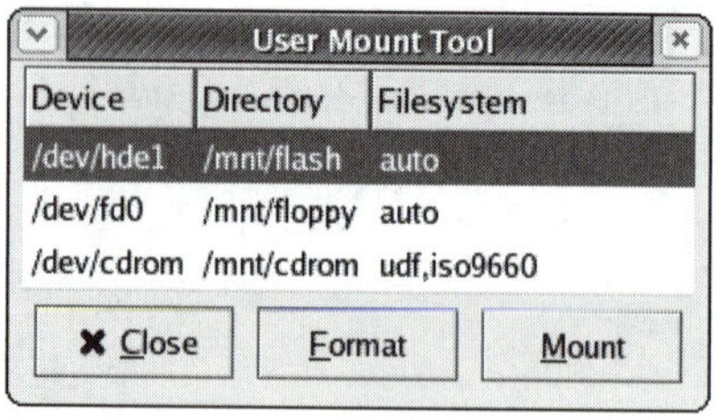

Figure 7-23

At this point, you can mount or unmount it by pressing the appropriate button and browsing its contents through the file manager.

5. You can try from a normal user terminal, as well:

```
$ mount /mnt/flash
$ ls -l /mnt/flash
total 2
drwxrwxr-x    4 eziodm      eziodm          2048 Nov  9 12:35 dcim
$ umount /mnt/flash
```

As an extra bonus, files stored in the CompactFlash card are owned by the user who mounted the device.

Using the su Command

We've already used the switch user command quite extensively to change the user account context within a terminal window. If you need to perform a lot of administrative work, it makes sense to open a terminal window, execute `su -` in it (to log in as root), and then keep that window open for admin tasks, for as long as you need it. Every time you need to run a command as root, just type it into *that* window, while you do all your other non-admin work in another window, as a normal user.

If you take this approach, it helps if you have some way to make the root shell terminal window visually distinct from the non-root shell window. This is effective, and very easy—you can create a special *root shell terminal* on your desktop, and give it distinctive features, such as a different title and color scheme.

Try It Out Creating a root Shell Launcher

First of all, while using a normal account, you need to create a new terminal profile called `root`. Here you'll give it a red background and a permanent "root shell" title.

1. Open a terminal window (choose Main Menu ➪ System Tools ➪ Terminal).
2. From the Edit menu, choose Profiles. . ., and then click the New button and type `root` as the new profile name (see Figure 7-24).

   Press Create to confirm.

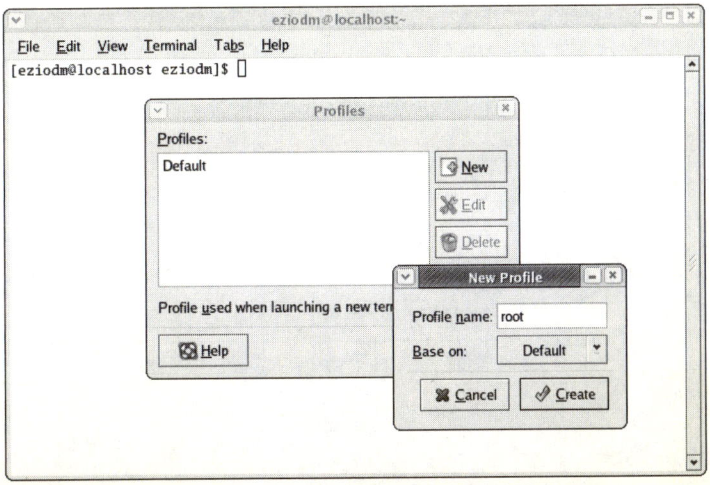

Figure 7-24

3. Now, in the Editing Profiles window, you can use your creativity to personalize the window used for root shells. For example, you can change the initial title to root shell, and set the color scheme to white-on-red, as shown in Figures 7-25 and 7-26.

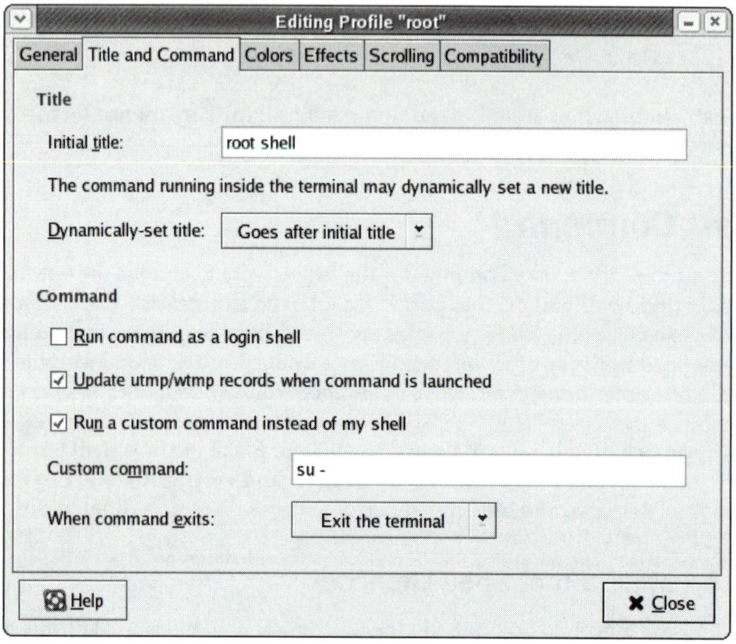

Figure 7-25

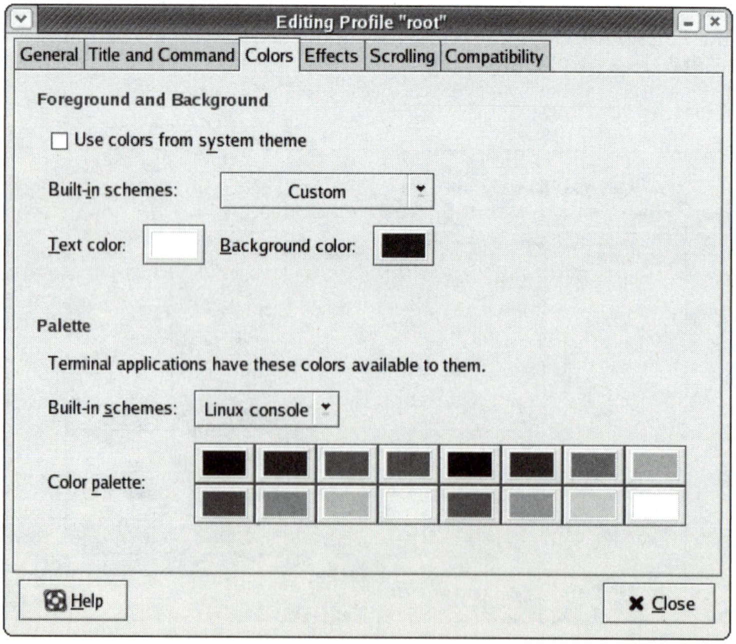

Figure 7-26

Whatever you decide to do, you *must* select the "Run a custom command instead of my shell" checkbox in the Title and Command tab, and the command *must* be `su -`. It is this that ensures that, whenever this profile is activated in the terminal, Linux will execute `su -`, and not your habitual shell.

By choosing a colored background, you create a root shell window that is clearly distinct from the others. Moreover, the title of this window will always contain the phrase "root shell," even if the application changes it.

Be sure to select Default as the Profile used when launching a new terminal in the Profiles window, otherwise every new terminal you open might be a root shell.

4. If you don't want to create a special launcher on your desktop or bottom panel, that's it: whenever you open a terminal window, you can choose File ➪ Open Terminal or File ➪ Open Tab and select the root profile instead of Default. Naturally, before having access to the root shell, you'll need to type the root password. (No matter how acquainted you get with your Linux system, it will never trust you completely).

5. If you want to create a *launcher* (that is, a personalized icon), click with the right mouse button on the desktop background and choose Create Launcher from the menu that pops up. The Create Launcher dialog box appears, as shown in Figure 7-27.

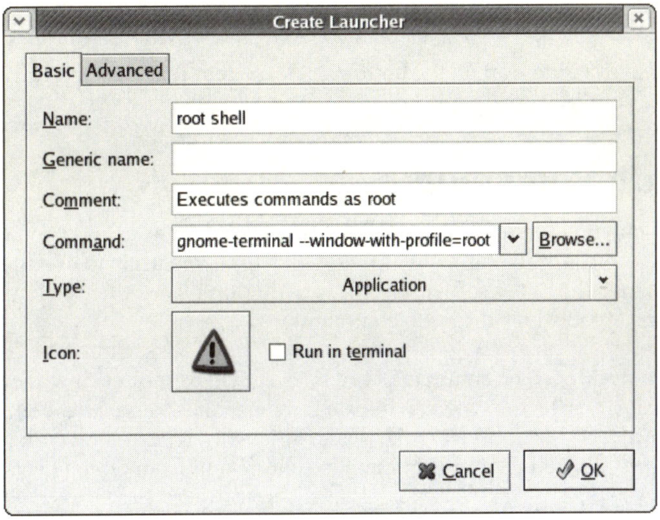

Figure 7-27

Fill in the window that appears as shown. It's important to get the spacing and double-hyphen right in the command line:

```
gnome-terminal  --window-with-profile=root
```

There is no need to go to the Advanced tab. The key here is that you start a new gnome-terminal with the root profile that you've just created. Therefore, this window will be different than the others.

When you press OK, a new icon will be created on the desktop.

6. Whenever you double-click the icon, a terminal window appears with the title and color scheme that you specified in Step 3 (the example in Figure 7-28 has white text on a red background). You'll need to type the root password. Once you're authenticated as root, you will be able to use this terminal to issue root commands.

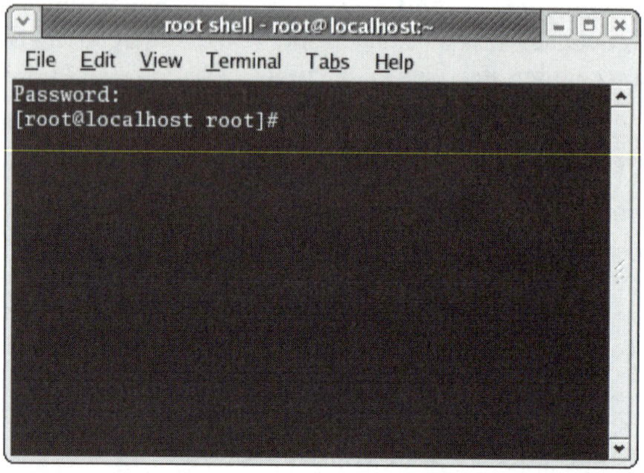

Figure 7-28

7. You can also drag the icon on the bottom panel so that it is always available. Be careful and administer your powers wisely.

Using the sudo Command

There are times when you execute the same administrative commands over and over again, and typing the root password becomes irritating. Other times, you trust some users to execute specific administrative tasks (for example, installing new software), and yet you don't want them to have the root password. These circumstances are ideal for the `sudo` command.

With `sudo`, you can decide which commands can be executed as root even when typed from an unprivileged shell. As a security measure, you can decide if the user has to type his own password before executing the command or if execution will take place right away. Moreover, you have the power to decide which parameters are allowed during command execution and from which hosts.

Configuring `sudo` means editing the `/etc/sudoers` file. It may appear difficult at first, and the output of `man sudoers` certainly looks awkward. However, the typical use scenarios are quite straightforward. First of all, `/etc/sudoers` should be properly locked before editing; therefore, it should always be edited through the `visudo` command. If you're not comfortable with `vi`, you can use a different editor by typing `EDITOR=gedit visudo` instead.

Once in the file, each line represents a different directive, and lines beginning with # are treated as comments and ignored. To allow eziodm to execute any command with root privileges, from any host and without typing the user's password, you can add a line like this:

```
eziodm ALL= NOPASSWD: ALL
```

This is how to read the line:

- The user account name is eziodm. You can specify several users in a row by separating them with commas, and you can specify groups instead of individual users by using the `%` prefix. For example, `%authors` would identify every user account belonging to the authors group.
- The first `ALL` indicates that the line is valid for every host. It could be a comma-separated list of computers (their hostname, or their IP address) on which this specification applies.
- `NOPASSWD` followed by a colon means that `sudo` will not prompt for the user's password before executing the command.
- The second `ALL` means that eziodm is allowed to execute any command as root. It can be a comma-separated list of commands, preferably with their full path and parameters, if any.

Allowing a user to execute any command without having to type the root password poses several security risks, especially on a shared computer, and it somewhat eliminates the distinction between root and non-root accounts. Here is a second and more restrictive example:

```
%authors ALL= /usr/bin/make install, /usr/bin/make uninstall
```

This means that any member of the authors group can execute either `/usr/bin/make install` or `/usr/bin/make uninstall` as root, but nothing else. `NOPASSWD` is missing, which means that `sudo` will prompt the user for the account's password before proceeding. Note that trying to execute `/usr/bin/make` alone will fail, and the same will apply for other programs called `make` located in a different path.

After deciding what goes into `/etc/sudoers`, the only thing that nonprivileged accounts have to do to execute a command as root is to type `sudo` right before it. In the following example, the user eziodm types `id` and `sudo id`, with two very different results:

```
$ id
uid=500(eziodm) gid=500(eziodm) groups=500(eziodm),504(authors)
$ sudo id
uid=0(root) gid=0(root)
groups=0(root),1(bin),2(daemon),3(sys),4(adm),6(disk),10(wheel)
```

Naturally, this works because eziodm is allowed to execute any command as root.

Compiling, Installing, and Running Software

If you need to compile software, it's usually sufficient to compile it as a normal user. Any well-behaved piece of software that requires compilation by a root user should warn you of such a requirement. The advice generally offered when extracting and compiling tarballs is to do so within the context of a normal account.

Extracting and compiling from within a normal (non-root) account is also a good *security* measure. For example, extracting from an archive from within the root account can get you into problems if the archive contains *absolute paths* instead of *relative* ones. Consider a tarball that contains a file called `/etc/passwd`: if you extract it as root, you could be in serious trouble because it will overwrite your user account file. But, if you extract from the safety of a normal user, you're using an account that is not allowed to overwrite the file, so you're protected from such disasters.

Better yet, you can extract and compile software with a non-root, non-personal account—then you won't even risk the possibility of messing up your home directory.

Immediately before the compiling phase, most modern programs require you to run a `configure` script. If this is the case (you can almost always find a `README` or `INSTALL` file or equivalent to get instructions from), installing the program with a non-root account becomes quite easy. Just run the script with the `--prefix` option, like this:

```
$ tar xzvf program_name-1.0.tar.gz
$ cd program_name-1.0
$ ./configure --prefix=$HOME/software/program_name-1.0
$ make
$ make install
```

If the program is well behaved, it will compile itself knowing that the installation directory is different than the default, typically `/usr/local`, `/usr`, or `/opt`. This allows you to install the necessary files to a place that you can write to.

If the program doesn't have a `configure` script, the solution may not be straightforward. In this case, carefully read the documentation that is included with the package (`INSTALL` and `README` files are good starting points) and, if all else fails, ask around or even contact the original developer.

Finally, we come to the first execution of the much sought after program.

Never run newly installed and unknown software as root!

This precaution is especially important if you haven't read the source code of the program and you're not certain about its features. At worst, you might damage your operating system installation, either by accidentally misusing the program or because the software you run has not been carefully written. In some extreme cases, it could even happen that the software you downloaded is *not* the one you wanted, or it will not behave as advertised.

To test-drive newly installed software, you can create a special user called swtest, for example, and switch to that account every time you run a new program for the first time. You'll have a chance to see the program in action, and possibly check swtest's home directory for added configuration files.

Who Is Logged In?

You know now that Linux is a multiuser system, and, consequently, it is possible for many remote users to be logged in to your Linux machine simultaneously, with each using their his account. But from where?

A traditional UNIX system would often have a (sometimes huge) number of *serial terminals* connected to it. Each terminal was basically just a screen with an attached keyboard (or maybe just a printer), capable of sending characters to the UNIX host and displaying characters received from it. Does this sound familiar? The term *terminal* is still used today to identify a window in which users run shells and type commands.

Although serial terminals can still be seen today, they've been largely replaced by network connections. Besides the computer itself, the network is the place from which most login requests are likely to come. In subsequent chapters of this book, you'll see how to manage networking and services that allow remote login. This feature in particular is really empowering and useful, but sometimes not desirable.

The following table contains a list of commands that you can use to find out who logs into your system and what they are doing when they're there. Even though these commands are some of the oldest of all UNIX commands, they are still very much in use today:

Command	Description
`Who`	Used to check who is logged in, and from where
`W`	Used to check who is logged in, and what they are doing (that is, what program they are running at the moment)
`Whoami`	Displays the username of the invoking user
`Last`	Used to check who logged in in the past
`Lastb`	If `/var/log/btmp` exists, shows a list of failed login attempts (disabled by default)

For further details, each command has its own manual page, accessible through the `man` command, for example with `man whoami`.

Summary

User accounts and groups play an important role in Fedora Core, just as they do in most other modern operating systems. You've seen in this chapter how the notion of a user account can be employed to provide many different users with simultaneous access to a system—each user having her own identity. Each user can have her own personal home directory, which (by default) is a subdirectory of `/home`.

From there, you can also devise systems of access rights, explicitly allowing or denying access to a file, directory, or executable, depending on the identity of the user. Indeed, you single out a special user account called root (which has very free administrative rights), and any number of other system accounts; and you are encouraged to create personal accounts for the people who use your system.

With a system that has a number of users, it becomes convenient to create groups of users and assign permissions to the groups. This makes the task of access management much more manageable and flexible. For example, you can set the access rights to a file to be dependent on the identity of the user. You can also assign special privileges to a group of users, and change the members of that group as often as necessary.

The information that describes all the users and groups on a system is contained in the files `/etc/passwd`, `/etc/shadow`, and `/etc/group`. There are a number of tools for managing the users and groups on the system—in particular, the graphical User Manager interface and the User Information Tool, and an array of flexible command line utilities:

- `su` and `id` for changing user and checking the user's identity
- `useradd`, `passwd`, `chfn`, `chsh`, `usermod`, and `userdel` for managing user accounts
- `groupadd`, `groupdel`, and `gpasswd` to managing groups

Having established the basics of users and groups (and having practiced creating and manipulating some users and groups), it's natural to examine how they can be used to implement some access policies. This chapter examined six strategies of file protection and sharing, starting with some simple scenarios and building up to a situation in which different groups of users require different access rights to the same set of files.

We stressed the advantages of working under a normal user account. You saw how easy it is to make errors when performing regular (seemingly harmless) tasks, and how these errors can cause a lot of damage if you're working as root. Working under a normal user account affords you some protection, and so it's worth avoiding the root wherever possible. You saw how to carry out administrative tasks in a normal user environment: mounting disks, executing sporadic root commands, and compiling and installing software locally.

Finally, the chapter noted a number of useful commands designed to check user activity on a Linux machine: `who`, `w`, `whoami`, `last`, and `lastb`.

The next chapter further expands the limits of your Fedora Core computer by connecting it to a network and making it fully interoperable with other servers.

Exercises

Try the following exercises to increase your skill level.

1. Fedora Core can automatically detect a number of digital cameras as if they were external USB disks or memory keys. Supposing that your camera is recognized as `/dev/sda1`, configure your system so that users can mount their cameras and access the pictures using `/mnt/digicam` as a mount point.
2. Configure `sudo` to allow eziodm to install new software packages with the following command and no need to type a password:

```
rpm -ivh packagename.rpm
```

8

Installing and Updating Software

As you would expect from a Linux distribution, Fedora 2 comes bundled with a vast array of software applications for your use. Major applications such as the OpenOffice productivity suite and Ximian Evolution e-mail client are installed as part of the installation, but a great number of other applications are not. This software may be stored on a CD, on the Internet, or anywhere else. This chapter looks at how you can get Fedora 2 applications and install them on your system.

The chapter discusses the following areas:

- The RPM and its advantages
- The RPM Package Management Tool
- RPM console commands
- RPM security features
- A few examples of RPM package installation

This chapter uses the terms RPM Package Management Tool, package management tool, Fedora package manager, and "Add and Remove Software" interchangeably to refer to the Package Management GUI provided by Fedora 2 (based on which variant scans best in natural language). The term `rpm` is used to refer to the RPM command line interface.

What Is RPM?

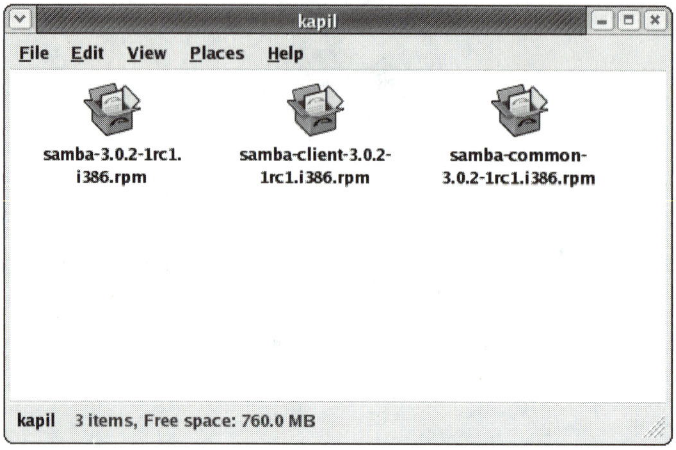

Figure 8-1

You can find more information about the background of RPM at `www.redhat.com` *and* `www.rpm.org/max-rpm/`.

The benefits of using RPM can be summarized as follows:

- **Simplicity:** RPM simplifies the task of installing software. RPM packages can be managed using the RPM GUI interface, or via the command line.
- **Upgrade ability:** RPM gives you the flexibility to upgrade existing packages without having to reinstall them. You can freshen and upgrade parts, or all, of your system automatically, with the minimum of fuss.
- **Manageability:** RPM facilitates managing software packages. It maintains a database of all the packages installed on the system, so you know exactly what you've got installed, what version it is, and when it was added.
- **Package queries:** RPM provides options to query packages for more details in different ways. You can search the package installed on the system. You can also find out what package a file belongs to. It helps in keeping track of all packages installed on your system.
- **Uninstalling:** RPM makes it easy to uninstall packages. This helps you keep the system clean.
- **System verification:** RPM also provides a feature to verify packages. In case of any doubt about file deletion, packages can be verified against the original package information using RPM. This checks all the files on the system with the package information and verifies that the files on the system are the same as those installed from the package originally.
- **Security:** RPM provides commands for the user to check the integrity of packages. Packages can be checked using `md5sum` to verify that they have not been corrupted or tampered with since they were created. RPM also provides functionality to verify a package provider's identity and package integrity using `gnupg` (very handy if you're downloading sensitive material from the Internet, because you want to be sure that you're installing what you think you're installing).

Now that you understand what RPM is, and what it can be used for, let's move on to consider how it works. RPM can be used in two different, yet complementary ways—from the desktop, using the GUI interface, and from the command line.

The RPM Package Management Tool

Fedora has added a lot of new features to its latest operating system (Fedora 2) to make it easier to manage. One of these new features is the *Package Management Tool*. This tool is a graphical user interface (GUI) designed for the management of package installation and removal. The GUI allows you to add and remove packages at the click of a mouse.

The Package Management Tool, also called Add and Remove Software, as accessed from the Main Menu, is able to manage only packages provided as part of Fedora 2. To install other RPMs from disk or download, you must navigate to the RPM in question and double-click on the file. This will load the Package Management Tool and skip you straight to the Install screen, bypassing the system-specific install options. Alternatively, you can install any RPM package by using the RPM command line utility, discussed later in this chapter.

Starting the RPM Package Management Tool

There are two ways to start the RPM Package Management Tool. From the Main Menu, select Main Menu ⇨ System Settings ⇨ Add/Remove Applications. Alternatively, from the command line you can type the following command:

```
$ system-config-packages
```

Either way, if you're logged in with privileges other than root privileges, you'll be prompted to enter the root password.

After you've authenticated as system root user with administrative privileges, you'll see the window shown in Figure 8-2.

Package Management Tool Functions

Fedora 2 Package Management Tool comes with two windows, each providing different functions. The first window is Add/Remove Software; the second window is Update System.

In the Add/Remove Software window, the package manager presents packages divided up into different categories, each containing different groups. The following table lists all the available package categories and package groups on a typical system. If you look through the entries on your machine, you'll find an explanatory note next to each one explaining what it does on your machine.

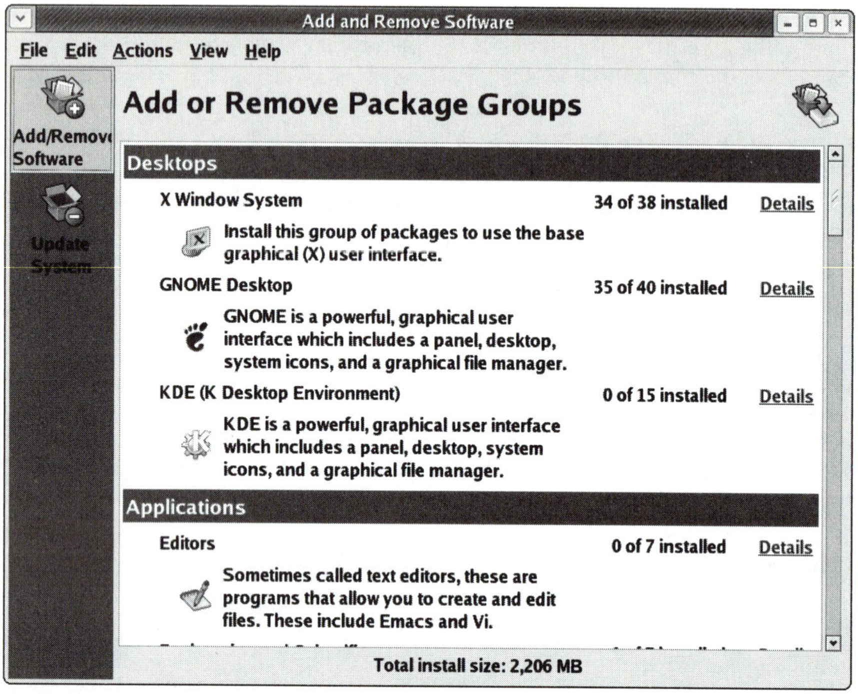

Figure 8-2

Package Category	Package Groups
Desktops	X Window System GNOME Desktop Environment KDE (K Desktop Environment)
Applications	Editors Engineering and Scientific Graphical Internet Text-based Internet Office/Productivity Sound and Video Authoring and Publishing Graphics Games and Entertainment
Servers	Server Configuration Tools Web Server Mail Server Windows File Server DNS Name Server FTP Server SQL Database Server News Server Network Servers

Package Category	Package Groups
Development	Development Tools Kernel Development X Software Development GNOME Software Development KDE Software Development
System	Administration Tools System Tools Printing Support
Miscellaneous	Compatibility Arch Development Support Compatibility Arch Support

You can view the details of any group of packages by clicking the Details link. See Figure 8-3 for details of each group.

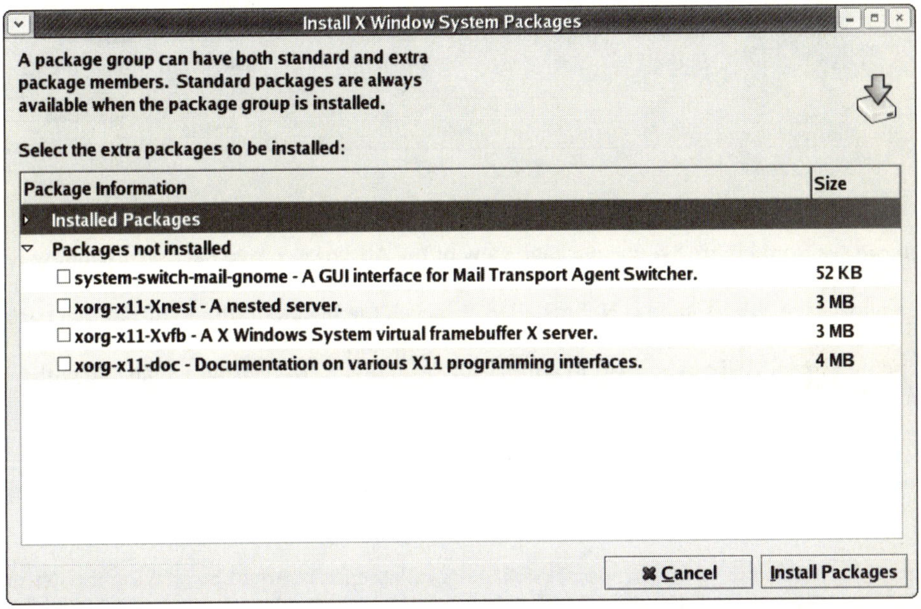

Figure 8-3

Each group may have Installed packages and Packages not installed. Installed packages are always available when a package group is installed—so you can remove it only from the Update System.

You can also change the view of the Add/Remove window by selecting View ➪ Package View from the Main Menu bar. See Figure 8-4 for the Package view of Add/Remove Software GUI.

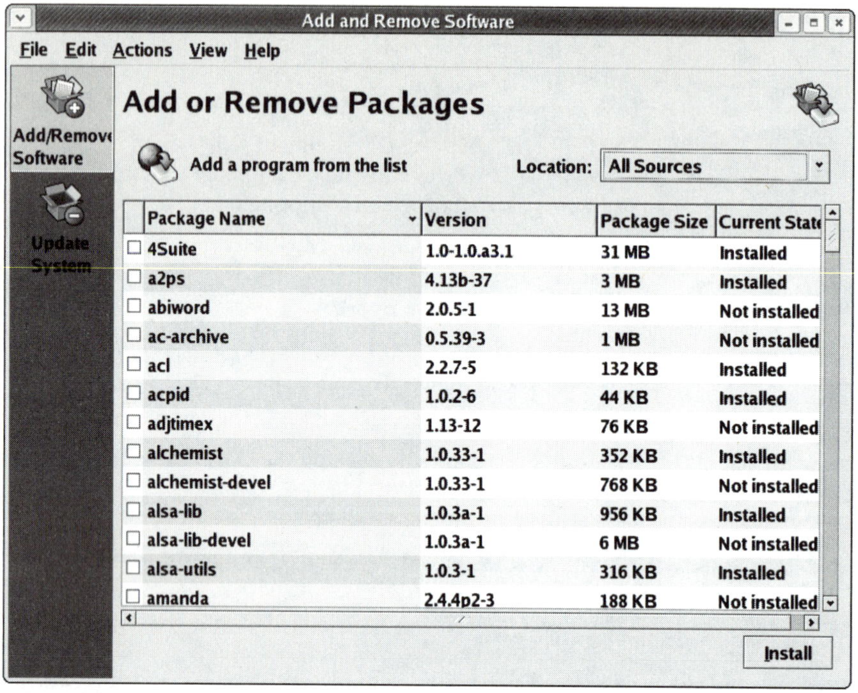

Figure 8-4

As you can see from Figure 8-5, the package view of the Add or Remove Packages window represents individual packages with Package Name, Version, Package Size, and Current state information. You can select any package, whose state is Not installed and click the Install button to install that package.

The Update System GUI can be used to remove any installed RPM packages available with Fedora 2. It provides a nice and easy graphical user interface to remove RPM packages from the system.

As you can see from Figure 8-6, the Package Management Tool presents packages divided up into different categories, each containing different groups. It will show only the categories for which the patches are available for removal.

You can view the details of any group of packages available for removal by clicking the Remove link. Details of each group of packages available for removal looks like those in Figure 8-5.

The Remove Packages window shows the Packages to be removed with their size. By default, all the installed packages will be checked for removal. To remove a selected package, uncheck the package and click the Remove Package button.

You can also change the view of the Remove Packages window by selecting View ➪ Package View from the Main Menu bar. The Package view of the Remove Packages GUI looks like Figure 8-6.

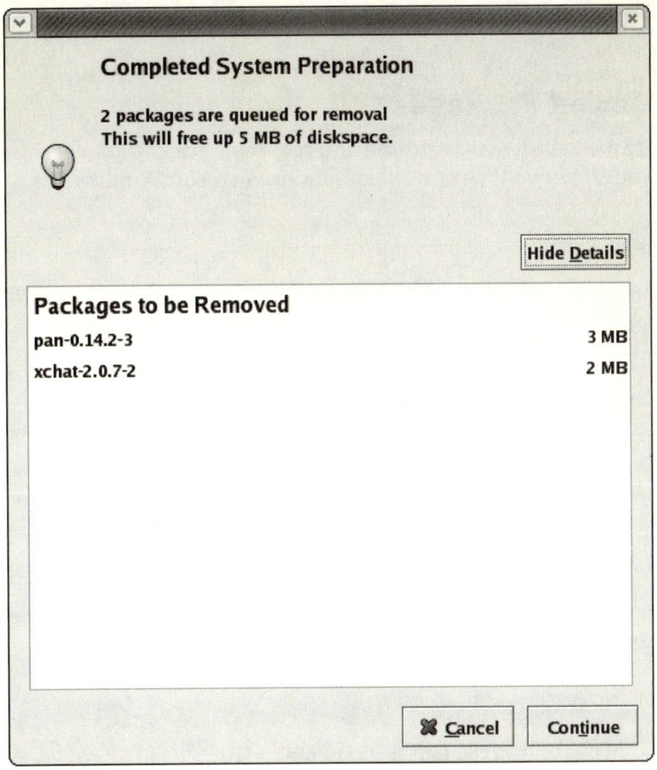

Figure 8-5

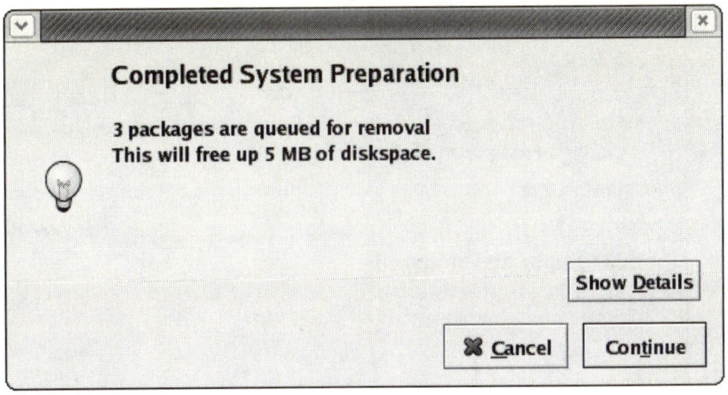

Figure 8-6

As you can see from Figure 8-8, the Package view of the Remove Packages window presents individual packages with Package Name, Version, and Package Size information. You can select any package and click the Remove button to uninstall the package.

To change the view of the Add or Remove Package and Remove Packages window, select View ➪ Group View from the Main Menu bar.

Adding and Removing Packages

The Package Management Tool makes adding and removing packages very simple. In fact, it's just as easy as using the Add/Remove Programs menu under Microsoft Windows.

Installing Packages

When you select any group using the RPM Package Management Tool interface, it automatically selects the standard packages (if any) that are needed for the category, as well as any dependent packages that it may have.

Dependent packages are packages needed for the main package to run properly. RPM checks for these before installing any new package. If they're not present, it adds them to the list of files to be installed. There's nothing unusual in this—Windows software also depends on other files (such as Dynamic Link Libraries, or DLLs), but it packages them all together for simplicity, while Linux leaves them separate for ease of updating, and bug-fixing.

To install packages, click on the Details button in the Add/Remove Software window under RPM Package Management Tool. You can customize the packages to be installed by selecting or deselecting checkboxes near the package names, as shown in Figure 8-7.

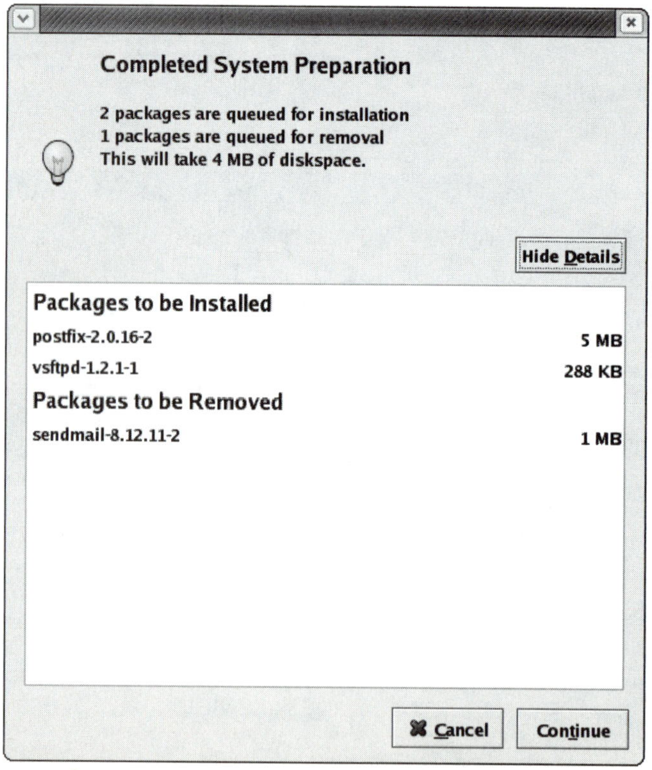

Figure 8-7

After you've made your selections in the preceding window, click the Install Packages button. The Package Management Tool will then calculate the disk space required for installing packages, as well as any dependencies, before displaying the dialog box shown in Figure 8-8.

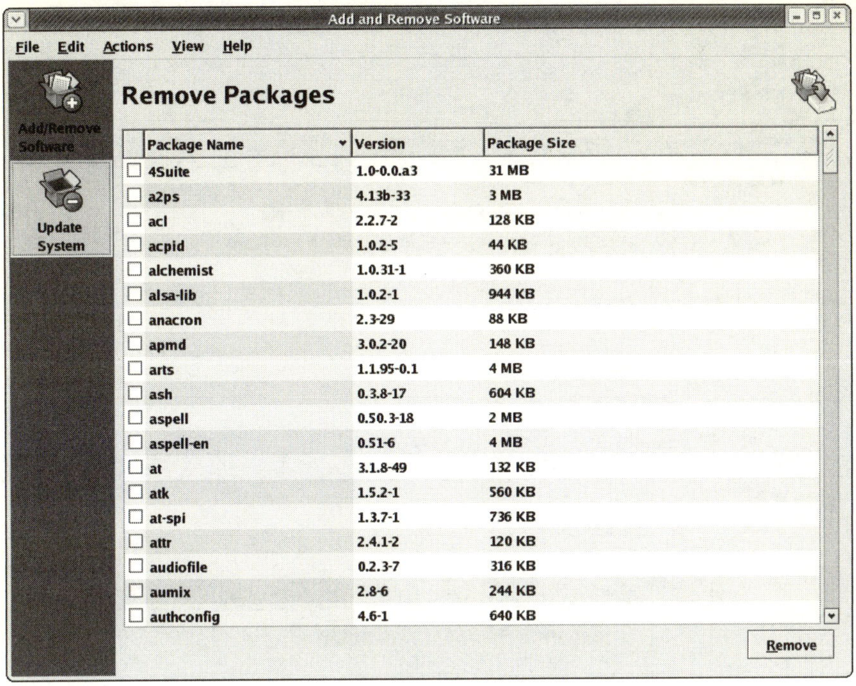

Figure 8-8

If you click the Show Details button shown in the preceding dialog box, you'll see a list of all the packages to be installed—with the disk space needed for each individual package. If you click the Continue button, the installation procedure starts. When the installation is finished, an Update Complete dialog box appears.

Removing Packages

Removing a package is also simple. To remove *all* packages installed within a package group, click the Remove link in the Update System window, which opens a dialog box as shown in Figure 8-9.

You can also remove any specific package by selecting the checkbox next to each package to be removed in the Remove Packages window.

Click the Remove Packages button shown in the preceding dialog box to continue with the package removal process. You will be presented with another dialog box, as shown in Figure 8-10.

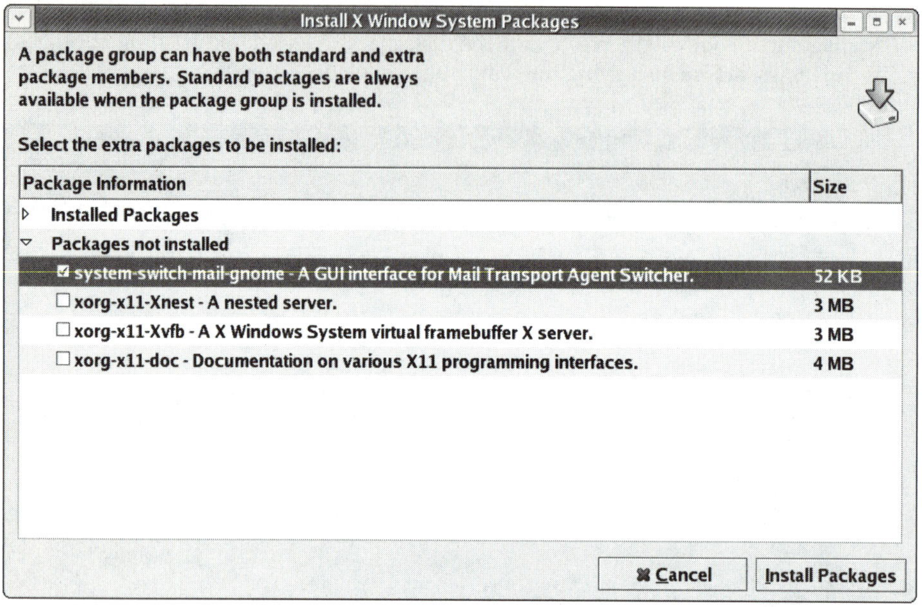

Figure 8-9

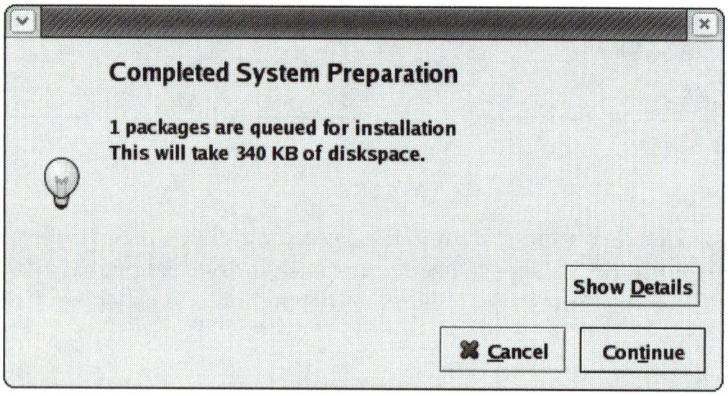

Figure 8-10

If you click the Show Details button shown in the preceding dialog box, you'll see a list of all the packages to be removed, with the disk space freed by each individual package removal, as shown in Figure 8-11.

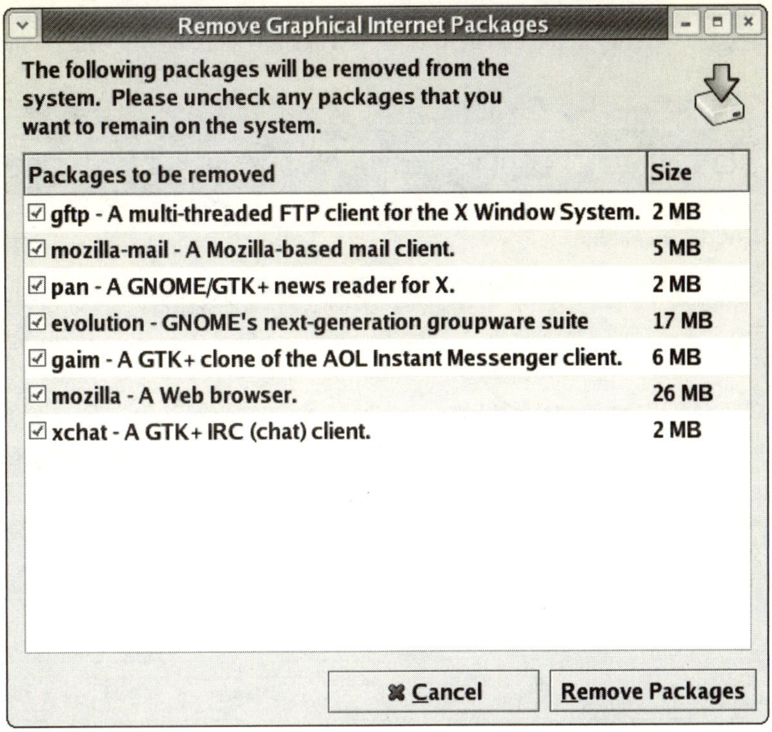

Figure 8-11

If you click the Continue button in the preceding dialog box, the uninstall procedure starts. When the uninstall is finished, an Update Complete dialog box appears, as shown in Figure 8-12.

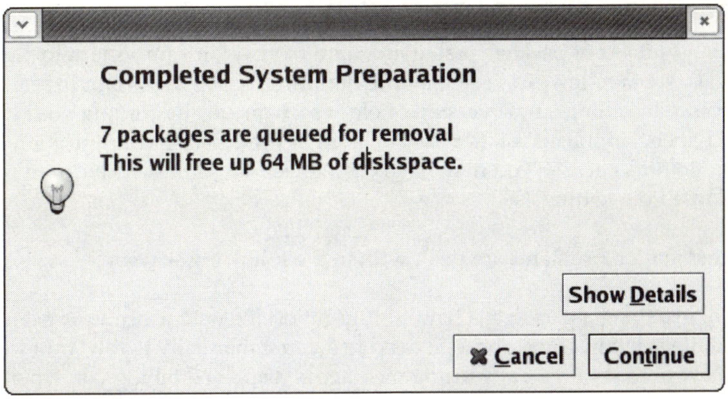

Figure 8-12

The Package Management Tool takes care of finding and removing any dependent packages that might also be installed, just as it did in the install routine. It will show you the following window.

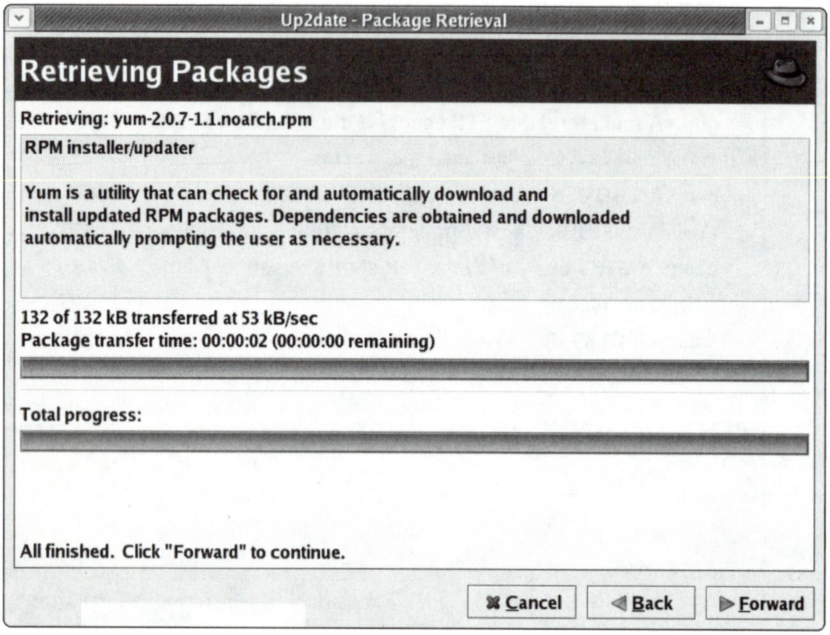

Figure 8-13

If this happens, you'll have to leave the package where it is, unless you want to delete the program that's using it first (in which case it will probably be removed anyway, as a dependent package).

Package Installation and Configuration Files

Before we leave the subject of package installation and removal, it's important to consider the topic of configuration files. What follows can seem a little daunting, so it's important to realize that this happens only rarely. If you're installing a new version of older software, or upgrading your existing version, there's a small chance that the installation will encounter pre-existing configuration files as it installs. This presents a dilemma because you may have customized those files, so it doesn't want to just overwrite them and lose your settings.

Therefore, the installation problems are dealt with in the following ways:

- If you're installing a package, a new configuration file with a `.rpmnew` extension is created. The old file is left in place, and you need to swap it manually if you want to take advantage of the new file's settings—a warning message is displayed telling you where the file is.
- If you're upgrading a package, the old configuration file is renamed with a `.rpmsave` extension, and the new file takes its place. Again, you are shown a warning message telling you this has taken place.

- If you're removing a package, and the tool detects that a configuration file has been modified, it warns you of this, and leaves a version of the file behind with a `.rpmsave` extension so it's still available if you should need it.

This situation isn't likely to occur very often, but you're aware of the issues now should you encounter it. Bear in mind the differences between how installs and upgrades handle configuration files. This knowledge will stand you in good stead as you move on to look at the command line package installer (RPM).

The RPM Command Line Tool

Up to now, we've talked about how to install and remove packages using Red Hat's graphical RPM Package Management Tool. While this tool is simple to use, it's lacking in functionality. For example:

- It cannot install packages using network, FTP, or HTTP connections.
- It does not show the location the files in a package are installed to.
- It lacks the capability to query for specific packages installed on the system.
- It does not provide full details of the RPM package, such as the vendor, build date, signature, description, and so on.
- It does not have a function to verify a package. That means it cannot compare information about files, such as size, MD5 sum, permissions, type, owner, and group installed from a package, with the same information from the original package.
- It does not show all the packages available in a product. So you won't always know if you've got the whole thing.

The *RPM Command Line Interface Tool* provides a solution to the package manager's limitations. RPM is very versatile and can be used to manipulate packages in a number of ways. The remainder of this section looks at some of the most common tasks you're likely to want to perform, and considers how best to do them.

*Complete details of all RPM's options can be found by typing **man rpm** at the command prompt; because there are so many options, only the most common are covered here.*

Querying Packages

Let's begin by discussing *querying* packages. RPM keeps a record of all the packages installed on your system in a database. By querying the database you obtain a complete list of all the packages that you've installed on your system. Should you want to, you can then go further and query each individual package for more details about it.

The syntax for a basic query is as follows:

```
rpm -q [options] <filename>
```

Try It Out — Querying RPM for Information About a Package

1. Open a terminal window (by selecting Main Menu ➪ System Tools ➪ Terminal).
2. Only a user with root privileges can perform RPM package operation. So, if you're not logged in as root, do so now, by using the `su` command:

```
$ su -
Password:
#
```

3. Change to the packages directory of CD 1 in your Fedora by inserting the CD and typing the following, once it has mounted:

```
# cd /mnt/cdrom/Fedora/RPMS/
```

4. Now, let's find the information for the Lynx package (Lynx is a text-based browser). To do this, type the following at the command line:

```
# rpm -qip lynx-2.8.5-15.i386.rpm
```

   Here, `-qip` represents the command options (discussed in more detail shortly), and `lynx-2.8.5-15.i386.rpm` is the RPM package file we're interested in. After a short while, you should see the following response:

```
warning: lynx-2.8.5-15.i386.rpm: V3 DSA signature: NOKEY, key ID 30c9ecf8
Name        : lynx                        Relocations: (not relocatable)
Version     : 2.8.5                            Vendor: Red Hat, Inc.
Release     : 15                           Build Date: Tue 17 Feb 2004 19:57:12
GMT
Install Date: (not installed)              Build Host: tweety.devel.redhat.com
Group       : Applications/Internet        Source RPM: lynx-2.8.5-15.src.rpm
Size        : 4841340                         License: GPL
Signature   : DSA/SHA1, Wed 17 Mar 2004 19:19:55 GMT, Key ID da84cbd430c9ecf8
Packager    : Red Hat, Inc. <http://bugzilla.redhat.com/bugzilla>
URL         : http://lynx.isc.org/
Summary     : A text-based Web browser.
Description :
Lynx is a text-based Web browser. Lynx does not display any images,
but it does support frames, tables, and most other HTML tags. One
advantage Lynx has over graphical browsers is speed; Lynx starts and
exits quickly and swiftly displays webpages.
```

Notice the warning in the first line? We'll explain it later in the chapter, when we cover verification.

   You can use this information to make sure you're installing what you think you're installing and to check that you've got the right version of software.

5. You can also use RPM to query a specific package installed on the system. Issue the following command as root:

```
rpm -qi lynx
```

Here, `-qi` represents the command options, and `lynx` is the RPM package filename we're interested in. After a short while, you should see the following response:

```
Name        : lynx                          Relocations: (not relocatable)
Version     : 2.8.5                              Vendor: Red Hat, Inc.
Release     : 15                             Build Date: Tue 17 Feb 2004 19:57:12
GMT
Install Date: Sat 15 May 2004 02:28:55 BST      Build Host: tweety.devel.redhat.com
Group       : Applications/Internet          Source RPM: lynx-2.8.5-15.src.rpm
Size        : 4869832                           License: GPL
Signature   : DSA/SHA1, Wed 17 Mar 2004 19:19:55 GMT, Key ID da84cbd430c9ecf8
Packager    : Red Hat, Inc. <http://bugzilla.redhat.com/bugzilla>
URL         : http://lynx.isc.org/
Summary     : A text-based Web browser.
Description :
Lynx is a text-based Web browser. Lynx does not display any images,
but it does support frames, tables, and most other HTML tags. One
advantage Lynx has over graphical browsers is speed; Lynx starts and
exits quickly and swiftly displays webpages.
```

6. Now issue the following command (still as root):

```
# rpm -qa
```

This command makes a query for all the packages that are installed on your system; you should get something like this in response:

```
setup-2.5.31-1
tzdata-2003d-1
bzip2-libs-1.0.2-10
e2fsprogs-1.35-4
.... switchdesk-gnome-3.9.8-18
nautilus-media-0.5.2-1
gpg-pubkey-4f2a6fd2-3f9d9d3b
lynx-2.8.5-15
```

7. Here's another example. You are likely to encounter situations in which you need to know about the package that owns a particular command on the system. For example, let's find out which package owns the command `/usr/bin/lynx`. To do this, type the following at the command line:

```
# rpm -qf /usr/bin/lynx
```

You should get the following response:

```
lynx-2.8.5-15
```

The lynx-2.8.5-15 package is used by the system whenever a user calls the command `/usr/bin/lynx`.

8. Finally, RPM also provides a command that allows you to get a list of all files contained in an RPM package. Let's find out what files are contained in a lynx package. Type the following:

```
# rpm -ql lynx
```

Here's the response you should get:

```
/etc/lynx-site.cfg
/etc/lynx.cfg
/etc/lynx.cfg.cs
/etc/lynx.cfg.ja
/etc/lynx.cfg.sk
/usr/bin/lynx
......
/usr/share/locale/sl/LC_MESSAGES/lynx.mo
/usr/share/locale/sv/LC_MESSAGES/lynx.mo
/usr/share/man/man1/lynx.1.gz
```

How It Works

When you query an RPM package file using RPM command line options, it displays the information such as name, version, release, group, summary, and description of the package. The exact type of query and the format of the resulting output depend on the command options that you specify:

- All five of the queries in the preceding example used `-q`. The `q` is to indicate that you're making a query.
- Steps 4 and 5 used `-qip`. The `p` indicates that you are querying a package, and the `i` indicates that you want to see the package information.
- In Step 6, we used `-qa`. That indicates that you are querying *all* currently installed packages.
- In Step 7, we used `-qf`. The `f` indicates that you wish to query the package that owns the specified file.
- In Step 8, we used `-ql`. The `l` indicates that you wish to query the list of files contained in the specified package.

RPM Package Security

RPM has had a number of releases over the years, and the latest versions (one of which is bundled with your system) have a few new features. One new feature of interest is that RPM now checks the *signature* of a package when querying, installing, or upgrading it.

Checking the signature of a package allows you to ensure that it is from a trustworthy source. All official Red Hat packages are signed by Red Hat using its GnuPG key, and RPM checks the package's GnuPG signature against the Red Hat GnuPG key to make sure the package is what it claims to be. If you do not have an appropriate key installed to verify the signature, you will get a warning message such as the following:

```
warning: lynx-2.8.5-15.i386.rpm: V3 DSA signature: NOKEY, key ID 30c9ecf8
```

The exact content of the warning message depends on the situation. For example, if RPM cannot verify the package's GnuPG signature, you will see the following error message:

```
error: V3 DSA signature: BAD, key ID 30c9ecf8
```

By contrast, if RPM cannot find the appropriate key to verify the signature of a package, you get this warning:

```
warning: V3 DSA signature: NOKEY, key ID 30c9ecf8
```

GnuPG signatures are digital signatures that are very hard to forge. Signatures are created with a unique secret key and can be verified by their recipient using a public key. A digital signature timestamps a document so that if anyone tries to tamper with it or modify it, the verification of the signature fails.

Fedora GNU Privacy Guard Keys

To install Red Hat's GNU Privacy Guard (GPG) keys on your installed system, issue the following command:

```
# rpm --import /usr/share/rhn/RPM-GPG-KEY-fedora-test
```

Or, use the following to install them from CD-ROM (make sure you've got the right one in the drive):

```
# rpm --import /mnt/cdrom/RPM-GPG-KEY-fedora-test
```

These commands install Red Hat's public GPG keys onto your system. You can also import other vendors' GnuPG keys in much the same way; just change the name of the file to the one that they've supplied to you.

To display a list of all GnuPG keys installed for RPM package verification on your system, issue the following command:

```
# rpm -qa gpg-pubkey
gpg-pubkey-4f2a6fd2-3f9d9d3b
gpg-pubkey-1cddbca9-3f9da14c
gpg-pubkey-30c9ecf8-3f9da3f7
gpg-pubkey-db42a60e-37ea5438
```

This will return a list of results. If you've installed the Fedora key, you should see the following listed among the results:

```
gpg-pubkey-30c9ecf8-3f9da3f7
```

You can get even more complete details of a Red Hat GPG key by executing the following command:

```
# rpm -qi gpg-pubkey-30c9ecf8-3f9da3f7
```

In the preceding command, note that `gpg-pubkey-30c9ecf8-3f9da3f7` *is the name of the Fedora GnuPG key, gathered from the output of the command* `rpm -qa gpg-pubkey`.

This produces the following response—quite detailed isn't it? Most importantly, it reveals the vendor's name and signing date, which is handy if you've got a key on your system but you aren't sure who it's from, or if it is still up-to-date:

```
Name        : gpg-pubkey                 Relocations: (not relocatable)
Version     : 30c9ecf8                        Vendor: (none)
Release     : 3f9da3f7                    Build Date: Sat 13 Mar 2004 00:20:37 GMT
```

```
Install Date: Sat 13 Mar 2004 00:20:37 GMT      Build Host: localhost
Group       : Public Keys                      Source RPM: (none)
Size        : 0                                   License: pubkey
Signature   : (none)
Summary     : gpg(Fedora Project (Test Software) <rawhide@redhat.com>)
Description :
-----BEGIN PGP PUBLIC KEY BLOCK-----
Version: rpm-4.3 (beecrypt-3.0.0)

mQGiBD+do/cRBACAF7Gv91v32uUrT4nZe+qKgLl59HmtvmaOzT4lInrF95Sget7p2TpnIqh5
H0x0VGpdoeNfHvlXCw+aP50mTJv91BYmLfelkTzokqpEU5YpqGOqa5BVjelnoK1VKOcXMB28
d79Gz9tn7friZN4SnyWbcSIA4C3dHNhsjifIYf0rywCg3y193N6jODa0VSGeeEb4whE2xccD
/i/rqk0MQmW6td2Dz2jTBaHxyf7FIcH18YDtwraDotBRxqGkTVyFGc1q7ZTrRsbzdjIfxbp2
C6GT2VJ5kHuRm9jf7JdW5fOhun+oLimRerTlrPmgz8qQRcqUm6fkmUsYufL1u7DdyfxX7jI2
ngkbAR+CsZ8Cj5JhBMeAXc/DWWhPA/4mzZ70hn1OrGLokzxNr4O7u1+n0thsxGN0qfuTNGIc
09UKCoAN42he7QjskIqiE7gLtLzx8elxVOK19tNcaAiLoqmtxlLQqB03pLy4V0tMP9QcWQET
bc67qTd1zASiefGjf364j41Qd+X9AqdyhUrnax3UgPD5IxilBp92Cw7Qi7QzRmVkb3JhIFBy
b2plY3QgKFRlc3QgU29mdHdhcmUpIDxyYXdoaWRlQHJlZGhhdC5jb20+iFsEExECABsFAj+d
o/cGCwkIBwMCAxUCAwMWAgECHgECF4AACgkQ2oTL1DDJ7Pgh8QCgqNNsb7xdW+UhzyZw+DEA
QF6e+q4AmwVus4u9REyd/aigK2RvrdtcsNy0iEYEExECAAYFAj+dpBoACgkQtEJp0E8qb9Ji
4QCfanY0CXnRwtBnm8GEMRNqgfGgcc0AnRunlejpJRxGPaRsmY/11stYl132iEYEEBECAAYF
Aj+e2SIACgkQKdW6JI31bQWWNQCfTKcX/7lerpwIVHcAILDduz9qxssAn1t46ERJ9EqsxJxS
FlN7oBPyNkt6
=R9He
-----END PGP PUBLIC KEY BLOCK-----
```

Verifying Fedora Signed Packages

Having installed Fedora's GPG keys, you can now verify official Fedora packages as being authentic. As an example, let's verify the Lynx package that you looked at earlier:

```
# rpm -K lynx-2.8.5-15.i386.rpm
lynx-2.8.5-15.i386.rpm: (sha1) dsa sha1 md5 gpg OK
```

If all goes well, you will see an `MD5 gpg OK` message. This proves that the signature of the package has been verified and that it has not been corrupted or altered.

Installing Packages

RPM provides other advantages over the RPM Package Management Tool because it can install packages from *any* source, including Red Hat distribution CDs, network locations, FTP, and HTTP.

The syntax for installing a package looks like this:

```
rpm -i [options] <package_filename>
```

Try It Out — Installing Packages Using RPM

1. First, let's install the Lynx Web browser that we've just verified is okay. You should already be logged in with root privileges, with the terminal window open and still in the Red Hat/RPMS directory of your mounted CD-ROM. From there, type in the following at the command line:

```
# rpm -ivh lynx-2.8.5-15.i386.rpm
```

The output you get depends on whether the Lynx browser is already installed. If it's not, you'll see the following:

```
Preparing...                ########################################### [100%]
   1:lynx                   ########################################### [100%]
```

But, if it's already on your machine, RPM won't attempt to install it again. Instead, you get the following message:

```
Preparing...                ########################################### [100%]
        package lynx-2.8.5-15 is already installed
```

2. Now, let's perform another installation to serve as an example; let's install a package that has dependencies. The *balsa* package is a GNOME e-mail client. If you try to install this using the same technique as before, you get a `failed dependencies` error message. Try it if you like:

```
# rpm -ivh balsa-2.0.17-1.i386.rpm
error: Failed dependencies:
        libesmtp >= 0.8.11 is needed by balsa-2.0.17-1
        libesmtp.so.5 is needed by balsa-2.0.17-1
        libltdl.so.3 is needed by balsa-2.0.17-1
```

3. As you can see from the output, RPM fails to install the package. Instead, it shows an error message indicating that the package `balsa-2.0.17-1.i386.rpm` has a dependency that is not met—namely, the packages `libesmtp.so.5` and `libltdl.so.3` are not installed. RPM provides the filename of the dependency but does not provide the package name to resolve it. This isn't very helpful, but Fedora provides an extra package that can be installed to get suggestions about package filenames to resolve dependencies.

   The package in question is currently called *rpmdb-fedora-1.92-0.20040421.i386.rpm*, but the name may differ slightly in your version (look on your CD-ROM for a filename beginning `rpmdb-` and that'll be it). Simply install it as you installed the previous packages:

```
#rpm -ivh rpmdb-fedora-1.92-0.20040421.i386.rpm
Preparing...              ########################################### [100%]
1:rpmdb-fedora           ########################################### [100%]
```

4. Now if you try to install the balsa package again, you get a message suggesting the location of the dependent file:

```
# rpm -ivh balsa-2.0.17-1.i386.rpm
error: Failed dependencies:
        libesmtp >= 0.8.11 is needed by balsa-2.0.17-1
        libesmtp.so.5 is needed by balsa-2.0.17-1
        libltdl.so.3 is needed by balsa-2.0.17-1
    Suggested resolutions:
        libesmtp-1.0.2-2.1.i386.rpm
        libtool-libs-1.5.6-1.i386.rpm
```

5. So, try again. This time, install the suggested packages libesmtp-1.0.2-1.i386.rpm and libtool-libs-1.5-8.i386.rpm first:

```
# rpm -ivh libesmtp-1.0.2-2.1.i386.rpm
Preparing...                ########################################### [100%]
   1:libesmtp               ########################################### [100%]
```

```
# rpm -ivh libtool-libs-1.5.6-1.i386.rpm
Preparing...                ########################################### [100%]
   1:libtool-libs           ########################################### [100%]
```

6. When that's complete, you can install the balsa package as follows:

```
# rpm -ivh balsa-2.0.17-1.i386.rpm
Preparing...                ########################################### [100%]
   1:balsa                  ########################################### [100%]
```

Alternatively, you could have installed them together on the same line, like this:

```
# rpm -ivh balsa-2.0.17-1.i386.rpm libesmtp-1.0.2-2.1.i386.rpm
Preparing...                ########################################### [100%]
   1:libesmtp               ########################################### [ 50%]
2:balsa                     ########################################### [100%]
```

7. Finally, it's worth mentioning that RPM packages can be installed directly from the Internet. You can use HTTP or FTP addresses to install directly. For example, if you wanted to install the vnc-server directly from the Fedora Web site, you'd type the following:

```
# rpm -ivh http://download.fedora.redhat.com/pub/fedora/linux/core/test/1.92/i386
/os/Fedora/RPMS/vnc-4.0-1.beta4.11.i386.rpm
```

How It Works

We've used the RPM command for installation, much as we did for querying earlier; this time, however, the options are slightly different. Each of the three install commands used the option `-ivh` here, which translates as follows:

- `i` indicates that you intend to perform an installation.
- `v` indicates that you want RPM to display "additional information," for example, to display package filenames while performing multiple package installations with one `rpm` command.
- `h` indicates that you want RPM to print hash (#) marks during the installation process to show the progress of the installation.

Removing Packages

Removing unwanted packages from your system is very important to save the disk space as well as reduce the system administration work such as maintaining patches, and so on. RPM makes package removal easy. It keeps a record of all the files installed by each package so you can easily clean your system by removing all the files associated with an unwanted package.

Try It Out Removing Packages Using the RPM

You probably don't actually need the vnc-server, lynx, and balsa packages on your system. So, here's how you go about removing them:

1. First, type the following to remove the vnc-server package:

```
# rpm -e vnc-server
```

2. Now do it again for Lynx:

```
# rpm -e lynx
```

3. Now, how about balsa? You've got dependencies here, so you need to progress carefully. If you try to remove libesmtp-1.0.2-2.1.i386.rpm before you remove balsa-2.0.17-1.i386.rpm, you'll get an error:

```
# rpm -e libesmtp
error: Failed dependencies:
        libesmtp.so.5 is needed by (installed) balsa-2.0.17-1
        libesmtp >= 0.8.11 is needed by (installed) balsa-2.0.17-1
```

As you learned in the previous example, `balsa-2.0.17-1` is dependent on `libesmtp.so.5`. So, if RPM were to remove `libesmtp.so.5`, `balsa-2.0.17-1` wouldn't work anymore. So RPM protects you from this: Any attempt to remove the `libesmtp` package throws an error.

You can, however, *force* RPM to remove `libesmtp`, even with balsa still installed. To do this, specify the `-nodeps` option in the RPM command:

```
# rpm --nodeps -e libesmtp
# rpm -e balsa
```

And it will remove the packages regardless. Let's look at the logic behind how this works.

How It Works

We used the `rpm` command to remove installed packages; this time we used the `-e` option to indicate that we're using RPM to remove a package.

Note that we didn't specify the full package filenames (`vnc-server-4.0-1.beta4.11.i386.rpm` *and* `lynx-2.8.5-15.i386.rpm`*) in the preceding commands; instead, we used the names of the packages themselves (vnc-server and lynx):*

```
# rpm -e vnc-server
# rpm -e lynx
```

We also used the `-nodeps` option to remove the `libesmtp` package. We don't recommend that you use this option for the installation or removal of packages, because the newly installed package will not work without having all of its dependent files installed. However, it's worth knowing about it in case you're confronted with a broken or corrupted package that you need to remove from your machine.

Upgrading Packages

Upgrading a package is similar to installing one. The only difference is in the processing that goes on in the background. When it upgrades a package, RPM *uninstalls* the old package and then *installs* a new one. It copies the new configuration file with a `.rpmnew` extension without touching the existing configuration file, if the existing configuration file has been changed since it was first created (that is to say if you, the user, has changed it from its defaults).

The syntax for a package upgrade using RPM is as follows:

```
rpm -U [options] <package_filename>
```

Let's go through the steps of upgrading the fetchmail remote mail retrieval and forwarding utility.

To upgrade the fetchmail package with the latest version (assuming that you've queried it and are satisfied that it is what it claims to be), execute the following command on the command line:

```
# rpm -Uvh fetchmail-6.2.5-1.i386.rpm
Preparing...                ########################################### [100%]
   1:fetchmail              ########################################### [100%]

Latest version of the Fedora packages can be downloaded from
http://fedora.redhat.com website.
```

Verifying Package Integrity

RPM provides one more useful piece of functionality—it allows you to compare information about your installed files with the same information from the original package. This helps when you need to check a file for changes, deletions, or data corruption.

You can verify a package in the following ways:

- To verify a particular file contained in a package, type the following:

```
# rpm -Vf /usr/bin/vncviewer
```

If the package owning the file has not been changed, corrupted, or deleted, you will not see any message.

- To verify an installed package against the RPM file, type the following:

```
# rpm -Vp vnc-4.0-1.beta4.11.i386.rpm
```

Again, if everything is okay, you will not see any message.

- If you try to verify a package that is *not* installed on the system, you will see a message such as the following:

```
# rpm -Vp lynx-2.8.5-15.i386.rpm
missing  c /etc/lynx.cfg
missing  c /etc/lynx.cfg.cs
...
missing    /usr/share/locale/sv/LC_MESSAGES/lynx.mo
missing  d /usr/share/man/man1/lynx.1.gz
```

- To verify all installed packages on your system, type the following:

```
# rpm -Va
```

With this command, you can compare all files installed by packages with the original packages.

> **For more details on RPM, see the project's Web page at** `www.rpm.org/max-rpm/`**.**

Building from Source

While RPM is an excellent, feature-rich, technology, it's not used universally, and you may occasionally find yourself needing to deal with uncompiled source packages in *Tape Archive (TAR)* or other compressed formats. Most of the packages' source code is usually available in `.tar` or `.tar.gz` format.

A binary package is a precompiled package, and comes ready to install. By contrast, you may also come across source code packages—these contain uncompiled code, and must be compiled before installation.

A source code is an uncompiled source of the software, which needs to be compiled on a specific platform to be able to install and use.

A TAR file is an archive file created using the `TAR` command on a Linux system. TAR archives were initially used to store files on magnetic tape but now commonly occur on all storage media.

TAR files are simply a method of sticking a number of smaller files together, so that a collection of files becomes one larger (easier to handle) file. This larger file can then be compressed using a program such as `gzip` to reduce its size. (This is similar to the way that Windows creates Zip files.)

The following table compares building software from source code to using a precompiled package in RPM format.

	RPM Package	**Source Code**
Ease of use	Very easy to install the software; easy to uninstall the package	Not an easy process because software source code needs to be compiled. Not easy to uninstall the package because it is difficult to find out the installation path of files and dependencies.
Usability	Limited to platforms such as Fedora, Red Hat Enterprise Linux, and so on	Widely used. Source code is available for all the open source platforms.
Management	Keeps track of package files and dependencies.	Difficult to keep track of the files and dependencies.
Flexibility	Less flexible. The package installation paths are predefined and have limited functionality to alter them.	Flexible. Packages can be compiled and installed anywhere on the system.
Control	Limited control-of-build process and installation.	High control-of-build process and installation.

Most of the applications are widely available in RPM package format and compressed source code format; many are only available in source code format. If the application is available in RPM as well as source code format, the one you choose depends on your personal preference.

It is always better to learn how to compile the source code into an installable application, in case it is only available in the source code format. In most cases, the applications' source code is available before they are ported to the rpm package. This gives you the advantage of upgrading to the latest version of the application.

In the next section, you download, compile, and install WGET, a utility to download files from the Internet. Fedora comes with the wget application, and you do not have to worry about compiling it from the source code. However, if you learn how to build an application from source code, you can update to the latest version of an application when it becomes available.

Installing Development Tools

Fedora comes with a set of development tools, which must be installed before you can compile any other application on the system. You must install the set of development tools, such as gcc, make, and Perl, to compile the source code on the system.

We will use the RPM Package Management applet to install development tools.

Try It Out Installing the Development Tools

Launch the RPM Package Management Tool by executing the command `system-config-packages` at the command prompt.

You will get an Add and Remove Software graphical interface. Browse through the entire package category until you find the Development category. Select the Development Tools package group by clicking Details, and then press the Install Packages button. It includes all the packages such as gcc, make, and so on required for building the applications from source (see Figure 8-14).

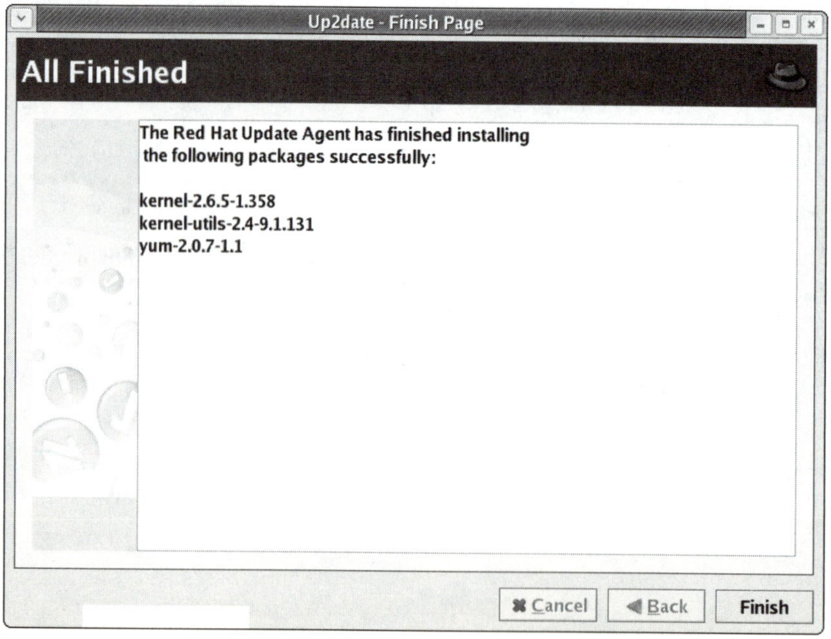

Figure 8-14

The Update process takes some time, but once finished, you can come out of the Package Management window and start building applications from source.

Building the Application

You will build a wget application as an exercise. You will download the source code, and compile and install the wget application. The entire process incorporates all the information you need to build any other application from source code.

Building an application from source code consists of many steps; the following steps are particularly important:

- Downloading the source code
- Configuring the source code
- Compiling the source code
- Installing the compiled application

Try It Out — Building the wget Application

To help you understand the process of building an application from source code, we will walk through the installation of a wget application, which is a non-interactive command line utility to retrieve files using HTTP, HTTPS, and FTP protocols.

The first step to build an application is to find a suitable directory in which to store the source code. The preferred choice is to use the `/usr/local/src` directory because it is separate from other operating system installation directories and can be used safely. You can also choose any other directory that is suitable to your operating system environment.

After you have decided the root source code directory, you should create a subdirectory where you can unpack the source code package. Some applications packages create their own directory to store source code files when unpacked, whereas others just dump the files in the current directory. So, let's create a subdirectory, *wget*, within the `/usr/local/src` directory.

```
# mkdir /usr/local/src/wget
```

Now you can change to the `/usr/local/src/wget` directory and download the wget application source code from `http://ftp.gnu.org/pub/gnu/wget/wget-1.9.1.tar.gz`.

You can download an application using your browser or from the command line using the preinstalled wget RPM package:

```
# mkdir /usr/local/src/wget
# cd /usr/local/src/wget
# /usr/bin/wget http://ftp.gnu.org/pub/gnu/wget/wget-1.9.1.tar.gz

--03:35:01--  http://ftp.gnu.org/pub/gnu/wget/wget-1.9.1.tar.gz
           => `wget-1.9.1.tar.gz'
Resolving ftp.gnu.org... 199.232.41.7
Connecting to ftp.gnu.org[199.232.41.7]:80... connected.
```

```
HTTP request sent, awaiting response... 200 OK
Length: 1,322,378 [application/x-tar]

100%[====================================>] 1,322,378     48.57K/s    ETA 00:00

03:35:28 (49.81 KB/s) - `wget-1.9.1.tar.gz' saved [1322378/1322378]
```

The next step is to uncompress the wget application source code's TAR archive.

```
# tar -kzxvf wget-1.9.1.tar.gz
wget-1.9.1/
wget-1.9.1/doc/
wget-1.9.1/doc/ChangeLog-branches/
wget-1.9.1/doc/ChangeLog-branches/1.6_branch.ChangeLog
wget-1.9.1/doc/ChangeLog
wget-1.9.1/doc/Makefile.in
.....
wget-1.9.1/ltmain.sh
wget-1.9.1/mkinstalldirs
wget-1.9.1/stamp-h.in
```

You must have noticed the various options used with the `tar` command to uncompress the TAR archive. Let's go through each option:

- The `k` switch forces the TAR not to overwrite the old files. This ensures that if there are any files with the same name already on the system, TAR will keep the old files as they are and not overwrite them. This is a safety measure to protect important files from a rogue package designed to destroy existing files on the system.
- The `z` switch filters the archive through `gzip`. It uncompresses the compressed TAR archive and makes it a normal TAR archive.
- The `x` switch extracts the files from the TAR archive.
- The `v` option is to verbosely list the files processed from the TAR archive.
- The `f` option specifies the TAR archive to use.

You now you have a directory, `wget-1.9.1`, which contains all the wget source code. You can now start the compilation process. Let's change to the `wget-1.9.1` directory and run the configure program, which configures the source code ready to be built on the system.

```
# cd wget-1.9.1
# ./configure --prefix=/usr/local
configuring for GNU Wget 1.9.1
checking build system type... i686-pc-linux-gnu
checking host system type... i686-pc-linux-gnu
checking whether make sets $(MAKE)... yes
checking for a BSD-compatible install... /usr/bin/install -c
checking for gcc... gcc
.....
config.status: creating src/config.h
config.status: executing default commands
generating po/POTFILES from ./po/POTFILES.in
creating po/Makefile
```

1. We executed the `configure` command with the prefix option to configure the source code. As shown, the configure script finds out the platform and operating system availability of compilers, tools, and libraries on the system where we are building the application. It also creates a Makefile, which will be used by the `make` command to compile the source code.

2. The `-prefix` option specifies a directory where the application files will be installed. It is good practice to specify the `-prefix` option with a directory to control where the custom build software will be installed. You can also run the configure script without specifying any option, and the script will use all the default options. We have specified `/usr/local` as the application install directory; all the files are installed under the `/usr/local` directory for better control. You can also specify any suitable path or directory with the `-prefix` option to install the application files.

> **You should always read INSTALL and README files supplied with the application before you start building the application. They will provide you with a better understanding of an application's features and build options.**

Now let's actually compile the source code by executing the `make` command to build the application.

```
# make
echo timestamp > stamp-h.in
cd src && make CC='gcc' CPPFLAGS='' DEFS='-DHAVE_CONFIG_H -
DSYSTEM_WGETRC=\"/usr/local/etc/wgetrc\" -DLOCALEDIR=\"/usr/local/share/locale\"'
CFLAGS='-O2 -Wall -Wno-implicit' LDFLAGS='' LIBS='-lssl -lcrypto -ldl '
prefix='/usr/local' exec_prefix='/usr/local' bindir='/usr/local/bin'
infodir='/usr/local/info' mandir='/usr/local/man' manext='1'
make[1]: Entering directory `/usr/local/src/wget-1.9.1/src'
gcc -I. -I.    -DHAVE_CONFIG_H -DSYSTEM_WGETRC=\"/usr/local/etc/wgetrc\" -
DLOCALEDIR=\"/usr/local/share/locale\" -O2 -Wall -Wno-implicit -c cmpt.c
........
make[1]: Entering directory '/usr/local/src/wget-1.9.1/util'
make[1]: Nothing to be done for `all'.
make[1]: Leaving directory `/usr/local/src/wget-1.9.1/util'
cd windows && make CC='gcc' CPPFLAGS='' DEFS='-DHAVE_CONFIG_H -
DSYSTEM_WGETRC=\"/usr/local/etc/wgetrc\" -DLOCALEDIR=\"/usr/local/share/locale\"'
CFLAGS='-O2 -Wall -Wno-implicit' LDFLAGS='' LIBS='-lssl -lcrypto -ldl '
prefix='/usr/local' exec_prefix='/usr/local' bindir='/usr/local/bin'
infodir='/usr/local/info' mandir='/usr/local/man' manext='1'
make[1]: Entering directory `/usr/local/src/wget-1.9.1/windows'
make[1]: Nothing to be done for `all'.
make[1]: Leaving directory `/usr/local/src/wget-1.9.1/windows'
```

3. The `make` command follows the instruction in Makefile, which was created by the configure script in the previous step, to build the source code. The `make` command will finish compiling the source code after a few minutes depending on the number of source files. The application will be ready, with all binaries, to be installed on the system.

4. Finally, install the compiled application into the /usr/local/ directory:

```
# make install
cd src && make CC='gcc' CPPFLAGS='' DEFS='-DHAVE_CONFIG_H -
DSYSTEM_WGETRC=\"/usr/local//etc/wgetrc\" -DLOCALEDIR=\"/usr/local//share/locale\"'
CFLAGS='-O2 -Wall -Wno-implicit' LDFLAGS='' LIBS='-lssl -lcrypto -ldl '
prefix='/usr/local/' exec_prefix='/usr/local/' bindir='/usr/local//bin'
infodir='/usr/local//info' mandir='/usr/local//man' manext='1' install.bin
make[1]: Entering directory `/usr/local/src/wget-1.9.1/src'
../mkinstalldirs /usr/local//bin
/usr/bin/install -c wget /usr/local//bin/wget
make[1]: Leaving directory `/usr/local/src/wget-1.9.1/src'
......
make[1]: Leaving directory `/usr/local/src/wget-1.9.1/po'
cd doc && make CC='gcc' CPPFLAGS='' DEFS='-DHAVE_CONFIG_H -
DSYSTEM_WGETRC=\"/usr/local//etc/wgetrc\" -DLOCALEDIR=\"/usr/local//share/locale\"'
CFLAGS='-O2 -Wall -Wno-implicit' LDFLAGS='' LIBS='-lssl -lcrypto -ldl '
prefix='/usr/local/' exec_prefix='/usr/local/' bindir='/usr/local//bin'
infodir='/usr/local//info' mandir='/usr/local//man' manext='1' install.man
make[1]: Entering directory `/usr/local/src/wget-1.9.1/doc'
../mkinstalldirs /usr/local//man/man1
/usr/bin/install -c -m 644 wget.1 /usr/local//man/man1/wget.1
make[1]: Leaving directory `/usr/local/src/wget-1.9.1/doc'
```

5. Following the preceding steps, you will now have the wget application installed under /usr/local directories. You will be able to execute the compiled wget application from the /usr/local/bin directory.

6. Let's check the wget application to see if it has been built and installed properly. You will find the wget binary executable under the /usr/local/bin directory because we specified this directory while configuring the source code. You can execute wget with the switch -version to verify that it is version 1.9.

```
$ /usr/local/bin/wget -version

GNU Wget 1.9.1

Copyright (C) 2003 Free Software Foundation, Inc.
This program is distributed in the hope that it will be useful,
but WITHOUT ANY WARRANTY; without even the implied warranty of
MERCHANTABILITY or FITNESS FOR A PARTICULAR PURPOSE.  See the
GNU General Public License for more details.

Originally written by Hrvoje Niksic <hniksic@xemacs.org>.
```

7. The existing wget application will continue to exist on your system in its original location (that is, /usr/bin). You can check the version of the original wget application as follows:

```
$ /usr/bin/wget -version
GNU Wget 1.9+cvs-stable (Red Hat modified)

Copyright (C) 2003 Free Software Foundation, Inc.
```

```
This program is distributed in the hope that it will be useful,
but WITHOUT ANY WARRANTY; without even the implied warranty of
MERCHANTABILITY or FITNESS FOR A PARTICULAR PURPOSE.  See the
GNU General Public License for more details.

Originally written by Hrvoje Niksic <hniksic@xemacs.org>.
```

It is your choice whether to keep both versions of an application. Typically, when you install a new version of an application, you should keep the old version until you have tested the new version for some time. That way, you can easily revert back to the old version of the application if something goes wrong with the new version.

How It Works

Finally, you have built your first application from source code. Building an application from source code is usually a straightforward process, but it varies from application to application:

```
# ./configure --prefix=/path/to/some/dir
# make
# make install
```

The preceding three commands build the source code as follows.

- The first command, `./configure -prefix=/path/to/some/dir`, finds out the platform, operating system, and development tools on your system, and also creates a Makefile, which the `make` command uses to compile the source code.
- The second command, `make`, compiles the source code. It follows the instruction in Makefile.
- The third command, `make install`, installs the binary application under the directory specified while executing the configure command (--prefix directory).

Building applications from source code gives you more control over the entire application building process, a choice to modify or optimize the source code, and also to select where to install the application. The process of building source code is generally straightforward, but you can run into source code compile problems. It is beyond the scope of this book to discuss these various situations, so please refer to *Beginning Linux Programming*, by Richard Stones, et al from Wrox Press for more details.

Keeping Systems Up-to-Date

One of the most difficult tasks of managing any operating system is to keep it up-to-date with the latest patches and updates. This task has become even more important due to growing security concerns and breaches. Fedora Linux makes this task much easier and manageable by providing a few tools to automate the patch management process. The following section discusses the up2date tool and the process of updating your system.

Up2date

Up2date is the default update tool available on Fedora Linux. It is an update agent to update the Red Hat Linux systems, and it is the same as the Red Hat Linux 9 up2date tool. Up2date provides a complete system to update RPM packages; it is available in command line as well as graphical interfaces.

When you run up2date, it matches the RPM list installed on the system with the RPM list on the Red Hat network and updates any new packages available. It is also intelligent enough to find out any dependencies and update them as necessary. Up2date can be started with the following command:

```
# up2date
```

> **You should start up2date as root user; otherwise, it will prompt for the computer's root password because up2date needs read/write access to the RPM database on the system and needs to be able to install RPM packages when requested.**

This command will start the up2date agent in GUI mode (see Figure 8-15).

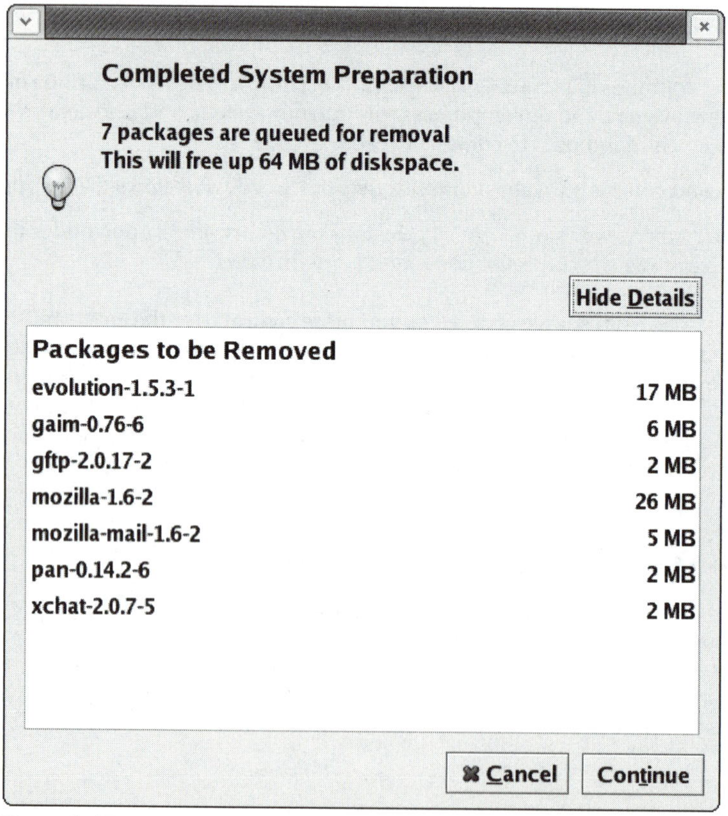

Figure 8-15

You can also start up2date as a command line interface to update any new RPM packages available from the Red Hat network. To do that, execute the following command:

```
# up2date -nox -u
```

The `-u` switch with the `up2date` command instructs up2date to completely update the system, and the `-nox` switch will instruct up2date to run all tasks on the command line interface without even trying to open the GUI. All available packages will be downloaded (and possibly installed, if you have configured Update Agent to do so) non-interactively.

Try It Out Update the System Using Up2date

Now that you have enough knowledge about the up2date agent and the update process, let's try this process out to update your system.

1. Start the up2date GUI interface by executing the following command as root user:

```
# up2date
```

   Click the Forward button to proceed to the next level.

2. You will be presented with the channels available for your system (see Figure 8-16). Select or deselect the channels, as required. By default, all channels will be selected.

A channel is a group that holds the details of packages for an operating system. Up2date will search a selected channel to find any updates for RPM packages.

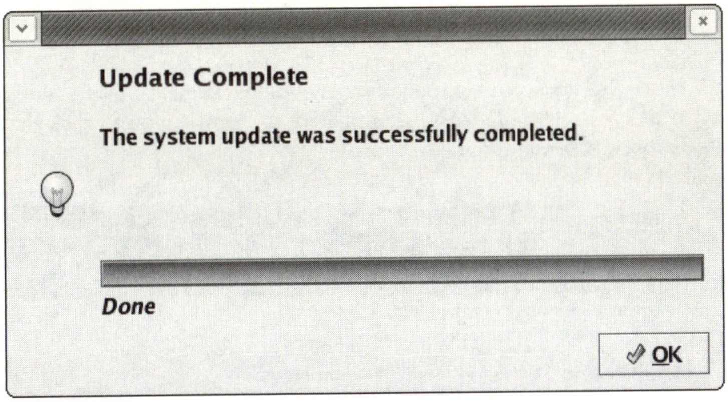

Figure 8-16

After you have selected the channels, click the Forward button. A few packages in the up2date configuration file should be skipped while updating the system. They are usually kernel RPM packages. If you want to check and update the kernel package updates (if available), select the packages in the next window.

> **Remember that updating the kernel can have some unknown effects on your system. You should update the kernel only when you are familiar with the new kernel and know how to revert back to the original kernel in case of problems.**

Click the Forward button after selecting or deselecting the required packages.

3. Up2date displays a list of all available updates for selection with details of each package. Select the packages to update and click the *Forward* button (see Figure 8-17).

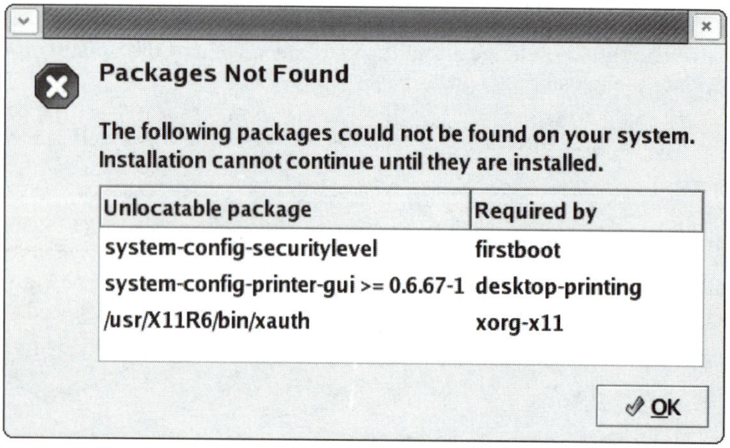

Figure 8-17

4. The update process takes some time to retrieve the packages from the repository, depending on the number of packages and size. Once finished, it prompts you to click the *Forward* button to continue as follows (see Figure 8-18).

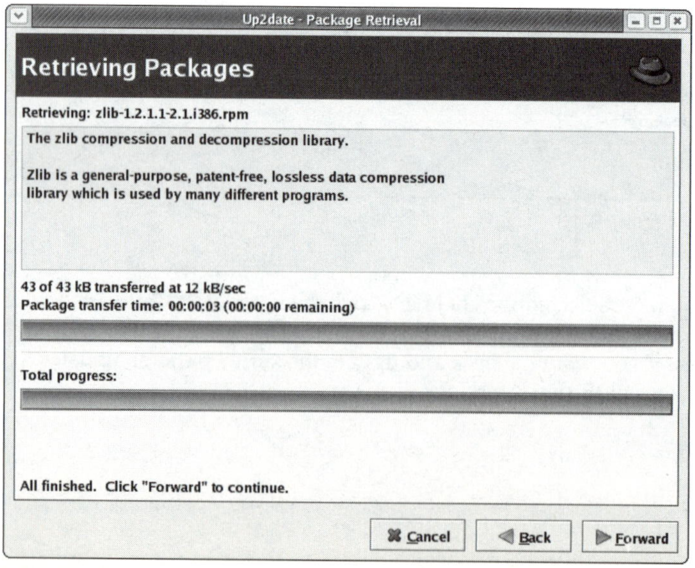

Figure 8-18

5. Up2date starts installing the downloaded packages and, once finished, again prompts you to click the Forward button.

6. At last, it displays the All Finished window to inform the user that all the selected packages have been updated successfully. The window looks like that shown in Figure 8-19.

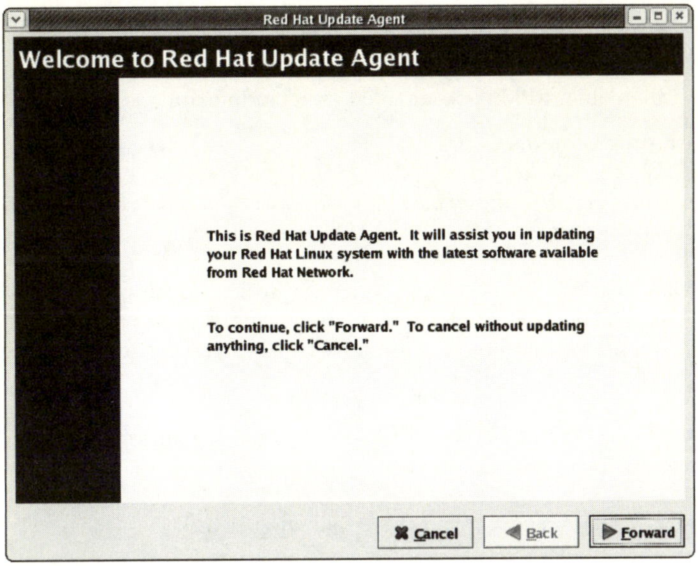

Figure 8-19

The benefits of keeping your system up-to-date with all available patches and upgrades include the following:

- Reduces the number of security attacks on the system. If your system is connected to the Internet, you will be faced with higher risks of security breaches if your system is not up-to-date with required patches.
- Increases the system uptime. Every operating system comes with some bugs, which can cause system crashes or downtime. Keeping the system up-to-date with all updates reduces the chance of a system crash.
- Provides new features available in new versions of applications.
- Provides more supported hardware available in the new version of the applications and kernel.

Yellow Dog Updater, Modified

Yellow Dog Updater, Modified (Yum) is an RPM package management utility to automate package management and maintenance. It provides automatic updates and package install/remove capabilities. Yum makes it easier to maintain a group of machines by automating the package management.

Yum's features include the following:

- Can work with multiple repositories, from where it can check for updates and download the required updates for the system.
- Uses a simple configuration file.
- Can correctly calculate the dependencies and deal with them automatically while installing/removing or updating packages.
- It is faster than other RPM package updates, including apt and up2date.
- Provides a simple interface.

A repository is a directory structure on the server side that contains RPM packages and Yum header information. A single server can host a number of Yum repositories.

Yum can be used as a server to host multiple Yum repositories, which can provide RPM packages to the clients, or as a client to manage RPM packages on the system. The `/usr/bin/yum-arch` program is available to build Yum RPM repositories, and the `/usr/bin/yum` program is available for client site package management.

We will discuss the Yum client in this chapter. You can find more information about Yum from the following resources:

You can find more information about Yum at the following URL:

```
http://linux.duke.edu/projects/yum/index.ptml
```

Or type the following command on the command line to view the Yum manuals:

```
man yum
man yum-arch
```

Configuring the Yum Client

Yum involves a client-side configuration file, `/etc/yum.conf`, and a binary program, `yum`. All the configuration parameters are defined in this file.

The `yum.conf` configuration file is located in `/etc/yum.conf` by default. It consists of two parts:

- A single Main section, which defines global configuration options
- One or more Server sections, where you define the repository you are planning to use

A default `yum.conf` file is provided with the Yum install. We will discuss the various options available in `/etc/yum.conf` file here.

Following is a typical configuration file (`/etc/yum.conf`):

```
[main]
cachedir=/var/cache/yum
debuglevel=2
```

```
logfile=/var/log/yum.log
pkgpolicy=newest
distroverpkg=redhat-release
tolerant=1
exactarch=1
retries=20

[base]
name=Fedora Core $releasever - $basearch - Base
baseurl=http://download.fedora.redhat.com/pub/fedora/linux/core/$releasever/$base
arch/os/

[updates-released]
name=Fedora Core $releasever - $basearch - Released Updates
baseurl=http://download.fedora.redhat.com/pub/fedora/linux/core/updates/$releasev
er/$basearch/

#[updates-testing]
#name=Fedora Core $releasever - $basearch - Unreleased Updates
#baseurl=http://download.fedora.redhat.com/pub/fedora/linux/core/updates/testing/
$releasever/$basearch/

#[development]
#name=Fedora Core $releasever - Development Tree
#baseurl=http://download.fedora.redhat.com/pub/fedora/linux/core/development/$bas
earch/
```

The main section of the `yum.conf` configuration file must exist, and the details of the configuration options follow. All options are in the format of option=value.

- `cachedir` defines the directory where Yum should store its cache and db files. It is `/var/cache/yum` in our case.

```
cachedir
```

- `debuglevel` defines the level of the logs. The valid levels are 0-10. In our case it is 2.

```
debuglevel
```

- `logfile` denies the location of the Yum log file. In our case it is `/var/log/yum.log`".

```
logfile
```

- `pkgpolicy` defines the package sorting order. The valid values are `newest` or `last`. The default value is newest, meaning when a package is available from multiple repository, Yum will install the most recent version of package found.

```
pkgpolicy
```

- The default value is `redhat-release` and it is used to determine the version of the distribution.

```
distroverpkg
```

- The default value is 1, which instructs Yum to be tolerant of the errors that arise while installing packages.

```
tolerant
```

- exactarch default value is 1, which instructs Yum to update only the architecture of packages that you have installed.

```
exactarch
```

Apart from the main section, the Yum configuration file also contains the server sections. Each server section defines the repository detail that you want Yum to use.

The default server sections for Fedora look like the following:

```
[base]
name=Fedora Core $releasever - $basearch - Base
baseurl=http://download.fedora.redhat.com/pub/fedora/linux/core/$releasever/$base
arch/os/

[updates-released]
name=Fedora Core $releasever - $basearch - Released Updates
baseurl=http://download.fedora.redhat.com/pub/fedora/linux/core/updates/$releasev
er/$basearch/
```

The first line of the server section of `yum.conf` defines the unique name of the repository by which it will be known. It must be a single word to identify the section. It should be in the form of [base], where "base" can be any single word.

The second line defines the descriptive name of the repository. It is in the form of name=value, where value can be any descriptive name by which the repository will be known.

The third line defines the location of the repository. It can contain any number of locations. It is in the form baseurl=location, where location is the actual URL of the repository.

For more information on Yum configuration, go to the Yum manual page by executing the following command on the command line:

```
man yum.conf
```

Or you can also find more information from the following URL:

```
www.phy.duke.edu/~rgb/General/yum_HOWTO/yum_HOWTO/index.html
```

Running the Yum Client

After you have set up the Yum configuration file on your system, you are ready to start using Yum to update your system. The Yum client provides various options to effectively handle package management.

Let's run Yum on the command line:

```
# yum
    Usage:  yum [options] <update | upgrade | install | info | remove | list |
            clean | provides | search | check-update | groupinstall | groupupdate |
            grouplist >

         Options:
          -c [config file] - specify the config file to use
          -e [error level] - set the error logging level
          -d [debug level] - set the debugging level
          -y answer yes to all questions
          -t be tolerant about errors in package commands
          -R [time in minutes] - set the max amount of time to randomly run in.
          -C run from cache only - do not update the cache
          --installroot=[path] - set the install root (default '/')
          --version - output the version of yum
          -h, --help this screen
```

As you can see, Yum shows all the available options when executing the `yum` command. We will discuss just often options to enable us keep our system "up2date."

You can execute Yum with an update option to update everything on the system, as follows:

```
# yum update
Gathering header information file(s) from server(s)
Server: Fedora Core 2 - i386 - Base
Finding updated packages
Downloading needed headers
Resolving dependencies
Dependencies resolved
I will do the following:
[install: kernel 2.4.22-1.2149.nptl.i686]
[update: binutils 2.14.90.0.6-4.i386]
[update: nscd 2.3.2-101.4.i386]
[update: xboard 4.2.7-1.i386]
[update: httpd 2.0.48-1.2.i386]
[update: glibc-devel 2.3.2-101.4.i386]
[update: glibc-common 2.3.2-101.4.i386]
[update: kernel-source 2.4.22-1.2149.nptl.i386]
[update: glibc 2.3.2-101.4.i686]
[update: glibc-headers 2.3.2-101.4.i386]
Is this ok [y/N]:
```

Yum will prompt you to verify the packages to be updated; enter **Y** at the prompt to process the update.

If you want to completely automate the update task, execute the Yum update command with the `-y` switch. Yum will assume "yes" to be the answer to any question asked during the update process.

```
# yum -y update
Gathering header information file(s) from server(s)
Server: Fedora Core 2 - i386 - Base
Finding updated packages
Downloading needed headers
Resolving dependencies
Dependencies resolved
.......
Running test transaction:
Test transaction complete, Success!
glibc-common 100 % done 1/19
glibc 100 % done 2/19
Stopping sshd:[  OK  ]
Starting sshd:[  OK  ]
glibc-headers 100 % done 3/19
binutils 100 % done 4/19
nscd 100 % done 5/19
xboard 100 % done 6/19
httpd 100 % done 7/19
kernel 100 % done 8/19
glibc-devel 100 % done 9/19
kernel-source 100 % done 10/19
Completing update for binutils  - 11/19
Completing update for nscd  - 12/19
Completing update for xboard  - 13/19
Completing update for httpd  - 14/19
Completing update for glibc-devel  - 15/19
Completing update for glibc-common  - 16/19
Completing update for kernel-source  - 17/19
Completing update for glibc  - 18/19
Completing update for glibc-headers  - 19/19
Kernel Updated/Installed, checking for bootloader
Grub found - making this kernel the default
Installed:  kernel 2.4.22-1.2149.nptl.i686
Updated:  binutils 2.14.90.0.6-4.i386 nscd 2.3.2-101.4.i386 xboard 4.2.7-1.i386
httpd 2.0.48-1.2.i386 glibc-devel 2.3.2-101.4.i386 glibc-common 2.3.2-101.4.i386
kernel-source 2.4.22-1.2149.nptl.i386 glibc 2.3.2-101.4.i686 glibc-headers
2.3.2-101.4.i386
Transaction(s) Complete
```

The update process will finish after some time depending on the number of package updates available.

Automating the Update

Yum also comes with a script to enable the automated update process. Once enabled, it runs the Yum automatically on a nightly basis. To enable Yum to automatically run every night, execute the following script:

```
# /etc/init.d/yum start
Enabling nightly yum update:                                    [  OK  ]
```

This script also provides other options. You can get a list of all the options by executing this script on the command line:

```
# /etc/init.d/yum
Usage: /etc/init.d/yum {start|stop|status|restart|reload|force-reload|condrestart}
```

The preceding script enables the cron entry in the `/etc/cron.daily/yum.cron` file.

If you want to disable the cron entry for Yum, execute the following command:

```
# /etc/init.d/yum stop
Disabling nightly yum update:                                   [  OK  ]
```

When you run Yum options for the first time, it takes some time to download all the package headers from the repository and store them in the `/var/yum/cache` *directory.*

The Advance Package Tool, APT

APT is an Advance Package Management Tool that was originally developed for Debian Linux. It has now also been ported to Fedora.

APT comes with the following utilities to manage the packages:

- `apt-get` is a command line tool to manage packages.
- `apt-cdrom` is a command line tool to manage CD-ROMs that are to be used as a package source.
- `apt-config` is an APT configuration query program.
- `apt-cache` is a program that performs a variety of operations on APT package cache.

You can get more information about the APT by typing the following command on the command line:

```
man apt-get
man apt-cdrom
man apt-config
man apt-cache
```

The apt-get utility must be executed as root user; otherwise, you will be prompted for the root password because it needs root access to access the RPM db and to install the RPMs on the system.

In the following section, we will try some of the apt-get commands that are useful in managing the packages.

```
# ant-get --help
apt 0.5.15cnc6 for linux i386 compiled on Apr  9 2004 10:38:19
Usage: apt-get [options] command
       apt-get [options] install|remove pkg1 [pkg2 ...]
       apt-get [options] source pkg1 [pkg2 ...]

apt-get is a simple command line interface for downloading and
installing packages. The most frequently used commands are update
and install.

Commands:
   update - Retrieve new lists of packages
   upgrade - Perform an upgrade
   install - Install new packages (pkg is libc6 not libc6.rpm)
   remove - Remove packages
   source - Download source archives
   build-dep - Configure build-dependencies for source packages
   dist-upgrade - Distribution upgrade, see apt-get(8)
   clean - Erase downloaded archive files
   autoclean - Erase old downloaded archive files
   check - Verify that there are no broken dependencies
   mirror-select - Select repositories and mirrors for use with apt

Options:
  -h  This help text.
  -q  Loggable output - no progress indicator
  -qq No output except for errors
  -d  Download only - do NOT install or unpack archives
  -s  No-act. Perform ordering simulation
  -y  Assume Yes to all queries and do not prompt
  -f  Attempt to continue if the integrity check fails
  -m  Attempt to continue if archives are unlocatable
  -u  Show a list of upgraded packages as well
  -b  Build the source package after fetching it
  -D  When removing packages, remove dependencies as possible
  -V  Show verbose version numbers
  -c=? Read this configuration file
  -o=? Set an arbitary configuration option, eg -o dir::cache=/tmp
See the apt-get(8), sources.list(5) and apt.conf(5) manual
pages for more information and options.
                       This APT has Super Cow Powers.
```

apt-get with the `-help` switch displays the usage information of the `apt-get` utility.

The apt-get update switch is used to resynchronize the package index files from their sources, which are specified in the `/etc/apt/sources.list` file. You should always execute apt-get with the update switch before you actually start updating the packages on your system so that APT knows of new package availability.

```
# apt-get  update
Get:1 http://ayo.freshrpms.net fedora/linux/1/i386 release [1993B]
Fetched 1993B in 0s (4426B/s)
Get:1 http://ayo.freshrpms.net fedora/linux/1/i386/core pkglist [1445kB]
Get:2 http://ayo.freshrpms.net fedora/linux/1/i386/core release [151B]
Get:3 http://ayo.freshrpms.net fedora/linux/1/i386/updates pkglist [214kB]
Get:4 http://ayo.freshrpms.net fedora/linux/1/i386/updates release [157B]
Get:5 http://ayo.freshrpms.net fedora/linux/1/i386/freshrpms pkglist [142kB]
Get:6 http://ayo.freshrpms.net fedora/linux/1/i386/freshrpms release [161B]
Fetched 1802kB in 33s (53.3kB/s)
Reading Package Lists... Done
Building Dependency Tree... Done
```

After updating the package indexes from the sources, you can start updating the packages on your system by executing apt-get with the upgrade switch.

Execute the following command to install the newest version of all the packages currently installed on the system from the source specified in the `/etc/apt/sources.list` file:

```
# apt-get upgrade
Reading Package Lists... Done
Building Dependency Tree... Done
The following packages will be upgraded
  gaim nmap nmap-frontend yum
The following packages have been kept back
  gthumb rhythmbox
4 upgraded, 0 newly installed, 0 removed and 2 not upgraded.
Need to get 3227kB of archives.
After unpacking 473kB of additional disk space will be used.
Do you want to continue? [Y/n] y
Get:1 http://ayo.freshrpms.net fedora/linux/1/i386/freshrpms yum 2.0.4-2.fd.fr
[139kB]
Get:2 http://ayo.freshrpms.net fedora/linux/1/i386/freshrpms gaim 1:0.75-1.fr
[2556kB]
Get:3 http://ayo.freshrpms.net fedora/linux/1/i386/freshrpms nmap 2:3.48-2.fr
[497kB]
Get:4 http://ayo.freshrpms.net fedora/linux/1/i386/freshrpms nmap-frontend
2:3.48-2.fr [35.4kB]
Fetched 3227kB in 54s (59.2kB/s)
warning: /var/cache/apt/archives/yum_2.0.4-2.fd.fr_i386.rpm: V3 DSA signature:
NOKEY, key ID e42d547b
Committing changes...
Preparing...                ########################################### [100%]
   1:nmap-frontend          ########################################### [ 25%]
   2:yum                    ########################################### [ 50%]
   3:gaim                   ########################################### [ 75%]
   4:nmap                   ########################################### [100%]
Done.
```

You will be prompted for the answer to continue with the download and installation of packages before you can actually download and install the packages. You can instruct APT not to ask any questions and automatically check, download, and upgrade any new versions of the packages by using the -y switch:

```
# apt-get -y upgrade
```

apt-get can also be used to install individual packages from the sources specified in /etc/apt/sources.list.

```
# apt-get install package-name
```

Here, install is the option that instructs apt-get to install the packages, and package-name is the name of the package to search on the sources and install, if available.

Using the Synaptic GUI Application

Synaptic is a front-end GUI for APT (Advance package tool). It makes the job of updating packages even easier. Before we can discuss the functionality of Synaptic, we have to install the Synaptic package.

Let's use the apt-get command line utility to install this package, as follows:

```
# apt-get install synaptic
Reading Package Lists... Done
Building Dependency Tree... Done
The following NEW packages will be installed:
  synaptic
0 upgraded, 1 newly installed, 0 removed and 2 not upgraded.
Need to get 528kB of archives.
After unpacking 1790kB of additional disk space will be used.
Get:1 http://ayo.freshrpms.net fedora/linux/1/i386/freshrpms synaptic 0.45-1.fr
[528kB]
Fetched 528kB in 9s (56.3kB/s)
Committing changes...
Preparing...                ########################################### [100%]
   1:synaptic               ########################################### [100%]
Done.
```

Once the Synaptic application is installed, you can either start the application from Main Menu ➪ System tools ➪ Synaptic Package Manager or by executing /usr/sbin/synaptic from the command line (see Figure 8-20).

Synaptic is used in the same way as the apt-get command line utility.

You should update the package list from the servers by clicking the Update List button. All sources are defined in the /etc/apt/sources.list file just as with the apt-get utility.

You can view the details of all upgradable packages by selecting Upgradable for Show filter (see Figure 8-21).

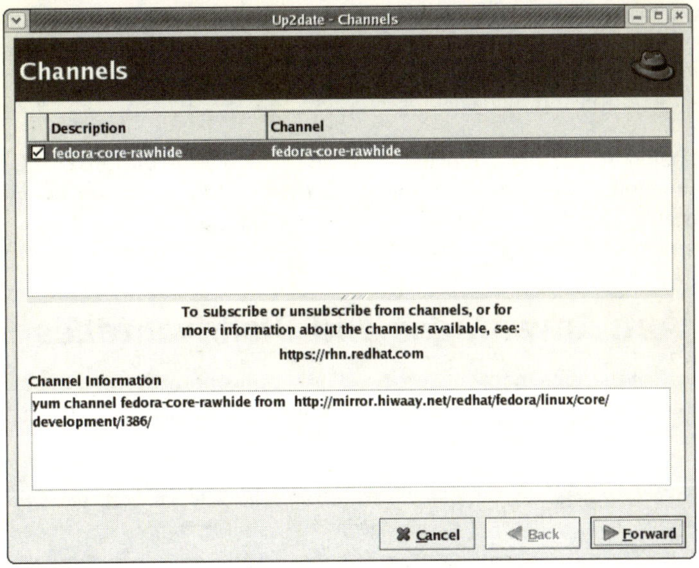

Figure 8-20

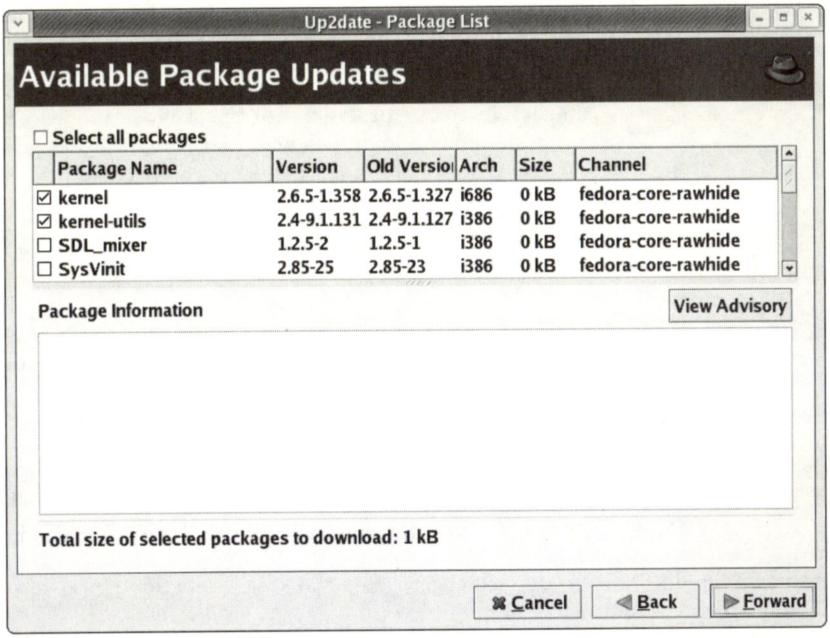

Figure 8-21

To update the system with all available packages, click the Upgrade all button. Upgrade all will upgrade only the packages that do not require any new package installation due to dependencies. Synaptic will save the upgrade task and will proceed with package upgrade only when you instruct it to do so by clicking the Execute button and then clicking Proceed.

To update the system with all dependencies, click the Dist Upgrade button. Dist Upgrade, in addition to performing the function of Upgrade all, automatically deals with dependencies and installs the new versions of all newly available dependencies. Dist Upgrade tasks are also saved and performed when you start the update process by clicking the Execute button and then Proceed.

Yum versus Apt: Advantages and Disadvantages

Both the Yum and Apt package managers are excellent applications designed to make the task of updating systems easy and manageable. Each has its advantages and disadvantages. The following table lists all the advantages and disadvantages of Yum and Apt.

Yum	Apt
Advantages	Yum has a small package list and therefore it is fast. It takes less time to download the package header information from the Internet. And Yum is based on Python, which makes it easy to inherit a lot of already developed code from up2date and Anaconda. Apt provides a clear indication of update process and estimated time left.
Disadvantages	Yum does not provide any indication about progress or estimated time left in update progress. Apt's package headers are larger than Yum's, and therefore it is slower than Yum. And Apt is based on C/C++ and cannot use up2date/Anaconda code.

Summary

This chapter provides the information you need to confidently add, remove, and upgrade packages on your system. You should now be able to do the following:

- Customize the packages installed on your system using the Package Management Tool.
- Install additional software directly from the RPM file, using the package manager.
- Query, install, remove, upgrade, and verify RPM files using the RPM command line interface.
- Ensure updated RPM files you receive from Red Hat are the real thing by checking their GnuPG signature file.
- Understand the basic principles behind uncompressing and installing source code packages available in TAR files on your system, so you'll know how to proceed with source code when an RPM file is not available.

- Understand how to keep your system up-to-date with patches and upgrades. You should also be able to appreciate the benefits of keeping your system up-to-date with the latest packages.
- Use Yum and Apt package management systems to keep your system up-to-date.

This chapter aimed to give you a good working knowledge of Red Hat's package management software. If you're interested in learning more, the following resources will be helpful:

- Red Hat RPM Documentation: `www.redhat.com/docs/manuals/linux/RHL-9-Manual/`
- Max RPM: `www.rpm.org/max-rpm/`
- Open source software portal: `http://freshmeat.net/`
- RPM search portal: `http://rpmfind.net/linux/RPM/`
- Yum project: `http://linux.duke.edu/projects/yum/`
- RPM package repository: `http://apt.freshrpms.net`

The next chapter takes a look at how to build and deploy some of the useful network applications, including Web server, FTP server, Print server, Mail Server, and DHCP server on a Fedora system.

Exercises

To build your skills even further, here is an exercise you can use to test yourself. The answers are provided in Appendix A, but keep in mind, there is always more than one way to accomplish a given task, so if you choose to do things a different way and the results display the way you want, more power to you.

1. Start the RPM Package Management Tool.
2. Install a package `ncftp`, an improved FTP client, using the RPM command line interface.
3. Display the RPM package information (for example, `ncftp`) on the command line.
4. Uninstall the same package, `ncftp`, using the RPM command line interface without verifying package dependencies.
5. Find a package that owns the file installed on your system (for example, `/bin/vi`).
6. Display the package information and list the files installed by a package (for example, `wget`) on your system before even installing it.
7. Use up2date to list the package updates available to download without using X.
8. Use yum help to find the option to check for package updates for your system, and then run the command to do the same.
9. Use APT to update the package indexes from the sources. In other words, use APT to check for updates from the RPM sources.

9

Building Networks

If you're going to share resources among computers efficiently, the use of networks is essential. Networking is a complex topic, but it's powerful, and these days it's indispensable. For example:

- At work, it's hard for many corporations to imagine life without the large networks that make files and services accessible to their employees.
- At home, if you've got a couple of computers, the convenience of having them networked together for sharing files is immeasurable. (Plenty of network professionals started out by tinkering with small home networks.)
- Networking is also what makes the Internet possible.

Linux is a popular choice these days when it comes to enterprise networking solutions. Linux networks are fast, reliable, secure, and cost effective. Google (`www.google.com`) provides one of the best examples of enterprise Linux networks. Google's search engine comprises more than 10,000 servers networked together to form one of the world's biggest distributed computing systems, and the world's largest commercial Linux cluster. The Stone SouperComputer is another (rather different) example of what is possible with Linux-based networking (see `http://stonesoup.esd.ornl.gov/`).

This chapter begins with a general discussion of networks, and the advantages of using Linux for building networks. Then, sections are devoted to each of the following services:

- Setting up a Web server, for hosting Web sites (or, if you're planning to develop Web sites, to test your sites as you build them)
- Setting up an FTP server, a place from which users can download files and/or upload files
- Setting up a Print server to manage printers and enable them to be shared among multiple users
- Setting up a File server to share files (for example, between Windows and Linux systems)

- Setting up a Mail server, for delivering e-mail to its final destination (for example, you could use an e-mail client on a Windows 2000 laptop and configure it to send and receive e-mail via a local Linux mail server)
- Setting up a DHCP server, which automatically assigns network settings to connected systems

You may choose not to read all of this chapter, but only the sections that relate to the services you're interested in. You probably won't need all these services on your Linux machine, and you're not obliged to set them all up. (In fact, there are good security reasons for choosing not to set up a service unless and until you *need* it to be there. Security is further discussed in Chapter 10.)

Moreover, these services all work independently of one another, so (for example) you don't have to set up an FTP server for your Web server to work. You can enable and disable any service just at the time you need it.

By default, Fedora 2 setup provides you the option to configure the firewall. If the firewall has been configured, you might face some problems accessing the services set up in this chapter. After setting up or configuring any of the services discussed in this chapter, you should always check the firewall settings and, if needed, open the ports to enable access to those services. Please refer to Chapter 10 of this book for more information about setting and configuring the firewall.

Networking

These days, networking is part of daily life. Whether you are sending e-mail from your desktop PCs or using the Internet for shopping, networking is at the heart of it. In fact, there are a number of different types of network:

- A local area network (LAN) is a network that covers a limited geographical area.
- A metropolitan area network (MAN) covers a geographic area such as a city or suburb.
- A wide area network (WAN) may span a wide geographic area, spread over many states or countries. The Internet is an example of a WAN.

To facilitate communication across these networks, you have *protocols*. A protocol is a standard language by which two (possibly dissimilar) systems can communicate. For example, TCP/IP is the protocol that allows different machines to participate together to make the Internet work.

For more information about Networking protocols such as TCP/IP, AppleTalk, X.25, Frame Relay, ISDN, PPP, SLIP, PLIP, and so on, try `www.tldp.org/LDP/nag2/index.html` *and* `www.tldp.org/HOWTO/Networking-Overview-HOWTO.html`.

Fedora Linux and Networking

Fedora 2 comes bundled with lots of networking applications and utilities that will help you meet your networking requirements. The following table categorizes and lists the networking applications that come with Fedora 2:

Application Type	Application Name	Description
Web server server.	httpd	The widely used Apache HTTP
FTP server	vsftp	A very secure FTP server.
File server	sambasambasamba-client	The SAMBA server provides file sharing between SMB-enabled machines (such as Windows and Linux machines). SAMBA client programs are designed to access SMB shares.
Print server	cups	CUPS printing service and the drivers to use it.
Mail server	sendmail	A widely used mail transport agent.
DHCP server	dhcp	A DHCP server and relay agent.

This chapter discusses some of these applications and helps you to get your Linux machine acting as a full-fledged network server.

Why Is Linux Good for Networking?

One of the most significant factors in choosing the hardware and software for a network is the *total cost of ownership (TCO)*. This is the cost of purchase, setup and configuration, and maintenance. If you sit down and analyze the requirements of different parts of network architecture, you'll quickly find that the free, open nature of Linux systems lends itself better to some parts of a network than others.

Linux is a particularly good choice for supporting network applications (such as file servers, Web servers, and mail servers):

- The cost of purchase (both of the operating system and the software itself) is low. Cost of setup should generally also be favorable, particularly given the advances both in recent releases of network applications and in Fedora 2 itself, and the vast body of knowledge in the open source community that is available via Web sites, news groups, and local Linux users' groups. (Many enterprise-level solutions companies such as Red Hat, IBM, Hewlett Packard, and Sun Microsystems have also started providing commercial-level support for Linux servers.)
- The stability and reliability of the operating system is also influential because an unstable or unreliable system brings maintenance costs. Linux is a good choice for network applications because it makes the grade in these areas. Moreover, Linux is ready for high-availability environments (see `www.ibiblio.org/pub/Linux/ALPHA/linux-ha`).
- Other factors influencing TCO include the scalability, flexibility, and security of the system:
    - By choosing a Linux operating system and open source networking applications, you have access to the source code of both the system and the application. This puts you in a position to adapt the applications to achieve whatever aims you need.

- ❑ You've already seen evidence in this chapter that Linux is capable of being deployed in both small- and large-scale networks.
- ❑ Red Hat Linux installs by default with a minimum of good-practice security, and can be further enhanced with a combination of open source security tools and good practice (see Chapter 10).

Linux is also great for services that can be replicated (for example, DNS). You can configure such machines cheaply, and replicate them. Then, if one machine fails, it should be possible to replace it cheaply. In the meantime, the replicate servers keep on working to provide the service.

By contrast, Linux is not a common choice for basic infrastructure, such as routers, hubs, and switches. While Linux is capable in this area, it's desirable only when the low cost of PCs is the major selection criteria. In a more business-critical role, where reliability will count for more than minimum purchase price, dedicated hardware is still the most popular choice.

You can find more information about TCO comparison between Fedora 2 and other UNIX flavors at `www.redhat.com/whitepapers/services/tco.pdf`.

Assumptions for Network Setup

In the demonstrations in this chapter, we've used a network setup that may not be the same as your own environment. You can choose your own server, connectivity devices (switch, hub, and direct cable connection), IP address scheme, and hostname to set up networking in a way that suits your own requirements. This section notes the network settings that we've used. To facilitate, an explanation of the terms used follows.

The *network topology* refers to the shape or layout of the network. It defines how different systems in a network are connected and communicate with each other. The ideal topology of a network depends on the size of the network, the requirements of its users, and the policies of the company or organization.

Figure 9-1 shows an ideal network topology.

This diagram shows a client machine (in the form of a Windows 2000 Professional laptop), and a server (running Fedora 2, and supporting some of the services described in this chapter. They are connected via an internal network, and protected from the Internet by a hub and a firewall.

Your network topology might look different. For example, if you have a smaller network, it's possible that you don't have a hub, and that your firewall is not a dedicated machine but a piece of software hosted by your Linux server machine. If you have only a single machine, it can double as both the server and client machines in this diagram (being a client of its own services).

Note that both the user's laptop and the server machine have been assigned an IP address—this is used to uniquely identify the computer (or other device) within a TCP/IP network. An IP address is a 32-bit binary address in the form of four decimal values. Each of these four decimals represents an 8-bit value (an octet), and is in the range 0 to 255. This format is known as *dotted quad notation.*

In fact, the TCP/IP network is divided into different class networks. The important classes are defined in the following table.

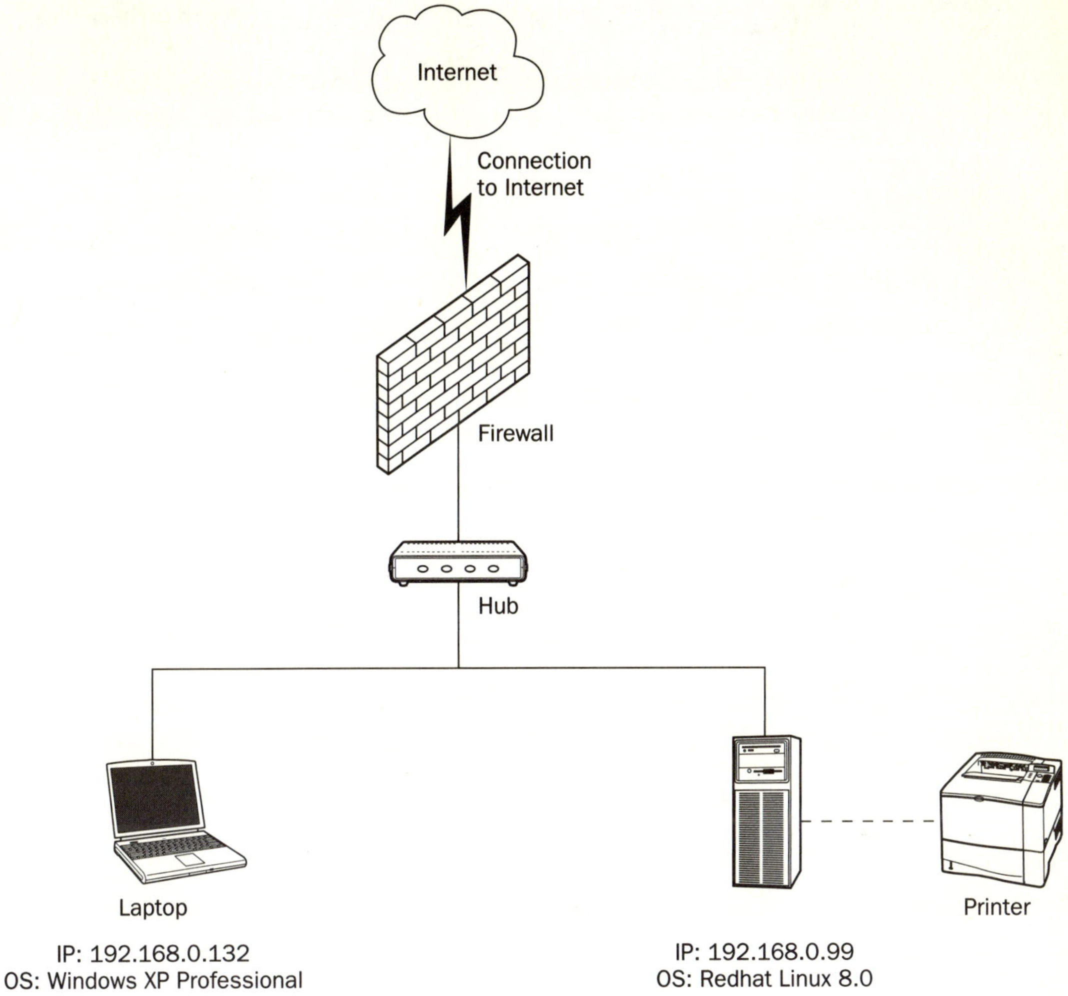

Figure 9-1

Class	Values	Description
Class A	1.x.x.x to 127.x.x.x	The first octet specifies the network number, and the remaining octets specify the host within the network. This class supports about 1.6 million hosts per network.
Class B	128.0.x.x to 191.255.x.x	The first two octets specify the network number, and the remaining octets specify the host within the network. This class supports 16,320 networks with 65,024 hosts each.

Table continued on following page

Class	Values	Description
Class C	192.0.0.x to 223.255.255.x	The first three octets specify the network number, and the remaining octets specify the host within the network. This class supports nearly two million networks with up to 254 hosts each.
Class D	224.0.0.0 to 239.255.255.255	These are reserved for multicast groups.
Class E	240.0.0.0 to 254.255.255.254	These are reserved for special purpose use.

The TCP/IP networks can also be divided by public and private IP addresses:

- Your Internet service provider (ISP) assigns you your public IP address. In fact, this IP address is allocated to the ISP by the Internet Assigned Numbers Authority (IANA—`www.iana.org`). It's your public IP address that identifies you on the Internet.
- Private IP addresses are those (like the addresses used in the preceding diagram) that identify a device within a private or non-Internet-connected network. Three TCP/IP network address ranges are reserved for use in private networks: 10.0.0.0–10.255.255.255, 172.16.0.0–172.31.255.255, and 192.168.0.0–192.168.255.255.

A *netmask* is a 32-bit string that hides the network part of an IP address, so that only the host (computer) part of the address remains. For example, the netmask 255.255.255.0 looks like an IP address, but in fact hides the first 24 bits of the IP address so that only the last 8 bits remain (recall that 255 is the decimal representation of the binary 11111111). The netmask 255.255.255.0 is commonly used for Class C IP addresses to reveal the specific host computer address publicly.

The following definitions will also be useful here:

- A *gateway* is a host that is connected to two or more physical networks, and allows messages to switch between them.
- The term *hostname* refers to the unique name of the machine, so that it can identify itself on the network.
- Finally, the *domain name system (DNS)* is a distributed database that translates domain names into IP addresses and vice versa. For example, DNS translates the domain name `www.linux4biz.net` to the IP address `66.103.135.76`.

With all that in mind, let's return to those two machines on our sample network—the Fedora 2 server machine and the Windows 2000 client laptop machine. Following are the network configuration settings we used for those two machines in this chapter.

The Fedora 2 server machine is set up as a firewall and router, and has Internet connectivity. Over the course of the chapter we'll show how it can be configured as a File server, Print server, DHCP server, FTP server, Web server, or Mail server.

Server	Value
Operating system	Fedora 2
IP address	`192.168.0.99`
Netmask	`255.255.255.0`
Hostname	`linux4biz`

The laptop is a simple client machine, designed for a user and (potentially) sharing resources with other similar machines on the network.

Setting	Value
Purpose	A Client laptop system to be used to share resources configured on a Linux server
Operating system	Windows 2000 Professional
IP address	`192.168.0.132`
Netmask	`255.255.255.0`
Hostname	`Win`

As we've said, your network topology, and the network configuration of your machine(s), may be different; but many of the principles in this chapter remain the same, and you should be able to get any of these services going regardless of your own environment.

We will assume that you have root access to the Fedora 2 server. The chapter uses the terms *Linux server* and *client* to refer to the Fedora 2 server machine and the Microsoft Windows 2000 client machine, respectively.

Setting Up a Web Server

When you want to publish Web pages on the Internet (or on an intranet), you use a *Web server*. In essence, a Web server is an application that does two things:

- It listens for page requests.
- When it receives a page request, it examines the request and responds with the page that was requested.

For example, when you use a Web browser to browse `www.wrox.com`, the browser turns this into a *request* message and sends it across the Internet to Wrox's own Web server. When the Web server receives this request, it processes it, works out what page you requested, puts that page together from whatever resources are necessary, and sends the page back to your browser in the form of a *response* message.

Of course, there are many different Web browsers in existence (including Mozilla, Opera, Internet Explorer, and others), and a great many types of Web server software also exist. To enable a browser to request pages from a Web server, they communicate using *Hypertext Transfer Protocol (HTTP)*—this is the standard protocol for the Internet. The request and response messages are composed using HTTP, and this is what allows *any* browser to request Web pages from *any* type of Web server.

> *By default, all Web servers listen for HTTP requests on port 80. Web servers also use port 443 to listen for requests made through secure HTTP connections, over the secure sockets layer (SSL), through a protocol called HTTPS.*

So, if you want to publish your own Web site, you'll need a machine with some Web server software. However, the chances are that if you build your own Web site, you probably won't want to expose it to the Internet from your *own* machine. There are security and maintenance issues to manage, and you'd need to buy enough hardware and bandwidth to handle all the page requests. More likely, you'd choose an ISP, and use its Web servers to host your Web site for you.

So, why would you want to install a Web server on your Fedora 2 Linux machine? Here are two scenarios:

- If you're building a Web site, you'll need a Web server so that you can test your site as you're developing it.
- Although you might not host an Internet site from your own machine, you might host an intranet site, a private Web site available only to other machines inside your private network. The demand for intranet pages is much more predictable than for Internet pages, and the security risks are not so significant.

This section shows you how to set up a Web server on your machine, configure it, and publish pages on it. From there, you'll soon be developing your own sites.

The Apache Web Server

As mentioned, a number of commercial and freely available Web servers are in existence. Among the commercial Web servers are offerings from Netscape, IPlanet, SunONE, Microsoft (the Internet Information Server, or IIS), and Zeus. Among the open source Web servers are Apache, thttpd, and Red Hat TUX.

Of all these, Apache is most widely used. At the time of writing, 66 percent of all Web sites are hosted on Apache Web servers (according to the Netcraft Web Server Survey, `www.netcraft.com/survey`)—the vast majority of them running on Linux or UNIX operating systems. Apache's popularity is due not only to its open source pedigree, but also to its highly competitive levels of performance, functionality, stability, flexibility, and security:

- Apache's flexibility comes from the fact that it is a modular Web server. That means that you can meet your requirements by plugging any number of external modules into the core httpd daemon. Of course, because it is open source software, you also have access to Apache's source code, which you can customize to fit your needs.

  Apache is also very scalable. You can run Apache on high-end hardware, and it's possible to increase the capacity of Apache Web servers by sharing the load across any number of servers. It's also very portable, being available for a number of operating systems.

- Apache's security is very good in comparison to other Web servers. Moreover, the Apache Foundation is extremely active in the continued defense of Apache from security problems, particularly in the form of announcements and patches.
- Apache performs very well—it boasts a highly optimized daemon for serving static content that dramatically outperforms its nearest rivals. Moreover, it rarely crashes and achieves extremely long up-times.
- Apache comes with detailed documentation, which helps to make the setup and configuration easy. And, because it's so popular, there's a wide network of support for Apache, in the form of mailing lists, newsgroups, and commercial vendors such as Red Hat.
- Apache development is active. The Apache Foundation is actively involved in development of new modules and new versions of Apache to make it reliable, stable, and secure.

Because you've already got Fedora 2, there's another good reason for choosing Apache as your Web server software—it's included as part of the Fedora 2 distribution. At the time of writing, the latest version of Apache is 2.0.49.

Installing Apache

As previously noted, Apache is a *modular* server—the core server provides the basic functionality, with extended features available in various modules. This makes it very flexible and easy to configure, because you have to configure only the modules you need. So, it's worth looking at how to control the installation and removal of these modules.

In fact, the different modules are contained in the different packages that you can install via the Package Management Tool. Recall that to start RPM's graphical interface, you can select Main Menu ➪ System Settings ➪ Add/Remove Applications, or type the following command at the command line:

```
$ system-config-packages
```

The Apache Web server packages are listed in the Web Server package group, which is found under the Servers category in the RPM Package Management Tool. If you look at the details of this package group, shown in Figure 9-2, you'll see that there are many packages listed.

Only one of these packages in the group is a Required Package—that's the httpd package that contains the base Apache Web server functionality. The remaining packages are all optional packages. The important packages are explained in the table that follows.

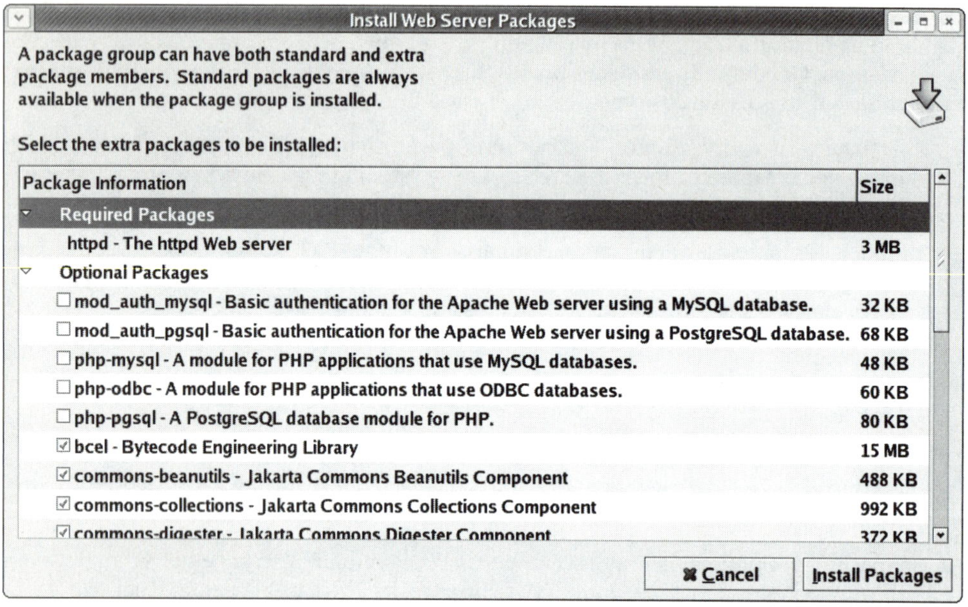

Figure 9-2

Package	Description
`httpd-manual`	Contains the documentation for the Apache Web server. After installation, you can access this documentation from the command line by typing `man httpd`.
`hwcrypto`	Provides support for hardware SSL acceleration cards. This package should be installed if you have hardware SSL acceleration cards, such as Ncipher Nforce, on your server.
`mod_ssl`	Provides an SSL interface to the HTTPS Web server, and enables the Apache Web server to support SSL. This package should be installed if you want to provide secure connections to your clients.
`php`	Provides the PHP module for Apache, which enables the Web server to serve PHP Web pages. This package is required if you want to host Web sites that contain pages written with the PHP scripting language.
`Webalizer`	Provides programs for Web server log file analysis. This package enables you to generate HTML usage reports for your Web site.

You can find out more about other Apache modules at the Apache Web site, `http://httpd.apache.org/docs-2.0/mod`.

You can choose whichever extra packages fit your requirements; it's definitely worth installing the `httpd-manual` package, and then you should choose whatever other packages fit your own requirements. Remember that you can re-launch the RPM at any time, and add or remove packages, as you need them.

When you've selected the packages you need, click the Install Packages button to begin the installation. During the installation, you'll be prompted to insert the distribution discs as they're required. The RPM will also inform you of any conflict between package dependencies.

The Apache Configuration Files

Apache's configuration information is contained in a select bunch of configuration files:

- The `/etc/httpd/httpd.conf` file is Apache's main configuration file.
- The `/etc/httpd/conf.d` directory contains configuration files for any installed modules (such as PHP, SSL, and so on).
- The `/etc/httpd/logs` directory is a symbolic link to `/var/log/httpd` directory, which contains all the Apache log files.
- The `/etc/httpd/modules` directory is a symbolic link to `/usr/lib/httpd/modules` directory, which contains all the Apache modules configured as dynamic shared objects.

Dynamic shared objects (DSOs) are modules that are compiled separately from the Apache httpd binary. They can be loaded on demand. There's more information on DSOs at `http://httpd.apache.org/docs-2.0/mod`.

- The `/etc/httpd/run` directory is a symbolic link to `/var/run`, which contains the process ID file (`httpd.pid`) of the httpd process.
- `/etc/rc.d/init.d/httpd` is a shell script, used for starting and stopping the Apache Web server.

Starting Apache for the First Time

You can start Apache using the Fedora Service Configuration GUI dialog box, or via the command line. Here's how to start Apache from the Service Configuration dialog box:

1. First, you need to fire up the Service Configuration GUI. To do this, click Main Menu ➪ System Settings ➪ Server Settings ➪ Services, or type the following at the command line:

```
$ system-config-services
```

The Service Configuration GUI will ask for root password if you started it as a normal user. When you do this, you get the Service Configuration dialog box, as shown in Figure 9-3.

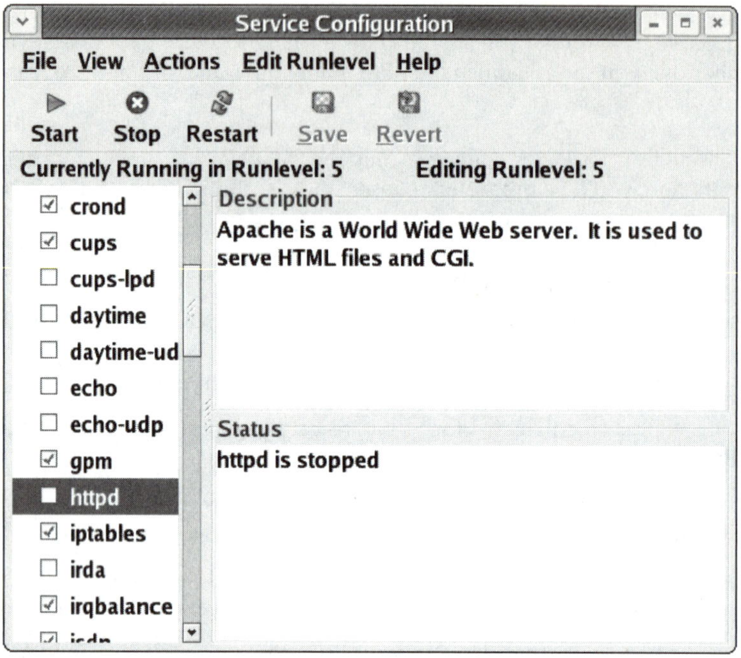

Figure 9-3

This dialog box contains a list of all the services that are supported on your computer. The check boxes indicate which of these services are started automatically when the machine boots up (as part of the `cron`). There are also Start, Stop, and Restart buttons so you can start and stop services manually.

2. Scroll down the list on the left of the dialog box, and select the entry for `httpd`. Check the status of the httpd service in the bottom-right of the dialog box; if it is `stopped` (as in the figure), click the Start button to start it.

   If you want it to start automatically next time you reboot your machine, select the check box, too. Then select File ➪ Save Changes to save the new settings. That's it; you can close the Service Configuration dialog box by selecting File ➪ Quit.

To control the Apache Web server from the command line, you can use the `service` command to fire the `httpd` script. Here's how you use it to start the Web server:

```
# service httpd start
Starting httpd:                                             [  OK  ]
```

If there are difficulties in starting the Web server, you'll find out about it here. For example, if you attempt to do this without root privileges, you'll get a message telling you that permission is denied. And here's another example:

```
# service httpd start
Starting httpd: httpd: Could not determine the server's fully qualified domain
name, using 192.168.0.99 for ServerName
                                                              [  OK  ]
```

Here, the message explains that the server's fully qualified domain name (FQDN) couldn't be determined, and that it's using the IP address (`192.168.0.99`) instead. If you get this message, it's because you have neither set up an FQDN for your Linux server, nor configured the `ServerName` configuration directive in the `httpd.conf` configuration file.

An FQDN is a unique name, consisting of a hostname and domain name that can be resolved to an IP address. For example, `www.linux4biz.net` *is a fully qualified domain name.*

Returning to the `httpd` script itself, there are similar switches for stopping or restarting the service:

```
# service httpd restart
Stopping httpd:                                                    [  OK  ]
Starting httpd:                                                    [  OK  ]
# service httpd stop
Stopping httpd:                                                    [  OK  ]
```

You can use a few other options with the `httpd` script. If you run the script without an option, the resulting usage message reveals all the available options:

```
# service httpd
Usage: httpd {start|stop|restart|condrestart|reload|status|fullstatus|graceful|
              help|configtest}
```

The `configtest` option is a particularly useful one. The configuration file is quite complex, so it's useful to check it for errors after you make changes to it. To do this, you use the `configtest` option:

```
# service httpd configtest
Syntax OK
```

Testing the Apache Web Server

Once you've started the Apache Web server, you should test it to see if it's working properly. To do that, use a Web browser to request a Web page from your server. There's a page provided by default for this purpose, and you can request it via the URL `http://localhost`. So, launch a Web browser (Main Menu ➪ Internet ➪ Mozilla Web Browser), and type this URL into the address box, as shown in Figure 9-4.

Configuring Your Web Server

It's a good idea to configure your Web server. Red Hat does provide a GUI tool, `apacheconf`, for configuring Apache, but it does not format the configuration file very well. Webmin (`www.webmin.com`—see Chapter 15) is an alternative Web-based software that you can use to manage most of the Linux services, including the Apache Web server. However, the following Try it Out section shows you how to do some basic configuration by editing the `httpd.conf` Apache configuration file directly.

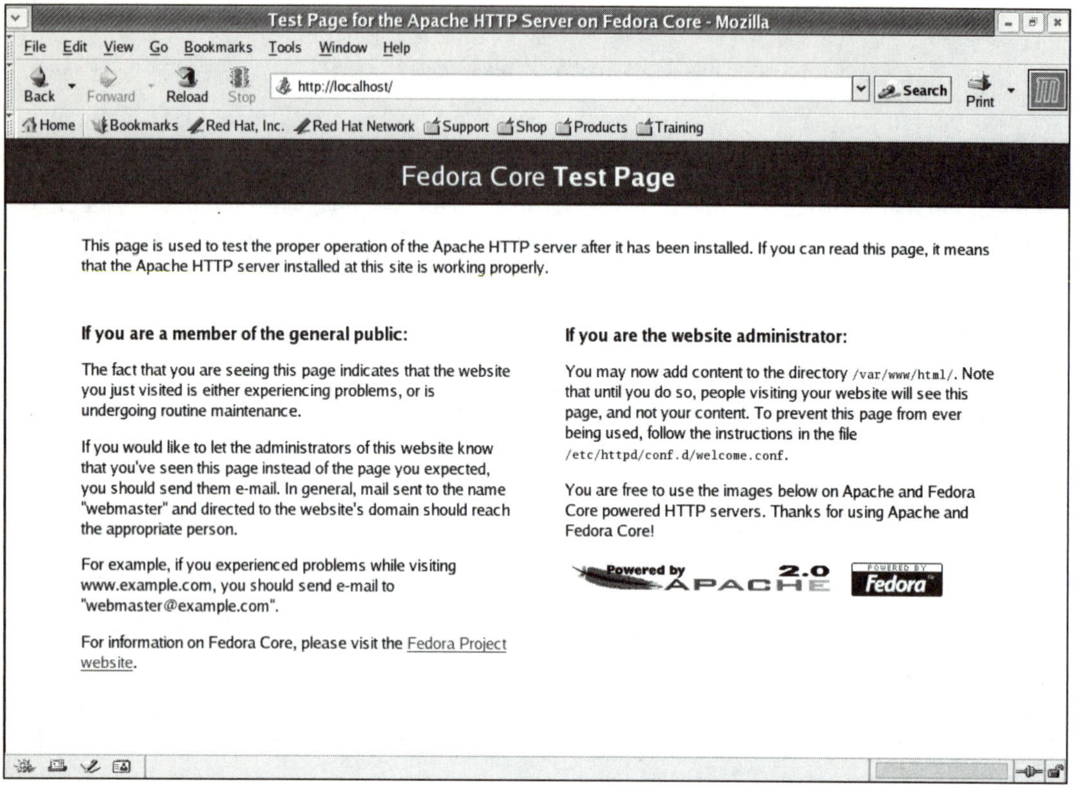

Figure 9-4

Try It Out — Configuring Your Web Server

We're going to configure the Web server by adjusting a couple of the settings to suit our needs.

1. Launch the `gedit` text editor (by selecting Main Menu ➪ Accessories ➪ Text Editor), or your favorite text editor. Use it to open the file `/etc/httpd/conf/httpd.conf`.
2. Select Search ➪ Find and use the resulting dialog box to find the word ServerAdmin in the file. The first occurrence should be the ServerAdmin directive, which looks like this:

```
# ServerAdmin: Your server address, where problems with the server should be
# e-mailed. This address appears on some server-generated pages, such
# as error documents. e.g. admin@your-domain.com
ServerAdmin root@localhost
```

   As you can see, the configuration file describes this directive very well. Change the e-mail address to your own e-mail address, or an address that you may have set up for Web site administration. For example:

```
# ServerAdmin: Your server address, where problems with the server should be
# e-mailed. This address appears on some server-generated pages, such
# as error documents. e.g. admin@your-domain.com
ServerAdmin webmaster@linux4biz.net
```

3. Now use the same technique to find the ServerName directive (you'll probably find that it's right after the ServerAdmin directive). Change this directive first by removing the leading hash (`#`) character. Then, if you have a registered DNS name, add it here (in place of the DNS name `test.linux4biz.net`, which is used here to demonstrate):

```
# ServerName gives the name and port that the server uses to identify itself.
# ...
ServerName test.linux4biz.net
```

   The server name you specify should be an FQDN (because it will need to be resolved to an IP address by DNS). If you haven't set up a DNS, you can enter the IP address allocated to the Linux server instead, like this:

```
ServerName 192.168.0.99
```

4. Save the `httpd.conf` file, and close it.
5. Restart the httpd daemon to reflect the changes. To do this, use Red Hat Services Configuration GUI, or the `httpd` command line script, as described earlier in this chapter:

```
# service httpd restart
Stopping httpd:                                            [  OK  ]
Starting httpd:                                            [  OK  ]
```

   Now browse to `http://localhost` again, to check that the Web server is still serving Web pages. You should see the Apache Test Page that you saw earlier in this section.

There are many configuration settings that you can control via the `httpd.conf` configuration file. For more information, refer to the Apache Web server documentation at `http://httpd.apache.org/docs-2.0/`.

Setting Up Your First Web Site

In the remainder of this section, we set up a simple Web site, which will be accessible on the network. This involves creating a simple HTML Web page, and saving it to a location on the hard disk that is used by the Web server to store published Web pages. Then, when a user requests the page, the Web server will be able to respond by retrieving it from this location and sending it to the requestor.

Try It Out Publishing Your First Web Page

1. Launch an editor (you can use a dedicated Web page editor such as Mozilla Composer if you have it installed; alternatively, `gedit` will do). Create a new file; call it `index.html` and save it in the directory `/var/www/html`.

2. Type some HTML into the file. For example:

```
<html>
<head>
  <title>Beginning Fedora 2  - Apache Test Page</title>
</head>
<body>
  <center>
    <h1>Beginning Fedora 2 - Apache Test Page</h1>
    This is the first page of your web site!
  </center>
</body>
</html>
```

3. Now open a browser and browse to the page using your server's FQDN address or IP address. (For example, the URL `http://test.linux4biz.net/index.html` is used to match the DNS name, but you might use something like `http://192.168.0.99/index.html`.) Your browser sends this request to the Web server listening for connections on port 80 by default. The Web server will serve the default Web site pages. Figure 9-5 shows the output you should see.

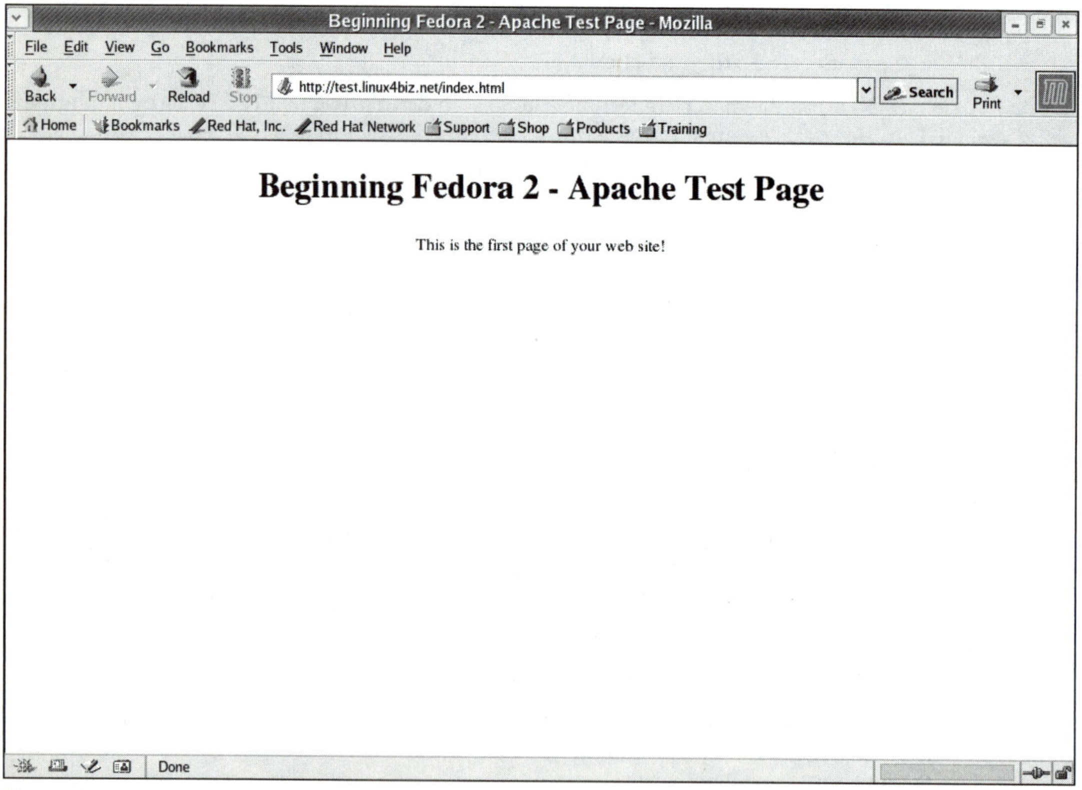

Figure 9-5

How It Works

In this example, we set up a simple Web page under Apache Web server's default root directory, `/var/www/html`, and tested it on an internal network. You can add more pages and directories under the `/var/www/html` directory, as explained in the previous example.

If you want to make your Web site available on the Internet, you need to connect your Web server to the Internet and assign it a public IP address, so that external users send page requests to it. You can also register a DNS so your Web site has a memorable name (so users don't need to refer to your Web site by its IP address).

By default, your Apache Web server hosts just one Web site (whose root is at `/var/www/html`). However, you can configure your Apache Web server to host as many Web sites as you like, and specify the root directory of each site to be whatever folder you wish.

If you want more information about acquiring and using Apache, try the URL `http://httpd.apache.org/`.

Installing SSL-Aware Apache

In the previous section, we installed an Apache Web server and also published a Web page. Apache also provides the functionality to host secure sites with the help of the mod_ssl module that requires OpenSSL software.

OpenSSL is an open source toolkit for secure communication between machines. Openssl supports SSL and Transport Layer Security (TLS) protocols. Fedora Linux comes with a preinstalled openssl toolkit. To check if the openssl is installed, use the RPM feature to check the installed packages, as shown in the following example:

```
# rpm -qi openssl
Name        : openssl                      Relocations: (not relocatable)
Version     : 0.9.7a                            Vendor: Red Hat, Inc.
Release     : 35                            Build Date: Thu 25 Mar 2004 15:38:19
GMT
Install Date: Fri 14 May 2004 02:11:09 BST      Build Host: tweety.devel.redhat.com
Group       : System Environment/Libraries   Source RPM: openssl-0.9.7a-35.src.rpm
Size        : 2597003                          License: BSDish
Signature   : DSA/SHA1, Thu 25 Mar 2004 20:11:22 GMT, Key ID da84cbd430c9ecf8
Packager    : Red Hat, Inc. <http://bugzilla.redhat.com/bugzilla>
URL         : http://www.openssl.org/
Summary     : The OpenSSL toolkit.
Description :
The OpenSSL toolkit provides support for secure communications between
machines. OpenSSL includes a certificate management tool and shared
libraries which provide various cryptographic algorithms and protocols.
```

To enable SSL in Apache Web server, we also require an Apache mod_ssl module. Once installed, Apache can be configured to serve secure pages on the HTTPS protocol. HTTPS is HTTP over SSL. HTTP and HTTPS have reserved ports of 80 and 443, respectively.

Now, let's install mod_ssl packages.

Installing the mod_ssl Package

This package (mod_ssl) provides an Apache interface to openssl to provide and enable the Apache Web server to support SSL. We will install this package now.

1. Start the RPM's graphical interface by selecting Main Menu ➪ System Settings ➪ Add/Remove Applications, or by executing `system-config-packages` on the command line as root user, like so:

```
# system-config-packages
```

2. Browse through all the categories until you get to the Servers category.
3. Click the Web Server group to open the details screen.
4. Select the mod_ssl package from the Extra Packages section and click Close and Update to install this package on the system (see Figure 9-6).

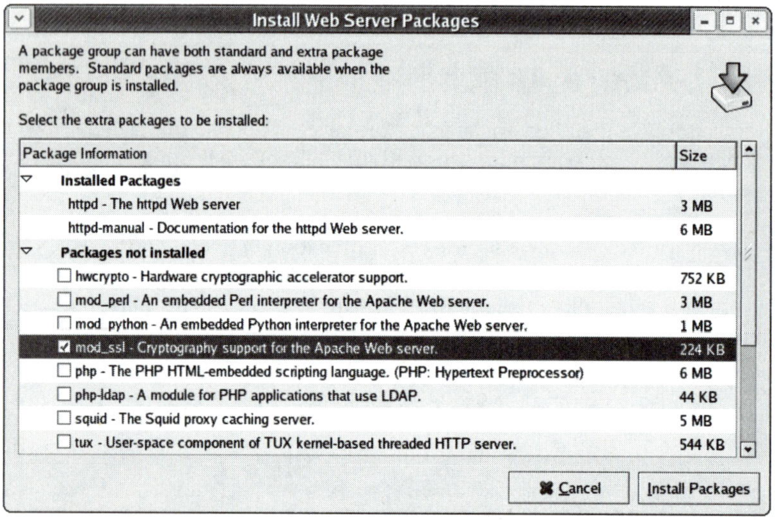

Figure 9-6

Follow all the instructions to install the mod_ssl package. After the mod_ssl module is installed, you have to configure Apache to use the SSL module.

Configuring Apache to Use SSL

You are halfway through making Apache SSL-aware by installing the mod_ssl package. We will now configure Apache to use SSL features.

Apache uses a configuration file `ssl.conf` for SSL, which is located under the directory `/etc/httpd/conf.d`. Apache's main configuration file `httpd.conf` includes the `ssl.conf` file by using an `include` directive in `httpd.conf`, as follows:

```
#
# Load config files from the config directory "/etc/httpd/conf.d".
#
Include conf.d/*.conf
```

The line in the `/etc/httpd/conf/httpd.conf` file includes all the configuration files that have a suffix of `.conf`.

Now, let's look at the important configuration of the `ssl.conf` file. Apache listens on port 80 for a plain HTTP request (http). Apache needs a different port to listen on the HTTPS protocol. The default port to run as a secure server is 443, and it can be configured by using the `Listen 443` configuration line in the `/etc/httpd/conf/httpd.conf` file.

Apache has to load a DSO module to enable the ssl feature. It can be done using the following line in the ssl configuration file.

```
LoadModule ssl_module modules/mod_ssl.so

Listen 443
```

The following lines will add the MIME types for downloading certificates and Certificate Revocation Lists (CRLs):

```
AddType application/x-x509-ca-cert .crt
AddType application/x-pkcs7-crl    .crl
```

You can set error and transaction logs with the following lines:

```
ErrorLog logs/ssl_error_log
TransferLog logs/ssl_access_log
```

The `SSLEngine` switch can be used to enabled or disable the SSL. The following line enables the SSL.

```
SSLEngine on
```

One of the requirements of ssl functionality is the ssl certificate and private key. To enable ssl functionality, you need to specify the ssl certificate file and ssl certificate key stored on the system, like so:

```
SSLCertificateFile /etc/httpd/conf/ssl.crt/server.crt
SSLCertificateKeyFile /etc/httpd/conf/ssl.key/server.key
```

The first line points the `SSLCertificateFile` to a `/etc/httpd/conf/ssl.crt/server.crt` certificate file. The second line points the `SSLCertificateKeyFile` to a private key for this certificate. `SSLCertificateFile` and `SSLcertificateKeyFile` can point to any ssl certificate and private key pair stored as a file on the system.

In the next section, we create a private key and certificate and configure it in Apache.

Generating Self-Signed Certificates

The first step in generating a certificate is creating a server's private key.

```
# openssl genrsa -des3 -out /etc/httpd/conf/ssl.key/testcert.key 1024
Generating RSA private key, 1024 bit long modulus
..................++++++
.++++++
e is 65537 (0x10001)
Enter pass phrase for /etc/httpd/conf/ssl.key/testcert.key:
Verifying - Enter pass phrase for /etc/httpd/conf/ssl.key/testcert.key:
```

Notice that the preceding command to generate a private key asks for the passphrase on the command line. A passphrase should not be easy to crack (avoid using your name or age, and so on), and should also be easy to remember. You will be required to provide the passphrase every time this private key is accessed. If you forget the passphrase, the private key will not be usable.

Here is the private key in Privacy Enhanced Mail (PEM) format, an encoding format that stores keys in a text format:

```
-----BEGIN RSA PRIVATE KEY-----
Proc-Type: 4,ENCRYPTED
DEK-Info: DES-EDE3-CBC,8174D67CB5871EDF

KGnYbuQH+BS9PclINlUo6ox8Yy6TEatMtfle6Zo8f9AB+ooRGOeOwuW84FhYyE2E
w7uXM/yxkyQ4jXHUD597SsqNdXcKX0YmQ5T+AqZ+mU1QmBRLJcT1JhkHrfFkdJ1W
bpNrJJDFtVfbKroyq7/hZqSkS6+VeVmfE67EfLJ2sGTrCq+FZDYT2TTQO0Ch1spW
kA0CX+zc+hEJudMxEDabQFmch+ueMt6dg7aCnE2IpF8Loqc1acvwtE8r7gXYumJe
R2arw/PZ/zY5Z8WbNKSgkclf6EhpzKFNRfSClECfc+9Rw/4F/rDkzYVjFAyAWxcX
uYiSVkAR3Pnlxj3BQtefMZbkVtsoPkIYpLQGlbn6wg/fzvWuPKvE635nyKsW68D7
ysTQn2V0pOFLy0wupuuSng2Hh5ZopD26XaCtk1425lRpORnyxTZfJF/DF8SmUqAJ
YuCRCsqVKeAZujCW2IqtNZsT2RAo1KWS0yh+ddDha82fxrtxLtgiLp0dcBwp5G4n
/9R6qAuMw/7gGym/NgerDjhVlwaJUPj+Dq2Ih4oqaQUhpfTm1LW3TRpx9pPe3fqy
eTe/jqV6I8IIpLnwbofSx8NLGmUs8ujz8FcCRRaPNbIB01QT2qhcnm2mvyx4nPhs
UTAF56/JRTJHxozOGwYuqFJpqeMxiJg4q5Ciw49n3Y0Do6O19m05hsvMzs6A7vr+
Whh5+ogYjEFQjsbuswCh9H6em8hqDXtXoGwv1fnzMUjzRZj8cUU4ffbtBuOs+SKG
PfLeqMFN2d0eKgVKezrHdpFf0n9pps0U14lxvyBkRrOUbaGe/WI/Wg==
-----END RSA PRIVATE KEY-----
```

The next step is to create a server's Certificate Signing Request (CSR). Before starting the certificate request creation process, you must have the following details ready:

- Country Name (2 letter code)
- State
- Locality Name (city)
- Organization Name
- Common Name (fully qualified domain name)

The common name is the domain name for which the certificate is required, such as `www.linux4biz.net`. The Organization Unit Name and E-mail Address are optional.

Execute the following command on a command line to create a CSR:

```
# openssl req -new -key /etc/httpd/conf/ssl.key/testcert.key -out
/etc/httpd/conf/ssl.csr/testcert.csr
Enter pass phrase for /etc/httpd/conf/ssl.key/testcert.key:
You are about to be asked to enter information that will be incorporated
into your certificate request.
What you are about to enter is what is called a Distinguished Name or a DN.
There are quite a few fields but you can leave some blank
For some fields there will be a default value,
If you enter '.', the field will be left blank.
-----
Country Name (2 letter code) [GB]:GB
State or Province Name (full name) [Berkshire]:London
Locality Name (eg, city) [Newbury]:London
Organization Name (eg, company) [My Company Ltd]:Linux4biz
Organizational Unit Name (eg, section) []:IT
Common Name (eg, your name or your server's hostname) []:test.linux4biz.net
Email Address []:hostmaster@linux4biz.net

Please enter the following 'extra' attributes
to be sent with your certificate request
A challenge password []:
An optional company name []:
```

You will be prompted for the private key's passphrase. The preceding command generates a CSR for the certificate, which can either be sent to the Certificate Authority, such as Verisign, or can be self-signed.

Following is the certificate request (CSR):


```
-----BEGIN CERTIFICATE REQUEST-----
MIIB1zCCAUACAQAwgZYxCzAJBgNVBAYTAkdCMQ8wDQYDVQQIEwZMb25kb24xDzAN
BgNVBAcTBkxvbmRvbjESMBAGA1UEChMJTGludXg0Yml6MQswCQYDVQQLEwJJVDEb
MBkGA1UEAxMSdGVzdC5saW51eDRiaXoubmV0MScwJQYJKoZIhvcNAQkBFhhob3N0
bWFzdGVyQGxpbnV4NGJpei5uZXQwgZ8wDQYJKoZIhvcNAQEBBQADgY0AMIGJAoGB
AK5ttW2rIFJicHu+xYkkX5CSXCfaVfnfBvSCtWcPEZ/zBBUAoHA9aHtmRZYWcmAf
Qest6TmWiH8StvnzzeJLxd8JseYds8u3pV4NVZZPYnkKHqC1Bns44hNTvJM39aUg
z2mFGlphECADkecEfqG94Xj+Vh2h3EtG8FJqjYSBzm+vAgMBAAGgADANBgkqhkiG
9w0BAQQFAAOBgQCbsi2Szxmyohz78S4KfhIVzwHRyxLPPXUu3AmJ9NWiP73Vg/nl
ocLys5/s/EbW0htUfT0szxMonzZbBLBB+LDXjyGWiDKsc7Arq+D2TBivEXO/67eS
l0dMthRnOaE3V8gOPMUGhBboR0muAzYgF0skwKs34pkZzFXvY1b61Y6hOg==
-----END CERTIFICATE REQUEST-----
```


We will self-sign the CSR by executing the following command on the command line:

```
# openssl x509 -in /etc/httpd/conf/ssl.csr/testcert.csr  -out
/etc/httpd/conf/ssl.crt/testcert.crt -req -signkey
/etc/httpd/conf/ssl.key/testcert.key -days 365
Signature ok
subject=/C=GB/ST=London/L=London/O=Linux4biz/OU=IT/CN=test.linux4biz.net/emailAddre
ss=hostmaster@linux4biz.net
Getting Private key
Enter pass phrase for /etc/httpd/conf/ssl.key/testcert.key:
```

Now, we will have a self-signed certificate in `/etc/httpd/conf/ssl.crt/testcert.crt` that looks like the following:


```
-----BEGIN CERTIFICATE-----
MIICnTCCAgYCAQAwDQYJKoZIhvcNAQEEBQAwgZYxCzAJBgNVBAYTAkdCMQ8wDQYD
VQQIEwZMb25kb24xDzANBgNVBAcTBkxvbmRvbjESMBAGA1UEChMJTGludXg0Yml6
MQswCQYDVQQLEwJJVDEbMBkGA1UEAxMSdGVzdC5saW51eDRiaXoubmV0MScwJQYJ
KoZIhvcNAQkBFhhob3N0bWFzdGVyQGxpbnV4NGJpei5uZXQwHhcNMDQwMjAxMDIw
NDExWhcNMDUwMTMxMDIwNDExWjCBljELMAkGA1UEBhMCR0IxDzANBgNVBAgTBkxv
bmRvbjEPMA0GA1UEBxMGTG9uZG9uMRIwEAYDVQQKEwlMaW51eDRiaXoxCzAJBgNV
BAsTAklUMRswGQYDVQQDExJ0ZXN0LmxpbnV4NGJpei5uZXQxJzAlBgkqhkiG9w0B
CQEWGGhvc3RtYXN0ZXJAbGludXg0Yml6Lm5ldDCBnzANBgkqhkiG9w0BAQEFAAOB
jQAwgYkCgYEArm21basgUmJwe77FiSRfkJJcJ9pV+d8G9IK1Zw8Rn/MEFQCgcD1o
e2ZFlhZyYB9B6y3pOZaIfxK2+fPN4kvF3wmx5h2zy7elXg1Vlk9ieQoeoLUGezji
E1O8kzf1pSDPaYUaWmEQIAOR5wR+ob3heP5WHaHcS0bwUmqNhIHOb68CAwEAATAN
BgkqhkiG9w0BAQQFAAOBgQCMkdagnNiHz+xrGpV9dWbgcB4fqllxkQwLkD0kbsYu
OixgHRNOWMl4GCxkrg3Jx/nVB6X0p6ayRIXbp2erxREK9hhIQBXo61sjmlzvc6Em
8/hGs9Xe+JD/TgNP2zsgXJMrdkhwvkAOJCsnMGNh6COJ3SkEc+L5jhYxmYfEVJkj
kg==
-----END CERTIFICATE-----
```


Installing Commercial Certificates

This section discusses how to get a commercial certificate and use it with Apache.

To get a commercial certificate from third-party Certificate Authorities, you follow the same procedure as used in generating a self-signed certificate.

Following are the tasks involved in getting a commercial certificate:

1. Create a server private key.
2. Generate a CSR using the private key, which can be sent to Certificate Authority to apply for as ssl certificate.
3. Receive and install a certificate from the Certificate Authority.

   Creating a private key and generating a CSR are the same as discussed in the last section. After the CSR is generated, it can be sent to the third-party Certificate Authority (CA). The CSR can be sent using a Web form on most of the CA's Web sites, such as Verisign and Thawte. The Certificate Authority will validate and verify all the certificate details and assign you a real certificate. Save this certificate in a file on the Apache Web server. In our case, save it in the `/etc/httpd/conf/ssl.crt/testcert.crt` file.
4. The last step is to install this certificate on Apache.

Make the following changes in the `ssl.conf` file to enable the newly received commercial ssl certificate. You have to follow the same procedure to use a self-signed certificate.

Change these lines in the `ssl.conf` file:

```
SSLCertificateFile /etc/httpd/conf/ssl.crt/server.crt
SSLCertificateKeyFile /etc/httpd/conf/ssl.key/server.key
```

to the following lines to use the new private key and certificate:

```
SSLCertificateFile /etc/httpd/conf/ssl.crt/testcert.crt
SSLCertificateKeyFile /etc/httpd/conf/ssl.key/testcert.key
```

Starting the Apache Web Server with ssl

After the ssl certificate is installed and configured on the system, you need to start or restart the Apache Web server with ssl.

We recommend that you check the Apache configuration file for errors using the `configtest` switch with the `apachectl` command, as follows:

```
# /usr/sbin/apachectl configtest
Syntax OK
```

To start the Apache server with ssl, issue the following command. Note that Apache will ask for the passphrase associated with the server's private key:

```
# /usr/sbin/apachectl startssl
Apache/2.0.49 mod_ssl/2.0.49 (Pass Phrase Dialog)
Some of your private key files are encrypted for security reasons.
In order to read them you have to provide us with the pass phrases.

Server www01.linux4biz.net:443 (RSA)
Enter pass phrase:

Ok: Pass Phrase Dialog successful.
```

Now, your ssl-enabled Apache Web server is up and running. In the next section, you publish your first secure Web page.

Launch an editor (you can use a dedicated Web page editor such as Mozilla Composer if you have it installed; alternatively, `gedit` will do). Create a new file—call it `indexsecure.html` and save it in the directory `/var/www/html`.

1. Type some HTML into the file. For example:

```
<html>
<head>
  <title>Beginning Fedora Linux - Secure Apache Test Page</title>
</head>
<body>
  <center>
    <h1>Beginning Fedora Linux - Secure Apache Test Page</h1>
    This is the first secure page of your web site!
  </center>
</body>
</html>
```

2. Now open a browser and browse to the page using your server's FQDN address or IP address. (For example, the URL `https://test.linux4biz.net/indexsecure.html` is used here to match the DNS name, but you might use something like `https://192.168.0.99/indexsecure.html`.) Your browser will send this request to the Web server listening for connections on port 443 by default. The Web server will serve the default Web site pages. Figure 9-7 shows the output you should see:

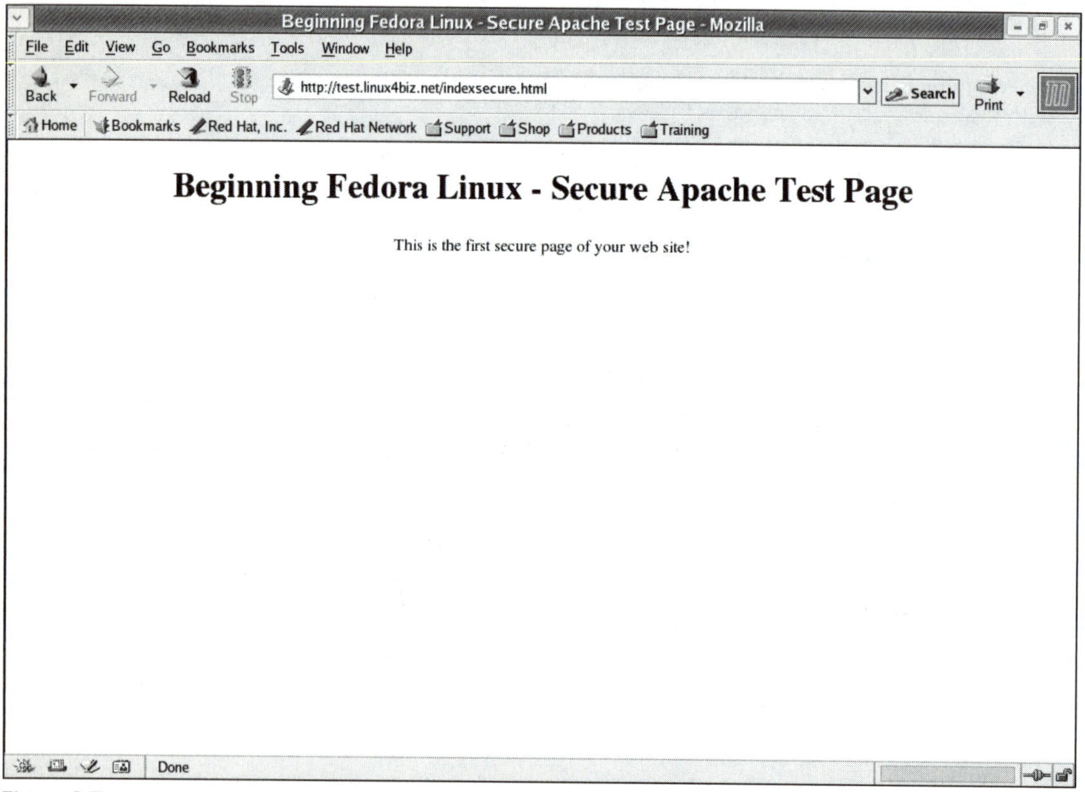

Figure 9-7

Notice the padlock in the bottom-right corner of the browser window. It is locked to show that the session between client browser and Web server is secure.

> **For more information about Apache, openssl, and mod_ssl, refer to the following Web sites:** `www.modssl.org`, `www.openssl.org`, **and** `www.apache.org`.

Setting Up an FTP Server

If you want to enable other users to download files from a location on your server's hard disk, and/or to upload files to that location, one solution is to install an *FTP server*. You can think of an FTP server essentially as an area of disk space that is used for storing files, plus the software and configuration required to allow other users to upload and download files. When users want to upload or download from your FTP server, they use a program called an *FTP client*.

These communications between FTP server and FTP client take place using the *File Transfer Protocol (FTP)*. FTP is a TCP protocol that is designed specifically for the transfer of files over a network, and it's one of the oldest Internet protocols still in widespread use. The availability of so many different FTP client programs, and the fact that many operating systems come with FTP software preinstalled, are indications of how relevant FTP still is today.

FTP is not considered a secure protocol because communication between the FTP client and server are unencrypted. Consequently, *Secure FTP (SFTP)* is also becoming popular (and, indeed, is part of the `openssh` package that comes with Fedora 2). You can also configure your FTP server in other ways, for example, by forcing users to log in, or by using access control lists (ACLs) to allow different rights to different groups of users.

> *You need to take security precautions if you plan to expose your FTP server on the Internet. There's also information on this subject, and on the FTP protocol in general, at RFCs 959 and 2577 (*`ftp://ftp.rfc-editor.org/in-notes/rfc959.txt` *and* `ftp://ftp.rfc-editor.org/in-notes/rfc2577.txt`*).*

In fact, many FTP servers still allow anonymous FTP access, which means that the FTP server allows any user to access its disk space and download its files. Anonymous FTP access is used mostly to enable users to access freely available documents and files via the Internet without access control.

In spite of the security issues, FTP remains popular—it's fast and easy to use, and it is the Internet standard protocol for file transfer.

FTP Servers in the Fedora Linux Distribution

A number of FTP servers are available for Fedora Linux 2:

- `vsftpd` is a simplified FTP server implementation. It is designed to be a very secure FTP server, and can also be configured to allow anonymous access. We explore `vsftpd` in this section.
- *TUX* is a kernel-based, threaded, extremely high-performance HTTP server that also has FTP capabilities. TUX is perhaps the best in terms of performance, but offers less functionality than other FTP server software. TUX is installed by default with Fedora 2.
- `wu-ftpd` is a highly configurable and full-featured FTP daemon that was popular in earlier versions of Red Hat Linux, but has since given way to the more security-conscious `vsftpd`.
- `gssftpd` is a kerberized FTP daemon, which means that it is suitable for use with the Kerberos authentication system.

All of these FTP servers ship as part of the Fedora Linux 2 distribution. However, we will consider only the first of these, `vsftpd`, here.

Installing the vsftpd FTP Server

The easiest way to install the `vsftpd` FTP Server package is via the RPM GUI Tool. After you've started the tool (for example, by selecting Main Menu ➪ System Settings ➪ Add/Remove Applications), find the FTP Server package group, which is listed under the Servers category. Check the Details.

You can click Details to see the package details. You will see that the package group contains only one package vsftpd—it's under the Required Packages banner (see Figure 9-8).

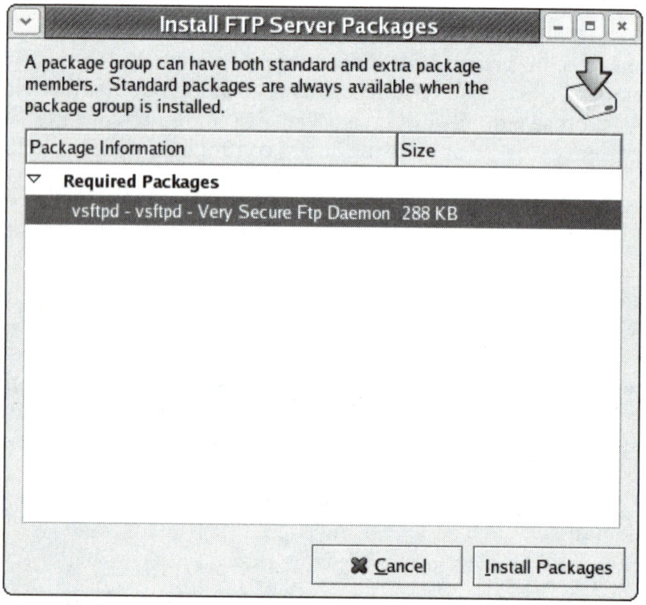

Figure 9-8

Click Install Packages to begin installation of the vsftpd FTP server. You'll be prompted to insert the Fedora 2 installation discs as necessary.

Starting Your FTP Server

To start the FTP service (and enable users to upload and download files), you can use the Service Configuration Tool. To launch the tool, select Main Menu ➪ System Settings ➪ Server Settings ➪ Services, or type the following command at the command line:

```
$ system-config-services
```

You'll be prompted for the root password, unless you're already logged on as root. To start the `vsftpd` FTP Server, select the `vsftpd` entry in the list and then click the Start button (see Figure 9-9).

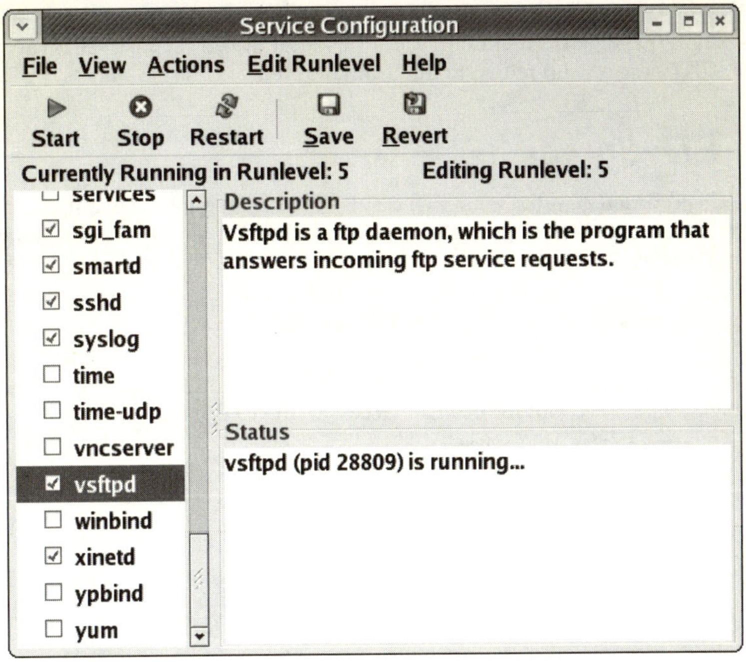

Figure 9-9

Again, if you want the FTP service to start automatically next time you reboot your machine, then select the check box to indicate so. Then select File ➪ Save Changes to save your new settings.

It's also possible to start and stop these FTP services from the command line, using the `service` command to start and stop the `vsftpd` script:

```
# service vsftpd start
Starting vsftpd:                                          [  OK  ]
# service vsftpd stop
Stopping vsftpd:                                          [  OK  ]
```

If you run the script without an option, the resulting usage message reveals all the available options:

```
# service vsftpd
Usage: vsftpd {start|stop|restart|condrestart|status}
```

Testing Your FTP Server

Now you've set up your FTP server and started the service, we'll adopt the role of the client to quickly test that the service is working. From a command line, issue the `ftp` command to start an FTP session, naming your FTP server as the server that you want to connect to:

```
$ ftp 192.168.0.99
Connected to 192.168.0.99 (192.168.0.99).
220 (vsFTPd 1.2.1)
Name (192.168.0.99:kapil):
```

Recall that 192.168.0.99 is the IP address of the Linux server. You should get a Name login prompt such as the one shown here—this is enough to confirm that the vsftpd server is running. Press *Ctrl+C* to terminate this FTP session and return to the command line.

Using Your FTP Server

Having installed and (briefly) tested your FTP server, you can begin to use it; this section demonstrates a few uses. There are a number of configuration issues to consider, and this section takes a look at five of the most important ones:

- Configuring for anonymous FTP server file download
- Configuring for anonymous FTP server file upload
- Creating a system account for per-user access to the FTP server
- Disabling local system user accounts
- Blocking FTP access for user accounts

It also shows you how to configure an FTP greeting banner.

Configuring an Anonymous FTP Server for File Download

Anonymous users cannot read from just *any* directory on your Linux server. By default, the vsftpd package creates a directory tree starting at /var/ftp, and enables anonymous read access to this directory and the directory structure beneath it.

To demonstrate this, let's start by placing a test file on the FTP server so that other users can download it. Then, let's adopt the role of one of these users, and run a client FTP session to access the FTP server, examine the contents of the FTP site, and download a copy of the test file.

Setting Up the FTP Server

All you need to do here is place some test content somewhere under the /var/ftp directory, so that other users can access it. The owner of the /var/ftp is the root account, and, by default, is the only one with permission to write to the directory. (Recall from Chapter 5 that the *owner*, *group*, and *others* can all have different privileges on a directory or file.)

To start, use a command line to switch to the root user:

```
$ su -
Password:
```

Place whatever content you want under the /var/ftp directory. For example, you can easily use a command such as echo to create a simple test file:

```
# cd /var/ftp/pub
# echo "This is the contents of a test file!" > test.txt
```

Here, we've created the file test.txt and placed it in the /pub subdirectory.

Using an FTP Client to Test Anonymous Read Access

Now you can test for anonymous read access by using an FTP client to try to grab a copy of this test file via an FTP connection. You can use any FTP client, and you can test from a Windows or Linux machine—provided the client machine can see the FTP server across a network. (You can even use your Linux server as a client, if you have only one machine.)

For example, in both Windows and Linux, you can use the `ftp` program at the command line. The following example uses the `ftp` program as FTP client to connect to the FTP server, examine the contents of the FTP site, and then download the file `test.txt`.

1. Start by connecting to the FTP server. When you're prompted for a username, specify `anonymous` (as shown) or `ftp` to indicate that you want anonymous access:

```
$ ftp 192.168.0.99
Connected to 192.168.0.99 (192.168.0.99).
220 (vsFTPd 1.2.1)
Name (192.168.0.99:kapil): anonymous
331 Please specify the password.
Password:
230 Login successful. Have fun.
Remote system type is UNIX.
Using binary mode to transfer files.
```

2. Now, you can start to examine the contents of the FTP site that are available to users with anonymous access. For example, the following uses the `ls` command to examine the contents of the FTP root directory (which happens to be the directory `/var/ftp` on the server):

```
ftp>ls
227 Entering Passive Mode (192,168,0,99,69,34)
150 Here comes the directory listing.
drwxr-r-x    2 0        0            4096 Feb 28 13:40 pub
226 Directory send OK.
```

This shows that the root directory contains just one subdirectory, called `pub`. Now, use `cd` to change to this directory, and list its contents:

```
ftp> cd pub
250 Directory successfully changed.
ftp> ls -al
227 Entering Passive Mode (192,168,0,99,56,125)
150 Here comes the directory listing.
drwxr-xr--x    2  0        0              4096 Feb 28 13:40 .
drwxr-xr-x     3  0        0              4096 Feb 27 19:15 ..
-rw-r--r--     1  0        0                22 Feb 28 13:30 test.txt
226 Directory send OK.
```

3. Now, we'll attempt to download the `test.txt` file we've just located. To do this, use the `get` command:

```
ftp> get test.txt
local: test.txt remote: test.txt
227 Entering Passive Mode (192,168,0,99,98,207)
150 Opening BINARY mode data connection for test.txt (22 bytes).
226 File send OK.
```

When the file is successfully downloaded, you should find it in your present working directory.

4. Finally, end the session:

```
ftp> bye
221 Goodbye.
$
```

For more information about anonymous FTP, refer to RFC 1635, which can be found at `ftp://ftp.rfc-editor.org/in-notes/rfc1635.txt`.

Configuring an Anonymous FTP Server for File Upload

In much the same way, anonymous FTP users can write only to the directories that you *allow* them to write to. By default, `vsftpd` does not allow users to upload to the FTP server at all; you must first configure the server to allow anonymous users write access to some directory.

So, we'll set up the FTP server for anonymous write access first; then we'll test it again using an FTP client.

Setting Up the FTP Server for Anonymous Write Access

There are four steps here. We'll need to create the folder, set the appropriate permissions, and then enable uploading in the FTP server configuration:

1. Create a writeable directory. Again, you'll need the root account for this. Create a directory called `/upload` (in the `/var/ftp/pub` directory):

```
# cd /var/ftp/pub
# mkdir upload
```

2. Set the permission of the `upload` directory so that it allows write-only access to anonymous FTP users (so that they can write to the directory but not to download from it—this restricts file sharing among FTP users). To do this, first use the `chgrp` command to change the group associated with the upload directory:

```
# chgrp ftp upload
```

Now, the *owner* of the folder is still root, but the directory's group is `ftp`—the set of FTP users. Now use the `chmod` command to assign read/write/execute access to the owner, write access only to the group, and deny access to other users:

```
# chmod -R u=rwx,g=wx,o-rxw upload
```

3. Finally, you must configure the `vsftpd` server to allow anonymous upload. To do this, simply edit the configuration file, `/etc/vsftpd/vsftpd.conf`. Open this file using `gedit` (or your favorite text editor), and locate the following lines:

```
# Uncomment this to allow the anonymous FTP user to upload files. This only
# has an effect if the above global write enable is activated. Also, you will
# obviously need to create a directory writable by the FTP user.
#anon_upload_enable=YES
```

   Just remove the leading hash (`#`) character in the last line, and save the file:

```
anon_upload_enable=YES
```

4. Restart the vsftpd service by using the Restart button in the Server Configuration dialog box, or typing the following at the command line:

```
# service vsftpd restart
```

That's it. Now you're ready to test this configuration.

Using an FTP Client to Test Anonymous Write Access

Let's test our configuration with another simple session on our FTP client:

1. Connect to the client and log in (with the username `anonymous` or `ftp`) as you did before:

```
$ ftp 192.168.0.99
Connected to 192.168.0.99 (192.168.0.99).
220 (vsFTPd 1.2.1)
Name (192.168.0.99:kapil): anonymous
331 Please specify the password.
Password:
230 Login successful. Have fun.
Remote system type is UNIX.
Using binary mode to transfer files.
```

2. Change to the `pub/upload` directory. Try to list its contents—you'll find that you can't because that's the way you configured the permissions on the `upload` directory:

```
ftp> cd /pub/upload
250 Directory successfully changed.
ftp> ls
227 Entering Passive Mode (192,168,0,99,95,148)
150 Here comes the directory listing.
226 Transfer done (but failed to open directory).
```

3. However, you can upload a file. To prove it, use the `put` command to upload a simple file, like this:

```
ftp> put uploadtest.txt
local: uploadtest.txt remote: uploadtest.txt
227 Entering Passive Mode (192,168,0,99,133,229)
150 Ok to send data.
226 File receive OK.
40 bytes send in 0.000101 secs (2.1e+02 Kbytes/sec)
```

4. Now you can close the FTP session:

```
ftp> bye
221 Goodbye.
#
```

Now you can go back to your FTP server and check the contents of the `/var/ftp/pub/upload` directory. You should find the `uploadtest.txt` file that was just uploaded from the client.

FTP Authentication via System Accounts

You've seen some examples using anonymous access to the `vsftpd` FTP server (via the `anonymous` or `ftp` username), but what happens if a user has a system account and tries to gain access? By default, `vsftpd` allows this, and gives the user access to their home directory this way. For example, suppose your system has an account for the user called kapil. This user can use an FTP client to log in and gain access to their home directory, `/home/kapil`, via `vsftpd`, like this:

```
# ftp 192.168.0.99
Connected to 192.168.0.99 (192.168.0.99).
220 (vsFTPd 1.2.1)
Name (192.168.0.99:none): kapil
331 Please specify the password.
Password:
230 Login successful. Have fun.
Remote system type is UNIX.
Using binary mode to transfer files.
ftp> ls
     ...lists contents of /home/kapil directory...
```

This can be useful if your situation demands it. For example, you could set a machine up as a dedicated FTP server and create an account for each user that needs to perform FTP:

```
# useradd -m -d /home/linux4biz
# passwd linux4biz
Changing password for user linux4biz.
New password:
Retype new password:
passwd: all authentication tokens updated successfully.
```

You assign each user his or her own individual FTP space.

Disabling Local System User Accounts for FTP

By default, these users would have the same permissions to read, write, and execute the contents of their home directory via FTP that they would have if they were accessing the directory by sitting at the computer. More importantly, authentication via FTP is not encrypted, so allowing FTP access via user accounts is actually *not* a good way to allow access to your system if you've got anything sensitive to protect.

Therefore, in most situations it's recommended that you *disable* FTP access via user accounts. This is easy to do—just change the appropriate setting in the configuration file, `/etc/vsftpd/vsftpd.conf`. When you open the file, locate the following lines:

```
# Uncomment this to allow local users to log in.
local_enable=YES
```

Change the directive to read as follows:

```
local_enable=NO
```

Then restart the vsftpd service using the Server Configuration dialog box, or by typing the following at the command line:

```
# service vsftpd restart
```

Now, if you try using an FTP client to gain FTP access via a system user account, you'll be refused:

```
$ ftp 192.168.0.99
Connected to 192.168.0.99 (192.168.0.99).
220 (vsFTPd 1.2.1)
Name (192.168.0.99:none): linux4biz
530 This FTP server is anonymous only.
Login failed.
```

Blocking FTP Access for User Accounts

Alternatively, you can deny FTP access to individual users (rather than to all users). You control this using the `/etc/vsftpd.ftpusers` file, which contains the list of users that are *not* allowed FTP access to the server.

To try this, first change the `local_enable` directive back from `NO` to `YES`, in `/etc/vsftpd/vsftpd.conf`, to enable FTP access via system accounts:

```
# Uncomment this to allow local users to log in.
local_enable=YES
```

Then, open the `/etc/vsftpd.ftpusers` file (using root privileges), add an account name at the bottom, and save the file. There's no need to restart the vsftpd service; changes to the `/etc/vsftpd.ftpusers` file take effect immediately.

Then use the account to try to gain FTP access via an FTP client:

```
# ftp 192.168.0.99
Connected to 192.168.0.99 (192.168.0.99).
220 (vsFTPd 1.2.1)
Name (192.168.0.99:none): linux4biz
331 Please specify the password.
Password:
530 Login incorrect.
Login failed.
```

Configuring an FTP Greeting Banner

Once you've installed the `vsftpd` FTP server, there are all sorts of ways you can configure it to behave as you want. Here's a simple example. You can change the default greeting message that the FTP server issues to clients on connection simply by changing the value of the `ftpd_banner` directive in `/etc/vsftpd/vsftpd.conf`. For example, try changing it to this:

```
# You may fully customize the login banner string:
ftpd_banner=Welcome to the Wrox Press FTP service.
```

Then restart the vsftpd service so that the change takes effect. Use your FTP client to log in to the FTP server, and you'll be greeted with this new message:

```
$ ftp 192.168.0.99
Connected to 192.168.0.99 (192.168.0.99).
220 Welcome to the Wrox Press FTP service.
...
```

For more information on the `vsftpd` FTP server, and all the configuration possibilities, refer to the man pages by typing `man vsftpd` and `man vsftpd.conf`. You can also find more information on the vsftpd FTP server at `http://vsftpd.beasts.org/`.

Setting Up a Print Server

If you want to share a single printer (or group of printers) among a number of users, what you need is a *print server*. The print server manages the print requests and puts them into a queue for processing. It can manage the following:

- Sharing of printers between many users
- Authentication, so that only permitted users can print to a given printer
- Print queues
- Configuration of many printers in a single location

This section examines how to configure your Linux machine as a print server for managing print jobs.

Fedora 2 provides the *Common UNIX Printing System (CUPS)* print server software package. CUPS is a printing service for UNIX-based platforms, capable of managing printer jobs and queues and supporting network printer browsing.

The Fedora 2 installation process should install the cups package by default. To check, launch the RPM (for example, using Main Menu ➪ System Settings ➪ Add/Remove Applications), locate the Printing Support package group (which is under the System category), click its Details button, and ensure that the CUPS package is under the Installed Packages heading (see Figure 9-10).

Click the Cancel button to exit this dialog box, and exit the Add and Remove software screen. If the CUPS package is not installed on your system, install it using the guidelines in Chapter 8.

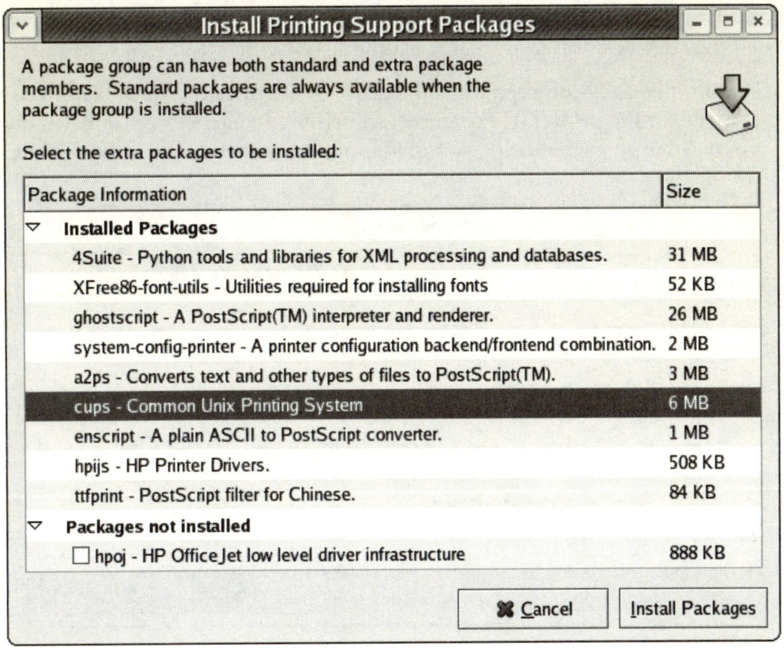

Figure 9-10

Installing a Printer

When you first install CUPS, you get a default set of sample configuration files at `/etc/cups`. However, it's easier to manage your printers using the Printer Configuration Tool that is provided by Red Hat. Each printer has its own *print queue*, so you configure the print server by using the Printer Configuration Tool to add a print queue for each printer.

1. To start the Printer Configuration Tool, select Main Menu ➪ System Settings ➪ Printing, or type the following command at the command line:

```
$ system-config-printer
```

   You are asked for the root password, unless you were already logged in with administrative privileges. The Printer Configuration window appears, as shown in Figure 9-11.

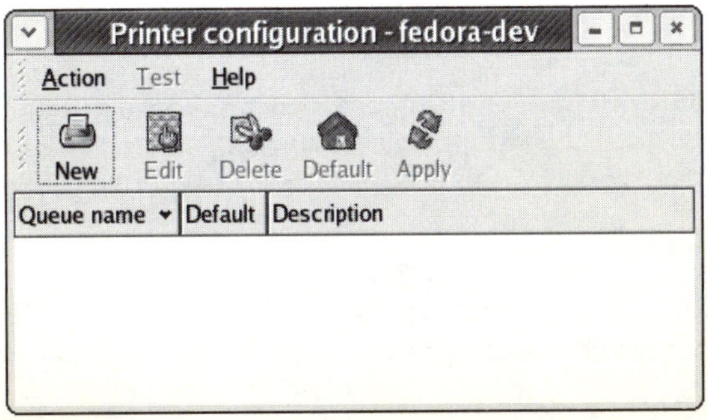

Figure 9-11

2. To add a print queue for a new printer, click the New button. This opens the Add a New Print Queue Wizard. Click Forward to get past the splash screen.

3. The first thing you're prompted for is the name of the print queue you want to add. Type a unique name for the printer (for example, something like `prntr_queue-1`). If you want, you can also type a description that helps you to identify the printer (see Figure 9-12). Click Forward.

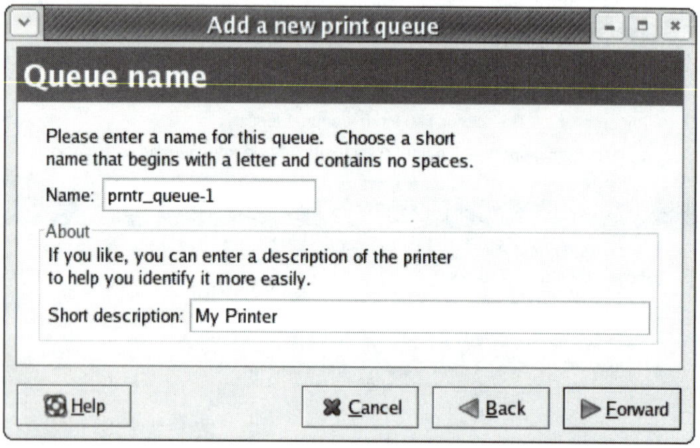

Figure 9-12

4. The next screen allows you to choose the queue type from the options in the table that follows.

Label	Type	Description
Locally connected	`LOCAL`	For a printer attached directly to your computer through a parallel or USB port
Networked CUPS	`IPP`	For a printer attached to a different CUPS system and accessible through TCP/IP
Networked UNIX	`LPD`	For a printer attached to a remote UNIX system and accessible through TCP/IP
Networked Windows	`SMB`	For a printer attached to a remote Windows system and accessible through a Samba share
Networked Novell	`NCP`	For a printer attached to a remote Novell Netware system
Networked JetDirect	`JETDIRECT`	For a printer connected directly to the network with its own IP address

This demonstration uses the `LOCAL` queue type. If you have a locally connected printer, select `Locally-connected`, and select a device from the list (such as `/dev/lp0`). Then click Forward.

If you have a networked computer, select one of the other options and follow the wizard to complete the configuration.

5. Next, you'll be prompted to select the make and model of your printer. When you've done that, click Forward, and the wizard confirms the details you've selected.
6. The new printer now appears in the printer list in the main window. You'll also see the dialog box shown in Figure 9-13.

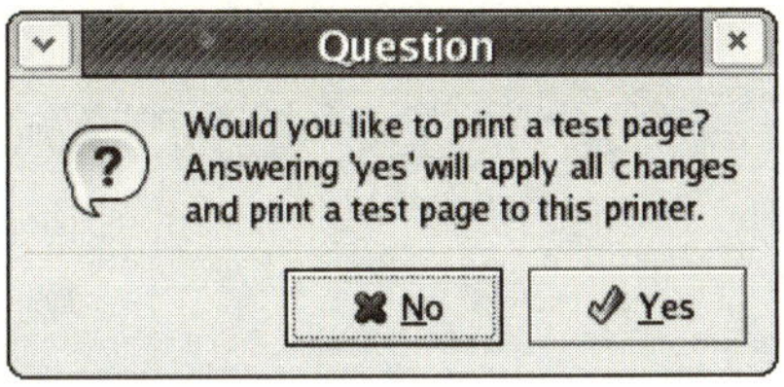

Figure 9-13

Click Yes to save the configuration changes to the `/etc/printcap` configuration file, restart the `lpd` printer daemon, and print a test page.

Configuring Printers

The Printer Configuration Tool provides a number of options for managing printers. For example, you can edit or remove the properties of a printer queue by selecting the queue and clicking Edit or Delete. You can also configure a particular printer to be the default by clicking the Default button. Whenever you make any changes, you must save them by clicking the Apply button (which also restarts the `cupsd` printer daemon to take account of your changes).

You can also test a printer from the Printer Configuration Tool, by choosing a printer and selecting any of the test configurations from the Test menu.

Starting (and Stopping) the Printer Daemon

To control the `cupsd` printer daemon, you can once again use the Service Configuration GUI. However, you may never need to do this manually—the service is configured to start automatically on system startup by default, and restarts automatically if you change its configuration via the Printer Configuration Tool.

If you do need to control the service manually, you can do it using the Service Configuration GUI (as described in other sections of this chapter—the service in question is called CUPS), or by using the `service` command at the command line to control the `cups` script:

```
# service cups
Usage: cupsd {start|stop|restart|condrestart|reload|status}
# service cups restart
Stopping cups:                                          [OK]
Starting cups:                                          [OK]
```

Printing from Applications

By default, all applications send printing requests to the default printer configured on the system, but, if more printers are available, the application's Print dialog box allows you to choose which print queue to send the job to.

For example, if you're printing a word-processed document from the OpenOffice OpenWriter application, you'd do so by selecting its File ➪ Print option from the menu bar. When you do that, you get a Print dialog box like that shown in Figure 9-14.

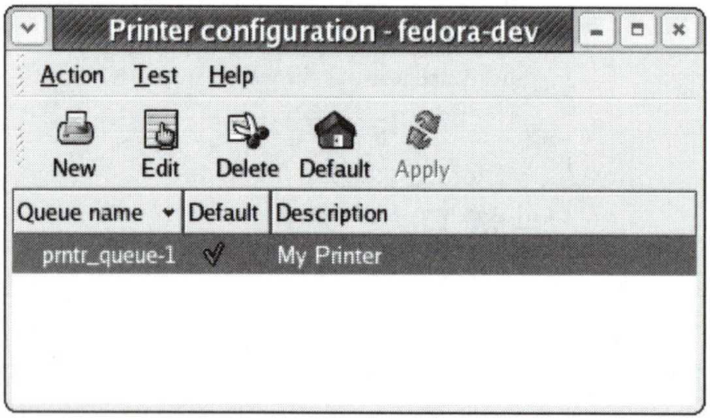

Figure 9-14

As you can see, the application offers you a list of printers to choose from. The list shown in Figure 9-15 includes an entry for the `prntr_queue-1` printer that we configured earlier. It also includes a Generic Printer entry; if you choose this, the application will send the print job to your default printer (the one that your machine is configured to use automatically).

You'll need to configure the default printer before you use if for the first time; you can do this through the OpenOffice Printer Setup Tool. Select Main Menu ➪ Office ➪ Openoffice.org Printer Setup, select the Generic Printer entry in that dialog box, and click the Properties button.

In the resulting Properties of Generic Printer dialog box, the default command in the Select Command section is `lpr`—this sends printer jobs via the `lpr` command to `/dev/lp0` as the default print queue. Change the command to `lpr -P` *`printername`*, where *printername* is the name you gave to your printer. Then click OK to save these settings.

Now you can return to your Writer application, select File ➪ Print, and select the Generic Printer option in the Print dialog box to send the job to that printer.

Creating Print Jobs at the Command Line

The `lpr` utility you've just seen can also be used to create print requests from the command line. For example, if you want to print a text document called `addresses.txt`, contained in the present working directory, you can do so by typing the following at the command line:

```
$ lpr addresses.txt
```

You can also examine and control existing print jobs via the `lpq` and `lprm` command line utilities of the CUPS software suite. The `lpq` command allows you to view the contents of the print queue, and can be used as follows:

```
$ lpq
ptntr_queue-1 is ready and printing
Rank      Owner    Job   File(s)                  Total Size
active    root       1   testprint.ps             15630 bytes
1st       kapils     2   (stdid)                  5761024 bytes
2nd       eziodm     3   (stdid)                  193536 bytes
3rd       eziodm     3   addresses.txt            1024 bytes
```

If you want to cancel a print job, use the `lprm` command. For example, to remove the job with `ID 838` from the print queue, issue the following command:

```
# lprm 838
```

Of course, if you try to cancel another user's print job and you don't have permission to do so, CUPS prevents you from canceling it. For example, suppose the user eziodm tried to cancel job 2 in the preceding list:

```
# lprm 2
lprm: You don't own job ID 2!
```

You can learn more about the CUPS printing system at `www.cups.org/`.

Setting Up a File Server

A *file server* is essentially a shared storage space. File servers are generally accessed across a network, and provide their users with a central location for file storage. Filesystems are also helpful when you need to share files with other users: you can simply place your file in a public directory on the file server, where other users can access it.

Like FTP servers, there are essentially two fundamental components to a file server: the *storage* space itself and the mechanism for accessing it. Whether you're working on a single machine at home, or as part of a large network in a major organization, you'll be using a filesystem to *store* your files; what a file server adds to this is the notion that the filesystem is a shared one, accessible by (possibly) many users.

A number of benefits can be gained by implementing a file server:

- It reduces administration cost. Instead of having important data stored on many individual PCs (all of which would require backing up), you can store *all* your important data in one place (on the file server). Then, only the file server needs regular backing up.
- It provides the opportunity to enforce a more controlled and focused security policy because the security policy needs to be applied only to the file server.

- It enables you to provide a more stable and reliable storage solution. It enables you to implement your storage solution on high-spec machines that provide high levels of uptime. Moreover, implementation of RAID or of mirrored SCSI disks (which help ensure data reliability) is more feasible on a central file server than on many PCs.
- There's also something to be gained in terms of cost of file storage (although this is less pertinent in these days of cheap storage). First, it makes best use of the available storage capacity by making it accessible to all users. Second, it provides a central repository from which common resources can be made available to all (eliminating the need for each user to store her own copy).

Once you've got a filesystem, what makes it a file server is the mechanism that enables the filesystem to be shared. There is plenty of software around for this purpose—Samba, the Network FileSystem (NFS), the Andrew filesystem (AFS), and Coda are all examples. Some of these are shipped as part of the Fedora 2 distribution. We'll focus on Samba here.

For more information on the others, see `www.nfsv4.org`, `www.transarc.com/Product/EFS/AFS/index.html`, *and* `www.coda.cs.cmu.edu`.

An Overview of Samba

Samba is an implementation of the Windows server message block (SMB) and CIFS protocols on UNIX. The Samba project was started by Andrew Tridgell, who wanted to mount his UNIX server disk space onto a DOS PC. When he'd solved the problem, Tridgell discovered that what he'd built was an implementation of the SMB protocol—a protocol for sharing files and other resources. Tridgell named his implementation Samba, and published version 1.0 in early 1992. Since that time, the Samba project has grown tremendously, and today Samba development is ongoing in the open source community.

So, Samba is a collection of programs that make it possible to share files and printers between computers equipped to use the SMB protocol—Windows by default, Linux/UNIX with Samba, and (more recently) Mac OS X. Samba is freely available under GNU General Public License, and is included as part of the Fedora 2 distribution.

This section looks at how to install Samba, perform some basic configuration, and set up a shared file server on a Linux machine. You'll also see how to use Samba to access a Linux-hosted file server from a Linux or Windows machine, and how to access a Windows-hosted file server from a Linux machine.

There should be enough in this section to get you started working with file servers in Linux. If you want to explore further with SMB and Samba, try `www.samba.org` (specifically, `www.samba.org/cifs/docs/what-is-smb.html`).

Installing SAMBA

Perhaps the easiest way to install the Samba software suite is via the RPM GUI Tool. After you've started the RPM, use the Package Management dialog box to locate the Windows File Server package group (which you will find under the Servers category). Click its Details button to see the package details. You will find packages for `samba` and `samba-client` under the heading Required Packages (see Figure 9-15).

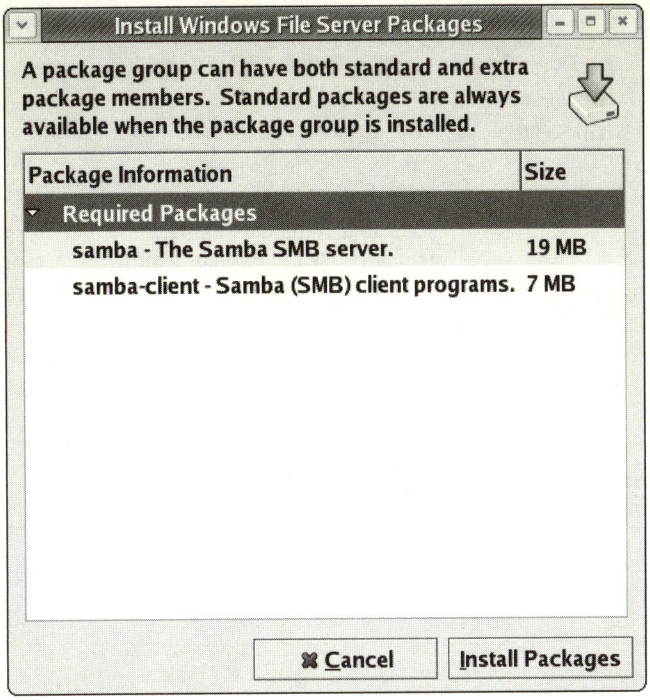

Figure 9-15

As you can see, there are two required packages: `samba` and `samba-client`. Click the Install Packages button to begin the installation of samba. You'll need the disk from your Fedora 2 distribution to complete the installation.

Starting and Stopping the Samba Service

As with other services you've seen, there are a number of ways to start and stop the Samba service. Once again, you can do so via the Service Configuration GUI Tool. To launch the Tool, select Main Menu ➪ System Settings ➪ Server Settings ➪ Services, or type the following command at the command line:

```
$ system-config-services
```

Then locate the smb service, as shown in Figure 9-16.

If the service is stopped (as shown in the Figure 9-18), start it by clicking the Start button. It's also a good idea to select the check box to configure the Samba service to start automatically whenever you boot up the system. For example, if you ever have to perform an emergency reboot on your file server, the automatic start configuration means that the file server is immediately available to users after the reboot. When you've done this, select File ➪ Save Changes to save your new setting.

Alternatively, you can stop and start smb service at the command line, using the `service` command to run the `/etc/rc.d/init.d/smb` script. Typing the script name at the command line like this reveals the possible usages:

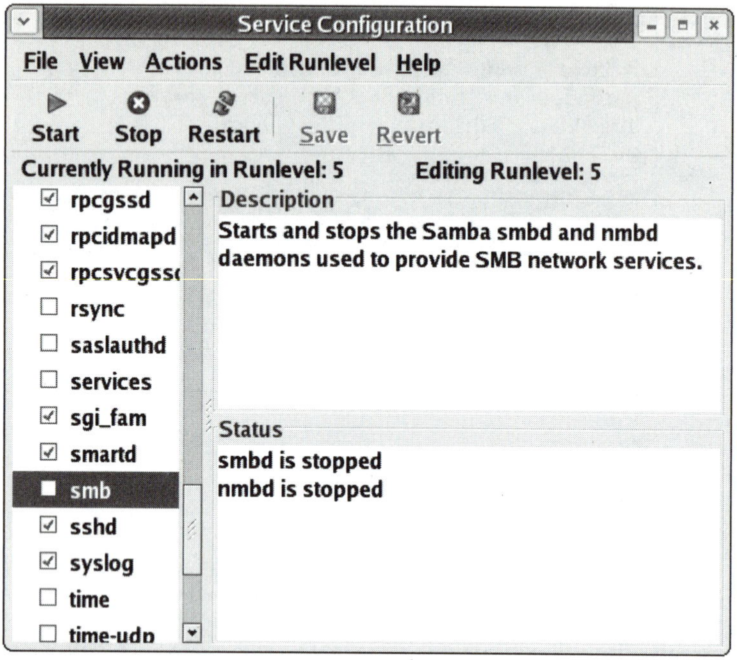

Figure 9-16

```
# service smb
Usage: /etc/rc.d/smb {start|stop|restart|reload|status|condrestart}
```

As you can see, it works in much the same way as the `httpd` and `vsftpd` scripts you saw in earlier sections of this chapter. So, to start the service, type the following:

```
# service smb start
Starting SMB services:                                     [  OK  ]
Starting NMB services:                                     [  OK  ]
```

This command starts both SMB and NMB (NetBIOS name server), which are both services related to Samba. To stop the service, type the following:

```
# service smb stop
Shutting down SMB services:                                [  OK  ]
Shutting down NMB services:                                [  OK  ]
```

You get the idea. Note, however, that this script allows you to control the service manually only. It doesn't allow you to configure the service to start automatically on boot-up—for that, you need the Service Configuration GUI.

Samba Configuration Files and Utilities

We won't take a look at every single item that is installed during the process described in the preceding subsection, but it is worth pointing out some of the most important files, both to give you an idea of

Samba's capabilities and because we'll be using some of these files and programs later in this section. Specifically of interest here are Samba's configuration files and programs.

Samba's configuration files are contained in the directory `/etc/samba`. The table that follows provides a brief description of the Samba configuration files that you'll find there.

Configuration File	Description
`smb.conf`	This is the main configuration file for Samba.
`Lmhosts`	This contains Samba's NetBIOS-to-IP address mappings.
`secrets.tdb`	This is the Samba secrets database. It stores private information such as the local SID and machine trust password. It is generated by the machine and cannot be read in a text editor.
`Smbusers`	This is a text file that maps your Linux system's users to various SMB-specific usernames.
`Smbpasswd`	This is an encrypted password file. The format of this file is very similar to that of the `passwd` file you met in Chapter 7. This file doesn't exist when you first install Samba, but is created when you add Samba users.

To work with file servers through Samba, you can use its many programs. The following table lists some of the most important utilities provided by Samba. They're all contained in the directory `/usr/bin`, and some of them are used later in this section.

Program	Purpose
`smbclient`	This is an FTP-like client, used to access SMB/CIFS resources on a file server.
`smbadduser`	This is a script, used for adding Samba users. It updates the `smbusers` and `smbpasswd` files.
`smbpasswd`	This changes a Samba user's SMB password. It is similar to the UNIX `passwd` command discussed in Chapter 7.
`smbmount`	This is used to mount an SMB filesystem.
`smbumount`	This is used to unmount an SMB filesystem.
`smbstatus`	This lists the current Samba connections.
`testparm`	This checks the `smb.conf` configuration file for correctness.
`nmblookup`	This is used to query NetBIOS names and map them to IP addresses in a network using NetBIOS over TCP/IP.

In addition, we'll also make use of the script `/etc/rc.d/init.d/smb`, which is used to start and stop the Samba file service.

Samba Configuration with SWAT

If you open the Samba configuration files using `gedit` (or any text editor), you'll see that the information and syntax used is rather complex. You can configure Samba by editing these files in a text editor, but if you're not familiar with it, it can be quite difficult and prone to error.

Samba provides a number of command line utilities for configuration, too, but perhaps the easiest way to configure Samba is by using the *Samba Web Administration Tool (SWAT)*. SWAT is a Web-based interface, which means that you can use it to configure and manage your Samba server through a Web browser—if you want, you can even do it remotely across a network or even across the Internet.

If you are thinking of using SWAT for remote Samba management, you should note that SWAT will transmit your username and password in clear text when you log in. Across an insecure connection, this presents the risk that an unwelcome visitor could sniff out your login credentials and use them to ill effect. To avoid this, you should use SWAT only from within a secure network. In fact, as you'll see it in the section "Starting the SWAT Service," shortly, SWAT's default configuration makes it available only at `http://localhost:901`.

Let's see how to install SWAT and start the SWAT service. When you've done that, you'll be ready to use SWAT to configure Samba and set up your file server for use.

Installing SWAT

Fedora 2's Package Management GUI Tool doesn't provide an option for installing the SWAT package. Instead, you must install this package via the RPM's command-line utility. The SWAT utility is made available through the `samba-swat` package. Here's how to install the `sambaswat` package at the command line:

1. Launch a terminal window, and switch to the root user account by using this command:

```
$ su -
```

2. Insert the appropriate Fedora 2 distribution disc. Change to the directory on the CD that contains the RPM package files:

```
# cd /mnt/cdrom/Fedora/RPMS
```

If you get a "No such file or directory" message, it's probably because the CD wasn't mounted automatically when you inserted it. In this case, mount the CD manually:

```
# mount /dev/cdrom
```

Then try the `cd` command again.

3. Use the `ls` command to find out the exact version of `samba-swat` contained on the disc. For example:

```
# ls samba-swat*.rpm
samba-swat-3.0.3-5.i386.rpm
```

4. Install the `samba-swat` package you've just found, by using the `rpm` command:

```
# rpm -ivh samba-swat-3.0.3-5.i386.rpm
Preparing...            ########################################### [100%]
   1:samba-swat         ########################################### [100%]
```

Alternatively, view the available package files on your disk by using the Nautilus file manager GUI to navigate to `/mnt/cdrom/Fedora/RPMS`. Locate the file matching the name `samba-swat-*.rpm`. Double-click this file to open the RPM GUI Tool, from which you can install the package.

Starting the SWAT Service

To start the SWAT service, take the following steps:

1. Launch `gedit` or your favorite text editor and open the file `/etc/xinetd.d/swat`. This is the configuration file for the SWAT service:

```
# default: off
# description: SWAT is the Samba Web Admin Tool. Use swat \
#              to configure your Samba server. To use SWAT, \
#              connect to port 901 with your favorite web browser.
service swat
{
        port            = 901
        socket_type     = stream
        wait            = no
        only_from       = 127.0.0.1
        user            = root
        server          = /usr/sbin/swat
        log_on_failure += USERID
        disable         = yes
}
```

2. Change the `disable` value, like this:

```
        disable         = no
```

3. Save the file, and close your text editor.

Note that this default configuration ensures that the SWAT service will be accessible only through the IP address `127.0.0.1`*, and on port 901. The IP address* `127.0.0.1` *is a special address known as the loopback address because requests to* `http://127.0.0.1` *are sent to the Web server on the same machine as the browser from which the request is made. Hence, by default, SWAT is available only from the file server machine itself, via* `http://127.0.0.1:901` *or* `http://localhost:901` *(as mentioned earlier in the chapter).*

4. Restart the xinetd service. (You must do this because SWAT runs as an xinetd service. The xinetd service is out of scope of this book, but it is enough to know that its purpose is to support Internet services such as SWAT.) To do this, first launch the Service Configuration GUI Tool by selecting Main Menu ➪ System Settings ➪ Server Settings ➪ Services (see Figure 9-17).

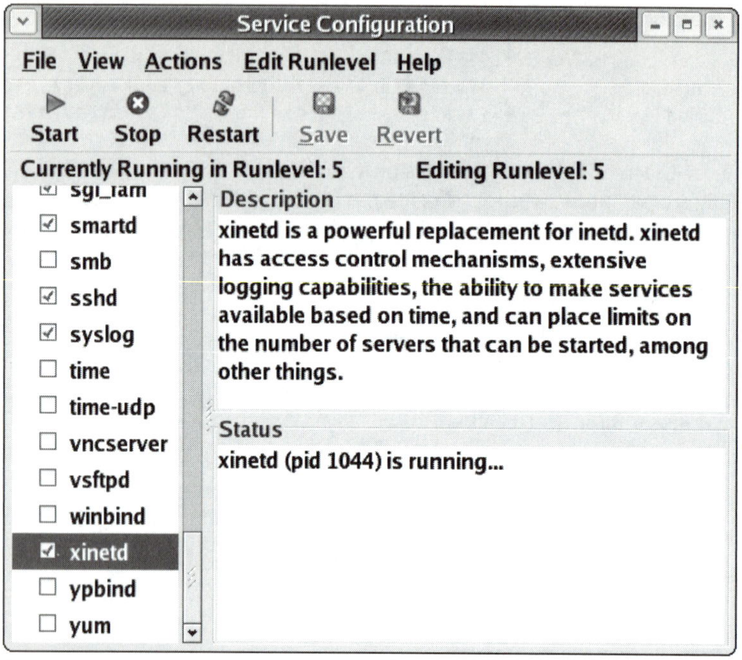

Figure 9-17

Then locate and select the service called `xinetd`, and click Restart. You'll get a dialog box to confirm that the restart was successful; then you can exit the tool by clicking Quit.

Using SWAT for the First Time

Now you can test SWAT. Open a browser on the Linux server and type in the URL `http://localhost:901`. You'll be prompted for a username and password—use the system's root username and password. You should see the SWAT HOME page.

This page contains the index of Samba's very comprehensive online documentation, where you can find out much more about Samba and SWAT. There are also eight buttons listed across the top of this page, which provide access to SWAT's various utilities:

- **HOME:** The home page of SWAT, and the first page that you see when you fire up the SWAT interface
- **GLOBALS:** For setting the global variable values of the `/etc//smb.conf` configuration file
- **SHARES:** For creating and deleting Samba shares, and setting Samba parameters
- **PRINTERS:** For creating and deleting Samba printer shares and setting printer parameters
- **WIZARD:** Like GLOBALS, this is also for setting various values in `/etc//smb.conf`

- **STATUS:** For viewing the Samba server's status, and starting and stopping Samba-related services
- **VIEW:** For viewing the content of the `/etc//smb.conf` configuration file
- **PASSWORD:** For adding, removing, enabling, and disabling Samba users, and for setting Samba users' passwords

So SWAT is up and running, and ready to use; the next task is to use it to configure the Linux machine as a file server. To do that, you'll make use of some of the features in the preceding list. Then, when you've set up the file server, you'll examine it from the client's perspective, by looking at how different clients use Samba to access the file server you've created.

Adding a Samba User

To grant a system account access to the Samba services, you can use SWAT's PASSWORD feature. Once you've logged into SWAT using the root username and password, click the PASSWORD button. In the Server Password Management section of the window that opens, enter the name of an existing account on the system, and supply a password. Then click the Add New User button. This adds an entry to Samba's `smbpasswd` configuration file, to indicate that this user has access to Samba's services.

Normal accounts that have access to the Samba services also have access to SWAT. However, only root users have access to the full range of SWAT's utilities; normal users are allowed to use only limited features contained in the HOME, STATUS, VIEW, and PASSWORD screens.

Creating and Configuring a Samba Share

Now you're ready to configure your Linux server as a file server, by creating a *share* (a dedicated directory on the server that will be accessible to other users). You can do all this using SWAT:

1. Create a directory, which we'll call `/share`, to be used for the file server. With root permission, you can do this at the command line using the following command:

```
# mkdir /share
```

2. If you haven't done so already, use the Mozilla browser (or your favorite Web browser) to browse to the SWAT home page at `http://localhost:901`, and log in using the root user account.

3. Click the GLOBALS toolbar icon. In the Base Options section, use the Workgroup field to enter the name of the workgroup that you want your server to appear in when clients use it. (If you haven't set up a workgroup, this is probably the default value, WORKGROUP). You should also name the service by entering a value in the server string field—it can be any string that you want your Samba clients to see. We'll stick with the default, Samba Server.

   Click Commit Changes to save your changes to the configuration files.

4. Now click the SHARES toolbar button at the top of the screen. We'll share our `/share` directory by giving it a *share name*; let's call it `linuxbox-share`. You should first check the entries in the drop-down list on this page, to ensure that your chosen share name hasn't already been used for a different share; then, enter the share name in the Create Share field.

Now click the Create Share button to create the share. This will present you with another screen in which you can specify the properties of your share. You will certainly need to set the path field to the path of your share directory (in this example, it's `/share`). You can also set a number of other fields, such as the following, for example:

- Set the read-only field to No to make it a writeable share.
- Set the browsable field to Yes, to allow the contents of the `/share` directory to be visible.
- Set the available field to Yes, to enable the share (that is, make it available to users).
- Add a comment to remind you what the share is for.

When you're done, click the Commit Changes button to commit these settings to the Samba configuration file.

If you like, you can click the Advanced View button in the SHARES screen to set further settings (for example, you can insert a space-delimited list of users into the valid users or invalid users text boxes, to control which users are allowed or denied access to the Samba share). You can also click the VIEW button to view the complete contents of the `/etc//smb.conf` *configuration file.*

5. Restart the Samba service so that the configuration changes can take effect. To do this, click the STATUS button and then click the Restart smbd button to restart the service. Wait for the page to reload, and then click the Restart nmbd button to restart that service, too.

Accessing the Share from a Windows NT/2000/XP Machine

Now that you have a Samba share configured on your Linux server, you can access it from a range of other machines on the network. To access the share from a Windows system, you can browse to it using Windows' Network Neighborhood, and even map it to a network drive using Tools ⇨ Map Network Drive.

Accessing the Share from Another Linux Machine

You can also access your Linux filesystem share from any SMB-equipped client machine (for example, from another Linux machine). To do this, the client machine can use functionality that is contained within the Samba client package. In fact, there are two different applications that you can use to access your Linux file share across the network from an SMB-equipped client machine:

- You can use the `smbclient` command, which provides an FTP-like interface to perform the same functions as FTP.
- If your client machine is a Linux machine, you can use the `smbmount` command to mount the remote smb share as a local directory.

To access an smb share via a remote machine, you will need to know the username and password of a Samba user account on the remote Samba server machine (such as the kapils account shown earlier).

The smbclient Utility

If you're using a client Linux machine to access your Samba share, you can do so using the `smbclient` utility. To do this for the share we've created here, run the following command at the command line:

```
$ smbclient //linuxserver/linuxbox-share -U kapils
added interface ip=192.168.0.114 bcast=192.168.0.255 nmask=255.255.255.0
Password:
Domain[WORKGROUP] OS=[Unix] Server=[Samba3.0.3-5]
smb: />
```

In the `smbclient` command, we needed to specify three things:

- The name of the file server
- The name of the share
- The name of the user we're using to access the share (that is, a user that we created using the SWAT facility's PASSWORD screen earlier in the section).

Note that you're prompted for a password. When the password authentication with the Samba server is successful, you will get an smbclient session, which looks similar to an FTP session. Now you can use all the available commands to work with the files in the remote filesystem:

```
smb: \>ls
temp1.txt      temp2.txt      temp3.txt
```

To get a list of all the commands you can use through the smbclient session, type **help** at the prompt:

```
smb: \>help
?      altname     archive     blocksize     cancel
cd     chmod       chown       del           dir
du     exit        get         help          directory
...
```

For more on using Samba shares via an smbclient session, see the documentation at `http://us3.samba.org/samba/ftp/docs/htmldocs/smbclient.1.html`. To exit the smbclient session, type **exit** at the `smb: \>` prompt.

The smbmount Utility (Mounting an SMB Share Locally)

The `smbmount` utility allows you to mount a (possibly) remote smb share on a client Linux computer. You can try this out if you have two Linux machines networked together—use the one with the Samba share as the server and the other one as the client. Alternatively, if you've got a single Linux machine, the machine acts as both file server and as a client of its own service.

The `smbmount` application uses a helper application called `smbmnt`, and the first thing to do is change the permissions on `smbmnt` so that your `smbmount` command can use it. By default, `smbmnt`'s permissions allow it to be used only by the root user of the machine on which it is running. Assuming you're using the client machine as a normal user, you'll need to use the root account to adjust these permissions, like this:

```
$ su -
Password:
# chmod s+u /usr/bin/smbmnt
```

You can check the new permissions, like this:

```
# ls -l /usr/bin/smbmnt
-rwsr-xr-x   1 root   root    491096   Jan 10  00.05   /usr/bin/smbmnt
```

Now you're ready to test smbmount. Change back to your normal user account, and create the directory onto which you want to mount the Samba share:

```
# exit
$ mkdir /home/kapils/mnt
$ mkdir /home/kapils/mnt/remote
```

Here, we're using the local kapils account on the client machine, and we've created a directory called `mnt/remote` underneath this user's home directory `/home/kapils`.

Now, run the `smbmount` command to mount the remote Samba share on the local directory:

```
$ smbmount //linuxserver/linuxbox-share /home/kapils/mnt/remote -o username=kapils
Password:
```

Here, *`linuxserver`* is the name of the Linux server that is hosting the Samba share, and `linuxbox-share` is the name of the share; `/home/kapils/mnt/remote` is the chosen mount point, and kapils is the name of the Samba user on the Linux server. You're prompted for the password of the Samba user.

When you've done this, and assuming the connection is good, you can navigate the contents of the Samba share as if they were contents of the mount point. For example:

```
$ ls /home/kapils/mnt/remote
temp1.txt      temp2.txt      temp3.txt
```

To unmount, you can use the `smbumount` command. However, like `smbmnt`, you may first need to use the client machine's root account to change the permissions on `smbumount`:

```
# chmod s+u /usr/bin/smbumount
```

Now you can safely unmount the share from your mount point using your normal user account:

```
$ smbmount /home/kapils/mnt/remote
```

Accessing NT Shares from a Linux Machine

What if you want to use a Linux client machine to access a filesystem hosted by a Windows server? In fact, you can access Windows NT shares in the same way that you access Linux shares.

For example, suppose you have a Windows NT machine called `winserver` that acts as a file server by hosting a share called `salesarchive`. You can treat the contents of this share as if it were part of the client machine's filesystem, by mounting it just as we did before.

First, you need a directory that will act as your mount point. For example, let's create a local directory called `sales`, under our user's home directory:

```
$ mkdir /home/kapils/mnt/sales
```

Next, use `smbmount` to mount the filesystem onto the mount point:

```
% su -
Password:
# smbmount //winserver/salesarchive /home/kapils/mnt/sales -o username=kapils
Password:
```

There are two points to note here. First, the normal user does not have permission to mount a filesystem, so you must change to root user before using `smbmount`. Second, the `smbmount` command itself requires that you specify a username and password. This username corresponds not necessarily to a user on the Linux machine, but to a network user that has permission to access the share.

Having achieved a connection, you can work with the files on the remote file server as if they were part of the local directory:

```
$ cd /home/kapils/mnt/sales
$ ls
sales2002Q2     sales2002Q3     sales2002Q4
sales2003Q1     salesnotes.txt
```

Your permissions on the contents of this folder will depend on the permissions assigned to the network user whose account you specified in the `smbmount` command. To unmount the share, use `smbumount` again:

```
# smbumount /home/kapils/mnt/sales
```

Accessing SMB/CIFS Shares Using Nautilus

You can even use the Nautilus file manager to access SMB/CIFS resources such as Windows and Linux Samba shares. To access Samba shares using Nautilus, first launch a Nautilus window (for example, by selecting Main Menu ➪ Run Program and typing **nautilus**).

Then type **smb:** in the Location bar. This will cause Nautilus to show you a list of all local domains and workgroups. From here, double-click the workgroup of your Windows machine, and then on the name of the Windows machine itself, to view all directory shares on that machine.

If you are connecting to smb shares that require a username and password, you can specify this information within Nautilus's Location bar. In this example, the Location bar with username and password should look like this:

```
smb://kapil:password@winserver/salesarchive/
```

After successful authentication, Nautilus shows you all the files under that share.

There's a lot to Samba, and we've covered only a little of the detail here. For more depth, take a look at Samba's software suite manual pages (using the `man` command), the SWAT documentation (on the HOME page of your SWAT tool), and the Samba official Web site (`www.samba.org`). You must always check your firewall settings for the SWAT port. Firewalls must be configured to open port 901 for SWAT.

Setting Up a Mail Server

For many of us, e-mail has become an essential part of life. When you send an e-mail, it is a *mail server* that is responsible for dispatching that mail to its intended destination; and at the other end, another mail server receives that message and passes it on to the appropriate mailbox.

A mail server can be configured to handle small home network e-mails or large, complex networks with hundreds of users. Many home users tend to use the mail server provided by their ISP. Many medium-to-large organizations host their own mail servers.

It's unlikely that you'll need to set up your own mail server, but in some situations there are good reasons for doing so:

- Your mail server will be on the same network as your client machine, so connection between your client machine and mail server will be much faster.
- If you have a dialup connection (rather than a dedicated Internet connection), having your own mail server allows you to work on your e-mail without ever having to connect manually to the Internet. You can configure your e-mail server to send and receive mail in batches, by connecting to the Internet at specified times.
- You can customize a mail server's security and monitoring rules, so that it alerts you if it receives a message that contains certain blocked words or if it detects unusual activity.

Hosting your own mail server comes with its burdens, too. There's the increased cost of support and maintenance, and the additional chance of being compromised (you're protected from this if you use an ISP's mail server). It's also more important to ensure that you keep your antivirus software up to date, and that it scans each e-mail. And there is a risk that your mail server will become an open relay SMTP server (another user uses your mail server as a gateway for sending mail).

So, there's much to consider, and debate of these issues is outside the scope of this book. However, if you do decide to host your own mail server, you won't be surprised to learn that the Fedora 2 operating system comes with a default mail server. It's called Sendmail.

What Is a Mail Server?

A mail server is a collection of applications that provide the functionality to manage the tasks of sending and receiving e-mail, and delivering e-mail to users' mailboxes. A mail server uses a number of different protocols to transfer e-mail from one system to other. Here's a brief description of these protocols:

- The *Internet Message Access Protocol (IMAP)* is a protocol used by an e-mail client application to access the remote e-mail mailbox. The main advantage of IMAP is that users can manage the e-mail messages on remote mailboxes instead of downloading the messages onto their local machine. For more information on IMAP, take a look at `www.imap.org/`.
- E-mail clients use the *Post Office Protocol (POP)* to download e-mail messages from a remote server and save them on their local machine. For more information on POP, refer to RFC 1939 at `www.rfc-editor.org/in-notes/rfc1939.txt`.

- The *Simple Mail Transfer Protocol (SMTP)* is used to send e-mails (this is in contrast with IMAP and POP, which are used to *receive* e-mails). Each e-mail message is transferred between remote e-mail servers using SMTP. Fedora 2 uses `Sendmail` as its default SMTP software.

E-mail Application Types

E-mail applications fall into the following three classes:

- **Mail User Agents (MUAs):** An MUA is an e-mail client, a program that is used to retrieve and manage e-mail messages via POP or IMAP protocols. Examples of MUAs on Linux systems include Pine, Mutt, Ximian's Evolution, and Mozilla Mail. Microsoft's Outlook is also an MUA.
- **Mail Transfer Agents (MTAs):** An MTA transfers e-mail messages between different machines using SMTP. During the course of its journey from source to destination, an e-mail message may transfer between several MTAs, hosted on different platforms. On Linux systems, `Sendmail`, `Postfix`, `Exim`, and `Qmail` are four different MTA applications. Fedora Core 2 uses `Sendmail` as its default MTA.
- **Mail Delivery Agents (MDAs):** An MDA is used to deliver e-mail messages to users' mailboxes. An MTA delivers messages to an MDA, which is then responsible for delivering it to the specified mailbox. Some MTAs (such as `Sendmail`) can also act as MDAs. On Linux systems, MDAs include `Sendmail`, `Procmail`, and `/bin/mail`. MDAs are sometimes also known as *LDAs (local delivery agents)*.

Why Sendmail?

This section looks at how to use and configure the Sendmail mail server. Sendmail is a widely used mail server, which (as stated) can act both as MTA and MDA, and is capable of serving the needs of home users as well as larger networks. It can be used to send e-mail via the Internet as well as locally (and hence can be used as a local intranet mail server), and the latest version provides many security features. Sendmail also comes with good documentation.

Installing Sendmail

As you'd expect, installing Sendmail is straightforward when you do it through the RPM GUI Tool. Once you've started the tool (for example, by selecting Main Menu ⇨ System Settings ⇨ Add/Remove Applications), you need to select the Mail Server package group (which you'll find under the Servers category). If you click the Details button, you'll see the package details (see Figure 9-18).

The sendmail package is selected by default as a Required Packages. Under the Optional Packages, you should also select the dovecot (an imap server) and sendmail-cf packages. The sendmail package will install the Sendmail MTA (the SMTP server), while the dovecot package installs the POP and IMAP services, and sendmail-cf provides the facilities for reconfiguring Sendmail. You can deselect all other packages. Click Install Packages to start the installation. As usual, you'll need the Fedora 2 distribution CDs handy to complete the installation.

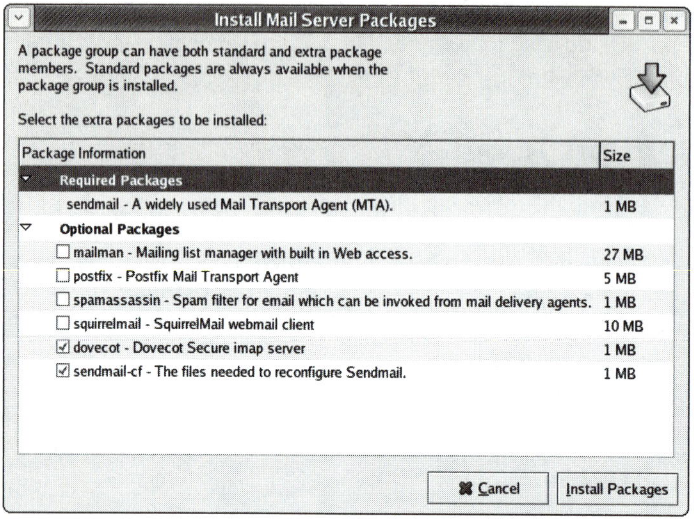

Figure 9-18

Configuring Sendmail

Sendmail is very flexible and provides a lot of options for handling e-mail. While this abundance of features brings a lot of advantages and flexibility, it also brings complexity. Some aspects of Sendmail's configuration are difficult to understand, and even experienced system administrators make mistakes. We will go through a simple configuration that should get Sendmail up and running and able to send e-mails. We assume you have already configured your Linux machine to connect to the Internet, as described in Chapter 3.

The default installation of Sendmail places the `sendmail` executable in the `/usr/sbin` (that is, `/usr/sbin/sendmail`). It also creates a symbolic link, `/usr/lib/sendmail`, which points to `/usr/sbin/sendmail`.

Sendmail's configuration files are contained within the `/etc/mail` directory. There are five configuration files of particular interest, as shown in the following table.

Configuration File	Purpose
`sendmail.cf`	This lengthy and complex file is the default main file used by Sendmail. Although you can read this document, you're not supposed to edit it; rather, you edit the source `sendmail.mc` file found in the same directory and then compile using the `m4` utility (see the section "Configuring Sendmail").
`access`	This file specifies which systems can use Sendmail for relaying e-mail. It allows you to restrict the access to the mail server by individual domains.

Configuration File	Purpose
`local-host-names`	This file specifies all aliases for your machine.
`domaintable`	This file specifies domain name mappings.
`virtusertable`	This file allows a domain-specific form of aliasing. It allows multiple virtual domains to be hosted on one machine.

If you look in the `/etc/mail` directory, you'll see that some of these files are stored in two formats:

- The `access`, `domaintable`, and `virtusertable` files are text files; they contain the configuration data that you specify to control how Sendmail works for you, and you can configure these files using a text editor such as `gedit`.
- The `access.db`, `domaintable.db`, and `virtusertable.db` files are database files. These contain the same data, in a database format that the Sendmail application can use.

Whenever you adjust the configuration contained in the text files, you must subsequently compile them into database format so that Sendmail can use the new configuration.

Here's a brief example. If you wanted to allow all the systems in `linux4biz.net` domain to use your e-mail server for relaying e-mail, you would add the following line in the `access` file:

```
# by default we allow relaying from localhost...
neptune.home            RELAY
localhost               RELAY
127.0.0.1               RELAY
linux4biz.net           RELAY
```

Then, you must convert the `access` text files to generate the `access.db` database file. To do this, use the `makemap` command:

```
# makemap hash /etc/mail/access.db < /etc/mail/access
```

This creates the `access.db` file (which is not human readable and can be used only by the Sendmail application).

Sendmail offers many configuration options to allow you to control almost every aspect of its behavior. We can't possibly cover them all here, but there are good resources on the Internet that will help you to set up your Sendmail installation the way you want it. A good place to start is `www.sendmail.org`.

A Simple Example Using Sendmail

To prove that Sendmail works, we'll demonstrate a little configuration of the Sendmail mail server. Then we'll see it in action, showing how it can act as an MTA—collecting incoming e-mails and filtering them into different mailboxes (according to the identity of the mail message's intended recipient).

We'll need to check the configuration of Sendmail, and then make sure all the necessary services are open. Then, to demonstrate, we'll masquerade as two different users, sending e-mails to each other across the system; and we'll see Sendmail in action, making sure that the messages get forwarded to the correct users' mailboxes.

Configuring Sendmail

By default, Sendmail listens for incoming mails only on the loopback IP address, `127.0.0.1`—and this allows SMTP connections between the Sendmail server and the *local* machine only. This is sufficient for this example because it involves only senders and recipients whose accounts are on the local machine.

However, you would need to change the following part of the `sendmail.mc` configuration file if you wanted to open up your Sendmail server to listen for incoming mails on other addresses:

```
dnl # The following causes sendmail to only listen on the IPv4 loopback address
dnl # 127.0.0.1 and not on any other network devices. Remove the loopback
dnl # address restriction to accept email from the internet or intranet.
dnl #
DAEMON_OPTIONS('Port=smtp,Addr=127.0.0.1, Name=MTA')dnl
```

Here, the `Port` parameter specifies the port on which the Sendmail server, acting as MTA, is to listen for messages (the default is `smtp`, which is port 25). If you want to make Sendmail listen for messages coming in from the Internet or across an intranet, you remove the `Addr` restriction:

```
DAEMON_OPTIONS('Port=smtp, Name=MTA')dnl
```

Alternatively, you can specify a specific IP address on which Sendmail should listen. For example:

```
DAEMON_OPTIONS('Port=smtp,Addr=192.168.0.99, Name=MTA')dnl
```

If you make changes to `sendmail.mc`, you must then compile them into the `sendmail.cf` file that Sendmail uses. To do this, you employ the `m4` utility, like this:

```
# m4 /etc/mail/sendmail.mc > /etc/mail/sendmail.cf
```

If you're stepping through this example for yourself, you can leave the `DAEMON_OPTIONS` directive as the default, so that Sendmail is listening only at `127.0.0.1`.

Starting the SendMail Service

You shouldn't need to start the Sendmail service because it is configured to start up automatically on system startup. You can check the service's status in much the same way as the other services we've mentioned in this chapter, via the Service Configuration GUI (Main Menu ⇨ System Settings ⇨ Server Settings ⇨ Services), where it is listed under the name sendmail (see Figure 9-19).

You can also start and stop the service manually at the command line by using the `service` command in the usual way, this time to control the `/etc/init.d/sendmail` script. For example:

```
# service sendmail
Usage: /etc/init.d/sendmail {start|stop|restart|condrestart|status}
# service sendmail restart
Shutting down sendmail:                                    [  OK  ]
Shutting down sm-client:                                   [  OK  ]
Starting sendmail:                                         [  OK  ]
Starting sm-client:                                        [  OK  ]
```

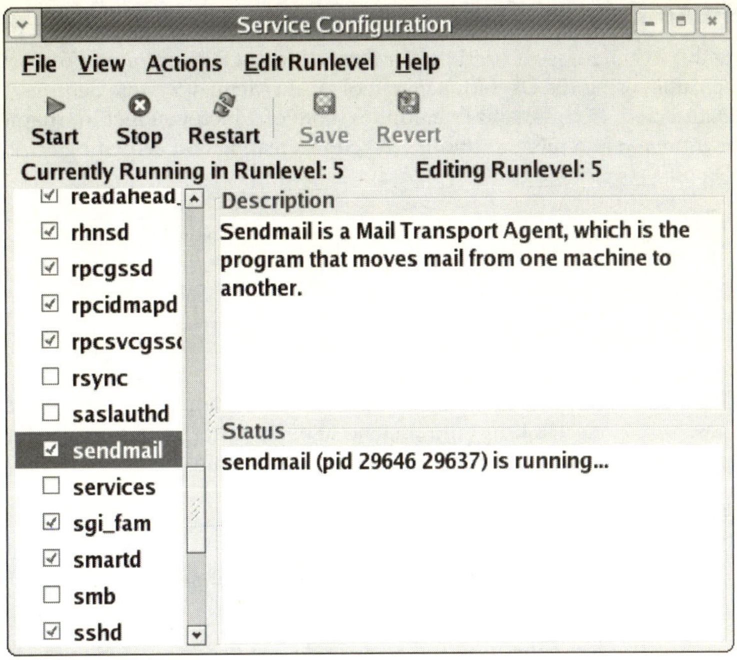

Figure 9-19

Testing the Configuration

If you change the Sendmail configuration, you can test the Sendmail connection by attempting to connect from a Windows machine on the same network. To do this, you can use the `telnet` command at the command prompt:

```
> telnet 192.168.0.99 25
220 linuxbox ESMTP 8.12.11/8.12.11; Fri, 21 May 2004 00:04:45 +0100
```

A response like the one shown here proves that Sendmail is listening on IP address `192.168.0.99`, port 25. In this response, `linuxbox` refers to the hostname of the server on which Sendmail is running. Sendmail automatically detects the hostname of the machine (this could be an FQDN or the machine's IP address). To disconnect from this port, type **quit**.

You should also look for the messages in Sendmail log file `/var/log/maillog` to troubleshoot any problem. When you start the sendmail daemon, the log file displays the following messages:

```
May 21 13:14:21 test sendmail[4040]: starting daemon (8.12.11):
SMTP+queueing@01:00:00
May 21 13:14:21 test sm-msp-queue[4049]: starting daemon (8.12.11):
queueing@01:00:00
```

Sendmail also logs many other messages, such as messages sent and other error messages in the `/var/log/maillog` log file.

Setting Up Some E-mail Clients

To demonstrate this in action; we'll need two or three different user accounts. You could create some fictional user accounts using the User Manager Tool (Main Menu ⇨ System Settings ⇨ Users & Groups) or the `useradd` and `passwd` command line utilities (both of which you met in Chapter 7). Here's a reminder of the `useradd` and `passwd` utilities in action, creating and activating an account for one of the authors of this book:

```
# useradd -c 'Mark Mamone' -s /bin/bash markm
# passwd markm
...
```

This example uses accounts markm and kapils; you can use different accounts if you like.

They also need to be configured with e-mail accounts on the system. The easiest way to do this is to log on as each of these users, one at a time (and pretend to be that user); and then use Ximian's Evolution e-mail client application to set that user up with an e-mail account.

If you're starting Evolution up for the first time, follow these steps:

1. You get the first screen of the Setup Assistant, and you should click Forward button to create an account.
2. In the Identity screen, enter your full name and e-mail address. (Evolution will accept only proper e-mail addresses here.)
3. In the first of two Receiving Email screens, select POP from the options in the Server Type field, and enter the IP address of your machine in the Host field. (This is the IP address of the POP3 server.) Enter the username, and set the Authentication Type to Password.
4. In the second Receiving Email screen, select Automatically check for new mail and specify the time interval between checks. Select Leave messages on server if you don't want messages deleted from the server after they've been downloaded to the mailbox.
5. In the next screen, Sending Email, change the Server Type to Sendmail (this selection is for delivery of mail messages by passing it to the Sendmail program on the local machine; the other option, SMTP, should be used for delivery of e-mails through a connection to a remote mail hub).
6. In the next screen, Account Management, enter the name of the account (it can be any name, but we'll just use the e-mail address here). Enable "Make this my default account."
7. In the final screen, select a time zone. Then click Next, and then Finish, to complete the setup.

If you *don't* get the Setup Assistant when you launch Evolution, you can enter all this information via the tabs in the Tools ⇨ Settings ⇨ Mail Accounts dialog box instead.

Demonstrating the Sendmail MDA

To summarize, so far you've done two things:

- ❑ You've set up the Sendmail application as a mail server, capable of listening for incoming mail messages on `127.0.0.1`, and filtering those messages into the correct mailbox so that the intended recipient can read them.

- ❑ You've created some users, configured their mailboxes, and set up each user to use the Evolution application as a mail client (to enable them to send messages and view the messages they've received).

In a moment, you can begin to test all this—for example, by logging in as kapils, sending a message to markm, and then logging in as markm to check that the mail message safely arrived.

Starting the POP3 Service

Before you can use Evolution to send a message, you must start the POP3 service. Fedora Core 2 provides a package called dovecot that provides imap as well as POP3 services. The default settings for dovecot only enable Internet Message Access Protocol (IMAP) and IMAP Secure (IMAPS) services. You can also configure dovecot to enable and serve POP3 service. To do that, take the following steps:

1. Open the dovecot configuration file `/etc/dovecot.conf` in your preferred text editor.
2. Scroll down the configuration file until you can see the following configuration lines:

```
# Protocols we want to be serving:
#  imap imaps pop3 pop3s
# protocols = imap imaps
```

   As seen from the preceding configuration snippet, dovecot only enables imap and imaps services by default.

3. To enable POP3 services on your system, uncomment the protocol line and add `pop3` at the end of this line, as follows:

```
protocols = imap imaps pop3
```

4. Save the file and start the dovecot service to implement the changes as follows:

```
Service dovecot start
Starting Dovecot Imap:                                    [  OK  ]
```

You can start the dovecot service to start imap or pop3 from the Service Configuration GUI (Main Menu ➪ System Settings ➪ Server Settings ➪ Services). First, select the check box next to the dovecot entry in the list to automatically start the dovecot service on boot-up, and then click the Start. button at the top of the window to start the dovecot service.

5. To test the pop3 service, connect to port 110 using telnet, as follows:

```
telnet 192.168.0.99 110
Trying 192.168.0.99...
Connected to 192.168.0.99.
Escape character is '^]'.
+OK dovecot ready.

If you get a OK message at the end of the telnet session, that means the service is
working OK.
```

Sending Mails

Log on to one of your accounts (for example, kapil), and launch the Evolution application by selecting Main Menu ⇨ Internet ⇨ Evolution Email. Then select File ⇨ New ⇨ Mail Message, and write a mail message to another account on the system (see Figure 9-20).

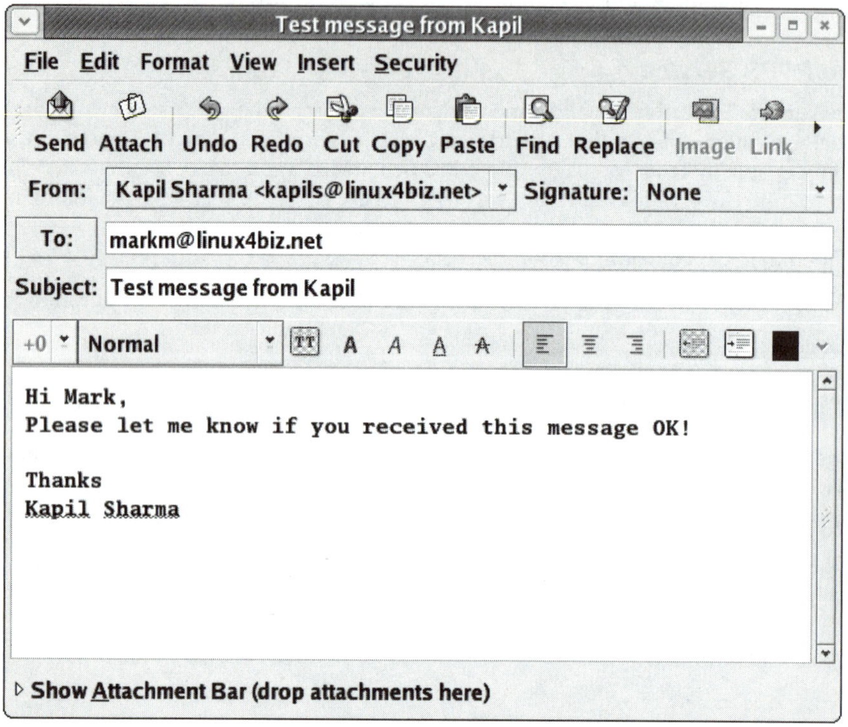

Figure 9-20

Click the Send button to send the message. You may be asked to provide your POP password; use the account's system password.

Receiving Mails

Now log out, and log in again as the user to whom you've just sent the message (markm, in this example). Launch the Evolution application again for this user, and click the Send/Receive button at the top of the Evolution window. This button launches a process that contacts the mail server and does two things:

- It queries the mail server for any new e-mail messages that have been sent to this account.
- It passes any newly composed mail messages to the mail server, so they can be sent on to the intended recipients.

You'll be asked to provide your POP password; use the account's system password. (If you have problems here, go back and check that the ipop3 service is enabled.) Then you'll see a Send & Receive Mail dialog box.

Allow the Send mail process to complete (as shown by the progress bar in the figure), and then click Cancel All to cancel the remaining jobs. In the Inbox section of your Evolution window, you should now see the test message that was sent here from the first account, as shown in Figure 9-21.

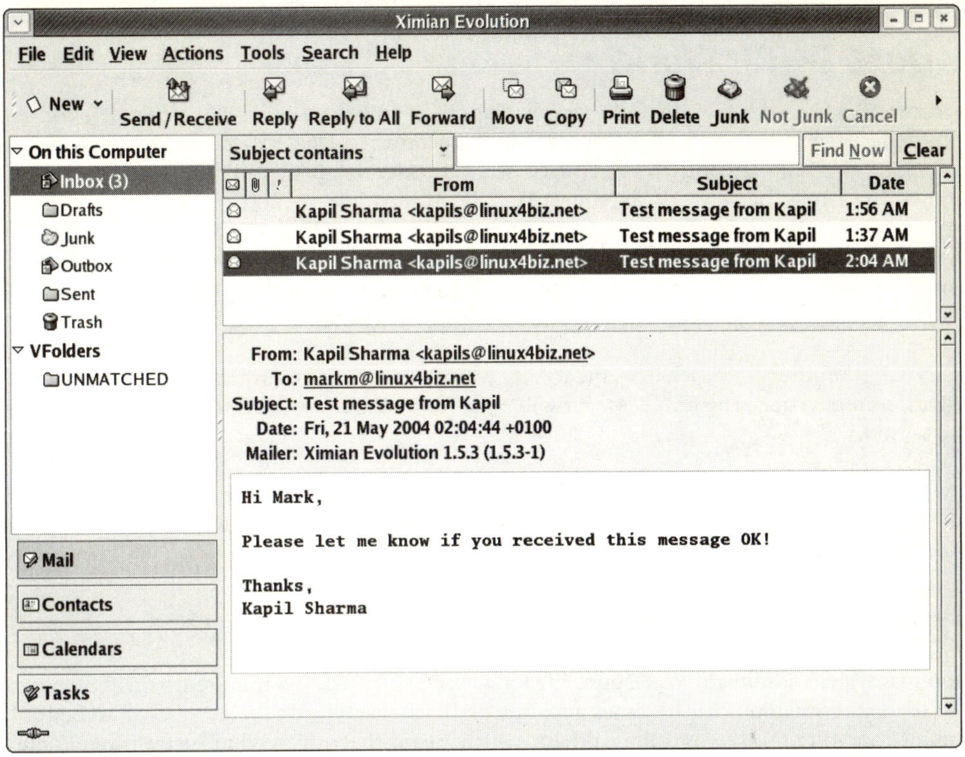

Figure 9-21

Feel free to experiment further with this, adding more mailbox addresses and hooking the Evolution application up to the Internet. You can also send and receive mail from Windows machines, using Microsoft Outlook. The same configuration settings should also suffice for Outlook; you'll need to set the server type to SMTP, which is the only option in Outlook for sending e-mails.

Setting Up a DHCP Server

You've already come across the Dynamic Host Configuration Protocol (DHCP), during the installation process in Chapter 1 in the "Setting the Network Parameters" section. In that step you are asked to choose between two options:

- You can specify the TCP/IP settings (IP address, netmask, default gateway, and DNS servers) explicitly.
- You can allow a DHCP server to dictate those settings.

This is what DHCP is all about. DHCP is a network protocol, whose purpose is to assign TCP/IP settings to client machines. By configuring a client machine to use DHCP, you're telling it that it must contact a DHCP server (on the network), and get its TCP/IP settings (IP address, netmask, default gateway, DNS servers) from there.

How Does DHCP Work?

The concept of DCHP is actually quite simple. Suppose you have a client machine that is configured to get its TCP/IP settings from a DHCP server—that machine is a *DHCP client*. At the time when the DHCP client requires a TCP/IP configuration (discussed in greater detail later in this section), it sends a broadcast message across the network, to request TCP/IP address information.

Elsewhere on the network, the DHCP server receives this request. It examines its IP pool (a pool of IP addresses that it is allowed to lend out to clients), and assigns one of these IP addresses to the client for a defined *lease* period. It sends this IP address, and other network configuration information, to the client.

The DHCP *client* then acknowledges the receipt of the network configuration information and sets up its network configuration. The DHCP server will not allocate the same IP address to other clients within the lease period.

So, when does a DCHP client need to request a TCP/IP configuration? The most obvious scenario is when the client is booting up and joining the network; it might also do so when its lease on the existing IP address expires, and it needs to ask for a new one.

The Benefits of DHCP

If you're a system administrator responsible for a network containing hundreds of computers, manual TCP/IP management quickly becomes a nightmare. Each machine on the network must be configured manually, and differently from all the others, which means that you need to keep a careful note of the TCP/IP configuration of each machine. The potential for error and time-consuming manual configuration tasks is great.

Implementing a DHCP server provides relief from this burden. It allows you to configure all client machines in exactly the same way—you just tell them all to use the DHCP server. It's also much more reliable than manual TCP/IP management because the DHCP server is designed to manage its IP pool and the lease periods so that you never get two machines using the same IP address at the same time.

In addition, a DHCP server provides a single central control for all TCP/IP resources. It allows IP addresses to be tracked and reserved. Critically, it facilitates performing cross-network changes—for example, if you need to change your gateway, or the range of allowed IP addresses, you can handle this smoothly and easily by updating *just* the DHCP central server configuration.

DHCP also provides the flexibility for mobile users with laptops who need to work in different offices. If a DHCP server controls each office's TCP/IP allocations, simply configure the laptop to request its TCP/IP settings from a DHCP server. Then, whenever you plug into any office network, your laptop will automatically ask the local DHCP server to serve up the appropriate network settings to allow you to get working.

The following section looks at how to set up a Linux machine as a DHCP server.

Installing the DHCP Server Packages

As you've probably already gathered, you need only one DHCP server per network. If you decide that you need a DHCP server, a Fedora 2 machine will suit your purposes. To configure your machine as a DHCP server, you need to install the appropriate package; you can do that via the RPM GUI.

To do this, launch the RPM GUI (Main Menu ➪ System Settings ➪ Add/Remove Applications); when the dialog box appears, select the Network Servers package group (which you'll find under the Servers category). Click the Details button to view the package details (see Figure 9-22).

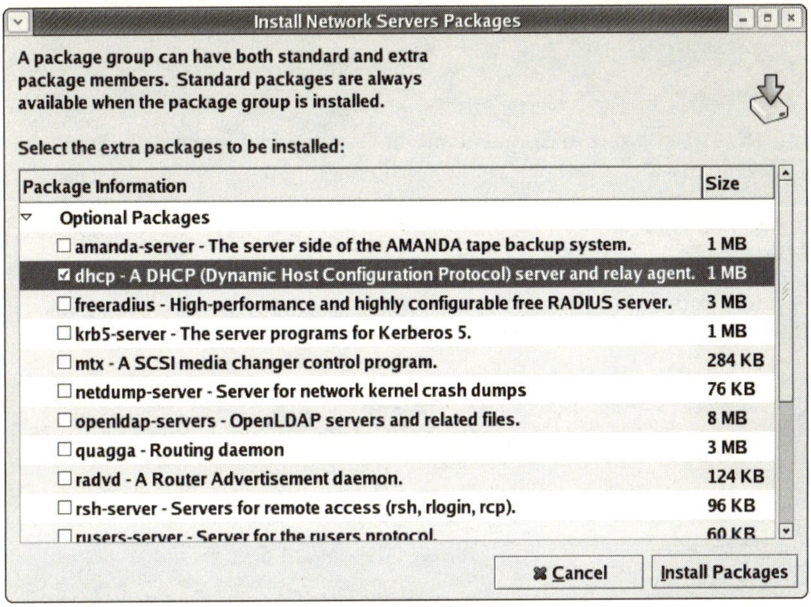

Figure 9-22

The package you need here is the one called dhcp—the others are not important for the purposes of installing a DHCP server (although you won't want to deselect them unless you're sure you're not using them for something else).

When you've selected dhcp, click Install Packages to start the installation. As usual, you'll need the Fedora 2 distribution CDs to complete the installation.

Configuring the DHCP Server

We will set up a simple DHCP configuration to provide clients with network information. The DHCP server can be configured using the default configuration file `/etc/dhcpd.conf`.

The DHCP server package comes with a sample dhcpd configuration file called `dhcpd.conf.sample`. Use this file as a starting point for the DHCP configuration. Make a backup of your existing `dhcpd.conf` file, and then copy the sample file in its place:

```
# cp /etc/dhcpd.conf /etc/dhcpd.conf.backup
# cp /usr/share/doc/dhcp-3.0.1rc12/dhcpd.conf.sample /etc/dhcpd.conf
```

Now open the `/etc/dhcpd.conf` file, using `gedit` or another text editor, and we'll edit it so it contains all the required options. A simple dhcp configuration file looks like this:

```
ddns-update-style interim;
ignore client-updates;
subnet 192.168.0.0 netmask 255.255.255.0 {
        option routers                  192.168.0.1;
        option subnet-mask              255.255.255.0;
        option domain-name              "linux4biz.net";
        option domain-name-servers      192.168.0.1;
        range dynamic-bootp             192.168.0.128 192.168.0.254;
        default-lease-time              21600;
        max-lease-time                  43200;
}
```

You can use hash (`#`) characters to comment out the lines you don't need, or simply delete them to keep the file tidy. Have a look at the settings in this example:

- The first two lines of the configuration file instruct the DHCP server not to accept dynamic DNS updates.
- The next line defines a subnet and netmask that are used to supply the DHCP information. After that, all the options are defined, as you can see in the following table.

Option	Description
`routers`	Specifies the default gateway.
`subnet-mask`	Specifies the default netmask.
`domain-name`	Specifies the default domain name.
`domain-name-servers`	Specifies the name servers for the network.
`range dynamic-bootp`	Specifies the range of IP addresses that the DHCP server is allowed to allocate to clients. In our example, all allocated IP addresses will lie in the range 192.168.0.128 to 192.168.0.254.
`default-lease-time`	Defines the default lease time, after which the client's DHCP configuration will expire, and the client must request a new DHCP configuration from the DHCP server. In this example, the DHCP lease will expire after six hours, unless the client asks for a specific time frame.
`max-lease-time`	Defines the *maximum* lease allowed to the client.

There are other options in the sample configuration file, `/usr/share/doc/dhcp-3.0.1rc12/dhcpd.conf.sample`*, that we won't discuss here. There's more about these options at the dhcpd.conf man page.*

The DHCP Lease Database

How does the DHCP server keep track of the IP addresses it has leased out? In Red Hat Linux 9 systems, this information is stored in the database file `/var/lib/dhcp/dhcpd.leases`. The data stored here includes a client identifier used by the client that requested the lease, the time and date of both the start and end of the lease, and the address of the Ethernet network interface card (NIC) that was used to retrieve the lease.

> **DHCP can recognize a server by the address of its Ethernet network interface card, which is unique. This address is also known as the *Media Access Control (MAC) address*.**

The DHCP server stores lease information for each recently assigned IP address automatically in the lease database, and you should not modify it by hand.

Starting the dhcpd Service

You can start the dhcpd service in the usual ways—using the Service Configuration GUI Tool, or the `/etc/rc.d/init.d/dhcpd` command line script.

In the Service Control GUI Tool (Main Menu ➪ System Settings ➪ Server Settings ➪ Services), the service you're interested in is called dhcpd (see Figure 9-23).

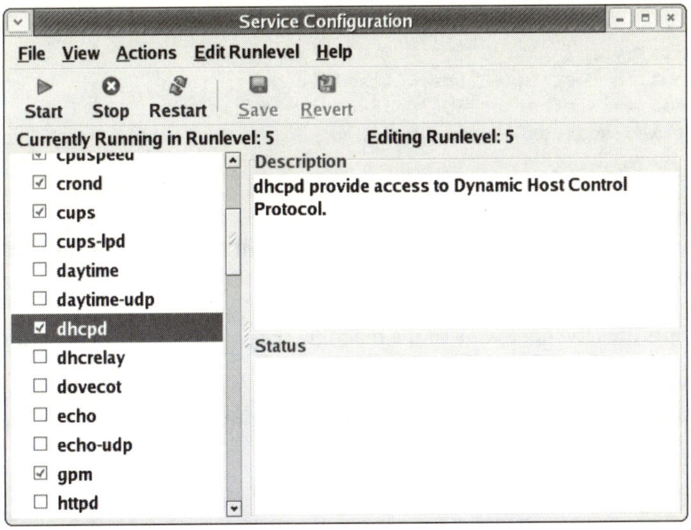

Figure 9-23

It's typical to select the check box so that the service starts automatically on startup. Don't forget to save your new settings using File ➪ Save Changes.

Alternatively, you can use the `service` command to control the `dhcpd` script:

```
# service dhcpd
Usage: /etc/init.d/dhcpd {start|stop|restart|condrestart|status}
# service dhcpd start
Starting dhcpd:                                             [OK]
```

Assigning Static IP Address Using DHCP

It's not always the best thing to have DHCP assign IP addresses dynamically. If you had a production server, such as a Web server or e-mail server, whose IP address changed every time its lease expired, it would be impossible for other machines on the network to find them. For servers and other machines like this, there are two alternatives:

- You can configure the machine with its own static IP address and TCP/IP information.
- Alternatively, you can configure the DHCP server to reserve fixed IP addresses for specific servers.

The second of these options is generally preferable because it means it's still easy to make global network configurations (such as changing the DNS server) in a single location (the DHCP server configuration).

To allocate a static IP address to a production server, you can add a `host` clause to the `/etc/dhcpd.conf`, as shown:

```
host emailserver {
        option host-name "test.linux4biz.net";
        hardware ethernet 00-20-18-8B-3F-9E;
        fixed-address 192.168.0.10;
}
```

Here, the first line defines the declaration for a single computer: `host` is a configuration option, and `emailserver` is a reference name for the computer that will be allocated a static IP address. You can use any reference name here, usually a name that reflects the purpose of the machine in question.

The second line specifies the hostname of the machine (`test.linux4biz.net`), and the third line defines the Ethernet hardware address.

You can find the Ethernet hardware address of a Linux machine by executing the following command on that machine:

```
$ /sbin/ifconfig
```

Check the first line of output; it should look something like this:

```
eth0      Link encap:Ethernet  HWaddr 00:D0:B7:0A:E7:41
```

You can find the Ethernet hardware address on a Windows machine by executing this command at the command prompt:

```
> ipconfig /all
```

In this case, search for the line that starts with the string `Physical Address`, under your Ethernet card description:

```
Physical Address. . . . . . . . . : 00-20-18-8B-3F-9E
```

The fourth line defines the static IP address to be assigned to the server whose hardware Ethernet address matches the one given.

It is recommended that you back up the `/etc/dhcpd.conf` file when you've finished your initial configuration, and keep it safe—just in case it gets corrupted or changed accidentally.

Installing and Configuring a DHCP Client

We've talked about how to configure the DHCP server, but what about the DHCP client? A default DHCP client software is installed on all Fedora 2 installations, and if you've configured your Linux machine to be a DHCP client, it's using that DHCP client program now.

If you want to configure a Linux machine to be a DHCP client, you can set this configuration either at installation or subsequently via the Network Configuration Tool. To launch the Network Configuration Tool, select Main Menu ➪ System Settings ➪ Network, or type the following command at the command line:

```
$ system-config-network
```

Under the Devices tab, select the Ethernet device and click Edit. Make sure the Activate device when computer starts option is enabled, and select the Automatically obtain IP address settings with dhcp option (see Figure 9-24).

Click OK when you're finished, and then Apply to apply the changes. The changes will take effect from the next reboot.

Configuring a Windows 2000 Machine to Use a DHCP Server

If you've got a Windows 2000 machine (for example, a Win2K laptop that you use both at home and at work), here's how to configure it to get its network settings from a DHCP server:

1. Click Start ➪ Settings ➪ Control Panel to open the Control Panel window.
2. Double-click Network and Dial-up Connections and then Local Area Connection.
3. Click the Properties button. In the resulting Local Area Connection Properties dialog box, highlight Internet Protocol (TCP/IP), and click Properties.
4. In the resulting Internet Protocol (TCP/IP) Properties dialog box, select Obtain an IP Address automatically and Obtain DNS server address automatically.
5. Click OK to confirm the changes, and then OK again to implement the changes. At this point, the DHCP client program will try to get address information from the DHCP server.

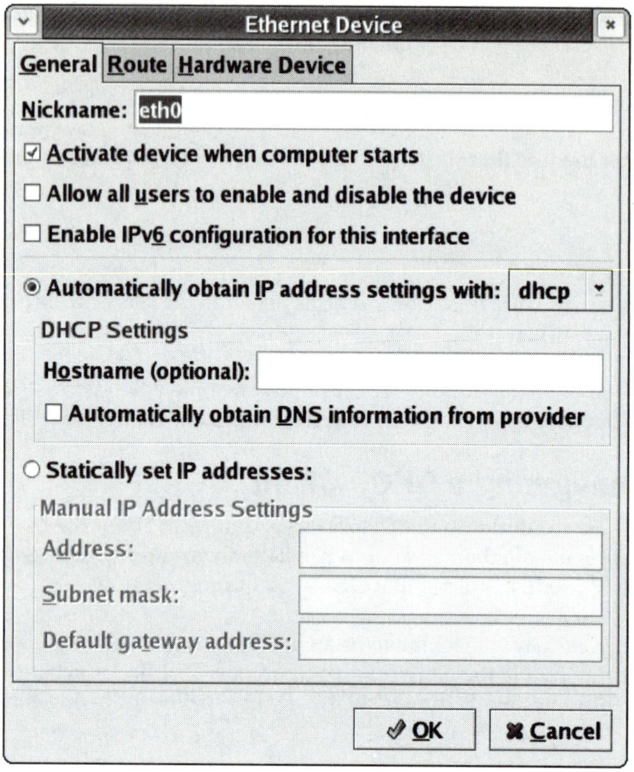

Figure 9-24

If you like, you can check the new IP address allocated by the DHCP server by executing the `ipconfig /all` command at the command prompt:

```
C:\>ipconfig /all
Windows 2000 IP Configuration
  Host Name . . . . . . . . . . . : my-win2k-laptop
  Primary DNS Suffix  . . . . . . :
  Node Type . . . . . . . . . . . : Hybrid
  IP Routing Enabled. . . . . . . : No
  WINS Proxy Enabled. . . . . . . : No
  DNS Suffix Search List. . . . . : linux4biz.net
Ethernet adapter Local Area Connection:
  Connection-specific DNS Suffix: linux4biz.net
  Description . . . . . . . . . . : Xircom CreditCard Ethernet 10/100 + Modem 56
  Physical Address. . . . . . . . : 00-80-C7-8B-C2-E3
  DHCP Enabled. . . . . . . . . . : Yes
  Autoconfiguration Enabled . . . : Yes
  IP Address. . . . . . . . . . . : 192.168.0.129
  Subnet Mask . . . . . . . . . . : 255.255.255.0
  Default Gateway . . . . . . . . : 192.168.0.1
  DHCP Server . . . . . . . . . . : 192.168.0.99
  DNS Servers . . . . . . . . . . : 192.168.0.1
  Lease Obtained. . . . . . . . . : 19 February 2003 09:01:21
  Lease Expires . . . . . . . . . : 22 February 2003 09:01:21
```

This allows you to see the TCP/IP information that the Windows DHCP client has acquired from the DHCP server. In the preceding output, the `DHCP Enabled` property is set to `Yes`, indicating that the Windows client machine is configured to get IP information from a DHCP server. The physical address of this machine (its MAC address, taken from its Ethernet card) is `00-80-C7-8B-C2-E3`; the DHCP server has leased the IP address `192.168.0.129` to the machine, and the lease will expire three days from when it was obtained.

Summary

This chapter covered six common services. It's unlikely that you'll need them all in a home computing environment, and it's certainly unlikely that you'll ever install all of these services onto a single machine, except to experiment with them. Most medium-size office environments will have at least some of these services, and in a production situation, you would often assign at least one dedicated machine to any of these services.

There are so many configuration options for all these services that we can't possibly cover them all here. There is a mass of useful information on the Web, both in formal documentation and on newsgroups, and you have the man pages, too. Here are just a few sites that provide more documentation and developments on some of the services discussed here:

- `www.sendmail.org`: the official sendmail Web site
- `fedora.redhat.com`: the official site for Fedora Linux
- `www.samba.org`: The official Web site for SAMBA
- `www.rfc-editor.org`: A searchable collection of all RFCs
- `www.isc.org/products/DHCP/`: The official site for DHCP
- `www.tldp.org/`: The Linux documentation Project site
- `www.linux4biz.net/writing.html`: Contains useful articles on Linux
- `www.linuxsecurity.com/`: A security news site for Linux

The next chapter delves further into systems security by looking at system and network security policies, software tools to detect and minimize the security threats, and virtual private networks (VPN).

Exercises

To build your skills even further, here is an exercise you can use to test yourself. The answers are provided in Appendix A, but keep in mind there is always more than one way to accomplish a given task, so if you choose to do things a different way and the results display the way you want, more power to you.

1. What do LAN, WAN, TCP/IP, PPP, and ISDN stand for?
2. Determine a Public Class C IP address and specify it with netmask.
3. Determine various IP ranges available to be used as Private IP addresses for your LAN.

4. Write down the steps to change the Apache 2 Web server port number from 80 to 81, on which Apache will listen for incoming requests.
5. Check the Apache Web server configuration file (`httpd.conf`) for syntax errors.
6. Restart the Apache Web server without affecting any connected clients.
7. Using the RPM command-line interface, determine the FTP server currently installed on your system.
8. Change the FTP greeting banner on your `vsftpd` server and test it.
9. Check the print queue using the command line utilities.
10. Check the Samba configuration file (`/etc/samba/smb.conf`) for correctness.
11. Check the mail queue on your Mail server.
12. What is the location of the DHCP server configuration file?

10

Security

Computer security is a vast topic, and detailed coverage is beyond the scope of this book. However, we will show you that, with a little planning and a few basic tools, you can secure your Fedora Core 2 Linux system against the most likely threats. Take the time to understand the basic principles of computer security, so you can be confident that your system is not vulnerable to accidental damage or malicious attack.

What Is Computer Security?

In a nutshell, computer security is about the protection of computing assets against threats such as theft, accidental loss, unauthorized access by a third party, and "denial of service" (whereby legitimate users of computing assets are prevented from using them). Computing assets include the following:

- Computer hardware
- Information stored on a computer (personal details, financial information, customer information, intellectual property, and so on)
- CPU, memory, storage, and network resources
- Computing services (Web sites, FTP, and print servers)

The concepts involved in computer security are straightforward. You need to identify what you want to protect and the threats you want to protect them from, figure out how much effort to put into your protection schemes, and, once you've implemented them, regularly test the effectiveness of your protection. The details of how this is done can get very technical, and really serious security requirements (such as government, banks, airlines, and so on) need highly advanced skills and equipment to address them. However, where the security requirements are more modest, such as those for the normal home or business user, they are within reach of the competent beginner.

The following sections show you how to enhance the security of your Fedora Core 2 Linux system.

Identifying What Is Valuable

The first step in planning the security of your Fedora Core 2 Linux system is to identify what you have on that system that is of value to you. You'll probably want to include the computer hardware itself (even though Fedora Core 2 Linux will happily run on machines considered by others to be nothing more than scrap), but the value of the information stored on the system is a little less clear.

To help you draw up a list, consider how much effort it would take to re-create information if it was lost, and what the impact would be if the information fell into the hands of an unauthorized person, possibly with malicious intent. Think about the confidentiality of your data.

Consider also the impact of unauthorized changes to your data; if you run a business, maybe your Web site gets hacked and displays prices twice that of your competitors, or perhaps someone does a "search and replace" operation on your homework essay and you don't check it before sending it in. Think about the integrity of your data.

Even if your data is secure, and hasn't been modified by unauthorized people, you and other authorized users still need to be able to access it. The only way of guaranteeing that your company's Web site won't get hacked is to unplug the computers on which it runs. So, availability of your data is important, too.

In some environments, performance of computer systems is critical. Transaction-processing systems need to meet expected response times for users; number-crunching systems need to get their calculations done in an acceptable time; Web servers need to respond quickly to requests from Web browsers. If your system has to perform well, but is subject to, or even taking part in, a denial-of-service attack, performance may be unacceptably low, so you'd better add performance to your list of things you want to protect.

Your list of valuable things that you want to protect will probably include personal information, such as your e-mail address book, financial information, and any confidential information belonging to third parties that you have an obligation to protect. In determining the value of something, it is helpful to try and work out how much time and effort would be required to re-create it. If, for example, your Fedora Core 2 Linux system was badly compromised, you might need to re-install everything from trusted CD-ROMs, and then validate application data as it is restored from backups.

Potential Threats

Now you've identified what you've got that's valuable; the next step in planning your system security is to identify the potential threats.

Despite what you may read in the press about hackers, the most common causes of data loss are *operator error* ("finger trouble") and *hardware failure*. Nevertheless, you should still consider unauthorized access, either locally or, if the machine is connected to some sort of network (LAN or the Internet), remotely, as another potential threat.

Hacking

A hacker typically starts his or her activities by attempting to connect to your system using various TCP port numbers to try and find out where your system is vulnerable. This process is known as *probing*. Of course, if the hacker is somewhere out there on the Internet, he can probe your system only when you are connected, which is why people with "always on" Internet connections, such as *x*DSL ("broadband"), need to pay particular attention to security. A secure system will simply ignore incoming probes so the potential hacker has no indication that there is anything using the IP address he picked to probe. (Note that not all probes indicate a threat—some ISPs also probe ports on their customers' systems.)

If your system does respond to a hacker's probes, the hacker's next step will be to identify what software is listening on the ports (for example, a Web server, FTP server, telnet, and so on) and try to exploit any security vulnerabilities in those programs. If the hacker is successful, he will be able to gain root access to your system, and may install modified versions of standard software that will allow him back in, or to use your system to launch attacks on other systems. Because vulnerabilities in software are found and fixed on a frequent basis, it is important to check regularly for known problems with any of the software you are running and obtain updates as soon as they become available. Fortunately, Fedora Core 2 makes this extremely easy through the Red Hat Network and the `up2date` command. We'll look at this later in the chapter.

Transferring Data

Transferring information over a network also opens up the possibility of eavesdropping—someone other than the intended recipient may intercept the information en route.

Physical Threats

Theft of computer equipment can be a big problem, especially for laptop users, and certain areas may suffer from environmental problems, such as flooding, that can damage computer equipment.

So, in summary your list of possible threats could look something like this:

- Operator error
- Hardware failure (particularly disk drives)
- Theft of equipment
- Unauthorized local access
- Unauthorized remote access
- Denial-of-service (DoS) attack
- Eavesdropping of network communications
- Damage due to environmental conditions

Worms, Viruses, and Trojans

Worms and viruses are examples of malicious code that an attacker may try to install on your system, either directly, or indirectly from a system that she has already compromised. The behavior of these programs varies from the relatively benign to serious security breaches. Worms can disrupt networks by overloading them as they replicate. Viruses can also do this, and may have a payload that causes the infected system to relay spam mail or participate in distributed denial-of-service attacks on high-profile Web sites. Trojans appear to be legitimate programs, but offer the attacker a "back-door" way to access the infected system bypassing normal security controls.

In all cases, infection is undesirable, and can be prevented by vigilant system administration—installing code and programs obtained from trusted sources only, limiting the open network ports to the minimum required for a server to do its job, and monitoring the server for unexpected network activity (for example, listening on unexpected network ports and high network traffic to unexpected Internet sites).

Countering the Threats

This section explores some of the options available to you to counter the threats already discussed.

Hardware

First, let's consider what you can do with the computer hardware to make your system more secure.

Physical Security of the Hardware

Physical security is really just a matter of common sense. Keep computer equipment, especially portable equipment such as laptops, secure. If the computer BIOS has the facility to configure a power-on password, use it. This at least will make it harder for someone to access your machine if it is stolen.

If you are unlucky enough to have your computer stolen, you have to rely on your backups to get back the information that you lost. You do have backups, don't you? You have tested them, haven't you?

The idea behind backing up your system is to allow you to *rebuild* it in case of some catastrophic event. This means that someone else can also build a copy of your system if they can get hold of your backups, so take care of the physical security of your backup media, too.

Hardware Failure

Pay attention to the environmental conditions that your computer is working in. Computers don't like to get hot, and excessive temperature can cause premature failure of heat-sensitive components, especially hard disk drives. There are ways of preventing the failure of a disk drive from causing loss of data, and these techniques rely on keeping the information on more than one physical disk.

The term *Redundant Array of Independent Disks (RAID)* is widely used to describe these solutions, and the *RAID level*, a combination of digits and sometimes letters, indicates how the information is stored on multiple disks.

RAID can be implemented in hardware (typically in the hard disk adapter) or in software. If you're interested in RAID, have a look at the Linux-ATA-RAID HOWTO and the Software-RAID HOWTO on your system's documentation resources, or online.

Common RAID levels are described in the table that follows.

RAID Level	Data Positioning
0	Data is broken up into equal size chunks (64Kb and 128Kb are common), and chunks are written to every disk in the array in turn (with four disks in the array, the first, fifth, ninth, . . ., chunks of data are written to the first disk; the second, sixth and, tenth to the second disk; and so on). This pattern of data placement is called "striping," and the size of each chunk of data is called the stripe width. This gives the best performance, but worst availability, because failure of any disk will result in the loss of some data.
1	Data is copied onto pairs of disks (mirrored). Good performance and availability, but it uses twice as much disk space.
5	Data is striped across multiple disks, and protected by parity information that is also striped across the disks. Good performance for reading, but writing can be slowed by the need to update parity information. Requires extra disk capacity to store the parity information.
7	Not really RAID at all, RAID 7 is also known as JBOD (Just a Bunch Of Disks). Here the information is not configured according to RAID, and your multiple disks are simply configured as one larger logical drive. It offers no fault tolerance advantages over simply using several disks individually.
10 (or 0+1)	Data is striped across multiple pairs of disks. Combines performance of RAID 0 with availability of RAID 1.

Whether RAID is suitable for you depends on how valuable you consider your information to be—a decision that only you can make. Even if you do go for a hardware or software RAID solution for your Fedora Core 2 Linux system, please don't make the mistake of thinking that you don't need to make regular backups. Even if you set up the most extreme combination of hardware and software RAID (using software RAID to mirror data between two hardware RAID arrays, giving you effectively four copies of the data on four separate physical hard disks), the `rm` command can still irreversibly delete all four copies in a fraction of a second.

Local Security

So, you've sorted out the physical security of your Fedora Core 2 system. You've enabled the BIOS password so that only those who know it can start the machine up in the first place, and you've taken care with the physical location so it won't get stolen and the disk drives will stay nice and cool. Should you be unlucky enough to suffer a disk drive failure, you're taking, and testing, regular backups so you're confident you can recover any lost information. What's next?

You'll recall from the previous section, "Potential Threats," that operator error was high on the list of potential threats. Computers have a nasty habit of doing exactly what you *tell* them to do, and not what you *want* them to do. So that this doesn't cause you too many problems, the trick is always to work with the lowest level of authority that you need to perform a particular task. Usually, this is *not* the root account.

Here's a little hypothetical example to demonstrate the potential pitfalls of using the root account for everyday tasks.

Suppose you need to maintain the contents of a directory called /home/foo/logs by deleting files that are more than 14 days old. You could write a simple script to do this:

```
#!/bin/bash
LOGDIR="/home/foo/logs"
cd $LGODIR
find . -mtime +14 -exec ls \{\} \;  # Use "ls" for testing, change to "rm" later
```

Unfortunately, there's a typo in the script (the fourth line should say cd $LOGDIR); this means that when the cd command is run, its argument is blank (because the misspelled variable $LGODIR is not defined). The cd command makes the current working directory the $HOME directory, not /home/foo/logs as you want. The find command then finds all the files below your $HOME directory (the current working directory) older than 14 days and deletes them. (Well, it will just list them at the moment—at least the test version of the script does not do anything dangerous). That's a pain if you're logged on as an ordinary user, but if you're logged on as root, this could well delete a lot of critical configuration information. (At least root's home directory on Fedora Core 2 Linux defaults to /root, which is a small mercy—on some other versions of UNIX, the default home directory for root is /, so running this flawed script on one of those could well wipe out the entire operating system.)

Passwords

The password that you use to authenticate yourself to the operating system when you log in is the only way you have of proving your identity, and thus keeping an intruder out. Your password is never stored on the Linux system (the operating system won't do it). Instead, a non-reversible mathematical function called a *hash* is used to combine your password with a random value (called the *salt*), and the hashed password is stored by the system. When you try to log in, the password you type is once again hashed with the same salt, and the result is compared to the one stored when the password was originally set. If the values are the same, it's fairly safe to assume that the password you typed is the same as the original one, and you are allowed in.

Now, you're probably thinking that someone could look at the stored hashed passwords and deduce the original passwords by reversing the hash function. However, the hash functions are chosen to make this reversal practically impossible. However, that doesn't stop someone who has access to the hashed passwords from using a program that guesses passwords to try and guess one.

Early versions of UNIX stored the hashed passwords with other user information in /etc/passwd. Because the user information needed to be accessible to everyone (so, for example, usernames could be shown in the output of ls -l), this also made the hashed passwords available to everyone. Modern versions of UNIX, including Fedora Core 2 Linux 9, avoid this problem by keeping hashed passwords in a separate file, called the *shadow password file*. On Fedora Core 2, this is /etc/shadow. Because the hashed passwords need to be accessible only to authentication programs that run with root authority, the shadow password file should be accessible only to the root user.

Choosing a Strong Password

Choosing a strong password really means to avoid weak passwords. Weak passwords are ones that can be guessed, either by humans or by password-cracking programs (that will quite happily try different permutations of words from password dictionaries for days on end without getting bored).

So, avoid passwords that can be found in a dictionary (in any language), or variations of these (for example, changing "is" to 1s, or os to 0s, or adding digits), passwords that someone who knows you may guess (name of family member or pet), or anything generated in a systematic way. Include punctuation and other symbols, and make use of the fact that Fedora Core 2 Linux 9 uses MD5 password hashes that allow passwords to be up to 15 characters long.

However, some characters shouldn't be included in passwords because they can be misinterpreted as terminal control characters and cause problems when logging in. Avoid @, #, *[backspace]*, and other control characters.

For example, here are some weak passwords:

- asdfghj (obvious keyboard pattern)
- oozyllak (pet's name spelt backwards)
- Pa55w0rd (trivial modification of a dictionary word)

These would have been strong passwords until they were published in this book:

- 14%-^^Ao-&
- Z&23vvO+%
- hjA+84ro*

However, make sure you can remember your password so you don't have to write it down. As soon as you do that, you're weakening it. A slip of paper under the keyboard is a dead giveaway.

Checking Passwords

The password-cracking programs that are useful to hackers are just as useful to you, as you can use them to identify weak passwords on your systems. Then you can get the offending users to change them before a hacker cracks them. One of the best known of these programs is simply called Crack. It requires a bit of work to build and install it, so we'll go through it step-by-step here.

Crack is a 2.5MB download. If you don't fancy downloading it, you can skip ahead to the section "Running Crack," and we'll catch up with you in a moment.

Try It Out Using the Crack Program

Before you begin setting up the Crack program, you need to make a home for it. It's best to create your own directories for programs that you build and install yourself (as opposed to installing from RPM packages) so they don't interfere with system-installed packages.

Crack doesn't require root privileges to run (but you do need to be root to get at the shadow passwords to feed Crack later on), so you'll download, configure, and build it as an ordinary, unprivileged user.

1. The first thing you'll do is create a home for Crack. Open a terminal window (Main Menu ⇨ System Tools ⇨ Terminal) and type the following commands at the prompt:

```
% cd
% pwd
% mkdir crack
```

The `cd` command on its own makes the current working directory the home directory for the user running the command. (This should be the current directory for a newly opened terminal session anyway, but we've included it here in case you're trying this out in an existing window.) The `pwd` command shows you the current working directory to confirm you're where you expect to be, and then the `mkdir` command creates a directory called `crack`. This is where you're going to install the Crack program.

2. Once you have a home for Crack, you need to get a copy of the program.

   The easiest way to download the Crack program is through the Mozilla Web browser. Start the browser, and then point it to `ftp://ftp.cert.dfn.de/pub/tools/password/Crack/`. You should be presented with a list of files in a directory. Click the file called `Crack_5.0a.tar.gz`, and when a dialog box appears asking you what you want to do, select Save to disk and click OK. Browse to the `crack` directory you've just created and click OK.

   If you have trouble connecting to the FTP site listed in the preceding paragraph, you can try `ftp://ftp.cerias.purdue.edu/pub/tools/unix/pwdutils/crack/` instead.

3. The next step is to unpack the downloaded file. The letters `.tar.gz` at the end of the file indicate that it is a tape archive (TAR) format file that has been compressed with GNU Zip. (You'll sometimes see `.tgz` at the end of a file to indicate the same thing.) You need to uncompress and "untar" the file.

   Go back to the terminal window and type the following commands:

```
% cd crack
% tar -xzvf Crack_5.0a.tar.gz
```

   The `tar` command extracts the files (`x` switch) from a compressed archive file (`z` switch) called `Crack_5.0a.tar.gz (-f Crack_5.0a.tar.gz)` and prints the filenames as they're extracted (`v` switch). Notice that the files go into directories under `c50a/` and that these directories are created as required (see Figure 10-1).

4. Now you need to make a few configuration changes to the Crack source code before it will build and run successfully on your Fedora Core 2 Linux system. First, you need to edit the Crack script. Change to the `c50a` directory and open `Crack` in the Gnome text editor by running these commands:

```
% cd c50a
% gedit Crack
```

5. A text editor window pops up. Scroll through the file to the section that says the following:

```
#
# now pick your compiler
#
```

   Fedora Core 2 Linux ships with the GNU C compiler called `gcc`, so the `gcc 2.7.2` section is what you need to use (even though you've got `gcc` version 3.2). Place `#` characters at the start of the lines for `vanilla unix cc` to turn them into comments (a process known as *commenting out* the code), and remove the same characters from the corresponding lines in the `gcc 2.7.2` section. You also need to use the `stdlib crypt()` routine, so remove the `#` from the start of the `LIBS=...` line.

   When you're finished, the modified Crack file should look like Figure 10-2.

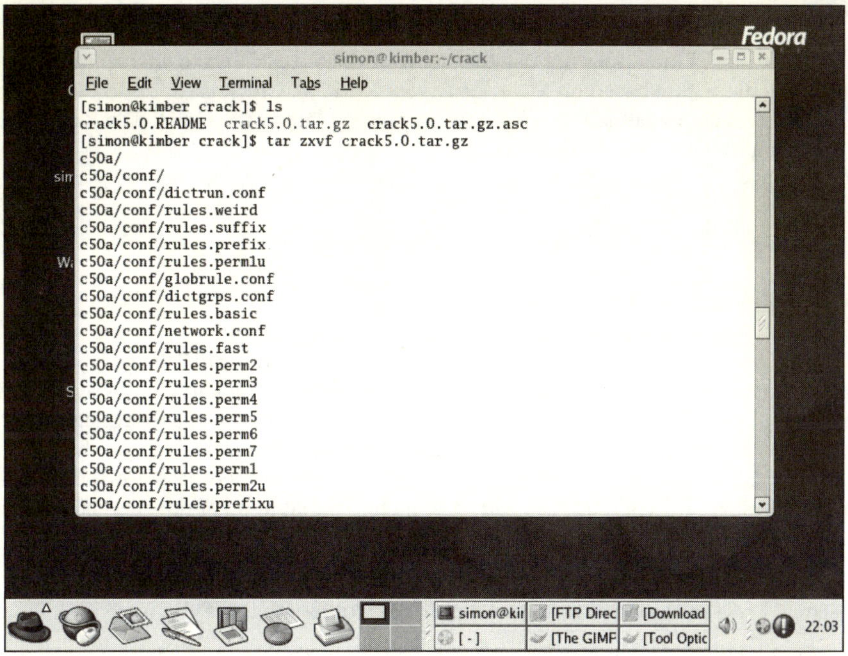

Figure 10-1

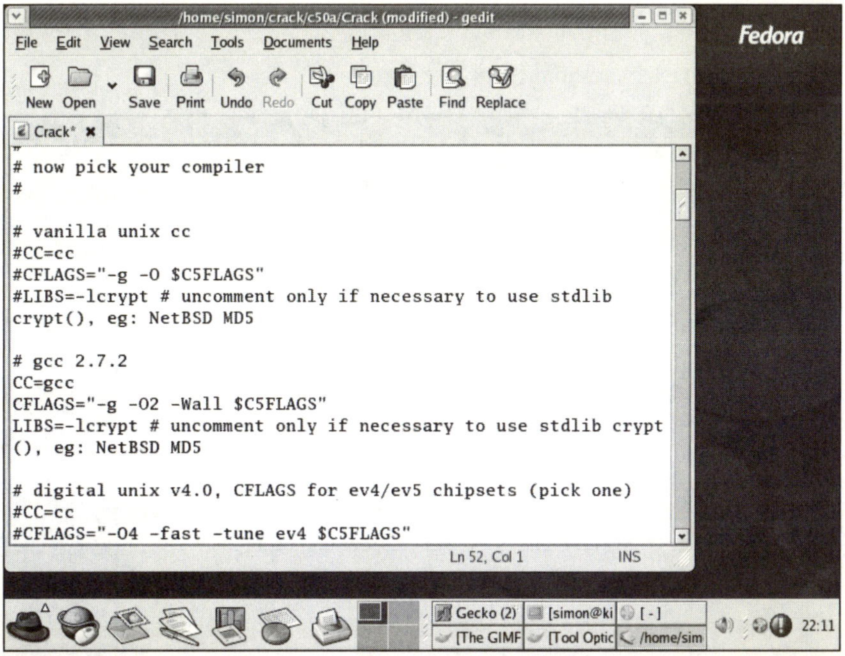

Figure 10-2

6. Save the changes and exit `gedit`.

7. Fedora Core 2 Linux does not use the standard DES algorithm to encrypt passwords, but uses a stronger algorithm based on Message Digest 5 (MD5). Crack is set up to use DES by default, so you need to change this. The following steps are given in the Crack 5.0a README file, so type them in at the command line prompt:

```
% mv src/libdes src/libdes.orig
% cd src/util
% cp elcid.c,bsd elcid.c
```

If asked to overwrite `elcid.c`*, answer* `y`.

8. There's one other small modification to make. The Fedora Core 2 9 shadow password file uses salts that contain characters that the shipped version of Crack interprets as invalid (because they're not in the list of valid characters). For the purposes of this exercise, we'll modify the routine that checks for the validity of the hashed passwords to accept these characters. The routine as shipped checks that each character in the *ciphertext* (hashed password) is in a list of allowed characters. We'll switch things around so it checks that none of the characters is in a list of disallowed characters.

   Edit the `elcid.c` source file by typing `gedit elcid.c`. Find the function `elcid_invalid(ciphertext)` and make the following three changes:

   - Change the name of the variable `validchars to invalidchars`.
   - Change the value of this variable to `!`.
   - Remove the `!` in the line starting `if (!strchr...` to reverse the sense of the logic.

   When you're finished, it should look like Figure 10-3.

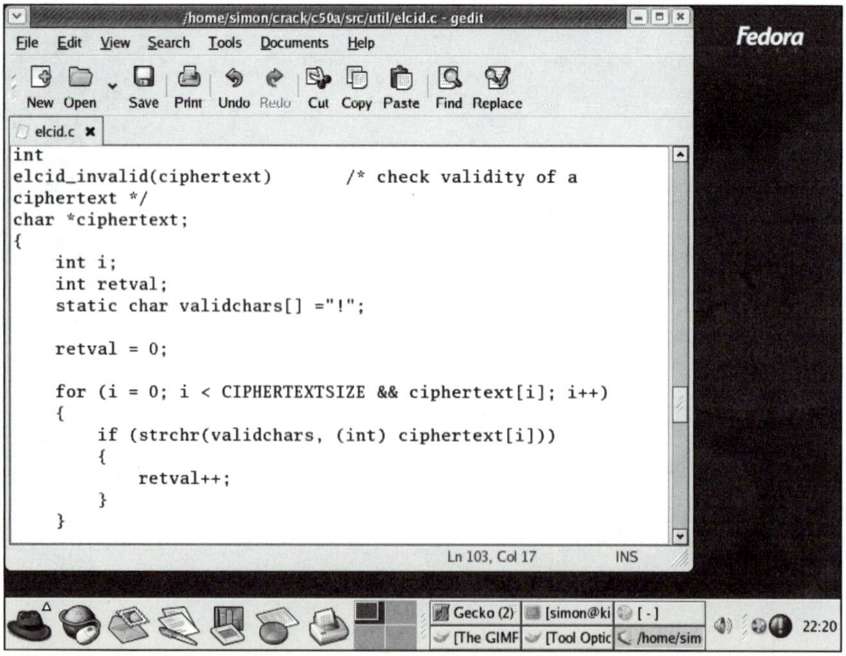

Figure 10-3

9. Save the changes and exit `gedit`.

10. Now you're ready to compile the Crack program. This is done by invoking the Crack script with the switch `-makeonly`. So, change the directory back to `$HOME/crack/c50a` and run the following command:

```
% ./Crack -makeonly
```

Note that you need to specify where to find the Crack program by giving the directory—`./` means the current directory. Unlike Microsoft Windows, Linux and other UNIX variants do not include the current directory on the search path unless explicitly told to do so. That's never a good idea for the root account, as you really want to be sure the root user is running programs in the correct system locations and not other programs lying around that happen to have the same name.

11. When Crack is invoked with the `-makeonly` option, it makes the required program files. Make sure that it finishes with the message `Crack: makeonly done`.

12. Next, you need to make the password dictionaries that Crack will use to try and guess the passwords on your system. Do this by running `./Crack -makedict`.

13. Again, make sure that this finishes with the message `Crack: makedict done`.

14. Before you can try out your newly built Crack program, you need to get it some passwords to work on. The information Crack requires is held on Fedora Core 2 Linux systems in `/etc/passwd` and `/etc/shadow`, and these need merging into a single file. Fortunately, there's a utility provided with Crack that will do just that for you.

15. Note that you must be root to read `/etc/shadow`, and because the merged file contains information useful to a potential hacker (the encrypted passwords from the shadow password file), you need to make sure that it too has restricted access. The best way to do this is to create an empty file with the correct permissions (by setting your umask), and then append the sensitive data to the file. (You could create the file with default permissions and then tighten them up, but there is a chance that someone could open the file before you've changed the permissions.) You'll change the ownership of the file back to the user under which you want to run Crack to avoid having to do that as root.

16. So, run the following commands to create the merged file that is suitable for Crack to work on:

```
% su root
# umask 077
# touch passwords.dat
# scripts/shadmrg.sv > passwords.dat
# chown user1 passwords.dat
# ls -l passwords.dat
# exit
```

17. All you have to do now is run the following command to start Crack guessing at the passwords your users have set to see if there are any weak ones:

```
% ./Crack passwords.dat
```

18. When you see the word `Done`, it doesn't mean that Crack has finished guessing passwords. (If passwords could be guessed that quickly, we might as well not bother with them at all!) What it does mean is that Crack has started a background process running that will spend the next

hours, or even days, guessing the passwords in the `passwords.dat` file and logging any matches that it finds. Use the following command to find the background process:

```
% ps -ef | grep crack
```

If you want to stop the background Crack process, the correct way to do this is to run the following:

```
$HOME/crack/c50a/scripts/plaster.
```

How do you find out how Crack is doing? Simply run the `Reporter` script that is in the same directory as the Crack program. To find out any passwords that have been guessed, type the following command in the command line window:

```
% ./Reporter -quiet
```

If you leave off the `-quiet` switch, you'll get some warning messages about locked accounts and accounts where there is no valid password. Expect several of these to show up, because accounts used for running system services such as printing and Web serving (such as `lpd` and `apache`) will normally be configured in this way to prevent anyone from logging in as those users.

A final word of warning when using Crack or any other password-cracking program: Make sure that you are authorized to do this by the appropriate person, preferably in writing.

Encryption and Verification

Encryption is the name given to the process of hiding the meaning of a piece of information by scrambling its content in some way to prevent unauthorized access to that information. Legitimate users of the encrypted information know how to unscramble it and recover its original form. Encryption is extremely useful for sending sensitive information across an insecure link (for example, Internet e-mail), and if you have used any secure Web sites (for example, online shops, Internet banking, and so on), you have already been using encryption that has been managed by your Web browser.

Verification is related to encryption. This is the process by which the recipient of some information can verify that the source of the information really is who they claim to be, and that the information has not been tampered with. (The information itself may or may not be encrypted). This is useful, too, where the recipient needs to be able to detect forged information (such as when downloading critical code updates from a Web site).

As is so often the case with security matters, a few words of caution are necessary. Encryption technology can be used for protecting a whole spectrum of information, from Granny's secret apple pie recipe to information that has a serious impact on national security. Different governments have different views on the relative importance of allowing individuals to use encryption to protect information and allowing law enforcement agencies access to the same information in detecting and preventing crime. It is up to you to find out whether your intended use of encryption is permitted, and whether there are any restrictions (for example, key length or key escrow requirements) that you must observe.

GNU Privacy Guard

We will look at using GNU Privacy Guard (GPG) to provide encryption and verification (or "signing") tools. You can find more comprehensive information about GPG at `www.gnupg.org`.

You will need to install the `gnupg` RPM; this is part of the Fedora Core 2 installation, so you should find the RPM on your install media if you need to install it.

Public Key Cryptography

GPG is based on public-key cryptography. Central to this technology is the creation of pairs of very large numbers, called *keys*. One key is kept secret; this is the private key. The other key is distributed to anyone who wants to send you information securely, or wants to verify that the information you are sending them is indeed from you and has not been tampered with. This second key is the public key.

When you want to send sensitive information to someone, you can encrypt it with their public key and send the encrypted version. Only someone who has the corresponding private key to the public key used to encrypt the information will be able to decrypt the encrypted information and recover the original contents. Similarly, if someone wants to send you some sensitive information, he or she can encrypt it with your public key and send it across an insecure channel, knowing that only someone with access to your private key could decrypt the encrypted information.

If the information is not sensitive, but you want to allow other people to verify that the information came from you and has not been tampered with, you can sign the information using your private key. Users of that information can verify the message using your public key and confirm that a) the information has not been tampered with, and b) it must have come from someone with access to your private key.

The very clever mathematics behind public key cryptography ensures that it is virtually impossible to break the encryption or signing schemes, but there are still weak points. There is the security of the private keys; if someone is able to get hold of your private key, then he will be able to decrypt information intended for your eyes only, and he will be able send out information that appears to come from you. The second weak spot is with the handling of public keys. If someone is able to convince you that her public key is really from someone else, then she will be able to read sensitive information that you have encrypted using the bogus public key and expect only the intended recipient to be able to access.

The designers of GPG have implemented safeguards to protect against both of these possibilities; your private key is protected by a *passphrase* (more than a password), and short signatures can be generated from public keys that can be compared (by telephone, for example) with the signatures the real owner of the key generates. Of course, GPG does not force you to use strong passphrases to protect your private key, nor does it force you to confirm public key signatures, but you need to do both if you are serious about the security of your information.

Try It Out Setting Up GPG

1. Use your Fedora Core 2 installation media to install the `gnupg` RPM.
2. After the `gnupg` RPM is installed, you need to generate your private and public key pair. You do this with the following command:

```
gpg --gen-key
```

3. The first time you run this, GPG creates a directory called `.gnupg` in your home directory, and populates it with a few files, and then prompts you for the information it needs to create the initial key pair. Note that if the `gpg` program is not run with root privileges, it is unable to pin memory pages containing potentially sensitive information and prevent them from being swapped out to disk (where the sensitive information could remain for some time). GPG detects this potential security problem and warns you about it when it starts. If you want to make this warning go away, turn on the set user ID bit on the `gpg` program by running the command `chmod +s /usr/bin/gpg` (as root), but you may feel that this introduces other security problems.
4. Here's an annotated log of a GPG key generation session:

```
[user1@kimber user1]$ gpg --gen-key
gpg (GnuPG) 1.2.3; Copyright (C) 2003 Free Software Foundation, Inc.
This program comes with ABSOLUTELY NO WARRANTY.
This is free software, and you are welcome to redistribute it
under certain conditions. See the file COPYING for details.
```

That's the disclaimer and copyright information. Now you get the warning about insecure memory because `gpg` is not setuid (so that the user ID it runs under is that of the user who invokes the program, rather than root).

```
gpg: WARNING: using insecure memory!
gpg: please see http://www.gnupg.org/faq.html for more information
```

Next, the `.gnupg` directory is created and some initial configuration files are created:

```
gpg: /home/user1/.gnupg: directory created
gpg: new configuration file `/home/user1/.gnupg/gpg.conf' created
gpg: WARNING: options in `/home/user1/.gnupg/gpg.conf' are not yet active during
this run
gpg: keyring `/home/user1/.gnupg/secring.gpg' created
gpg: keyring `/home/user1/.gnupg/pubring.gpg' created
```

5. Now on to the key generation proper. The first question is about the kind of key you want. Because you'll want to encrypt and sign information, choose option 1 (the other two allow you to sign information, but not encrypt it).

```
Please select what kind of key you want:
   (1) DSA and ElGamal (default)
   (2) DSA (sign only)
   (5) RSA (sign only)
Your selection? 1
```

6. Now you're asked for the length of the key. Longer keys are stronger and take more effort to break, but also take more CPU time to use. The default key length of 1,024 bits is fine for most requirements:

```
DSA keypair will have 1024 bits.
About to generate a new ELG-E keypair.
              minimum keysize is  768 bits
              default keysize is 1024 bits
    highest suggested keysize is 2048 bits
What keysize do you want? (1024)


Requested keysize is 1024 bits
```

7. You can set an expiry date for your key if you wish. Short key lifetimes limit the amount of damage someone can do if they manage to steal your private key, but increase the amount of effort required to regenerate and redistribute a new key every time the old one expires. Here, accept the default of not setting an expiry date.

```
Please specify how long the key should be valid.
         0 = key does not expire
      <n>  = key expires in n days
      <n>w = key expires in n weeks
      <n>m = key expires in n months
      <n>y = key expires in n years
Key is valid for? (0)


Key does not expire at all
Is this correct (y/n)? y
```

8. When you distribute your public key, others need to be able to identify the key as yours. Here you are asked for identification information that will be encoded with the key. This cannot be changed without regenerating the key, so make sure it is correct:

```

                         You need a User-ID to identify your key; the software
constructs the user id
from Real Name, Comment and Email Address in this form:
    "Heinrich Heine (Der Dichter) <heinrichh@duesseldorf.de>"

Real name: Father Christmas


Email address: santa@northpole.org


Comment: Santa Claus


You selected this USER-ID:
    "Father Christmas (Santa Claus) <santa@northpole.org>"

Change (N)ame, (C)omment, (E)mail or (O)kay/(Q)uit? o
```

9. The key that is generated is not stored on disk, existing in memory only while `gpg` is running. (This is why `gpg` warns that the memory is insecure and may be swapped out to disk, which would result in a copy of the private key being on disk). Instead, the private key is encrypted with a passphrase and the encrypted version is stored on disk. That way, even if someone gets access to the disk, he cannot use your private key unless he knows (or can guess) your passphrase. Your choice of passphrase, therefore, has a direct impact on the security of the information you protect with GPG; a weak passphrase (one that is short or uses natural language) increases the chances of your private key being compromised, which defeats all the encryption and signing mechanisms.

```
You need a Passphrase to protect your secret key.

Enter passphrase:

Repeat passphrase:
```

10. GPG now has all the information it needs to generate the key—apart from some random data. The busier your system is, the quicker the truly random data can be generated. You may have to help the system along by wiggling the mouse, typing on the keyboard, and generating some disk I/O (for example, by tar'ing some files to `/dev/null` with `tar -cf /dev/null /usr`).

```
We need to generate a lot of random bytes. It is a good idea to perform
some other action (type on the keyboard, move the mouse, utilize the
disks) during the prime generation; this gives the random number
generator a better chance to gain enough entropy.
+++++++++.+++++++++++++++++++++++++++++++++++.+++++++++++++++++++++++++.++++++++++
.++++++++++++++++++++++++++++++++++..++++++++++.+++++>.+++++.++++>+++++...+++++

Not enough random bytes available.  Please do some other work to give
the OS a chance to collect more entropy! (Need 215 more bytes)
We need to generate a lot of random bytes. It is a good idea to perform
some other action (type on the keyboard, move the mouse, utilize the
disks) during the prime generation; this gives the random number
generator a better chance to gain enough entropy.
+++++++++++++++++++++++++++++++++++++++++++++.+++++.+++++++++++++++..++++++++++++++
++++++++++++++++..++++++++++..++++++++++++++++++++++++...>+++++...................
...............+++++^^^^^
```

11. After a few minutes, GPG is finally happy that it has enough entropy (randomness) and your key pair is created. Because you've just generated the key yourself, GPG marks the key as "trusted" (meaning you are confident that the key has come from the person it claims to have come from). The fingerprint of your public key is also displayed. Other people may ask you for this if they receive your public key and want to check that it is genuine (as they should) before trusting it.

```
gpg: /home/user1/.gnupg/trustdb.gpg: trustdb created
public and secret key created and signed.
key marked as ultimately trusted.

pub  1024D/4B366142 2004-03-23 Father Christmas (Santa Claus) <santa@northpole.org>
     Key fingerprint = 300C 0CED 818F D302 BA11  DA7B 26FE 1D0B 4B36 6142
sub  1024g/8DBED907 2004-03-23
```

12. As soon as you've created your key, it is a good idea to create a revocation certificate that allows you to revoke your public key should you lose your private key, or suspect that it has become compromised. You can publish this revocation certificate in the same way that you publish your private key to let others know that they should no longer use your revoked public key, either because you won't be able to decrypt the encrypted information (you've lost the key), or the encrypted information won't be secure (your private key is compromised). You will still be able to use your private key to decrypt information encrypted with the public key, but others will not be able to use your revoked public key to encrypt new information destined for you.

The revocation certificate is created with the following command:

```
gpg --output revoke.asc --gen-revoke santa
```

This generates an output file called `revoke.asc` that contains the certificate created by the revocation function (`--gen-revoke`) for the key whose user identifier matches `santa`. Here's the output from a typical session, starting as before with a warning about insecure memory:

```
gpg: WARNING: using insecure memory!
gpg: please see http://www.gnupg.org/faq.html for more information
```

Now GPG shows you the key it has found that matches the partial identifier you gave it on the command line (`santa`) and asks if you want to create a revocation certificate for this key. Answer `y` (yes).

```
sec  1024D/4B366142 2004-03-23   Father Christmas (Santa Claus) <santa@northpole.org>

Create a revocation certificate for this key? y
```

13. You can specify a reason code for the revocation, and add a plain text explanation if you wish:

```
Please select the reason for the revocation:
  0 = No reason specified
  1 = Key has been compromised
  2 = Key is superseded
  3 = Key is no longer used
  Q = Cancel
(Probably you want to select 1 here)
Your decision? 1

Enter an optional description; end it with an empty line:
> Rudolph knows my private key passphrase.
>


Reason for revocation: Key has been compromised
Rudolph knows my private key passphrase.
Is this okay? y
```

14. GPG now needs to get your private key. As previously mentioned, GPG does not store your private key as it is on disk, but, instead, encrypts it using the passphrase you provided when the key was created. To use the key, you need to provide the same passphrase again:

```
                You need a passphrase to unlock the secret key for
user: "Father Christmas (Santa Claus) <santa@northpole.org>"
1024-bit DSA key, ID ABCD0123, created 2004-03-23

Enter passphrase:

ASCII armored output forced.
Revocation certificate created.
```

15. You now have your revocation key. GPG is not quite finished; it provides a few helpful words of advice:

```
Please move it to a medium which you can hide away; if Mallory gets
access to this certificate he can use it to make your key unusable.
It is smart to print this certificate and store it away, just in case
your media become unreadable.  But have some caution:  The print system of
your machine might store the data and make it available to others!
```

16. While you're copying important files to a removable medium (for example, floppy disk or CD-ROM), you should copy your (encrypted) secret key. If you lose this, you will not be able to decrypt any information encrypted with that private key's corresponding public key. You must take great care to ensure the security of this copy of your secret key because it is extremely valuable to anyone who wants to intercept encrypted messages intended for you, or who wishes to masquerade as you by sending messages that have been signed with your private key.

Key Management

So, you have created a key pair (comprising one secret key that you must keep absolutely secret and a public key). What now? You must give your public key to other people so that they can use it to encrypt information in a way that only you can decode, and you need to get hold of other people's public keys so that you can encrypt information you want to send to them. The place where you keep all these keys is called a *keyring*. You will have two keyrings: one for public keys (yours and other people's), which is stored in `~/.gnupg/pubring.gpg`, and the other for secret keys (yours only—you should never get other people's secret keys), which is stored in `~/.gnupg/secring.gpg`.

Exporting Your Key

You can use several methods to publish your public key:

- Put it on a Web site
- E-mail it directly to people who you want to communicate securely with
- Upload it to a public key server

The first two require that you translate your public key into a format that is compatible with communication methods (cut and paste from a Web browser and e-mail) that cannot reliably transfer binary data. You can use GPG to do this with a command like this:

```
gpg --armor --output mypublickey.asc --export santa
```

The `--armor` option tells GPG that you want an "ASCII armored" format output, which encodes the output so that it contains only 7-bit ASCII characters, and is therefore much less likely to be corrupted by being sent through various e-mail systems. The other options tell GPG where you want the output saved (`mypublickey.asc`), that you want a public key to be exported (`--export`), and the partial key name (`santa`) that GPG can search your public keyring for.

The file GPG creates will look like this:

```
-----BEGIN PGP PUBLIC KEY BLOCK-----
Version: GnuPG v1.2.3 (GNU/Linux)

mQGiBEBjWm0RBACuIwiEu/FWae/Ibe61kt3al6EOv0pASN1MNFPpXsLpEQAYAK8u
LiLLkZldPXv9mcFeQhXtTVlLPiHXfogiYDCgRFn0xhS688PkrMtzr3JKDLa8mR+B
...
PFreOnho9tDXhACfSnCz6ZaCHmQTVXmnjrDD5e63DM0AningrYxnw1iSqYcQTvwE
e7Mbo7Cf
=YbQy
-----END PGP PUBLIC KEY BLOCK-----
```

If you make this file available to other people (putting it on a Web server, e-mailing it, and so on), they will be able to import your public key into their public keyrings and use it to either send you encrypted information, or verify information that you have signed.

The other way of distributing your public key is to upload it to a *key server*. There is a network of public key servers that people can upload their public keys to and can search for and download other people's public keys from. If you add your key to this network (by sending it to just one of the servers, which will replicate it to the others in due course), anyone will be able to search for your key and download it to their own public keyrings to use in the ways previously described.

You can specify the host name of the keyserver you wish to use, and the protocol required to talk to it, on the GPG command line with the `--keyserver` option. However, the default GPG configuration file `~/.gnupg/gpg.conf` already contains a keyserver entry:

```
keyserver hkp://subkeys.pgp.net
```

So, if you do not specify a keyserver on the command line, GPG will use this one. The keyserver URL specifies the HTTP Keyserver Protocol, hkp://, rather than the more familiar HTTP protocol http://, and for this to work, you need to be able to make outgoing connections on TCP and UDP port number 11371. Make sure whatever port filtering or firewalling you have in place allows outgoing connections on port 11371 (UDP and TCP) before trying to use GPG to talk to keyservers using the HKP.

To send your public key up to the network of keyservers, you simply run the following command:

```
gpg --send-key santa
```

Doing so should result in the following message:

```
gpg: success sending to `subkeys.pgp.net' (status=200)
```

Importing Keys

You have just seen how you can make your public key available to other people, and they can use exactly the same methods to publish their keys for you to use. If you receive someone's public key in an armored ASCII format (for example, a block of unintelligible text starting "-----BEGIN PGP PUBLIC KEY BLOCK-----"), you can import the key into your public keyring with a command like this:

```
gpg --import somefile.asc
```

where *somefile.asc* is the name of the file containing the armored ASCII text. Output will look something like this:

```
gpg: key 01234567: public key "Owner Name <email@somehost.net>" imported
gpg: Total number processed: 1
gpg:               imported: 1
```

Now use the following command:

```
gpg --list-keys
```

You should see the newly imported public key on your public keyring. (You can use the `--list-secret-keys` command to show the keys that are on your secret keyring.)

If you want to search the keyserver for a public key, use the `--search` option. For example, to find the public key for John Doe, use the following command:

```
gpg --search "John Doe"
```

This will search the keyserver listed in the `gpg.conf` file for public keys that match the name John Doe. Any keys that are found are displayed, ten at a time, on the screen. You can type *n* and press enter to display the next group of ten keys, or *q* to quit. If you find the key you are looking for in the list, you can type its index number (displayed next to the key), and GPG imports the key into your public keyring.

A Matter of Trust . . .

One of the problems with public key cryptography, where public keys are exchanged by parties that wish to communicate securely, is how the parties ensure that the public keys they use really are the public keys of the intended recipient of the encrypted information, and not the public key of an imposter who wants to gain unauthorized access to that information. To be really sure, a user of a public key should check the key fingerprint with the key's owner to confirm that the key is the right one. This is the best method to use within small groups, but for larger groups of users who want to communicate with each other, having every user check the key fingerprint of every other user becomes impractical.

In these situations, you can make use of the principle of trusted keys. If someone has verified the fingerprint of another person's public key and is confident that the key is genuine, they can sign the key with his or her own key, and in doing so, certify that the key is genuine. If you now receive a copy of the key (by downloading from a keyserver), you will be able to see that someone else has signed the key as well as the originator, and if you trust that other person to have verified the key properly, you can decide that the key is genuine without having to verify the fingerprint yourself.

To see what signatures have been attached to a public key, use the `--list-sigs` command:

```
gpg --list-sigs santa
```

The output will contain lines starting with `sig` that indicate signatures that have been added to the key. (For an explanation of the fields following the `sig` tag, see the `gpg` man page.)

If you want to sign someone else's public key to say that you think it is genuine, you must first check the fingerprint with the owner of the key and make absolutely sure that they are who they are claiming to be and that the fingerprints match (use `gpg --fingerprint <keyid>` to see a key's fingerprint). Once you have done that, and you are satisfied that the key is genuine, you can edit the key to add your signature:

```
gpg --edit-key Rudolph
```

Then use the `sign` command. Here's an example:

```
gpg --edit-key Rudolph
gpg (GnuPG) 1.2.3; Copyright (C) 2003 Free Software Foundation, Inc.
This program comes with ABSOLUTELY NO WARRANTY.
This is free software, and you are welcome to redistribute it
under certain conditions. See the file COPYING for details.


pub  1024D/01234567  created: 1998-12-25 expires: 2004-12-25 trust: -/-
(1). Rudolph Reindeer (Red Nose) <Rudolph@northpole.org>
```

GPG has told you which key(s) it has found that match your search string (`Rudolph`). Now you can issue the `sign` command:

```
Command> sign

             pub  1024D/01234567  created: 1998-12-25 expires: 2004-12-25 trust: -/-
 Primary key fingerprint: 0000 1111 2222 3333 4444  5555 6666 7777 8888 9999

     Rudolph Reindeer (Red Nose) <Rudolph@northpole.org>
```

Because the public key has an expiry date, GPG asks you if you want your signature to expire at the same time. It is sensible to answer "yes" to this.

```
This key is due to expire on 2004-12-25.
Do you want your signature to expire at the same time? (Y/n) y
```

GPG now asks you how carefully you have checked the key you are about to sign. It is important to answer this question truthfully; misleading answers undermine the entire trust model behind Public Key exchange in this way:

```
How carefully have you verified the key you are about to sign actually belongs
to the person named above?  If you don't know what to answer, enter "0".

    (0) I will not answer. (default)
    (1) I have not checked at all.
    (2) I have done casual checking.
    (3) I have done very careful checking.

Your selection? (enter '?' for more information): 2
Are you really sure that you want to sign this key
with your key: "Father Christmas (Santa Claus) <santa@northpole.org" (ABCD0123)

I have checked this key casually.
```

GPG asks you to confirm that the information you have entered is correct, and that you really do want to sign the public key. If you answer `y`, you are prompted for the passphrase for your secret key and, if this is correct, the public key you are editing is signed.

```
Really sign? y

               You need a passphrase to unlock the secret key for
user: "Father Christmas (Santa Claus) <santa@northpole.org" (ABCD0123)
1024-bit DSA key, ID ABCD0123, created 2004-03-25

Enter passphrase:
```

If you want to confirm that your signature has been added to the key, you can use the `check` command at GPG's `command>` prompt:

```
Command> check


uid  Rudolph Reindeer (Red Nose) <Rudolph@northpole.org>
sig!3       01234567 2002-12-25   [self-signature]
sig!2       ABCD0123 2004-03-26   Father Christmas (Santa Claus)
<santa@northpole.org>
```

Everything seems okay, so you can quit from the GPG program, which will ask you whether to save the changes you have made or not before exiting.

```
Command> quit

Save changes? y
```

You can use the `--send-keys` command to send this updated key back up to the keyservers so that others can see that you have verified the identity of the key and signed it.

Encrypting and Decrypting Information

Having all these keys on your public keyrings is of no use unless you can use them to encrypt information in such a way that only the intended recipient can decrypt the information. The `--encrypt` GPG command is used to encrypt a file (or `stdin`, if no filename is specified). When encrypting information, you need to specify one or more public keys with the `--recipient` *<keyname>* option (repeating once for each different recipient); only the holders of the private keys corresponding to these public keys will be able to decrypt the encrypted data. It is useful also to specify where to put the encrypted data with the `--output` *<filename>* option, and note that this will be a binary file (unsuitable for sending via e-mail), unless you also specify the `--armor` option.

If, for example, you want to e-mail a sensitive document called `proposal.doc` to `bill@mywork.com` and `ben@yourwork.com`, and you have the public keys for the recipients in your public keyring, you can use the following command:

```
gpg --output proposal.gpg --armor --encrypt --recipient bill@mywork.com --recipient
ben@yourwork.com proposal.doc
```

This creates an armored ASCII file called `proposal.gpg` that can be safely e-mailed to the two recipients, safe in the knowledge that it won't get corrupted in transit and cannot be read by anyone other than the intended recipients. As an added bonus, GPG also compresses the data, so the size of the e-mail is reduced. (Compressing the data before encrypting it also makes it harder to use cryptanalysis to decrypt the contents of the encrypted document.)

Your recipients can use the `--decrypt` GPG command to decrypt the encrypted document you sent them and recover the original form. They would use a command like this:

```
gpg --output proposal.doc --decrypt proposal.gpg
```

And they would be prompted for the passphrase associated with their private key, which would have to be supplied correctly before the document is decrypted.

Where to Go from Here

If you are going to be working with e-mail and encrypted documents a lot, you will find it tedious to have to use the GPG command line to encrypt and decrypt documents you send and receive. Fortunately, a number of tools and plug-ins are available that make GPG functions available from within popular e-mail packages. Go to `www.gnupg.org/(en)/related_software/frontends.html#mua` for descriptions of the various tools and plug-ins, and links to the Web sites where you can obtain them.

Monitoring Security

There are several ways to monitor the security of your Fedora Core system that enable you to spot security breaches and other potential problems.

System Logs

The Fedora Core system maintains several log files that record system activity. Most of the interesting ones reside in `/var/log`.

/var/log

The table that follows describes the most important log files that you will find in `/var/log`.

File in /var/log	Contents	View with
`Btmp`	Record of all bad login attempts. Updated by login program if it exists.	`lastb` command
`Cron`	Messages sent to `syslogd` from the `cron` daemon (which schedules jobs on UNIX systems).	Normal text-viewing tools
`Dmesg`	Kernel messages (from `boot`).	Normal text-viewing tools
`Lastlog`	Last login times for all users.	`lastlog` command
`Messages`	Messages sent to `syslogd` with level of info or higher, except those from `mail`, `cron`, or authentication-related messages.	Normal text-viewing tools
`Secure`	Messages sent to `syslogd` from `authpriv` (that is, authentication and security messages that should be visible only to privileged users).	Normal text-viewing tools
`Wtmp`	Record of all logins and logouts.	`last` command

Note that several of these files are maintained by the kernel logging daemon `syslogd`*. The behavior of this daemon is controlled by the configuration file* `/etc/syslog.conf`*, and you can customize it if you don't like the defaults (which are pretty good). For more information on configuring* `syslog`*, check its man page.*

The files `/var/log/btmp` *and* `/var/log/wtmp` *are updated only if they exist (that is, the programs that update these files won't create them for you). The default Fedora Core 2 installation has* `/var/log/wtmp`*, so all logins and logouts are logged, but not* `/var/log/btmp`*.*

A diligent system administrator will regularly review the contents of these log files, either using tools such as `gedit`, if the file is a plain text file, or the appropriate command, such as `last` or `lastlog` if the file contains formatted data. However, regularly trawling through log files for the occasional message of significance is very tedious. Fortunately, an automated tool called `logwatch` takes away much of the tedium. Even better, Red Hat includes a sensible default setup so it's up and running out of the box.

logwatch

Fedora Core 2 has a tool called `logwatch` that can search through log files for interesting messages and summarize them elsewhere. We will look at the default configuration provided with Fedora Core 2 here.

The configuration files for `logwatch` are in `/etc/log.d`. The main configuration file is called `logwatch.conf`, and here are the default contents:

```
########################################################
# This was written and is maintained by:
#  Kirk Bauer <kirk@kaybee.org>
#
# Please send all comments, suggestions, bug reports,
#  etc, to kirk@kaybee.org.
#
########################################################

# NOTE:
#  All these options are the defaults if you run logwatch with no
#  command-line arguments. You can override all of these on the
#  command-line.

# You can put comments anywhere you want to. They are effective for the
# rest of the line.

# this is in the format of <name> = <value>. Whitespace at the beginning
# and end of the lines is removed. Whitespace before and after the = sign
# is removed. Everything is case *insensitive*.

# Yes = True = On = 1
# No = False = Off = 0

# Default Log Directory
# All log-files are assumed to be given relative to this directory.
# This should be /var/log on just about all systems...
LogDir = /var/log

# Default person to mail reports to. Can be a local account or a
# complete email address.
MailTo = root

# If set to 'Yes', the report will be sent to stdout instead of being
# mailed to above person.
Print = No
# if set, the results will be saved in <filename> instead of mailed
# or displayed.
#Save = /tmp/logwatch

# Use archives? If set to 'Yes', the archives of logfiles
# (i.e. /var/log/messages.1 or /var/log/messages.1.gz) will
# be searched in addition to the /var/log/messages file.
# This usually will not do much if your range is set to just
# 'Yesterday' or 'Today'... it is probably best used with
# Archives = Yes
# Range = All

# The default time range for the report...
# The current choices are All, Today, Yesterday
```

```
Range = yesterday

# The default detail level for the report.
# This can either be Low, Med, High or a number.
# Low = 0
# Med = 5
# High = 10
Detail = Low

# The 'Service' option expects either the name of a filter
# (in /etc/log.d/scripts/services/*) or 'All'.
# The default service(s) to report on. This should be left as All for
# most people.
Service = All
# If you only cared about FTP messages, you could use these 2 lines
# instead of the above:
#Service = ftpd-messages  # Processes ftpd messages in /var/log/messages
#Service = ftpd-xferlog   # Processes ftpd messages in /var/log/xferlog
# Maybe you only wanted reports on PAM messages, then you would use:
#Service = pam_pwdb    # PAM_pwdb messages - usually quite a bit
#Service = pam       # General PAM messages... usually not many

# You can also choose to use the 'LogFile' option. This will cause
# logwatch to only analyze that one logfile.. for example:
#LogFile = messages
# will process /var/log/messages. This will run all the filters that
# process that logfile. This option is probably not too useful to
# most people. Setting 'Service' to 'All' above analyizes all LogFiles
# anyways...
```

As you read through the file, you see that most of the lines are comments (because they start with the # sign, and that's a widely used way of introducing comments in most script and configuration files). So, out of all those lines, the only entries that are in effect are the following:

```
LogDir = /var/log
MailTo = root
Print = No
Range = yesterday
Detail = Low
```

These are highlighted in bold in the example. If you consult the man page for `logwatch` (run the command `man logwatch`), you can see that `logwatch` will check the log files in `/var/log`, looking for entries from the previous day, and e-mail a report containing a low level of detail to root.

If you've run your system for a few days and checked root mail, you'll have seen messages from `logwatch`—so how is this happening? Scheduling of unattended jobs on Fedora Core 2, and most other UNIX versions, is handled by the *cron daemon*. This daemon looks for files containing information about when and what to run in the directories `/var/spool/cron` and `/etc/cron.d`, and in the file `/etc/crontab`. On Fedora Core 2, the `/etc/crontab` file is the one that is configured by default.

If you examine the contents of this file, you see a few lines of environment information, and some other lines starting with numbers:

```
SHELL=/bin/bash
PATH=/sbin:/bin:/usr/sbin:/usr/bin
MAILTO=root
HOME=/

# run-parts
01 * * * * root run-parts /etc/cron.hourly
02 4 * * * root run-parts /etc/cron.daily
22 4 * * 0 root run-parts /etc/cron.weekly
42 4 1 * * root run-parts /etc/cron.monthly
```

The numbers specify when `cron` should run the command described by the rest of the line. There are five fields, which are, from left to right, minute, hour, day of month, month, and day of week. Where an asterisk is used, this means "I don't care." So the four scheduled jobs in the default Fedora Core 2 crontab are run at times shown in the table that follows.

Scheduled Time	Interpretation
01 * * * *	01 minutes past each hour
02 4 * * *	04:02 every day
22 4 * * 0	04:22 every Sunday (1=Monday, 2=Tuesday, and so on; Sunday=0 or 7)
42 4 1 * *	04:42 on the 1st day of every month

The jobs are essentially similar; run the `run-parts` script as `root` and pass the name of a directory (for example, `/etc/cron.hourly` for the job run at 1 minute past each hour). The `run-parts` script simply runs every executable file it finds in the directory that it is given (except files ending in the characters ~ or `,`, and a few other exceptions). If you look in the `/etc/cron.daily` directory, you'll see a file called `00-logwatch`, which is a symbolic link to the `logwatch` command.

All this means that, at 04:02 every day, the root user will be mailed a message containing summaries of important information entered into various log files in `/var/log` the previous day. This is all set up for you when Fedora Core is installed, but now that you know how it works, you can adjust the configuration to suit your own requirements. If, for example, you'd like more information in the messages, you can simply edit `/etc/log.d/logwatch.conf` and change the `Detail = Low` line to `Detail = High`. Maybe you'd like the message to be sent at 00:15 instead. Just delete the file `00-logwatch` from `/etc/cron.daily` (so the 04:02 daily cron job no longer runs) and add the following line to `/etc/crontab`:

```
15 00 * * * root /usr/sbin/logwatch
```

It's as simple as that.

System Integrity

Once a hacker has gained access to a system, she will often want to install modified versions of system files to ensure their continued access and to gather more information that will help her achieve her objectives. If your security analysis has identified this threat as one you need to consider, you need to have some means of identifying when your system may have been compromised in this way, so you can take remedial action (restore the compromised file from a trusted backup).

But if you're checking the system for modified files, you'll not only identify files modified by intruders, you'll also identify files that may have been inadvertently modified by authorized individuals, or that have become corrupt due to hardware problems (such as bad blocks appearing on disk drives).

Tripwire

Tripwire is an open source *system integrity checker* that is available for Fedora Core. It is a useful weapon in the system administrator's armory, so this section will take you through obtaining it and setting it up. Note that when Tripwire scans the system to detect changes, it's doing a lot of work and will hit the processor(s) and file I/O hard.

Try It Out — Downloading, Configuring, and Running Tripwire

1. Tripwire is available in RPM format for Fedora Core, which makes installation very straightforward. It's available on the Fedora Core 2 CD-ROMs, but as an interesting exercise, you'll try using the `rpm` command's built-in FTP and HTTP client. You'll use the `rpm` command to download and install the Tripwire RPM with a single command. Open a terminal window, switch to the root user, and type in the following command (all on one line):

You'll need to change the httpproxy IP address and httpport port number to suit your Internet connection (omit them if you don't need to go through a proxy server to access the Internet).

```
# rpm -iv --httpproxy 10.4.65.2 --httpport 3128 http://download.fedora.us/fedora/
fedora/1/i386/RPMS.testing/tripwire-2.3.1-18.fdr.3.1.i386.rpm
```

   The command also assumes that you're running on an Intel architecture machine. If not, you will need to download the source RPM and build the package yourself.

   After a few minutes (depending on the speed of your Internet connection), you should see the message "Preparing packages for installation . . ." followed by "tripwire-2.3.1-18," and be returned to the command prompt.

2. You can confirm that the Tripwire package was installed by running the following command:

```
# rpm -q tripwire
```

   If all is well, you'll get the package version information back; if not, you'll get a message saying "package tripwire is not installed" (in which case, just download the RPM in the conventional way, and try again).

3. Now that Tripwire is installed, you can configure its policies and complete the setup. Before diving in to the configuration, take time to read the README file in `/usr/share/doc/tripwire-2.3.1`, and the `twintro` and `twpolicy` man pages to familiarize yourself with the required configuration tasks. These can be divided into three distinct steps:

    - Setting up the policy file
    - Initializing the Tripwire database
    - Configuring Tripwire to run periodically and report system integrity violations

    Let's begin with the policy file. Tripwire's policy file defines which files and directories Tripwire should monitor for changes, and what changes are significant. For some files, such as those in `/bin/login`, any change in file contents, modification date, or ownership is suspicious, but you'd expect them to be accessed frequently. Other files, such as log files, are expected to grow in size, but not change ownership.

    The policy file that is installed with the RPM in `/etc/tripwire/twpol.txt` tells Tripwire to monitor many files that probably don't exist on your system, so you'll get lots of spurious error messages when you run an integrity check. What you really need to do is edit the policy file so that files and directories that don't exist aren't monitored, and conversely, if files and directories that do exist are commented out in the policy file, they are reinstated. It would be tedious to do this by hand, so let's use our newfound knowledge of Perl to write a script to do it for us.

4. The algorithm you need to employ is straightforward. If you find a line that looks like an instruction to Tripwire to check a file or directory (optional white space, string beginning with `/`), you should check that the file or directory exists. If not, comment out the line to prevent Tripwire from generating an error.

    Similarly, if you find a line in the policy file that looks like a commented-out file (optional white space, `#`, optional white space, string beginning with `/`), check if the file or directory exists. If it does, you'll remove the comment to reinstate the file.

5. We'll write the script as a filter, so it reads configuration lines from `STDIN` and writes to `STDOUT`. Any lines that don't look like either of the types of line you're interested in are passed through unmodified.

    Here's the script (we hope your new knowledge of Perl will give you an idea of the structure being employed, even if the details are still a bit beyond you—they'll come with practice):

```
#! /usr/bin/perl -w

# Filter for Tripwire policy file. Looks for lines that
# start with optional whitespace and a filename, and
# comments them out if the file does not exist. Also
# looks for commented out lines containing filename and
# removes comment if they do exist.

$Additions = 0;
$Removals = 0;
# Read each line from stdin into the $line variable
while ($line = <STDIN>) {
  # Look for lines that match a pattern (the Perl
  # pattern matching characters are enclosed in [])
```

```
    # start with optional white space [ ^\s* ]
    # then a '#' [ # ]
    # then more optional white space [ \s* ]
    # then a string starting with '/' that doesn't
    # contain white space [ \/\S+ ]
    #
    # The last part of the pattern is enclosed in ()
    # so that if the pattern matches, we can access
    # this part through the $1 variable.
    #
    # This pattern matches a commented out entry/
    if ( $line =~ /^\s*#\s*(\/\S+)/ ) {
     # Found commented out entry. If the file exists,
     # strip off the comment character.
     if ( -e $1 ) {
       $line =~ s/^\s*#//;
       $Additions++;
     }
    # Now look for a line that's like the above but
    # without the '#' comment character.
    } elsif ( $line =~ /^\s*(\/\S+)/ ) {
     # Found entry that starts with "  /". If file
     # does not exist, then comment out entry.
     if ( ! -e $1 ) {
       $line = "# " . $line;
       $Removals++;
     }
    }

    # Output the line (whether modified or not)
    print $line;
}
# Print the statistics on STDERR, so they won't get redirected by >
print STDERR "Number of additions: $Additions\n";
print STDERR "Number of removals: $Removals\n";
```

6. Create a text file containing this script and call it `/usr/local/bin/cleanpol.pl`, and make it executable by running the following command:

Depending on the examples you've followed earlier in the book, you may need to acquire root privileges at this point.

```
# chmod +x /usr/local/bin/cleanpol.pl
```

7. Now you can use this Perl script to produce a customized Tripwire policy file:

```
# cd /etc/tripwire
# mv twpol.txt twpol.txt.orig
# /usr/local/bin/cleanpol.pl <twpol.txt.orig \ >twpol.txt
...
Number of additions: 38
Number of removals: 125
```

This little script saves you from making 163 manual changes to the Tripwire policy file! (The number of changes made on your system will vary depending on which packages you have installed.) You can review the changes that were made with the `diff` command:

```
diff twpol.txt.orig twpol.txt
```

8. Now, use `gedit`, or your favorite text editor, to review the contents of the updated `/etc/tripwire/twpol.txt` file. In particular, there may be a problem with the line defining the policy for `/sbin/e2fsadm`. If the `cleanpol.pl` script uncommented this line, the note `tune2fs?` at the end of the line is treated by Tripwire as a relative path to a file, and the policy file is rejected. Simply delete this note, as in the following:

```
/sbin/e2fsadm     -> $(SEC_CRIT) ; tune2fs?
```

becomes

```
/sbin/e2fsadm     -> $(SEC_CRIT) ;
```

9. The next step is to initialize the Tripwire database. This is done by running the `twinstall.sh` script in `/etc/tripwire`:

```
# ./twinstall.sh
```

This script asks you to enter site and local passphrases (a term used to describe a long "password"), generates encryption keys, and cryptographically secures the configuration and policy files to prevent unauthorized changes:

```
[root@rh9 tripwire]# ./twinstall.sh

----------------------------------------------
The Tripwire site and local passphrases are used to
sign a variety of files, such as the configuration,
policy, and database files.

Passphrases should be at least 8 characters in length
and contain both letters and numbers.
See the Tripwire manual for more information.

----------------------------------------------
Creating key files...

(When selecting a passphrase, keep in mind that good passphrases typically
have upper and lower case letters, digits and punctuation marks, and are
at least 8 characters in length.)

Enter the site keyfile passphrase:
Verify the site keyfile passphrase:
Generating key (this may take several minutes)...Key generation complete.

(When selecting a passphrase, keep in mind that good passphrases typically
have upper and lower case letters, digits and punctuation marks, and are
at least 8 characters in length.)

Enter the local keyfile passphrase:
```

```
Verify the local keyfile passphrase:
Generating key (this may take several minutes)...Key generation complete.

---------------------------------------------
Signing configuration file...
Please enter your site passphrase:
Wrote configuration file: /etc/tripwire/tw.cfg

A clear-text version of the Tripwire configuration file
/etc/tripwire/twcfg.txt
has been preserved for your inspection. It is recommended
that you delete this file manually after you have examined it.


---------------------------------------------
Signing policy file...
Please enter your site passphrase:
Wrote policy file: /etc/tripwire/tw.pol

A clear-text version of the Tripwire policy file
/etc/tripwire/twpol.txt
has been preserved for your inspection. This implements
a minimal policy, intended only to test essential
Tripwire functionality. You should edit the policy file
to describe your system, and then use twadmin to generate
a new signed copy of the Tripwire policy.
```

10. The final step in initialization is to run the command `tripwire -- init`. You are prompted for the local passphrase; then Tripwire scans all the files listed in the configuration file and gathers baseline data against which all future scans are run. This may take several minutes, so be patient:

It is vital that you are confident the system is in a sound state before initializing the database, otherwise there's little point in using Tripwire. After the database is initialized, it's a good idea to put a copy on write-once media (for example, CD-ROM) so that it cannot be altered:

```
# tripwire --init
Please enter your local passphrase:
Parsing policy file: /etc/tripwire/tw.pol
Generating the database...
*** Processing Unix File System ***
Wrote database file: /var/lib/tripwire/rh9.twd
The database was successfully generated.
```

Setting Up Tripwire to Run Automatically

You've already seen how `logwatch` is set up to run automatically every day at 04:02. You can easily set up Tripwire to run at the same time.

Create a two-line script called `/etc/cron.daily/run-tripwire` containing the following lines:

```
#!/bin/sh
/usr/sbin/tripwire --check
```

Make sure the script is owned by root and has permissions of `500 (r-x------)` so it is executable only by root. This script invokes Tripwire and gets it to check the system's integrity according to the rules in the policy file, and using the database you just created as its baseline. When `cron` runs this script at 04:02 every day, its output is sent to root (or whomever is configured in the `MAILTO` variable in `/etc/crontab`).

Updating the Tripwire Database

We'll test the script by running it now. Type `/etc/cron.daily/run-tripwire` on the command line as root, and check that Tripwire runs successfully. Carefully examine the output produced; you should see that Tripwire has spotted the addition of the `run-tripwire` script to `/etc/cron.daily` and flagged it as a critical change.

To stop Tripwire from reporting this change (which you made and know is okay) as a policy violation every time it runs, you need to update Tripwire's database. You do this by running `tripwire --update`, specifying a Tripwire report file that you wish to use for the update. To see what files are available, run `ls -ltr /var/lib/tripwire/report`; choose the last report listed, as this will be the most recent one.

The command to run (all on one line) is then as follows:

```
# tripwire --update --twrfile /var/lib/tripwire/report/rh9-20030209-040304.twr
```

Replace the report filename with the most recent `.twr` file on your system. This will produce a text file and start `vi` for you so you can edit the file. Each proposed database update is tagged with `[x]`, and if you don't want the update to be made, simply delete the `x`. If we don't want to use `vi`, add `--visual gedit` to the command, and Tripwire starts the graphical editor instead.

When you exit the editor, you're asked for the local passphrase, and then updates are applied to the database. Subsequent Tripwire integrity checks should no longer warn you about the change to `/etc/cron.daily`.

Network Security

Virtually all Fedora Core 2 systems will be connected to other computers via a network at some time. This may be a permanent connection through a network adapter to a local area network (LAN), an "always on" connection to the Internet, or a dial-up connection to an Internet service provider that is active only when required. Whatever the connection, you need to make sure that a hacker cannot use it to gain access to your system, or mount a denial-of-service attack that prevents legitimate use of your computing resources. This section looks at some of the techniques that you can use to secure your system and make life hard for the potential hacker.

Unless you are connected to an isolated network where every machine is secure and trusted, you must assume that all the information you send and receive across the network can be intercepted by a third party (someone other than you and the intended recipient of the information).

Network Services

One way a hacker may try to gain unauthorized access to your system is by exploiting weaknesses in the network services that you are running on your Fedora Core system. These are programs—often run in the background with no controlling terminal (called *daemons* in UNIX, and *services* in Microsoft Windows)—that provide services to other computers. Examples include file transfer protocol (FTP), Web, Network File System (NFS), and print servers.

Enabling and Disabling Services

The first and easiest way of reducing your vulnerability is to disable all the services that you don't need. In particular, you need to be very careful about older services that send sensitive information (such as usernames and passwords) across the network without any form of encryption (in plain text). Also, services that gratuitously hand out information about your system should be avoided where possible.

The following table will help you to decide which services you need to run.

Service	TCP/UDP Port Number	Description	Fedora Package	Security Level	Run It?
Echo	7	Sends received characters back to sender.	xinted	None	No (unless you really need to debug remote terminal problems).
Daytime	13	Sends current data and time as ASCII string back to sender.	xinetd	None	No. Use NTP for time synchronization. It is more accurate and has better security features.
Chargen	19	Generates continuous stream of ASCII characters for testing terminals.	xinetd	None	No (unless you really need to debug remote terminal problems).
FTP	20 (data) 21 (control) Random ports > 1023	File Transfer Protocol. Transfers files between systems.	vsftp or wu-ftp	Weak. Usernames and passwords are sent in plain text. Anonymous FTP gives access with no password.	No. Use `sftp` instead.

Service	TCP/UDP Port Number	Description	Fedora Package	Security Level	Run It?
SSH	22	Secure Shell. Allows remote system to access command shell on local machine.	openssh-server	Good. Data is encrypted and connections can be authenticated to verify identity of remote system.	Only if remote access to command line is required.
Telnet	23	Allows remote system to access command shell on local machine.	telnet-server	Weak. Usernames and passwords are sent in plain text.	No. Use `ssh` instead.
SMTP	25	Simple Mail Transfer Protocol. Used to transfer mail between systems.	sendmail or procmail	Weak. Mail is transferred in plain text.	Only if mail needs to be handled locally. Encrypt sensitive information before e-mailing.
Time	37	Sends current time (in seconds since 00:00 on 1st January 1970) back to sender.	xinetd	None.	No. Use NTP for time synchronization. It is more accurate and has better security features.
Finger	79	Gives information about local system or users to remote machine.	finger-server	None.	No.
HTTP	80	Hypertext Transfer Protocol. Used by Web servers	httpd	Depends on server configuration.	Only if Web server needs to run on system.
Auth (identd)	113	Identification protocol. Allows remote system to identify user of a particular IP address.	pident	Supports DES encryption of returned information.	Only if required to access specific public services (for example, some FTP and Internet Relay Chat sites).

Table continued on following page

Service	TCP/UDP Port Number	Description	Fedora Package	Security Level	Run It?
sftp	115	Secure File Transfer Protocol. FTP-like file transfer using SSH protocol.	openssh-server	Good. Transfers are encrypted and systems may be authenticated.	Only if file transfers are required.
NNTP	119	Network News Transfer Protocol. Used to transfer USENET news groups.	inn	Depends on server configuration.	Only if newsgroup server needs to be run on the system.
SMB (netbios)	137, 138 & 139	Server Message Block. Allows Fedora servers to interoperate with Microsoft Windows clients.	samba	Depends on server configuration, but note that Samba versions up to and including 2.2.8 have a serious security vulnerability.	Use non-vulnerable versions if interoperation with Microsoft Windows clients is required.
HTTPS	443	Secure HTTP.	httpd	Depends on server configuration.	Only if Web server needs to be run on the system.
rsh, rlogin	514	Allows remote machine to run commands or access command prompt on a local machine without supplying a password.	rsh-server	Weak. Relies on Domain Name Server (DNS) to identify remote system, so is exposed if DNS is compromised.	No.
LPD	515	Allows remote machines to send print jobs to local printers.	cups	Weak. Information is passed over the network without encryption.	Only run if your system has printers you want to share.

Service	TCP/UDP Port Number	Description	Fedora Package	Security Level	Run It?
NFS	2049 (requires portmapper to be listening on port 111)	Network File System. Allows other machines to access filesystems remotely.	nfs-utils	Weak. Information is passed over the network without encryption.	Only use to access information that is not sensitive.

Having decided which services are required, you need to make sure they are started, and make sure that any of the undesirable services are stopped. This is done through the Red Hat Service Configuration application. As an example, we'll use the Red Hat Service Configuration application to turn off the lpd and portmapper services because our theoretical demonstration machine doesn't have any printers attached to it (so there's no point in running lpd), and we're not using NFS or NIS (so there's no point in running portmapper).

Try It Out — Running the Service Configuration Application

1. Start the Service Configuration application by choosing Main Menu ➪ System Settings ➪ Server Settings ➪ Services, or typing `redhat-config-services` at the command prompt.
2. If you're not logged on as root (and you shouldn't be), you'll be prompted for the root password in the dialog box shown in Figure 10-4.

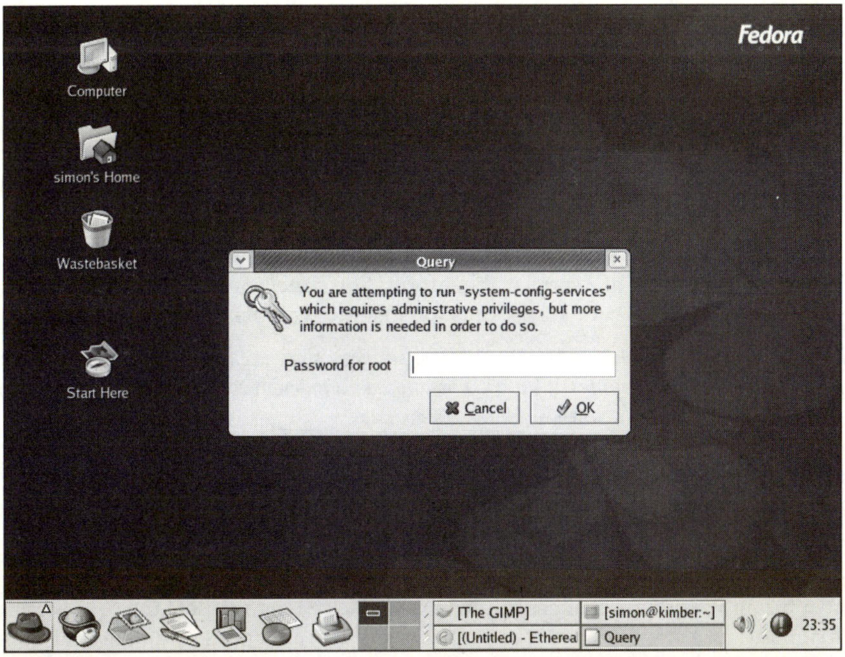

Figure 10-4

3. Now the service configuration menu appears, as shown in Figure 10-5.

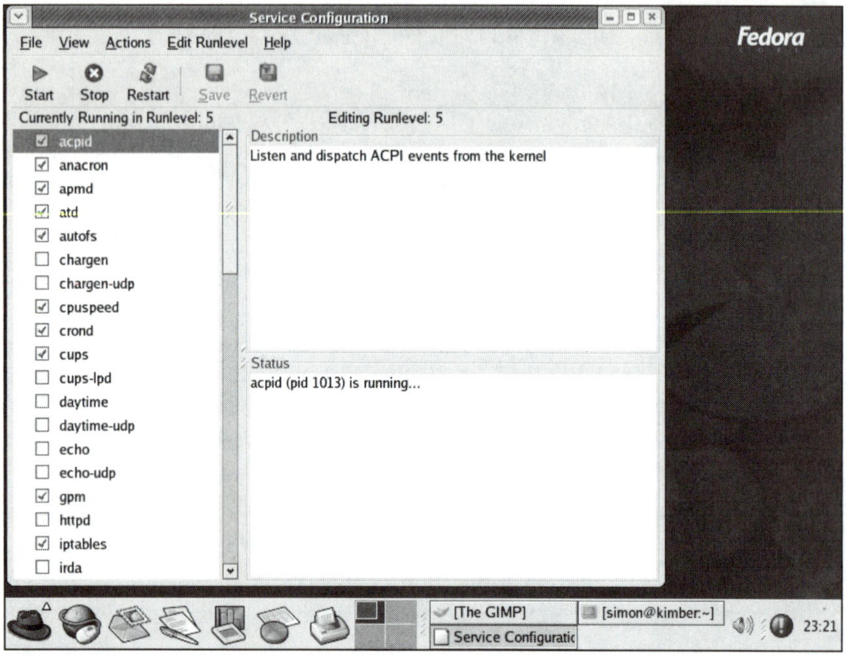

Figure 10-5

In the Service Configuration window, there are a few important things to note. First, the status line immediately below the toolbar icons shows you that the system is running in Runlevel 5, and that this is the runlevel that is being edited. (A runlevel is a particular state of the operating system, characterized by a set of processes that are started. If you haven't changed the system runlevel, you'll be editing the default, which is just what you want. For more information on runlevels, see the man pages for `inittab` and `telinit`. Be careful if you experiment with these because mistakes could render your system unbootable, forcing you to boot from CD-ROM to correct the problem.)

4. If you click the name of a service, the information panels on the right of the window will show a brief description of what the service is for, together with its status.

Not all services represented here represent external services; some are internal daemons vital for the smooth running of your computer. It's a good idea to take a moment to read through all the descriptions here and start to familiarize yourself with what's available.

5. Scroll through the list of services, and clear the check boxes next to lpd and portmapper, as these are two services that do allow remote connections to your system and that are enabled by default, but probably aren't needed in the majority of cases.

   When you make a change to any of the services, the Save button is no longer grayed out. When you're happy with the changes you've made, click Save to update the configuration files. Note that this does not actually start or stop any services; all it does is update configuration files so that next time the runlevel that is being edited is entered, the right services are started, and when it is being left, the right services are stopped. If you want to make the change effective immediately, highlight the service and click the Start, Stop, or Restart button on the toolbar according to what you want to do.

xinetd

You may have noticed in the table of services and their daemons presented earlier that several services (such as echo, daytime, and chargen) appear to be provided by the same service, namely `xinetd`. This isn't a typo—`xinetd` does provide these, and it also looks after a whole lot more.

The `xinetd` service is an enhanced version of the standard UNIX `inetd` (Internet daemon) program, which manages incoming connections to many different services (it is sometimes called a "super server"). It is a long-running service (usually started when the system boots) that listens for incoming TCP/IP connections on ports that it has been told about in its configuration file. When a connection request arrives, `xinetd` checks that the connection should be allowed, and then starts the appropriate server (if required) to handle the connection. This section takes a brief look at some of the configuration options `xinetd` has that relate to system security.

The main configuration file of `xinetd` is `/etc/xinetd.conf`. Figure 10-6 shows the default contents of this file.

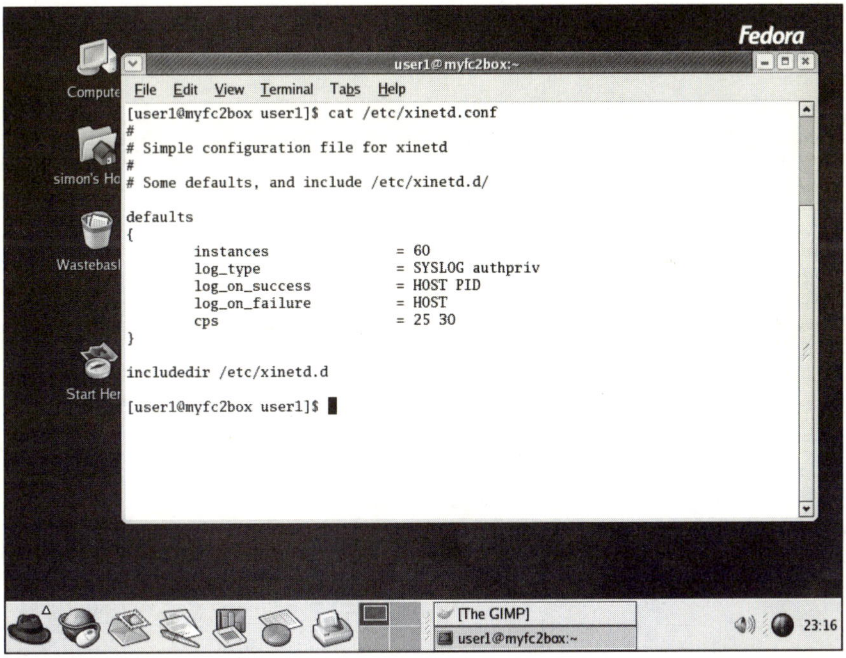

Figure 10-6

This file simply sets up some sensible default values that apply to all services managed by `xinetd` (by placing them inside `defaults { }`), and then tells `xinetd` to read configuration information from all the files in `/etc/xinetd.d`. The table that follows lists the meanings of the default values.

Value	Meaning
`instances = 60`	No more than 60 instances of each subserver will be started.
`logtype = SYSLOG authpriv`	Service log output is sent to `syslogd` using the `authpriv` facility (so that the output is logged to a file that can be read only by privileged users).
`log_on_success = HOST PID`	Logs remote host address and process ID (if there is one) when a service is started or exits.
`log_on_failure = HOST`	Logs remote host address when a service fails to start (with the reason for the failure).
`cps = 25 30`	Allows maximum connection rate of 25 connections per second (first number) and disables service for 30 seconds (second number) if this rate is exceeded.

Monitoring Services

It is useful to be able to check what services are running on your Fedora Core 2 system, especially what ports they are listening on. Before a remote machine can make a connection to your local machine, some process on your local machine has to be ready to receive network packets (listening) sent to its port number.

You can use a couple of tools to identify what ports are listening on your machine: `netstat` and `nmap`.

netstat

The `netstat` program is a multipurpose utility for reporting on all things relating to networks. You invoke it with the flags shown in the following table.

Flag	Meaning
`-t`	TCP
`-u`	UDP
`-l`	Port sockets in state of "listening"
`-n`	Show numeric values for hosts and ports
`-p`	Show process ID that owns sockets

```
# netstat -nutlp
Active Internet connections (only servers)
Proto Recv-Q Send-Q Local Address  Foreign Address State  PID/Program name
tcp    0    0 127.0.0.1:32769 0.0.0.0:*   LISTEN 718/xinetd
tcp    0    0 0.0.0.0:6000   0.0.0.0:*   LISTEN 979/X
tcp    0    0 0.0.0.0:22    0.0.0.0:*   LISTEN 704/sshd
tcp    0    0 127.0.0.1:25   0.0.0.0:*   LISTEN 832/sendmail
udp    0    0 0.0.0.0:68    0.0.0.0:*      772/dhclient
```

```
udp      0     0 10.4.65.253:123 0.0.0.0:*         803/ntpd
udp      0     0 127.0.0.1:123   0.0.0.0:*         803/ntpd
udp      0     0 0.0.0.0:123     0.0.0.0:*         803/ntpd
```

This lists the TCP and UDP sockets that are ready to receive incoming data (connections in the case of TCP and datagrams for UDP). You can see that this machine is listening on four TCP/IP ports, which are the numbers after the ":" in the Local Address column (22 for ssh, 25 for incoming mail, 6000 for X11 and 32769 for the xinetd "super" server). It will also accept datagrams on port 68 (DHCP client) and 123 (Network Time Protocol service).

Three TCP/IP addresses appear in this local address column: `0.0.0.0` means that the server is listening on all addresses, `127.0.0.1` is the machine's loopback address, and `10.4.65.253` is the address of the machine's Ethernet card (leased from a DHCP server).

If you leave out the `-l` flag, `netstat` shows you all the active connections. If you leave out the `-n` flag, `netstat` looks up port names in `/etc/services` and host names using DNS, giving symbolic output. Try varying the flags to see what information is returned.

You can check the output of the `netstat` command to make sure that you don't have any programs listening on TCP or UDP ports that you're not expecting. The `-p` flag, which gets `netstat` to print out the Process ID (PID) and name of the process that opened the socket, is very useful for identifying "rogue" programs, perhaps modified by an intruder, that are listening on unexpected ports. (Of course, if you've got Tripwire set up and you're running regular scans, you'll quickly identify a program modified by an intruder.)

nmap

The `nmap` program takes a different approach to the problem of identifying which ports are being listened to (are "open" in `nmap` parlance) on a machine. It sends special packets to ports on the machine in question, and listens for the response. This enables it to deduce whether the port is open, closed, or even being blocked by a firewall (more on that later). The `nmap` program isn't installed by default, but it is on the Fedora Core CD-ROMs, so you may need to install it if you want to try these examples.

First, by way of example, let's get `nmap` to see what ports are open on our machine. We'll use the flags `-sUT` to tell `nmap` we want it to scan both TCP and UDP ports, and accept the defaults for everything else (including the port range, which is 1 to 1023, because these are the ports that privileged services use, plus others that are mentioned in `/etc/services`).

Here's the output from a test system:

```
# nmap -sUT localhost
Starting nmap V. 3.00 ( www.insecure.org/nmap/ )
Interesting ports on rh9 (127.0.0.1):
(The 3064 ports scanned but not shown below are in state: closed)
Port      State     Service
22/tcp    open      ssh
25/tcp    open      smtp
68/udp    open      dhcpclient
123/udp   open      ntp
6000/tcp  open      X11

nmap run completed -- 1 IP address (1 host up) scanned in 3 seconds
```

It has identified the same ports as netstat did, with the exception of xinetd listening on tcp/32769. Port tcp/32769 is not listed by nmap because it is not in the range 1 to 1023, nor is it listed in /etc/services, so it won't get scanned by default. If we used the -p flag to specify port numbers (for example, added -p 1-65535 to the command line to have all ports scanned), then the open port is found and listed with unknown in the service column.

Notice that nmap needs to be told which host to scan the ports on, suggesting that it can be used to scan for open ports on remote machines. The nmap program is capable of scanning for open ports on a range of remote machines, even choosing addresses at random. However, it is wise to get written permission from the owners of systems before scanning their ports because this action may be seen as a prelude to illegal hacking activity. After all, it is just like walking past a row of parked cars and trying the doors on each one to see if they're locked. If a policeman caught you doing that, you'd have a hard time explaining that you were just looking for unlocked cars so you could tell the owners to be more careful.

IP Traffic

Capturing and analyzing network traffic is surprisingly easy. Many tools are available that enable users with sufficient privileges to record the headers and contents of network packets into files on disk and analyze the contents later. With broadcast network media, such as Ethernet, every machine on a network segment receives all the packets, regardless of who the packet is addressed to. Typically, the receiving network card discards packets not addressed to it, but most network cards can be configured to operate in "promiscuous" mode, which allows them to receive and process packets regardless of their intended destination. (Ethernet *switches*, as opposed to *hubs*, have intelligence and effectively create a series of point-to-point Ethernet links, instead of sending all packets to all machines. This not only improves security, but it can also improve performance.)

We'll use a utility called tcpdump (from the RPM package of the same name) to demonstrate just how easy it is to capture data not destined for your machine. (As with nmap, make sure you have permission to do this if you're going to try it on a network that you don't own.)

Our theoretical test setup is this. There are three machines, all connected to a 10/100 Ethernet hub, and all on a private subnet 192.168.1/24 (that's shorthand for a subnet 192.168.1.0 with a netmask of 255.255.255.0, that is, 24 bits). Fred (192.168.1.1) is a Windows machine that we'll use as a Telnet client, Bob (192.168.1.2) is a Linux server we'll be telnetting into, and Kate (192.168.1.3) is our Fedora Core 2 machine. On Kate, we su to root and type the following:

```
# tcpdump -i eth0 -l -q -X src or dst port 23
```

This tells tcpdump to listen to all packets on interface eth0 (-i eth0), buffer the output line-by-line (-l), not to print lots of header information (-q) but do print the packets in ASCII (-X), and show only packets where the source or destination port is 23—the Telnet port (src or dst port 23). We'll get an acknowledgment:

```
tcpdump: listening on eth0
```

This shows that tcpdump is logging all Telnet packets it sees on the network segment connected to eth0.

Now we go to Fred, our Windows machine, and telnet from there to Bob, our Linux server. As soon as we do, we see the packets being logged by tcpdump, even though that's running on a machine that's not the destination for the packets!

```
12:11:51.070377 fred.3335 > bob.telnet: tcp 0 (DF)
0x0000   4500 0030 317b 4000 8006 3342 0a04 4101  E..01{@...3B..A.
0x0010   0a04 4102 0d07 0017 24e6 7419 0000 0000  ..A.....$.t.....
0x0020   7002 2000 26f7 0000 0204 05b4 0101 0402  p...&...........
12:11:51.070826 bob.telnet > fred.3335: tcp 0 (DF)
0x0000   4500 0030 0000 4000 4006 a4bd 0a04 4102  E..0..@.@.....A.
0x0010   0a04 4101 0017 0d07 f267 5575 24e6 741a  ..A......gUu$.t.
0x0020   7012 16d0 e838 0000 0204 05b4 0101 0402  p....8..........
```

If you look carefully at the packet log, you can find the Password prompt and see what the user typed in response. The password has been highlighted to make it easier to see, but hackers don't need that much help—they'll probably use an automated password sniffer that'll decode the packets for them:

```
12:12:02.265222 bob.telnet > fred.3335: tcp 10 (DF) [tos 0x10]
0x0000   4510 0032 9d51 4000 4006 075a 0a04 4102  E..2.Q@.@..Z..A.
0x0010   0a04 4101 0017 0d07 f267 55fc 24e6 746e  ..A......gU.$.tn
0x0020   5018 16d0 2c48 0000 5061 7373 776f 7264  P...,H..Password
0x0030   3a20                                     :.
12:12:02.465557 fred.3335 > bob.telnet: tcp 0 (DF)
0x0000   4500 0028 4a7b 4000 8006 1a4a 0a04 4101  E..(J{@....J..A.
0x0010   0a04 4102 0d07 0017 24e6 746e f267 5606  ..A.....$.tn.gV.
0x0020   5010 21a8 0941 0000 2020 2020 2020    P.!..A........
12:12:03.180919 fred.3335 > bob.telnet: tcp 1 (DF)
0x0000   4500 0029 4b7b 4000 8006 1949 0a04 4101  E..)K{@....I..A.
0x0010   0a04 4102 0d07 0017 24e6 746e f267 5606  ..A.....$.tn.gV.
0x0020   5018 21a8 a337 0000 6620 2020 2020    P.!..7..f.....
12:12:03.218203 bob.telnet > fred.3335: tcp 0 (DF) [tos 0x10]
0x0000   4510 0028 9d52 4000 4006 0763 0a04 4102  E..(.R@.@..c..A.
0x0010   0a04 4101 0017 0d07 f267 5606 24e6 746f  ..A......gV.$.to
0x0020   5010 16d0 1418 0000 65fd 01ff fb05    P.......e.....
12:12:03.423073 fred.3335 > bob.telnet: tcp 1 (DF)
0x0000   4500 0029 4c7b 4000 8006 1849 0a04 4101  E..)L{@....I..A.
0x0010   0a04 4102 0d07 0017 24e6 746f f267 5606  ..A.....$.to.gV.
0x0020   5018 21a8 9736 0000 7220 2020 2020    P.!..6..r.....
12:12:03.423232 bob.telnet > fred.3335: tcp 0 (DF) [tos 0x10]
0x0000   4510 0028 9d53 4000 4006 0762 0a04 4102  E..(.S@.@..b..A.
0x0010   0a04 4101 0017 0d07 f267 5606 24e6 7470  ..A......gV.$.tp
0x0020   5010 16d0 1417 0000 6465 6420 4861    P.......ded.Ha
12:12:03.555199 fred.3335 > bob.telnet: tcp 1 (DF)
0x0000   4500 0029 4d7b 4000 8006 1749 0a04 4101  E..)M{@....I..A.
0x0010   0a04 4102 0d07 0017 24e6 7470 f267 5606  ..A.....$.tp.gV.
0x0020   5018 21a8 a435 0000 6520 2020 2020    P.!..5..e.....
12:12:03.555354 bob.telnet > fred.3335: tcp 0 (DF) [tos 0x10]
0x0000   4510 0028 9d54 4000 4006 0761 0a04 4102  E..(.T@.@..a..A.
0x0010   0a04 4101 0017 0d07 f267 5606 24e6 7471  ..A......gV.$.tq
0x0020   5010 16d0 1416 0000 0d0a 0869 6e3a    P..........in:
12:12:03.699442 fred.3335 > bob.telnet: tcp 1 (DF)
0x0000   4500 0029 4e7b 4000 8006 1649 0a04 4101  E..)N{@....I..A.
0x0010   0a04 4102 0d07 0017 24e6 7471 f267 5606  ..A.....$.tq.gV.
0x0020   5018 21a8 a534 0000 6420 2020 2020    P.!..4..d.....
```

This is what we mean when we say that the Telnet protocol sends passwords in plain text across the network. If that network uses broadcast media, every machine on the same network segment as the sender receives the unencrypted password on its network interface. Most of the time, the other machines will just ignore this data, but all it takes is one of them to be running a promiscuous mode packet logger such as `tcpdump` and all the passwords sent by `telnet` can be captured. FTP suffers from a similar vulnerability. Fortunately, there are secure alternatives to both Telnet and FTP (`ssh` and `sftp`, respectively) that encrypt all data they send over the network using strong encryption techniques so the eavesdropper is not able to glean any useful information from the packets.

Another packet analyzer that can be installed from the Fedora Core 2 CDs is called Ethereal. This has a graphical front end that makes it much easier to set up filters and interpret the contents of packets. (There is also a character-based version called `tethereal` that does not require X Windows). When Ethereal is started (as root, by simply typing `ethereal` at the command prompt once the `ethereal` and `ethereal-gnome` RPMs have been installed, of course), the main window opens. The Capture ➪ Start menu option opens another window where you can set capture options (see Figure 10-7).

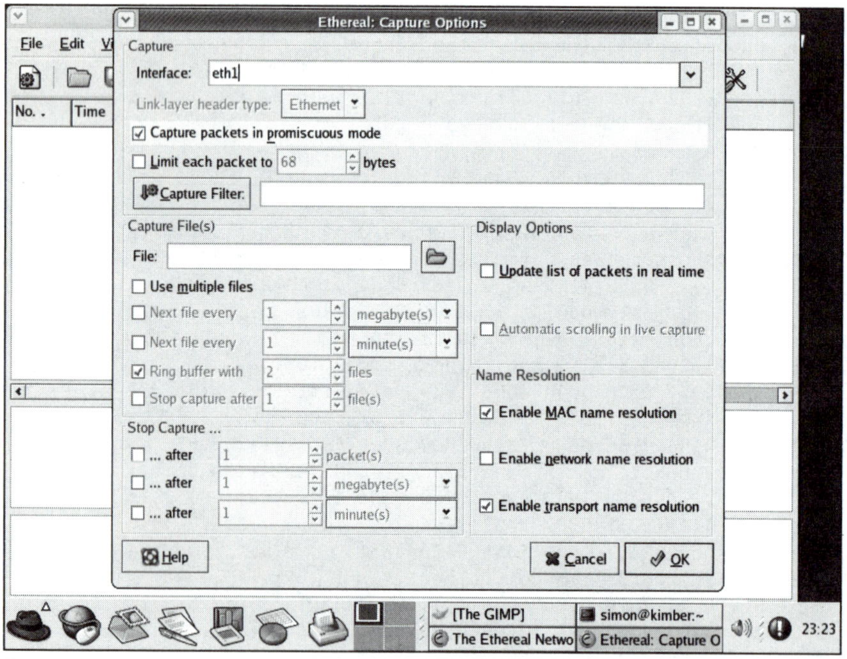

Figure 10-7

Note the check box to put the interface (`eth0`) in promiscuous mode, so packets not intended for this machine can be captured. Once capturing is running, another window is updated continuously with packet counts, as shown in Figure 10-8.

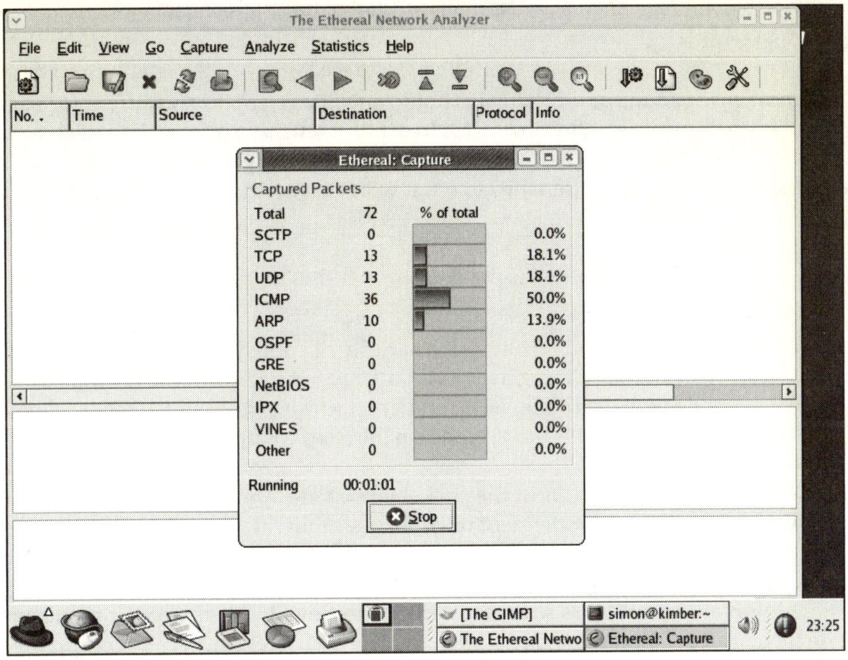

Figure 10-8

With the options chosen in the example capture window, the main display is also updated in real time, as demonstrated in Figure 10-9.

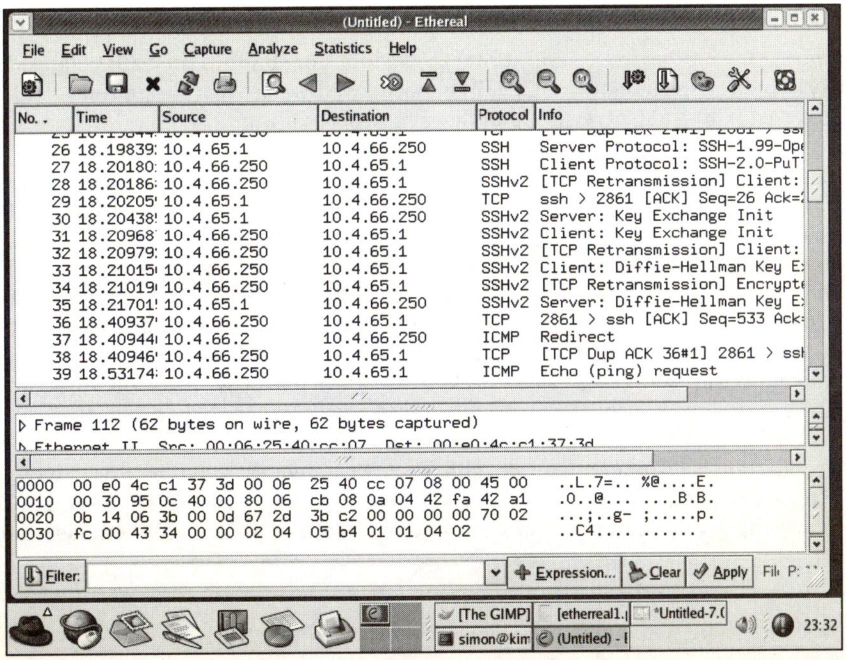

Figure 10-9

This example shows the start of an `ssh` session between two machines. This time, you won't be seeing any plain text passwords.

The point of showing `tcpdump` and Ethereal is not to encourage you to go sniffing for packets on networks, but rather to illustrate just how easy it is to capture sensitive information such as passwords that are sent across broadcast networks, such as Ethernet. However, if you make sure that you use protocols such as `ssh` and `sftp` that encrypt sensitive data, it won't matter if someone is capturing the packets you send.

Firewalls

Firewalls are another useful tool for improving the security of your system. They come in different varieties, but all do essentially the same thing: network traffic passing through the firewall is analyzed, and the decision about what to do with the traffic (let it through, throw it away and tell the sender, throw it away and don't tell the sender, and so on) is made based on the rules configured by the firewall administrator.

Some firewalls analyze network traffic at the packet level; these are called *packet filters*. They can work with any network traffic, but can implement only fairly simple rules based on the contents of the packet header (typically where the packet came from, where it's going to, and what flags are set). Other firewalls understand more about the higher-level protocols used for e-mail and Web browsing. They can perform more complex tasks such as scanning e-mail attachments for viruses, or requiring users to authenticate themselves before allowing access to certain Web sites. In a typical corporate environment, the protection provided by simple packet filtering firewalls is enhanced with more sophisticated firewalls and proxies that can analyze the contents of the packets as well as their headers.

Because the Linux kernel has built-in packet filtering capabilities, we'll look at how we can configure these to enhance the security of our Fedora Core system.

Network Connections

Before exploring the mechanics of configuring the Fedora Core built-in firewall, you need to understand how network connections work. For TCP/IP connections, there are two basic protocols: Transmission Control Protocol (TCP) and Universal Datagram Protocol (UDP).

TCP is a connection-oriented protocol. This means that when two machines wish to communicate via TCP, their TCP stacks negotiate a connection and the application (such as a Web browser talking to a Web server using HTTP) and TCP ensure that packets are delivered to the application in the right order, with no duplicates. The mechanism for setting up a connection involves the exchange of TCP packets between the systems that have different flags set in their headers. First, the client (that's the machine that wants to establish a connection) sends the server (the machine the client wants to connect to) a TCP packet with the SYN flag set. The server replies with a packet whose header has both the SYN and ACK flags set, and when the client receives this packet, it sends one back with just the ACK bit set. From this point on, the connection is established, and the client and server can exchange packets.

When the connection is no longer required, either party can request that it be closed by sending the other end a TCP packet with the FIN flag set. The recipient replies with a packet that has the ACK flag set, and then performs whatever termination steps are required by the application. When this is done, a packet with the FIN flag set is sent back to the end that initially requested the connection to be closed. When this is acknowledged with a packet where the ACK bit is set, the connection is finished.

UDP is a much simpler, connection-less protocol. All that happens here is that the originator sends the UDP datagram to the recipient, and the network layer tries its best to deliver it. Unlike TCP, delivery is not guaranteed, and datagrams traveling over long distances may go by different routes and, therefore, arrive out of order at the other end. All the logic for synchronizing client and server, or retrying failed packets, has to be handled by the application code.

It is important that you understand the differences between TCP and UDP when configuring firewalls. With TCP, the direction of the connection (incoming, where the client is remote and the server is on your machine, or outgoing, where the client is local and the server is remote) is determined by the exchange of SYN, SYN+ACK, and ACK packets at the start of the connection, but with UDP, there is no connection, so incoming and outgoing simply refer to the direction of the packet.

Configuring the Fedora Core Firewall

Configuring the Fedora Core firewall is very straightforward. Start the Security Level Configuration application by choosing Main Menu ➪ System Settings ➪ Security Level, or by typing `redhat-config-securitylevel` at the command prompt. If you are not logged on as root, and you haven't recently supplied the root password to enable you to update system-wide settings, you'll be prompted to do that before the Security Level Configuration starts. When it does, you'll see the window shown in Figure 10-10.

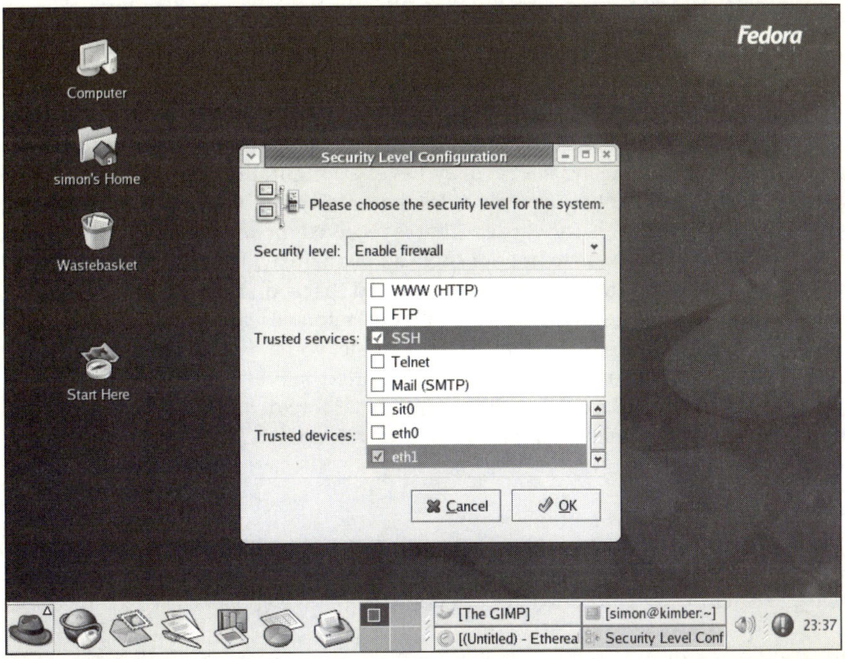

Figure 10-10

Under the Security Level drop-down list, the options are Enable Firewall and Disable Firewall. If you choose Disable Firewall, the other options are disabled, and when you click on the OK button and click the Yes button on the Warning dialog, any firewall configuration is removed and your system is completely open to any packets sent to it on any network interface. For obvious reasons, this is not recommended.

If you choose Enable Firewall, you can "trust" (that is, allow incoming connections) on five different services by checking the box next to the service name:

- **WWW (HTTP):** Used for remote Web browser connections to your local Web server
- **File Transfer Protocol (FTP):** Used for transferring files, but sends passwords in plain text
- **SSH - Secure Shell (SSH):** Used for encrypted and authenticated remote shell and file transfer
- **Telnet:** Allows users to log in remotely
- **Mail (SMTP):** Allows other machines to send our machine e-mail messages

Note that this configuration only affects *incoming* connections, that is, when it is the remote machine that initiates the connection. The Fedora Core 2 firewall configuration does not affect *outgoing* connections, that is, when it is your local machine that initiates the connection.

The bottom half of the Security Level Configuration application window shows the available network devices. You can choose to "trust" (that is, not restrict the traffic on) a device by checking the box next to the device name. Trusted network devices ignore any restrictions you may place on the services you trust. For example, if you trust only SSH, but also trust the `eth0` device, incoming Telnet or FTP connections will still be accepted on the `eth0` interface (provided you have the FTP and Telnet servers correctly configured to handle incoming connections).

The example in Figure 10-10 shows a system where SSH and `eth1` are trusted. This means that incoming SSH connections will be accepted on any interface, and all incoming packets are accepted on `eth1`. There is one significant drawback to using the Security Level Configuration application to configure your packet filtering firewall; both configure only rules that selectively block incoming network traffic. Outgoing traffic and traffic that is forwarded (that is received on one network interface and sent out on another) by your Fedora Core system are not checked in any way. This means that, should you have a system behind your firewall that has been compromised (hacked or maybe infected by a virus), it is free to transmit whatever it likes through your firewall. It is a good idea to configure your firewall to block selected outgoing and forwarded traffic, too. For example, you may want to force all Internet access for machines behind the firewall to be handled by secure proxy servers. You can do so by blocking outgoing Internet access for all machines except the proxy servers. More detailed firewall configuration like this is done with the `iptables` command, so let's look at how to do that.

iptables

This section is a brief introduction to setting up customized security beyond what is possible with the GUI tools provided by Red Hat. It's not meant to be comprehensive, as everyone's needs are different, and it'd be impossible to cater to them all. However, we hope it will give you a taste of the tools available.

Blocking and allowing traffic based on direction (incoming or outgoing) and port number gives some degree of control over network traffic, but there are situations when you need finer control. For example, you may want to run a Web server that can be accessed only from machines within your department, and not from machines elsewhere. Or you may want to prevent users on certain machines from being able to FTP files from your machine while allowing others to do so. The firewalling code in Fedora Core 2 is perfectly able to cope with these situations, and far more complex ones, but you have to roll up your sleeves and configure it from the command line.

This is where the `iptables` command comes in. It is used to manipulate the kernel's packet filtering tables, so you can fine-tune the firewall settings to your environment.

Imagine your Fedora Core machine has two network interfaces: `eth0` has the IP address `192.168.1.1` and `eth1` has the IP address `192.168.10.1`. Both interfaces have netmasks of `255.255.255.0`. You're running a Web server listening on port 80, and an FTP server that uses ports 20 and 21. You need to allow machines with IP addresses starting with `192.168.10` access to the Web server, but nobody else. You also need to allow all machines in the `192.168.1.0` network access to the FTP server, except `192.168.1.57`. How do you configure this?

The first thing to do is look at the existing firewall configuration. Log on to the machine and switch to the root user. Run the following command to get a verbose listing of the current firewall rules:

```
# iptables -L -v
```

Rules are grouped together into *chains*. There are three default chains:

- `INPUT`, which handles incoming network packets destined for processes on the local machine
- `OUTPUT`, which handles outgoing network packets produced by the local machine
- `FORWARD`, which handles packets that arrive on one interface and leave on another (meaning the local machine is forwarding them).

If you have enabled the Fedora Core 2 firewall, you will see that the `INPUT` and `FORWARD` chains are linked to a user-defined chain called `RH-Firewall-1-INPUT`. The rules in the `RH-Firewall-1-INPUT` are those that the Security Level Configuration application created in response to your trusted service and trusted device selections.

To set up your machine to meet the specifications, clear out (or *flush*) the existing rules with the following command:

```
# iptables -F
```

You can use this command to delete the named user-defined chain:

```
# iptables -X name
```

You're going to be dealing only with packets coming into your machine in this example, so you'll be configuring rules in the `INPUT` chain. Your first step is to configure the default behaviors—or Policy—for the `INPUT` chain so that if it receives a packet that doesn't match any rules, it drops (discards) it. This is the most security-conscious approach because it means that everything is blocked unless you explicitly allow it. The command to set the policy on the `INPUT` chain to `DROP` is as follows:

```
# iptables -P INPUT DROP
```

As soon as you type that in, all incoming network packets are dropped, so before you do so, make sure that you're logged in to the machine on the console. If not, you'll lose your connection to the machine and won't be able to get it back.

You could also have used `REJECT` *instead of* `DROP` *as the policy. This would result in a message being sent back to the sender of a blocked packet informing them that the port is not reachable. This is polite, and could prevent a hapless user from continually retrying a connection attempt that will never work. However, it also confirms your presence to a would-be hacker. The policy of* `DROP` *silently discards the incoming packet, so your would-be hacker won't even know there's anything listening at your IP address. Of course, this is valid only if you never respond to any requests—once you've responded to one, you've given the game away.*

Now, you need to allow machines with IP addresses on the `192.168.10/24` network access to the Web server. This is listening on TCP port 80. You'll add a rule that says to accept any packet arriving on interface `eth1` from a machine in the `192.168.10/24` network that is destined for port 80. The syntax for this is as follows:

```
# iptables -A INPUT -p tcp -s 192.168.10/24 -i eth1 --dport 80 -j ACCEPT
```

- `-A INPUT` means append the rule to the `INPUT` chain.
- `-p tcp` means match packets for the TCP protocol.
- `-s 192.168.10/24` means match packets with a source address in the `192.168.10/24` network.
- `-i eth1` means match packets on the `eth1` interface.
- `--dport 80` means match packets with a destination port of 80.
- `-j ACCEPT` means jump to the `ACCEPT` target (that is, allow the packet through).

You don't have to specify the network interface, but doing so will prevent someone spoofing an IP address on the wrong network from gaining access.

Your second requirement is to allow FTP access to hosts in the `192.168.1/24` network attached to `eth0`, except `192.168.1.57`. You do this as a pair of rules; the first is a specific rule to block FTP access from `192.168.1.57`, and the second is a more general rule that allows the others in. Because packets are passed to rules in order, you want to place your more restrictive rules first to ensure that they match. So, your two new rules are created with the following:

```
# iptables -A INPUT -p tcp -s 192.168.1.57 --dport 20:21 -j DROP
# iptables -A INPUT -p tcp -s 192.168.1/24 -i eth0 --dport 20:21 -j ACCEPT
```

If you view your tables with the following command, you'll see our rules . . . eventually:

```
# iptables -L -v
```

If DNS is configured on your machine, you'll find that all the DNS queries time out because you've blocked all the DNS traffic. So, you need to add some more rules to allow important network traffic through:

```
# iptables -A INPUT -p all -s nameserver --dport domain -j ACCEPT
```

(Replace *nameserver* with the TCP/IP address of your name server.) Now your name server queries should work again. Here's what the rules look like:

```
# iptables -L -v
Chain INPUT (policy DROP 26 packets, 2276 bytes)
 pkts bytes target   prot opt in   out   source          destination
  0    0 ACCEPT   tcp -- eth0  any   192.168.10.0/24    anywhere      tcp dpt:http
  0    0 DROP    tcp -- any  any   192.168.1.57     anywhere      tcp dpts:ftp-data:ftp
  0    0 ACCEPT   tcp -- any   any   192.168.1.0/24    anywhere      tcp dpts:ftp-
data:ftp
  0    0 ACCEPT   all -- any   any   nameserver     anywhere      tcp dpts:domain


Chain FORWARD (policy ACCEPT 0 packets, 0 bytes)
 pkts bytes target   prot opt in   out   source          destination

Chain OUTPUT (policy ACCEPT 1190 packets, 430K bytes)
 pkts bytes target   prot opt in   out   source          destination
```

Once you've configured your rules, you need to make sure that they work as expected. In this example, you could try FTP and Web server access from different hosts to see that they were allowed or blocked, as required. When you're happy with the rules, save them so they will be reactivated if the machine is rebooted. Do this with the following command:

```
# service iptables save
```

Virtual Private Networks

Virtual Private Networks (VPNs) are widely used to connect two trusted networks via a third network that is not trusted. A typical example is a company that needs to give some of its employees secure access to internal network resources from their own homes. This is possible using dedicated communications lines between the office and the employees' homes, but such lines are usually expensive. A VPN solution only requires the office and employees' homes to be connected to the Internet, which is usually a much cheaper alternative.

Tunneling

Tunneling is the name given to the technique of transporting information between two endpoints across a transmission medium where the information being transported is hidden from the transmission medium. The diagram in Figure 10-11 illustrates this.

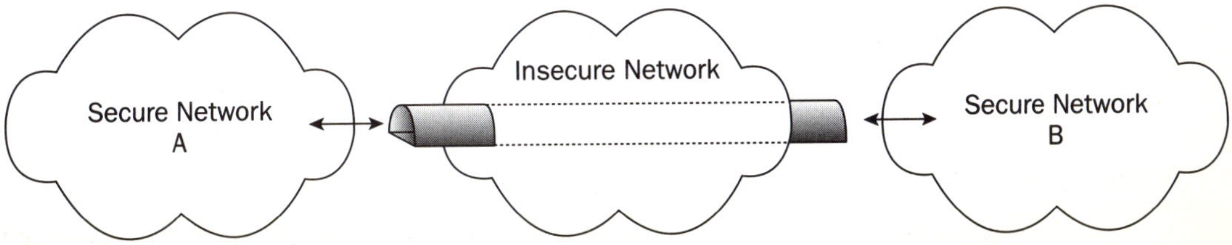

Figure 10-11

In the diagram, the two endpoints are called Secure Network A and Secure Network B; however, in real life, the endpoints could just as well be host systems instead of networks. The problem that you are trying to solve is that you want to transfer information between the two secure networks, but do not trust the network path in between (for example, because it is the Internet).

The diagram shows how you solve the problem by creating a tunnel between the two networks. Information leaving Secure Network A is encoded before it enters the tunnel in such a way that only Secure Network B can decode it, and Secure Network B can also verify that the information could have come only from Secure Network A. (It is possible to create a tunnel that does not have these security features, but this is not often done).

When you create tunnels and use them in this way, you are creating Virtual Private Networks (VPNs). The next few pages look at how you can set up VPNs using your Fedora Core 2 system in common scenarios.

When talking about VPNs, the terms "client" and "server" have a rather loose interpretation. Once a VPN tunnel is established, it is a peer-to-peer connection, with both ends performing identical roles. In this section, the "client" is taken to be the end that makes the initial request to set up a VPN tunnel, and the "server" is the end that responds to the request.

Working with Microsoft VPN Servers

This section shows you how to set up your Fedora Core 2 system so that it can connect to a Microsoft VPN server (for example, you may have such a server in your office and wish to connect to it from your home).

You must make sure you have permission from the owner of the VPN server to connect your Fedora Core 2 system to it. When your VPN tunnel is up and running, your machine effectively becomes part of the secured network behind the VPN server. If you are also connected to the Internet (which is very likely, as that is probably how you are accessing the VPN server), the firewall configuration on your machine is the only thing between the Internet and the secured network.

Point-to-Point Tunneling Protocol

The tunneling protocol you will be configuring here is the Point-to-Point Tunneling Protocol (PPTP). Some Microsoft Windows versions also support Layer 2 Tunneling Protocol (L2TP) tunnels. With PPTP tunnels, there are two paths between the endpoints. A control session is created using TCP on port 1723, and the tunneled data is sent using the Generic Route Encapsulation (GRE) protocol, which is protocol number 47. (See the file `/etc/protocols` for a list of protocols—you are probably already familiar with ICMP, TCP, and UDP, which are protocol numbers 1, 6, and 17, respectively.)

The protocol number for GRE is important if you have any sort of firewall or port filtering between your machine and the VPN server (which you certainly should). You will need to ensure that the TCP connection on port 1723 and the GRE protocol are allowed by your firewall before you will be able to get a VPN tunnel working.

MPPE and MPPC

Microsoft uses its own encryption algorithm, Microsoft Point-to-Point Encryption (MPPE—described in RFC 3078), along with its own compression algorithm, Microsoft Point-to-Point Compression (MPPC—described in RFC 2118). Unfortunately, at the time of this writing, support for these protocols is not included in the Fedora Core 2 release, so if you want to connect your system to a Microsoft VPN server, you will have to add MPPE and MPPC support yourself.

The first place to look for the necessary MPPE and MPPC packages is `http://pptpclient.sourceforge.net/`. This is the home of a Point-to-Point Tunneling Protocol (PPTP) Client that is released under the GNU General Public License. By the time you read this, there may be specific instructions and RPM packages for Fedora Core 2. In any case, there is a lot of very helpful information on this site, and it is well worth a visit.

Another place to look for the patches required to add MPPE support to Fedora Core 2 is at `www.polbox.com/h/hs001/`.

From here, you can download the appropriate kernel patch (for example, linux-2.6.1-mppe-mppc-0.98.patch.gz for the 2.6.1 kernel). As the name implies, this file is a patch for the kernel source code, so you will need to install the kernel-source-2.6.1-1.65 RPM package and the utilities required to build the kernel. Be warned: This requires about 2GB of space in `/usr/src`. If you have not got enough space in `/usr`, you can create a new filesystem and mount it under `/usr/src` before installing the kernel source RPM.

Patching the Kernel

After you have installed the kernel source RPM, you are ready to patch the kernel. Change to the directory where you saved the downloaded file, and extract the patch with the following command:

```
gzip -d linux-2.6.1-mppe-mppc-0.98.patch.gz
```

This will uncompress the file and you will have a new file without the `.gz` filename extension. Switch to the root user and apply the patch with the following commands:

```
su
patch -d /usr/src/linux-2.6.1-1.65 -Np1 < linux-2.6.1-mppe-mppc-0.98.patch
```

You should see output similar to this as the patch modifies the kernel source files:

```
patching file drivers/net/Kconfig
Hunk #1 succeeded at 2313 (offset 17 lines).
patching file drivers/net/Makefile
Hunk #2 succeeded at 103 (offset 1 line).
patching file drivers/net/ppp_generic.c
patching file drivers/net/ppp_mppe_crypto.c
patching file drivers/net/ppp_mppe_crypto.h
patching file drivers/net/ppp_mppe_mppc_comp.c
patching file include/linux/ppp-comp.h
```

Now type

```
exit
```

to return to your nonprivileged shell prompt.

Now decide where you want to build the new kernel. This should be a directory under your home directory. Use the following commands to create the directory and set up an environment variable (`$BD`) that will save you some typing and reduce the chance of errors. (In the example, the build directory is set to `/home/user1/build/kernel`; change this to suit your system.)

```
mkdir -p /home/user1/build/kernel
BD="/home/user1/build/kernel"
```

Now change the directory to the top of the source tree and configure the kernel by running these commands:

```
cd /usr/src/linux-2.6.1-1.65
make O=$BD menuconfig
```

This brings up a character-based menu that can be used to configure the kernel (see Figure 10-12).

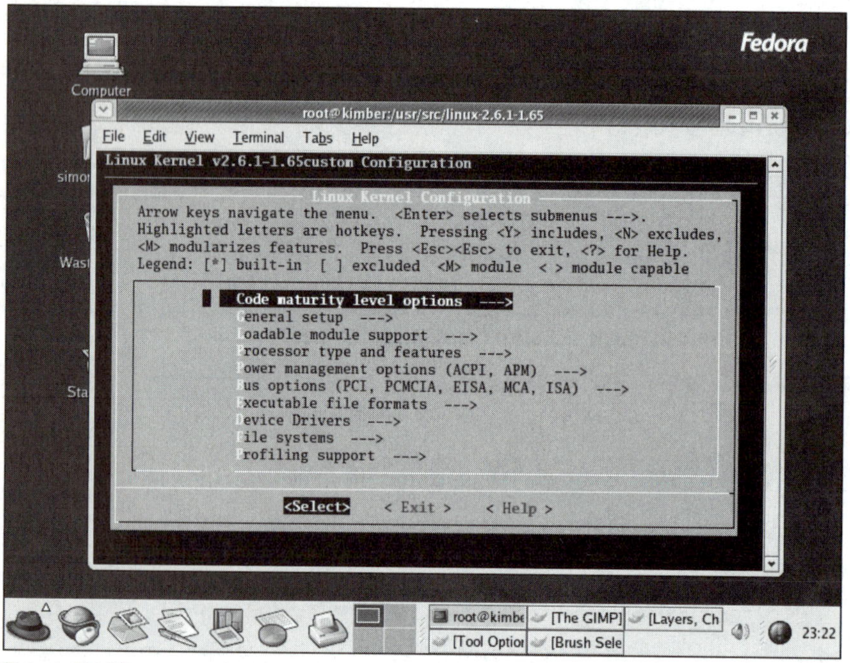

Figure 10-12

Navigate through the menus as follows: Device Drivers ➪ Networking Support.

Scroll down the list of devices until you find Microsoft PPP compression/encryption (MPPC/MPPE). Type **M** to have this built as a kernel module (see Figure 10-13).

Press Escape repeatedly to exit back up through the menus, and answer Yes when you are asked if you want to save your new kernel configuration.

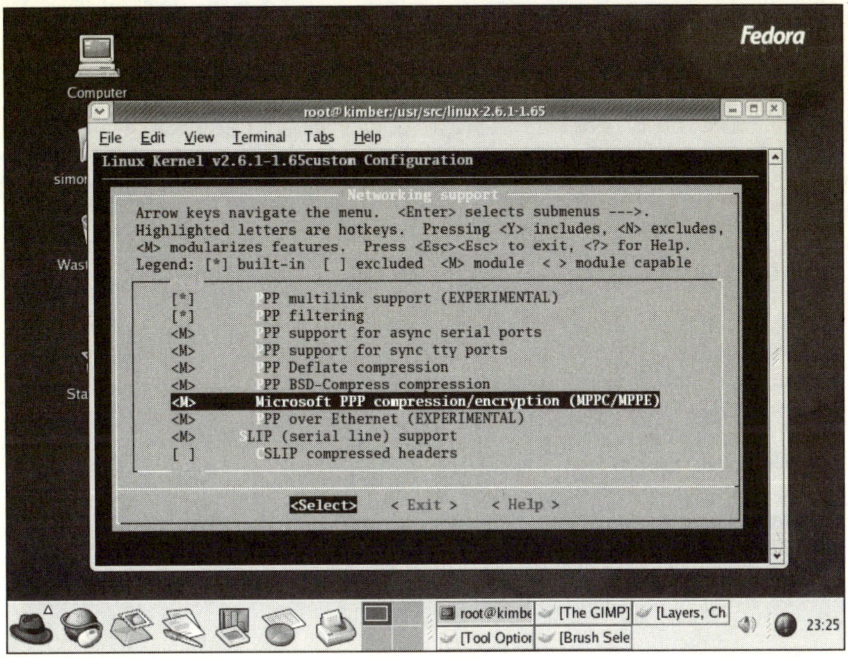

Figure 10-13

Building the Kernel

Now build the kernel with this command:

```
make O=$BD
```

This starts the kernel build process that takes quite some time (up to an hour, depending on the speed of your hardware). The name of each object file is listed as it is compiled, along with any error or warning messages from the compiler. If all the objects are built successfully, they are linked together to form a new kernel.

The next step is to build the modules. You do this with the following command:

```
make O=$BD modules
```

Finally, the modules need to be installed. Root authority is required for this because the modules are written to a directory that is not writeable by unprivileged users.

```
su
make O=$BD modules_install
```

Using the New Kernel

Having built the patched kernel and built and installed the modules (including the one that provides MPPE and MPPC support), you can now copy the kernel image and map file (essential for booting) to `/boot`, and configure GRUB (refer to Chapter 1 for more information on using GRUB) to boot the new kernel for you.

The location of the kernel image depends on your machine architecture. There are different subdirectories under the arch directory for each supported hardware architecture. Assuming you are running on 32-bit, Intel-compatible hardware, the kernel image will be called `arch/i386/bzImage`.

```
cp $BD/arch/i386/boot/bzImage /boot/vmlinuz-2.6.1-1.65custom
cp $BD/System.map /boot/System.map-2.6.1-65custom
```

Configuring GRUB is simply a matter of editing the configuration file `/boot/grub/grub.conf`, copying the stanza that defines the kernel that you currently boot your Fedora Core system with, and modifying the title and kernel definitions. If, for example, your current Fedora Core 2 boot stanza is

```
title Fedora Core 2
    root (hd0, 1)
    kernel /vmlinuz-2.6.1-1.65 ro root=LABEL=/ rhgb
    initrd /initrd-2.6.1-1.65.img
```

Create a new stanza like this:

```
title Fedora Core 2 with MPPE MPPC support
    root (hd0, 1)
    kernel /vmlinuz-2.6.1-1.65custom ro root=LABEL=/ rhgb
    initrd /initrd-2.6.1-1.65.img
```

After all this work, you can reboot your system and choose your new kernel.

Testing Kernel MPPE and MPPC Support

Now that you are up and running with the new kernel, you need to test that the MPPE/MPPC support module can be loaded by the kernel.

First, define an alias so that the PPP daemon can load the module using the name `ppp_compress_18` by adding the line

```
alias ppp_compress_18 ppp_mppe_mppc
```

to `/etc/modprobe.conf`, and then running the following command:

```
modprobe ppp_compress_18
```

(You will need to be root to do both of these.) Check that the `ppp_compress_18` module is loaded by running the following:

```
lsmod | grep ppp
```

You have just a couple more tasks before you can try and connect to a VPN server.

Checking for MPPE Support in pppd

PPTP VPN tunnels use the Point-to-Point Protocol (PPP) daemon (`pppd`) to transport TCP/IP packets, so `pppd` must also have support for MPPE. Full details of how to check and update `pppd` can be found at http://pptpclient.sourceforge.net. Essentially, the checking process is simply to see if the string mppe appears in the pppd executable, as follows:

```
strings /usr/sbin/pppd | grep -ic mppe
```

This command counts how many times the string mppe occurs in the /usr/sbin/pppd executable and displays the result. If it is zero, pppd does not have MPPE support and needs upgrading.

If you need to upgrade, download the latest ppp 2.4.2 i386.rpm update from http://pptpclient.sourceforge.net, and then use rpm --upgrade to upgrade your currently installed PPP RPM.

```
rpm --upgrade ppp-2.4.2_cvs_20040102-1.i386.rpm
```

Setting Up a VPN Client Connection

Now you need the PPTP client (pptp-linux RPM package) itself and (optional, but recommended) the graphical configuration tool (the pptp-php-gtk RPM package). Both of these can be obtained from http://pptpclient.sourceforge.net, so download and install them now.

After the pptp-php-gtk package is installed, you can access the graphical configuration tool by clicking the Red Hat icon, and then choosing System Settings ➪ More System Settings ➪ PPTP Client. If you are not running as root (and you should not be), you will be prompted for the root password before the main pptp-php-gtk-setup window appears. The window is split into two parts; the top part shows the status of each tunnel you have defined, and the bottom part contains entry fields where you can define tunnels (see Figure 10-14).

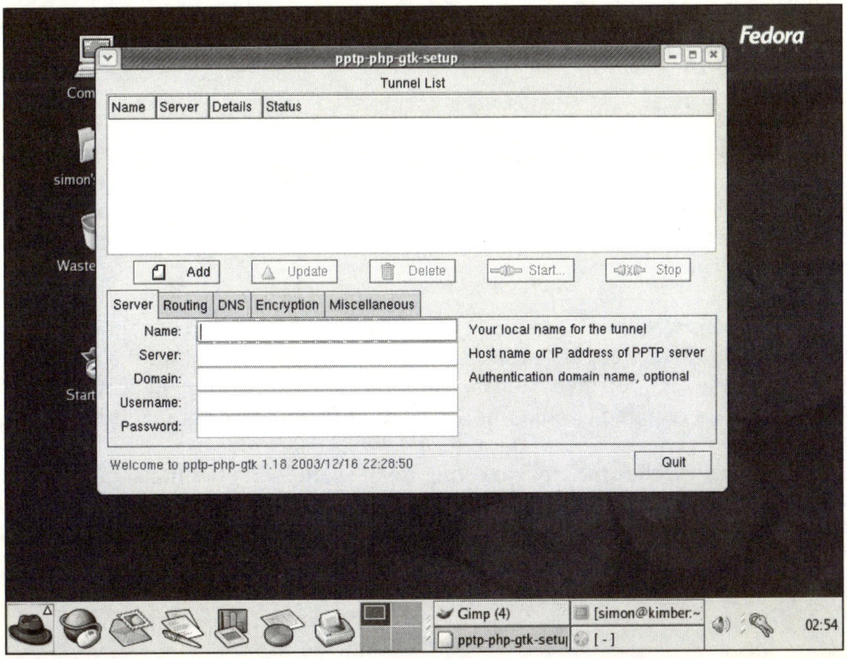

Figure 10-14

The first thing to do is fill in the fields on the Server tab. The example in Figure 10-15 shows how you would set up a server called MyWorkplace where the IP address of the remote VPN server is `172.20.1.1`, the Windows username is mylogin, and the password is secret. (A Windows domain name is not needed to log in to this particular server, but if you do need to supply one, there is a field to put it in.)

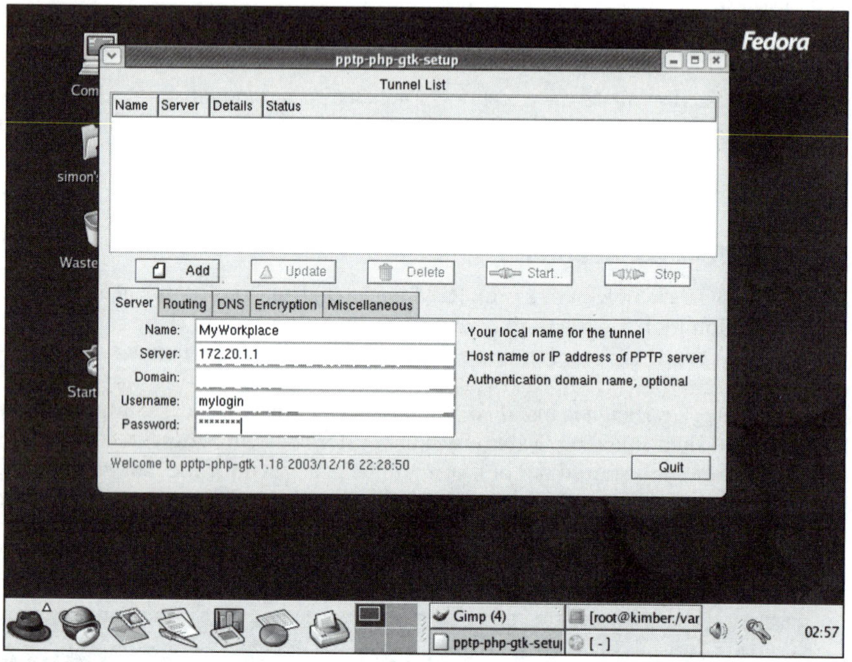

Figure 10-15

After defining the server, you must configure the routes. Click the Routing tab, and you will see four routing options. You want to set up a route from your machine to all the addresses in the `172.20.1.0/24` network via the tunnel, so this is a "Client to LAN" type routing requirement (because your machine—the client—needs a route to a LAN). Select the Client to LAN radio button, and then click the Network Routes button (see Figure 10-16).

Another window opens where you can define the required routes. Fill in the Network information (in the format network address/network mask bits, that is, `172.20.1.0/24` for the network `172.20.1.0` with netmask `255.255.255.0`), give it a name, and click the Add button. Repeat these steps for all the network routes that are required (see Figure 10-17), and then click the Close button.

Back in the main window, click the DNS to configure the name server options. In this example, the remote VPN server tells the client the IP addresses of the name servers to use during the PPP link setup phase, so you simply need to check the Automatic box (see Figure 10-18). This causes the PPTP client to change the `/etc/resolv.conf` file using information provided by the remote VPN server when bringing the link up and restore it from a saved copy when taking the link down again.

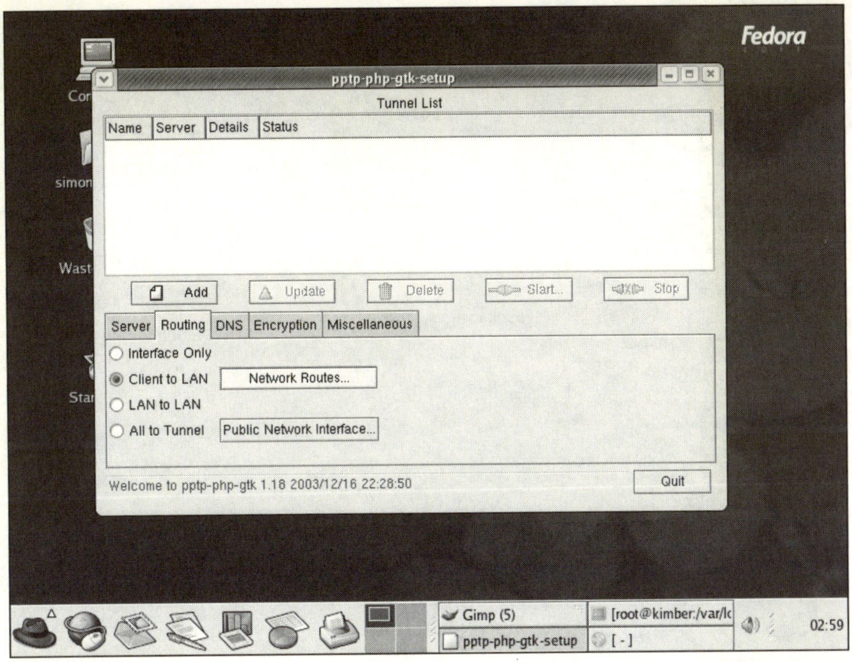

Figure 10-16

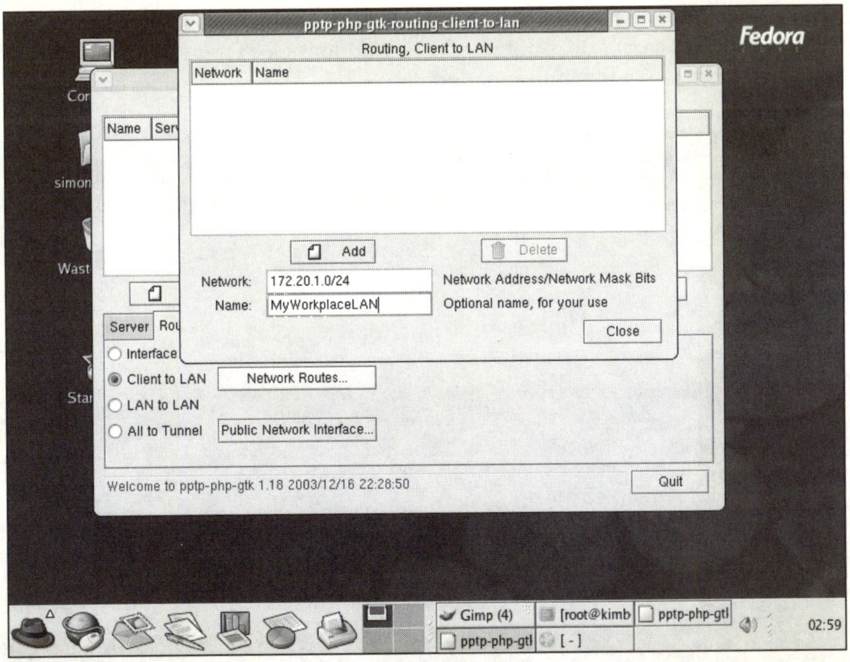

Figure 10-17

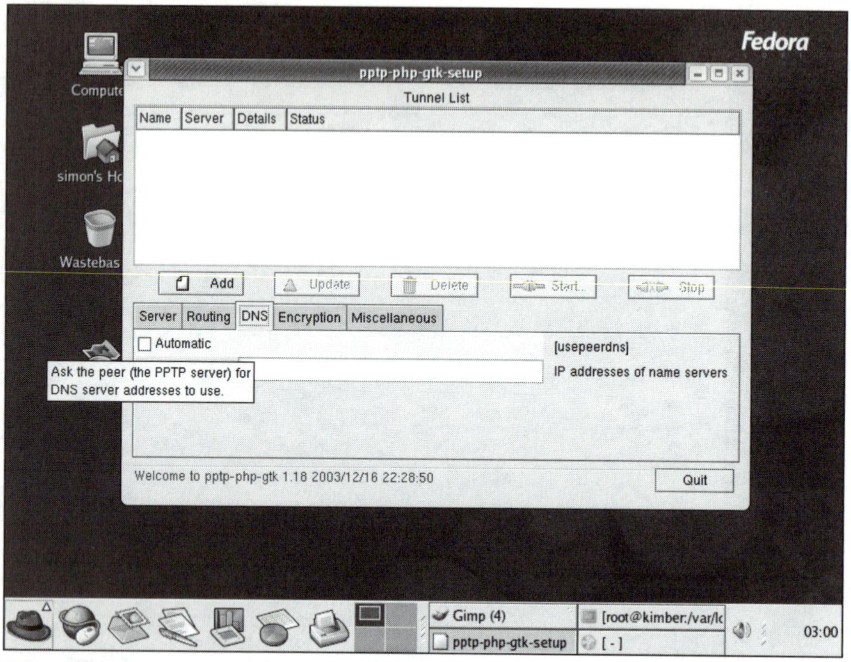

Figure 10-18

The next tab is the Encryption tab. Here you can set the encryption options to suit the remote VPN server. Our example VPN server does not require any options (see Figure 10-19), but you may find that you need to force MPPE to get the tunnel started.

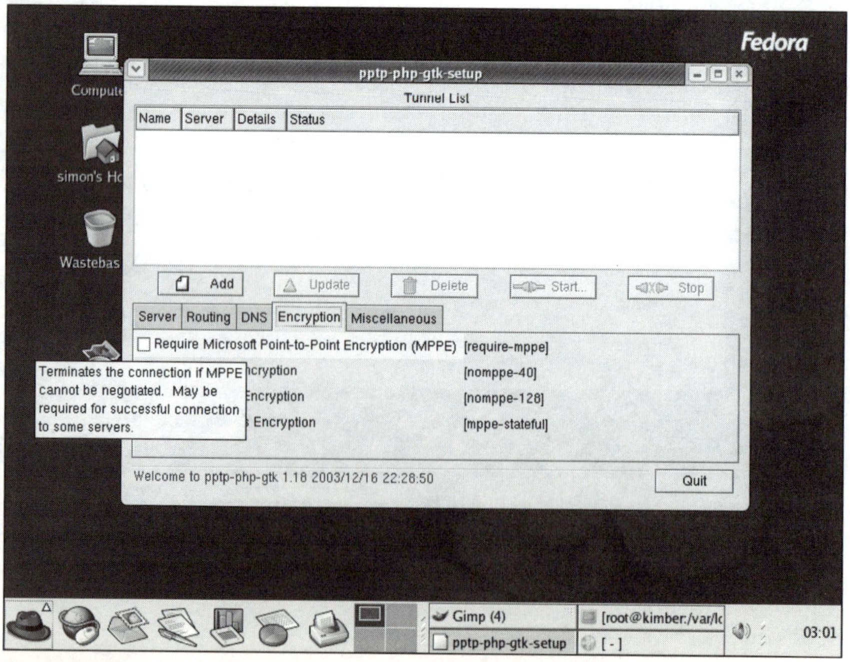

Figure 10-19

The last tab is the Miscellaneous tab (see Figure 10-20). You do not usually need to set any options here, but if you are having trouble starting your tunnel, enabling connection debugging may be helpful.

After you have entered all the information for your tunnel, click the Add button and a new entry appears in the list in the top part of the window. (What is happening behind the scenes is that the files containing PPP authentication information, `/etc/ppp/chap-secrets` and `/etc/ppp/pap-secrets`, are updated, a file is created in `/etc/ppp/peers` with your connection information, and the configuration file `/etc/ppp-php-gtk/tunnels` is updated.)

Now you are ready to test the tunnel. Click the line representing your tunnel in the list at the top of the screen, and then click the Start button (see Figure 10-21).

A new window opens and shows you progress messages as `pptp-php-gtk` tries to start your tunnel (see Figure 10-22).

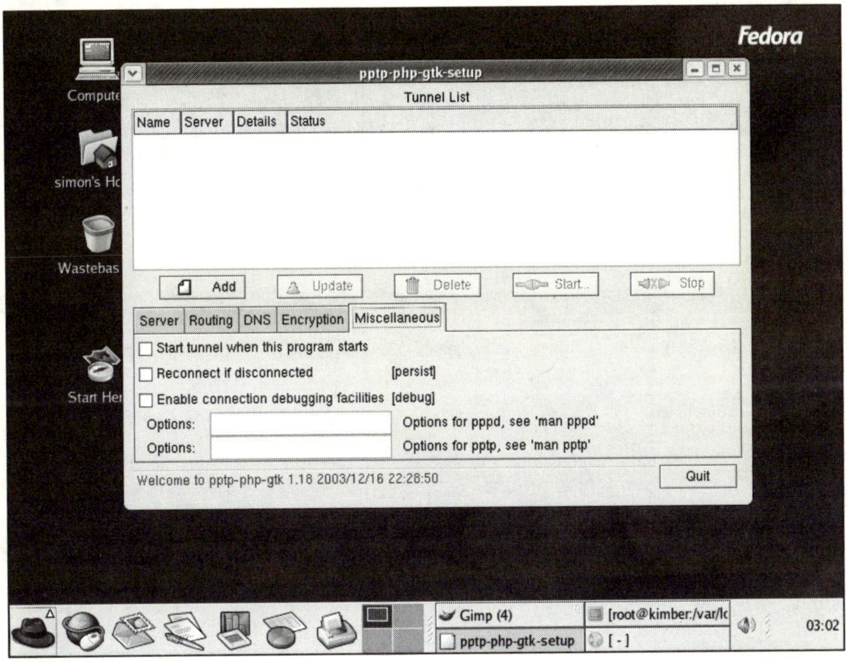

Figure 10-20

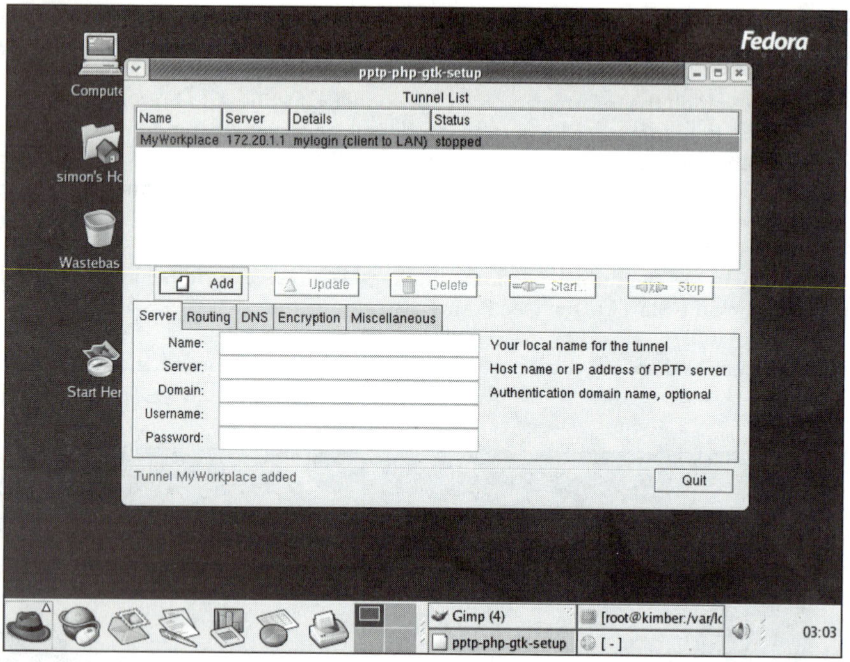

Figure 10-21

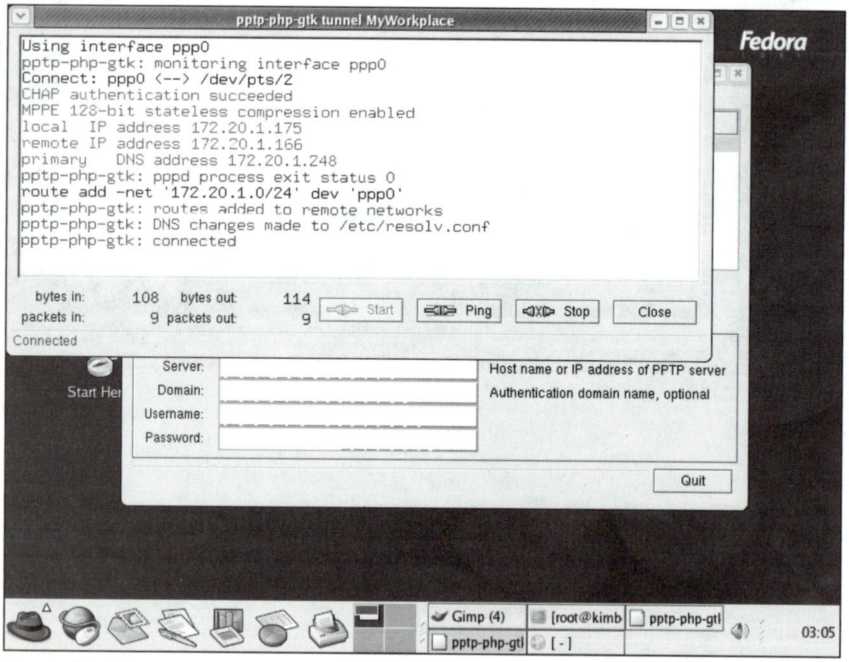

Figure 10-22

All being well, the pptpclient creates a PPP interface (ppp0, in this example), makes a connection to the remote VPN server, and passes the data coming from the tunnel to the PPP daemon, which decrypts them and unencapsulates the TCP/IP packets within. DNS information is provided by the remote VPN server when the link is established (the primary DNS address 172.20.1.248), and the pptp-php-gtk application uses this to change /etc/resolv.conf. The application also adds the network route that we asked it to.

Working with Microsoft VPN Clients

You have seen how, with a little bit of work, you can use your Fedora Core 2 system to connect to a remote Microsoft VPN Server. What if you want to do things the other way around, and have your Fedora Core 2 system as the VPN Server and allow Microsoft Windows clients to connect to you? For this you need a PPTP server. This section will use PoPToP, the PPTP Server for Linux.

The first thing to do is visit www.poptop.org. Here you can read about PoPToP and follow links to the SourceForge download sites. When you get to the SourceForge site, click the Files link at the top of the text frame to go to the list of files. Here you should find RPM packages for the latest stable release (pptpd-1.1.3-4.i386.rpm) and the latest beta test release (pptpd-1.1.4-b4.i386.rpm). Note that these are for the Intel-compatible platform; if you are running on something else, you will need to download the source code and build from that.

Download and install the RPM package (latest stable if you will be running a production server, or the beta test one if you prefer and stability is not crucial). Add the following line to /etc/modprobe.conf:

```
alias net-pf-47 ip_gre
```

You need to specify the IP addresses to be used by the local PPTP server and remote clients, and this is done with the localip and remoteip options in /etc/pptpd.conf. Note that each simultaneous connection to your PPTP server requires a unique IP address, so make sure you specify enough remote IP addresses to meet your needs. (Each connection can, however, share the same local IP address). See the comments in /etc/pptpd.conf for information on how to configure ranges of IP addresses. Add the following line to this file to tell pptpd where to find the ppp options file:

```
option /etc/ppp/options.pptpd
```

The options file, /etc/ppp/options.pptpd, provides the options for pptpd to pass on to pppd. (Note that this is different from the file /etc/ppp/options.pptp, which specifies the PPP options to use when you are acting as the PPTP client). Add the following lines:

```
refuse-pap
refuse-eap
refuse-chap
refuse-mschap
require-mschap-v2
require-mppe
nomppe-stateful
nomppe-40
```

The first few lines prevent the PPP daemon started by `pptpd` from negotiating the following with the remote client:

- Password Authentication Protocol (`refuse-pap`)
- Extensible Authentication Protocol (`refuse-eap`)
- Challenge Handshake Authentication Protocol (`refuse-chap`)
- Microsoft CHAP v1 (`refuse-mschap`)

The next lines require the remote client to agree to the following:

- Microsoft CHAP v2 (`require-mschap-v2`)
- Microsoft Point-to-Point Encryption (`require-mppe`)
- Prevent negotiation of stateful MPPE (`nomppe-stateful`) or 40-bit MPPE encryption keys (`nomppe-40`)

If the client does not agree to all of these during the initial negotiation, the connection is dropped.

The final configuration file to edit is `/etc/ppp/chap-secrets`. This is where you list the usernames and passwords that the remote machines must supply to authenticate with you and bring up a VPN connection. Add a new line, containing four fields separated by white space.

- The first field (client) is the username that the remote machine must supply.
- The second field (server) must match the name of the server, as specified with the "name" option in `/etc/ppp/options.pptpd`.
- The third field (secret) is the password that the remote machine must supply.
- The fourth field (IP address) is the IP address of the remote client—specify "*" to allow the client to have any IP address (from the range(s) allowed by the `remoteip` option in `/etc/pptpd.conf`).

With all these changes made, you can start `pptpd` with the following command:

```
service pptpd start
```

Set up your Microsoft Windows clients per the instructions in the "client configuration" section of the documentation on the PoPToP Web site and you're done.

ssh and Friends

There are many times when a system administrator needs to work with remote systems (systems where access is via some sort of network connection, rather than a directly attached terminal), either logging in to a shell to run interactive commands, transferring files between systems, or running commands non-interactively, without needing to supply a password. The most popular protocols for these tasks—Telnet for interactive login, FTP for file transfer and rlogin for automated logins—all have a major weakness: they are insecure. Telnet and FTP both send passwords across the network connection in plain text, where they can easily be intercepted, and rlogin is vulnerable to an attacker who makes their system appear to be one that the remote system trusts (sometimes called "spoofing").

Fortunately, there are widely supported, secure alternatives to these insecure protocols. This section explores using `ssh` for running remote commands, and `scp` and `sftp` for transferring files. All three of these commands use the SSH protocol to transfer information securely over a network link that may not be trusted. This protocol supports a variety of options to ensure that the systems at each end of a link are who they claim to be (thus preventing spoofing attacks), and to encrypt the information flowing across the link so that even if it is intercepted, an attacker will not be able to understand it. As a bonus, the SSH protocol also compresses the data it sends, and this generally speeds things up (except perhaps where you have a very slow machine and a fast network).

Try It Out Using ssh to Set Up a Secure Connection

You will use `ssh` to make a secure connection either between two separate systems, if you have them available, or between client and server running on the same system. We will assume that both systems are running Fedora Core 2, but if this is not the case, you should be able to adapt the following steps to suit your setup.

1. Check that the client machine (the one you will be connecting *from*) has the `ssh` client program installed by running the following command:

```
rpm -q openssh-clients
```

You should get a brief message showing you the version of the `openssh-clients` package that is installed. If you get a message saying "package openssh-clients is not installed," you should install it from your Fedora Core 2 installation media now.

2. Check that the server machine (the one you will be connecting *to*) has the `sshd` server program installed by running the following command:

```
rpm -q openssh-server
```

As in the previous step, you should get a message listing the version of the package that is installed. If you get a message saying that the package is not installed, install it now from your Fedora Core 2 installation media.

3. Try using `ssh` to connect from your client machine to your server by running the command

```
ssh servername
```

where *servername* is the hostname or IP address of your target server. Use `localhost` if you only have one system at your disposal. You should receive a message similar to the following:

```
The authenticity of host 'bach (192.168.1.1)' can't be established.
RSA key fingerprint is dc:29:c6:8e:03:96:f3:44:9f:21:fe:c4:d0:46:d7:27.
Are you sure you want to continue connecting (yes/no)?
```

This message is telling you that the server you have connected to has provided a public key to your client to prove its identity (an RSA key in this example), but your client has no record of this key. Are you sure that you have connected to the right server? What if an attacker is spoofing the identity of your target server? Type **no** at the prompt and press Enter to abort the connection because, at the moment, you are not sure that you have connected to the right server.

4. The way to be sure that you are connecting to the right server is to obtain the fingerprint of its public key by an independent route that you trust. If you are the system administrator for the

remote system, you need to log on to it via a locally attached terminal and find out the fingerprint. Here's how to do this:

Log in to the server (you do not have to be root to do this; an unprivileged login is sufficient) and run the following command:

```
ssh-keygen -l
```

You will be prompted for the name of the file containing the key. On a Fedora Core 2 system, the default location for the SSH RSA public host key is `/etc/ssh/ssh_host_rsa_key.pub`, so type this in at the prompt. (Version 2 of the SSH protocol uses RSA keys by default, but it may be configured to use DSA keys, in which case the public key file you should use is `/etc/ssh/ssh_host_dsa_key.pub`. If you are using version 1 of the SSH protocol, the public key file to use is `/etc/ssh/ssh_host_key.pub`.) The `ssh-keygen` command calculates the fingerprint of the key in this file and displays it. You should get an output similar to this:

```
[user1@bach user1]$ ssh-keygen -l
Enter file in which the key is (/home/user1/.ssh/id_rsa):
/etc/ssh/ssh_host_rsa_key.pub
1024 dc:29:c6:8e:03:96:f3:44:9f:21:fe:c4:d0:46:d7:27 /etc/ssh/ssh_host_rsa_key.pub
```

Make a note of this fingerprint—you don't have to worry about security because this is the fingerprint of the server's *public* key, and this should be known to any system that wants to use the SSH protocol to connect to it.

If you are not the system administrator for the remote server, you should really ask the person who is to confirm the public key fingerprint.

5. Now that you have obtained the server's public key fingerprint without using a network connection that may be secretly diverted to an attacker's system, you can try to connect again from the client system. Rerun the following command:

```
ssh servername
```

You will get the same warning message about the authenticity of the server you are connecting to, but this time you *can* verify the fingerprint and be sure you are connecting to the right server. (Only a system with the right private key installed on it will be able to generate the public key that has the right fingerprint, so, as with all asymmetric key encryption systems, the strength of the security depends on how well the private key is protected).

Check that the fingerprints match and type **yes** at the prompt to continue connecting. You will receive a message saying that the host has been permanently added to the list of known hosts, and then be prompted for your password. Type in your password and press Enter to log in. Whereas the Telnet protocol would have sent your password in plain text over the network for any eavesdropper to see, the SSH encrypts your password to keep it safe.

Try out a few simple commands. Everything you type and all the responses back from the server are compressed and encrypted, so you can be reasonably sure that they are secure. Log out as you would with a Telnet session (that is, type **exit** or **logout** at the shell prompt).

6. The list of known hosts is maintained in two locations on the client system. There is a system-wide list stored in `/etc/ssh/ssh_known_hosts`, and each user has his or her own list in `$HOME/.ssh/ssh_known_hosts`. The contents of these lists can be queried using the `ssh-keygen -l` command as before, so do this now to examine the contents of `$HOME/.ssh/ssh_known_hosts` (on the *client* system) You should see an entry that corresponds to the *server* that you have just connected to.

7. If you frequently have to connect to remote systems to run interactive commands, or if you need to automate remote commands, it is very useful not to have to type in a password every time you connect to the remote system. The `rsh` and `rlogin` commands allow you to do this, but they are insecure (because they rely on looking up the hostname of the client system from its IP address, and this can be spoofed). In these next few steps, you will see how `ssh` can give you the same capability, but in a much more secure way.

   Just as the SSH client uses a server's public key to authenticate that server (that is, to verify that the system it is communicating with really is the right one), the SSH server also needs to authenticate the identity of a client by using the client's public key if it is to allow a user to log in from that client without requiring a password.

   How does an SSH client get a public key? The answer is by using the `ssh-keygen` utility that you have already used. Each user on a system can use this utility to generate a public and private key pair for the SSH client to use in authenticating itself with an SSH server. Run the following command to generate an RSA public and private key pair for your SSH client to use:

```
ssh-keygen -t rsa
```

   You will be prompted to enter the name of a file in which to store the private key. This defaults to `$HOME/.ssh/id_rsa`, so just press Enter to accept this.

   Next, you will be prompted for a passphrase. You can choose not to have a passphrase by just pressing Enter, but this means that anyone who gets hold of the file containing your private key will be able to masquerade as you and connect to remote systems using your login without requiring a password. If you do use a passphrase (strongly recommended), your private key file is useless to anyone else, unless they can guess your passphrase. So, enter a strong passphrase (that is, one that contains mixed case letters, punctuation, and numbers, but is not so complex that you cannot remember it without having to write it down).

   After confirming your passphrase by typing it in a second time, the RSA key pair is generated. The private key is stored in the file you specified, and the public key is stored in the file whose name is the name of your private key file with `.pub` appended to it.

   The overall dialog should look like this:

```
[user1@bach user1]$ ssh-keygen -t rsa
Generating public/private rsa key pair.
Enter file in which to save the key (/home/user1/.ssh/id_rsa):
Enter passphrase (empty for no passphrase):
Enter same passphrase again:
Your identification has been saved in /home/user1/.ssh/id_rsa.
Your public key has been saved in /home/user1/.ssh/id_rsa.pub.
The key fingerprint is:
26:56:72:0a:4f:24:45:e0:a9:88:c5:67:ca:c5:cc:87 user1@bach
```

8. Now that you have a public key, you need to install it on the *server* system(s) that you wish to connect to without being prompted for your password. The SSH server will look in the file `$HOME/.ssh/authorized_keys` (if this file is not writeable by anyone other than the owner) and try to match up the credentials being presented by your SSH client with the public keys of the systems you have installed in this file. If there is a match, you will be able to connect without supplying a password.

Copy the *public* key only to the server by running this command and entering your password on the remote system (*server*) when prompted.

```
scp $HOME/.ssh/id_rsa.pub server:temp.key
```

(Don't worry about the syntax of the `scp` command yet—we will explore it in more detail later. All you need to know at this point is that this command will copy your public key to a file called `temp.key` in your `$HOME` directory on the remote system called *server*.)

Now log in to the remote server (using `ssh`), and run these commands to add your client's public key to the list of host systems from which you want to log in without being prompted for a password:

```
cd
cat temp.key >> .ssh/authorized_keys
chmod 600 .ssh/authorized_keys
```

9. Log out from the server system and try to log back in again using `ssh`. Instead of being prompted for your user password on the remote server, you should now be prompted for the passphrase for the RSA private key you have just generated and saved. Type in your passphrase and you should be logged in to the remote server, without needing to enter your password on that server. Log out from the remote server.

   You are probably not impressed with this. Instead of having to type in your user password on the remote system, you now have to type in the passphrase for your private key, which is probably much longer than the password. You will have to do this each time you connect, unless you use another part of the SSH suite to automate this task: the `ssh-agent`. This program takes care of supplying authentication details to SSH client programs as required, so you only have to supply your private key passphrase once (typically when you first log on to your SSH client system).

10. You can now start the `ssh-agent`. The agent outputs strings on stdout when it starts that should be evaluated by the shell to set two environment variables (`SSH_AUTH_SOCK` and `SSH_AGENT_PID`), which tell the SSH client programs how to communicate with the agent. (The agent tries to work out whether the shell requires C-shell or Bourne-shell syntax, but it can be forced either way by using the `-c` or `-s` flags, respectively).

    Start the SSH agent and set the environment variables by running the following command:

    ```
    eval `ssh-agent`
    ```

    You should get a message showing the process ID of the `ssh-agent` process that has just started, and the two environment variables previously mentioned will be set to appropriate values. Check this by running the following command:

    ```
    env | grep SSH
    ```

11. With the agent running, all that remains is to add private keys to the agent so that it can supply them to SSH clients, as required. Do this with the `ssh-add` program. Run with no arguments, `ssh-add` adds the private keys stored in the files `$HOME/.ssh/id_rsa`, `$HOME/.ssh/id_dsa`, and `$HOME/.ssh/identity` (used by SSH Version 2 RSA, SSH Version 2 DSA, and SSH Version 1 protocols, respectively). This is usually all that is required, so just run the following command:

    ```
    ssh-add
    ```

If you protected your private key(s) with passphrases, `ssh-add` will prompt you to enter these.

You can see what private keys have been added to the agent by running the following:

```
ssh-add -l
```

Remove individual keys with the following:

```
ssh-add -d
```

Remove all keys with the following:

```
ssh-add -D
```

12. Now that the SSH agent is able to perform functions that require your private key on behalf of SSH clients, you can (at last) log in to the remote servers (where you added your *public* key to the `$HOME/.ssh/authorized_user` file) without having to enter your password.

Run the following command:

```
ssh servername
```

where *servername* is the name of the remote system that knows your public key, and this time you should be logged on straight away. You can also give `ssh` a command to run on the remote system:

```
ssh servername date
```

This will cause `ssh` to run the `date` command on the remote system and then exit.

13. There is one last trick that `ssh` can do that is worth a mention in this briefest of introductions to SSH, and that is the ability to forward X11 connections over a secure channel. Many organizations do not allow X11 traffic on their networks because it is insecure (the client-server traffic is not encrypted in any way, so it is vulnerable to eavesdropping), and it also consumes a lot of bandwidth. The `ssh` program addresses both of these issues by compressing and encrypting the X11 protocol traffic between client and server. All that is needed is for the `DISPLAY` environment variable to be set when the `ssh` command is run.

If you have a graphical login (you are running an X11 server on your system and the `DISPLAY` environment variable is set), you can run a command such as

```
ssh servername xterm
```

to open an `xterm` session on the remote server.

Copying Files

There are two programs in the OpenSSH suite that copy files between systems; `scp` (secure copy) is like the insecure `rcp` (remote copy) program, and `sftp` (secure FTP) is like the insecure `ftp` program. The syntax of these two programs is similar to that of the insecure ones that they replace, so getting used to them should not be a problem. For example, suppose you wanted to copy a file called `/home/user1/data1` from a machine called `tangerine` to the `/data/incoming` directory on your local machine. The syntax for the `rcp` command to do this is as follows:

```
rcp tangerine:/home/user1/data1 /data/incoming
```

Using `scp`, the syntax is as follows:

```
scp tangerine:/home/user1/data1 /data/incoming
```

To compare, you might use the `ftp` program to connect to a remote system called `caesar` and send files in a local directory called `/app1/archive` to a directory called `/app1/backup` on the remote system using commands like this:

```
$ ftp caesar
(Enter username and password when prompted.  These are sent in plain text across
the network).
ftp> lcd /app1/archive
ftp> cd /app1/backup
ftp> binary
ftp> prompt
ftp> mput *
ftp> bye
```

With `sftp`, the commands are very similar:

```
$ sftp caesar
(Enter password or passphrase when prompted.  This is not sent across the network).
sftp> lcd /app1/archive
sftp> cd /app1/backup
sftp> put *
sftp> exit
```

The man pages for `scp` and `sftp` have more details on these commands.

Security Enhanced Linux

Security Enhanced Linux (SELinux) is a new feature of Fedora Core 2. As such, it is changing rapidly, and there are few tools available to help the beginner configure their system. The information in the following section may, therefore, become outdated before the rest of the book.

What Is SELinux?

SELinux is a version of Linux that has been developed by the U.S. Government's National Security Agency (NSA) that incorporates some of its research into computer security issues and implements "Mandatory Access Controls" (more on this later). Fedora Core 2 supports SELinux and comes with a usable default configuration that can be customized to suit your requirements.

SELinux enhances security by restricting the access users and processes have to files, directories, and other objects (for example, network interfaces) according to a set of security policies. A key feature of the SELinux security model is that all users are treated in the same way, including the root user; no user can bypass the security policies. This is what makes the access controls *mandatory*. (It is quite possible for the root user to be denied access to a file if such access would violate the security policy).

Traditional (that is, not Security-Enhanced) Linux systems are only as strong as their weakest point. Once the root account is compromised, an attacker has complete control over the machine. Figure 10-23 illustrates how dangerous this can be. The attacker (1) exploits a weakness (for example, an error in the configuration or a programming error) in one of the publicly accessible services running on the traditional Linux system. A successful attack allows them to gain root access (2). With root access, the attacker can do anything they wish, such as modifying Web pages (3) or using the compromised system to relay "spam" e-mail (4).

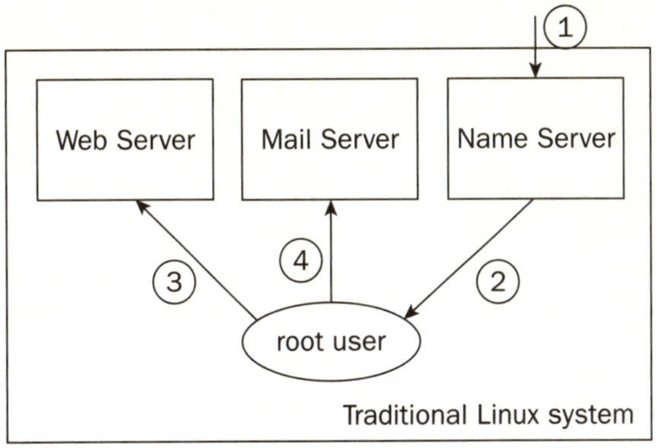

Figure 10-23

In an SELinux system, the three services in the example (Web, Mail, and Name servers) are given different "types" (as indicated by the heavy lines in the Figure 10-24). The security policy rules are defined so that the server processes are only allowed to access the objects (files, directories, devices, and so on) they need to perform their task. This effectively constrains each service to run within its own box on the diagram. Should an attacker successfully compromise a vulnerable service (1), they are severely restricted as to what they can do with that access (2).

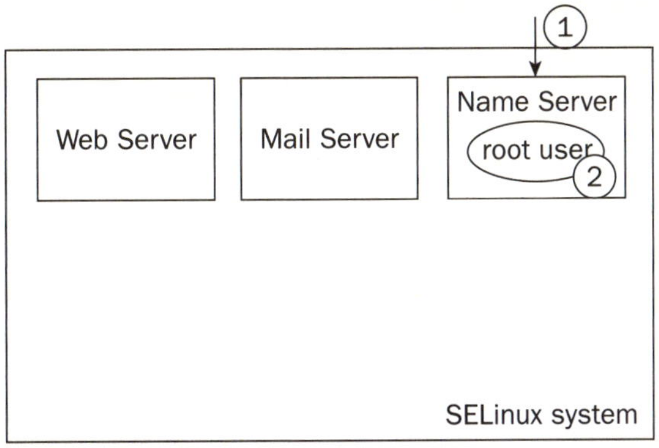

Figure 10-24

So SELinux does not particularly help with removing vulnerabilities from specific programs, but it does much to limit the damage caused if a vulnerable service is compromised and offers tighter control over who can make changes to configuration files.

If you like analogies, here's one that may help. You can think of an SELinux system as being like a ship whose hold is divided up into separate watertight compartments, with locked doors in between. If the ship gets a hole, one compartment might flood, but the doors will prevent other compartments from being affected, and the ship stays afloat. On an SELinux system, a successful attack on one service does not allow other services to be affected. A traditional Linux system, however, is like a ship with a single large hold; put a hole in it and the ship will sink.

Do I Need SELinux?

Now that you understand a little about what SELinux can do for you, you can decide if it is appropriate for your situation. As in all security matters, the decision comes down to whether the benefit of SELinux's ability to enforce access controls outweighs the cost of implementing SELinux (in terms of the extra work required to learn about, set up, and maintain the security configuration).

If, for example, you have a Fedora Core 2 system that is running several services (such as the ones used in the preceding illustrations) that are accessible from the Internet, SELinux may offer considerable benefits to you. If, however, you are running a Fedora Core 2 system on a trusted network providing just a single service, the SELinux may be less appropriate.

SELinux Basics

SELinux introduces some new terms and concepts for the Fedora Core 2 system administrator. These are explained in the following table.

Term	Meaning
Subject	A process, program, or user that can perform an action.
Object	A file, directory, device, and so on, on which one or more subjects can perform actions.
Type	A security attribute that SELinux attaches to a subject or object. (In other implementations, processes are given "domains" rather than "types.")
Context	A collection of security attributes associated with a subject or object. Contexts for files are set by "labeling" them with a security context. Such security contexts are persistent (that is, they are not changed by reboots and so on). A context comprises three values: the user identity, the role, and the type (or domain). These values are displayed separated by colons (:), as in the following example: `system_u:system_r:ntpd_t` This example has a user identity of `system_u`, a role of `system_r` and a type of `ntpd_t`.

Term	Meaning
Policy	A set of rules that define the permitted behavior of the system, including what actions subjects can perform on objects, what roles a user can have, and what transitions are allowed between domains. The default configuration of SELinux on Fedora Core 2 contains nearly 300,000 rules. (Fortunately, these are generated automatically from human-readable configuration files found in `/etc/security/selinux/src/policy` using Makefiles).
Security Identifier (SID)	An integer that maps to a security context. The SELinux code automatically assigns these integers and uses them to speed up the process of making security decisions (comparing the security contexts of a subject and object and deciding whether to allow or deny the access).
User Identity	The SELinux user space is different to the Fedora Core 2 user space. For example, a system may have 100 login users defined, but just three SELinux users (an ordinary user, an application administrator, and a system administrator).
Role	Users are authorized for a set of roles (through a User Identity), and these roles are checked against the security context of an object to determine what actions a user can perform.
Enforcing mode	SELinux denies actions that are not permitted by the security policy. This is the mode that SELinux needs to be operating in to provide enhanced security to your Fedora Core 2 system. The `/etc/sysconfig/selinux` file controls what mode SELinux will start in at the next boot. The command `setenforce 1` turns on enforcing mode on a running system. The command `sestatus` shows the current mode SELinux is running in.
Permissive mode	SELinux logs actions that it would deny in enforcing mode using syslog, but the action is allowed (so there is no additional security compared to a non-SELinux system). This mode is there to help with the configuration of the security policy. The command `setenforce 0` turns on permissive mode on a running system.

New and Updated Commands

There are several new commands for managing the new SELinux security environment. You have already been introduced to the `setenforce` command that can be used to change the mode that SELinux is operating in. Other useful new commands include `chcon`, for changing the context of a file or directory, and `newrole`, for switching the current shell to a different role (a sort of `su` command for the SELinux environment).

Many commands in Fedora Core 2 have been updated to make them SELinux aware, and there are also several new commands for managing the new security model. Often, the updated commands have a `-Z` or `--context` switch to show the SELinux context information in the output.

Try It Out Finding the Security Context

To find out the security context of your current shell, run the following command:

```
id --context
```

(Or `id -Z`, if you prefer.)

To find out the security context of the files in the current working directory, run the following command:

```
ls --context
```

(Again, `ls -Z` works, too.)

To see what security contexts the processes running on your machine have, run the following command:

```
ps -e --context
```

(Or `ps -e -Z`.)

Changing the SELinux Policy Rules

Anyone who is contemplating changing the SELinux policy should read the document "Confguring the SELinux Policy" by Stephen Smalley (you can find this at `www.nsa.gov/selinux/papers/policy2-abs.cfm` in a variety of formats). This document is an excellent introduction to the concepts found in SELinux, and the last section contains examples of adding users, permissions, and programs, as well as the more advanced tasks of creating new domains, types, and roles.

Where to Find Out More

Many useful sources of information on SELinux exist on the Internet; only a few are listed here:

- `www.nsa.gov/selinux`—U.S. Government National Security Agency (the creators of SELinux)
- `www.crypt.gen.nz/selinux/faq.html`—The Unofficial SELinux FAQ
- `fedora-selinux-list@redhat.com`—Fedora SELinux mailing list

Security Awareness

The final part of this chapter deals with "softer" security concerns, such as maintaining awareness of security issues.

Security Alerts

Security problems with software are found and fixed on an almost daily basis. It is important to be aware of any security vulnerabilities that affect software you have running on your system as soon as they are discovered. Perhaps the easiest way to do this is to subscribe to a security alert service. Red Hat provides its own through the Red Hat Network, and it is very useful because you will be notified only of problems that affect the RPMs that you have installed on your system. You'll also get notified immediately if there's an update to a Red Hat supplied RPM that you've just installed.

In addition to the Red Hat Network, many Web sites offer useful security information. A few of them are described in the following subsections.

Red Hat Errata Web Site

Red Hat provides another Web site (`www.redhat.com/apps/support/errata`) that you can use to check out security-related fixes for the packages that you have installed. From this page, you can access Security Alerts, Bug Fixes, and Enhancements for all currently supported releases of Fedora Core. There's also a link to the Red Hat Security Resource Center, where you can subscribe to a monthly security newsletter and find links to other, security-related resources.

Computer Emergency Response Team (CERT)

The Software Engineering Institute of Carnegie Mellon University runs the CERT Coordination Center. Their web site, `www.cert.org`, provides a wealth of up-to-date information about security problems. You can also subscribe to a mailing list so that you receive security alerts by e-mail.

Bugtraq

Bugtraq is a mailing list for the detailed discussion of computer security issues. You can access the Bugtraq archives at `www.securityfocus.com`, and find several mailing lists to which you can subscribe. Click the Mailing Lists button on the toolbar, and then click on the `[ info ]` link to the mailing list of interest. A pop-up window that includes instructions on how to subscribe appears.

Mailing lists you might want to check out include the following:

- `bugtraq`
- `focus-linux`
- `linux-secnews`

Logging Out

It is vital that whenever you leave a computer system that you logged into (such as your Fedora Core server, or your online banking Web site), you log out again. If you do not, there is a risk that someone else can come along and take over your connection, accessing the system as you without having to go to the trouble of cracking passwords or intercepting network traffic.

Checking Site Certificates, Signatures, Checksums, and So On

With increasing awareness of security issues, more and more online resources (Web sites, RPM downloads, and so on) are authenticated in some way. When you access these resources, you may have an opportunity to verify their authenticity. This may be a pop-up window from your Web browser, or a checksum for an RPM. Whatever mechanism exists, you should always use it to check that the Web page you are accessing or the RPM package you are about to install, is the genuine article, and has not been tampered with by anyone else.

Where to Find Out More

You can download the Official Fedora Core Security Guide from `www.redhat.com/docs/manuals/linux`. This is a good read for people who need a deeper understanding of security issues surrounding their Fedora Core systems. There are also lots of good Linux HOWTOs that cover security-related topics. Check out the Security-HOWTO and Firewall-HOWTO, for starters.

Summary

Security is largely a matter of commonsense. Different people value different things, so there is no single security configuration that will be exactly suited to everyone. However, Fedora Core does a pretty good job "out of the box," so most security work will be in fine-tuning your setup to meet particular requirements, rather than urgent actions required to fix glaring security holes.

The most important points for you to try and remember are as follows:

- Choose strong passwords.
- Avoid using insecure protocols such as Telnet and FTP, if possible.
- Do use secure protocols such as `ssh` and `sftp`, wherever possible.
- Disable network services that are not required.
- Configure Tripwire to monitor the integrity of your system on a regular basis.

If you can do all of these things, you can confidently use your Fedora Core 2 system on the Internet, knowing that you're as secure as you reasonably can be, and that all but the most determined hackers will go in search of an easier target elsewhere.

Exercises

You have a Fedora Core 2 system that is to function as a Web proxy server. Client machines are on the `192.168.1/24` network. The Internet connection is via a router on the `172.20.5/24` network. Your proxy server has two network interfaces: `eth0` is `192.168.1.100` and `eth1` is `172.20.5.17`. Both interfaces use a subnet mask of `255.255.255.0` (24-bits). Assume that the network routes and proxy services (`squid` and `named`) are correctly configured.

1. Design firewall rules (using `iptables`) to implement the following requirements.
   a. No incoming connections are allowed on the `172.20.5.17` interface.
   b. The only permitted outgoing connections on the `172.20.5.17` interface are for DNS, FTP, HTTP, and HTTPS traffic from the proxy server.

c. Two machines (IP addresses `192.168.1.201` and `192.168.1.155`) are to be allowed to connect using SSH.

d. All other machines in the `192.168.1/24` network are allowed to connect on port 3128 only (the port that the Squid Web proxy server is listening on) and port 53 (for DNS queries).

e. Allow ICMP traffic.

f. All other connections (incoming or outgoing) must be blocked.

g. Log attempts by machines on the `192.168.1/24` network to use Telnet or FTP to access the proxy server.

2. Make sure your rules will be applied each time the system boots.

3. After your proxy server has been running for a while, a new requirement is identified. Machines on the `192.168.1/24` network need to be able to make PPTP connections to an external VPN server with an IP address of `10.1.3.97`. Update the `iptables` rules to satisfy this requirement. (Assume that IP forwarding is enabled on your proxy server).

11

Advanced System Administration

Previous chapters of this book have dealt exclusively with the Personal Desktop version of Fedora Core, but you still need to perform a number of administrative tasks to keep your system running well; system administration is not limited to full multiuser servers. We have already discussed how to install the operating system and how to use it for day-to-day operations. Now it's time to explore the more advanced administrative aspects of managing a Linux system. More specifically, this chapter focuses on the following tasks:

- Examining important configuration files and the information they contain
- Analyzing system log files to track problems
- Backing up and archiving
- Installing new applications from source code

By understanding the rationale for performing these tasks, as well as how to actually implement them, you will get a better feel for how the operating system works and how to manage it properly. As you will see, Linux provides you with the capability to control and administer nearly all aspects of its operation, including the core part of the system, the kernel.

We will start by looking at the system configuration, including how to find the information you need and how to modify it to suit your requirements.

System Configuration

What do you think of when you hear the term "system configuration?" If you were to pose that exact same question to a group of people, you would most likely get entirely different responses. System configuration encompasses such a broad area of system administration that it is difficult to cover all aspects. And so, we will concentrate on configuration related to users and login, hardware, booting up and startup services, networking, and security. Even though numerous applications will allow you to manipulate system configuration through a graphical interface, you will have better control of the system if you know where the configuration information is stored and how to modify it manually when necessary.

Depending on the operating system, the configuration information is stored in different locations. For example, Microsoft Windows stores most configuration data in the Registry, while Mac OS stores it in separate binary files in a special `Preferences` folder. Where does Linux store the configuration details? For the most part, Linux, by which we mean the core components as well as individual applications, stores the information in *plain text* files in the `/etc` directory or in one of its subdirectories. This gives it a number of advantages over the other operating systems:

- You can read and edit the information easily with a text editor.
- You can back up the files consistently.
- You can maintain version control, thereby keeping track of all changes.

Unfortunately, because each component or application stores its configuration information individually in a separate file, there are bound to be differences in syntax between them. However, a majority of the files have a syntax that is easy to understand, as you will see in a moment.

Example: Finding the DNS Server

For example, perhaps you entered a DNS server address when you were installing the operating system in Chapter 1. That DNS server address forms part of the system's configuration, and its value is stored in the appropriate configuration file under the `/etc` directory hierarchy.

If you take a look at the `/etc` directory, you'll see that there are quite a lot of configuration files there. Which one contains the DNS server configuration? If you know the DNS server address, one way to find out is to use the `grep` command to search for the file that contains that address. For example, if you used the primary name server address `192.168.1.1`, you can find the correct configuration file via the following command:

```
# grep -ri 192.168.1.1 /etc
/etc/resolv.conf:nameserver 192.168.1.1
```

The output from this command points you in the direction of the file `/etc/resolv.conf`—in fact, it is this file that holds all the DNS server information. You can take a look at this file using a text editor such as `gedit`:

```
# gedit /etc/resolv.conf
```

You'll see that it is simply a text file with the following format:

```
nameserver 192.168.1.1    ## primary
nameserver 192.168.1.2    ## secondary, etc.
```

Let's take a look at some more configuration files.

Configuration Files

We mentioned that a large number of configuration files are contained in the `/etc` directory hierarchy. They're stored in a tree structure.

We can't possibly mention them all here, but in the next few pages we will cover some of the configuration files that you're most likely to find important. You should take some time to explore these files to see what information they contain, either using the `cat`, `more` or `less` commands, or an editor of some sort; just be careful not to accidentally modify or delete any information.

/etc/X11/xorg.conf

The `xorg.conf` configuration file (named XF86Config in previous versions of Red Hat Linux) controls specific aspects of the X Window system (X11) server, from keyboard and mouse to monitor. This file is essential if X11 is to work properly on your system.

> *While it is generally possible to modify configuration files by hand, we recommend that you don't try it with this one because its configuration is quite difficult. It is best to use the following Fedora Core GUI applications to manipulate the information in this file:*
>
> - `system-config-display` *(Main Menu ➪ System Settings ➪ Display)*
> - `system-config-keyboard` *(Main Menu ➪ System Settings ➪ Keyboard)*
> - `system-config-mouse` *(Main Menu ➪ Preferences ➪ Mouse)*

/etc/aliases

The `aliases` configuration file contains aliases for mail users and is used by the `sendmail` application discussed in Chapter 9. For example, you can set up an alias such that all mail sent to the alias `mickeymouse` is forwarded to the system administrator:

```
mickeymouse: root
```

Whenever you modify this file manually, you must also run the `newaliases` application (located in `/usr/bin`) for the changes to take effect.

> *The* `postfix` *mail transport application, an alternative to* `sendmail`*, has a similar configuration file, which is located at* `/etc/postfix/aliases`.

/etc/bashrc and /etc/csh.cshrc

These two configuration files set the defaults (file creation masks/permissions, shell prompts, and so on) that are used by all `bash` and `csh` shell users upon starting a new shell.

/etc/crontab

This file is a configuration file for the *cron daemon* (`crond`), which allows you to execute *automated tasks*, tasks that run unattended at specified times. Once a minute, the cron daemon checks for changes in the `crontab` file (and also in the `/etc/cron.d` directory and the `/var/spool/cron` directory), and reloads them into memory as necessary.

The following is a `crontab` entry that records the system load averages into a file every hour from 8:00 pm until 11:00 pm on Mondays:

```
min hour   day  mon  weekday  command
00  20-23 *    *    01       /usr/bin/uptime >> /var/log/load.log
```

You don't need root privileges to set up automated tasks using the `crontab` application. Any user can edit his or her own `crontab` entries via the command `crontab -e`. There's more about the cron daemon in Chapter 6.

/etc/default/useradd

This file sets the default parameters that are used whenever a new user is created. For example, if you want all new users to have the C shell by default, you would change the `SHELL` directive in the `useradd` configuration file, so that it reads as follows:

```
SHELL=/bin/csh
```

/etc/fstab

The `fstab` file contains the *filesystem table*, which is a table of all disk partitions and their mount points and default mount options. You can use this file to tell Linux about any and all filesystems to which the machine has access.

/etc/group

This configuration file lists the group names and group IDs (GIDs) of all the groups of users known to the system. Groups are important in Fedora Core—indeed, every user must be associated with at least one group. See Chapter 7 for a more detailed discussion of users and groups.

If you don't want to deal with this file directly, you can use the `system-config-users` GUI application (Main Menu ➪ System Settings ➪ Users and Groups).

/etc/grub.conf

The `grub.conf` configuration file is used at the time you start your system (unless you specified LILO). When you start your system, the first program that runs is the *grand unified bootloader* (GRUB). The GRUB is responsible for transferring control to the Linux kernel. The `grub.conf` file found in the `/etc` directory is, in fact, a symbolic link to the file `/boot/grub/grub.conf`—which, in turn, specifies the path to the kernel and the root partition.

Here is an example of what you might find in a `grub.conf` file:

```
title Fedora Core (2.6.5-1.358)
      root (hd0,0)
      kernel /boot/vmlinuz-2.6.5-1.358 ro root=LABEL=/ rhgb
      initrd /boot/initrd-2.6.5-1.358.img
```

In Chapter 12, when we build our own custom kernel, we will modify the `grub.conf` file to point to our new kernel.

/etc/hosts

The hosts file allows you to set up aliases for local and remote hosts. This is a very powerful feature that can simplify host name lookups. For example, if you wanted to force all of your users to go to www.google.com when they enter google, simply add this record to the hosts file:

```
216.239.53.99 google
```

The IP address 216.239.53.99 is one of many IP addresses assigned to www.google.com. You can use the ping command to verify that the alias has taken effect:

```
$ ping google
PING www.google.com (216.239.53.99) from 192.168.254.2: 56(84) bytes of data.
64 bytes from www.google.com (216.239.53.99): icmp_seq=1 ttl=45 time=72.5 ms
...
```

Note that this will not work properly with network applications that perform their own DNS lookups, such as the Lynx text browser.

/etc/hosts.allow and /etc/hosts.deny

The hosts.allow file specifies (by name or IP address) the hosts that are allowed access to local TCP/IP services. By default, all other hosts are denied access. Or, you can specifically list the hosts for which you want to deny access in the hosts.deny file.

Suppose you want to control access to your server through the telnet protocol. Specifically, suppose you want to allow access only to remote users from the host www.wrox.com and to local users. To achieve this, you would specify this line in hosts.allow:

```
telnetd: LOCAL, 192.168.1., www.wrox.com
```

And specify this line in hosts.deny:

```
telnetd: ALL
```

All entries listed in hosts.allow take precedence over any entries in hosts.deny.

Note that you can use this access control mechanism only if tcp_wrappers *(the* /usr/sbin/tcpd *server) is enabled for that specific service. See the* xinetd.d *entry later in this section for more information.*

/etc/init.d

This is a symbolic link to a directory that contains a number of *startup scripts*. The startup scripts perform a number of functions, including initialization of network connections and startup of server daemon processes. For example, the file /etc/init.d/crond implements functionality to start, stop, restart, and reload the cron daemon.

Not all of the scripts in this directory are executed when you start the system. Rather, execution is governed by the system's *run level*. We discussed run levels in Chapter 2—as you'll recall, the run levels (0–6) are represented by the directories /etc/rc.d/rcX.d. Each of these directories contains symbolic links to the chosen scripts in the init.d directory. If you want a particular application or process to run within a particular run level, you can simply add a symbolic link to that application to the corresponding run level directory.

/etc/inittab

The inittab configuration file is probably the single most important file in the system—it controls the initialization process that occurs when you start the system. It is responsible for starting the init process. It contains a line to set the default run level to be used:

```
id:3:initdefault:
```

This line sets the run level to 3 (see Chapter 2 for more information on the different run levels). If you want to start your system with an X Window system interface, you can simply change this to run level 5:

```
id:5:initdefault:
```

/etc/issue and /etc/issue.net

The issue and issue.net configuration files contain the text that is displayed when you start a terminal session. Typically, this message contains the Fedora Core release number and the kernel identification. The only difference between these two files is that issue.net is displayed only to remote users who log in to the system, whereas the contents of issue are displayed to local users only.

/etc/ld.so.conf

This file contains a list of directories in which shared libraries (*.so) can be found. The information in this file is used by the ldconfig application to create the necessary links and cache to these libraries, so that development tools (such as the dynamic linker) can find them. You need to run ldconfig whenever you add, remove, or change the entries in this file.

/etc/logrotate.conf

This file contains information that controls the rotation of log files and is used in conjunction with the logrotate application.

The main reasons for rotating log files are to keep them organized and to limit their size. If you don't control the size of your log files, your backups take longer, and you also run the risk of your disk space filling up unexpectedly.

Moreover, when something goes wrong with the system, examination of the log files often helps to trace the cause of the problem. But if the log files get too large, this examination process becomes more difficult—and finding the problem is like searching for the proverbial needle in a haystack.

So the idea is that you rotate your log files periodically, or when a log file reaches a specified size. The logrotate application (located in /usr/sbin) does the work; to do so it uses the rotation time interval or file-size limits specified in logrotate.conf.

In fact, the /etc/cron.daily directory contains a simple script called logrotate, which invokes the following command to rotate the logs:

```
/usr/sbin/logrotate /etc/logrotate.conf
```

If you look at the crontab file, you will see that all the scripts in cron.daily are configured to run at 4:02 AM every day:

```
02 4   *   *   *   root   run-parts /etc/cron.daily
```

/etc/modprobe.conf

The modprobe.conf configuration file (named modules.conf in Red Hat Linux 9) tells the kernel (or more specifically, the modprobe and depmod applications) which modules to load on demand.

For example, if you want to use the tulip driver to handle your Ethernet/network card, you add the following line to the modprobe.conf file:

```
eth0 tulip
```

Of course, this assumes that the tulip driver (tulip.ko) exists in the /lib/modules/2.6.5-1.358 directory; this directory contains the modules for the Linux kernel 2.6.5-1.358. You can use the following command to check that the driver exists:

```
# find /lib/modules/ -name 'tulip.ko'

/lib/modules/2.6.5-1.358/kernel/drivers/net/tulip/tulip.ko
```

Chapter 12 discusses the modular nature of the Linux kernel, and the Linux Loadable Kernel Modules (LKM).

/etc/passwd

The passwd configuration file stores the account information (including the username, full name, and path to the home directory and default shell) for every user on the system. You can use the system-config-users application (Main Menu ➪ System Settings ➪ Users and Groups) if you do not feel comfortable modifying the contents of this file. See Chapter 7 for more information on adding users and groups.

/etc/rc

The rc file and the files in the rc.d directory control what applications and services run at specific run levels. The rc.d directory contains a number of subdirectories—each subdirectory represents a run level from 0–6. These subdirectories, in turn, contain symbolic links to startup scripts in the init.d directory (see the previous entry for init.d).

The rc file itself is responsible for starting and stopping services when a run level changes.

/etc/resolv.conf

We discussed the resolv.conf file at the beginning of this chapter.

/etc/security

The security directory contains a list of configuration files that impose restrictions on various resources. This includes information about who can log in and from which location(s) they can log in, the privileges that console users are given, and resource limits for all users.

For example, if you want to increase the hard limit for resources allocation (that is, the number of file descriptors) to all users from 1024 to 8192, you could add the following lines to `limits.conf`:

```
*       soft    nofile  1024
*       hard    nofile  8192
```

This change, along with the following change to `/etc/pam.d/login`, will allow users to increase their file descriptor limits:

```
session    required     pam_limits.so
```

At this point, users can increase their limits up to their allocated hard limits by issuing the following command:

```
$ ulimit -n unlimited
```

Typically, you would increase resource limits for users and processes that are under a heavy and constant load, such as the Web server process.

/etc/shadow

If shadow passwords are enabled, the `shadow` configuration file contains encrypted passwords for all users listed in the `passwd` file. This is a more secure approach because the `shadow` file is readable only by root. See Chapter 7 for more information on users and passwords.

/etc/shells

This file can be used to list all the valid shells on the system. The `chsh` command, which allows users to change their default shell, makes use of this list. Historically it has been used to restrict access: network services such as FTP daemons have required users logging in to have a valid shell. With no valid shell, access is denied.

/etc/skel

The `skel` directory contains a list of files that will be copied to a user's directory when the user is first created. This allows you to provide each user with a set of default resources, such as scripts, and configuration and data files.

/etc/sysconfig

The `sysconfig` directory is critical. It consists of important configuration files used by various applications, including hardware and network configuration applications and tools.

For example, consider the information stored within the `/etc/sysconfig/network` file and the files in the `/etc/sysconfig/network-scripts` directory. This information specifies how the system is connected to an external network. Or, take a look at the `hwinfo` file, which keeps track of the system hardware and devices, and the `iptables` configuration file, which lists the firewall rules.

/etc/sysctl.conf

This is a highly powerful configuration file that allows you to configure kernel parameters at runtime. For example, to increase the number of file descriptors system-wide from 8,192 to 32,768, you would insert the following entry into this file:

```
fs.file-max=32768
```

Some of these kernel parameters can also be changed by modifying the relevant files in the /proc directory.

/etc/syslog.conf

The syslog.conf configuration file is the main driver for the syslogd daemon, which is responsible for logging information. For example, take a look at the following entry in the configuration file:

```
*.info;mail.none;authpriv.none;cron.none        /var/log/messages
```

This directive instructs the syslogd daemon to log all messages that have a severity level greater than that of an "information-only" message (with the exception of mail, authentication, and cron-related messages) to /var/log/messages.

Various administrative log files are examined later in this chapter, including the /var/log/messages log file previously mentioned.

/etc/xinetd.conf

Finally, the xinetd.conf configuration file configures the services provided by the xinetd daemon, which include FTP and telnet. In fact, the xinetd.d directory contains a configuration file for each service. Each of these configuration files looks something like this:

```
service telnet
{
  flags           = REUSE NAMEINARGS
  protocol        = tcp
  socket_type     = stream
  wait            = no
  user            = root
  server          = /usr/sbin/tcpd
  server_args     = /usr/sbin/in.telnetd
  log_on_failure += USERID
}
```

We discussed the tcp_wrappers application as a means to implement access control earlier in this section. Incidentally, the preceding configuration file uses tcp_wrappers, as signified by the /usr/sbin/tcpd server setting. This server provides the access control for each incoming request and, if the request is successful, invokes the application specified by the server_args argument—telnet daemon in this case.

The next section looks at the various administrative log files so you can better understand what is happening with your system.

Logging

One of the best features of UNIX-based operating systems is their extensive support for logging, and in Fedora Core the same is true. Most of the system's core components, including the kernel as well as other services and applications, such as `telnet` and `ftp`, write the status of their significant actions to specific text files. You can use this information to get a snapshot of the system to see what is going on at any given time. Viewing the contents of these log files enables you to find the following:

- What is happening as the system boots
- If a device failed to initialize at boot time
- When a user logged in and from what address
- Any suspicious security alerts, such as failed logins
- If a user tried to send e-mail to a particular address
- All e-mail received, from whom, and at what time
- Status of all cron jobs

Your role as the system administrator is to use this information to properly maintain your system and take any corrective actions, if necessary. There is no point in having all of this valuable information at your fingertips if you do not make good use of it. For example, if you notice from the log files that a particular user is repeatedly trying to telnet in from a specific unknown location and is unsuccessful, you can most likely assume that a hacker is trying to gain entrance to your system. At this point, you can take some decisive actions. You can use the `hosts.deny` file that was discussed in the previous section to deny complete access to that particular service for the specific host or address, and also try to inform the hacker's Internet service provider of the malicious activities.

Viewing Logs

Log files are plain text files, much like the configuration files you saw earlier in this chapter. You can find most of the system log files in one directory, `/var/log`, so keeping track of them is rather easy. The following table lists some of the more important files that you will find in this directory.

File	Description
`boot.log`	Boot messages
`Cron`	crond messages
`Maillog`	All e-mail-related messages
`Messages`	All informational messages except for cron, mail, and secure
`Secure`	Secure authentication messages

You can use either the `cat`, `more`, or `less` utilities from the command line or the System Logs GUI application (by selecting Main Menu ➪ System Tools ➪ System Logs) to view the contents of these plain text log files. Here is an example:

```
# more /var/log/messages
May 22 21:22:02 localhost syslogd 1.4.1: restart.
May 22 21:22:02 localhost syslog: syslogd startup succeeded
```

```
May 22 21:22:02 localhost kernel: klogd 1.4.1, log source = /proc/kmsg started.
May 22 21:22:02 localhost syslog: klogd startup succeeded
May 22 21:22:02 localhost kernel: Linux version 2.6.5-1.358
(bhcompile@bugs.build.redhat.com) (gcc version 3.3.3 20040412 (Red Hat Linux
3.3.3-7)) #1 Sat May 8 09:04:50 EDT 2004
May 22 21:22:02 localhost kernel: BIOS-provided physical RAM map:
May 22 21:22:02 localhost kernel:  BIOS-e820: 0000000000000000 - 000000000009fc00
(usable)
May 22 21:22:02 localhost kernel:  BIOS-e820: 000000000009fc00 - 00000000000a0000
(reserved)
May 22 21:22:02 localhost kernel:  BIOS-e820: 00000000000e0000 - 0000000000100000
(reserved)
May 22 21:22:02 localhost kernel:  BIOS-e820: 0000000000100000 - 000000000c000000
(usable)
May 22 21:22:02 localhost kernel:  BIOS-e820: 00000000fec00000 - 00000000fec01000
(reserved)
May 22 21:22:02 localhost kernel:  BIOS-e820: 00000000fee00000 - 00000000fee01000
(reserved)
May 22 21:22:02 localhost kernel:  BIOS-e820: 00000000fffc0000 - 0000000100000000
(reserved)
...
```

You can also view the `messages` log file using the System Logs GUI application (under System Tools); it shows a list of log files on the left side, and the contents of the selected log file on the right side (see Figure 11-1).

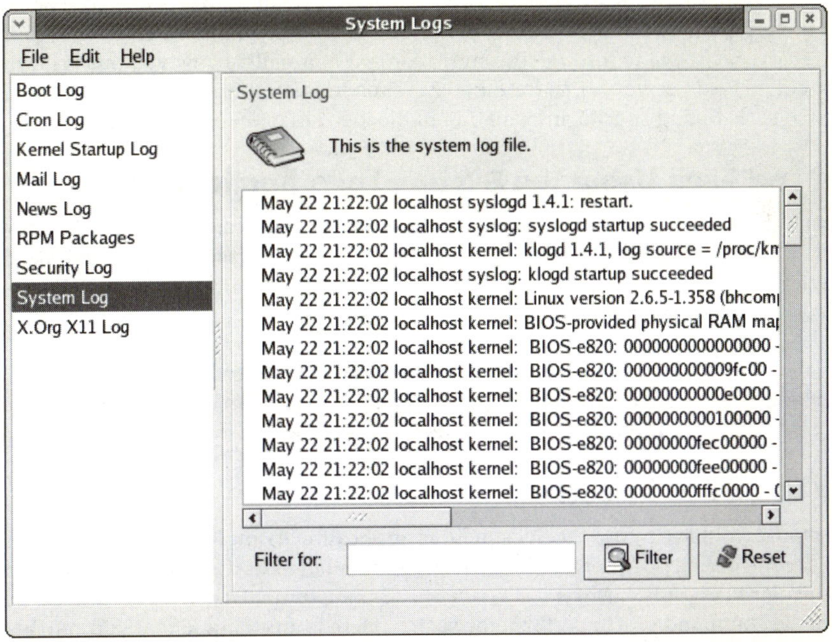

Figure 11-1

Go ahead and experiment with the other log files to see what type of information is logged. Simply select a log file from the left side, and its contents will be shown in the right frame. Unfortunately, this application does not allow you to add other log files to the menu; you are limited to the ones listed.

Application-Specific Log Files

We have found a number of system log files in `/var/log`. However, a number of applications, such as Web servers and database servers, store their log files in other locations. How do you go about finding them? First, you should read the individual application's documentation, or its manual pages, for more details. Usually, the manual page will have a `FILES` section that will list all files used by the application, including configuration and log files. If you cannot locate the files in this manner, you should look for any application-specific subdirectories in `/var/log` or even in the `/etc` directory. If that too proves unsuccessful, the best bet is to proceed to the application installation directory and try to find any files or subdirectories that contain the word `log` in their filename, like so:

```
# find /usr/local/thttpd -name '*log*' -print
```

Here, we are looking for any possible log files or directories in the `/usr/local/thttpd` directory; this is the installation directory for the `thttpd` Web server.

Searching Log Files

As you look through the various log files, you may soon realize that it is very difficult to keep track of failures and other alerts because of the large amount of information that is logged. For example, you may want to keep track of all login failures or certain hardware problems. To do this, you could schedule some time every day to wade through the entire content manually. However, this is far from efficient, and you could instead use your time for other system administration–related tasks. Or, you could use simple search tools to find specific information in the log files quickly and easily.

Searching Log Files Using the System Logs Application

The System Logs application also provides a filtering option (you can see it at the bottom of the window in Figure 11-2)—this allows you to search for specific words or phrases within a log file. For example, try selecting the System Log, typing the word **fail** into the Filter for textbox; click the Filter button to execute the search. We found a few error messages.

The application found seven entries from the System Log file that contained the word "fail." In addition, it also highlighted entries where it found the word "failed;" you can configure what words trigger this effect by using the application's Edit ⇨ Preferences ⇨ Alerts option.

Searching Log Files Directly

Of course, you don't have to use the System Logs application to analyze or search a log file. You can also examine a log file directly by viewing it in a text editor (such as `gedit`), and using its search capability to find particular keywords, such as `fail`, `error`, `denied`, or `unable`. Or, you can use the `grep` command from the command line to perform the search. Here is an example that you can use to search the `messages` log file for all occurrences of the string `fail`:

```
# grep -i fail /var/log/messages
May 22 21:22:05 localhost kernel: There is already a security framework
initialized, register_security failed.
May 22 21:22:05 localhost kernel: Failure registering capabilities with the kernel
May 22 21:29:17 localhost mdmpd: mdmpd failed
May 22 21:31:49 localhost gconfd (root-2686): file gerror.c: line 225
(g_propagate_error): assertion `src != NULL' failed
May 22 22:42:24 localhost kernel: There is already a security framework
initialized, register_security failed.
May 22 22:42:24 localhost kernel: Failure registering capabilities with the kernel
May 22 22:43:09 localhost mdmpd: mdmpd failed
...
```

As you can see, these results are nearly identical to the output produced by the System Logs application; in both cases, we found seven entries that contained the word "fail." However, having the capability to search for particular log entries from the command line affords you great flexibility and convenience. For example, you could do the following:

- Write a simple shell script to periodically check for certain keywords in the log files, and send a report of this search to the administrator. In fact, there are already a number of applications that do this, including Todd Atkins' swatch, which is available from `http://swatch.sourceforge.net`.
- Build a Web interface to these log files, which allows you to view warnings and suspicious activity from other computers on a local network. In fact, we will build our own such application, which you can find on the bonus online chapter (posted at `www.wrox.com`).

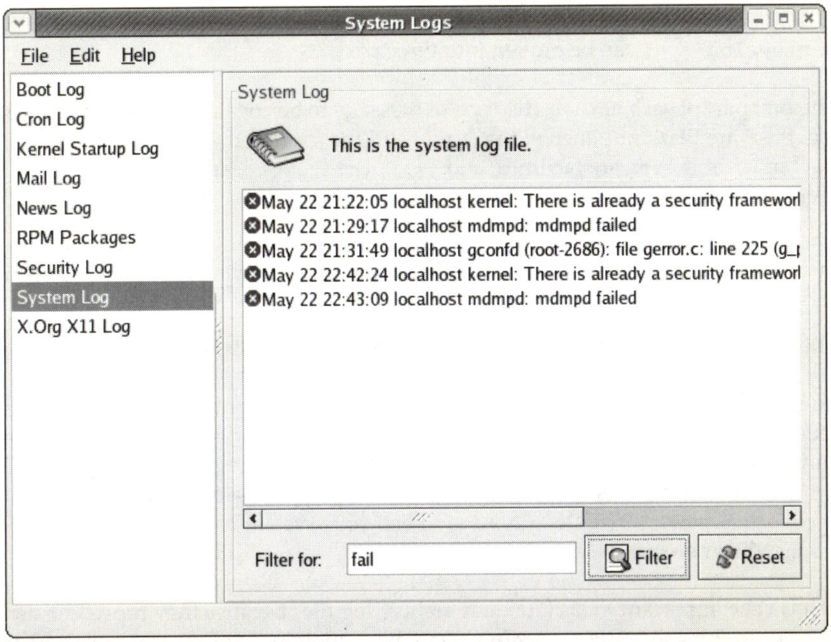

Figure 11-2

Understanding the Logging Process

This is all great, but how do all of these messages get in the various log files, especially when these messages are all being generated by different applications? In fact, we discussed this briefly in the first section of this chapter, when we looked at the `syslog.conf` configuration file. Let's look more closely at this subject now.

The magic behind the entire logging process is the *syslogd daemon*. The syslogd daemon acts as a switchboard for messages of all types, produced by various services, daemons, and system software processes. More specifically, the daemon process listens for messages on a UNIX domain socket, `/dev/log`, and routes them according to the rules specified in the `syslog.conf` configuration file.

> *There is one interesting detail to note. The kernel does not communicate with the syslogd daemon directly. Instead, the kernel injects messages into another daemon,* klogd, *which is designed specifically to handle messages from the kernel. Eventually, however, the klogd daemon communicates with syslogd, and the messages get routed to the intended destination.*

Here are a few sample entries that you might find in a typical `syslog.conf` configuration file:

```
kern.*                                    /dev/console           ## tty
kern.crit                                 @dev2                  ## dev2 host
*.info;mail.none;authpriv.none;cron.none /var/log/messages      ## file
authpriv.*                                | /usr/local/bin/audit ## app.
mail.*                                    /var/log/maillog       ## file
cron.*                                    /var/log/cron          ## file
*.emerg                                   *                      ## all users
*.alert                                   root,johnson           ## users
```

Each entry in `syslog.conf` can be broken into three parts:

- The first part of each entry is the type of message to be considered. For each type of message to log, there are two components: the *facility* and the *level*. In the preceding examples, `kern`, `mail`, `authpriv`, and `cron` are facilities, and `crit`, `info`, `emerg`, and `alert` represent the different logging levels.
- The second part is the destination to which the message should be sent. Valid destinations include files, terminals, logged-in users, applications (via pipes), and even remote `syslogd` servers.
- The third column simply represents user-defined comments, which are optional.

As you can see, the `syslogd` application is a very powerful and flexible logging mechanism. Most of the types of messages that you would ever want to see are already configured by default when you install the operating system. However, you should monitor the logs on a regular basis for any possible problems, either using the search techniques discussed in the previous section or by using other specialized applications, such as `swatch`. That way, you can keep your system running safely and efficiently, and intervene only when necessary.

Of course, it is very important to back up and archive log files because they represent a snapshot in time of the system's activity and status. Therefore, the next section looks at several tools and applications that allow you to archive your data safely.

Backing Up and Archiving

The one task that is overlooked by a majority of users who operate their own personal systems, whether running Linux or any other operating system, is backing up and archiving necessary data and resources. Yet, this same task is thrust upon most system administrators and operators who manage multiuser servers. So, before moving ahead, you should understand what the terms *backup* and *archival* really mean. Do they refer to the same process or are they two completely different tasks? For most people, the two terms are synonymous because they are often discussed together in most books, magazines, and other documentation. In reality, however, they have different connotations and purpose.

A *backup* is a copy of a resource kept elsewhere in case the existing resource fails or corrupts in some way; it allows you to get back up and running quickly. For example, you would typically want to back up the operating system and all of the configuration files, so you can quickly recover in case of a fatal system crash. Backups are typically optimized for speed of recovery of a system or application. On the other hand, an *archive* is a copy of a resource that you may need, but you don't want it cluttering up your main system. The resource could be an old file that you don't use anymore, or it could be a snapshot of a frequently changing resource that was taken at a particular point in time. You would typically want the ability to retrieve portions of data, such as a specific file or an exact system log from a certain date, from an archive.

Backing up and archiving are usually mentioned together in the same breath, mainly because one common practice involves *taking backups and archiving them*. However, confusing the two tasks will lead to requirements for both processes being poorly served. And so, this chapter considers the purpose and process of each task separately.

What Tools Do You Use?

Linux comes with a vast assortment of applications and utilities to back up and archive resources quickly and easily. There are tools available for bundling individual files and directories, mirroring disk partitions and filesystems, and performing network backups. However, to keep things simple, we'll use the `tar` application for a majority of this section. Some of the other useful utilities and tools are discussed briefly at the end of the section.

The `tar` application, which stands for **t**ape **ar**chive, is a traditional UNIX tool for bundling and distributing files. It is best suited for single-user systems or systems with a small amount of data because it lacks the sophisticated features of more complex backup and archival applications. `tar` works by taking a specified set of files and serializing them into one big stream that consists of the file headers (name, owner, file creation date) and contents. You can store this data stream in a file on a filesystem or removable media, or even directly onto a magnetic tape. One of the main advantages of `tar` is its support across many operating systems, ranging from Linux to Windows and the Mac OS. For example, the highly popular WinZip application for Microsoft Windows and the Stuffit application for both Windows and Mac OS can deserialize tar files without any problem. The implications of this type of portability are huge; you can recover resources from your saved backups and archives on other operating systems even if you are having problems with your Linux system.

Creating Backups

As discussed previously, there is a distinct difference in process and purpose between backing up and archiving. Backups are generally used for disaster recovery. In a typical computing environment, you can run into all types of unfortunate situations where you lose precious data, but having a good quality backup—a copy of a resource from a previous point in time—will help you get back up and running with ease. Here are a few of these situations.

You could accidentally delete a file critical to the performance of the system, such as a configuration file or even the kernel itself. Imagine what would happen if you deleted the critical `/etc/passwd` file. No one would be allowed to log in to the system. But, if you could quickly recover this important file from a previous backup, you would be back in business in no time. Actually, this is one of the more practical reasons why you should not be logged in as the system administrator (root user) on a regular basis; you will have the necessary privileges to modify or remove just about any file on the system.

If, for example, you are the main system administrator for a corporation that deals with daily financial transactions, it is paramount for the systems to be running all of the time. What if you experience a serious hardware failure that wipes out all of your financial applications? If you had meticulously backed up the most recent versions of the applications, their license keys, and configuration, you could get the system working properly with only a minimum loss of business. On the other hand, had you not backed up this information, you would have to find all of these applications from the original distributions, install and configure them on the system, and make sure all of the patches are up to date. This could take a very long time, which would translate into a serious loss of business.

These are just examples of two types of failures. Unfortunately, there are plenty of other less dramatic instances that you could experience, where you could save precious time and money by making sure you back up all of your critical applications and files. And so, this section discusses various issues related to backups, including the following:

- What data needs to be backed up?
- What medium should you use for backups?
- How do you create and verify backups?
- How often do you need to back up your data?

What Do You Need to Back Up?

This is a very hard question to answer and depends highly on your needs and requirements. On a typical Linux system, you will find the operating system, its configuration and log files, any special applications that you install, their licenses and configuration, and users' personal data. Of course, this is a very simplistic view; you probably have a lot more information and data that is specific for your needs. But, based on this list and your specific requirements, you need to ask yourself just one question: What resources do I need to get the system up and running quickly in case of a disaster of some sort?

Most likely, your answer may have included the operating system, configuration files, and all of the specially installed applications and their related resources. However, if you have not updated the original operating system with patches and other updates to core applications, you don't need to back it up; you can possibly install it from the original distribution and restore the system configuration from saved backups. On the other hand, if you have made a lot of changes to the original system, you will save a lot of time and unnecessary headache by simply backing up the entire operating system, including all of the configurations.

Your specially installed applications are a completely different matter, altogether. Because these applications and their related data are either critical for your business or your everyday needs, you definitely should back them up. Why go through the hassle of installing all of these applications and their patches from the original medium when you can simply restore them from backups quickly and easily?

In addition, you should also consider the speed with which you can recover these resources when needed. For example, if you have access to a high-speed network attached storage (NAS) server with an extremely large storage capacity, you might consider even backing up critical resources that you can install from their original distribution. This will allow you to restore everything in one fell swoop very quickly without the hassle of dealing with different media.

And, finally, other resources such as users' personal data and server log files are important, but are not critical for the running of the system. Sure, it is very useful to know who accessed your Web server at what time—which you can see from the Apache Web server log file—but if you lose a few days worth of data, it will not significantly hurt you. Having said that, however, these resources should be archived on a periodic basis; see the next section on archiving for more information. Your users will not be too thrilled if they lose all of their files.

What Medium Should You Use for Storing Backup Files?

We have talked about what you need to back up, but what medium do you use to actually store these resources? Various types of media are available for backing up data, everything from floppy disks and magnetic tapes to CD-ROM, DVD, and hard disks, as well as network storage. The following table illustrates some of the advantages and disadvantages of each type of media.

Medium	Advantage	Disadvantage
Removable disks (Zip, USB Flash)	Convenient.	Low capacity, not supported on all operating systems, more expensive than floppy disks, and only somewhat reliable.
Magnetic tapes	Inexpensive, high capacity; ideal for unattended backups.	Sensitive to heat and electromagnetic fields, relatively slow, and drives are expensive.
CD-ROM, DVD	Inexpensive, DVD has high capacity; reasonably fast.	CD-ROM has low capacity; multiple DVD standards.
Hard disk/Network storage	Very fast, no media to load, and relatively inexpensive.	Stored backups in system are vulnerable to same risks as the system itself.

You need to assess the cost and benefits of what medium to choose based on the answers to the following three questions:

- How long will you be storing the backups?
- How frequently do you envision accessing the backups and restoring data?
- What are you willing to pay for the medium and its associated writing device?

You should typically lean toward optical media, such as CD-ROM or DVD, if you are intent on storing backups for a long period of time. On the other hand, all magnetic media are sensitive to environmental factors, including heat and electromagnetic fields, and typically have a much shorter shelf life than optical media. Optical media also tend to be much less expensive than all other media, costing only pennies for nearly 700MB of storage capacity.

However, hard disks and dedicated network storage servers are ideal for recovering data quickly from saved backups. You should stay away from storing backups in an internal hard disk that is physically located in the same machine as the operating system, as you run the risk of the same problem wiping out the system and the backup. A better solution might include setting up a standalone disk array, formatted as VFAT or NTFS, that can be used by all Linux machines in your network to store backups using SAMBA (see Chapter 9 for more information). In addition, by formatting this disk array as VFAT or NTFS, you can access the same disk array with most versions of the Windows operating system, as well. Needless to say, while hard disks and network storage servers provide great performance, they are also much more expensive than all other media.

How Do You Create a Backup?

Now that you have an idea of what backups are, what types of resources you should back up, and where you should back them up to, it is time to look at some examples. In this section, you learn more about `tar`, especially how to create an archive and restore from an existing archive.

Creating a tar Archive

Let's start with a simple example:

```
# tar -cWPhf etc-200403101335.tar /etc
```

The `tar` application will recursively iterate through all the files and subdirectories within `/etc` and create an archive named `etc-20040310.tar` in the current directory. The meaning of the word "archive" here is different than the purpose and process of *archiving*, as defined at the top of this section. The `-c` and `-W` switches are used to ask `tar` to create an archive and verify it after creation, storing the final archive in the file specified by the `-f` switch. If an error occurs during the creation of a backup file (so that the file becomes corrupted in some way), that backup file is as good as useless. If you've taken the care to generate regular and systematic backups, and you find that backup is corrupted when you ultimately turn to it in need, you're unlikely to be very happy. Therefore, it's a good idea to check the validity of each backup at the time you create it, so that you can rest assured that the backup file will not let you down if you ever need to use it.

The `-P` switch forces `tar` to keep the leading `/` (slash) from filenames; all files will be stored as `/etc/` instead of the default `etc/`. Not specifying this switch would cause `tar` to fail during the verification phase because it would not be able to find files starting with `etc/` in the current directory.

We did not discuss the very important `-h` switch in the previous paragraph. By default, `tar` archives symbolic links (also known as shortcuts on other platforms) as is, which is not much help if you were to lose the original. The `-h` switch, on the other hand, forces `tar` to archive the original files pointed to by the symbolic links.

And finally, you might be wondering why we named our archive `etc-200403101335.tar`. It is very important for you to choose a proper naming convention for your backups because doing so allows you to distinguish one backup from another. This one uses the folder name followed by the date and time (March 10, 2004, 1:35 PM), which allows you to see the date of the backup simply by looking at the archive name.

What if you want to see the files that `tar` is archiving? Simple, add a `-v` (verbose) switch to the preceding command, like so:

```
# cd /
# tar -cvWhf etc-200403101339.tar /etc
tar: Removing leading `/' from member names
etc/
etc/sysconfig/
etc/sysconfig/network-scripts/
etc/sysconfig/network-scripts/ifup-aliases
...
Verify etc/shadow
Verify etc/gshadow
Verify etc/lilo.conf.anaconda
Verify etc/fstab.REVOKE
```

As `tar` archives each file, you will see it listed on your screen. You can use the `-v` switch with any syntax to enable verbose output. Also notice how `tar` removed the leading `/` (slash) from the file names because the `-P` switch was not specified.

Restoring from a tar Archive

How do you restore files from a `tar` archive? You can simply do the following:

```
$ tar -zvf etc-200403101339.tar
etc/
etc/sysconfig/
etc/sysconfig/network-scripts/
etc/sysconfig/network-scripts/ifup-aliases
...
```

The `tar` application creates a directory called `etc` in your *current* working directory, along with all the files and subdirectories that were archived. We use the `-f` switch to specify the `tar` archive from which to restore, the `-z` switch to force restoration mode, and the `-v` switch to enable verbose output.

If you don't want to extract all the files, or are not sure what files are contained in an archive, use the `-tf` switches first to look at the files in the archive:

```
$ tar -tvf etc-200403101339.tar
```

Then, you can extract a specific file, like so:

```
$ tar -f etc-200403101339.tar -vx etc/shadow
```

By default, `tar` overwrites existing files with files from the archive. This is typically not a problem unless you perform the extraction or restoration in the directory where the original file or directory resides. For example, if you were to invoke the following set of commands, the file `etc/shadow` from the archive would overwrite the original file `/etc/shadow`:

```
# cd /
# tar -f etc-200403101339.tar -vx etc/shadow
```

You can use the `-k` switch to force `tar` not to follow this behavior:

```
$ tar -f etc-200403101339.tar -vxk etc/shadow
```

Other tar Facilities

The `tar` application has other options, such as the ability to *compress* archives, to *include* files from multiple directories, and to *exclude* certain files. Here is another example:

```
# tar -cvPhzf mysystem-200403121800.tar.gz /etc /usr/local /home
```

Here, `tar` will include configuration files from `/etc`, custom applications from `/usr/local`, and users' personal data from `/home` into a `gzip` compressed archive, `mysystem-200403121800.tar.gz`. No verification will be performed because the `-W` switch is not compatible with compression.

You should make it a habit to store all of your specially used and custom-built applications in a separate directory hierarchy, so it is easy to back up these resources quickly without having to remember a long list of disparate directories. The `/usr/local` directory is quite popular for this purpose among UNIX users, developers, and administrators.

You can restore this compressed archive by using the `-z` switch again:

```
$ tar -zxvf mysystem-200403121800.tar.gz
```

Saving a Backup to CD-ROM

Over the last several years, there has been a great explosion in the number of CD writers installed in personal computers, as prices have been severely reduced across the board. This is terrific for us, as we can use a CD writer to back up our data and resources to a CD-ROM, providing us with an inexpensive and stable backup solution.

Configuring the CD Writer

CD writers come with many interfaces: parallel port, IDE, SCSI, USB, and FireWire. Because IDE writers are by far the most widely used, we will deal with them exclusively in this section; a similar procedure applies for all other types of writers, as well. Linux uses the `ide-cd` kernel module to communicate with IDE CD writers; this module comes with most recent Linux 2.6 distributions. See if you have the module installed by using the following:

```
# find /lib/modules/`uname -r` -name 'ide-cd.ko' -print
/lib/modules/2.6.1-1.65/kernel/drivers/ide/ide-cd.ko
```

Kernel modules and this command syntax are described in great detail in the Chapter 12. The kernel will load the module on demand at boot time when it detects the presence of the CD writer.

Creating the ISO9660 Image

Burning a CD-ROM involves two distinct steps: the first is to create an ISO9660 image and then burn that image to the disk. First, we will use the `mkisofs` command to create the image:

```
# mkisofs -o mysystem-200403121800.iso \
  -V MySystem-2004-03-10-1800 \
  -J -R -v mysystem-200403121800.tar.gz
INFO:   UTF-8 character encoding detected by locale settings.
        Assuming UTF-8 encoded filenames on source filesystem,
        Use -input-charset to override.
mkisofs 2.01a27 (i686-pc-linux-gnu)
Writing:   Initial Padbock                        Start Block 0
Done with: Initial Padbock                        Block(s)    16
...
Total translation table size: 0
Total rockridge attributes bytes: 269
Total directory bytes: 0
Path table size(bytes): 10
Done with: The File(s)                            Block(s)    11909
Writing:   Ending Padblock                        Start Block 11940
Done with: Ending Padblock                        Block(s)    28
Max brk space used 6024
11968 extents written (23 MB)
```

The `-o` switch specifies the ISO9660 image name, the `-J` switch enables Joliet filenames for Windows compatibility, the `-R` switch preserves filenames and permissions, the `-V` switch specifies the volume identification, and the `-v` switch enables verbose output.

If you cannot get the `mkisofs` application to work, you may not have it installed on your Linux system. In that case, simply insert either the DVD or the first CD-ROM from the distribution, wait a few moments, and invoke the following commands:

```
# rpm -hvi /mnt/cdrom/Fedora/RPMS/mkisofs-2.01-0.a27.3.i386.rpm
# rpm -hvi /mnt/cdrom/Fedora/RPMS/cdrecord-2.01-0.a27.3.i386.rpm
```

You will need the `cdrecord` application to actually burn the image to disc, as you will see next.

Testing the Image

Before you burn the ISO9660 image to disc, you can view its contents by mounting it to a filesystem directory via a loopback device, like so:

```
# mount -t iso9660 mysystem-200403121800.iso /mnt/cdrom -o loop
$ ls -ls /mnt/cdrom
total 1245
1245 -rw-r--r--    1 root     root      1274545 Mar 12 18:01 mysystem-
200403121800.tar.gz
```

This mounts the image in the `/mnt/cdrom` directory. You can treat the image like a regular filesystem, using commands such as `ls` and `cat` to view individual directories and files. When you are finished checking the contents, you can unmount the image, like so:

```
# umount /mnt/cdrom
```

And burn the image to disc.

Burning the Image to CD-ROM

Now that the image has been tested, you can burn it onto a CD-ROM with the following:

```
# cdrecord dev=ATAPI -scanbus
Cdrecord-Clone 2.01a27-dvd (i686-pc-linux-gnu) Copyright (C) 1995-2004 Jrg
Schilling
Note: This version is an unofficial (modified) version with DVD support
Note: and therefore may have bugs that are not present in the original.
...
Using libscg version 'schily-0.8'.
scsibus0:
        0,0,0     0) 'LG      ' 'CD-RW CED-8080B ' '1.07' Removable CD-ROM
        0,1,0     1) *
        0,2,0     2) *
        0,3,0     3) *
        0,4,0     4) *
        0,5,0     5) *
        0,6,0     6) *
        0,7,0     7) *
# cdrecord -v -eject -speed=8 dev=ATAPI:0,0,0 mysystem-200403121800.iso
```

The `cdrecord` command with the `-scanbus` argument returns a list of all the CD-ROM devices attached to the system. You pass the device number from the list to the `cdrecord` command, in addition to the speed and ISO9660 image to burn the image to the disc; the `-eject` switch forces the CD writer to eject the tray after the burn is finished.

Restoring from CD-ROM

Later on, if you want to restore a file from a backup stored on the CD-ROM, you would mount the disk and extract the necessary file or files directly from the disk, like so:

```
# mount /dev/cdrom /mnt/cdrom
$ tar -zxvf /mnt/cdrom/mysystem-200403121800.tar.gz
```

Or, you can extract a single file:

```
$ tar -zf /mnt/cdrom/mysystem-200403121800.tar.gz -vx /etc/shadow
```

Frequency of Backups

Having considered *how* to archive, you now need to think about *how often* you need to perform backups. The frequency with which a certain resource should be backed up depends on several issues, namely the following:

- How often does the resource change making the old backup outdated?
- How much data can you afford to lose?

For example, financial institutions cannot afford to lose *any* data, so transaction data must be backed up as the transactions occur, for replay later if necessary. Unfortunately, this can be expensive, and in many other situations, it is possible and optimal to back up daily or weekly. Fortunately, frequent backups don't necessarily have to consume a lot of space because most backup applications support *incremental backups*. An incremental backup is different than a full or complete backup, in that it archives only those files that have been added or changed since the last full backup.

Finally, how do you create incremental `tar` archives that contain files that have only been added or modified since a specific date? Luckily, the newer versions of `tar` have an `-N` switch, which allows you to do this:

```
# tar -cvWPhf etc-200403121830.tar /etc -N 01/01/04
```

This will archive files that have been added or modified after January 1, 2004. As you can see from all of these examples, `tar` is a very flexible and powerful archival tool, but one that is not designed to archive arbitrary files located in various directories throughout the system. For that purpose, you use the `cpio` application, which is briefly explained toward the end of this section.

But now, we will look at the process of archiving resources and information—a process that has an entirely different purpose than backups.

Archiving

People are creatures of habit; they like to keep things around whether they need them or not. Take a good look around your Linux system. You will most likely find a ton of resources that you may no longer need, including old log files, copies of previous system configuration files, source code for applications that you are no longer using, or outdated personal data. Obviously, you don't want to go out and delete all of these resources on a whim because you might really need them at a later time. For example, what if you need to determine the Web server utilization rate for the last three years to plan for the future? You would need to take a look at all of the old Web server log files during that time period to determine this information. Or, what if you want to see how you built a certain application with an older set of development tools so you could use the same procedure with an updated version of the tools? You certainly would not want to spend the time to rediscover the techniques that you followed.

On the flip side, deleting these types of resources not only removes clutter from your system, but also frees up valuable disk space that you could use to store other more important resources. You will be surprised at just how much space all of these older resources consume. The answer to this dilemma is to archive the data and information in a safe place, away from the main system. That way, you can always retrieve any of the information when needed, while keeping your system clean and up-to-date.

Remember again the distinction between backups and archiving. *Backups* allow you to recover critical resources so you can get up and running quickly in case of a disaster. *Archiving* data serves another purpose completely, namely long-term storage of data and resources that you may need at a later time. In fact, a common practice among system administrators involves archiving old backups. As you back up necessary information on a periodic basis, the older backups are no longer significant or entirely useful. But there is a chance, however slim, that you could need older versions of these resources at some time.

What Sort of Things Do You Need to Archive?

We have briefly mentioned a list of possible resources that are prime candidates for archiving, namely old or outdated log files, configuration files, source code for special applications, and personal data. This list is just the tip of the iceberg; as you look around, you will find other files that can safely be archived as well.

How do you determine what to archive? Unfortunately, there is no single answer that will cover every possible scenario and environment. But, here are a few examples that illustrate some of the resources you should or should not archive. For example, corporate entities may be required by law to archive financial, legal, or medical records for a particular period of time; a copy of the corporate financial accounts can be archived at a particular date to read-only media. On the other hand, you may not want to archive source code to applications that you can easily download from online repositories, such as Perl or Python (see Chapter 12 for more information on managing your system with Perl).

However, a reasonably efficient overall technique is to use the `find` command to determine all files that have not been modified in more than six months and archive them, deleting them from the system in the process, if necessary. If you use this automated technique, along with a manual list of special files, you will be assured of archiving a broad range of data and resources.

What Medium Should You Use for Archiving?

Because backup and archival are similar and related processes, you can use much the same criteria used for assessing media for backups and apply them to archiving, as well; namely, the following:

- The length of time you need to store the archive
- The frequency with which you are likely to access the archive
- Whether to create a permanent archive or a temporary one
- The price you are willing to pay for the media

You should especially consider the first and last points in the preceding list. Because archives are typically stored for a longer period of time than up-to-date backups, you can have a number of archives on your hands at any given time. So cost is a very important factor. Optical media, such as CD-ROM and DVD, are ideal for the archiving process because they fit both of these criteria very well. However, you should feel free to look through the table of media in the backup section and decide for yourself what media best fits your needs and requirements.

How Do You Archive a Resource?

You can use `tar` in much the same manner as before; the main difference is that you will be using it to archive data as opposed to backing it up.

Here is a slightly more advanced example that uses the `find` command in conjunction with the `xargs` command to pass a list of files that have not been accessed in *six months or more* from the user's home directories to `tar` for archival:

```
# find /home -atime +180 -print | \
  xargs tar -cvPhz -f home-180-200403101335.tar.gz
```

The find command finds all files in /home that have not been accessed in 180 days or more, using the -atime switch. Those filenames are then passed to the xargs command via a pipe; notice the vertical | (bar) character. The xargs command d invokes tar, with our standard set of switches, passing these file names as arguments. See Chapter 13 for more examples that illustrate find and xargs in action.

It's worth taking a little time to learn to use the find command well. With mastery of the find command's options, you can develop a very powerful and effective backup and archival strategy; see the manual page for find for more information on the various options.

Other Backup and Archival Tools

For simplicity, we've exclusively used tar as the application of choice for both simple backups and archiving. However, you can use other useful applications, namely cpio and dump. The cpio archiving application allows you to easily specify disparate files and directories to backup or archive by specifying them on the command line. On the other hand, dump makes it easy for you to back up entire filesystems, although the resulting file is far from portable even across other UNIX platforms.

cpio

Early versions of tar had their share of limitations. For example:

- They could not create archives that spanned multiple (tape) volumes.
- They could not handle all types of files.
- They could not compress the archives on the fly.
- They could not handle bad areas on a tape.

Over time, tar has improved greatly, and these issues are no longer relevant. However, the limitations of early versions of tar were also the motivation behind the development of the cpio archiving tool. At this point in time, there are few differences in functionality between tar and cpio, except for the syntax, so you should use the one that you prefer.

Creating a cpio Archive

Let's look at an example of cpio in action:

```
# find /etc -print | cpio -vo > etc-200403101335.cpio
cpio: /etc: truncating inode number
/etc
cpio: /etc/sysconfig: truncating inode number
/etc/sysconfig
cpio: /etc/sysconfig/network-scripts: truncating inode number
/etc/sysconfig/network-scripts
cpio: /etc/sysconfig/network-scripts/ifup-aliases: truncating inode number
/etc/sysconfig/network-scripts/ifup-aliases
...
```

Here, the find command finds a list of all the files and subdirectories in /etc, and they are passed to the cpio command, which creates the archive on the filesystem. The -o switch asks cpio to create the archive, while the -v (verbose) switch gives you verbose output (just as it did for the tar command).

Selective Archiving

As you can see, passing filenames in this manner to `cpio` allows you great flexibility in selecting what files to archive and what not to archive. For example, take a look at this:

```
# find /home -name '*.p[lm]' -print | cpio -vo > perl-200403151335.cpio
cpio: /home/dwilliams/lib/CGI/Lite.pm: truncating inode number
/home/dwilliams/lib/CGI/Lite.pm
/home/gundavaram/bin/ckmail.pl
cpio: /home/mellett/lib/Tie/Handle.pm: truncating inode number
/home/mellett/lib/Tie/Handle.pm
...
```

Here, we ask `find` to locate all Perl application files that end with either a `.pl` or `.pm` extension, and send that list to `cpio`.

Restoring from a cpio Archive

You've learned how to create `cpio` archives, but not yet how to restore them. In fact, it is a rather easy process. Here's an example that restores data from a `cpio` file:

```
# cpio -vi < perl-200403151335.cpio
cpio: /home/dwilliams/lib/CGI/Lite.pm not created: newer or same age version exists
cpio: /home/gundavaram/bin/ckmail.pl not created: newer or same age version exists
cpio: /home/mellett/lib/Tie/Handle.pm not created: newer or same age version exists
11 blocks
```

As you can see, by default `cpio` does *not* create the files if the destination file is newer than the archived file or has not been modified. If the existing file is older than the archived file, `cpio` overwrites that file with the archived version. You can change this behavior with the `--unconditional` switch:

```
# cpio -vi --unconditional < perl-200403151335.cpio
```

Or better yet, if you want to simply restore the archive to another location, use the following syntax:

```
# cpio -vi -d --no-absolute-filenames --unconditional --force-local < perl-
200403151335.cpio
```

What if you don't want to extract all of the files, but only a single file? First, you can use the `--list` option to get a list of all the files in the archive:

```
# cpio -vi --list < perl-200403151335.cpio
-rw-rw-r--   1 dwillia  eng     0 Mar 14 03:07 /home/dwilliams/lib/CGI/Lite.pm
-rwx------   1 gundava  eng  5112 Mar 12 03:35 /home/gundavaram/bin/ckmail.pl
-rw-rw-r--   1 mellett  eng     0 Mar 14 03:07 /home/mellett/lib/Tie/Handle.pm
11 blocks
```

Then, use the `-E` switch to extract a specific file:

```
# cpio -vi -E /home/gundavaram/bin/ckmail.pl < perl-200403151335.cpio
```

We hope this brief introduction to cpio has provided you with a chance to learn more about this powerful archival solution. In summary, both tar and cpio have similar functionality, although the manner in which you specify the files to archive is different. The final backup application to be discussed in this chapter is dump, which is quite different than either tar or cpio.

Archiving with dump

What if you want to back up an entire partition, or filesystem, incrementally, complete with the correct ownership, permissions, and creation and modification dates? You could certainly use the tar and cpio tools, but they would be far from efficient because you must determine what has been modified and when. However, dump understands the layout of the filesystem, but can only work with certain types, notably ext2 and ext3. Unfortunately, the dump format is not at all portable. With tar and cpio, there is a good chance that another UNIX system can read and process their archives, but with dump, there is little chance at all. As a result, dump is sensible for backups, but not for archiving files.

In addition, dump is designed to perform incremental backups, recognizing up to ten backup levels. When you use dump, you need to assign a backup level from 0 to 9. The strategy is to perform a full, or complete, backup first—this is referred to as a level 0 backup. Then, periodically, you can perform incremental backups at different levels. If you are curious as to how dump keeps track of modified files, take a look at the /etc/dumpdates configuration file, which looks like the following:

```
/dev/hda2 0 Wed Mar 10 13:30:00 2004
/dev/hda2 9 Thu Mar 11 13:30:00 2004
```

For example, if you later back up at level 9, dump archives files that have been modified since the last backup at level 8 or lower. With this type of strategy in place, you can simply recover the entire system from several sets of backups: the full backup plus a series of incremental backups.

Creating a dump Archive

Let's look at an example:

```
# dump -0 /dev/hda2 -u -f /data/backup/hda2-200403101430-0.dmp
DUMP: Date of this level 0 dump: Wed Mar 10 14:30:00 2004
DUMP: Dumping /dev/hda2 (/home) to /data/backup/hda2-200403101430-0.dmp
DUMP: Added inode 8 to exclude list (journal inode)
DUMP: Added inode 7 to exclude list (resize inode)
DUMP: Label: /home
DUMP: mapping (Pass I) [regular files]
DUMP: mapping (Pass II) [directories]
DUMP: estimated 40720 tape blocks.
DUMP: Volume 1 started with block 1 at: Wed Mar 10 14:30:03 2004
DUMP: dumping (Pass III) [directories]
DUMP: dumping (Pass IV) [regular files]
DUMP: Closing /data/backup/hda2-200403101430-0.dmp
DUMP: Volume 1 completed at: Wed Mar 10 14:30:36 2004
DUMP: Volume 1 43190 tape blocks (42.18MB)
DUMP: Volume 1 took 0:00:30
DUMP: Volume 1 transfer rate: 1439 kB/s
```

```
DUMP: 43190 tape blocks (42.18MB) on 1 volume(s)
DUMP: finished in 30 seconds, throughput 1439 kBytes/sec
DUMP: Date of this level 0 dump: Wed Mar 10 14:30:00 2004
DUMP: Date this dump completed:  Wed Mar 10 14:30:36 2004
DUMP: Average transfer rate: 1439 kB/s
DUMP: DUMP IS DONE
```

This performs a level 0 backup of the `/dev/hda2` partition to the specified file. The `-u` option is very important because it asks `dump` to update the `/etc/dumpdates` file. It's important to remember to label your backups properly, whether you are archiving your data onto hard disk or onto other media. This allows you to find your backups quickly if disaster ever strikes.

Compressed Archives

Like `tar`, `dump` also supports compression on the fly. By specifying either the `-j` (bzlib) switch or the `-z` (zlib) switch, followed by a compression level from 1 to 9, you can enable compression. Here is an example:

```
# dump -0 /dev/hda2 -u -z9 -f /data/backup/hda2-200403111430-0.dmp
DUMP: Date of this level 0 dump: Thu Mar 11 14:30:00 2004
DUMP: Dumping /dev/hda2 (/home) to /data/backup/hda2-200403111430-0.dmp
DUMP: Added inode 8 to exclude list (journal inode)
DUMP: Added inode 7 to exclude list (resize inode)
DUMP: Compressing output at compression level 9 (zlib)
...
DUMP: Wrote 44940kB uncompressed, 29710kB compressed, 1.513:1
DUMP: DUMP IS DONE
```

Incremental Backups

After a full backup, you should typically perform a series of incremental backups, like so:

```
# dump -9 /dev/hda2 -u -z9 -f /data/backup/hda2-200403121430-9.dmp
DUMP: Date of this level 9 dump: Fri Mar 12 14:30:00 2004
DUMP: Date of last level 0 dump: Thu Mar 11 14:30:00 2004
DUMP: Dumping /dev/hda2 (/home) to /data/backup/hda2-200403121430-9.dmp
...
```

Restoring from a dump Archive

You can decide to do a partial restore, selecting a set of specific files, or a full restore. To do a full restore, however, you need to create and mount the target filesystem, like so:

```
# mke2fs /dev/hda2
# mount /dev/hda2 /home
# cd /home
# restore -rvf /data/backup/hda2-200403101430-0.dmp
Verify tape and initialize maps
Input is from file/pipe
Input block size is 32
```

```
Dump   date: Wed Mar 10 14:30:00 2004
Dumped from: the epoch
Level 0 dump of /home on localhost.localdomain:/dev/hda2
Label: /home
Begin level 0 restore
Initialize symbol table.
Extract directories from tape
Calculate extraction list.
Make node ./lost+found
Make node ./dwilliams
Make node ./dwilliams/.gnome2
Make node ./dwilliams/.gnome2/accels
Make node ./dwilliams/.gnome2/share
...
```

This restores the dumped archive. The `-r` asks `restore` to rebuild the filesystem, the `-v` switch turns on verbose messages, and the `-f` option specifies the dump file. In turn, you could restore the incremental backups in much the same manner. You need to make sure that you restore the dumps in the order they were created, starting with the lowest-level dump, typically level 0.

What's Next?

In summary, backing up and archiving data and resources is critical for quickly recovering from possible disasters. Linux comes with a vast assortment of applications and tools to make archiving a convenient process. There are tools available for mirroring partitions and files, performing network backups, such as Amanda, as well as backups to CD-ROM. Once you decide on a backup and archival strategy, you should investigate these tools to determine the application that is best suited for your requirements.

Next, let's shift gears a bit and talk about building applications from source code. Say, for example, you find a really powerful backup or archival application. After looking at its documentation, you realize, to your disappointment, that it does not come with a pre-built binary package for Linux, but only source code. How do you go about building it? Proceed to the next section to find out more.

Building from Source

So far in this book, the applications have all been installed from precompiled binary Red Hat Packet Manager (RPM) packages. You've seen how quick and easy it is to install, modify, and uninstall programs from precompiled binaries. However, many applications are also available as (uncompiled) source code, typically in a compressed archive of some sort (for example, `.tar.gz` or `.tar.bz2`).

Many applications are made available in both formats (RPM and uncompiled source), and if you want to install such an application, you have a choice about which format to use—building applications via source code or installing prebuilt binary RPM packages. In this situation, it's not clear which method is preferable; it comes down to personal preference. The following table summarizes the levels of difficulty and control involved.

Action	Binary RPM	Source Code
Ease of installation	High	Low to high; dependent on environment
Ease of un-installation	High	Low to high
Control of build process and installation	Low	Medium to high

The RPM keeps track of dependencies, giving you the ability to upgrade or uninstall a package quite easily. While an RPM package tends to install the files contained in the package in disparate locations throughout the system, it is possible to use the `--prefix` and `--relocate` options to force RPM to install the files in specific directories. But, if you want even more control over the installation process, you should build the application from source code.

Of course, there are also many applications for which there is no RPM package—only the uncompiled source code is made available. If you want to install an application of this type, you have no choice but to produce the application yourself, by building and compiling the source code on your system.

In the next section, we'll download, build, and install version 2.0.17 of the `gFTP` application, an FTP client application with a graphic user interface, from its source code. Fedora Core comes prebuilt with version 2.0.17 of the gFTP application, so you don't have to worry about upgrading the application. However, by learning how to build the application from its source code now, you can update to the latest version when it becomes available.

Installing Development Tools and Libraries

Before starting to build your first application from source code, you need to install the appropriate development tools and code libraries. First, you need to have certain development tools installed, including `make` and `gcc` for initiating the build process and to compile the `C` source code, respectively. Second, you need to install the X Window system and GNOME software development libraries. The gFTP application uses these libraries to create a rich GNOME-compliant user interface. We'll use the RPM applet to install these required packages.

Try It Out Installing the Development Tools

1. Launch the RPM applet (either from the Main Menu ➪ System Settings ➪ Add/Remove Applications menu, or by executing the `system-config-packages` application from the command line).

2. As you peruse the list of package categories, you will see the Development package category toward the end. Click Development Tools, which bundles the `make` and `gcc` packages, as well as the X Software Development and GNOME Software Development package groups, and press the Update button (see Figure 11-3).

   The installation process takes some time, but once it's finished, you can start your application-building process.

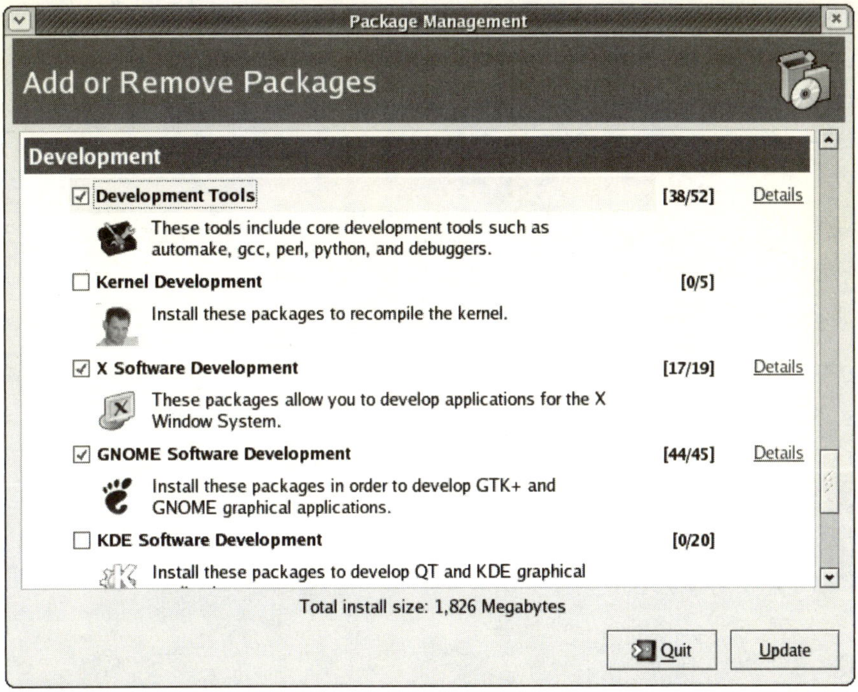

Figure 11-3

Building the Application

As you will soon see, the entire process of building and installing the gFTP application is limited to three simple steps. You can apply these same techniques when building other applications from source code, as well.

Try It Out Compiling the gFTP Application

1. Determine the root source directory where you will be *building* any and *all* applications. A good directory to choose is `/usr/local/src` because it is separate from the standard operating system installation directories. Remember, you need to be logged on as the root user to have the necessary privileges to create and modify files in this directory.

2. Once you have decided on the root source directory, you should create a subdirectory where you will unpack the source code for the application. Some source code packages when unpacked create a directory to hold all of their files, while others just dump the files into the current directory. Take this step to ensure that you do not end up with source code files cluttered all over the `/usr/local/src` root directory:

```
# mkdir /usr/local/src/gftp
```

3. Obtain the source code for gFTP from the following URL: `www.gftp.org/gftp-2.0.17.tar.gz`.

Notice that the source code is distributed as a compressed `tar` archive. You can download it using a Web browser, or by using the `wget` program, like so:

```
# cd /usr/local/src/gftp
# wget http://www.gftp.org/gftp-2.0.14.tar.gz
--02:13:47--  http://www.gftp.org/gftp-2.0.17.tar.gz
           => 'gftp-2.0.17.tar.gz'
Resolving www.gftp.org... 18.244.0.188
Connecting to www.gftp.org[18.244.0.188]:80... connected.
HTTP request sent, awaiting response... 200 OK
Length: 1,931,750 [application/x-gzip]

100%[====================================>] 1,931,750 356.05K/s ETA 00:00

02:13:53 (339.65 KB/s) - 'gftp-2.0.17.tar.gz' saved [1931750/1931750]
```

4. Uncompress and untar the archive:

```
# tar -zkxvf gftp-2.0.17.tar.gz
gftp-2.0.17/
gftp-2.0.17/po/
gftp-2.0.17/po/zh_CN.po
gftp-2.0.17/po/Makevars
...
gftp-2.0.17/README.html
gftp-2.0.17/INSTALL
gftp-2.0.17/ABOUT-NLS
gftp-2.0.17/ChangeLog
gftp-2.0.17/COPYING
gftp-2.0.17/ChangeLog-old
```

The `-k` switch forces `tar` to keep any existing files; it will not overwrite existing files with files from the archive. This is for your own safety and ensures that you will not lose any important files in case you are exposed to a rogue package that was designed to destroy existing files.

5. We now have a directory called `gftp-2.0.17`, which contains all of the source code for the gFTP application. Let's get into that directory and run the `configure` program, which configures the source code for building on your system.

```
# cd gftp-2.0.17
# ./configure --prefix=/usr/local
creating cache ./config.cache
checking for non-GNU ld... /usr/bin/ld
checking if the linker (/usr/bin/ld) is GNU ld... yes
checking for a BSD compatible install... /usr/bin/install -c
checking whether build environment is sane... yes
checking whether make sets ${MAKE}... yes
checking for working aclocal-1.4... found
checking for working autoconf... found
checking for working automake-1.4... found
checking for working autoheader... found
checking for working makeinfo... found
checking host system type... i686-pc-linux-gnu
checking for gcc... gcc
...
```

```
creating config.h
creating po/POTFILES
creating po/Makefile
```

As you can see, the configure command does a lot of work, trying to determine what type of system you have and what tools are available. We have asked the configure application to use the /usr/local prefix when it is time to install the application. In other words, all of the files that we need to install will be installed in various subdirectories under /usr/local. This allows you to control where you store all of your custom-built application's data and files.

6. Now, you are ready to compile. Simply invoke the make command:

```
# make
make  all-recursive
make[1]: Entering directory '/usr/local/src/gftp/gftp-2.0.17'
Making all in intl
make[2]: Entering directory '/usr/local/src/gftp/gftp-2.0.17/intl'
make[2]: Nothing to be done for 'all'.
make[2]: Leaving directory '/usr/local/src/gftp/gftp-2.0.17/intl'
Making all in docs
make[2]: Entering directory '/usr/local/src/gftp/gftp-2.0.17/docs'
Making all in sample.gftp
make[3]: Entering directory
        '/usr/local/src/gftp/gftp-2.0.17/docs/sample.gftp'
make[3]: Nothing to be done for 'all'.
make[3]: Leaving directory '/usr/local/src/gftp/gftp-2.0.17/docs/sample.gftp'
make[3]: Entering directory '/usr/local/src/gftp/gftp-2.0.17/docs'
make[3]: Nothing to be done for 'all-am'.
make[3]: Leaving directory '/usr/local/src/gftp/gftp-2.0.17/docs'
make[2]: Leaving directory '/usr/local/src/gftp/gftp-2.0.17/docs'
Making all in lib
make[2]: Entering directory '/usr/local/src/gftp/gftp-2.0.17/lib'
gcc -DHAVE_CONFIG_H -I. -I. -I.. -I/usr/include/glib-2.0
    -I/usr/lib/glib-2.0/include   -D_REENTRANT -I../intl
    -DSHARE_DIR=\"/usr/local/share/gftp\"
    -DLOCALE_DIR=\"/usr/local/share/locale\"
    -g -O2 -c bookmark.c
...
make[2]: Leaving directory '/usr/local/src/gftp/gftp-2.0.17'
make[1]: Leaving directory '/usr/local/src/gftp/gftp-2.0.17'
```

The make command follows the instructions specified in Makefile (which was customized to the system by the configure program) to build the application. In this case, there are only a small number of C source files that need to be compiled. So after a few minutes, make finishes and we have our application.

7. Install the compiled application into /usr/local:

```
# make install
Making install in intl
make[1]: Entering directory '/usr/local/src/gftp/gftp-2.0.17/intl'
if { test "gftp" = "gettext-runtime" || test "gftp" = "gettext-tools"; } \
   && test 'no' = yes; then \
  /bin/sh ../../mkinstalldirs /usr/local/lib /usr/local/include; \
  /usr/bin/install -c -m 644 libintl.h /usr/local/include/libintl.h; \
```

```
      @LIBTOOL@ --mode=install \
        /usr/bin/install -c -m 644 libintl.a /usr/local/lib/libintl.a; \
      if test "@RELOCATABLE@" = yes; then \
        dependencies='sed -n -e 's,^dependency_libs=\(.*\),\1,p'
          < /usr/local/lib/libintl.la | sed -e "s,^',," -e "s,'\$,,"'; \
        if test -n "ependencies"; then \
          rm -f /usr/local/lib/libintl.la; \
        fi; \
      fi; \
    else \
      : ; \
    fi
    ...
    make[2]: Leaving directory '/usr/local/src/gftp/gftp-2.0.17'
    make[1]: Leaving directory '/usr/local/src/gftp/gftp-2.0.17'
```

8. Let's check to see that the new version of the gFTP application has been built and installed properly. Because you asked the `make` program to install the application and its related files in `/usr/local`, you will find the gFTP binary executable in `/usr/local/bin`. You can execute the application with the `-version` switch to verify that it is indeed version 2.0.17, like so:

```
$ /usr/local/bin/gftp --version
gFTP 2.0.17
```

The existing version continues to exist on your system in its original location, `/usr/bin`, which you can see for yourself:

```
$ /usr/bin/gftp --version

gFTP 2.0.17
```

It is up to you to decide whether you want to keep both versions around. Typically, when you install a new version of a software application, you should keep the older version around until you have had the chance to test the new version for some period of time. That way, you can always revert back to the original version if the newer version of the application is problematic.

Before you build any application from its source code, you should spend some time reading through the README and INSTALL files, as well as looking at some of the source code. That way, you can get a better handle on the application's features and limitations.

You have compiled and built your first application straight from source code; the process was quite straightforward for this application, although it will vary somewhat from application to application:

```
# ./configure --prefix=/some/dir
# make
# make install
```

By building applications in this manner, you have more control over the entire process and can decide how to modify or optimize the code and select where and how to install its components. For the most part, the building process is not difficult. Sometimes, however, you may run into difficulties getting the code to compile. It is beyond the scope of this book to discuss these various situations, so please refer to *Professional Linux Programming*, by Neil Matthew and Richard Stones, for more details.

Summary

This chapter covered various administrative aspects of the Linux operating system, including system configuration and log files, backup and archival procedures, and building applications from source code.

The chapter started out with system configuration files. Unlike other operating systems, where the system configuration is stored in some binary format or other, Linux and most other UNIX derivatives store their configuration information in plain text files. This allows you to easily see and edit this configuration without much effort, and makes it easier for you to back up these files as part of your full or incremental backup procedures.

We then proceeded to look at log files. As you may have seen, the core Linux components, such as the kernel, as well as other services and applications, log all types of information to these text files. If you pay close attention to the content in these log files, you can find and diagnose all types of issues from hardware failures to security alerts.

System configuration and log files are very important aspects of your operating system. For you to keep your Linux system running even when faced with a severe crash, you need to implement a useful backup strategy. We discussed all types of backup and archival strategy, including what tools to use; how, when, and where to back up; and what types of issues you need to watch for.

The chapter finished with an explanation of how to compile applications from source code. There will be many occasions where you will find an application in source code form only; no binary RPM package may be available. You can use the various development tools with the techniques discussed in the chapter to build applications. In fact, the same strategy and techniques can be used to build the most complex application of them all: the Linux kernel (covered in Chapter 12).

Exercises

1. Create a `crontab` entry to record the system load averages to a log file every 15 minutes, but only on Monday through Friday, from 8:00 a.m. to 6:00 p.m. Hint: Take a look at the following online resource to learn more about the `crontab` format: `http://www.opengroup.org/onlinepubs/007908799/xcu/crontab.html`.
2. Search the System Log file from the command line for other possible problems, such as warnings, errors, and failures.
3. Modify `syslog.conf` to log FTP-related messages to another file, such as `/var/log/ftp.log`. Hint: Each entry in `syslog.conf` has three separate components: the messages to be considered, the destination, and any user-defined comments.
4. Find all compressed tar archives within the `/usr/local` directory hierarchy and archive them to an ISO image so you can burn them to a CD-ROM and then delete them to free up disk space.
5. Try to build and install the `enscript` application from its source code. This application converts ASCII files to PostScript and also supports a number of options to customize the PostScript output. For example, you can use `enscript` to print your scripts and other source code in an easy-to-read two-column format with line numbers. Hint: Read the `INSTALL` and `README` documents that come with the package for any special instructions.

12

Rebuilding the Linux Kernel

The Linux *kernel*, as you may already know, is at the heart of the Linux operating system. One of the main responsibilities of any operating system kernel is to provide an interface to the underlying hardware; the kernel handles all communications between applications and hardware. In addition, the kernel implements and oversees a variety of tasks, including the following:

- Process creation, scheduling, and termination
- Interprocess communication
- Memory management (paging, swapping, and mapping)
- Access and security control

You can loosely categorize the kernel into two main components: *device drivers* and *device-independent subsystems*. The device drivers implement the actual communications with the physical hardware, whereas the subsystems mediate access to hardware resources by providing each and every process with fair access (known as *scheduling*). These components are typically not built into the core kernel, but are instead separate executable objects, or *Linux Kernel Modules (LKM)*, that can be loaded and unloaded as needed. In other words, the Linux kernel is modular in nature and is not one large monolithic entity; it can be configured and built as a monolithic kernel, however, as you will see in a minute.

In this chapter, you learn enough about the Linux kernel to understand how the kernel works on the surface. You will do this by building a small, lean, monolithic kernel—one that has a minimal set of device drivers—that is ideal for use in routers and firewalls. You probably will not want to use this kernel on your desktop or laptop machine on a day-to-day basis. However, you can try this out now (to see how easy it is) and then reinstate the default kernel shipped with Fedora afterward. Then, if you ever need to build a dedicated router or firewall machine, you'll know how.

Before building the actual kernel, however, let's discuss the rationale for building a new version of the kernel and its associated advantages.

Why Rebuild the Kernel?

You might wonder why you would ever need to rebuild or configure the kernel because modules that are not required will not be loaded by the core kernel. That is entirely true. However, there are a number of reasons to manipulate the kernel:

- The kernel provided by the standard distribution is generic in nature—it is capable of running on most Intel x86 hardware but not optimized for any particular configuration. You may want to optimize the kernel for your *particular* hardware for better performance.
- Certain device drivers are built directly into the kernel itself, and you may want to remove these drivers for security and performance reasons.
- You may want to add support for your particular hardware devices directly into the kernel.

Now, let's build our very own version of the Linux kernel.

Initializing the Kernel

Before you start to work with the kernel, you must perform two important tasks. First, you need to install the necessary kernel source packages, and second, you need to back up the current kernel and related files so you can revert back to the original version of the kernel quickly.

Let's install the necessary kernel headers and sources.

Try It Out Initializing the Kernel

1. Open the RPM applet (either from the Applications ➪ System Settings ➪ Add/Remove Applications menu, or by executing the `system-config-packages` application from the command line).
2. Select the `Kernel Development` package group from the `Development` category, and press the Details button to install the necessary packages (see Figure 12-1). If you installed the necessary development tools and libraries to build gFTP in Chapter 11, the `Development Tools`, `X Software Development`, and `GNOME Software Development` package groups will be shown as installed. However, if you did not build gFTP, you will need to select the `Development Tools` package group, in addition to `Kernel Development`, to build the kernel.

   The `Kernel Development` package group installs the kernel source code in the `/usr/src/linux-2.6.5-1.358` directory.
3. Before you can start to configure the kernel, you must back up the existing kernel. That way, if something goes wrong, you can always revert to the original kernel.

   The kernel and its related files, but *not* the modules, are stored in the `/boot` directory, or partition, if you have set it up that way. You would back up this directory with the following:

```
# tar -zcvf /root/boot-2.6.5-1.358.20040518.tar.gz /boot
```

   Use a combination of the kernel version along with the current date to name the compressed `tar` archive; this provides you with a unique identifier. If you get in the habit of compiling kernels on a regular basis, this naming convention will allow you to quickly identify which archive to use for recovery, if necessary.

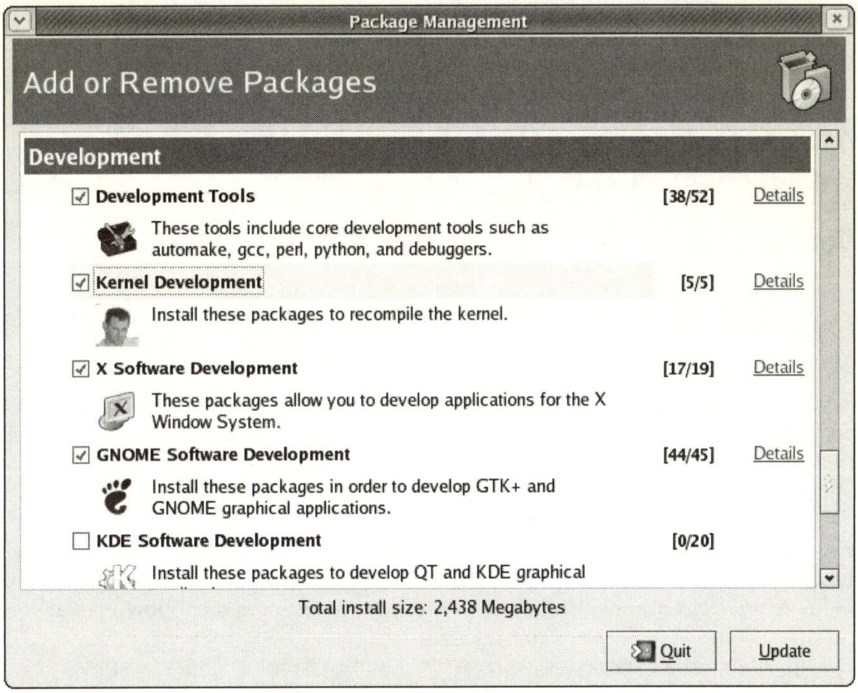

Figure 12-1

Now that you have backed up the kernel, it would be nice to create a book disk as well, so you can use it to boot into the system and replace the kernel if something goes horribly wrong. However, unlike previous versions of Red Hat Linux, the Linux kernel used in Fedora version 2.6 has reached the point where it does not fit on a standard floppy disk. Fortunately, you have other options. You can simply use the Fedora Linux installer in rescue mode if you ever run into a problem. Or, you can use one of the many slimmed-down versions of Linux available online to create a boot disk; my personal favorite is `tomsrtbt`. Insert a clean floppy disk into the drive and enter the following set of commands:

```
# wget http://www.tux.org/pub/distributions/tinylinux/tomsrtbt/tomsrtbt-
2.0.103.tar.gz
# tar -zxvf tomsrtbt-2.0.103.tar.gz
# cd tomsrtbt-2.0.103
# ./install.s
```

```
Don't forget to READ the FAQ.

Insert a blank writable 3.5" floppy diskette then strike ENTER.

About to fdformat /dev/fd0u1722
Double-sided, 82 tracks, 21 sec/track. Total capacity 1722 kB.
Formatting ... done
Verifying ... done
About to dd floppy image
```

```
3444+0 records in
3444+0 records out
About to verify floppy image
Succeeded!
```

This essentially installs the kernel and other required files to the floppy disk, so you can use this disk to boot into your system at any time.

How It Works

The `/boot` directory holds the kernel and related files. If you look around at the contents of this directory, you will see a file called `vmlinuz-2.6.5-1.358` (or something similar). This is the kernel.

If you are using Fedora Core 2, your kernel is probably v2.6.5-1.358. In the Linux kernel's versioning scheme, the first digit (2, in this case) represents the major version, and the second digit (6, in this case) represents the minor version. If the minor version number is odd, the kernel is a beta version; otherwise, it is from a release/production branch. The third number (5, in this case) is the kernel patch number, and the final number is the package number.

By contrast, the kernel modules are stored in the directory `/lib/modules/2.6.5-1.358`. If you take a look at the contents of this directory, you'll see that a large number of modules are available. If you are curious to know the exact number of modules here, you can execute the following statement:

```
# find /lib/modules/`uname -r` -name '*.ko' -print | wc -l
    989
```

You can use the `find` command to locate all the modules (that is, files with a `.ko` extension) in the `/lib/modules` directory associated with the system kernel. Instead of hardcoding the kernel version, you used the `uname` command with the `-r` switch, which returns the system's kernel version.

You are now ready to work with the kernel.

A Small, Lean Kernel

You will build a small, lean monolithic kernel that is ideal for use in routers and firewalls. Unlike the "regular" kernel that you would typically use in a desktop computer or laptop, a kernel designed for a router or firewall has to have very specific characteristics:

- It has to be lean so you don't use up a lot of resources.
- It has to be monolithic; it should not have the capability to load or unload modules.
- It should disable support for any hot swappable devices, floppy drives, and multimedia components.
- Advanced networking features should be enabled.

Looking at these characteristics, you might wonder why you would want to disable support for the floppy drive, for example. You certainly do not want any intruders who have potential physical access to this router or firewall server to introduce any files or executables into your server. By disabling the floppy drive altogether, you don't have to worry about this.

Keep these characteristics in mind, and you will end up with a kernel that is lean, secure, and optimized for network performance.

Try It Out Building a Kernel

1. First, you need to change your current directory to /usr/src/linux-2.6.5-1.358:

```
# cd /usr/src/linux-2.6.5-1.358
```

2. From there, you can use the following commands to run the X Window-based kernel configuration editor:

```
# make xconfig
  HOSTCC  scripts/basic/fixdep
  HOSTCC  scripts/basic/split-include
  HOSTCC  scripts/basic/docproc
  SHIPPED scripts/kconfig/zconf.tab.h
  ...
  HOSTCXX scripts/kconfig/qconf.o
  HOSTLD  scripts/kconfig/qconf
scripts/kconfig/qconf arch/i386/Kconfig
#
# using defaults found in /boot/config-2.6.5-1.358
#
```

After a short time, you'll see the configuration editor appear. The dialog box that you see on your screen will not resemble the one shown in Figure 12-2 until you change the display view to tree view; click the last button on the toolbar.

If you don't have the X Window system installed, you can use a text-based editor by executing the following command:

```
# make menuconfig
```

As you can see from Figure 12-3, the text-based editor looks a bit different, but supports all of the same configuration options.

For the rest of this configuration section, you will use the X Window configuration editor.

3. From the configuration editor, you can enable or disable a multitude of options and kernel modules. In this example, we plan to build a monolithic kernel; therefore, you need to disable loadable module support. To do this, expand the `Loadable module support` option—this brings up the `Enable loadable module support` option. Click the small checkbox to the right of the option to disable it.

If you look through some of the other options, you'll notice the presence of a great number of choices, laid out in a hierarchical manner. Deselecting an option (by clicking) disables all the options listed below. In some cases, however, you will have to manually deselect all the options below the main category one item at a time.

4. That's just the first setting. Now, go through the rest of the configuration—you can always jump around from one option to another with the mouse.

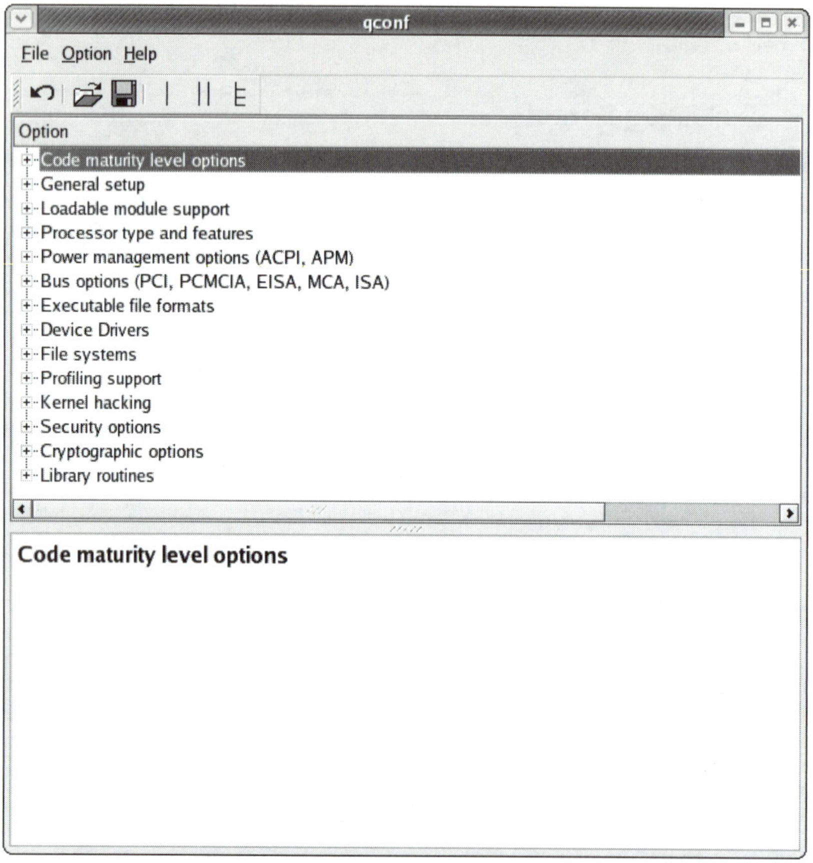

Figure 12-2

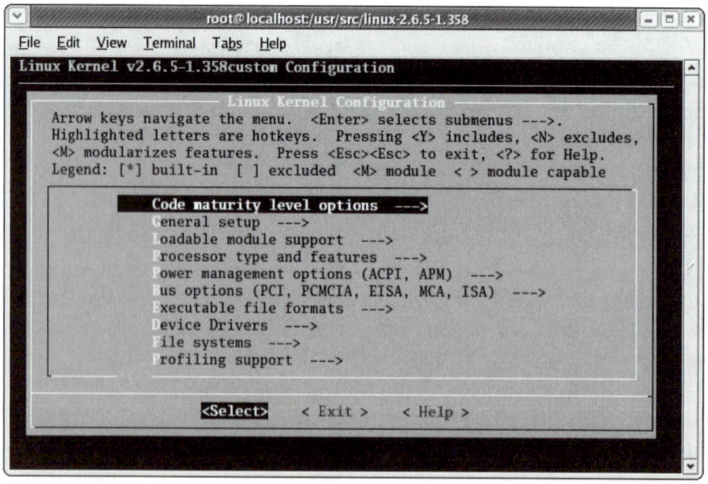

Figure 12-3

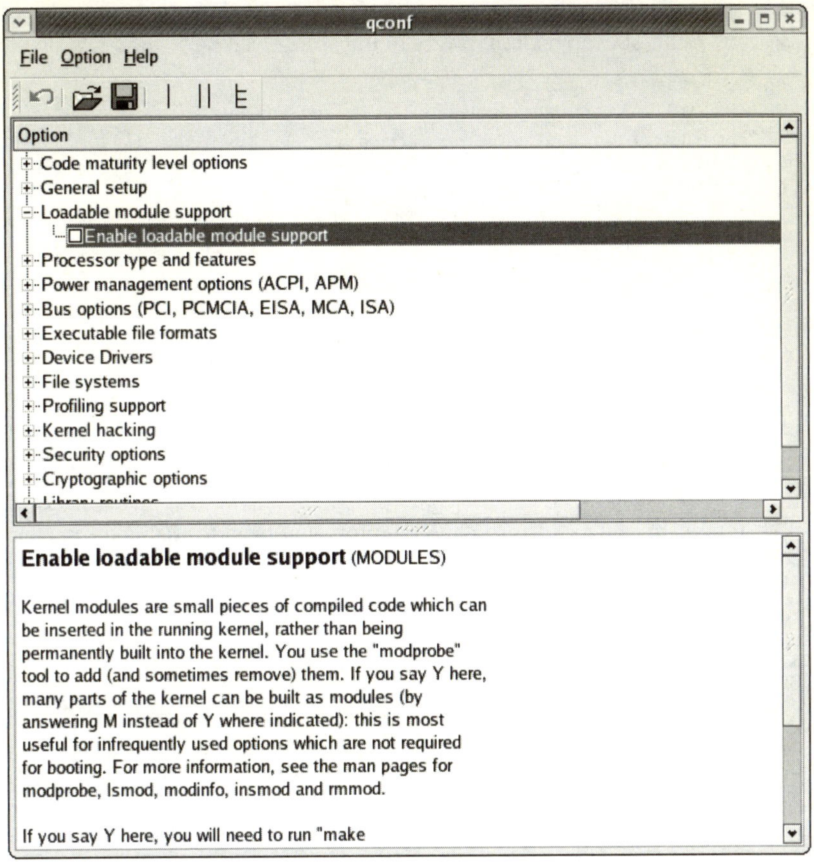

Figure 12-4

Use the following recipe, which lists settings that need to be changed only; each following bold-faced option represents a section with further options in the kernel configuration:

```
Code maturity level options
    - Prompt for development and/or incomplete code/drivers       OFF

Loadable module support
    - Enable loadable module support                               OFF

Processor type and features
    - Processor family                                Select from List
    - Generic x86 support                                          OFF
    - HPET Timer Support                                           OFF
    - Symmetric multi-processing support                           OFF
    - Toshiba Laptop support                                       OFF
    - Dell laptop support                                          OFF
    - /dev/cpu/microcode - Intel IA32 CPU microcode support        OFF
    - /dev/cpu/*/msr - Model-specific register support             OFF
    - /dev/cpu/*/cpuid - CPU information support                   OFF
    - High Memory Support                                          OFF
```

You can determine the processor name and type for your machine by simply searching for the string `CPU:` in the startup boot messages in the `/var/log/messages` log file, like so:

```
# grep CPU /var/log/messages
May 22 21:22:02 localhost kernel: Initializing CPU#0
May 22 21:22:02 localhost kernel: CPU 0 irqstacks, hard=02345000 soft=02344000
May 22 21:22:03 localhost kernel: CPU: L1 I cache: 16K, L1 D cache: 16K
May 22 21:22:03 localhost kernel: CPU: L2 cache: 128K
May 22 21:22:03 localhost kernel: Intel machine check reporting enabled on CPU#0.
May 22 21:22:03 localhost kernel: CPU: Intel Celeron (Mendocino) stepping 05
May 22 21:22:10 localhost kernel: microcode: CPU0 updated from revision 0x0 to 0x3, 
date = 05051999
```

Based on this information, you should select a processor family that is most closely related to your hardware configuration:

- If you are using a system with multiple processors, you may want to enable the options italicized in the preceding code, which, in turn, activate source code responsible for utilizing multiple processors.
- If you are using a Toshiba or Dell laptop, you need to enable the respective options from the preceding list.

Let's continue with the recipe:

```
Power management options (ACPI, APM)
    - Power Management support                                        OFF
    - ACPI (Advanced Configuration and Power Interface) Support
        - ACPI Support                                                OFF
    - CPU Frequency Scaling
        - CPU Frequency Scaling                                       OFF

Bus options (PCI, PCMCIA, EISA, MCA, ISA)
    Legacy /proc/pci interface                                        OFF
    ISA support                                                       OFF
    PCMCIA/CardBus support                                            OFF

Executable file formats
    Kernel support for MISC binaries                                  OFF
```

If you are using a laptop, you might want to examine the options listed within the `Power management options` section; you will see a number of options that, when enabled, will enable your laptop to conserve power more efficiently.

As you will soon see, the Linux kernel supports a vast variety of hardware, from ATA and SCSI to USB and Bluetooth. Because you are looking to create a lean and minimal kernel, you will disable most of this hardware support as you proceed with configuring `Device Drivers`:

```
Device Drivers
    - Memory Technology Devices (MTD)
        - Memory Technology Device (MTD) support                      OFF
    - Parallel port support
        - Parallel port support                                       OFF
```

```
- Block devices
    - Normal floppy disk support                                    OFF
    - Compaq SMART2 support                                         OFF
    - Compaq Smart Array 5xxx support                               OFF
    - Mylex DAC960/DAC1100 PCI RAID Controller support              OFF
    - Loopback device support                                       OFF
    - Network block device support                                  OFF
    - Support for Large Block Devices                               OFF
- ATA/ATAPI/MFM/RLL support
    - ATA/ATAPI/MFM/RLL support
        - Enhanced IDE/MFM/RLL disk/cdrom/tape/floppy support
            - Include IDE/ATAPI FLOPPY support                      OFF
            - CMD640 chipset bugfix/support                         OFF
            - PCI IDE chipset support
                - RZ1000 chipset bugfix/support                     OFF
                - Generic PCI bus-master DMA support                OFF
- SCSI device support
    - ALL OPTIONS                                                   OFF
- Multi-device support (RAID and LVM)
    - Multiple devices driver support (RAID and LVM)                OFF
- Fusion MPT device support
    - Fusion MPT (base + ScsiHost) drivers                          OFF
- I2O device support
    - I2O support                                                   OFF
```

You start off by disabling support for the parallel port and the floppy disk. Unless you have a very specific peripheral that requires the parallel port, there is no point in enabling this feature. The floppy disk support, on the other hand, is to enhance the security of your kernel; you don't want users who have access to the physical hardware, where you will run this version of the kernel, to load or extract sensitive information from the system via an easy-to-use floppy disk.

Next, you assume that a typical router machine will have an ATA/IDE setup. So, you disable the drivers for SCSI devices. If your configuration requires support for SCSI devices, enable the necessary options. However, you should be aware that this will increase the size of the kernel greatly.

And finally, before moving on to the next piece of configuration, you should note that the CMD640 and the RZ1000 chipsets have design flaws that could lead to corruption on 486 and Pentium motherboards. If you have a newer machine, you can safely disable these fixes, as previously shown.

On to networking devices:

```
                                                   (continued from above)
- Device Drivers
    - Networking support
        - Networking support
            - Networking options
                - IP: Virtual Server Configuration
                    - IP virtual server support (EXPERIMENTAL)      OFF
                - 802.1d Ethernet Bridging                          OFF
                - 802.1Q VLAN Support                               OFF
                - The IPX protocol                                  OFF
```

```
            - Appletalk protocol support                        OFF
        - IrDA (infrared) subsystem support                     OFF
        - Bluetooth subsystem support                           OFF
        - TUX: Threaded linUX application protocol ...          OFF
        - Network device support
            - Bonding driver support                            OFF
            - EQL (serial line load balancing) support          OFF
            - Ethernet (10 or 100Mbit)
                - Sun Happy Meal 10/100baseT support            OFF
                - Sun GEM support                               OFF
                - 3COM cards                                    OFF
                - HP 10/100VG PCLAN (ISA, EISA, PCI) support    OFF
                - EISA, VLB, PCI and on board controllers       OFF
            - Ethernet (1000 Mbit)
                - ALL OPTIONS                                   OFF
            - Ethernet (10000 Mbit)
                - Intel(R) PRO/10GbE support                    OFF
                - S2IO 10Gbe Xframe NIC (S2IO)                  OFF
            - FDDI driver support                               OFF
            - Wireless LAN (non-hamradio)
                - Wireless LAN drivers (non-hamradio) ...       OFF
            - Fibre Channel driver support                      OFF
    - IrDA (infrared) support
        - IrDA subsystem support                                OFF
    - Bluetooth support
        - Bluetooth subsystem support                           OFF
- ISDN subsystem
    - ISDN support                                              OFF
```

This configuration should be relatively easy to understand. We have disabled support for the IPX and AppleTalk network protocols. If you need your router to interact with other servers that communicate via these protocols, you should enable them.

Next, disable all Ethernet cards, except for cards that contain the DEC tulip chip; this is not shown here, but is evident in the configuration. Most of the SMC and Linksys cards on the market utilize this chip, so the configuration should work without a hitch for cards manufactured by these companies. However, if you have a network interface card from another vendor who may not use this specific chip, you should first determine the chip being used:

```
# grep eth0 /var/log/messages
May 22 01:44:14 localhost network: Bringing up interface eth0:  succeeded
May 22 01:44:28 localhost kernel: eth0: ADMtek Comet rev 17 at 0xe83ec00,
00:20:78:10:BD:C8, IRQ 11.
```

You can then look up the specific chip at `http://web.archive.org/web/20030602115200/www.scyld.com/page/support/network/` to determine whether a corresponding driver exists. If this does not yield any success, you can try to determine whether the default Fedora kernel detects your specific card. If it does, you can use the `lsmod` command to see what kernel module is being loaded to handle the card, and then enable that option in the configuration. This is trickier than it sounds because you must determine the correct module from a list of all the loaded modules.

Now, let's move on to input devices and other character devices:

```
                                        (continued from above)
- Device Drivers
    - Input device support
        - Joystick interface                                    OFF
        - Event interface                                       OFF
        - Gameport support                                      OFF
        - Serial port line discipline                           OFF
        - Joysticks                                             OFF
        - Touchscreens                                          OFF
        - Misc                                                  OFF
    - Character devices
        - Non-standard serial port support                      OFF
        - Serial drivers
            - 8250/16550 and compatible serial support
                - Console on 8250/16550 and compatible ...      OFF
                - Extended 8250/16550 serial driver options     OFF
        - Crash Utility memory driver                           OFF
        - IPMI
            - IPMI top-level message handler                    OFF
        - Watchdog Cards
            - Watchdog Timer Support                            OFF
        - Intel/AMD/VIA HW Random Number Generator support      OFF
        - Double Talk PC internal speech card support           OFF
        - Siemens R3964 line discipline                         OFF
        - /dev/agpgart (AGP Support)                            OFF
        - Direct Rendering Manager (XFree86 4.1.0 and ...)      OFF
        - ACP Modem (Mwave) support                             OFF
    - I2C support
        - I2C support
            - I2C device interface                              OFF
            - I2C Algorithms
                - I2C PCF 8584 interfaces                       OFF
```

We won't discuss support for all of this hardware here because most of the devices are not common in personal desktop systems. In summary, we disable support for joysticks and gameport and serial ports because these are not typically used in a system that is serving as a network router or firewall.

We are not done with device drivers just yet. Let's look at one final section dealing with graphics, multimedia, and USB devices:

```
                                        (continued from above)
- Device Drivers
    - Misc devices
        - Device driver for IBM RSA service processor           OFF
    - Multimedia devices
        - Video for Linux
            - Video for Linux
                - ALL OPTIONS                                   OFF
            - Radio Adapters
                - ALL OPTIONS                                   OFF
        - Digital Video Broadcasting Devices
            - DVB For Linux                                     OFF
```

```
- Graphics support
    - Support for frame buffer devices                              OFF
    - Console display driver support
        - VGA text console (NEW)
            - Video mode selection support                          OFF
        - MDA text console (dual-headed) (EXPERIMENTAL)             OFF
- Sound
    - Sound card support                                            OFF
- USB support
    - Support for Host-side USB
        - EHCI HCD (USB 2.0) support                                OFF
        - USB Modem (CDC ACM) support                               OFF
        - USB Printer support                                       OFF
        - USB Mass Storage support                                  OFF
    - Aiptek 6000U/8000U tablet support                             OFF
    - Wacom Intuos/Graphire tablet support                          OFF
    - KB Gear JamStudio tablet support                              OFF
    - Griffin PowerMate and Contour Jog support                     OFF
    - MicroTouch USB Touchscreen Driver                             OFF
    - X-Box gamepad support                                         OFF
    - ATI USB RF remote control                                     OFF
    - Microtek X6USB scanner support                                OFF
    - DABUSB driver                                                 OFF
    - USB IBM (Xirlink) C-it Camera support                         OFF
    - USB Konica Webcam support                                     OFF
    - USB OV511 Camera support                                      OFF
    - USB Philips Cameras                                           OFF
    - USB SE401 Camera support                                      OFF
    - USB STV680 (Pencam) Camera support                            OFF
    - USB W996[87]CF JPEG Dual Mode Camera support                  OFF
    - USB KLSI KL5USB101-based ethernet device support              OFF
    - USB Pegasus/Pegasus-II based ethernet device support          OFF
    - Multi-purpose USB Networking Framework                        OFF
    - USB Serial Converter support
        - USB Serial Converter support                              OFF
    - EMI 6|2m USB Audio interface support                          OFF
    - Texas Instruments Graph Link USB ...                          OFF
    - USB LCD driver support                                        OFF
    - USB LED driver support                                        OFF
    - Cypress USB thermometer driver support                        OFF
```

You start by turning off drivers from the `Multimedia devices`, `Graphics support` and `Sound` sections. Then, you step through the USB `support` section and quickly disable any and all USB multimedia devices, such as digital cameras and scanners. For now, USB modems and network interface cards, which are italicized, have also been disabled. If you are using such devices, however, you should enable them.

We are all done with device drivers. Are you surprised at the amount of support for the vast number of hardware devices? These drivers are bundled with the Fedora kernel. If you have a specific device that is not listed here, you should check the manufacturer's Web site, as you will most likely find it there.

Moving on to filesystems:

```
File systems
    - Second extended fs support                                         OFF
    - Reiserfs support                                                   OFF
    - JFS filesystem support                                             OFF
    - XFS filesystem support                                             OFF
    - Minix fs support                                                   OFF
    - Quota support                                                      OFF
    - Kernel automounter support                                         OFF
    - Kernel automounter version 4 support (also supports v3)            OFF
    - CD-ROM/DVD Filesystems
        - UDF file system support                                        OFF
    - DOS/FAT/NT Filesystems
        - DOS FAT fs support                                             OFF
    - Pseudo filesystems
        - HugeTLB file system support                                    OFF
    - Miscellaneous filesystems
        - Apple Extended HFS file system support                         OFF
        - Compressed ROM file system support                             OFF
        - FreeVxFS file system support (VERITAS VxFS(TM) ...)            OFF
        - QNX4 file system support (read only)                           OFF
        - System V/Xenis/V8/Coherent file system support                 OFF
        - UFS file system support (read only)                            OFF
    - Network File Systems
        - NFS file system support                                        OFF
        - NFS server support                                             OFF
        - SMB file system support (to mount Windows shares etc.)         OFF
        - CIFS support (advanced network ...)                            OFF
        - NCP file system support (to mount NetWare volumes)             OFF
    - Partition Types
        - Advanced partition selection                                   OFF
    - Native Language Support
        - Base native language support
            - Codepage 737 (Greek)                                       OFF
            - Codepage 775 (Baltic Rim)                                  OFF
            - Codepage 850 (Europe)                                      OFF
            - Codepage 852 (Central/Eastern Europe)                      OFF
            - Codepage 855 (Cyrillic)                                    OFF
            - Codepage 857 (Turkish)                                     OFF
            - Codepage 860 (Portuguese)                                  OFF
            - Codepage 861 (Icelandic)                                   OFF
            - Codepage 862 (Hebrew)                                      OFF
            - Codepage 863 (Canadian French)                             OFF
            - Codepage 864 (Arabic)                                      OFF
            - Codepage 865 (Norwegian, Danish)                           OFF
            - Codepage 866 (Cyrillic/Russian)                            OFF
            - Codepage 869 (Greek)                                       OFF
            - Simplified Chinese charset (CP936, GB2312)                 OFF
            - Traditional Chinese charset (Big5)                         OFF
            - Japanese charsets (Shift-JIS, EUC-JP)                      OFF
            - Korean charset (CP949, EUC-KR)                             OFF
            - Thai charset (CP874, TIS-620)                              OFF
            - Hebrew charsets (ISO-8859-8, CP1255)                       OFF
            - Windows CP1250 (Slavic/Central European Languages)         OFF
            - Windows CP1251 (Bulgarian, Belarusian)                     OFF
```

Older versions of Red Hat Linux, as well as Linux from other distributors, used the famous ext2 filesystem. However, almost all of the new generation of Linux distributions, including Fedora Core, use the ext3 filesystem, which is more efficient, reliable, and is backward compatible with ext2. As a result, let's disable support for all other filesystems:

```
Kernel hacking
    - Kernel debugging                                       OFF
    - Sleep-inside-spinlock checking                         OFF

Security options
    - Enable different security models                       OFF
```

You disable the different security models, most notably Security Enhanced Linux, or SELinux, because it is not yet stable under Fedora Core.

5. Before you save the configuration, take a quick look at all of the options once again, making sure that any devices and functionality that you need are enabled. When you have finished going through the options, select the Save option from the File menu, and then choose Exit to save the configuration and exit from the editor.

6. We are not quite done yet! Unfortunately, the configuration editor does not properly disable some of the features that we decided that we don't need. So, go ahead and launch the editor as specified in Step 2 and disable the following options:

```
 - Device Drivers
    - SCSI device support
        - SCSI device support                                OFF
    - I2C support
        - I2C support                                        OFF
    - Multimedia devices
    - Video for Linux                                    OFF
```

Save the configuration and exit.

7. Only a few more changes are required. First, you must edit the Makefile contained in the /usr/src/linux-2.6.5-1.358 directory, by changing the identifier assigned to the EXTRAVERSION variable, as follows:

```
EXTRAVERSION = -1.358router
```

The -1.358 corresponds to the package number (the last part of the kernel identifier: 2.6.5-1.358), and router is what we've added to distinguish this configuration of the kernel from other configurations. Therefore, our kernel will be installed as 2.6.5-1.358router.

8. Next, you need to create an empty modules directory associated with your kernel, despite the fact that you are building a monolithic kernel. The Makefile assumes that a modules directory exists, or else the compiler will complain with an error message and terminate:

```
# mkdir /lib/modules/2.6.5-1.358router
```

9. The first step in actually building the kernel is to clean up any remnants of old code, temporary object files, and other unnecessary files:

```
# make clean
```

10. Now, build the kernel:

```
# make bzImage
  CHK     include/linux/version.h
  UPD     include/linux/version.h
  SYMLINK include/asm -> include/asm-i386
  SPLIT   include/linux/autoconf.h -> include/config/*
  HOSTCC  scripts/basic/fixdep
  HOSTCC  scripts/basic/split-include
  HOSTCC  scripts/basic/docproc
  HOSTCC  scripts/conmakehash
  ...
  LD      .tmp_vmlinux1
  KSYM    .tmp_kallsyms1.S
  AS      .tmp_kallsyms1.o
  LD      .tmp_vmlinux2
  KSYM    .tmp_kallsyms2.S
  AS      .tmp_kallsyms2.o
  LD      vmlinux
  AS      arch/i386/boot/bootsect.o
  LD      arch/i386/boot/bootsect
  AS      arch/i386/boot/setup.o
  LD      arch/i386/boot/setup
  AS      arch/i386/boot/compressed/head.o
  CC      arch/i386/boot/compressed/misc.o
  OBJCOPY arch/i386/boot/compressed/vmlinux.bin
  GZIP    arch/i386/boot/compressed/vmlinux.bin.gz
  LD      arch/i386/boot/compressed/piggy.o
  LD      arch/i386/boot/compressed/vmlinux
  OBJCOPY arch/i386/boot/vmlinux.bin
  HOSTCC  arch/i386/boot/tools/build
  BUILD   arch/i386/boot/bzImage
Root device is (3, 1)
Boot sector 512 bytes.
Setup is 2554 bytes.
System is 1146 kB
Kernel: arch/i386/boot/bzImage is ready
```

11. Next, install the new kernel and related files in `/boot`:

```
# make install
make[1]: `arch/i386/kernel/asm-offsets.s' is up to date.
  CHK     include/linux/compile.h
Kernel: arch/i386/boot/bzImage is ready
sh /usr/src/linux-2.6.5-1.358/arch/i386/boot/install.sh 2.6.5-1.358router
arch/i386/boot/bzImage System.map ""
```

12. This step doesn't apply if you followed the recipe previously listed because you disabled loadable module support (back in Step 3). However, if you were configuring a kernel in which loadable module support was enabled, this would be the right time to build and install the loadable modules:

```
# make modules
# make modules_install
```

13. Now, check your kernel to see how it compares in size with the original kernel. Remember, our goal was to build a small and lean kernel:

```
$ cd /boot
$ ls -s vmlinuz*
   0 vmlinuz@
1176 vmlinuz-2.6.5-1.358
1156 vmlinuz-2.6.5-1.358router
```

As you can see, you've reduced the size of the kernel slightly, but because it is monolithic, it already includes all of the modules that we enabled during configuration.

14. The final step in the build process is to modify the boot loader configuration, as written by the installer. First, determine the device identification for the root partition, like so:

```
$ grep '/' /etc/mtab
/dev/hda1 / ext3 rw 0 0
```

15. Next, edit the `/etc/grub.conf` file, where you will see the following:

```
title Fedora Core (2.6.5-1.358router)
        root (hd0,0)
        kernel /boot/vmlinuz-2.6.5-1.358router ro root=LABEL=/
        initrd /boot/initrd-2.6.5-1.358router.img
```

Simply replace the `root` argument, like so:

```
        kernel /boot/vmlinuz-2.6.5-1.358router ro root=/dev/hda1
```

16. Now reboot. If the kernel was built and installed successfully, you will see two options in the GRUB bootloader screen when your system starts up Fedora Core `2.6.5-1.358` and Fedora Core `2.6.5-1.358router`. If you choose the first option, your system will boot up using the original kernel. Otherwise, the system will boot using the lean and optimized kernel that you have just built.

Reverting to the Original Kernel

Unfortunately, if you made any mistakes, or if certain bugs in the source code manifested themselves during the build or compile processes, you may have a situation where the system will fail to boot. In such a case, you have three options that you can try, starting from the easiest to the most difficult:

- Boot from the original kernel through the GRUB bootloader screen.
- Boot from the floppy disk.
- Boot from the Fedora Core CD-ROM #1 in rescue mode.

The first option of booting from the GRUB bootloader is by far the easiest and should allow you to boot properly into the system. Simply select the original kernel from the list and the kernel will load, assuming that this kernel was not overwritten when you built the customized kernel. This is possible only if you failed to give your lean kernel a different identifier, such as `2.6.5-1.358router`.

Once you are in the system, you can try to restore an older version of the `/boot` partition from the tar archive, like so:

```
# cd /
# mv boot boot.notworking
# tar -zxvf /root/boot-2.6.5-1.358.20040315.tar.gz
```

Then, try to reboot the system and see what happens.

If this option does not work, insert the floppy boot disk that you created earlier into the machine and start up your system. This is a very reliable option because a slimmed-down kernel is itself stored on the floppy disk. If you can get into the system, you should again attempt to restore the `/boot` partition:

```
# mkdir /mnt/sysimage
# mount /dev/hda1 /mnt/sysimage
# cd /mnt/sysimage
# mv boot boot.notworking
# tar -zxvf root/boot-2.6.5-1.358.20040315.tar.gz
```

Finally, if both of these options fail to start up your system, you should boot your system in rescue mode using either the Fedora Core DVD or the Rescue CD-ROM. Once you see a splash screen, enter the following command at the prompt:

```
linux rescue
```

Eventually, you will see the following message:

```
The rescue environment will now attempt to find your Linux installation
and mount it under the directory /mnt/sysimage. You can then make any
changes required to your system.  If you want to proceed with this step choose
'Continue'. You can also choose to mount your filesystem
read-only instead of read-write by choosing 'Read-Only'.
If for some reason this process fails you can choose 'Skip'
and this step will be skipped and you will go directly to a
command shell.
```

Choose Continue, at which point the Fedora Core installer mounts your filesystems in the `/mnt/sysimage` directory in read-write mode; you will be able to add and delete files. If this process is successful, you will be able to access your `/boot` partition via `/mnt/sysimage/boot`. You can do even better and make the `/mnt/sysimage` directory your root partition by using the `chroot` command:

```
# chroot /mnt/sysimage
```

Now, try to restore the original `/boot` partition and see if you can boot into your system.

Summary

The Linux kernel is the core component that communicates with the hardware and provides an interface between applications and hardware. Because you have the entire source code available to you, you can build the kernel to suit almost any need. In this chapter, you built a lean, mean, and optimized kernel suitable for use in routers and firewalls.

13

Managing Your System with Perl

You may have already heard of the *Perl* programming language, perhaps in the context of back-end Web applications. If you've ever come across the ubiquitous term *CGI-Perl*, or references to the `.pl` file suffix in URLs as you surfed the Web, you've rubbed shoulders with Perl before. Over the years, Perl's popularity has grown with the proliferation of Web applications. But what exactly is Perl for?

Perl is a high-level (yet relatively easy-to-use) programming language that is particularly suited to development of various types of applications, including networking tools, database management applications, system administration utilities, and (of course) Web applications.

As you continue your journey with Linux, you will probably find that you want to take more and more control over the way that your system works. As this happens, you'll also find the features offered by Bash shell scripts increasingly limiting. The Perl programming language will help you get the flexibility you'll crave—the vast majority of professional Linux systems administrators use Perl as their preferred method for maintaining their systems. They find its power and flexibility invaluable.

The best way to do a job is often to look at how the professionals do it, and follow in their footsteps. But, it's often not easy when you start out. Perl was built for power and flexibility, but not necessarily for immediate comprehensibility or beginner's ease of use (that's what the shell's for).

Nevertheless, this book would not be complete without a glimpse at the world of Perl, so this chapter gives you a few examples of how it can be used to make your life easier. This chapter is rather unlike the others in this book; it's not going to try and teach you key skills that you can take away and use with little or no additional guidance because to give you that much understanding of Perl would require a 300-page chapter. Instead, the intention is to give you a chance to experiment with these examples, and give you a feel for the Perl technology as a whole.

If and when you begin to feel yourself constrained by the limitations of the shell, the information and examples here should enable you to make an informed decision as to whether Perl is the right choice for you.

This chapter looks at the following:

- Perl installation
- The Comprehensive Perl Archive Network (CPAN)
- A number of demonstration Perl script applications (four large examples and half a dozen smaller ones)

Finally, it touches on a larger, more comprehensive, Perl application—a Web-based systems administration assistant—which you can use to assist you in your day-to-day administrative tasks. (In fact, this application is further discussed in Chapter 15, and you can download its code from `www.wrox.com`.)

If you have difficulty getting started, you can supplement the information in this chapter with a good online Perl tutorial. For example, we recommend the Tutorials section of the `www.perl.com` Web site. At the time of writing, this was at `www.perl.com/cs/user/query/q/6?id_topic=74`, but if this should change, you can access it from the Main Menu, by selecting Resources and scrolling down to the Tutorials option.

What Is Perl?

A large variety of programming languages exists for Linux, ranging from simple shell scripting variants such as csh and bash, to high-level interpreted languages, such as Perl, Tcl, and Python, to the most hardcore of them all, C and C++. Naturally, each has its own advantages and disadvantages, which you can see in more detail at The Great Computer Language Shootout, at `www.bagley.org/~doug/shootout/`.

Perl bridges the gap nicely between the two extremes, the simple and the hardcore, by supporting some of the best of both breeds' features. For example, Perl allows you to write applications that interact with the shell, execute commands, and process the output with the same ease of use and rapid development that is seen with shell scripting. You can use a simple editor to write your program and then run it without worrying about linking and compiling it, which is the case with the advanced compiled languages such as C and C++. On the other hand, Perl also supports advanced programming constructs, complex data structures, and a higher level of security, as found in high-level compiled languages, but commonly lacking in scripting languages.

Let's look at a hypothetical example that illustrates these points better. Say you decide to develop an application that needs to monitor hard disk partitions and alert an administrator if the amount of available space drops below 10 percent. The application must also determine which users are occupying the most space and send them an e-mail urging them to clean up by listing their 15 largest files. What would happen if you were to try to develop this using a shell scripting language, such as bash? First, you would start out using the `df` command, which returns a report of the disk space usage. The report could be something like the following, depending on how your machine is partitioned:

```
Filesystem           1K-blocks      Used Available Use% Mounted on
/dev/hda1              3020140   1582492   1284232  56% /
/dev/hda5              7684844   1280812   6013656  18% /data
/dev/hda2              3020172   2637411    229341  92% /home
none                     94868         0     94868   0% /dev/shm
```

You would then need to extract the percentage values from this report, which is more difficult than it seems; most shell scripting languages don't support this type of text manipulation directly. As a result, you would need to use a language such as *sed* or *awk* to get at the data that you are looking for. Both sed and awk are languages designed specifically for pattern matching and transformation and are used extensively in shell scripting. Once you determine that the `/dev/hda2` partition (the `/home` filesystem) exceeds the 90 percentage usage threshold, you would need to calculate each user's individual usage and determine their largest files. How would you do that?

You would need to get a list of all the users' home directories in the filesystem, most likely using the `ls` command, and then iterate through each one using a loop of some sort. As you go through each directory, you would issue the `du` command to get a list of all the files and their sizes, like so:

```
3656    /home/postgres/base/1
3656    /home/postgres/base/16975
4       /home/postgres/base/16976/pgsql_tmp
1128708 /home/postgres/base/16976
1136024 /home/postgres/base
140     /home/postgres/global
82024   /home/postgres/pg_xlog
12      /home/postgres/pg_clog
1218232 /home/postgres
```

The most difficult part of this process is to keep track of each user's usage and his or her files, both the name and the size. Why is this difficult? Shell scripting languages have very primitive support for complex logic operations and data structures. You would need to come up with an alternative mechanism to temporarily store this individual data, and then process and sort it once you finish going through all the users' directories. The final part of the application would involve sending an e-mail, both to the offending users and the administrator, using the `mail` or `sendmail` commands.

You may have noticed that we glossed over the section regarding sed and awk here. There's a reason for this—shell scripting languages allow you to develop scripts that invoke shell commands easily and without much effort. In addition, the development cycle is rather simple; you use an editor to modify and debug the script and then simply execute it from the command line. On the other hand, shell scripts fall apart when you need to implement any type of complex logical operations or store relational or structured data because shell scripting languages were not designed for this purpose.

On the flip side, how would you fare if you developed this application using Perl? You would retain some of the advantages of shell scripting, but also have access to more advanced language features. Because Perl allows you to interact with the shell, you can use the `df` command to get the disk usage report, and then use pattern-matching expressions to easily parse and extract the percentage values. If you find a partition that exceeds the threshold value, you can use the internal `readdir` function, along with a `for` loop, to iterate through all of the main directories on that filesystem. Perl integrates well with the underlying operating system to abstract certain functions on all supported platforms. This allows you to use a function such as `readdir` to get a list of all the files in a particular directory, whether you are using Linux or Mac OS X.

For each directory, you can use the `df` command, as you did before, to get a list of all the individual files and their sizes and then store them in a complex data structure. Once you finish iterating through all the directories, you can use Perl's `sort` function to sort and order the information in the data structure to determine the offending users and their largest files. At that point, you can send an e-mail to the administrator and the necessary users, either using the external `mail` or `sendmail` commands, or a Perl extension such as `Mail::Send`. Typically, you would want to use an extension, instead of an external shell command, because it is more efficient and allows you to better implement the desired functionality. You'll actually see how to write this application in Perl later in the chapter, after looking through some simpler examples first.

Detailing the advantages or disadvantages of developing a similar application in a compiled language, such as C or C++, is beyond the scope of this chapter. However, if you are interested in a high-level overview, a language such as C provides more control (memory management) and typically better performance, but at the expense of development time and difficulty.

The next sections take a more in-depth look at the advantages and disadvantages of Perl. This will allow you to evaluate for yourself what Perl has to offer.

Advantages

As previously discussed, Perl provides a good mixture of features and performance that lies somewhere between a scripting language and a compiled language. To understand this better, here are some specific advantages of Perl:

- Perl provides great flexibility in developing applications. Perl does not force you to use any specific style or paradigm, but instead allows you to express your ideas and thoughts in the way that you choose. In fact, one of Perl's mottos is, "There is more than one way to do it."
- Perl is extensible. You can write modules or libraries in Perl to extend Perl's functionality and make them available for reuse in other projects. The CPAN holds hundreds and thousands of freely available extensions to interface and communicate with various utilities, applications, Internet services, and database engines.
- Perl is highly portable and runs on a large number of hardware and software platforms, including most known UNIX/Linux platforms, Windows, Mac OS, OS/2, VMS, and even Palm. Programs that don't use platform-specific functionality, such as pipes in UNIX, or OLE/COM in Windows, will work unchanged across platforms.
- Perl supports powerful regular expressions for pattern matching. You can use these expressions to search for patterns or specific strings in a body of text.
- Perl has a strong developer community, which is very active in implementing extensions, fixing bugs, and providing technical support.
- Perl is free for both commercial and non-commercial use.

Disadvantages

Like any other programming language, Perl does have its share of disadvantages:

- The flexibility that Perl provides can sometimes mesmerize developers into producing hard-to-maintain code. Because there are so many different ways to solve the same problem, it's easy to come up with a solution that no one else can follow, especially if your documentation isn't up to snuff.

- Perl has weak exception handling abilities that make it difficult for you to handle any errors that crop up during the execution of your script—for example, if a file isn't where it's supposed to be, or if write-access to one of your disks isn't permitted.

However, for the most part, Perl is perfectly capable of doing the tasks required of it in a sensible and organized way.

Installation

Perl, along with a number of useful modules, is installed by default on your Linux system. We will use the terms "extension" and "module" interchangeably because they have much the same meaning in Perl. If you want to check what version of Perl is installed, use the `perl` command with the `-v` option:

```
$ perl -v

This is perl, v5.8.3 built for i386-linux-thread-multi

Copyright 1987-2003, Larry Wall

Perl may be copied only under the terms of either the Artistic License or the
GNU General Public License, which may be found in the Perl 5 source kit.

Complete documentation for Perl, including FAQ lists, should be found on
this system using `man perl' or `perldoc perl'.  If you have access to the
Internet, point your browser at http://www.perl.com/, the Perl Home Page.
```

At the time of this writing, 5.8.3 is the latest version of Perl available. If, for some reason, you do not have Perl installed on your system, you can use the `rpm` application to install it directly from the Fedora distribution. Place the first CD-ROM into the drive, wait a few moments for it to load, and type the following:

```
# rpm -hvi /mnt/cdrom/Fedora/RPMS/perl-5.8.3-5.i386.rpm
```

If you want to be on the cutting edge, you can even download the latest copy of Perl and build it, in much the same way that we compiled the `gFTP` application in Chapter 11; you need to install the Development Tools packages as specified in the chapter. Simply type the following into a terminal (each line represents a different command, and you'll need root privileges for it to work):

```
# cd /usr/local/src
# wget http://www.perl.com/CPAN/src/latest.tar.gz
# tar -zxvf latest.tar.gz
# cd perl-5.8.3
# ./Configure
# make
# make test
# make install
```

Make sure to read the `INSTALL` file, which provides more instructions on how to compile and build Perl. While you're at it, you should also read the obligatory `README` file for any last-minute changes, bug fixes, and so on.

Installing Extensions

Once you have installed Perl, you can use the CPAN extension to install any other extensions or modules that you may need for development. The CPAN extension automates the process of retrieving the necessary source code from The Comprehensive Perl Archive Network, uncompressing, configuring, and building it into an extension. Fortunately, the CPAN extension is installed by default with Perl, so you don't have to spend time tracking down and building this valuable extension.

Suppose, for example, you need an extension to send e-mail from a Perl program. Your first step should be to go to CPAN and check to see if such an extension exists. You can do this by pointing your browser to `http://search.cpan.org` and entering *Send Mail* into the search field. You will see a number of e-mail related modules that match the criteria. Traverse down the list and you should see the `Mail::Send` extension that was briefly discussed earlier; the `Mail::Send` extension is actually part of the `MailTools` package, as you will see in the installation example that follows. Now, log in as root and use the CPAN extension to install the module:

```
# perl -MCPAN -e shell

/usr/lib/perl5/5.8.3/CPAN/Config.pm initialized.


CPAN is the world-wide archive of perl resources. It consists of about
100 sites that all replicate the same contents all around the globe.
Many countries have at least one CPAN site already. The resources
found on CPAN are easily accessible with the CPAN.pm module. If you
want to use CPAN.pm, you have to configure it properly.

...
```

The `-M` switch asks Perl to load the CPAN extension, which implements, among other things, a function called `shell`. This function is responsible for providing a user interface, or a shell, where you can search for and install modules. You can execute this function by using the `-e` switch. As you will see later, you can also use this switch to execute arbitrary pieces of Perl code from the command line.

The first time you use the CPAN shell, it will ask you a number of questions, including where to store the sources and what CPAN mirror to use. You should be able to simply choose the default answers and continue. Once inside the shell, use the `install` command with the name of the extension to start the process of installation:

```
cpan> install Mail::Send
CPAN: Storable loaded ok
CPAN: LWP::UserAgent loaded ok
Fetching with LWP:
  ftp://mirrors.kernel.org/pub/CPAN/authors/01mailrc.txt.gz
Going to read /root/.cpan/sources/authors/01mailrc.txt.gz
Fetching with LWP:
  ftp://mirrors.kernel.org/pub/CPAN/modules/02packages.details.txt.gz
...
Running make for M/MA/MARKOV/MailTools-1.61.tar.gz
Fetching with LWP:
  ftp://mirrors.kernel.org/pub/CPAN/authors/id/M/MA/MARKOV/MailTools-1.61.tar.gz
```

```
CPAN: Digest::MD5 loaded ok
Fetching with LWP:
  ftp://mirrors.kernel.org/pub/CPAN/authors/id/M/MA/MARKOV/CHECKSUMS
Checksum for /root/.cpan/sources/authors/id/M/MA/MARKOV/MailTools-1.61.tar.gz ok
Scanning cache /root/.cpan/build for sizes
MailTools-1.61/
MailTools-1.61/t/
...
MailTools-1.61/ChangeLog
MailTools-1.61/MANIFEST

  CPAN.pm: Going to build M/MA/MARKOV/MailTools-1.61.tar.gz

Checking for Net::SMTP...ok
Checking for Net::Domain...ok
Checking for IO::Handle...ok
Checking if your kit is complete...
Looks good
Writing Makefile for Mail
cp Mail/Mailer/rfc822.pm blib/lib/Mail/Mailer/rfc822.pm
cp Mail/Cap.pm blib/lib/Mail/Cap.pm
cp Mail/Header.pm blib/lib/Mail/Header.pm
...
  /usr/bin/make  -- OK
Running make test
...
All tests successful.
Files=7, Tests=93,  3 wallclock secs ( 1.56 cusr +  1.11 csys =  2.67 CPU)
  /usr/bin/make test -- OK
Running make install
Installing /usr/lib/perl5/site_perl/5.8.3/Mail/Mailer.pm
Installing /usr/lib/perl5/site_perl/5.8.3/Mail/Send.pm
...
Installing /usr/share/man/man3/Mail::Field::AddrList.3pm
Installing /usr/share/man/man3/Mail::Field.3pm
Writing /usr/lib/perl5/site_perl/5.8.3/i386-linux-thread-multi/auto/Mail/.packlist
Appending installation info to /usr/lib/perl5/5.8.3/i386-linux-thread-
multi/perllocal.pod
  /usr/bin/make install  -- OK

cpan> exit
Lockfile removed.
```

The entire installation process is simple and straightforward. And you can get more information on all of the commands that the CPAN shell supports by issuing the `help` command. If, however, you don't want to use the shell, you can download the source directly from CPAN and build it yourself. This will provide you with a bit more control, but you need to make sure to install any prerequisite modules that are needed by the extension that you are building before hand. If you do use the shell, it is intelligent enough to install these modules for you automatically, provided that the module authors followed certain conventions for specifying prerequisites.

You have now looked at what Perl is, how it compares to other programming languages, what its advantages and disadvantages are, and how to install it. The next step is to actually learn the language.

Learning Perl

As previously mentioned, learning an entire language within a span of 10 to 15 pages is rather difficult, but you can certainly learn enough of the language to develop useful applications. You will learn by studying three example applications: one that lists the system users, another to send e-mail from the command line, and the last one to archive system load average data. These examples illustrate how to accomplish the following:

- Create a Perl program
- Store and access different types of data
- Process input and output
- Implement logic operations
- Find patterns or strings
- Interact with external applications

This section finishes by actually designing the disk usage application that we looked at earlier. By implementing this reasonably advanced application, you can see for yourself how well you understand some of the concepts behind Perl development. Let's start!

How to Start

You have seen examples of shell scripts throughout the book, which look something like the following:

```
#!/bin/sh

...

exit;
```

Perl programs have a similar structure:

```
#!/usr/bin/perl

##++
##   hello.pl: This is so cool, my first Perl program, can you believe it?
##--

$city    = 'Manchester';    ## Scalar variable: store Manchester in $city
$country = 'England';       ## Scalar variable: store England in $country

print "Hello, welcome to my home in $city, $country!\n";  ## Print message

exit (0);                   ## Hooray, success!
```

After you've saved this code in a file (`hello.pl`, for example), you can execute the program in one of two ways. You can invoke the Perl interpreter manually and pass the filename to it, as follows:

```
$ /usr/bin/perl hello.pl
```

Or, you can ask the shell to execute it for you:

```
$ chmod +x hello.pl
$ ./hello.pl
```

In the first case, you manually call upon the interpreter to execute the code. In the second case, however, the shell will execute the interpreter, feeding to it the program. This will work only if the program meets two specific conditions. The initial line of the program must start with `#!` and specify the path to the interpreter, in this case `/usr/bin/perl`. And the user executing the program must have the execute permission enabled.

Why don't you try running this program? What do you get as the output? As you look at this rather trivial program, you should be aware of a few details. First, each statement, defined as a single logical command, ends with a semicolon. This tells Perl that the statement is complete. Second, everything starting from the # character to the end of the line represents a comment. You should make it a point to add comments that describe the thoughts and logic behind your code, especially if you are implementing something that might be difficult for other people, or even yourself, to understand at a later time. And, finally, Perl ignores white space and empty lines in and around statements, so you should use a liberal amount of white space to align variable declarations and indent code. This will make it easier for other developers to read and understand your code.

Now, let's look at our first main application. Each application is designed to illustrate a set of Perl's key features. Before tackling the application, these features are explained, including their significance and how you can use them later to build your own programs.

Application 1: Who Can Get In?

The first task is to build a simple application to open the `/etc/password` configuration file and display each user's login name and associated comment. If you don't remember the format of this file (which was discussed in Chapter 7), here is how it looks:

```
sravanthi:x:500:500:Sravanthi:/home/sravanthi:/bin/bash
dcheng:x:501:501:David Cheng:/home/dcheng:/bin/bash
dzhiwei:x:502:502:David Zhiwei:/home/dzhiwei:/bin/bash
sliao:x:503:503:Steve Liao:/home/sliao:/bin/bash
```

Each record in the file consists of seven fields, starting with the login, and followed by the password, user id, group id, comment (typically the full name), home directory, and the default shell. We are interested in extracting the first and fifth fields.

By understanding the code behind this application, you will learn how to open a text file, read its contents, access certain pieces of information, and display the formatted results. These tasks are critical for everyday development, because most administrative applications will rely on opening, reading from, and writing to one file or the other.

```
#!/usr/bin/perl

##++
##   list_users.pl: display list of users and their comments
##--
```

```
use strict;                                    ## "strict" mode

my (@data);                                    ## Pre-declare array

open (FILE, '/etc/passwd')                     ## Open the file
    || die "Cannot open file: $!\n";

while (<FILE>) {                               ## Read each record
    @data = split (/:/, $_, 7);                ## Separate the elements
    print "$data[0], $data[4]\n";              ## Print login, comments
}

close (FILE);                                  ## Close file
exit  (0);                                     ## Exit application
```

Perl provides you with flexibility to develop applications in the manner that you choose; it imposes very few restrictions. Take, for example, the declaration of variables. By default, you don't have to pre-declare variables before using them in the program. Once you refer to a new variable, it is automatically instantiated and has an undefined value until you provide it with a set value. Unfortunately, this is not good programming practice and should be avoided because it makes finding errors in your code very difficult if something goes wrong.

Lucky for users, Perl comes with the `strict` pragma, which, when enabled, requires you to pre-declare variables before using them and forces you to avoid symbolic references and bareword identifiers Later examples look at the latter two requirements, but what exactly is a *pragma*? A pragma is either an internal module, an outside extension, or a combination of the two that specifies the rules that Perl should follow when processing code.

Using strict

This brings us to the first line of our application. The `use` function imports functionality from an external module into your current application. You call on this function with the `strict` argument to enable the `strict` pragma. That is all that is needed to force you to pre-declare variables from here on. As a side note, if you look in the Perl extensions directory, typically `/usr/lib/perl5/5.8.3`, you will see the file `strict.pm`; this is the file that will be loaded.

Next, use the `my` function to declare, or localize, the `@data` array. An *array* is simply a data type, represented by the leading at-sign character, that you can use to store a set of scalar (single) values in one variable. You will use this array to store all of the individual elements for each record in the file, including login and comment.

Opening the File

We proceed to open the configuration file, `/etc/password`, using the `open` function. This function takes two arguments, the first being the file handle that you want to use and the second the path to the file. Think of the handle as a communications channel through which you can read data from the file. If the `open` function executes successfully, which means that the file exists and you have the necessary permissions, it returns a positive (true) status.

In Perl, a status of true is represented by a defined non-zero value, and a status of false is identified with an undefined or zero value or a null string.

If you cannot open the file, call the `die` function with a specific error message to exit from the program. Notice the `$!` expression within the double-quoted message string. *Expressions that start with the dollar sign represent scalar variables*. You can use a scalar variable to store a single value, whether it is a character, number, a text string, or even a paragraph of content. However, the `$!` is a special Perl scalar variable that holds the latest error message, returned by either a system function call or a user-defined procedure. Typical messages for failure to open a file include "Permission denied" and "No such file or directory."

Look again at the entire line that is trying to open the file, and think of it as two separate statements separated by the logical `OR` operator, `||`. The second statement will be executed only if the first statement is false, if the file cannot be opened. We are using a convenient shortcut, but you can just as easily rewrite that code as follows:

```
if (!open (FILE, '/etc/passwd')) {
    die "Cannot open file: $!\n";
}
```

The exclamation point in front of the open function call will negate the status returned by the function. In other words, it will convert a true value into a false, and vice versa. So, only if the entire expression within the main parentheses is true will you end up calling the `die` function to terminate your program. And that will happen if the open function returns a false status.

You can also write the same statement like this:

```
if (open (FILE, '/etc/passwd')) {     ## Success
    ## Read file
    ## Parse records
    ## Print output
} else {                              ## Failure!
    die "Cannot open file: $!\n";
}
```

This should be easy enough to understand by now; if the `open` function returns true, you process the file or else you exit. Now, you are ready to read data from the file. But, how do you know how many records to read? Simple, use a `while` loop to iterate through the file, reading one record at a time, until there are no more records to be read. And for each record retrieved from the file, Perl executes the block of code inside the loop.

Reading Records

The expression located inside of the parentheses after the `while` command controls when the loop will terminate; the loop will continue until this expression evaluates to a false value. The strange-looking expression is the one responsible for reading a line from the `FILE` filehandle and storing it in the default Perl variable, `$_`. When there are no more lines to be read, Perl returns an undefined value, or `undef`, for short. Once this happens, the expression evaluates to a false value and the `while` loop stops.

Whenever you see such an expression—an identifier of some sort enclosed between a less-than and a greater-than sign—you should know that Perl is reading data from the filehandle represented by that identifier. You can store each record read from the file in a variable other than `$_` by doing the following:

```
while ($line = <FILE>) {
    ...
}
```

Inside the loop, you see two statements. These are responsible for pulling out the different elements from each record and displaying the login and comment.

Extracting the Elements

The `split` function separates a piece of text into multiple elements, based on a specified delimiter, and returns an array. It takes three arguments: the delimiter, the input string, and the maximum number of elements. Notice that the delimiter is enclosed within a set of backslash characters; this is an example of a regular expression, commonly known as *regex*. You can use regular expressions to specify a pattern to match, as opposed to a simple one-character delimiter. Regular expressions are covered in more detail in "Application 3: What Is My System Load?"

The last two arguments to the `split` function are optional. If the input string is not specified, Perl uses its default variable, `$_`. This is something you should be aware of. A large number of Perl functions operate on this default variable, so it is very convenient. You have seen two examples of it already: reading records from a filehandle and now the `split` function. Last, but not least, if you don't specify a maximum number of elements, you won't see a difference a majority of the time. However, there will be occasions when the last element in the text string is null, in which case, `split` strips and removes this element. To be on the safe side, you should specify the number of elements that you expect to get back, so there are no surprises.

Once the `split` function returns the elements, store them in the `@data` array. Each item in an array is associated with a specific position or index, starting at index zero. You can access a specific element in an array by specifying its associated index within brackets. Use the `print` command to display the first and sixth elements to the terminal, followed by a newline.

Repeat this process for all the records in the file. Once the `while` loop terminates, close the file using its filehandle and exit from the application. This completes your first major Perl application.

The Output

Go ahead and run the program. What do you see? You will most likely see output like the following:

```
$ perl list_users.pl
root, root
bin, bin
...
sravanthi, Sravanthi
dcheng, David Cheng
dzhiwei, David Zhiwei
sliao, Steve Liao
```

The application itself seems to work properly, but there are a few flaws that should be fixed. First, there is no need to see a list of the default system users, users created by the Linux installation. Second, it would make for a good display if the two pieces of information were neatly aligned into columns.

Who Can Get In? Take 2

We will change the application somewhat to implement the new features discussed in the preceding paragraph, namely ignoring system users and fixing the display format. Ignoring system users from the output is not difficult, but is not fully precise. How do you tell the difference between a system user and a regular user? There is no one distinct flag or marker that identifies a system user. However, system users are typically, but not always, allocated a user identification number less than 500, so we will use that as the main criteria.

The display format must also be fixed. Fortunately, there is the `pack` function, which you can use to pad each data element with a certain number of spaces, thereby creating columns that are aligned. Let's look at the new version of the application:

```
#!/usr/bin/perl

##++
##   list_users_plus.pl: display list of users and their comments
##   in neat columns
##--

use strict;                                  ## Enable "strict" pragma

my (@data);                                  ## Pre-declare variables

open (FILE, '/etc/passwd')                   ## Open the file
    || die "Cannot open file: $!\n";

while (<FILE>) {                             ## Read each record
    @data = split (/:/, $_, 7);              ## Separate the elements
    if ($data[2] < 500) {                    ## Ignore UID less than 500
        next;
    }

    print pack ("A16A*", $data[0], $data[4]), "\n";  ## Print
                                                     ## login, comments
}

close (FILE);                                ## Close file
exit  (0);                                   ## Exit application
```

The code has changed very little. If you find a user identification number less than one hundred, you use the `next` command to start the next iteration of the `while` loop. As a result, the `print` command never gets executed and the record doesn't display.

You can also combine the `next` command and the conditional check into one statement, like so:

```
next if ($data[2] < 500);
```

You will most likely see this abbreviated syntax in a number of Perl programs. It is convenient and easy to use. However, you cannot use this syntax if you need to execute a block of code based on a specific condition.

Formatting the Output

Next, use the `pack` command to create a string based on a specific template configuration and a set of values; these comprise the first and subsequent arguments, respectively. The `A16A*` template instructs `pack` to create a 16-character ASCII padded string using the first value from the list, followed by a string containing all other remaining values. When you execute this program, you will see the following much improved output:

```
sravanthi         Sravanthi
dcheng            David Cheng
dzhiwei           David Zhiwei
sliao             Steve Liao
```

You have already learned much about Perl, including the following:

- Using its `strict` pragma
- Declaring and using variables
- Implementing `while` loops
- Reading data from text files
- Formatting output for display

The next section looks at more Perl syntax and constructs, including how to use the `Mail::Send` module to send e-mail.

Application 2: Send a Quick E-Mail

How many times have you wanted to send a quick e-mail, without having to use a full-fledged e-mail client? Linux provides you with a few applications that allow you to read and send e-mail from the command line, such as `mail`. But we are not interested in those at the moment. Instead, let's develop a useful Perl application that serves much the same purpose, namely the ability to send e-mail. In the process, you will learn how to check code for errors, accept input from the user, implement regular expressions, and use external modules and view their built-in documentation. Here is the application:

```
#!/usr/bin/perl

##++
##   send_email.pl: send e-mail messages from command-line
##--

use Mail::Send;                                  ## Import/use Mail::Send
use strict;                                      ## Enable "strict" pragma

##++
##   Let's purposely inject two errors in this program so we can
##   understand the debugging process:
##      - remove semicolon at end of line
##      - spell $email as $emale
##--

my ($emale, $answer, $subject, $message)

print "*** E-Mail Sender Application ***\n\n";  ## Display header

##++
```

```
##   Prompt for recipient's e-mail address, checking for validity.
##--

while (1) {
    print "Enter recipient's e-mail address: ";
    $email = <STDIN>;                          ## Read from standard input
    chomp $email;                              ## Remove trailing newline

    next if (!$email);                         ## Repeat loop if no $email

    print "You entered $email as the recipient's address, accept [y/n]: ";
    chomp ($answer = <STDIN>);                 ## Different style
    last if ($answer eq 'y');                  ## Exit loop if $answer=y
}

##++
##   Prompt for subject and message body.
##--

print 'Subject: ';
chomp ($subject = <STDIN>);

print "Enter message, type Control-D (CTRL-D) to end:\n";

while (<STDIN>) {                              ## Read from standard input
    $message .= $_;                            ## Concatenate to $message
}

##++
##   Set defaults if empty.
##--

$subject ||= 'No Subject';
$message ||= 'No Body';

##++
##   Print summary and ask for confirmation.
##--

print "*** E-Mail Summary ***\n\n";
print "To: $email\n";
print "Subject: $subject\n";
print "Message:\n\n$message\n";

print 'Do you want to send the message [y/n]: ';
chomp ($answer = <STDIN>);

if ($answer eq 'n') {
    print "Aborting.\n";
    exit (0);
}

##++
##   Send message
```

```
##--

my ($mail, $fh);

$mail = new Mail::Send;                    ## Create new object

$mail->to ($email);                        ## Call its function/method
$mail->subject ($subject);

$fh = $mail->open();                       ## Returns filehandle
print $fh $message;                        ## Print body to filehandle
$fh->close();                              ## Close filehandle

print "Message sent.\n";

exit (0);
```

You can save this application in `send_email.pl` and proceed to run it, like so:

```
$ perl send_email.pl
syntax error at send_email.pl line 15, near ")

print"
Global symbol "$email" requires explicit package name at send_email.pl line 23.
Global symbol "$email" requires explicit package name at send_email.pl line 24.
Global symbol "$email" requires explicit package name at send_email.pl line 26.
Global symbol "$email" requires explicit package name at send_email.pl line 28.
Global symbol "$email" requires explicit package name at send_email.pl line 58.
Global symbol "$email" requires explicit package name at send_email.pl line 78.
Execution of send_email.pl aborted due to compilation errors.
```

Perl is telling you there are errors in the code. The first error is at or around line 15. The second set of errors claim that we are using the `$email` variable without pre-declaring it first. Take a look at the code. You should see that we purposely left out the semicolon at the end of line 12 and declared a variable called `$emale` instead of `$email`. The line numbers that Perl reports in the errors may not always be exact, due to the manner in which it parses the code, so you should check the entire area around the reported error for any possible bugs.

Fixing Errors and Checking Syntax

If you are getting other errors, you may have forgotten to install the `Mail::Send` module properly, as shown in the section "Installing Extensions" earlier in the chapter. It is also possible that you may have made a mistake in typing the code. Fix the broken code in the application, adding the necessary semicolon and correcting the misspelled variable:

```
my ($email, $answer, $subject, $message);
```

Let's run it again, but before doing so, check its syntax and structure. You can use Perl's `-w` and `-c` options, which report warnings and check syntax, respectively, to check the status of your code, like so:

```
$ perl -wc send_email.pl
send_email syntax OK
```

If there are no problems with the code, Perl returns the output previously shown. You should make it a point to check the syntax of your applications in this manner before running them, so that you can catch possible errors quickly.

Loading External Modules

You saw the `use` command in the first application, `list_users.pl`, when we discussed the `strict` pragma. Here, we import the `Mail::Send` extension, so we can use its functionality to send e-mail. You can find this module at `/usr/lib/perl5/site_perl/5.8.3/Mail/Send.pm`; the `.pm` extension stands for Perl Module. Most CPAN extensions include built-in documentation, which you can view by using the `perldoc` application.

```
$ perldoc Mail::Send
```

This documentation provides you more information on what the extension does and how to use it. You can also use `perldoc` to get information on virtually any Perl command. In this application, the `chomp` command is used to remove the end-of-line character, also referred to as the *record separator*. To see more information on `chomp`, including examples, you can type the following:

```
$ perldoc -f chomp
```

Let's go back to the code. We pre-declare the variables that we intend to use in the program and print out a header for the user. You don't have to declare all of the variables in one place; you can declare them as you go.

Getting Recipient's E-Mail Address

The real core of the program starts now. We wrap a block of code inside a `while` loop that will run until we explicitly break out. Remember, the expression that follows the `while` command determines how many times the loop executes; as long as the expression is true, the loop continues to run. In this case, a static expression with a value of 1 always evaluates to true, so the loop never stops.

Our job inside the loop is to ask the user for the recipient's e-mail address. If the user doesn't enter an address or accidentally makes a mistake in typing, this provides him or her the ability to enter it again. Repeat this process until the user is satisfied and affirmatively confirms the address, at which point you jump out of the loop using the `last` command.

Notice how input is accepted from the user. Doesn't the syntax look similar to that used in `list_users.pl` to read data from a file? In fact, you can use the `<filehandle>` expression to read a line of data from any defined filehandle. The standard input (`STDIN`) filehandle is established at program startup time and allows you to read data from the user, terminal, or input stream. In addition to the `STDIN` filehandle, you have access to `STDOUT` (standard output), `STDERR` (standard error), and `DATA`. You can use `STDOUT` to write output, `STDERR` to write diagnostic messages, and `DATA` to read data stored within a Perl application. As a side note, whenever you use the `print` command to display a message, Perl writes it to the standard output stream.

Once the user enters the recipient's e-mail address and presses the Enter key on his or her keyboard, the trailing newline is actually captured as part of the input. You use the `chomp` function to cleanly remove this end-of-line character from the input, as stored in the `$email` variable. If you don't remove it, you will have a difficult time determining if the user entered an address because `$email` will still evaluate to true, as it would have a length of at least 1 (from the newline character).

Checking the E-Mail Address

Next, check to see if `$email` is false, which would occur if the user did not enter an address, and if so, you simply execute the loop again. This provides the user another chance to enter the address. However, if an address was entered, you ask the user for confirmation and exit from the loop. An advanced application might also check the validity of the e-mail address, but we are not doing it here. If you are interested in adding such functionality, you should install the `Email::Valid` module, as shown in the section "Installing Extensions," and then change this application in the following manner:

```
#!/usr/bin/perl

use Mail::Send;                              ## Import/use Mail::Send
use Email::Valid;                            ## Import/use Email::Valid
use strict;                                  ## Enable "strict" pragma

...

while (1) {
   ...

   next if (!$email);                        ## Repeat loop if no $email

   if (!Email::Valid->address ($email)) {   ## E-Mail address is not valid
       print "The e-mail address you entered is not in a valid format.\n";
   }

   ...
}

...

exit (0);
```

Use the `address` function, defined in the `Email::Valid` module, to check whether the specified e-mail address conforms to the RFC 822 specification, Standard for the Format of ARPA Internet Text Messages. The function simply checks the syntax; there is no way to determine whether a specific address is deliverable without actually attempting delivery.

Getting Subject and Message Body

Continuing on with the program, we ask the user to enter the subject and the body of the message. Use a `while` loop to allow the user to enter as much content as desired. Each time through the loop, take the content that is entered (`$_`) and append it to the existing content in `$message`, using the concatenation `.=` operator. If the user presses *Ctrl+D* at any point, the shell ends the input stream, at which point the `while` loop terminates.

Then, we perform a few routine tasks. First, assign default values to the subject and body of the message in case they were not entered. The `||=` operator is very useful and is a shortcut for the following:

```
if (!$subject) {               ## or:
    $subject = 'No Subject'    ## $subject = 'No Subject' if (!$subject);
}
```

Second, print out all of the information entered by the user and ask whether he or she wants to continue with the message. If not, exit from the application. Otherwise, use the `Mail::Send` module to send the e-mail.

Sending the Message

If you look at the built-in documentation for the `Mail::Send` module, you will see several small examples on how to use the module. These examples look very similar to the code that you are about to look at. `Mail::Send` is a module that provides an object-oriented interface to its functionality. If you have done any C++ or Smalltalk application development, you know exactly what this means. If not, think of object-oriented programming (OOP) as a clean way to implement a data structure—the object—that contains not only data, but also associated functions to manipulate that data.

We call the `new` function, typically known as the constructor, in `Mail::Send` to create a new instance of the object. You can use this instance to invoke defined functions (or methods) in the object. First, we call the `to` and `subject` methods to specify the recipient and subject, respectively. Then, we invoke the `open` method to obtain the filehandle associated with the mail transport mechanism. By default, `Mail::Send` uses the `sendmail` application to send the message. If you don't have `sendmail` installed on your Linux system, or need to use an external SMTP server from within a firewall environment, you can specify the server address in the `open` method:

```
$fh = $mail->open ('smtp', Server => 'smtp.someserver.com');
```

Unfortunately, this is not explained in the built-in documentation. If you look at the module's code, you will find that `Mail::Send` actually calls the `Mail::Mailer` module to send the e-mail. And `Mail::Mailer` can use `sendmail`, `qmail`, or an SMTP server as the transport mechanism. Whatever arguments passed to the `open` method here are simply passed on to `Mail::Mailer`.

The last action we have to take is to write the body content to this filehandle using the `print` command and then close the filehandle. This sends the message, at which point we display a status message and exit.

Sample User Session

Let's run through the application to see how it looks. Figure 13-1 shows the application in use.

Developing this application has shown you how to accept and validate user input and how to load and use external modules. There are literally hundreds of Perl extensions available through CPAN, so learning how to use them properly is extremely valuable. Whenever you need to build a new application, you should make it a habit to browse through CPAN to see if there is a module that might help you. If one exists, all you have to do is look at the built-in documentation, determine how to interface with the module, and you are on your way to building an excellent application in no time.

Until now, you have learned quite a bit about Perl and how to use it. However, you have not looked at the two features of the language that are probably the most powerful, namely regular expressions and the ability to interact with the system environment. Application 3 looks at an interesting application that uses both of these features.

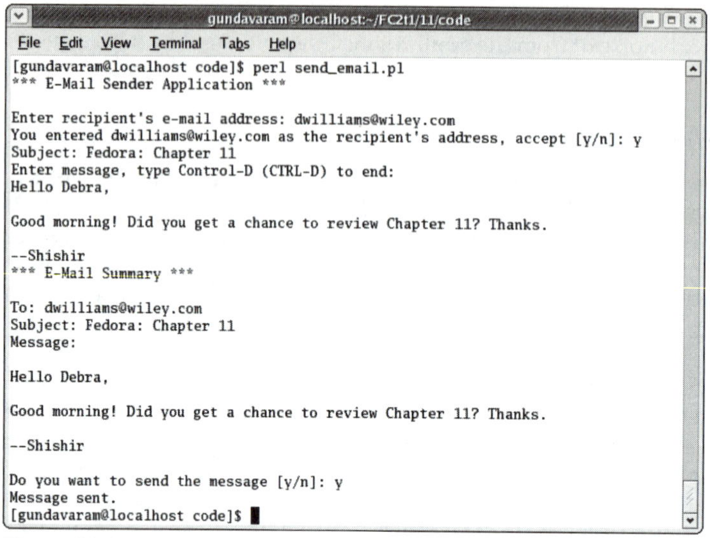

Figure 13-1

Application 3: What Is My System Load?

In a typical single-user environment, where the system administrator is also the only user, you don't have to pay much attention to administering, monitoring, and optimizing the operating system. However, the situation is completely different with a multiuser system; the stakes are higher as more people are dependent on the system running well. You can use a number of diagnostic applications to keep tabs on the system. Take, for example, the `uptime` program, which returns a number of useful pieces of information, including how long the system has been up and running, the number of users currently logged on, and the load averages for the past 1, 5, and 15 minutes:

```
23:15:42 up 54 min,  3 users,  load average: 0.33, 0.29, 0.36
```

If you want to optimize the system, you should typically keep track of system activity and metrics over a certain period of time. This activity can include the number of users logged in, what applications they are running, the average system load, and how much memory is being consumed. This allows you to analyze the data and look for specific patterns. You may find, for example, that a large spike occurs in the system load every Monday morning before the weekly engineering meeting. Then, you can determine how to best handle the issue: don't run other jobs on Monday mornings, add more RAM, or upgrade the processor.

In that vein, we will create an application to archive the system load averages and the number of active users. However, for any data analysis to be effective, you need to have enough data that captures a variety of conditions. The best way to do that is to set up a cron job to automatically run this application every hour Monday through Friday, like so:

```
00 * * * 1-5  /home/gundavaram/uptime_monitor.pl /home/gundavaram/uptime.log
```

Even though the application is only ten lines long, you will still learn enough advanced Perl development techniques to make it worthwhile. More specifically, you will learn how to invoke an external program, retrieve its output, extract certain information from it and write the formatted output to a log file. Because there are so many useful utilities and programs that exist for Linux, the ability to interact with these tools from within Perl will empower you to develop some very interesting applications.

Here is the code.

```
#!/usr/bin/perl

##++
##   uptime_monitor.pl: archive system load averages to file
##--

use strict;                                    ## Enable "strict" pragma

my ($file, $uptime, $users, $load1, $load2, $load3);
$file   = $ARGV[0] || '/var/log/uptime.log';   ## Path to log file
$uptime = `/usr/bin/uptime`;                   ## Store output from uptime

##++
##   Parse the output of the uptime command and store the numbers of
##   users and the three system load averages into: $users, $load1,
##   $load2 and $load3.
##--

$uptime =~ /(\d+) +user.+?(\d.+?), +(.+?), +(.+)/;
$users  = $1;
$load1  = $2;
$load2  = $3;
$load3  = $4;

##++
##   We can also write the above like this:
##
##     $uptime =~ /(\d+) +user.+?(\d.+?), +(.+?), +(.+)/;
##     ($users, $load1, $load2, $load3) = ($1, $2, $3, $4);
##
##   or even:
##
##     ($users, $load1, $load2, $load3)
##         = $uptime =~ /(\d+) +user.+?(\d.+?), +(.+?), +(.+)/;
##--

##++
##   Store the data in a log file; open modes:
##
##     >> = append, > = write, < (or nothing) = read
##--

open (FILE, ">>$file") || die "Cannot append uptime data to $file: $!\n";
print FILE join (':', time, $users, $load1, $load2, $load3), "\n";
close (FILE);

exit (0);
```

One note, before discussing the code: Our application accepts a command line argument and uses its value to determine where to archive the load average data. This provides the flexibility to archive the data to different files without modifying the code at all. If you were curious as to the significance of the /home/gundavaram/uptime.log file in the preceding crontab entry, now you know that it refers to the log file.

Getting the Command Line Argument

A user can specify arguments and information to any Perl application through the command line, and Perl makes them available to you through the special @ARGV array. You don't necessarily have to use these arguments in your application, but they are there in case you need them. Here is a simple program that illustrates how command line arguments are processed:

```
#!/usr/bin/perl

##++
##   print_args.pl: display all command-line arguments
##--

use strict;

for (my $loop=0; $loop <= $#ARGV; $loop++) { ## $#ARGV returns the
    print "\$ARGV[$loop] = $ARGV[$loop]\n";  ## last index of the
                                             ## array
}

exit (0);
```

You are looking at the for loop in action. You should use this construct when you know exactly how many times you want a loop to execute. This is very different than a while loop, where you may not know how many times it should run; all you know is that once the loop meets some specific criteria, it should stop. You iterate through the @ARGV array, one element at a time, displaying its value. Go ahead and run the program, like so:

```
$ perl print_args.pl how are you this is a test
$ARGV[0] = how
$ARGV[1] = are
$ARGV[2] = you
$ARGV[3] = this
$ARGV[4] = is
$ARGV[5] = a
$ARGV[6] = test
```

You can treat the @ARGV array as you would any other array, accessing a specific element by specifying its index. Look back at the main application where you get the first command line argument, $ARGV[0], and use it:

```
$file = $ARGV[0] || '/var/log/uptime.log';
```

What do you think we are trying to do? If you remember, this clever one-line statement is identical to the following if-then block:

```
if ($ARGV[0]) {
    $file = $ARGV[0];
} else {
    $file = '/var/log/uptime.log';
}
```

We use the value passed to us from the command line as the path to our log file, storing it in `$file`, but only if it is defined and has a true value. Otherwise, we use the `/var/log/uptime.log` as our default log file. We mentioned Perl's flexibility in the beginning of this chapter. This is just a simple example that illustrates it. If you don't feel comfortable using the one-line technique, you can always use the longer, but more clear, group of code shown previously. If you are more adventurous, you can also use the following:

```
$file = ($ARGV[0]) ? $ARGV[0] : '/var/log/uptime.log';
```

You've just seen three different techniques for performing the same task. Perl does not force you to use one approach over another; you are free to use whichever one you feel comfortable with.

Invoking the uptime Command

We can now invoke the `uptime` system command to get the load average data that we're looking for. You will be quite surprised when you see how easy it is to communicate with external applications from within Perl. We simply need to enclose either the command to execute or the path to an application, along with any necessary command line arguments, within a set of *backticks*. Perl then spawns a shell to execute the application and returns its output. In this case, we store that output in the `$uptime` variable.

We are about to venture off on a long detour to better understand the intricate process of communicating with external applications. If you are not interested in learning about these techniques now, you can safely jump to the section "Back to Our Program" and come back to this material at a later time.

Pipes

The *backtick* approach is very easy to use and quite convenient. However, it should be used only when you know that the output generated from the invoked application is small. Imagine what would happen if an application generates megabytes and megabytes of output? Perl would then have to store all this information in memory, which could cause quite a problem. So, Perl provides an alternative to communicate with applications, via a pipe. For example, say you wanted to retrieve the list of currently logged-in users; here is how you would do it:

```
#!/usr/bin/perl

##++
##   current_users.pl: display list of current users
##--
use strict;

open (MYPIPE, '/usr/bin/w |') || die "Cannot create pipe: $!\n";

while (<MYPIPE>) {          ## Read one line at a time into $_
    print;                  ## Equivalent to: print $_;
}

close (MYPIPE);
exit  (0);
```

If you quickly glance at this program, you may think that we are simply iterating through a file and displaying each record. However, that is not the case. Instead, we are opening a pipe to the `/usr/bin/w` command, reading it, and displaying its output:

```
23:16:35 up 55 min,  3 users,  load average: 0.13, 0.24, 0.34
USER     TTY      FROM          LOGIN@   IDLE   JCPU   PCPU WHAT
root     :0       -             22:26   ?xdm?   5:43   2.34s /usr/bin/gnome-session
root     pts/0    :0.0          22:27    0.00s  1.23s  0.03s w
root     pts/1    :0.0          23:02    6:42   0.64s  0.23s -bash
```

You may have seen examples of pipes throughout this book. Here is an example that finds the number of occurrences of the word "perl" in all of the files located in the `/etc` directory:

```
# grep -d skip perl /etc/* | wc -l
     67
```

When the shell sees this, it executes the `grep` command, finding all lines that contain the word perl, and then passes that output to the `wc` command as input. In other words, the output of the first command gets passed to the second as input. We are doing something very similar in our program, as well. However, if you look at the previous code line with the `open` command, you will see that there is nothing specified after the *pipe* (the vertical bar) character. Where is the output going? To the `MYPIPE` filehandle, like this:

```
$ /usr/bin/w | MYPIPE
```

By reading data from the `MYPIPE` filehandle, you are in effect reading the content produced by the `/usr/bin/w` program. The main advantage here is that you can read the content a line at a time, which is not only more efficient, but provides you with better control. In a similar fashion, you can also use a pipe to send data to another application as input, as in the following example:

```
#!/usr/bin/perl

##++
##   sort_numbers.pl: send list of numbers to /bin/sort to get sorted list
##--

open (MYPIPE, '| /bin/sort -g') || die "Cannot create pipe: $!\n";
print MYPIPE "100\n50\n30\n70\n90\n60\n20\n80\n10\n40\n";
close (MYPIPE);

exit (0);
```

Notice the location of the pipe; it's on the left side rather than the right side. This means that we are sending our output through the `MYPIPE` filehandle to another application as input. More specifically, we are passing a series of unordered numbers to the `sort` command, which produces the following output:

```
$ perl sort_numbers.pl
10
20
30
40
50
```

```
60
70
80
90
100
```

Unfortunately, once you send information to the external application as input, you have no control over the output that it produces; the output is typically sent to the standard output stream.

The system Command

What if you want to interact with a program that doesn't care about its input or output? Take, for example, a script that starts a server of some sort, or an editor, which might open an empty window. Perl provides the `system` command, which you can use to invoke an application.

Let's look back at the `send_email.pl` program in the previous section for a moment. Imagine how convenient it would be for the user if he or she could enter the body of the message in an editor? You can use the `system` command to open an editor, saving the contents in a temporary file. Then, you can read the content from the file and pass it to the `Mail::Send` module, as follows:

```
#!/usr/bin/perl

use Mail::Send;                  ## Import/use Mail::Send
use POSIX;                       ## Import/use POSIX
use strict;                      ## Enable "strict" pragma
...

print 'Subject: ';
chomp ($subject = <STDIN>);

print "Enter the message in an editor, save and exit when you are done:";

##++
##   Call POSIX::tmpnam() to determine a name for a temporary file,
##   which we'll use to store the content of the message.
##--

my $file = POSIX::tmpnam();      ## For example: /tmp/fileTwFpXe

system ("/usr/bin/gedit $file"); ## Open the editor; Perl will wait until
                                 ## user finishes, at which point a temp.
                                 ## file is created by the editor.

{
    local $/ = undef;            ## Undefine record separator

    if (open (FILE, $file)) {
        $message = <FILE>;       ## Reads ENTIRE content from file, as
                                 ## there is no record separator

        close (FILE);
    }
}
```

```
unlink $file;                    ## Delete temp. file; ignore status

...

exit (0);
```

We won't discuss this code snippet in detail, but I we hope you get the general idea. As you can see from all of these examples, communicating with external applications via backticks, pipes, and the system command is reasonably straightforward, yet extremely powerful. You can interact with any application, whether it is a system program, a script of some sort, or a compiled application.

Parsing Load Averages

Now comes the most difficult part of the application. We briefly talked about regular expressions earlier in the chapter. However, we have yet to really use them in a program, with the exception of the simple regex in `list_users.pl`. In this application, we need to extract the number of users and the load averages from the output generated by the `uptime` command. Although you can use many techniques to accomplish this task, regular expressions are by far the best and easiest way to handle it.

Regular Expressions

What is a regular expression? Simply defined, a regular expression is a set of "normal" characters and special syntactic elements (metacharacters) used to match patterns in text. You can use regular expressions in all types of text-manipulation tasks, ranging from checking for the existence of a particular pattern to finding a specific string and replacing it.

Substitutions from the Command Line

Suppose you have a large set of HTML files that contain, among other information, your company's physical address. Soon after you create these files, you move to a new location and have to change the address in all of the files. How would you do it? One tedious way would be to manually replace the address in each and every file, but that's not realistic. However, armed with Perl and its regex support, you can get this task done in no time.

Take a look at the following HTML file. Everything is left out except for the company address that we are interested in modifying:

```
<HTML>
...
MechanicNet Group, Inc.<br>
43801 Mission Blvd., Suite 103<br>
Fremont, CA 94539
...
</HTML>
```

We want to change this address to read as follows:

```
<HTML>
...
MechanicNet Group, Inc.<br>
7150 Koll Center Parkway, Suite 200<br>
```

```
Pleasanton, CA 94566
...
</HTML>
```

There are several ways to tackle this job. It would be beyond the scope of this chapter to discuss each approach, so we will concentrate on one technique that is compact, versatile, and easy to use:

```
$ perl -0777 -p -i.bak -e \
's/43801 Mission Blvd., Suite 103<br>\s*Fremont, CA 94539/7150 Koll Center Parkway,
Suite 200<br>\nPleasanton, CA 94566/gsi' *.html
```

That's it, and we didn't even have to write a full-fledged program! We are running the Perl interpreter from the command line, passing to it several arguments, including a piece of code that performs the actual substitution. The `-0` switch sets the record separator to the octal number `777`. This has the same effect as assigning an undefined value as the separator because the octal value 777 is not legal. By doing this, we can match strings that span multiple lines. How, you ask? Typically, the default record separator is the newline character; each time you read from a filehandle, you will get back exactly one line:

```
$record = <FILE>;     ## One line
```

However, if the record separator is undefined, one read will *slurp* the entire file into a string:

```
local $/ = undef;     ## $/ = record separator; special Perl variable
$record = <FILE>;     ## Entire file
```

This is convenient because you can search for strings or patterns without having to worry about line boundaries. However, you should be careful not to use this technique with very large files, as you might exhaust system memory. On the other hand, if you need to match only a single string or pattern, you can safely ignore this switch.

Next, the `-p` switch creates an internal `while` loop that iterates over each record from each of the specified files, storing the content in the default Perl variable, `$_`. If you look at the far right of the one-line statement, you will see the list of files that Perl will process. Remember that because the record separator is undefined, `$_` will contain the contents of the entire file, as opposed to just one line.

The `-i` switch asks Perl to modify each of these files in-place, moving the original to another file with the same name but with the `.bak` extension. If you don't want to create a backup copy of each file, you can simply remove the `.bak` after the `-i` switch. And, finally, the `-e` switch specifies the Perl code that should be executed for each record read from a file. If you want more information on all of the command line switches accepted by the interpreter, you should look at the `perlrun` man page.

Here is the code that performs the substitution:

```
s/43801 Mission Blvd., Suite 103<br>\s*Fremont, CA 94539/7150 Koll Center
Parkway, Suite 200<br>\nPleasanton, CA 94566/gsi;
```

This is technically equivalent to

```
$_ =~ s/43801 Mission Blvd., Suite 103<br>\s*Fremont, CA 94539/7150 Koll
Center Parkway, Suite 200<br>\nPleasanton, CA 94566/gsi;
```

as regular expression operators, including `s//`, work on the default Perl variable, `$_`, if another scalar variable is not specified. Whenever you see the `=~` or `!~` operators, you should automatically think of regular expressions. You can use these operators to compare a scalar value against a particular regular expression.

The `s//` operator replaces the left side of the expression with the value on the right side. For example, if you want to substitute the ZIP Code `94539` with `94566`, you would use the following:

```
s/94539/94566/;
```

We are simply substituting literal values here. But, in our main example, we are using regex metacharacters in the substitution pattern. These metacharacters have a special significance to the regex processing engine. Take a look at the `\s` token followed by the asterisk. The token matches an occurrence of white space; white space includes a regular space character, tab, newline, or carriage return. We use the asterisk as the token's multiplier, forcing the regex engine to match the token—in this case, the white space—zero or more times. Other than this metacharacter, the rest of the expression is simply a set of literal characters.

And, finally, let's look at the expression modifiers that follow the substitution operator. Each of the three characters, `g`, `s`, and `i`, has a special significance:

- The `g` modifier enables global substitution, where all occurrences of the original pattern are replaced by the new string.
- The `s` modifier forces the engine to treat the string stored in the `$_` variable as a single line.
- The `i` modifier enables case-insensitive matching.

Only a small subset of metacharacters is supported by the Perl regex engine. We won't cover them all here, so take a look at the documentation provided by Perl and *Beginning Perl,* by Simon Cozens with Peter Wainwright, by Wrox Press.

Substitutions in Many Files

What if you have many HTML files spread around in multiple directories? Can you use the one-line Perl statement discussed previously to find and replace the old address with the new one? Yes, you can use the `find` command in conjunction with the `xargs` to process all the files:

```
$ find . -name '*.html' -print0 | xargs --verbose --null \
perl -0777 -p -i.bak -e \
's/43801 Mission Blvd., Suite 103<br>\s*Fremont, CA 94539/7150 Koll Center
Parkway, Suite 200<br>\n Pleasanton, CA 94566/gsi'
```

This example uses the `find` command to find all the files with an `.html` extension in the current directory and all underlying subdirectories. These files are sent as input, via the pipe, to the `xargs` command, which takes them and passes them as arguments to the ensuing `perl` command.

In summary, we have looked at just one regular expression metacharacter, along with a useful Perl technique for manipulating text easily and quickly from the command line. That alone should convince you of the power of regular expressions. Next, we will continue on with our main application, using the knowledge gained here to parse the relevant information from the output generated by the uptime command.

Back to Our Program . . .

Are you ready to handle a much more advanced regex? Let's dissect the one used in our main application to extract the number of users and the load averages (see Figure 13-2).

You can liken the process of crafting a regex to putting together a jigsaw puzzle piece by piece. To jog your memory, look once again at the `uptime` output:

```
23:15:42 up 54 min,  3 users,  load average: 0.33, 0.29, 0.36
```

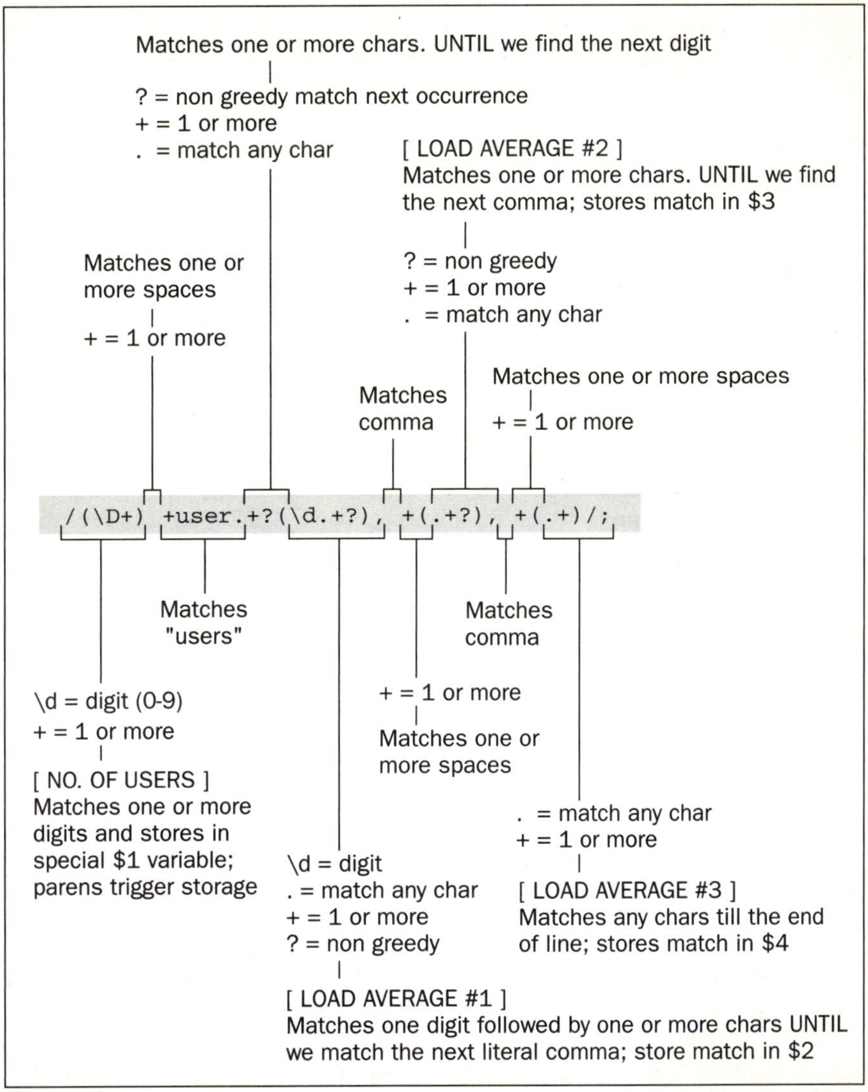

Figure 13-2

The first piece involves extracting the number of users. The easiest way to do this is to find the number that precedes the literal word *user*. You don't need to start your search from the beginning of the input string; you can create your expression to match from anywhere in the string. And once you find the number of users, you must store this value somewhere. Do this by enclosing the information you are interested in within a set of parentheses (see the expression in the preceding figure). This forces Perl to save the matched information in a special variable, `$1`.

Next, we need to get at the three load averages. You can use a variety of different expressions, but the simplest is to proceed through the output, starting from the string *user* and stopping when you find the next numerical digit. Once you find this number, store all the characters from that point forward until the next comma; this is the first load average that gets stored in `$2`. Then, ignore this comma as well as the following space, and obtain the next load average. And, finally, extract the final load average by matching everything from the current point to the end of the line.

At first glance, regular expressions are difficult to comprehend. But, as you practice more and more, they will get much easier to handle, and you will be able to implement all types of parsers, from finding errors in log files to extracting content from Web sites.

Archiving to File

Once you have the four pieces of information that you are interested in, you archive this data to a log file. You use the `open` command to open the file, but with a little twist. Notice the two leading greater-than signs in front of the filename; this tells Perl to open the file in *append* mode. Then, use the `join` command to create a string containing the current timestamp and the `uptime` information, delimited by the colon character.

To accurately analyze this type of information over time, you also need to have a timestamp associated with each data point. For this purpose, use the `time` command, which simply returns the number of non-leap seconds since the epoch—on UNIX systems, this is 01/01/1970. Try the following to get a feel for these types of timestamps:

```
$ perl -e 'print time, "\n"'
1079335147
$ perl -e 'print scalar localtime 1079335147, "\n"'
Sun Mar 14 23:19:07 2004
```

There are a large number of Perl extensions that you can use to manipulate timestamps, in addition to the built-in `localtime` command.

Last but not least, you write the delimited string to the file using the `print` command. Then, close the file and exit.

You have read quite a number of new techniques in this section, ranging from accepting command line arguments to interacting with external applications and designing regular expressions. It is not easy to understand all of this material at first glance, so take some time to go through the material a number of times. In addition, you should refer to the built-in documentation as well as to other resources, such as *Beginning Perl,* by Simon Cozens and *Professional Perl,* by Peter Wainwright et al, from Wrox Press for more detailed coverage.

The next section implements the disk usage application that was covered at the beginning of the chapter. You should use this application as a benchmark to see how well you understand the techniques presented up to this point.

Application 4: Disk Usage Monitor

We spent a considerable amount of time and space discussing and analyzing a hypothetical disk usage monitoring application earlier in the chapter. You have learned quite a bit of Perl since that discussion, so in this section, you actually implement the application. To summarize, the application must be able to perform the following tasks:

- Monitor specified filesystems for available disk space.
- Determine user directories that exceed a certain quota limit if available disk space falls below a specified threshold.
- Find the 15 largest files for each user directory that exceeds the quota limit.
- Send an e-mail message to the offending user listing the largest files.

In discussing this application, we will not dissect the code in extreme detail as we have done with the three previous programs. Instead, you will see a block of code and a brief description of its functionality, highlighting any new constructs or syntax. But first, Figure 13-3 illustrates an e-mail message that is typically produced by this application if the quota usage thresholds are reached.

Here is the code:

```
#!/usr/bin/perl

##++
##   disk_usage.pl: monitor disk usage and alert users via e-mail
##--

use Mail::Send;                                    ## Load Mail::Send
use strict;                                        ## Use strict pragma;
                                                   ## must declare all vars.

##++
##   Declare constants/global variables
##--

our ($DF, $DU, %FILESYSTEMS, $QUOTA, $NO_FILES); ## Pre-declare global
                                                 ## variables

$DF          = '/bin/df';                        ## Path to df command
$DU          = '/usr/bin/du -ab';                ## Path and options to du

##++
##   The following three constants store (1) the filesystems to check and
##   their maximum allowable usage thresholds, (2) max user's disk quota,
##   50 MB and (3) the number of files to process, 15. You should change
##   these values to suit your requirements and system configuration.
##--
```

```
%FILESYSTEMS = ('/home1' => 90, '/home2' => 85);
$QUOTA       = 1_024_000 * 50;                ## Use _ to make large
                                              ## numbers more readable
$NO_FILES    = 15;

##++
##   Start main program
##--

print STDERR "Disk usage check in progress, please wait ...\n";

my    ($percent, $filesystem);
local *PIPE1;                                 ## Pre-declare/localize
                                              ## filehandle

open (PIPE1, "$DF |") || die "Cannot create pipe: $!\n";

while (<PIPE1>) {                             ## Read line into $_
    if (/(\d+)%\s+(.+)\s*$/) {                ## Match against $_ variable
        ($percent, $filesystem) = ($1, $2);   ## Store matches

        if (exists $FILESYSTEMS{$filesystem} &&      ## Does this element
                                                     ## exist in hash?
            $percent >= $FILESYSTEMS{$filesystem}) {

            print STDERR ">> $filesystem has $percent usage <<\n";
            process_filesystem ($filesystem); ## Invoke subroutine
        }                                     ## with $filesystem as arg.
    }
}

close (PIPE1);
exit  (0);
##++
##   End of main program, subroutines follow ...
##--
```

We start out by defining a set of *constants*, variables whose values will not change over the life of the program, using the `our` command. The `our` command allows you to define variables that have a global scope and can be accessed in subroutines. By using a constant, as opposed to a literal value, you can change its value easily without having to search and replace various instances of the actual value throughout the program.

One of the constants you should take note of is `%FILESYSTEM`, a data type that you have not seen so far. It is an *associative* array, commonly referred to as a *hash*, but is very different than a regular array. You can think of a hash as an array that is indexed by an alphanumeric *key*, rather than an ordered number. Each hash element has two scalar components: the key and an associated value. This application uses a hash to associate filesystems with their corresponding disk usage thresholds. For example, you can access the threshold value for the `/home1` filesystem by using the following syntax:

```
$home = $FILESYSTEMS{'/home1'};
```

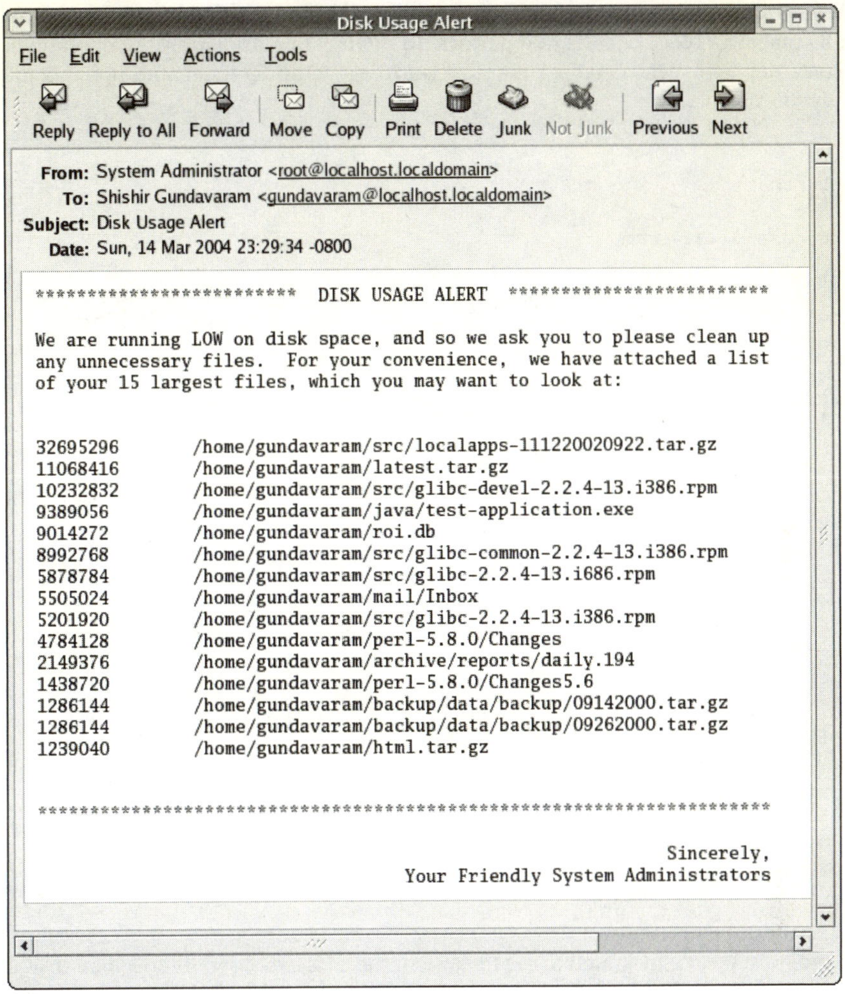

Figure 13-3

After initialization, we proceed to use a pipe to interact with the `df` system command, which, in turn, produces and returns a disk usage report. Then, we iterate through each line of the report and extract the usage percentage and filesystem name with a regular expression. Based on the regex dissection performed in the previous section, can you understand this expression? We start our search toward the end of the input string, looking for one or more numerical digits followed by a percent sign. The numerical value will be stored in `$1` and represents the usage percentage. Then, we match one or more white space characters and proceed to extract and save the remaining portion of the string in `$2`; this is the filesystem name. The trailing `$` metacharacter allows us to anchor a regex to the end of the string.

Only if the line of input matches the regex do we proceed with the rest of the code. For each filesystem, we check to see if it exists in the hash and if the usage value exceeds the specified threshold. Only in that case do we print a diagnostic message and invoke the `process_filesystem` subroutine to process each user's individual directory.

You can use subroutines, also known as functions, methods, and procedures, to make your code more modular. By placing a block of code that performs a distinct operation or set of operations in its own unique "container," you can keep the program clean, easy to understand, and possibly more efficient. Look at this subroutine:

```
##++
##   Subroutines
##--
sub process_filesystem
{
    my    $filesystem = shift;           ## Argument; read from @_ array
    my    ($dir, $path, $files);         ## Pre-declare other variables
    local *DIR;                          ## Pre-declare/localize filehandle

    opendir (DIR, $filesystem)           ## Open specified filesystem
        || die "Cannot open filesystem $filesystem: $!\n";

    while ($dir = readdir (DIR)) {       ## Get each user's directory
        next if ($dir =~ /^\./);         ## Ignore dirs. that start with .

        print STDERR "- Processing $dir directory ...\n";

        $path  = "$filesystem/$dir";     ## Add full path to user's dir
        $files = process_dir ($path);    ## Invoke subroutine

        ##++
        ##   Send e-mail to user only if he/she has exceeded quota limit.
        ##--

        send_email ($dir, $files) if (ref $files);
    }

    closedir (DIR);                      ## Close directory
}
```

The main program passes the name of the filesystem that has exceeded its specified disk usage threshold as an argument to this subroutine. Perl stores subroutine arguments in the special `@_` array—analogous to the `$_` default variable. We use the `shift` command to remove the first element from this array and store its value in `$filesystem`. However, if you don't feel comfortable using `shift` on an "unseen" array to obtain the argument, you can use either one of the following two statements:

```
my $filesystem = shift @_;               ## Remove first element from @_
my $filesystem = $_[0];                  ## Argument; access index 0
```

Next, we call the `opendir` function to open the filesystem's root directory, in much the same manner as we would open a text file. We proceed to iterate through the directory, getting a subdirectory name each time we invoke the `readdir` command. You should be aware that each subdirectory, in turn, represents a user's home directory. Because `readdir` returns only the subdirectory name, we use the `$filesystem` value to construct the entire path to the directory and pass it to the `process_dir` subroutine.

The `process_dir` subroutine traverses through all of the user's files and returns a hash reference containing the list of the largest files, but only if the user has exceeded the quota value as defined by the `$QUOTA` constant. If we do end up getting back a list, we would call the `send_email` subroutine to send a warning e-mail message to the user.

We have not talked about references at all in this chapter. You can use references to create complex data structures using the three basic data types that you are familiar with, namely scalars, arrays, and hashes. We will look at references in more detail as we discuss this application:

```
sub process_dir
{
    my    $dir = shift;                        ## Argument; from @_ or $_[0]
    my    ($min, %files, $size, $file, @sorted);
    local *PIPE2;                              ## Localize filehandle

    ##++
    ##   Open a pipe to the /usr/bin/du command, with the -ab arguments;
    ##   this is defined by the $DU constant. The -a switch returns sizes
    ##   for all files, not just directories, and the -b switch returns
    ##   the sizes in bytes -- instead of the default unit blocks.
    ##
    ##   Sample output:
    ##   140      /home/postgres/global
    ##--

    open (PIPE2, "$DU $dir |") || die "Cannot create pipe: $!\n";

    $min   = 0;                                ## Keep track of smallest file
    %files = ();                               ## Initialize hash

    while (<PIPE2>) {                          ## Read record for file
        ($size, $file) = /^(\d+)\s+(.+)\s*$/;  ## Get the size and file
                                               ## from du

        last if ($file eq $dir);               ## End loop if we are finished
        next if (-d $file);                    ## Ignore if file is directory

        if ($size > $min) {
            $files{$file} = $size;             ## Store each file and size

            ##++
            ##   If we have more than 15 files in the %files hash, then
            ##   we sort the values based on the file size and delete the
            ##   file with the smallest size. At any given time, we will
            ##   have only that number of files in the hash.
            ##--

            if (scalar keys %files > $NO_FILES) {
                @sorted = sort { $files{$a} <=> $files{$b} } keys %files;
                $min    = $files{ $sorted[1] };

                delete $files{ $sorted[0] };   ## Delete smallest file
            }
```

```
        }
    }

    close (PIPE2);                              ## Close pipe
    return ($size >= $QUOTA) ? \%files : 0;     ## Return list only if user
                                                ## exceeded quota
}
```

This is the most complicated piece of code to date in this chapter. The task in this subroutine is to locate and return files from a specific user's home directory that occupy the most disk space. The actual number of files to process is specified by the `$NO_FILES` constant defined at the beginning of the program—15, in this case.

First, we create a pipe to the `du` command to get a list of each and every file and its associated size from the specified directory. We then iterate through this list one file at a time, ignoring all directories, with the exception of one. That is the directory that has the same path as the user's home directory. This signifies the end of the output, so we exit from the loop.

Looking inside the loop, we check to see if the size of the current file is greater than the minimum size, which is initially zero. If so, we store the file and its size in the hash, and then immediately determine the number of files currently stored in the hash. You don't want to store more than 15 files at any given point. If the number exceeds 15, you need to remove the file with the smallest size.

The technique to remove this file from the hash is a simple one. You use the `sort` command to sort the hash by file size and store the sorted sizes in the `@sorted` array. Next, reset the minimum file size to the second smallest size, so that from here on, you store only the files that are larger than this value. And then, you finally remove the smallest file from the hash using the `delete` command. Repeat this process for all of the files, at which point you will be left with the 15 largest files, unless there are less than 15 files in the directory. After the loop terminates, you return the list of these files, but only if the user's total directory size is greater than the defined quota.

You should note a few things, to note however. The first is the `sort` command and its syntax. The `sort` command expects to receive an array as input and returns the sorted array as output:

```
@array  = (100, 50, 25, 75);
@sorted = sort { $a <=> $b };  ## @sorted = (25, 50, 75, 100);
```

Your objective is to get the list of files in the `%files` hash ordered by their size, so you can remove the file with the smallest size. Unfortunately, `sort` cannot directly work with hashes, so you must do things a bit differently. You can use the `keys` command to return an array of all the hash keys (filenames):

```
@files = keys %files;          ## @files = ("/home/postgres/global", ...);
```

Then, pass this array to the `sort` command, but you need to change the logic of the sort expression to make sure that you get back an array based on the file size and not the filename. The expression within the braces determines what is sorted and how it is sorted. The `sort` command takes two values from the input at a time, internally labeled `$a` and `$b`, and compares them. In this case, `$a` and `$b` represent filenames, so you use these to access their respective file sizes in the hash, which are then compared. After `sort` finishes its job, it returns an array of filenames sorted by file size.

Next, you need to familiarize yourself with is the `return` command. You can use the `return` command to return a value or set of values back to your caller. However, the `return` command, as shown in the subroutine, is a shortcut for the following:

```
if ($size >= $QUOTA) {
    return \%files;             ## Return reference to a hash
} else {
    return 0;
}
```

Remember, an associative array and a regular array allow you to store multiple elements. If you were to return one of these data types from a subroutine, they would not be returned as one entity, but instead as multiple scalar variables. To avoid this, you take a reference of the hash by using the \ prefix; now it is returned as one single entity. Of course, if you return a reference to a hash in this manner, you must *de-reference* it outside before you can access elements in the hash. We discuss this process after we look at the following `send_email` subroutine:

```
sub send_email
{
    my ($user, $files) = @_;
    my ($mail, $list, $fh);

    $mail = new Mail::Send;              ## Creates new Mail::Send object
    $list = '';                          ## String to hold list of files

    $mail->to ($user);
    $mail->subject ('Disk Usage Alert');

    $fh = $mail->open();

    map { $list .= pack ("A15A*", $files->{$_}, $_) . "\n" }
               sort { $files->{$b} <=> $files->{$a} } keys %$files;

    ##++
    ##   This is a here document. It allows us to output large blocks
    ##   of a text at once; it prints until it finds the
    ##   'Message' delimiter.
    ##--
    print $fh <<Message;

*************************  DISK USAGE ALERT  *************************

We are running LOW on disk space, and so we ask you to please clean up
any unnecessary files.  For your convenience,  we have attached a list
of your $NO_FILES largest files, which you may want to look at:


$list


**********************************************************************
```

```
                                                              Sincerely,
                                          Your Friendly System Administrators

Message

    $fh->close();
}
```

Most of the code in this subroutine should be familiar to you by now; it is nearly identical to the `send_email.pl` application. The `process_filesystem` subroutine passes the username and the hash reference to this subroutine to build and send the e-mail warning message. We are making one critical assumption here, namely that the user's e-mail address is the same as his or her home directory name. If you are adventurous, you can modify the code a bit from `list_users.pl` to match the home directory to the username, and thus the e-mail address.

If you look at the code carefully, you will see one very cryptic-looking statement. You should read it from right to left, instead of left to right. First, we use the `sort` command to sort the files in descending order; compare the position of `$a` and `$b` here to the sort expression in the `process_dir` subroutine. We pass the resulting array to `map` to build a string that lists the files and sizes in a tabular format.

To make this statement easier to understand, it is broken up into a simpler syntax here:

```
@keys   = keys %$files;
@sorted = sort { $files->{$b} <=> $files->{$a} } @keys;

foreach $key (@sorted) {
    $list .= pack ("A15A*", $files->{$_}, $_) . "\n";
}
```

That's it for the application, but we are not done with Perl just yet. The next section implements a Web-based system administration application that you can use to monitor your system. But more significantly, it illustrates how easy it is to design and develop a comprehensive application in Perl.

And Finally . . .

Perl, when used correctly, can make your administrative life a great deal easier, especially when used in conjunction with other tools and technologies. As a demonstration of this and, we feel, an appropriate ending to this Perl chapter, we'd like to touch upon a small application we've written and included in the code download (from `www.wrox.com` for this book).

It's a simple systems administration assistant, with a graphical user interface that we hope you might find a use for when you're working on your system. To install it, simply run the `sysadmin-install.pl` script that's in the download. It will install a `thttpd` server and the necessary code files. Once it's up and running, it looks something like t Figure 13-4.

This is covered in more detail in Chapter 15, and there's a downloadable blow-by-blow account of how it was put together available from the Wrox Web site.

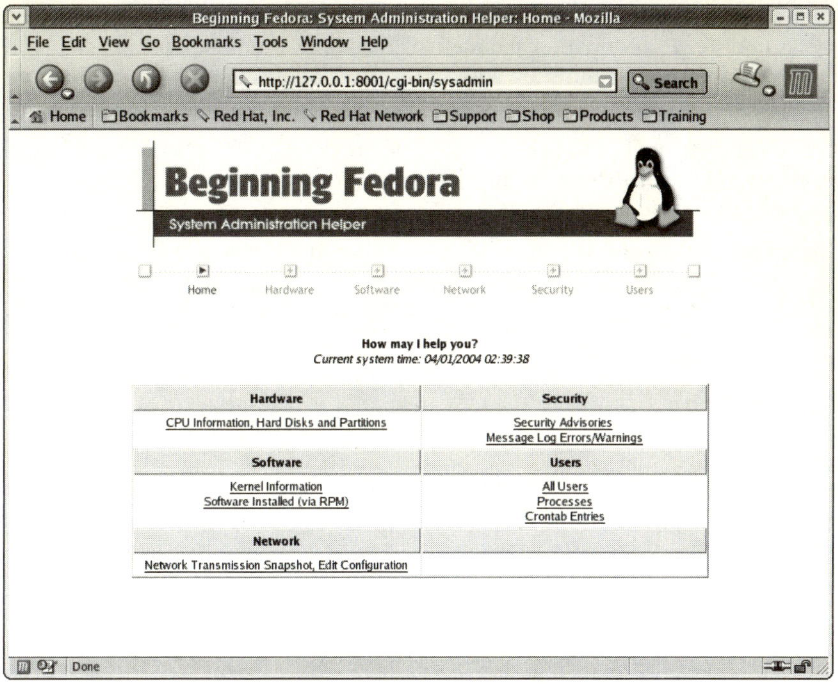

Figure 13-4

Summary

In this chapter you looked at how to administer and manage your Linux systems using Perl. You were introduced to the basic principles of function and syntax, before swiftly moving on to more practical topics, such as interacting with your system and using Perl to facilitate your day-to-day administration by automating common and tasks.

We'll end our coverage of Perl here, although you'll meet it again in the coming chapters, where it is utilized to facilitate a number of examples.

Exercises

1. Try to install the `XML::RSS` Perl module. As you will see in the bonus chapter, we use this module in our `sysadmin` application to parse an RSS data stream that contains the latest security headlines.
2. Change the `hello.pl` program to display your own hometown.
3. Implement an application that is similar to `list_users.pl` to display the system groups: the gid followed by the group name. Hint: The group information is stored in `/etc/group`.

4. Write a small snippet of code to invoke the `lsmod` command and display its output. The `lsmod` application shows information about all loaded kernel modules. Hint: Try to use either backticks or a piped open to communicate with the external application, as you will reuse this code in the next question.

5. Extend the snippet of code you wrote for the previous question to display only the kernel module name and its size. There are many ways to accomplish this task, but using a regular expression will garner you bonus points.

6. Change the Disk Usage Monitor application to send the system administrator, or `root@localhost.localdomain`, a copy of the warning message. Hint: Use the `perldoc` command to learn more about the `Mail::Send` module and its functionality.

14

Contributing to the Fedora Project

The Introduction of this book discussed what the Fedora Project is all about and how it is different than a typical Linux distribution. If you have forgotten, Fedora is a Red Hat–sponsored, community-supported, open source project. In fact, the motto of the project is, "*Openness. Participation. Quality. Change. Disagreement. Opportunity. Community.*" That is wonderful, but how exactly does this impact you? Quite simply, you have the power to help improve the Project on many fronts, from finding and reporting bugs to contributing new code and patches to writing tutorials and documentation. And that is the type of power and flexibility that you don't have with most other Linux distributions.

This chapter examines the development, testing, and release process for the Fedora Project and how you can possibly make contributions. The chapter begins with a look at the available mailing lists to learn about and find potential issues and then moves on to using the Fedora bug tracking system to submit bug reports. Then, you learn how to submit patches, bug fixes, and documentation to the Project. Unfortunately, at this time, the public-facing Fedora development infrastructure, most notably the source code repository, is still in its infancy and is not available. As a compromise, however, we will play around with the GNOME source code repository, so you can get a feel for interacting with a repository. You can use this knowledge to contribute to the Fedora Project when the necessary infrastructure becomes a reality.

Communicating with Users and Developers

For a project the size of Fedora to be a success, there needs to be a large number of casual users, testers, and developers all working in parallel, communicating with each other, and reporting their experiences. Fortunately, the Project coordinators, which include Red Hat staff and management, set up a number of avenues that allow for this type of interaction, ranging from mailing lists and Internet Relay Chat (IRC) channels to publicly available bug tracking mechanisms.

Mailing Lists

Mailing lists are a wonderful medium for communicating with a wide variety of people, from the casual new user to the core developer, all from the comfort of your favorite e-mail client. Using the mailing lists, you can do the following:

- Follow discussions of Fedora users and testers
- Learn of possible problems with Fedora releases
- Pick up tips on how to solve certain issues
- Receive announcements of new software
- Contribute your knowledge and solicit suggestions from other users about your specific obstacles

A number of Fedora-related mailing lists are available, and you can find more information at `www.redhat.com/mailman/listinfo`.

The following table lists a number of Fedora-related mailing lists.

List Name	Description
`fedora-announce-list`	Announcements of Fedora Core changes and events
`fedora-list`	For users of Fedora Core releases
`fedora-test-list`	For testers of Fedora Core test releases
`fedora-devel-list`	For developers
`fedora-docs-list`	For participants of the docs project
`fedora-desktop-list`	For discussions about desktop issues, such as user interfaces, artwork, and usability
`fedora-config-list`	For discussions about the development of configuration tools

If you want to subscribe to a specific mailing list shown in the preceding table, you can send an e-mail to `<listname>-request@redhat.com`, where `<listname>` is the name of the list, with the word *subscribe* in the subject. You should be aware that most of these lists generate a tremendous amount of traffic, which might fill up your mailbox rather quickly. If you are not quite ready for this type of barrage, you can always peruse the list archives via a Web interface at the URL mentioned. Unfortunately, the Web interface will *not* allow you to post messages to the list.

Now that you know how to get involved with the mailing lists, you should spend some time reading through the recently archived messages. You will not only gain a much deeper insight into the Fedora releases, but might also find solutions to any problems or issues you are experiencing.

As you can see, Fedora users are discussing a wide number of issues; this is pretty typical for the Fedora lists. If you are interested in posts on a specific problem that you may be experiencing, you can use the search form to see whether other users have run into something similar. If you cannot find any relevant posts, you can post a new message to the list. With the number of people reading the lists, including Fedora developers, you will most likely receive a response indicating a possible solution or workaround. And if you don't receive a response, at the very least, your post will be archived for other users to find at a later time.

The next step is to check whether someone has filed a formal bug report with the Project that is similar in nature to the problem you are experiencing. You can do this using the Fedora bug tracker.

Bug Tracker

As you may have guessed, a bug tracker (also known as an *issue* or *defect tracker*) is an application that allows project staff to keep track of not only bugs, but also requests, enhancements, and whatever else circulates throughout the project. In this respect, a bug tracker is very different than a mailing list; every issue is typically tracked from submission to resolution.

Here is an overview of the typical defect tracking process. When a defect is found, a tester records the bug into the tracker, along with any necessary steps to reproduce the problem. At this point, a project manager gets involved to determine whether the defect is valid and, if so, assigns responsibility to a single developer or a staff of developers. The developer is then responsible for fixing the problem and notifying the project manager, who will then certify the resolution and close out the issue.

A plethora of commercial and open source bug tracking applications are available, most of which have very similar functionality and interfaces. This section looks at one system, Bugzilla, which is used by Fedora, as well as the KDE and GNOME projects. Go ahead and look at a random bug submitted against the Fedora Core 2 test 2 release, so you have a better understanding of what a typical bug report looks like. Go to the following:

```
https://bugzilla.redhat.com/bugzilla/long_list.cgi?buglist=119854
```

As you can see, a typical bug report contains a lot of valuable information, including the hardware platform and the product, version, and component where the user experienced the problem, as well as all of the problem details.

Try It Out Filing a Bug Report

1. Perhaps you are experiencing crashes when exiting from the Evolution e-mail client on Fedora Core 2 release. Before you file a new bug report, go to `https://bugzilla.redhat.com/bugzilla/easy_enter_bug.cgi`.

   Use the form you find at this URL to search for possible bug reports that are similar in scope to the problem you are experiencing.

   Because you cannot find any bugs that are similar in scope to your problem, continue on to the next step to create a Bugzilla account, from which you can file a bug report.

2. Create a Bugzilla account by going to `https://bugzilla.redhat.com/bugzilla/createaccount.cgi`.

   All you need to do is enter your name and a legitimate e-mail address. Bugzilla creates an account and sends a randomly generated password via e-mail.

3. After you have the necessary Bugzilla authentication credentials, you can log in to the bug tracker. Once there, proceed to the product selection page to start the bug submission process: `https://bugzilla.redhat.com/bugzilla/easy_enter_bug.cgi?action=second`.

   Select Fedora Core from the component menu on the left-hand side, and then click the Submit button at the bottom of the page to continue to the next step.

4. You need to select a component. Luckily, the evolution component is easily found. However, in cases where you cannot find the component that matches your application, you can use the `rpm` command, with the `-qif` switches, to determine the associated component, like so:

```
# rpm -qif /usr/bin/evolution | grep 'Source RPM'
Group: Applications/Productivity     Source RPM: evolution-1.5.3-1.src.rpm
```

   The component name is the string noted by Source RPM without the version information.

5. Now, choose the version and platform. Go ahead and select `test1` as the Fedora version and your hardware as the architecture—typically `i386`, `i586`, `i686`, or `athlon`. Then, press the Submit button to enter the bug description.

6. Enter the summary, version release, description, reproducibility, steps to reproduce, and the severity level for the bug. The following table provides an example.

Field	Value
Summary	Evolution client crashes on exit
Version Release	1.5.3-1
Description	Evolution client crashes every time on exit with error 2
Reproducibility	Every time
Steps to Reproduce	1) Launch the evolution client, and 2) try to exit from the application
Severity Level	High: crashes, loss of data, severe memory leak

7. Click the Open Bugzilla Entry Form button and then the Commit button on the ensuing page to submit the bug report. As the Fedora developers investigate your bug and change the status of the bug from NEW to VERIFIED to ASSIGNED, and then, one hopes, to RESOLVED and CLOSED, you will receive e-mail messages from Bugzilla. You can then log in and see more information about the progress of the bug.

To recap, bug tracking applications allow project staff to quickly understand and analyze the state of the development process because they can track the issues that have been raised, the components or subsystems that are involved, the severity level of the issues, and how the issues have been resolved. If you are interested in setting up your very own bug tracker, take a look at the Request Tracker application, which is covered in Chapter 15.

Now that you know a bit about the Fedora development process, the next section covers source code control and the concept of code repositories, so you can actually take a look at the code behind the Fedora Core operating system.

Accessing the Source Code

A source code repository, or source control system, is exactly what its name indicates, a repository where source code is maintained. It is invaluable to prevent developers from tripping on each other's changes, especially if the development team is large, as is the case with Fedora Core, GNOME, and other high-profile open source projects. In a typical source control system, each developer connects to the repository and checks out a copy of the current version of the code to a local destination, where he or she can work on that code independently from others. Once the developer makes changes to the code, he or she can commit them back into the repository, where the new versions can be picked up by other developers at a later time. In cases where multiple developers commit different changes to the same set of files around the same time frame, the repository server tries to merge the changes together automatically. This merging is not always successful, in which case the developers are notified and are responsible for performing the merge manually.

This section looks at the Concurrent Versions System (CVS), which is a powerful source control system that comes with nearly all Linux distributions. The Fedora Project intends to provide a public CVS source code repository from where you can check out the operating system code. However, at the time of this writing, the repository has not been set up and there is no timeline for such an implementation. Therefore, we will look at the GNOME project and its CVS repository. More specifically, we will connect to the repository, check out code for the gnome-common and gnome-pkgview modules, build and install them, and then work on creating a simple patch.

Connecting to the Repository

You must install the `cvs` client application before you can connect to any CVS repository. However, if you followed the procedure and built the gFTP application in Chapter 11, you already have the necessary application installed. Otherwise, follow the instructions specified in the "Installing Development Tools and Libraries" section in that chapter to install the necessary development applications and tools. After you have finished the installation, issue the following commands from the command line:

```
# export CVSROOT=':pserver:anonymous@anoncvs.gnome.org:/cvs/gnome'
# cvs login
Logging in to :pserver:anonymous@anoncvs.gnome.org:2401/cvs/gnome
CVS password: (leave it blank)
```

The `CVSROOT` environment variable is very important, as you need to set it to the host name and the directory path of the CVS repository that you intend to connect to. Then, you issue the `cvs` login command to force the `cvs` client application to connect to the `anoncvs.gnome.org` repository. If the client connects successfully, it asks you for a password. Because you are connecting to the repository in anonymous read-only mode, you don't need a password, so leave it blank. That's all there is to it.

Checking Out Source Code

Before you check out any source code, you should make it a habit to store that code in a separate location, away from all of your other personal files. That way, you can be assured of not accidentally mixing your personal files with the source code, especially if you have the access to commit files to the repository.

In this section, we will retrieve the `gnome-common` and `gnome-pkgview` GNOME packages. The `gnome-pkgview` application is simple in that displays the list of installed GNOME applications and their version numbers. You might be wondering why we are checking out the `gnome-common` package. It is needed to properly build `gnome-pkgview`.

Now, it's time to get some source code:

```
# cd /usr/local/src
# mkdir gnome
# cd gnome
# cvs -z9 co gnome-common gnome-pkgview
cvs checkout: Updating gnome-common
U gnome-common/.cvsignore
U gnome-common/AUTHORS
...
U gnome-common/support/vasprintf.c
U gnome-common/support/vsnprintf.c
cvs checkout: Updating gnome-pkgview
U gnome-pkgview/.cvsignore
U gnome-pkgview/AUTHORS
...
U gnome-pkgview/src/pkgview-cursor-utils.h
U gnome-pkgview/src/pkgview.h
```

The `cvs co` command, where `co` is short for checkout, is used to check out certain modules, as defined by the remote CVS repository. In this case, we ask the repository for the `gnome-common` and `gnome-pkgview` modules. Use the `-z9` switch to ask the server to compress the files before transmission; the client decompresses them on our side. This reduces the amount of data that is transmitted and is especially suited for low-bandwidth connections.

Building Modules

Now that you have the source code, you can build the `gnome-pkgview` application. But before doing so, you need to install the GNOME Development Libraries. Again, see the "Installing Development Tools and Libraries" section in Chapter 11 for more information. First, let's install the `gnome-common` package:

```
# cd gnome-common
# ./autogen.sh --prefix=/usr/local
checking for autoconf >= 2.53...
  testing autoconf2.50... not found.
  testing autoconf... found 2.59
...
config.status: creating doc-build/gnome-doc-common
Now type 'make' to compile Gnome Skeleton
# make
# make install
```

Now let's install our main `gnome-pkgview` application:

```
# cd ../gnome-pkgview
# ./autogen.sh --prefix=/usr/local
# make
# make install
```

We were able to successfully build a GNOME application based on the latest, bleeding-edge code, directly from the source code repository. Figure 14-1 illustrates this application in action.

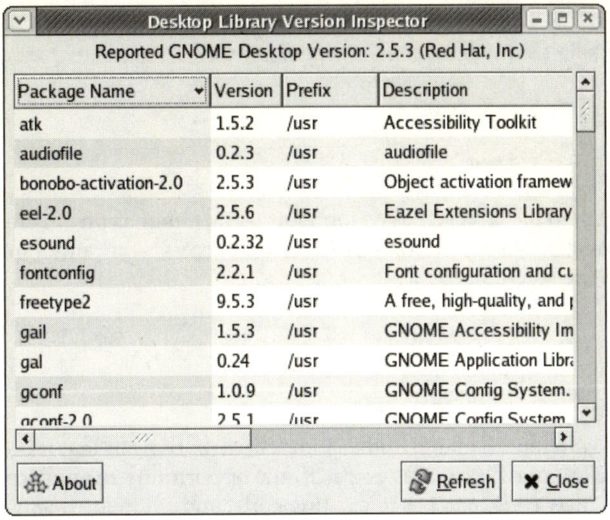

Figure 14-1

Once the Fedora Project opens up the public repository, you will be able to build the latest versions of the kernel, as well as other applications whenever you feel the need to do so.

Creating a Patch

Now that you have the source code at your disposal, you can modify it, whether to implement a new feature or to fix a bug. Because it is beyond the scope of this chapter to dwell on application development, let's make a small and inconsequential change to the `gnome-pkgview` application. That way, you can learn how to make a patch.

First, let's add a simple line to `about-box.c`:

```
/* This is it, this is the change. Nothing but a comment */
```

Then, use the `cvs diff` command to make a patch:

```
# cvs diff -u about-box.c > about-box.patch
```

The patch file looks like this:

```
Index: about-box.c
===================================================================
RCS file: /cvs/gnome/gnome-pkgview/src/about-box.c,v
retrieving revision 1.6
diff -u -r1.6 about-box.c
--- about-box.c 6 Jan 2004 19:43:00 -0000       1.6
```

```
+++ about-box.c 6 Apr 2004 10:43:29 -0000
@@ -2,6 +2,8 @@
 #include <config.h>
 #include "about-box.h"

+/* This is it, this is the change. Nothing but a comment */
+
 void create_about_box ( void ) {

         GdkPixbuf *pixbuf;
```

You can send this patch to the GNOME development team, either as an attachment via the bug tracker, or as an e-mail message. Because you don't have commit access, you cannot make the change to the actual source code in the repository.

Summary

The Fedora Project is different than most other Linux distributions in that it is a community-supported, open source project. This model provides you with the opportunity to enhance the distribution by contributing bug reports, new code, patches to existing code, and even documentation and tutorials.

15

Where to Now?

Throughout this book, we have examined the Linux operating system in detail, covering everything from its history and installation to everyday administration and even an introduction to programming in Perl. But Linux has much more to offer; we have only scratched the surface of what is possible. Hundreds of open source applications can run on Linux. Whether exciting games, office productivity applications, or sophisticated development tools, you will be able to find software that meets your needs. Therefore, this chapter's main goal is to give you a taste of this vast frontier of the open source movement.

This chapter is broken into three sections:

- The first section gives a brief snapshot of where to look for resources online, what you will find, and a summary of widely used licensing schemes.
- The second section discusses several administration applications that you can use on a daily basis to monitor and optimize your Linux system.
- The third section will be particularly exciting if you are interested in development. It looks at a number of programming languages, development utilities, and database engines that can be used effectively with Linux.

For each of the applications covered in this chapter, we examine the reason for using the application, where to obtain it, and how to install it properly on your system.

Before looking at the applications themselves, let's review the various documentation and online resources you can use to find the applications and utilities that will best meet your needs.

Online Resources and Licensing Schemes

It seems that more than ever these days, there is a proliferation of information on Linux and open source—discussions on the open source initiative, articles on whether open source is good or bad, and references to the success of Linux. However, the best resources on Linux arguably can be found at the *Open Source Development Network (OSDN)*. OSDN is a network of a number of Web sites, including the famous Slashdot.org, SourceForge.net, and Freshmeat.net.

Software Resources

Suppose you are in the mood to play a game of Battleship—the game where you try to sink your opponent's ships—but you are not sure if a version exists for Linux. How do you find out? Just head to Freshmeat.net and search for "Battleship," and see what you get. Figure 15-1 shows what your search results might yield.

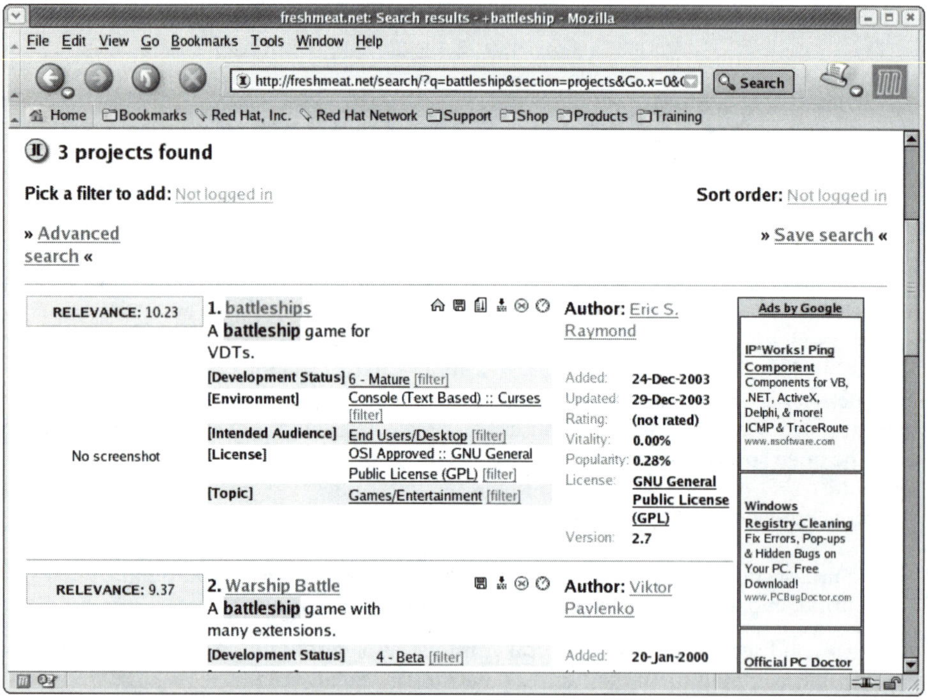

Figure 15-1

This is just an example. Go ahead and search for other software that you may be interested in; you will be pleasantly surprised at how much software you find. In addition to Freshmeat.net, you can also search for software at its sister site, SourceForge.net, as well as freshrpms.net, rpmfind.net and also at the GNOME and KDE project Web sites at `www.gnome.org/softwaremap/list` and `http://apps.kde.com`.

Documentation Resources

If you're looking for information on how to perform a particular task (for example, how to set up a Wireless LAN or how to implement software RAID), you can do worse than visit the Linux Documentation Project (`www.tldp.org`). Here you will find documents referred to as *HOWTOs*—each HOWTO contains concise, to-the-point instructions on how to perform a particular task. The following table gives a few examples of HOWTO documents.

Document	Description
Cable modem	Answers basic questions on how to connect your Linux box to a cable modem or cable Internet provider
Diskless	Describes how to set up a diskless Linux box
Infrared	Provides an introduction to Linux and infrared devices, and how to use the software provided by the Linux/IrDA project
KickStart	Briefly describes how to use the KickStart system to rapidly install large numbers of identical Linux boxes
Software-RAID	Describes how to use Software RAID under Linux
Wireless	Explains how to set up Wireless in Linux, compatibility problems, something about geographic requirements, and more

As you acquire more and more of these resources, whether software or documentation, you will find that most of them are governed by some form of license. The next section takes a look at some of the more common licenses.

Open Source Licenses

For all of the advantages of open source software—such as freely available source code and reduced cost of ownership—the licensing requirements sometimes seem to get in the way. The problem is that there are so many open source licenses out there that it is difficult to keep track of them all.

But help is at hand. You can find more information on a variety of open source licenses at Google's Web Directory: `http://directory.google.com/Top/Computers/Open_Source/Licenses/`.

Dozens of licenses are listed here, and we cannot possibly examine all of them in this chapter. However, we will look at three that are widely used:

- The GNU General Public License (GPL)
- The GNU Lesser General Public License (LGPL)
- The original BSD License

To comprehend the requirements imposed by these licenses, you need to have a good understanding of what is really meant by the term *open source*. An open source software application or utility is one that typically provides the user complete access to its source code, and the right to produce derived works and to distribute them without restriction.

The GNU GPL and GNU LGPL Licenses

Both the GNU GPL and the GNU LGPL fall into the category of *copyleft licenses*. These licenses permit unrestricted modification and redistribution, on condition that either all or portions of derivative works retain the same terms as the original license. These licenses were created to assure developers that any software they develop and distribute would always remain "free" and open source (here, "free" refers to rights rather than to financial matters).

Let's consider the Battleship example for a moment. Suppose you did go looking for a *Battleship* application, and that you found an application that is licensed under the GNU GPL. Having found it, you can certainly play the game as much as you want; you can also distribute it to your friends, and even burn it onto a CD-ROM and sell it; the license entitles you to charge enough to reasonably cover your packaging and distribution costs.

Here's the crux, though. Suppose you want to *change* the application (by adding some interesting artificial intelligence algorithms, for example) and distribute the new version only in compiled form, so that your algorithms remain closed, or proprietary. If you did that, you would be in violation of the GPL because you tried to redistribute the modified application without making the source code available. Remember, you can change the application, but if you do, you must release the *entire* source code, including the code that you added or modified, under the terms of the original license. This ensures that the Battleship game always remains open source, even as developers add and modify its feature set.

The GNU LGPL has one exception to this: You can use any code libraries licensed under the LGPL within your own proprietary code, and you're not obliged to release your *entire* software under the original license. For example, suppose the Battleship game contains a set of libraries, licensed under the LGPL, that display the game board and accept input from the user. Under the LGPL, you can incorporate these into your own version of the Battleship game (thereby saving time and money), but you would not be required to release your *entire* application under the terms of the LGPL.

The BSD License

The BSD license is a lot simpler and much easier to understand than the GPL variety. Unlike the GPL, whose main purpose is to ensure that derivative works remain free for everyone, the BSD license encourages people to use and distribute software. More specifically, the BSD license allows you to use, modify, and distribute the source code or binary form of the software without restriction, as long as the original license is included.

System Administration Applications

This section looks at a number of system administration applications, each of which implements a different set of functionality. Though there are plenty of administration, monitoring, and tracking applications that come with the standard Fedora Core distribution, the ones discussed here are very powerful and a little bit different.

The sysadmin Application

You may remember that we first mentioned the sysadmin application in Chapter 13. As an example of the power and flexibility of Perl, we've put together a small System Administrator Helper application, for which we hope you may find a use. It's not as complex and functional as the others being introduced in this chapter, but in many ways this is a strong point—it shows you the bare-bones information about your system that you'll need to refer back to time and time again.

To install the System Administration Helper, simply download the files from the `www.wrox.com` Web site, where they form part of the book's code download. There are two .tar.gz files, and a .pl installation script. Once you've got the files on your machine (probably in `/usr/local`), simply run the installation script and follow the instructions provided.

You'll be asked to specify a username and password. Make a note of these, as you'll need to supply them every time you log in to the application.

When you load the System Administration Helper in your browser, you should see something like that shown in Figure 15-2.

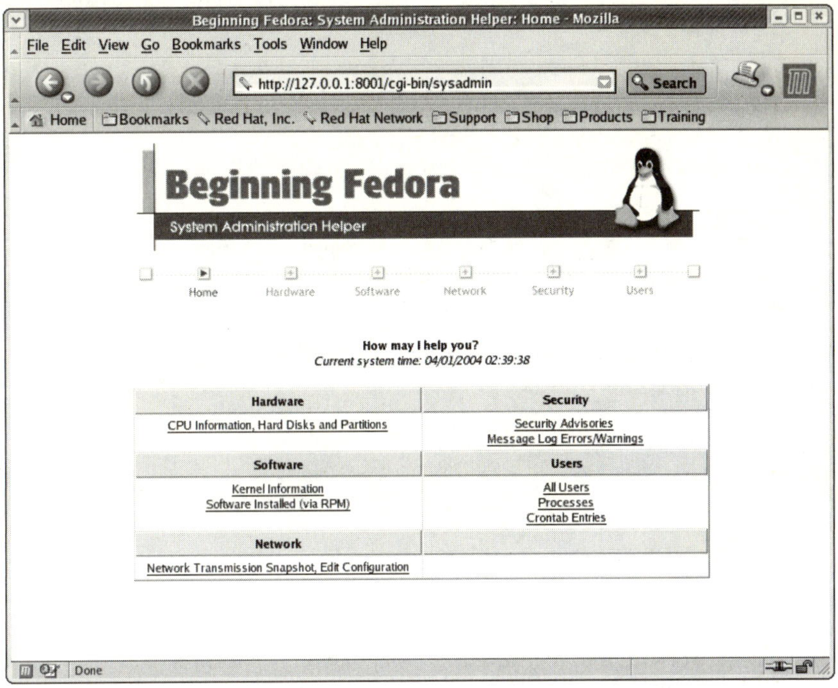

Figure 15-2

The application presents you with information about your Hardware, Software, Network, and User settings, together with a list of the latest Linux Security vulnerabilities that have been detected, and may apply to your system. Many of these headings contain subsections that you can use to further explore and configure your system. Try it and see.

This application uses its own thttpd Web server. This is started automatically as part of the install, but for security reasons isn't configured to run all the time (it runs only until your machine is shut down). So, before browsing to the program, you'll need to start the server by issuing the command `/etc/init.d/thttpd start` *from the command line.*

The GNOME Workstation Command Center

You may remember the Perl systems administration applications from the previous chapter. If you imagine that application with a few more features, and converted into a standalone GNOME application that can be run from the desktop, you have a fairly good idea of the *GNOME Workstation Command Center* (or GWCC). Figure 15-3 illustrates GWCC in action.

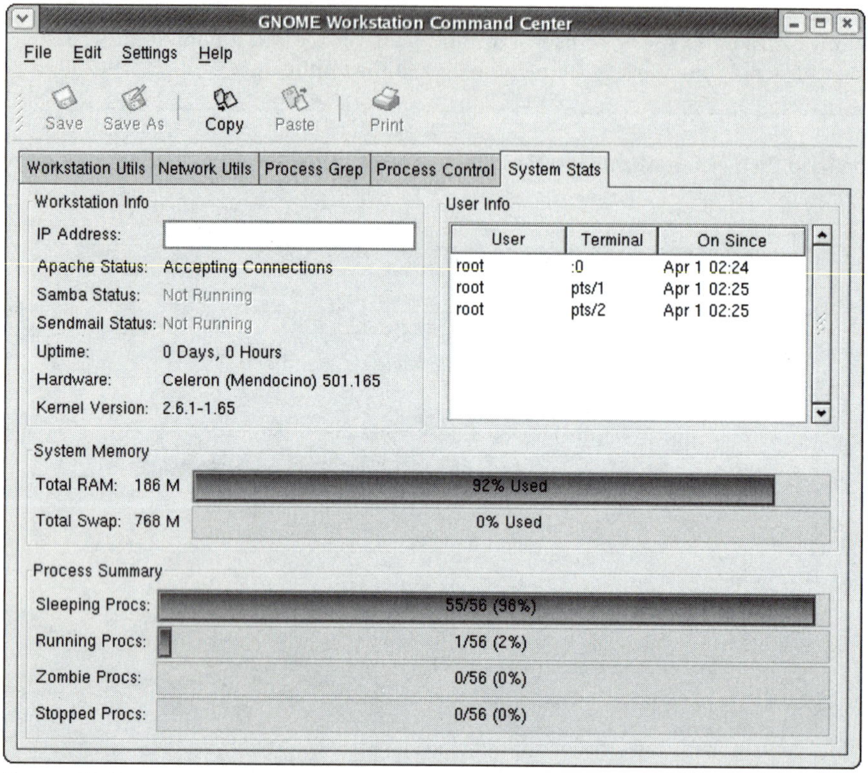

Figure 15-3

You can use GWCC to show network activity and connections, view current processes, monitor disk usage, and invoke network utilities. Because it is a standalone application (and does not rely on the existence of a Web server running in the background), you can conveniently use this application at any time without having to worry about possible security issues.

If you want to give this application a try, download the binary RPM package from one of the following sites on SourceForge.net:

```
http://gwcc.sourceforge.net
http://sourceforge.net/projects/gwcc/
```

To install the package, you can use the `rpm` command with the `-hvi` switches from the command line, like so:

```
# rpm -hvi gwcc-0.9.8-1.i386.rpm
```

Then you can execute it using the command `/usr/bin/gwcc`. Its convenience and small memory footprint may convince you to have it running all the time.

Webmin

GWCC and our sysadmin tool are definitely nice and useful applications. But now, you are about to get a look at the king of them all—*Webmin*. Before reading what Webmin can do, take a look at Figure 15-4.

Look at all of those features! Webmin, like our sysadmin application, provides a Web interface to a variety of system administration tasks. For example, you can use Webmin to do the following:

- Configure the Apache Web server
- Manipulate MySQL databases
- Modify Sendmail configuration
- Install RPM packages
- Set DNS client information
- Edit user information
- View system and network status

And that's just a small subset of Webmin's capabilities.

Figure 15-4

You might be surprised to learn that Webmin is also written in Perl. If you are interested in developing Perl applications, a look through Webmin's source code will provide you with a good learning experience. In addition, Webmin implements its own Web server rather than using an external one such as Apache or thttpd. This can be a double-edged sword. Because the server and the applications are closely tied together, there is better integration and a higher level of security. You do not have to worry about taking the time to learn how to manually install or configure any extra components. Unfortunately, this type of integration can be a security risk as well, albeit a small one. The widely used Web servers, such as Apache, are being used and abused by a large community of users, hackers, and developers on a regular basis, so any bugs or security holes found are typically fixed very quickly. On the other hand, you can't depend on the same amount of response and support by the smaller number of Webmin developers, and rightly so. Having said that, however, there are no outstanding security issues with Webmin at the time of writing this chapter.

You can download a compressed TAR archive or binary RPM package from the following:

```
www.webmin.com
www.webmin.com/download.html
```

Once you've downloaded it, you can install it in much the same manner as GWCC. Webmin is one application that you should thoroughly use because it will teach you a lot about your Linux system and how to maintain it properly.

RT: The Request Tracker

Now let's shift gears a bit and cover a different type of administration application. If you are the administrator for a multiuser system, no doubt, you will receive all types of requests from your users, such as the following:

- Can you give me more disk quota?
- I accidentally deleted my presentation. Can I get it back?
- I need to be able to log in from home. Can I?
- Can I install the latest version of Java?

If you get a lot of these requests, it soon becomes very difficult to keep track of who asked what and when. This is where the *Request Tracker* comes to the rescue. RT is a ticketing system/bug tracker that allows you to manage requests from users by storing them in a central repository, assigning priorities, and keeping track of resolutions and dates.

If you haven't guessed it already, RT is also written in Perl. You can download the source code and documentation from the following:

```
www.bestpractical.com/rt/
www.fsck.com/rtfm/
```

To install, follow the instructions specified in the second URL listed. Unfortunately, the installation process can get a bit laborious because you need to have a Web server and the MySQL database engine installed. (Web server installation is covered in Chapter 9, and MySQL is discussed at the end of this chapter.) However, after you have RT installed and are using it actively, you will wonder how you ever managed as an administrator without it.

Development Applications

If you're interested in developing your own applications, or if you simply enjoyed the material in Chapter 13, this section is for you. It looks at a number of development tools, including editors and integrated development environments (IDEs), and several programming languages.

jEdit

Before you can start to write code, you need a good and useful editor. The standard Fedora Core distribution comes with a whole slew of text editors, including `vi`, `gedit`, and `emacs`. However, you should also take a look at jEdit, which touts itself as the "open source programmer's text editor."

jEdit has a number of interesting features, including autoindenting of code, syntax highlighting for languages, and special plug-ins that extend the core functionality of the editor. These plug-ins implement, among other features, connections to FTP servers to transfer files, access to the external shell, and support for interfacing with project management applications. You can see some of these features in Figure 15-5.

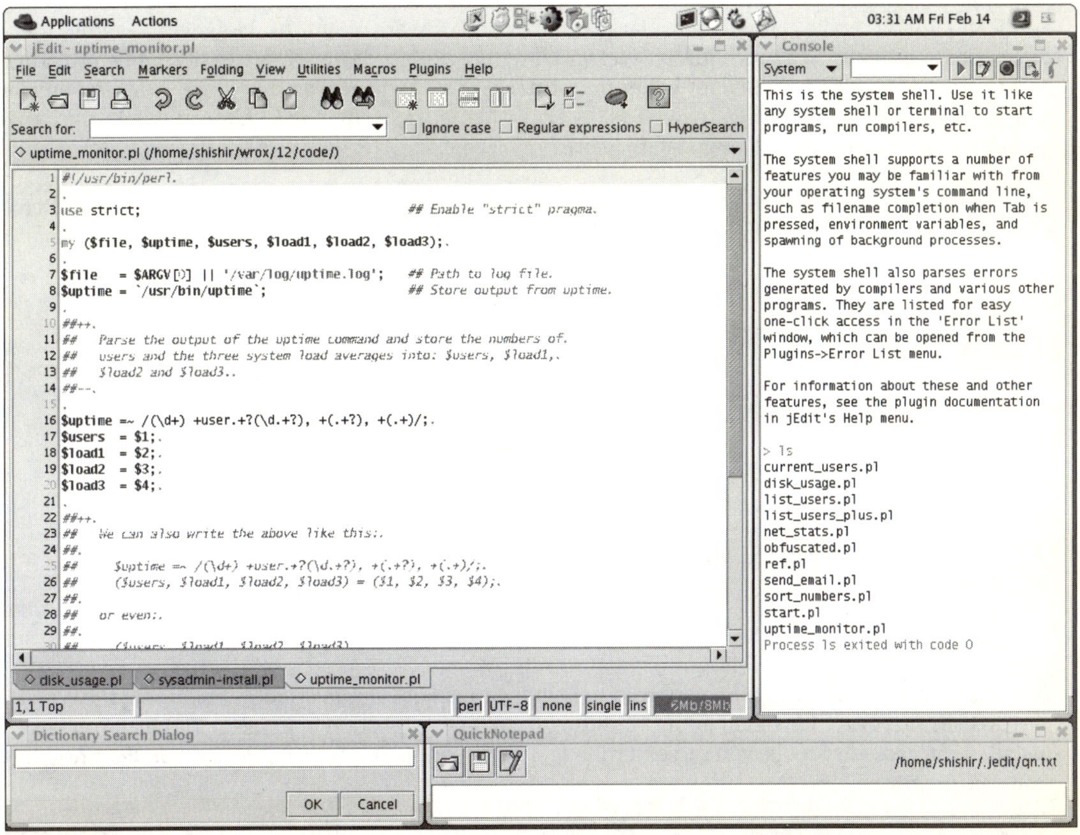

Figure 15-5

If you're ready to download and try this editor, you can download the binary RPM package from the following:

```
www.jedit.org
www.jedit.org/index.php?page=download
```

You can use the `rpm` command to install the application from the command line.

Note that before you can use the editor, you need to make sure that you have the Java language compiler installed on your system. You can do this by downloading the Java 2 Standard Edition (J2SE) Runtime Environment from either Sun Microsystems at `http://sun.java.com` *or from IBM DeveloperWorks at* `www.ibm.com/developerworks/java`*; the IBM version is more optimized for Linux..*

Then, go ahead and type **jedit** and you are on your way to developing some cool applications.

Developing C/C++ Applications

We discussed Perl and how to develop applications with it in Chapter 13. The C programming language is similar to Perl, in both syntax and operation. It too has high-level constructs, can produce efficient applications, and can be compiled on a large number of hardware platforms. However, C allows the developer to program at a much lower level and interface with hardware more easily, while providing greater control and the potential for better performance. This is the reason that other programming languages, such as Perl and Python, as well as the Linux kernel are written in C. Unfortunately, this power also makes C a more difficult language to learn.

Most of the software applications that you will see at Freshmeat.net and SourceForge.net are written in C (or its object-oriented counterpart, C++). Here's a simple program written in C to give you a taste:

```
[ number.c ]

#include <stdio.h>

int main(void)
{
   int number;

   printf ("Enter a number: \n");
   scanf("%d", &number);
   printf("You entered %d, am I correct?\n", number);

   return (0);
}
```

For you to compile this program, you need to install various development tools, including the *gcc compiler,* which are covered in detail in the "Building from Source" section in Chapter 11. Once you have installed the necessary tools, you can enter the following commands to compile and run the preceding example program:

```
$ gcc -o number number.c
$ ./number
Enter a number: 79
You entered 79, am I correct?
```

This creates a binary executable called `number`. For example, the `*.exe` files that you see on the Windows platform are examples of binary executables that have been created by a compiled language, such as C or C++. In fact, this is one of the major differences between Perl and C; Perl is an *interpreted* language, so the interpreter has to parse the program code each time it is run. By contrast, C and C++ are *compiled* languages—you compile the code into binary some time before it is needed.

To make C and C++ development easier, you can use one of the various integrated development environment (IDE) applications in existence. These types of tools provide you with a single integrated interface from which to edit, compile, link, and debug your applications, eliminating the need to jump between your editor, your command line, and your debugger. Take a look at the *Anjuta DevStudio* in action in Figure 15-6.

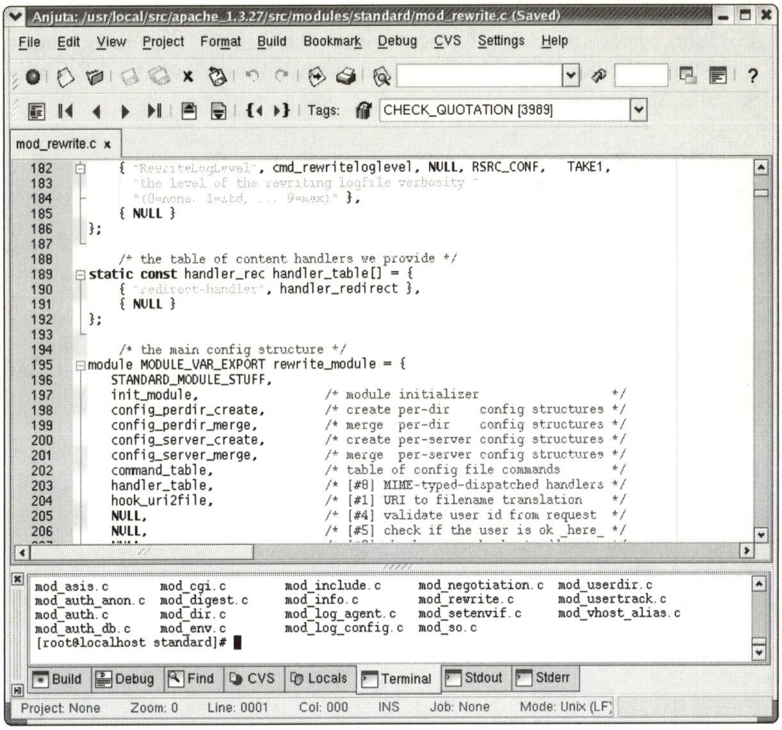

Figure 15-6

You can download this IDE in binary RPM package format from the following Web sites:

```
http://anjuta.org
http://anjuta.sourceforge.net
```

Then, you can install it using the `rpm` command. You will need to play with the IDE for a while before you start to feel comfortable with its functionality. And once you are ready to develop serious C or C++ applications, you can find a host of resources and helpful tutorials on the Web, including the following sites:

```
www.cs.cf.ac.uk/Dave/C/CE.html
www.desy.de/gna/html/cc/Tutorial/tutorial.html
```

Developing Python Applications

What is it with these scripting languages anyway, with names such as Perl and Python? *Python* is an object-oriented interpreted language that shares many similarities with Perl, such as the following:

- High-level syntax and constructs
- Complex data types, such as arrays and hashes
- Powerful regular expression support
- Large source code, module, and extension repository
- Active community of developers

There is a fierce rivalry between Perl and Python users, each claiming that their language is better. You might want to read the following two columns where each author tries to make a case for why one language is superior to the other:

```
www.linuxjournal.com/article.php?sid=3882
www.perl.com/pub/a/language/versus/python.html
```

In reality, these two languages support much the same functionality. The choice of language boils down to which syntax you prefer. Take a look at this example, which is identical in functionality to the `list_users.pl` example in Chapter 13:

```
[ list_users.py ]

#!/usr/local/bin/python

import sys

try:
    file = open('/etc/passwd', 'r')
except IOError, err:
    sys.stderr.write("Cannot open file: %s\n" % err.strerror)
    sys.exit(1)

for line in file:
    if line.find(':') != -1:
        data = line.split(':')
        print "%s, %s" % (data[0], data[4])

file.close()
```

In fact, the majority of the Fedora Core installation scripts and GUI applets are written in Python, so it is likely that the interpreter and most necessary libraries should already be installed on your system.

To find documentation, tutorials, and examples of Python scripts and modules, visit the Python home page and the Vaults of Parnassus (the equivalent to Perl's CPAN):

```
www.python.org
www.vex.net/parnassus/
```

Although the development cycle for creating applications using a scripting language is often simpler than for using a compiled language, you can nonetheless still use an IDE to improve your efficiency. The Komodo IDE by ActiveState is one that you can use with both Python and Perl (see Figure 15-7).

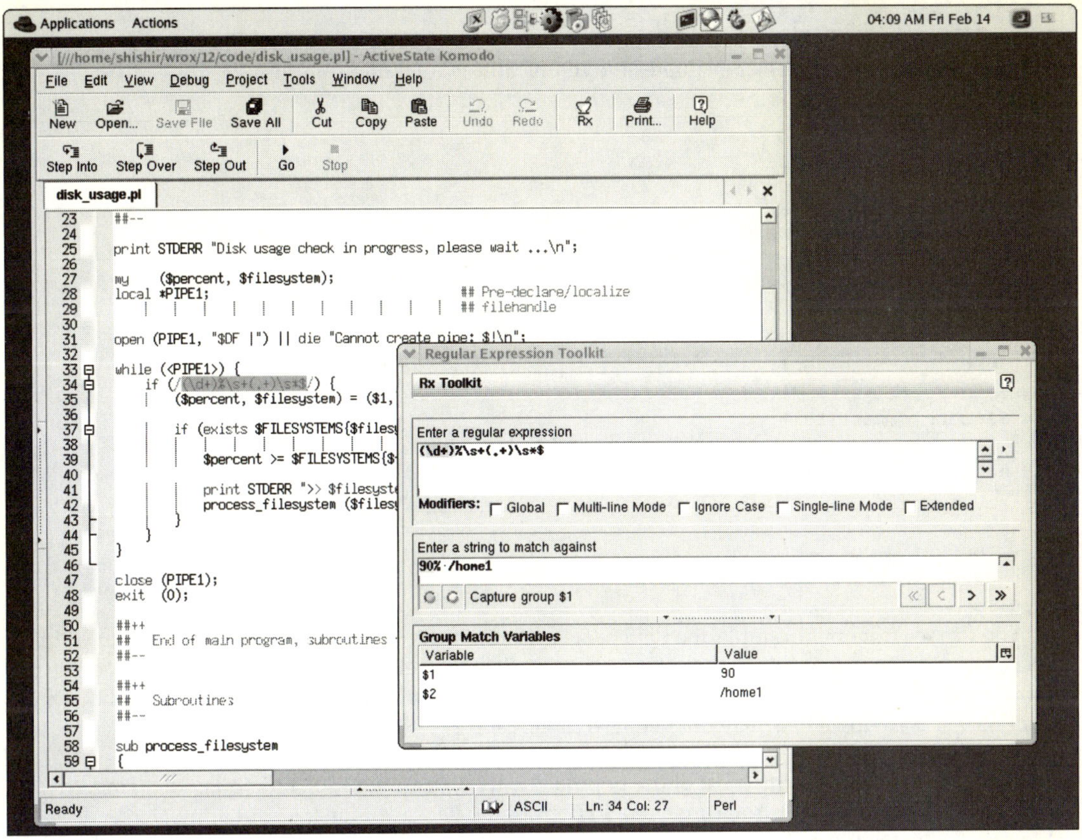

Figure 15-7

You can find Komodo at `www.activestate.com/Products/Komodo/`.

Komodo is a commercial application that costs $29 for a single user license at the time of this writing. Having said that, it is well worth the cost and can save you a lot of valuable time when developing large-scale applications.

PHP: Hypertext Preprocessor

Have you ever wanted to develop Web applications? The *PHP Hypertext Preprocessor* (or just PHP) is a cross-platform scripting language. It was designed primarily for Web development, although it can be used for other purposes as well.

To understand how PHP works, it might help to compare it to the Perl sysadmin application. The sysadmin application keeps all of the HTML code in separate templates and uses Perl's `HTML::Template` module to replace specially marked tokens with dynamic values on the fly. This allows you to keep the logic separate from the display semantics.

With PHP, on the other hand, you take the opposite approach. You can embed PHP code within the HTML, and the PHP processor evaluates it dynamically. Here is an example:

```
[ time.phtml ]

<html>
<head>
  <title>Simple Time Example</title>
</head>
<body bgcolor="#FFFFFF">
<?php

$hour   = date("G");
$minute = date("i");
$second = date("s");

echo "<font>$hour:$minute:$second</font>\n";

?>
</body>
</html>
```

As you can see from this example, the PHP code is enclosed within a special `<?php ... ?>` tag; within each page, you can use as many of these tags as you want. Some developers prefer this approach because they can keep the display and logic in one place, without fear of misplacing or deleting the additional dependent files. It boils down to a matter of personal preference.

Fortunately, PHP comes with most of the popular Linux distributions, including Fedora Core, so it is just a matter of installing it. You can install PHP from the Package Management applet located at Main Menu ➪ System Settings ➪ Add/Remove Applications. If you click the Web Server option (which is in the Servers category) and examine its Details, you will see a number of packages selected, including mod_perl, mod_python, mod_ssl, php, squid, tux, and webalizer. Because we will not use most of these tools, we will install only the PHP-related packages shown in Figure 15-8.

Click the Install Packages button to install the packages; when installation is complete, you will have a PHP-enabled Apache Web server. You can refer to Chapter 9 for more information on how to configure the Web server.

PHP supports a very large amount of functionality that allows you to build all types of Web applications, from dynamically generated graphics to database manipulation. Many resources are available to help you make the most of PHP's power. For example, you can find extensive documentation on PHP at its Web site:

```
http://conf.php.net
www.php.net
```

You could also try *Beginning PHP4,* by Chris Lea et al., from Wrox Press.

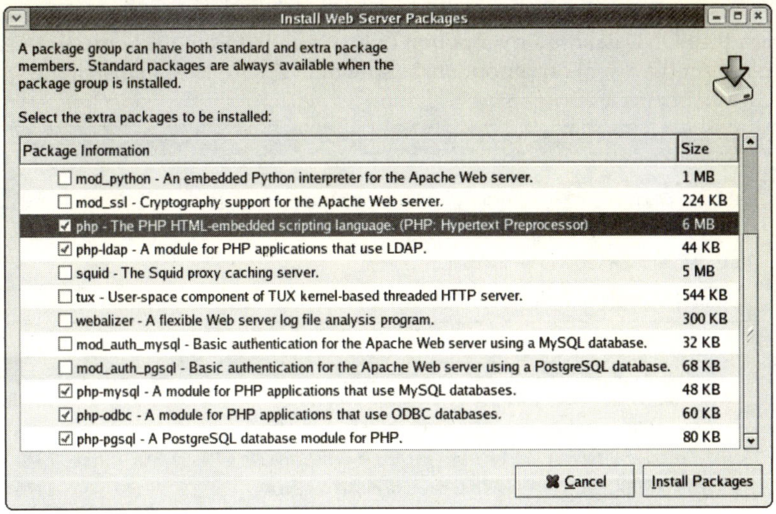

Figure 15-8

We have discussed C, C++, Perl, Python, and PHP, but these represent only a small number of the available programming languages. Others, such as Tcl, Ruby, and Smalltalk, are also quite popular. You can really pick and choose which one suits your needs, but you should be aware of the following:

- If you are intent on learning a language, learn one that provides access to developers who are familiar with the language, so you can avoid some of the common programming pitfalls.
- Look at as many examples as possible, and search for any available modules or extensions to cut down on your development effort.
- PHP has a smaller learning curve than Perl. For limited Web applications, PHP is preferable, although Perl and Python are more flexible and have a much wider scope.
- You should typically not tackle C or C++ if you are new to development; it is better to start with Perl or Python and move up when you are ready.

We mentioned database manipulation in the context of PHP Web applications. But what database do we use? Certainly, Oracle and Sybase are not released under any of the open source licenses, but MySQL is.

MySQL Database Engine

MySQL is probably the most widely used open source database engine. Although it does not support some of the enterprise database features found in Oracle or Sybase, such as online (hot) backups, sophisticated transactions, and an internal procedural language, it has more than enough functionality and power to suit most applications. Best of all, it is released under the GPL license, which means you can use it free of charge for both commercial and non-commercial applications.

You can find the MySQL installers, as well as documentation and information on support plans, at `www.mysql.com`.

MySQL also comes with the Fedora Core distribution. To install it, launch the Add and Remove Software applet and click the SQL Database Server option (which you'll find in the Servers category). Click the Details tab and select the mysql-server option, as shown in Figure 15-9, to install the application.

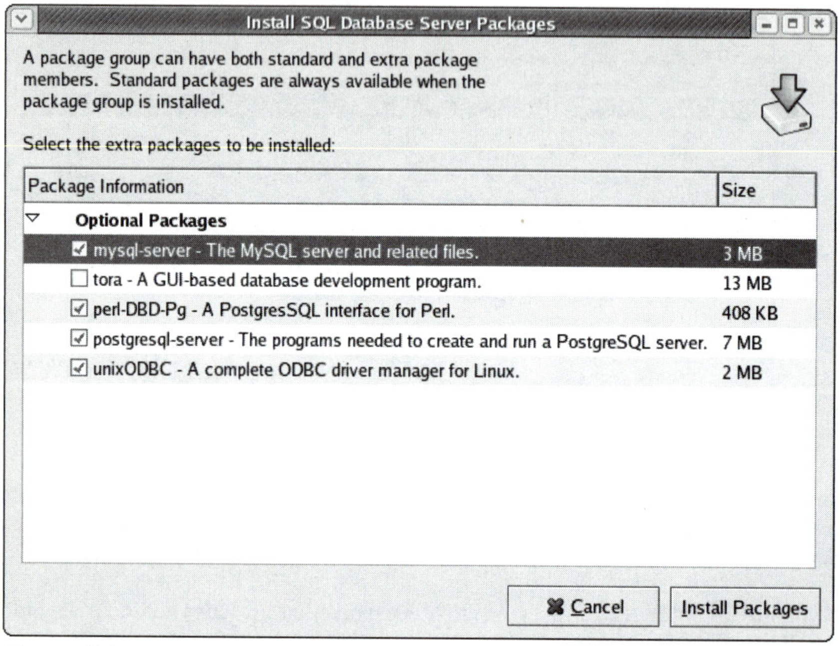

Figure 15-9

After you have installed MySQL, you can enter the following commands as the root user to start the server and view a list of the database users stored in the internal user table:

```
# /etc/init.d/mysqld start
# mysql mysql
mysql> select * from user;
...
mysql> \q
```

The `select` query that you see is an example of Structured Query Language (SQL). Most of the commercial relational database systems, including Oracle, Sybase, Informix, as well as open source alternatives MySQL and PostgreSql, allow you to use SQL to manipulate the database. You can find more information on SQL at the following:

```
http://sqlzoo.net/
www.w3schools.com/sql/sql_intro.asp
```

If you want to avoid learning SQL, you can use one of the many database administration GUI tools that exist—such as *Aqua Data Studio*, available from `www.aquafold.com`.

Figure 15-10 illustrates the convenience of this application.

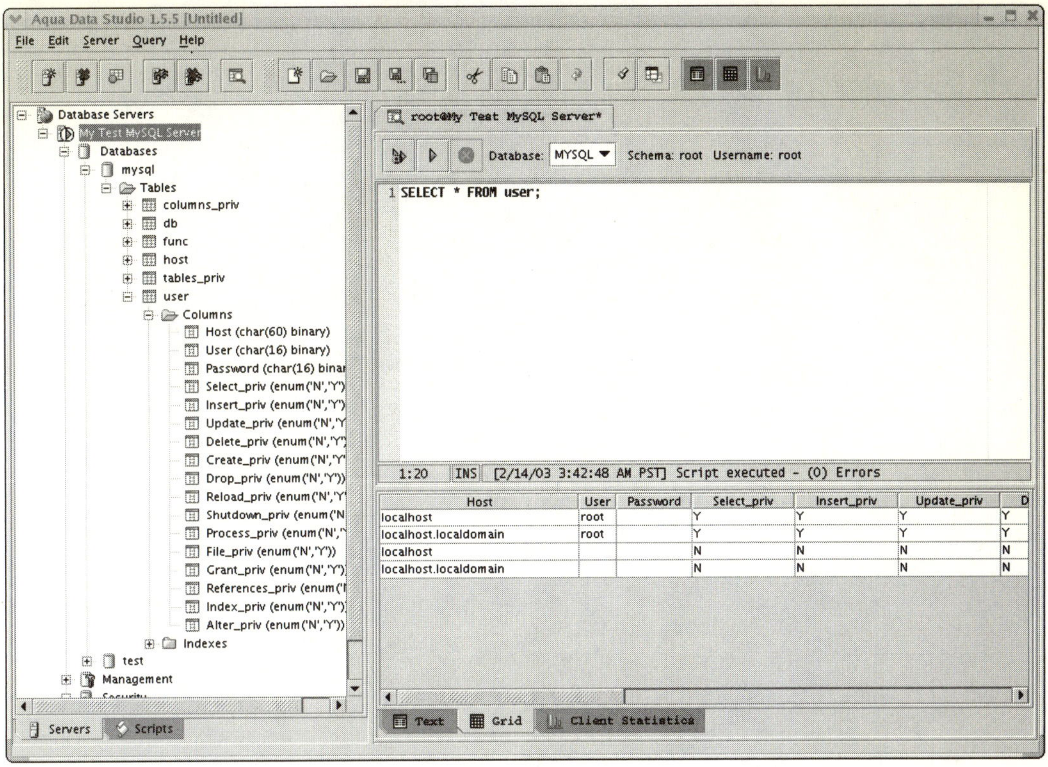

Figure 15-10

When you installed MySQL from the Add and Remove Software applet, you may have noticed a listing for the PostgreSql database server. While this database engine is not used as widely as MySQL, it is designed for the enterprise and supports many features that are found in Oracle and Sybase but are lacking in MySQL. Feel free to investigate and learn more about this application.

Summary

We hope you enjoyed the brief tour of some of the more intriguing and useful open source applications and utilities. However, we have covered just the tip of the iceberg; there is a vast amount of software out there that you can use to your advantage. Most of this software is not only free from a financial standpoint, but comes packaged with the entire source code. You can modify this source code to fix bugs, optimize functionality, and add new features. Moreover, even if you are not in a position to make these types of changes, you will at least have some peace of mind knowing that it is possible.

Installing and configuring your Linux system is just the beginning. You should take some time to explore all of the resources presented in this chapter. Surf over to `www.osdn.com`, search for your favorite applications, and download and test them out. Eventually, you will reach a point where you'll want to implement your own open source software or modify one that exists to suit your needs. Then, you can decide on what programming language to use and how to develop an application. The bottom line is that you will be able to make your operating system run the way you want it to.

A

Answers to Exercises

Chapter 1

1. If you add new hardware to your system, how do you configure it?

A. Fedora comes with Kudzu, a hardware auto-detection and configuration tool, installed by default. Kudzu runs at boot-up and detects changes in the system's hardware configuration. Once it detects new or removed hardware, it gives you the option of configuring the added or removed hardware.

2. When you switch on a computer on which you've installed a dual-boot system, the boot loader will show you two options to boot into. If you do not choose, it will boot the system into the default choice. How do you change the default choice?

A. Fedora uses the *grub* boot-loader. Grub can be configured to specify one of the dual-boot choices to be the default. You need to modify the appropriate configuration file, which in this case is `/boot/grub/grub.conf`. Here is a typical `grub.conf` file:

```
# grub.conf generated by anaconda
# --TEXT DELETED--
#boot=/dev/hda
default=0
timeout=10
splashimage=(hd0,1)/boot/grub/splash.xpm.gz
title Windows 2000
    rootnoverify (hd0,0)
    chainloader +1
title Fedora Core (2.6.1-1.65)
    root (hd0,1)
    kernel /boot/vmlinuz-2.6.1-1.65 ro root=LABEL=/ rhgb
    initrd /boot/initrd-2.6.1-1.65.img
```

The `default` parameter determines which of the two operating systems is the default for booting up. The `title` sections indicate the two options; you can see a title section for Microsoft Windows and another one for Fedora. The first title option is numbered 0, the second one 1, and so on. Since the default parameter is set to 0—that is, the title corresponding to Microsoft Windows—the system will boot up into Windows if you don't pick one of the choices at boot time. You could change the `default` parameter to 1, which would cause Fedora to boot up by default. *Caution*: Be very careful when editing the `grub.conf` file, as you may render your system unbootable if the file becomes corrupted. Refer to the grub man page for further details on configuring grub.

Chapter 2

1. Change the wallpaper (the background) on your desktop.

A. Either right-click on the desktop and select Change Desktop Background or click on the Main Menu (the Red Hat icon at the bottom-left corner of the screen), selecting Preferences ➪ Control Center and clicking on Desktop Wallpaper.

2. Locate a file called `magic` on the system. Hint: You can use the `locate` command to do this.

A. Just type **locate magic**, and the `locate` command will print a list of file names with the word *magic* in them. You may also use the Search Tool, invoked from the Main Menu by choosing Search for Files.

3. Check your system's load average.

A. You can find the load average of the system with the `uptime` command. Review the section on monitoring the system (in Chapter 2) to learn more.

Chapter 3

1. What are the different services running on your machine?

A. You can access details of services configured on your system from the Main Menu by choosing System Settings ➪ Server Settings ➪ Services.

2. Determine the Ethernet address of your network card.

A. Use the `ifconfig` command with the `-a` option to determine the Ethernet address of the Ethernet card. Note that the Ethernet address is different from the IP address; the Ethernet address is the hardware address of the card and remains the same if you install the card on a different machine. The `HWaddr` field in the output of ifconfig displays the Ethernet address.

3. Web sites use cookies to track your use of the site. Determine which sites are using cookies to track you.

A. From the Mozilla Web browser, choose Edit ➪ Preferences ➪ Privacy & Security ➪ Cookies. On the panel displayed, click the Manage Stored Cookies button. This lists the cookies currently used by various sites to track your browsing activity.

Chapter 4

1. Create a very simple home page using the word processor as part of Office and then save it as an HTML file so it can be easily viewed by both Microsoft and Netscape browsers.

A. Use Writer but make sure you set the HTML Compatibility options to HTML 3.2 before saving to disk as a HTML file.

2. Use the browser shipped with Fedora to open the HTML home page that you created in Exercise 1.

A. In the Mozilla Browser, use the File ➪ Open menu option to open the HTML file from disk.

3. Using a tool provided with Fedora, extract tracks from one of your favorite music CDs and save them to an electronic format that can be played from disk without the need to have the CD loaded in the CD drive.

A. Use the CDPARANOIA command line utility with a command line of `cdparanoia -B -w "1-"` to extract the tracks to the current working directory.

4. Considering that the files you extracted in Exercise 3 can take up valuable disk space, use a Fedora utility to compress them into a single archive and thus free up some disk space.

A. Use the file-roller utility to create an archive that contains the .WAV files extracted in exercise 3.

Chapter 5

1. Calculate the size of all files under the `/etc` directory.

A. The `du -ah /etc` command prints the size of all files under the `/etc` directory. The `-a` option to the `du` command prints the sizes for all files in the subdirectories, rather than just the size of the directory and subdirectories. The `-h` option prints the output in a human-readable form, indicating the size of the files in bytes, kilobytes, or megabytes. Refer to the `du` man page for more options.

2. Create a file called `story.txt` containing the following line of text:

```
The quick brown fox jumps over the lazy dog
```

Use the `sed` command to change the contents of the file to the following:

```
The quick brown dog jumps over the lazy fox
```

A. The following commands will modify the content of the file as desired:

```
$ sed -e 's;dog;fox;' simple.txt > temporary.txt
$ sed -e 's;brown fox;brown dog;' temporary.txt > simple.txt
```

The first `sed` command substitutes the word *dog* for the word *fox*. This is redirected to a file called `temporary.txt`. This file will now contain the text "The quick brown fox jumps over the lazy fox". The second `sed` command needs to convert only the first occurrence of *fox* into *dog*. Therefore it replaces the two words *brown fox* with the words *brown dog*, resulting in the text "The quick brown dog jumps over the lazy fox".

3. Use the `find` command to list files that are greater than 500KB in size created by users of the system.

A. Users' files are typically stored under the `/home` directory. Because you need to search files belonging to other users, you will need to assume root privileges either by using the `su` command or by logging in as root before executing the `find` command. The `find` command line for obtaining the list of files greater than 500KB created by users is as follows:

```
# find /home -type f -size +500k
```

The `-type f` option indicates that we are looking for files (not directories or other filesystem objects). The `-size` option indicates that our search criterion is the size of files, and `+500k` indicates that we are searching for files larger than 500KB.

Chapter 6

1. List the complete command lines of all the processes belonging to the root user.

A. The command `ps -auxww` lists the complete command lines of all processes running on the system. This output can be filtered using the `grep` command by piping the output of the `grep` command to the `ps` command. The final command line would then be `ps -auxww | grep root`.

2. Modify the command prompt to display the current working directory.

A. The command prompt can be set by modifying the `PS1` variable. The macro for indicating the current directory is `\w`. Therefore, the following command will set the prompt to the current working directory:

```
$ export PS1='[\w] '
```

3. Use `cron` to run the `date` command once every 15 minutes.

A. Using the `crontab -e` command, edit the crontab entries. Add the following line to have the `date` command executed once every 15 minutes:

```
0-59/15 * * * * /bin/date > /tmp/date.out
```

The line above will cause `cron` to execute the `date` command every 15 minutes and send the output to the file `/tmp/date.out`.

4. Write a shell script that will maintain a log of users logged on to the system. Logging should happen every 5 minutes.

A. The following shell script when saved to a file and executed will log the list of current users of the system every 5 minutes into the file `/tmp/users.out`. Remember to set executable permissions for the shell script file using the `chmod` command (e.g., `chmod +x filename`).

```
while true; do sleep 300; date; who; echo "============"; done

>>/tmp/users.out
```

Chapter 7

1. Fedora Core can automatically detect a number of digital cameras as if they were external USB disks or memory keys. Supposing that your camera is recognized as `/dev/sda1`, configure your system so that users can mount their cameras and access the pictures using `/mnt/digicam` as a mount point.

A. First, create /mnt/digicam with the following command:

```
mkdir /mnt/digicam
```

Then edit /etc/fstab and add the following line:

```
/dev/sda1     /mnt/digicam     auto     noauto,user,kudzu     0     0
```

2. Configure sudo to allow eziodm to install new software packages with the following command and no need to type a password:

```
rpm -ivh packagename.rpm
```

A. Edit /etc/sudoers and add the following line:

```
eziodm        ALL = NOPASSWD: /bin/rpm -ivh
```

Chapter 8

1. Start the RPM Package Management Tool.

A. To start the RPM Package Management Tool, select System Settings ➪ Add/Remove Applications from the Main Menu.

You can also start the RPM Package Management Tool from the command line by typing the following:

```
$ system-config-packages
```

2. Install a package ncftp, an improved FTP client, using the RPM command line interface.

A. Find out the ncftp packages from the Fedora distribution and execute the following command at the command line:

```
rpm -ivh ncftp-3.1.7-2.i386.rpm
/etc/security/selinux/file_contexts: No such file or directory
Preparing...                ########################################### [100%]
   1:ncftp                  ########################################### [100%]
```

3. Display the RPM package information (for example, ncftp) on the command line.

A. To display the RPM package information on the command line, execute the following on the shell prompt:

```
   rpm -qip ncftp-3.1.7-2.i386.rpm
Name        : ncftp                        Relocations: /usr
Version     : 3.1.7                             Vendor: Red Hat, Inc.
Release     : 2                             Build Date: Tue 17 Feb 2004
10:21:31 GMT
Install Date: (not installed)               Build Host:
tweety.devel.redhat.com
Group       : Applications/Internet         Source RPM: ncftp-3.1.7-2.src.rpm
Size        : 1077786                          License: Distributable
Signature   : DSA/SHA1, Wed 17 Mar 2004 19:15:02 GMT, Key ID da84cbd430c9ecf8
```

```
Packager    : Red Hat, Inc. <http://bugzilla.redhat.com/bugzilla>
URL         : http://www.ncftp.com/ncftp/
Summary     : An improved FTP client.
Description :
Ncftp is an improved FTP client. Ncftp's improvements include support
for command line editing, command histories, recursive gets, automatic
anonymous logins, and more.
```

4. Uninstall the same package, `ncftp`, using the RPM command line interface without verifying package dependencies.

A. To uninstall the rpm, execute the following command:

```
rpm -e --nodeps ncftp
```

5. Find a package that owns the file installed on your system (for example, `/bin/vi`).

A. To find a package that owns the file `/bin/vi`, execute the following command on the shell prompt:

```
rpm -qf /bin/vi
```

6. Display the package information and list the files installed by a package (for example, `wget`) on your system before even installing it.

A. To list the packages owned by a packages like `wget`, execute the following command on the shell prompt:

```
rpm -qpil wget-1.9.1-5.i386.rpm
Name        : wget                         Relocations: (not relocatable)
Version     : 1.9.1                             Vendor: Red Hat, Inc.
Release     : 5                             Build Date: Thu 11 Mar 2004
16:24:47 GMT
Install Date: (not installed)               Build Host:
tweety.devel.redhat.com
Group       : Applications/Internet         Source RPM: wget-1.9.1-5.src.rpm
Size        : 1210725                          License: GPL
Signature   : DSA/SHA1, Wed 17 Mar 2004 18:52:55 GMT, Key ID da84cbd430c9ecf8
Packager    : Red Hat, Inc. <http://bugzilla.redhat.com/bugzilla>
URL         : http://wget.sunsite.dk/
Summary     : A utility for retrieving files using the HTTP or FTP protocols.
Description :
GNU Wget is a file retrieval utility which can use either the HTTP or
FTP protocols. Wget features include the ability to work in the
background while you are logged out, recursive retrieval of
directories, file name wildcard matching, remote file timestamp
storage and comparison, use of Rest with FTP servers and Range with
HTTP servers to retrieve files over slow or unstable connections,
support for Proxy servers, and configurability.
/etc/wgetrc
/usr/bin/wget
/usr/share/doc/wget-1.9.1
/usr/share/doc/wget-1.9.1/AUTHORS
/usr/share/doc/wget-1.9.1/MAILING-LIST
/usr/share/doc/wget-1.9.1/NEWS
.......
```

```
/usr/share/locale/zh_CN/LC_MESSAGES/wget.mo
/usr/share/locale/zh_TW/LC_MESSAGES/wget.mo
/usr/share/man/man1/wget.1.gz
```

7. Use up2date to list the package updates available to download without using X.

A. Execute the following command on the shell prompt:

```
up2date -nox -l
```

8. Use yum help to find the option to check for package updates for your system, and then run the command to do the same.

A. Read the yum manual by executing the following command on the shell prompt:

```
man yum
```

To find the package update using yum, execute the following command on the shell prompt:

```
yum list update
```

9. Use APT to update the package indexes from the sources. In other words, use APT to check for updates from the RPM sources.

A. To check the package updates using `apt-get`, execute the following command on the shell prompt:

```
apt-get update
```

Chapter 9

1. What do LAN, WAN, TCP/IP, PPP, and ISDN stand for?

A. These abbreviations stand for the following:

- **LAN:** Local Area Network
- **WAN:** Wide Area Network
- **TCP/IP:** Transmission Control Protocol / Internet Protocol
- **PPP:** Point-to-Point Protocol
- **ISDN:** Integrated Services Digital Network

2. Determine a Public Class C IP address and specify it with netmask.

A. `192.168.1.10` with a netmask of `255.255.255.0` is a Public Class C IP address.

3. Determine various IP ranges available to be used as Private IP addresses for your LAN.

A. Following are the Private IP ranges available to be used in your LAN:

- 10.0.0.0–10.255.255.255
- 172.16.0.0–172.31.255.255
- 192.168.0.0–192.168.255.255

4. Write down the steps to change the Apache 2 Web server port number from 80 to 81, on which Apache will listen for incoming requests.

A. Following are the steps to change the Apache port number to listen for inkling requests:

a. Open the `/etc/httpd/conf/httpd.conf` file in your preferred editor.

b. Search for the following configuration line: *Listen 80*

c. Change this line to the following: *Listen 81*

d. Save the file.

e. Restart the Apache Web Server using the service command as follows: `service http restart`

5. Check the Apache Web server configuration file (`httpd.conf`) for syntax errors.

A. To check the `httpd.conf` configuration file for syntax errors, use the following command: `service httpd configtest`.

6. Restart the Apache Web server without affecting any connected clients.

A. To restart the Apache Web Server without affecting any connected client and without any downtime on the Web site hosted on Apache Web Server, use the following command: `service httpd graceful`.

The `graceful` option restarts the Apache httpd daemon without aborting currently open connections.

7. Using the RPM command-line interface, determine the FTP server currently installed on your system.

A. You can find out any RPM package installed on your system by using the following command: `rpm -qi vsftpd`.

If you can't remember the exact name of the package, you can also search for a package using the following command to display the list of packages installed on your system with *ftp* in their package names: `rpm -qa|grep ftp`.

Once you learn the name of the package, you can get more information about that package using the `rpm -qi [`*`package name`*`]` command.

8. Change the FTP greeting banner on your `vsftpd` server and test it.

A. To change the ftp banner on your vsftpd server, follow these steps:

a. Open the `vsftpd` configuration file `/etc/vsftpd/vsftpd.conf` in your preferred text editor.

b. Find the following configuration directive: `#ftpd_banner=Welcome to blah FTP service`.

c. Uncomment and change the preceding configuration directive to look something like the following: `ftpd_banner=Welcome to the Wrox Press FTP service`.

d. Save the configuration file and restart the `vsftpd` service as follows: `service vsftpd restart`.

9. Check the print queue using the command line utilities.

A. You can check the print queue on the print server using the `lpq` command line utility as follows: `lpq -a`.

10. Check the Samba configuration file (`/etc/samba/smb.conf`) for correctness.

A. The SAMBA package comes with a command line utility called `testparm` to check the SAMBA configuration file. Execute the command on the command line to check the `/etc./samba/smb.conf` file as follows: `testparm`.

11. Check the mail queue on your Mail server.

A. Execute the `mailq` command on the command line as follows: `mailq`.

12. What is the location of the DHCP server configuration file?

A. The location of the DHCP configuration file is `/etc/dhcpd.conf`.

Chapter 10

Scenario: You have a Fedora Core 2 system that is to function as a Web proxy server. Client machines are on the `192.168.1/24` network. The Internet connection is via a router on the `172.20.5/24` network. Your proxy server has two network interfaces: `eth0` is `192.168.1.100` and `eth1` is `172.20.5.17`. Both interfaces use a subnet mask of `255.255.255.0` (24-bits). Assume that the network routes and proxy services (`squid` and `named`) are correctly configured.

1. Design firewall rules (using `iptables`) to implement the following requirements.

a. No incoming connections are allowed on the `172.20.5.17` interface.

b. The only permitted outgoing connections on the `172.20.5.17` interface are for DNS, FTP, HTTP, and HTTPS traffic from the proxy server.

c. Two machines (IP addresses `192.168.1.201` and `192.168.1.155`) are to be allowed to connect using SSH.

d. All other machines in the `192.168.1/24` network are allowed to connect on port 3128 only (the port that the Squid Web proxy server is listening on) and port 53 (for DNS queries).

e. Allow ICMP traffic.

f. All other connections (incoming or outgoing) must be blocked.

g. Log attempts by machines on the `192.168.1/24` network to use Telnet or FTP to access the proxy server.

The solutions given here are just some of the many possible sets of `iptables` *rules that will meet the stated requirements. If you are going to try these out on a remote machine (that is, one where you have to connect via a network), you run the risk of blocking your own connection that you are using to configure* `iptables` *and therefore not being able to correct the problem.*

One way to prevent yourself from being locked out is to set up an `at` *job that will disable the firewall in, say, 15 minutes so that if your connections do get blocked, you will have to wait only 15 minutes at most before being able to reconnect and fix the problem. The command to do this is:*

```
echo "/sbin/service iptables stop " | at now + 15 minutes
```

The system will respond with a message similar to this:

```
job 11 at 2004-05-20 17:43
```

Now you can set up your `iptables` *rules, remembering to save them frequently with this command because they will get cleared when the* `at` *job runs.*

```
service iptables save
```

(Alternatively, you can edit the file `/etc/sysconfig/iptables-config` *and set the* `IPTABLES_SAVE_ON_STOP` *variable to* `yes` *and remove the* # *from the start of the line where it is set). If you are happy with the firewall configuration and want to stop the* `at` *job from running, use the following command:*

```
atrm job#
```

where `job#` *is the job number you were given when you set up the* `at` *job (11 in the preceding example).*

A. Deal with each firewall chain (`INPUT`, `OUTPUT`, and `FORWARD`) separately. For each chain, start by flushing the existing firewall rules set up by the system-config-securitylevel application, and set the default policy to DROP.

```
# INPUT chain

iptables -F INPUT               # Flush existing rules
iptables -P INPUT DROP          # Default policy set to DROP

# Accept incoming SSH connections on eth0 from 192.168.1.155.
# There is one rule for TCP and a similar one for UDP.
# Use the state module (-m state) so that the rule matches only
# new connections (--state NEW).
iptables -A INPUT -p tcp -i eth0 -s 192.168.1.155 --dport ssh \
-m state --state NEW -j ACCEPT
iptables -A INPUT -p udp -i eth0 -s 192.168.1.155 --dport ssh \
-m state --state NEW -j ACCEPT

# As previous pair of rules but for different source IP address
iptables -A INPUT -p tcp -i eth0 -s 192.168.1.201 --dport ssh \
-m state --state NEW -j ACCEPT
iptables -A INPUT -p udp -i eth0 -s 192.168.1.201 --dport ssh \
-m state --state NEW -j ACCEPT

# Accept incoming connections on port 3128 from 192.168.1/24 network
iptables -A INPUT -p tcp -i eth0 -s 192.168.1/24 --dport squid -j ACCEPT
iptables -A INPUT -p udp -i eth0 -s 192.168.1/24 --dport squid -j ACCEPT

# Accept incoming connections on port 53 from 192.168.1/24 network
iptables -A INPUT -p tcp -i eth0 -s 192.168.1/24 --dport domain -j ACCEPT
iptables -A INPUT -p udp -i eth0 -s 192.168.1/24 --dport domain -j ACCEPT
```

```
# Allow ICMP packets
iptables -A INPUT -p icmp -j ACCEPT

# Log unauthorized attempt to use Telnet or FTP
iptables -A INPUT -p tcp -i eth0 -s 192.168.1/24 --dport telnet -j LOG
iptables -A INPUT -p udp -i eth0 -s 192.168.1/24 --dport telnet -j LOG
iptables -A INPUT -p tcp -i eth0 -s 192.168.1/24 --dport ftp -j LOG
iptables -A INPUT -p udp -i eth0 -s 192.168.1/24 --dport ftp -j LOG

# Accept packets on any interface that are related to established connections
iptables -A INPUT -m state --state ESTABLISHED,RELATED -j ACCEPT
#
#
#
# OUTPUT chain
#
iptables -F OUTPUT
iptables -P OUTPUT DROP

# Allow outgoing packets on any interface that are part of established connections
iptables -A OUTPUT -m state --state ESTABLISHED,RELATED -j ACCEPT

# Allow outgoing packets on eth1 for HTTP, FTP, HTTPS and DNS.  Using the
# multiport match extension reduces the number of rules to two (one for
# UDP the other for TCP).  Note that the service name used by DNS is "domain".

iptables -A OUTPUT -p udp -i eth1 -m multiport --dports http, ftp, ftp-data, \
          https, domain -j ACCEPT
iptables -A OUTPUT -p tcp -i eth1 -m multiport --dports http, ftp, ftp-data, \
          https, domain -j ACCEPT

# Allow proxy to send ICMP packets
iptables -A OUTPUT -p icmp -j ACCEPT



# FORWARD chain

# The proxy server should not forward any packets, so drop everything.
iptables -F FORWARD
iptables -P FORWARD DROP
```

2. Make sure your rules will be applied each time the system boots.

A. Your customized `iptables` rules are saved to the file `/etc/sysconfig/iptables` by running the following command: `service iptables save`.

Rules in `/etc/sysconfig/iptables` are applied when the system boots and the `iptables` service starts. It is a good idea to make a backup of this configuration file.

3. After your proxy server has been running for a while, a new requirement is identified. Machines on the `192.168.1/24` network need to be able to make PPTP connections to an external VPN server with an IP address of `10.1.3.97`. Update the `iptables` rules to satisfy this requirement. (Assume that IP forwarding is enabled on your proxy server).

A. PPTP connections use TCP port 1723 and the GRE protocol (protocol number 47). Add the following rules to the rules defined in Exercise 1:

```
# FORWARD chain
#
# Additions for PPTP support.  These two rules specify the interfaces
# so that the PPTP control traffic on port 1723 is only forwarded in
# one direction - the VPN server
iptables -A FORWARD -p tcp -i eth0 -o eth1 -d 10.1.3.97 --dport 1723 -j ACCEPT
iptables -A FORWARD -p tcp -i eth1 -o eth0 -s 10.1.3.97 --sport 1723 -j ACCEPT

# Pass GRE traffic between networks.
iptables -A FORWARD -p gre -j ACCEPT
```

Chapter 11

1. Create a `crontab` entry to record the system load averages to a log file every 15 minutes, but only on Monday through Friday, from 8:00 a.m. to 6:00 p.m. Hint: Take a look at the following online resource to learn more about the `crontab` format: `http://www.opengroup.org/onlinepubs/007908799/xcu/crontab.html`.

A. If you came up with the following `crontab` entry, you are absolutely correct:

```
# min hour  day  mon  weekday  command
*/15  08-18 *    *    01-05    /usr/bin/uptime >> /var/log/load.log
```

2. Search the System Log file from the command line for other possible problems, such as warnings, errors, and failures.

A. Use the extended form of `grep`, or `egrep`, to specify a regular expression that will search for a number of errors in one fell swoop:

```
# grep -Ei 'fail|warning|error|bad|refused' /var/log/messages
```

Of course, you could have split this command into five separate commands, such as:

```
# grep -i fail    /var/log/messages
   # grep -i warning /var/log/messages
   ...
```

But using the regular expression allows you to get an aggregate listing of possible issues. You can learn more about regular expressions in Chapter 13.

3. Modify `syslog.conf` to log FTP-related messages to another file, such as `/var/log/ftp.log`. Hint: Each entry in `syslog.conf` has three separate components: the messages to be considered, the destination, and any user-defined comments.

A. This one is easy to solve; it can be done with one line:

```
ftp.*        /var/log/ftp.log       ## log FTP messages
```

4. Find all compressed tar archives within the `/usr/local` directory hierarchy and archive them to an ISO image so you can burn them to a CD-ROM and then delete them to free up disk space.

A. You can accomplish this task in a number of ways. Two approaches are represented here:

```
# mkisofs -o source-200403121800.iso \
                 -V SourceCode-2004-03-10-1800 \
                 -J -R -v \
                 `find /usr/local -name '*.tar.gz'`

   # find /usr/local -name '*.tar.gz' | xargs --verbose \
               mkisofs -o source-200403121800.iso \
                       -V SourceCode-2004-03-10-1800 \
                       -J -R -v
```

5. Try to build and install the `enscript` application from its source code. This application converts ASCII files to PostScript and also supports a number of options to customize the PostScript output. For example, you can use `enscript` to print your scripts and other source code in an easy-to-read two-column format with line numbers. Hint: Read the `INSTALL` and `README` documents that come with the package for any special instructions.

A. The procedure to build `enscript` is identical to the one that we used to build the `gFTP` application:

```
# cd /usr/local/src
   # wget http://www.iki.fi/mtr/genscript/enscript-1.6.4.tar.gz
   # tar -zxvf enscript-1.6.4.tar.gz
   # cd enscript-1.6.4
   # ./configure --prefix=/usr/local
   # make
   # make install
```

If you cannot get `enscript` to install but want to use the program, you can install the binaries from the Fedora Core distribution. Simply insert the DVD or the first CD-ROM from the distribution and enter the following command:

```
# rpm -hvi /mnt/cdrom/Fedora/RPMS/enscript-1.6.1-25.i386.rpm
```

Or you can install it using the Main Menu ➪ System Settings ➪ Add/Remove Application applet.

Chapter 13

1. Try to install the `XML::RSS` Perl module. As you will see in the bonus chapter, we use this module in our `sysadmin` application to parse an RSS data stream that contains the latest security headlines.

A. You can use the CPAN shell to install `XML::RSS`, like so:

```
# perl -MCPAN -e shell
   cpan> install XML::RSS
```

2. Change the `hello.pl` program to display your own hometown.

A. This is a rather trivial change. Simply modify the `$city` and `$country` variables:

```
$city    = 'Indianapolis';
   $country = 'US';
```

3. Implement an application that is similar to `list_users.pl` to display the system groups: the gid followed by the group name. Hint: The group information is stored in `/etc/group`.

A. As you will see, this code is nearly identical to `list_users.pl`, with the exception of three lines. See if you can identify the differences:

```
#!/usr/local/bin/perl

    use strict;                                  ## Enable "strict" pragma

    my (@data);                                  ## Pre-declare variables

    open (FILE, '/etc/group')                    ## Open the file
            || die "Cannot open file: $!\n";

    while (<FILE>) {                             ## Read each record
            @data = split (/:/, $_, 4);              ## Separate the elements

        print pack ("A16A*", $data[2], $data[0]), "\n";  ## Print
                                                           ## gid, group
      }

    close (FILE);                                ## Close file
    exit  (0);                                   ## Exit application
```

4. Write a small snippet of code to invoke the `lsmod` command and display its output. The `lsmod` application shows information about all loaded kernel modules. Hint: Try to use either backticks or a piped open to communicate with the external application, as you will reuse this code in the next question.

A. Since Perl allows us to communicate with external applications and tools using a number of techniques, we will look at the three most popular ones. First, we'll start with backticks:

```
$lsmod = `/sbin/lsmod`;
        print $lsmod;
```

Next, we'll look at the piped open:

```
open (MYPIPE, '/sbin/lsmod |') || die "Cannot create pipe: $!\n";

    while (<MYPIPE>) {         ## Read one line at a time into $_
            print;                 ## Equivalent to: print $_;
    }

    close (MYPIPE);
```

And finally, we'll end with the `system` command:

```
system ('/sbin/lsmod');
```

5. Extend the snippet of code you wrote for the previous question to display only the kernel module name and its size. There are many ways to accomplish this task, but using a regular expression will garner you bonus points.

A. We will look at two solutions, both of which use the piped open to communicate with the `lsmod` application. The first example uses a regular expression to extract the first two columns, while the second example uses the `split` command to do the same.

```
use strict;                             ## Enable "strict" pragma

   open (MYPIPE, '/sbin/lsmod |') || die "Cannot create pipe: $!\n";

   my $record;

   while (<MYPIPE>) {                   ## Read a line into $_
       ($record) = /^(\S+\s+\S+)/;      ## Grab the first two columns
       print "$record\n";               ## and store in $record
   }

   close (MYPIPE);
   exit  (0);
```

If you don't want to use a regular expression, you can also use the `split` command, which we have used in multiple examples:

```
#!/usr/local/bin/perl

   use strict;                          ## Enable "strict" pragma

   open (MYPIPE, '/sbin/lsmod |') || die "Cannot create pipe: $!\n";

   my ($module, $size);

   while (<MYPIPE>) {                   ## Read a line into $_
           ($module, $size, undef)
            = split (/\s+/, $_, 3);     ## Split into three, ignore last set
                                         ## Format and print info.
         print pack ("A16A*", $module, $size), "\n";
   }

    close (MYPIPE);
    exit  (0);
```

6. Change the Disk Usage Monitor application to send the system administrator, or `root@localhost.localdomain`, a copy of the warning message. Hint: Use the `perldoc` command to learn more about the `Mail::Send` module and its functionality.

A. Before we get to the answer, here is how you would use the `perldoc` command to get documentation on the `Mail::Send` module:

```
$ perldoc Mail::Send
```

Now to the code. The Disk Usage Monitor application uses the `send_email` subroutine to send e-mail, so that is where we need to add some extra code:

```
sub send_email
 {
        ...
```

```
        $mail  = new Mail::Send;          ## Creates new Mail::Send object
        $list  = '';                      ## String to hold list of files
        $admin = 'root@localhost.localdomain';

        $mail->to ($user);
        $mail->cc ($admin);               ## CC to administrator
        $mail->subject ('Disk Usage Alert');

        $fh = $mail->open();

        ...
}
```

Index

Symbols and Numerics

A

C

D

G

H

J

K

N

O

T

U

GNU General Public License

Version 2, June 1991
Copyright © 1989, 1991 Free Software Foundation, Inc.
59 Temple Place — Suite 330, Boston, MA 02111-1307, USA

Everyone is permitted to copy and distribute verbatim copies of this license document, but changing it is not allowed.

Preamble

The licenses for most software are designed to take away your freedom to share and change it. By contrast, the GNU General Public License is intended to guarantee your freedom to share and change free software — to make sure the software is free for all its users. This General Public License applies to most of the Free Software Foundation's software and to any other program whose authors commit to using it. (Some other Free Software Foundation software is covered by the GNU Library General Public License instead.) You can apply it to your programs, too.

When we speak of free software, we are referring to freedom, not price. Our General Public Licenses are designed to make sure that you have the freedom to distribute copies of free software (and charge for this service if you wish), that you receive source code or can get it if you want it, that you can change the software or use pieces of it in new free programs; and that you know you can do these things.

To protect your rights, we need to make restrictions that forbid anyone to deny you these rights or to ask you to surrender the rights. These restrictions translate to certain responsibilities for you if you distribute copies of the software, or if you modify it.

For example, if you distribute copies of such a program, whether gratis or for a fee, you must give the recipients all the rights that you have. You must make sure that they, too, receive or can get the source code. And you must show them these terms so they know their rights.

We protect your rights with two steps: (1) copyright the software, and (2) offer you this license which gives you legal permission to copy, distribute and/or modify the software.

Also, for each author's protection and ours, we want to make certain that everyone understands that there is no warranty for this free software. If the software is modified by someone else and passed on, we want its recipients to know that what they have is not the original, so that any problems introduced by others will not reflect on the original authors' reputations.

Finally, any free program is threatened constantly by software patents. We wish to avoid the danger that redistributors of a free program will individually obtain patent licenses, in effect making the program proprietary. To prevent this, we have made it clear that any patent must be licensed for everyone's free use or not licensed at all.

The precise terms and conditions for copying, distribution and modification follow.

Terms and Conditions for Copying, Distribution and Modification

0. This License applies to any program or other work which contains a notice placed by the copyright holder saying it may be distributed under the terms of this General Public License. The "Program", below, refers to any such program or work, and a "work based on the Program" means either the Program or any derivative work under copyright law: that is to say, a work containing the Program or a portion of it, either verbatim or with modifications and/or translated into another language. (Hereinafter, translation is included without limitation in the term "modification".) Each licensee is addressed as "you".

   Activities other than copying, distribution and modification are not covered by this License; they are outside its scope. The act of running the Program is not restricted, and the output from the Program is covered only if its contents constitute a work based on the Program (independent of having been made by running the Program). Whether that is true depends on what the Program does.

1. You may copy and distribute verbatim copies of the Program's source code as you receive it, in any medium, provided that you conspicuously and appropriately publish on each copy an appropriate copyright notice and disclaimer of warranty; keep intact all the notices that refer to this License and to the absence of any warranty; and give any other recipients of the Program a copy of this License along with the Program.

   You may charge a fee for the physical act of transferring a copy, and you may at your option offer warranty protection in exchange for a fee.

2. You may modify your copy or copies of the Program or any portion of it, thus forming a work based on the Program, and copy and distribute such modifications or work under the terms of Section 1 above, provided that you also meet all of these conditions:

   a) You must cause the modified files to carry prominent notices stating that you changed the files and the date of any change.

   b) You must cause any work that you distribute or publish, that in whole or in part contains or is derived from the Program or any part thereof, to be licensed as a whole at no charge to all third parties under the terms of this License.

   c) If the modified program normally reads commands interactively when run, you must cause it, when started running for such interactive use in the most ordinary way, to print or display an announcement including an appropriate copyright notice and a notice that there is no warranty (or else, saying that you provide a warranty) and that users may redistribute the program under these conditions, and telling the user how to view a copy of this License. (Exception: if the Program itself is interactive but does not normally print such an announcement, your work based on the Program is not required to print an announcement.)

   These requirements apply to the modified work as a whole. If identifiable sections of that work are not derived from the Program, and can be reasonably considered independent and separate works in themselves, then this License, and its terms, do not apply to those sections when you distribute them as separate works. But when you distribute the same sections as part of a whole which is a work based on the Program, the distribution of the whole must be on the terms of this License, whose permissions for other licensees extend to the entire whole, and thus to each and every part regardless of who wrote it.

Thus, it is not the intent of this section to claim rights or contest your rights to work written entirely by you; rather, the intent is to exercise the right to control the distribution of derivative or collective works based on the Program.

In addition, mere aggregation of another work not based on the Program with the Program (or with a work based on the Program) on a volume of a storage or distribution medium does not bring the other work under the scope of this License.

3. You may copy and distribute the Program (or a work based on it, under Section 2) in object code or executable form under the terms of Sections 1 and 2 above provided that you also do one of the following:

   a) Accompany it with the complete corresponding machine-readable source code, which must be distributed under the terms of Sections 1 and 2 above on a medium customarily used for software interchange; or,

   b) Accompany it with a written offer, valid for at least three years, to give any third party, for a charge no more than your cost of physically performing source distribution, a complete machine-readable copy of the corresponding source code, to be distributed under the terms of Sections 1 and 2 above on a medium customarily used for software interchange; or,

   c) Accompany it with the information you received as to the offer to distribute corresponding source code. (This alternative is allowed only for noncommercial distribution and only if you received the program in object code or executable form with such an offer, in accord with Subsection b above.)

   The source code for a work means the preferred form of the work for making modifications to it. For an executable work, complete source code means all the source code for all modules it contains, plus any associated interface definition files, plus the scripts used to control compilation and installation of the executable. However, as a special exception, the source code distributed need not include anything that is normally distributed (in either source or binary form) with the major components (compiler, kernel, and so on) of the operating system on which the executable runs, unless that component itself accompanies the executable.

   If distribution of executable or object code is made by offering access to copy from a designated place, then offering equivalent access to copy the source code from the same place counts as distribution of the source code, even though third parties are not compelled to copy the source along with the object code.

4. You may not copy, modify, sublicense, or distribute the Program except as expressly provided under this License. Any attempt otherwise to copy, modify, sublicense or distribute the Program is void, and will automatically terminate your rights under this License. However, parties who have received copies, or rights, from you under this License will not have their licenses terminated so long as such parties remain in full compliance.

5. You are not required to accept this License, since you have not signed it. However, nothing else grants you permission to modify or distribute the Program or its derivative works. These actions are prohibited by law if you do not accept this License. Therefore, by modifying or distributing the Program (or any work based on the Program), you indicate your acceptance of this License to do so, and all its terms and conditions for copying, distributing or modifying the Program or works based on it.

6. Each time you redistribute the Program (or any work based on the Program), the recipient automatically receives a license from the original licensor to copy, distribute or modify the Program subject to these terms and conditions. You may not impose any further restrictions on the recipients' exercise of the rights granted herein. You are not responsible for enforcing compliance by third parties to this License.

7. If, as a consequence of a court judgment or allegation of patent infringement or for any other reason (not limited to patent issues), conditions are imposed on you (whether by court order, agreement or otherwise) that contradict the conditions of this License, they do not excuse you from the conditions of this License. If you cannot distribute so as to satisfy simultaneously your obligations under this License and any other pertinent obligations, then as a consequence you may not distribute the Program at all. For example, if a patent license would not permit royalty-free redistribution of the Program by all those who receive copies directly or indirectly through you, then the only way you could satisfy both it and this License would be to refrain entirely from distribution of the Program.

   If any portion of this section is held invalid or unenforceable under any particular circumstance, the balance of the section is intended to apply and the section as a whole is intended to apply in other circumstances.

   It is not the purpose of this section to induce you to infringe any patents or other property right claims or to contest validity of any such claims; this section has the sole purpose of protecting the integrity of the free software distribution system, which is implemented by public license practices. Many people have made generous contributions to the wide range of software distributed through that system in reliance on consistent application of that system; it is up to the author/donor to decide if he or she is willing to distribute software through any other system and a licensee cannot impose that choice.

   This section is intended to make thoroughly clear what is believed to be a consequence of the rest of this License.

8. If the distribution and/or use of the Program is restricted in certain countries either by patents or by copyrighted interfaces, the original copyright holder who places the Program under this License may add an explicit geographical distribution limitation excluding those countries, so that distribution is permitted only in or among countries not thus excluded. In such case, this License incorporates the limitation as if written in the body of this License.

9. The Free Software Foundation may publish revised and/or new versions of the General Public License from time to time. Such new versions will be similar in spirit to the present version, but may differ in detail to address new problems or concerns.

   Each version is given a distinguishing version number. If the Program specifies a version number of this License which applies to it and "any later version", you have the option of following the terms and conditions either of that version or of any later version published by the Free Software Foundation. If the Program does not specify a version number of this License, you may choose any version ever published by the Free Software Foundation.

10. If you wish to incorporate parts of the Program into other free programs whose distribution conditions are different, write to the author to ask for permission. For software which is copyrighted by the Free Software Foundation, write to the Free Software Foundation; we sometimes make exceptions for this. Our decision will be guided by the two goals of preserving the free status of all derivatives of our free software and of promoting the sharing and reuse of software generally.

NO WARRANTY

11. BECAUSE THE PROGRAM IS LICENSED FREE OF CHARGE, THERE IS NO WARRANTY FOR THE PROGRAM, TO THE EXTENT PERMITTED BY APPLICABLE LAW. EXCEPT WHEN OTHERWISE STATED IN WRITING THE COPYRIGHT HOLDERS AND/OR OTHER PARTIES PROVIDE THE PROGRAM "AS IS" WITHOUT WARRANTY OF ANY KIND, EITHER EXPRESSED OR IMPLIED, INCLUDING, BUT NOT LIMITED TO, THE IMPLIED WARRANTIES OF MERCHANTABILITY AND FITNESS FOR A PARTICULAR PURPOSE. THE ENTIRE RISK AS TO THE QUALITY AND PERFORMANCE OF THE PROGRAM IS WITH YOU. SHOULD THE PROGRAM PROVE DEFECTIVE, YOU ASSUME THE COST OF ALL NECESSARY SERVICING, REPAIR OR CORRECTION.

12. IN NO EVENT UNLESS REQUIRED BY APPLICABLE LAW OR AGREED TO IN WRITING WILL ANY COPYRIGHT HOLDER, OR ANY OTHER PARTY WHO MAY MODIFY AND/OR REDISTRIBUTE THE PROGRAM AS PERMITTED ABOVE, BE LIABLE TO YOU FOR DAMAGES, INCLUDING ANY GENERAL, SPECIAL, INCIDENTAL OR CONSEQUENTIAL DAMAGES ARISING OUT OF THE USE OR INABILITY TO USE THE PROGRAM (INCLUDING BUT NOT LIMITED TO LOSS OF DATA OR DATA BEING RENDERED INACCURATE OR LOSSES SUSTAINED BY YOU OR THIRD PARTIES OR A FAILURE OF THE PROGRAM TO OPERATE WITH ANY OTHER PROGRAMS), EVEN IF SUCH HOLDER OR OTHER PARTY HAS BEEN ADVISED OF THE POSSIBILITY OF SUCH DAMAGES.

END OF TERMS AND CONDITIONS

Wiley Publishing, Inc.
Linux CD Mail-In Offer

If you do not have access to a PC with a DVD drive, we are offering the complete set on CD-ROMs for a nominal shipping-and-materials fee. If you'd like the CDs sent to you, please follow the instructions below to order by phone, online, or by coupon.

For each ordering method, please use ISBN: 0774577867 and Promo Code: BF2WX when prompted. For orders shipping within the U.S., the cost is $13.50 (U.S. funds). For orders outside the U.S., the cost is $20.00 (U.S. funds).

Terms: Void where prohibited or restricted by law. Allow 2–4 weeks for delivery.

To order by phone:

1. Call toll free in the United States — 1-877-762-2974. International customers, dial 1-317-572-3994.
2. Give the operator the appropriate ISBN and Promo Code. Please have your credit card ready.

To order online:

1. Go to `www.wiley.com`.
2. Use the Product Search feature to search for Fedora 2 CD multipack.
3. Place your order through the shopping cart using the appropriate ISBN and Promo Code.

To order by coupon:

1. Complete the coupon below.
2. Include a check or money order for $13.50 (U.S. funds) for orders shipping within the U.S. or $20.00 (U.S. funds) for orders outside the U.S.
3. Send it to us at the address listed at the bottom of the coupon.

Name ______________________________

Company ______________________________

Address ______________________________

City ____________ **State** ________ **Postal Code** ________ **Country** ____________

E-mail ____________________ **Telephone** ____________

Place where book was purchased ______________________________

❑ Check here to find out what we're up to by joining our email list—a convenient way to receive news about our products and events as well as about special discount offers.

Return this coupon with the appropriate US funds to:

Wiley Publishing, Inc.
Customer Care
Fedora 2 CD multipack, 0774577867 Fulfillment Promo: BF2WX
10475 Crosspoint Blvd.
Indianapolis, IN 46256

Terms: Wiley is not responsible for lost, stolen, late, or illegible orders. For questions regarding this fulfillment offer, please call us at 1-877-762-2974 or 1-317-572-3994.